P9-APF-045

Becoming a Secondary School Science Teacher

FIFTH EDITION

Leslie W. Trowbridge
Professor Emeritus of Science
Education
University of Northern Colorado

Rodger W. Bybee
Associate Director
Biological Sciences
Curriculum Study
The Colorado College

Merrill Publishing Company
A Bell & Howell Information Company
Columbus   Toronto   London   Melbourne

Dedication

This fifth edition of *Becoming a Secondary School Science Teacher* is dedicated to Dr. Robert B. Sund (coauthor of the first two editions) who died in 1979. Dr. Sund was a professor in the Department of Science Education at the University of Northern Colorado for nineteen years and senior author of the second edition. He wrote prolifically for the college level, producing books on pedagogy, teaching activities, and Piagetian psychology. In addition, he authored books for children in elementary science from kindergarten to grade six.

Dr. Sund was a superb teacher and demonstrated by word and deed the attributes of effective instruction. He was loved by his students and highly respected by his colleagues. He is sorely missed.

Leslie W. Trowbridge
Rodger W. Bybee

Cover Photo: Jim Whitmer

Published by Merrill Publishing Company
A Bell & Howell Information Company
Columbus, Ohio 43216

This book was set in Melior.

Administrative Editor: Jeff Johnston
Developmental Editor: Linda James Scharp
Production Editor: Victoria M. Althoff
Art Coordinator: Mark Garrett
Cover Designer: Russ Maselli
Photo Editor: Gail Meese

Copyright © 1990, 1986, 1981 by Merrill Publishing Company. All rights reserved. No part of this book may be reproduced in any form, electronic or mechanical, including photocopy, recording, or any information storage and retrieval system, without permission in writing from the publisher. "Merrill Publishing Company" and "Merrill" are registered trademarks of Merrill Publishing Company.

The first and second editions of this book were published under the title *Teaching Science by Inquiry in the Secondary School.* Copyright © 1973, 1967, by Bell & Howell Company. Substantial portions of Chapter 5, "The Psychology of Development and Groups," were published in *Piaget for Educators* by Rodger W. Bybee and Robert B. Sund, copyright © 1982, 1976, by Bell & Howell Company.

Photo Credits: pp. 70, 254 by the National Science Teachers Association; pp. 74, 236, 388, 407 by Lloyd Lemmerman/ Merrill; pp. 117, 146 by Jean Greenwald/Merrill; p. 164 by Andy Brunk/Merrill; p. 177 by David Strickler; pp. 194, 234, 386 by Paul Conklin; p. 209 by Bruce Johnson/Merrill; pp. 211, 258 by Kevin Fitzsimons/Merrill; p. 259 by Linda Scharp/Merrill; p. 398 by Merrill; p. 400 by Tom Hubbard; p. 403 by Larry Hamill/Merrill.

Library of Congress Catalog Card Number: 89–62284
International Standard Book Number: 0–675–21166–2
Printed in the United States of America
1 2 3 4 5 6 7 8 9—94 93 92 91 90

PREFACE

The Fifth Edition of *Becoming a Secondary School Science Teacher* contains many improvements over previous editions. In response to the changing needs of prospective secondary school science teachers, several chapters have been extensively revised and updated. We have addressed both the theoretical and the practical aspects of teaching science in secondary schools.

Throughout the book, we have incorporated the science-technology-society (S-T-S) theme and the constructivist approach to teaching and learning. The S-T-S theme is becoming a major curriculum emphasis and should be a consideration for any school science program in the 1990s. Constructivism refers to a concept of learning that assumes students actively construct their understanding of phenomena. Through experience they develop conceptual schemes that they use to interpret events and objects. Anomalous events and objects require students to reconstruct basic conceptual schemes. In science teaching, we try to encourage students to develop more adequate, that is, scientific, explanations of the world.

Chapter 10 which describes the use of microcomputers in science classrooms has been updated to provide insights into how computer technology may be used more effectively in science teaching. Both hardware and software changes are discussed, and projections that schools can consider in planning their microcomputer teaching program or hardware capabilities are emphasized.

We continue to highlight the importance of demonstration and laboratory work in science classes. Up-to-date information on safety practices has been emphasized. Use of students as laboratory assistants, both to provide for teacher assistance and as a learning experience for students has been discussed.

Understanding and making effective use of objectives for science teaching is a continuing area of importance. Not only is the cognitive domain stressed but also the equally important areas of psychomotor and affective objectives have been addressed.

Throughout the book, stress is placed on the need to consider all aspects of human development as part of the students' education in the sciences. Also, recognition is given to the important responsibility of serving the needs of the large percentage of students in our middle and senior high schools who are not necessarily college bound but who will become the future backbone of society. These students must become scientifically and technologically literate citizens to be able to participate fully in the complex society in which we live.

The original chapter on curriculum has been divided into two chapters. Chapter 16 discusses middle/junior high school courses of study, and Chapter 17 addresses high school curricula. The middle school is currently the fastest growing innovation in education, yet it is also the most neglected level. We think the middle school deserves special attention.

Instruction is another emphasis in contemporary education. Chapter 18, "Models for Effective Science Teaching" has been expanded to include an array of different instructional models that you might encounter. An extended presentation of one instructional model forms part of the chapter.

We conclude the book with a chapter describing the S-T-S theme. The significance of the S-T-S theme is only beginning to be recognized. In the 1990s, global problems, such as biodiversity, ozone depletion, and deforestation will demand increased attention by science educators. We believe this chapter provides an excellent introduction to the S-T-S theme.

To place the information on science teaching in a practical setting, we again include guest editorials from persons who have taught, are teaching, or are students in science teaching methods classes.

This textbook is primarily designed for the undergraduate pre-service teacher of science. However, many of its features make the book valuable for graduate students in courses dealing with instructional methods and curriculum development as well as for workshops and institutes in which pedagogical topics in science teaching are discussed. Also, experienced, practicing science teachers will gain much useful information in the "Investigating Science Teaching" and "Teaching Science Activities" sections of the book.

The authors have had extensive experience in public school teaching and have also been involved with teacher education for many years. The feedback from practicing teachers has enabled us to produce a textbook which we believe is close to the concerns of secondary school science teachers.

Robert B. Sund, to whom this book is dedicated, was senior author on the first two editions. He died in the planning stages of the third edition. His influence on teaching methods and philosophy is still strong in this edition. We wish to acknowledge his valuable contributions to this textbook and to science education.

We would like to thank the reviewers who provided suggestions for this revision: George J. Frangos, California University of Pennsylvania; Thomas R. Koballa, University of Texas, Austin; Cheryl L. Mason, San Diego State University; Joseph D. McInerny, The Colorado College; Janet Carlson Powell, The Colorado College; and Richard Sloop, Frostburg State College. We also wish to acknowledge the contributions of C. Yvonne Wise, Biological Sciences Curriculum Study, and Dorothee Trowbridge.

Science teaching at the secondary level continues to be a challenging experience. In today's educational climate, science teaching once again returns to full prominence. It is an exciting time to be or to become a science teacher. The future holds much promise for well-prepared, dedicated science teachers. The responsibilities of the professional science teacher do not diminish, but grow more significant each year. We extend our good wishes, and hope that you enjoy a satisfying career in the profession of science teaching.

Leslie W. Trowbridge
Rodger W. Bybee

CONTENTS

CHAPTER 1

Becoming a Science Teacher

If you are reading this sentence, you are in the process of becoming a science teacher. As with other important issues in your life, you no doubt struggled with this decision. While deciding, you probably gathered information on the options—you might have explored the science major, talked to friends and parents, conferred with your college advisor, and even visited your high school science teacher. With all the facts in mind, you decided to become a science teacher. Thinking all was settled, you went to work on your science major and began taking education courses. For a time, most aspects of your career choice seemed resolved. Now you are taking a course to learn about specific aspects of science teaching; soon you will be student teaching; in the foreseeable future, you will have your first job as a science teacher.

All of this is exciting. But: now you have an entirely new set of questions about your career! "How do I teach science?" "Am I qualified to teach science?" "What do I need to know?" "What science do I teach to middle school or senior high school students?" "What is science teaching like?" "What are the problems facing science teachers today?" Constantly emerging questions and concerns on science teaching are part of the process.

Some of your questions have answers; others depend on your specific talents, personality, knowledge, enthusiasm, and many other important, but elusive, qualities. Obviously, we cannot answer all of these questions in this chapter or this book. We can provide some information and direction. In addition, we can suggest activities that will help clarify your own answers about your strengths and weaknesses and the realities and possibilities of science teaching. The best way to begin is by completing Activity 1–1, "Investigating Science Teaching: How I See Myself as a Science Teacher," at the end of this chapter.

■ Am I Qualified to Teach Science?

This question is difficult to answer with a simple yes or no, because of the adjective *qualified*. Traditionally, persons have "qualified" to be science teachers by completing a set of educational requirements. In this sense most individuals can be qualified for teaching. But there is more to teaching science than fulfilling a set of requirements and, in fact, there is more to teaching science than being able to talk about science. Some of the dimensions of science teaching addressed in the activity "Investigating Science Teaching: How I See Myself as a Science Teacher" are identifiable in the following discussion.

Understanding Science and Technology

The science teacher should have a good background in science, including a broad general knowledge in the areas of her major. These statements seem obvious. In the 1990s, however, you will also need to have an understanding of technology because our society and the experience of your students are strongly oriented toward technology. You should have an understanding of the many relationships between science and technology. In the past, science teachers and textbooks presented technology as "applied science"; that is, the enterprise of science resulted in knowledge that was applied to human problems. Although this statement is generally accurate, in some cases, scientific advances must wait until technology is developed. Technology can also be viewed as an area of study. Like science, technology also has products and processes that form the basis of study.

In addition to having scientific and technological knowledge, the science teacher is required to apply this knowledge in new situations she has not considered, to use basic science concepts to analyze problems presented by students, and to synthesize knowledge so that she may answer questions accurately. So, you should be well-informed and be able to use your scientific knowledge in many ways. An understanding of science and technology does not automatically qualify you to teach science; other skills are necessary.

Organizing Science Instruction

Science teachers should be prepared, organized, and have a direction and purpose for their teaching. There is no substitute for a well-prepared lesson. At one time or another, most science teachers have tried to teach without preparation. More often than not, the lesson was not very effective. As you begin organizing your science program, try to establish the "big picture" by determining the sequence of your program for the year. You may wish to break the year into units and the units into individual lessons. This simple procedure will give you a sense of overall organization. However, there is more to teaching methods than organization.

Effective science teachers use a variety of teaching methods, choosing the best for each lesson. Always keep in mind the simple questions: "What do I want to teach?" and "How can I best teach it?" The answers to these questions will direct you to different teaching methods. Complete Activity 1–2, "Investigating Science Teaching: The What and How of Science Lessons," at the end of this chapter.

Understanding Students

Imagine that you are ready to begin your first lesson. The students are sitting at their desks, waiting for you to teach them about science. Question: Do the students in front of you already have any science concepts? The answer is *yes*. The students you will be teaching have lived 12 to 16 years. Through formal and informal experiences, the students have developed ideas about the events and objects in their perceived world. They have also placed labels on many of those events and objects. In this regard, you should

remember three points: (1) students have concepts about their world, (2) many of these concepts are inadequate when compared to scientific explanations or concepts, and (3) these concepts of the natural world influence what and how students will learn about science.[1] David Ausubel summarized this when he wrote: "If I had to reduce all of educational psychology to just one principle, I would say this: The most important single factor influencing learning is what the learner already knows. Ascertain this and teach him accordingly."[2]

Organizing Science Instruction

Science teachers usually approach instruction as though students are "empty vessels" to be filled with facts, information, and concepts about the world. This perception of how students learn is inaccurate. It is more accurate to say that students construct their explanations of the world through a personal process in which sensory data are given meaning in terms of prior knowledge. In order for learning to occur, the adequacy of current student conceptions must be challenged, and appropriate time and opportunities must be provided so students can reconstruct newer and more adequate explanations. Ways to facilitate this process of learning will be explored in later chapters. How is this process of learning different from what you currently understand about student learning? Review your response to Activity 1–2, "The What and How of Science Lessons," at the end of this chapter.

Personalizing Science Teaching

The effective science teacher realizes the importance of interpersonal relations. This section relates directly to the portion of the first "Investigating Science Teaching" activity on perceptions of students. One of the important findings in regard to helping others is that objectivity has a negative correlation with effectiveness; that is, if students are treated as objects, the relationship becomes impersonal. In our endeavors to become significant to our students, we have occasionally treated them as insignificant people. No one becomes significant to someone else, whether students, fellow teachers, or friends, if he is made to feel insignificant. You become significant to others by treating them with integrity, sincerity, and openness.[3] Some of the best science teachers make a conscious effort to regard each student positively, to understand her as a human being, and to help her grow in every way possible. In these situations, students learn science; in fact, they probably learn more science because of the interpersonal rapport. If you become a significant person to your students, the final reward is yours; you cannot help another person without becoming a better science teacher in the process.

Personalizing your relationship with students can include many things, such as a greater understanding of the pupils, devising different tasks for different students, individual evaluation, varied questioning, or the use of different materials and equipment. Effective communication is the idea that covers, in one way or another, most of the important aspects of personalizing science teaching.

Take time to talk to the students. To personalize the interaction, present yourself as you are: you are not a science curriculum, a textbook, or the Grand Inquisitor. You are a person. Be open; let your students see you as an individual beyond the confines of the classroom or scientific subject. This approach can be made individually, with a group, or with the whole class, on field trips, in the halls, at lunch, or during individual work in class. At the same time, you must reciprocate by listening to the students and discussing topics that interest them.

Listening unhurriedly, responsively, and empathetically will enhance your personal relationship with students because the message, "I care," comes through. There is an abundance of literature showing that many students need caring relationships before they are set to memorizing science facts. Through listening you can also gather information that will help students learn science. You need not be a psychologist to pick up some of the personal messages that say, "I'm happy," "My self-image is low," "I don't like school," or "I like you."

Talking and listening to the students is a subtle and important way of recognizing the adolescent's growing need for identity. It also enhances the learning relationship and increases the teacher's efficiency in facilitating the student's understanding of science.

Recognizing Personal Meaning in Teaching Science

Imagine two middle school lessons about the life cycles of organisms. In the first lesson the students read about mealworms. In the second, a container of mealworms is given them and they are allowed to explore the tiny organisms. There are numerous "Oohs," "Ahhs," "I can't touch this," "It squirmed," "Look at my worm back up!" and other exclamations that indicate the students' feelings about the experience.

The second lesson provides an experience that is physically close, that is less abstract, and that is emotionally involved with the subject. There is little problem in extending this exercise into areas such

as designing experiments, reaction to stimuli, and the life cycle of mealworms. Both lessons convey the material; however, the second would probably be more effective in teaching the concepts because there were physical and psychological involvement and personal meaning.

Many contemporary science curricula are inquiry- or discovery-oriented. For the most part the "discovery" is of science facts and concepts; physical involvement with materials through laboratory activities provides the primary teaching method for presenting these facts and concepts. The next step in the teaching task is incorporating the affective dimension of discovery; that is, the discovery of the personal meaning of these facts and concepts for the individual. If the perceptions of the student are considered, it is obvious that learning science is easier when students are interested and involved. For example, you have been motivated to read this chapter because it has some personal meaning. Your motivation to read this book is fairly clear—you are becoming a science teacher and you want to know how to be as effective as possible. What is said in this book, then, has some personal meaning for you.

Personal meaning has two aspects: (1) the physical closeness of the materials, and (2) the psychological interest that the individual has in the materials. To state this idea succinctly: learning science is enhanced when there is personal involvement with materials and organisms. Usually, science teachers have started with content and assumed that personal meaning would emerge. This progression, as it turns out, may or may not occur. It is also possible to begin with interest, motivation, and personal meaning, and structure the content on these experiences while still teaching scientific concepts. Feelings and emotional involvement can be used to the teacher's advantage in developing science concepts and processes.

Realizing Your Role as Decision Maker in the Science Classroom

Imagine that you are about to begin a chemistry lesson on pollution. Your plan is to demonstrate how the common air pollutants, sulfur dioxide (SO_2) and sulfur trioxide (SO_3), are produced when coal and oil containing sulfur are burned. Then you plan to show how sulfur trioxide (SO_3) can react with water vapor (H_2O) to form sulfuric acid. You have some sulfuric acid on the demonstration desk so that you may show the students the corrosive power of this acid. As you begin your demonstration, you accidentally knock over the beaker containing the acid. It spills onto the papers and books on the desk. What would *you* do? Take a moment and think about the situation.

Who Me?! A Science Teacher?

Laurel Hall
Science Education Student-Geology, Carleton College,
Northfield, Minnesota

"Teaching science? Me? You've got to be nuts." This would have been my reaction a few months ago; however, today my response is just the opposite: science teaching is a plausible career for me. Why the change of opinion in such a short time? The answer is simple: after seriously evaluating my interests and goals, with respect to possible careers, I found that teaching would allow me to incorporate and use more of them. The next step was to discover what education is and what methods are used. This step was achieved through a science methods course where I actually observed and participated in various teaching activities of a class at a local junior high school. The career experience in this field has had an important positive effect on my knowledge and opinions of the educational system, besides showing me some of the realities of science teaching.

I have always been interested in helping people learn; my past working experience as a camp counselor, recreational leader, and YMCA swimming instructor and coach is evidence of this interest. However, teaching in the educational system did not appeal to me; I felt that I would become very bored with teaching the same thing to several classes year after year. Yet, with my recent finding that education was a career possibility and that many of my goals and interests could be combined with it, I began to take a new look at education and saw it as a challenge as long as my adolescent biases toward the educational system could be eradicated.

I entered the education program still unsure of what teaching science entailed. I soon found out that my preconceived biases toward the educational system, based on my own public school experiences, were not universally true. The elimination of these biases was the major factor in altering my opinion of the system. Now, instead of looking at the system as hopeless, I see myself as an agent of change: I can set an example and hope others will follow. I can challenge myself to improve, change, and alter lessons, activities, and methods to counteract any boredom in myself and in the students and to communicate with more students.

Through a science methods course, I learned about education, the variety of methods that can be used to attain objectives, and some of the realities of teaching. From these new views, I can see that teaching can be a much tougher occupation than I had previously expected. It involves many time-consuming activities such as developing new units, changing lesson plans, improving activities, keeping up-to-date on recent developments in the specific area of science, and keeping enthusiasm at a high level. Yet, it is through these same time-consuming processes that the rewards of teaching are to be found: for example, communicating with those who previously did not understand or care, introducing students to new and interesting ideas and techniques, developing within the students an enthusiasm for continued learning, and watching them develop into individuals. Thus, if I decide to take up science teaching as a career, I expect to know periods of hardship, frustration, and feelings of hopelessness; but in my opinion, the rewards are more important and are worth the toil and trouble that are a part of my career.

Suppose you have just finished an activity investigating the effects of continental glaciers. You begin a film on the subject. As soon as you turn off the lights, Melvin, the class clown, starts his act. You are fairly (but not absolutely) certain it is Melvin making funny noises and muffled comments. What would *you* do? Take a moment to think about this situation.

You could consult this textbook for the answer. You could call your methods teacher for an answer. You could ask the science supervisor in your district for an answer. You could do any number of things, most of which would help only in the unlikely event that the same situation recurred. The one certainty in these and all other real classroom situations is that you will have to decide what to do and respond in the best way possible. Your role as a science teacher will be to combine your knowledge and perceptions of classroom situations with your understanding of the students and then to decide on appropriate action. One of the major problems of science teachers is that they do not realize this central role of decision making. You must adapt the textbook, the curriculum, and the inquiry method to the events that occur in teaching situations.

Look back to the opening question "Am I qualified to teach science?" This question still cannot be answered with a direct yes or no. But you have started thinking about what it means to become a science teacher. How well do you understand science? How are you at organizing instruction in science? Can you personalize science teaching? How can you include personal meaning as a part of science lessons? Do you realize what your role will be in the science classroom? These questions and many more will emerge as you continue the process of becoming a science teacher. It is not our purpose, nor should it be yours, to try to answer these questions now. So, let us go on to another important question.

■ What Is Science Teaching Like?

Most individuals entering the teaching profession are concerned about daily happenings in the school. In one form or another they ask, "What is science teaching like?" When asked to further clarify the question, they want to know what the science programs are like, what teachers talk about, what it is like actually being in front of a class, and the concerns of other science teachers. If you complete Activity 1–3, "Investigating Science Teaching: A First Lesson" at the end of this chapter, and "Teaching Science Activity: An Introduction to Scientific Inquiry" on page 438, some of these questions will be answered. In addition, the next sections give glimpses into many different schools, science programs, and science teachers. The short vignettes are from a series of case studies funded by the National Science Foundation and completed as part of a larger evaluation of science education. The case studies were completed by individuals who spent time at different schools, observing and participating in the various activities of science teachers.[4] Although we realize that virtually all schools, science programs, and teachers differ, the case studies present some perspectives of actual science programs, some insights into teacher conver-

sations, and some perception of what science teaching is actually like.

Junior High School Science Programs

This section characterizes two junior high school science programs from the same science district. The district is located in mid-California (Western City is the name used in the case study), a region where much of the population is involved in agriculture. Student background and interest are diverse due to the large Black and Hispanic populations. This comparison of junior high school science programs points out how differently science can be taught at the same grade level and within the same district.[5]

Case Study 3

Science instruction at both schools is offered at the discretion of the building principal. If the principal had no interest in science, the science program at either school would fail to exist. As a consequence, the science program at both schools is a minimal program and is only as complete and thorough as the teachers who instruct in the program make it. The following observations (made during site visits) tell the story.

At Junior High School I, the "science room" is almost bare. There are some bulletin boards but they, too, have only a few items about earth tacked on them. The storeroom is badly supplied. There are three microscopes that are in semioperable condition, a few unlabeled chemicals, a few pieces of broken glassware (thistle tubes, test tubes), a Fisher burner, and a Bunsen burner. There is no evidence of any packaged kits (such as I.P.S. kits) or other pieces of equipment that would indicate that the students would have some experience with hands-on equipment. The desks and only a few tables are available in the room. The principal is making a great effort to upgrade this area.

The "science room" at Junior High School II is not in the same condition as the science room at Junior High School I. Although the walls are still relatively bare, the closets are filled with I.S.C.S. (Florida State Science Program) packaged kits. There are ample supplies of glassware, hardware, and chemicals normally used in a junior high school science class. The collection of rocks and minerals is minimal, as is the preserved animal collection. Relatively speaking, the science room is much better supplied and organized at Junior High School II than the science room at Junior High School I.

The science program at Junior High School II has been well established by the instructor (one of the participants in the State University Project), who has been at Junior High School II for three years. He follows a course of study that he has developed over the years and continues to modify it, utilizing the I.S.C.S. materials as time goes on. His counterpart at Junior High School I, on the other hand, appears to flounder in the science area. At Junior High School I, a considerable amount of time is spent studying earthquakes. ("Since we live in an area that is earthquake-prone, I feel the students should spend some time studying earthquakes.") Besides earthquakes, there is not much evidence of other science topics being discussed nor is there any evidence of students having an opportunity to get their hands on any equipment.

Because the science program at the junior high school level is left up to the individual schools and the respective science teachers, there is a wide range of areas and approaches that are used by the science teachers. Some science teachers in Western City have attended NSF institutes and are well versed in a variety of programs (I.P.S., I.C.I.S., I.S.C.S.) but do not use the materials exclusively. A great number of science teachers in the district are not aware of these planned science curricula and their packaged equipment and, as a consequence, do not use them.

The teachers, when asked about their major concerns about the science program at their respective schools, responded accordingly:

Junior High School I

The students lack discipline. They make little or no effort to learn. They would rather talk and delay the teaching process. They are the ones that will suffer the most.

Junior High School II

The biggest problem at the school is absences. The students don't seem to care. They would much rather be somewhere else. Discipline is not as much of a problem here as is the lack of supplies and equipment. I always have to be on the lookout for equipment.

These expressed concerns by two faculty members from different schools are not necessarily the two most pressing concerns in the district. Other teachers in the same schools have voiced concern about such things as:

1. Lack of administrative support for their programs
2. Lack of supplies and equipment
3. The continued use of outdated books
4. Large classes
5. Lack of student motivation
6. Lack of parental interest in their children

7. Lack of adequate facilities to conduct their programs

In the same conversations, when the science teachers were asked to describe a typical day in their science classes, the following is typical of the description made:

The kids come into class as soon as the bell rings. We check their homework (this is done for purposes of reinforcement). We present a short lecture (at least twenty minutes) on a given topic. We make an assignment for the following day. On Fridays, we schedule quizzes based on the last four days of work.

It is true that the description above is a rough approximation of a "typical day" in a science class, but it is important to note that science teachers at both Junior High Schools I and II made approximately the same statement in response to the question about a typical day in a science class. Field observations would indicate that their descriptions are not far from wrong.

Finally, the extent of intra-school communication for purposes of sharing ideas with other science teachers and for purposes of borrowing or trading equipment is nonexistent in W.C.S.D. This especially is true of the science area. The specialist from the City Central office makes little, if any, effort to call the science teachers together at least once a year. There are no in-service workshops offered by the City Central office and this in turn makes it very difficult to establish dialogue among or between any of the science teachers in the district.

High School Science Programs

This case study was completed in a small city on the plains east of the Rocky Mountains. The name used for the school was Fall River.[6]

Case Study 1

The high school science program consists of eighteen courses. Despite lenient graduation requirements, enrollments are high. The courses are staffed with an impressive group of teachers, most of whom have advanced degrees in the disciplines and have attended National Science Foundation institutes.

The biology program has the largest enrollment and staff. All students who elect biology take a one-semester introductory course, after which they can choose one or more follow-up courses in ecology, plant structure and function, social biology, microbiology, heredity, and animal anatomy. Some students fail or opt out of biology after the introductory course. An advanced placement course in biology is also offered.

The content of the introductory course is largely the same, regardless of who teaches it. The text used is from the Biological Sciences Curriculum Study (green version). The instructional methods are largely lectures, laboratory investigations, review sheets, and occasionally films and guest speakers. Although the BSCS text emphasizes developing students' interest and heuristic inquiry, the classroom instruction at Fall River High tends to be formal, didactic, and organized. Almost the entire text is covered. This is a large quantity of material for one semester, but it provides the background needed for the more specialized follow-up courses. In the ecology course, for example, the students review the relevant BSCS chapters and then go on to more specialized texts. They participate in simulations designed to show the relationship between values and environmental processes. Topics covered include ecology and the law, mountain ecosystems, and the food chain. Laboratory investigations are conducted on photosynthesis and chromatography, as are field investigations in small ecosystems near the school building. The students conduct independent research on biomes.

Although the other follow-up courses are not so directly related to the environment, a strong environmental consciousness pervades the entire department and has been adopted by many of the students who participate in Earth Club. When asked about the principles that underlie the program, three teachers made the following statements:

The purpose is to make them better citizens, help them understand the issues in society that are related to science, help them make better decisions. Like, I ask them how much longer they're going to be able to drive up and down Main Street. I don't try to impose my own view on them, but I do try to make them think.

You can't separate our values and science anymore. When we talk about population growth or genetics, controversial issues come in. I tell them they should learn the material, if only so they can determine their own futures.

The person just can't be an effective citizen unless he can read and understand political issues that have scientific overtones. . . . The average citizen has to have the awareness and appreciation of how his actions affect the environment and what is likely to happen, depending on the choices he makes now.

In addition to the notion of developing environmental consciousness, the teachers believe their purpose is to provide a strong and diverse academic experience that puts the students in touch with the major body of knowledge in biology and the processes used to arrive at it. One teacher reported, "Any systematized body of knowledge is part of the foun-

dation of civilization. It's part of their responsibilities as citizens to be aware of it. Science has applications in all their lives."

The biology program is not without its rough edges. Students in the introductory course fail in higher proportions than from other courses. Most teachers are determined to hold to their standards, however. Based on previous experience, they are convinced that students will take the easiest possible path, dilute the content of the course, and make the follow-up course structure impossible. The teachers feel that any student who makes the effort can pass.

Another serious problem is lack of space and facilities. There are two well-equipped laboratories, but sometimes four sections must share them in a single class period. Therefore, the teachers have to coordinate classes so that, while one section is doing lab work, the other teacher must lecture in a classroom designed for physics. No space is available for advanced laboratory preparations. They look back wistfully on the year they had a teacher's aide.

Not having the facilities lowers my interest and energy and influences what I teach. The situation has discouraged every bit of open-ended inquiry I've got. A question comes up from the class and I think of an investigation that would be related, but there we are in the physics room, so I lecture.

About forty percent of each graduating class go to college. A greater proportion of students follow a traditional college-preparatory course of study. Most of this group take chemistry in the junior year. The chemistry classes are packed, but it is unclear whether the high enrollment is due to students' scientific curiosity, the genial personality and showmanship of the teacher, or the abundance of A grades. Although there was some complaint from the best students that the class "wasn't tough enough . . . didn't go too deep into chemistry," the instructor primarily wants

them to be interested in science and to master the basic material in the field. I feel like anybody can learn at the level I teach them. The kids who are really interested then can go off on their own and learn more.

The text *Modern Chemistry* is used, but the approach is traditional. The greatest amount of class time is spent in lectures and laboratory experiments. The laboratory areas are well-equipped for a basic program, but the teacher longs for materials that would support more advanced work. The laboratories are terribly overcrowded and the teacher worries that someone will be injured in an accident.

The physics course is taught by a man with experience and impressive credentials—advanced degrees in physics and math, several NSF training institutes including training in the use of both Physical Science Curriculum Study (PSSC) and Harvard Project Physics (HPP). His laboratory is well-equipped and under his leadership the science program has always received a healthy share of the school budget. He now uses HPP in his three sections of physics. For several years PSSC was used but "NSF backed a real loser with that one." He found that few students were capable of learning the PSSC materials, enrollment dropped, and the physics program was jeopardized. He decided to change over to the HPP course and textbook, which are somewhat less theoretically and mathematically rigorous and more appealing to larger segments of the school population. A few students and parents complained. One parent stated:

> I've been very disappointed with the district for watering down the courses. There used to be a really strong physics program (under PSSC) but then (the teacher) decided he needed to accommodate the low to middle achiever so he threw out the good program and came up with this other one that is less comprehensive. It really hurts the well-motivated kids.

In answering a question about the purpose of science education, the physics teacher spoke of his own philosophy:

> In recent years I've wondered if you could justify it. Earlier I would have said that physics was a part of cultural knowledge, something enormously practical, like all science having something philosophically to offer the public, and intellectual integrity which could carry over into politics and society.
>
> Now I don't know. We live in a technological society so it is necessary to propagate information to some parts of the society. But for the general person in high school who will eventually go into business or become a homemaker they really don't need to know about physics, except in a very superficial way. If you want a kid to know how to change a tire, you teach him about levers ... I'm a good sailor and I apply my knowledge of physics, but other people are better sailors and have no physics background.
>
> That is too pessimistic. Let me state it this way. Everyone deals with nature. Every high school student knows a great deal of physics and the teacher merely encourages him to abstract his knowledge to form more general and sometimes more useful patterns of thought. If the student can deal with ideas in the abstract, he learns this before going to college and can thereby make a sounder choice of careers. He may not do better than another competent college student, but he has had the benefit of guidance and proven academic discipline. Finally, and this is important for all ability ranges of students, a sense of being at home in the universe must be transmitted. The physical world and the technology of man must be dealt with as an important part of the total culture he is to inherit.

In addition to the more traditional rack of three courses, the science program includes a great variety of offerings: astronomy, archaeology, geology, conceptual physics, electronics (less mathematical than the physics course), introduction to chemistry (a student-centered laboratory program using discovery techniques and emphasizing the process of science) and space science (a rather easy course for students who have a previous failure or little interest in science).

The man responsible for several of these courses is a former geologist who runs his classes very informally, trying to structure each one around the interests and questions of the students. Environmental consciousness appears strongly in his course as well. In the course description for geology he wrote:

> Our study of geology will be centered around the following concepts: Geology, the study of the earth, is essentially an environmental science.... Man ... must learn to function in harmony with the earth environment.... Citizen roles dictate an understanding of the environmental problems confronting man, solutions to these problems, and the responsibilities of citizens and government to work toward their solutions.

These objectives are not mere educational cant. During his classes, this philosophy is never far off, injected even into a presentation on the physical properties of minerals.

In his courses, perhaps more than those of others, scientific methods are given prominent attention. In the archaeology class he listed the following among his objectives.

> Demonstrates an understanding of the process of identifying and defining a scientific problem or question to be investigated ... of proposing a logical test of a hypothesis ... of testing the effects of variables and controlling relevant variables ... the ability to synthesize data from several sources to arrive at generalizations or conclusions ... withhold judgments or conclusions until adequate information has been validated.

In interviews he spoke of his frustration (shared by several other teachers) with both students and the district administration:

I have also had to modify my practices for kids who can't assimilate material from lectures and films. When you have such a large range of student abilities it becomes difficult to come up with a satisfactory compromise. I've had students who were five to six times behind in reading ability. This shows up not just in their ability to read but in their ability to sit in class and listen and understand.... We're just trying to come to grips with the student who isn't interested in science and we have quite a number of them. This is hard for us because we have always been interested in science. In the past even if you weren't interested in science you knew you had to take it because it was important. Now the public is questioning the value of science, for some good reasons. Sometimes it has appeared that science has been misused. People are upset with the high costs of science, particularly the space program. What they don't realize is that this enjoyable society has been brought about by basic research.... I spend a lot of time in class emphasizing the benefits of doing basic research. Like last year when the senate was upset by the studies that were trying to figure out why people fall in love. That may seem silly but perhaps the results of that might help us solve our social problems....

I always thought that the main goal of education was teaching kids, now I find out that the main goal is management. We want more money, so does every other department in the school. I have some opinions about the amount of money they spend on athletics. I'm biased. I'm in the minority.... Some teachers are no longer interested because of frustration. You can try and try, but you never get any recognition or monetary reward for your efforts. It doesn't gain anything to innovate or analyze or revise or evaluate.

There seems to be a gap between teaching and learning in the science program at Fall River. The teachers are interested in students and extremely well-prepared in the sciences. The curriculum is strong. Instruction is effective. Yet the students are not very involved in study. One teacher responded to a request for the names of the serious science students by asking, "What serious science students?" Independent study, research, and free-time participation in scientific activities are rarities. One of the highest achieving seniors explained her motives for taking an advanced science course as "a way to get some college credits out of the way."

Here is a second view of high school science. This program is from a large high school in a major city in the Pacific Northwest. The name used to identify the school is Hardy.[7]

Case Study 2

The natural science program at Hardy is strong. It is paced by an active biology program team-taught by three full-time and one part-time teacher. Currently 472 students (93 percent of sophomore enrollment)[8] are enrolled in a laboratory course led by the department chairman. The classrooms are filled with science artifacts (birds, weather maps, rocks, specimens, snakes, etc.) and the spirit of the group can be portrayed by two episodes: an open session with students one day after school to discuss the implications for science of the presidential election and a weekend assault on the walls separating the three biology rooms, resulting in open portals that central adminstration had stalled on for nearly two years.

Probably 80 percent of the class time is spent by students working on experiments and three tracks (developed locally) are provided, depending on student ability. The course is patterned after college science courses and seems difficult for many of the students. However, teacher enthusiasm and interest seem to rub off on students and they rate the course as very good. Marine biology, human physiology, mushrooms, and wildflowers are other courses offered as part of this strong program. Exactly which courses will be offered a given semester depends a great deal on student interest. A college-style registration procedure is used and if a given course doesn't "fill" (i.e., isn't selected by more than twenty-five students), then it may not be offered. Conversely, sections are added if student interest is high.

During the semester following the site visit, the life science enrollment was as follows:

Biology II	250
Molecular Biology	29
Marine Biology	53
Wild Flowers/Edibles	34
Human Physiology	53

Apparently some of those students in the first semester of biology opt for more specialized courses the second semester.

The first year of chemistry is currently taken by 146 students (27 percent of junior enrollment) and is taught as a laboratory science. The five sections of chemistry are handled by the physics teacher and a chemistry teacher who also teaches biology. The CHEM Study texts are used and the course is viewed by students and teachers as primarily a college-preparatory course. A third semester of general chemistry and a semester of organic chemistry are offered if enough students register for these courses.

Physics may be taken in either the junior or senior year and currently sixty-eight students (13 percent of senior enrollment) are enrolled. About half of the group are girls, which is seen by students and teachers as a result of changing female roles. Counselors, parents, and friends are relaxing their attitude that advanced science is only for males. The course has some laboratory components, but in general is

===== REFLECTING ON SCIENCE TEACHING =====

Instructional Programs

After reading the case studies of science programs, discuss the following questions with other students in the methods class.

1. How much freedom do you think science teachers have to design and teach their program?
2. What were some of the expressed concerns of science teachers?
3. How could science programs differ so greatly within a single district?
4. What are your concerns about science teaching? Are they similar to those expressed by the teachers in the case studies?

---

taught more like a mathematics class; that is, explain concepts, assign problems, correct problems, discuss difficulties. This routine is interrupted occasionally by exams or experiments, but the "doing of problems" dominates over the "doing of science" found in the other classes. The class is clearly for the academically elite and the teacher sees no need to try to increase enrollments. At one time the PSSC and the ECCP courses were used, but this year the Holt-Rinehart-Winston book, *Modern Physics*, is being tried and will probably become the district-wide text for next year.

The rest of the science program includes a semester of geology and a science seminar. The geology situation portrays quite well some of the current problems in the school. Because of staff cutbacks, the assistant principal was teaching one section of geology this fall. After two weeks of school, a displaced junior-high teacher was assigned by the district office to teach mathematics and science. He took over the geology class along with several mathematics classes and the assistant returned to full-time administration. The new teacher was encountering some difficulties in the class because students were irritated by the changes. In fact, in one class there were four teachers during the first month of school.

An adjunct to the science program is a popular horticulture program offered in the Industrial Arts department. In a temporary building and greenhouse located about two blocks from the main building, 113 students were enrolled in environmental horticulture. The course meets the state requirements for a laboratory science, but although it is considered a strong program by the science teachers, there seems to be very little interaction between it and the rest of the science program. It has grown through the efforts of an active teacher whose academic home is industrial arts.

The science program is strong and surviving, but it is being subjected to many challenges: transfer teachers, declining budgets for texts and equipment, and competition from the "basics." It may be seriously affected if subjected to many more problems.

Conversations with Science Teachers

In this section, comments from the teachers' lounge are used to point out some issues in science education. The observations are from a case study made in a greater Boston high school.[9]

The Role of the Experiment in Science Teaching

STEVE: (Looking through a workbook of experiments David has been using in his class) The trouble with a lot of this stuff is that it is so obvious. Even when you have done the experiment, you only know what you knew already.

DAVID: Maybe it's obvious to you, but it isn't always obvious to these kids. To some of them maybe, but not to all of them. Sometimes they do know what is going to happen in the experiment, but they only know it vaguely; they haven't really thought it out.

Like this morning we were talking about that experiment where you float a cork in water, then push an upturned glass down on top of it. They did the experiment and saw what happened. When I asked why the cork went down, one girl just said "gravity." Well, you can see what she means; it does involve gravity, but that's not an explanation of what you see happening.

STEVE: Yes, but you can't say that's exciting. Floating corks in water. I want to get these kids interested in science. I want experiments you can do that set them all off saying, "Wow! How did that happen?" Something that really challenges and excites them. (Looking at the book) Finding out 20 percent of the air is oxygen, that's no challenge. Why not just tell them. You shouldn't just have to do an experiment for everybody, only if it excites them or triggers them off.

DAVID: But before you can work on these dramatic experiments they have got to know scientific procedures and appreciate the methods. All this week I've been emphasizing the five stages of writing a lab report and getting them to appreciate the difference between observation and explanation. Those are not things you can just tell anybody. You have to do it several times and it takes practice. And for most of them, writing a scientific report is not something they are used to

=========== REFLECTING ON SCIENCE TEACHING ===========
The Role of Experiments

This conversation identified several important concerns of science teachers.

1. What is the role of experiments and laboratory work in science teaching?
2. Should science teachers start with theory and then point out applications? Or, should they start with applications and then develop theory?
3. What is the science teacher's obligation toward science-related social issues?

These case studies and this textbook cannot offer direct answers to these questions. You will have to work some of them out for yourself.

---

doing; in fact, some of them have got so used to multiple choice tests that it is an effort for them to write complete sentences.

STEVE: Maybe you are right. I think teaching them rigor and method is a useful thing to do. The danger, though, is that you end up just pacifying them. The science that is going to affect their lives isn't the five stages of writing a lab report. It is nuclear power, pollution, recombinant DNA research. Those are the things I want them to know about, and I want them to be able to pursue things for themselves, not just because they are in a course or a textbook.

Methods of Teaching

Teaching methods is an issue that emerged in several conversations among members of the cluster teams. The "conversation" reported here has been assembled from various fragments and so lacks the authenticity of others reported in this section. We hope it is no less true. We have done our best to illustrate accurately what we think is an important emerging issue.

CIVICS TEACHER: I feel constrained by the forty-minute period and the pressures of working in a building that is really only a heap of classrooms. I'd like to be able to get out more with the students and get to do more things.

SCIENCE TEACHER: I don't agree. I think almost the most important thing for the students to learn is the discipline of working in the classroom. When they come here at the beginning of the year they are all up in the air and we have got to bring them down. You've got to get order and discipline before you can give it up.

CIVICS TEACHER: By this time of year (March) they should have learned some sort of classroom discipline. The problem is that enforcing it starts to become an end in itself. You begin to forget about what you are trying to teach and just think about keeping a neat, orderly class.

SCIENCE TEACHER: I don't just think of discipline as keeping

an island of sanity in my class, whatever happens in the rest of the school. I don't think you can separate discipline in class from the discipline of the subject. In science especially, where you have expensive equipment and valuable things around, you have to learn certain ways of behaving, and learning those ways of behaving are (sic) part of learning the subject.

SECOND SCIENCE TEACHER: I'd like to get out of the classroom more because there are a lot of things I want to do that you can't very easily do in school. I think really the only way to get students to appreciate the significance of things like environmental pollution is to get them out of the classroom looking at it.

ENGLISH TEACHER: My classroom is important to me. I can't imagine a better place for doing the kind of teaching I want to do. Going outside the classroom on some occasions might have advantages. I'd like to have students going out to interview people, for example. But what they do in the classroom (which is mainly writing) has got to remain at the center of everything else for me.

CIVICS TEACHER: Sometimes I feel limited by the expectations the students have of me as their teacher. For most of them the range of things they will allow in a teacher is very limited and this makes it very hard to start anything new or different. The experience I have had in the past of working a lot outside school has shown me that you can have quite a different kind of relationship with students once you get them out of the school building.

ENGLISH TEACHER: I don't want a different kind of relationship. I want to be the kind of teacher I am.

A Key Issue: How to Motivate Students.
    Discipline is not a major issue for teachers in the high school. The school shows no signs of a faculty under siege from the students. The teachers come into the teachers' lounge at break relaxed and talkative. The corridors and classrooms seem free of the usual signs of vandalism. Between classes, students move in groups rather than as masses. The police rarely visit the school, and then only by invitation.
    If you ask the teachers about discipline, they

tell you about the problem of getting students interested in the subject, rather than how they handle confrontation. Incidents that do arise seem mainly to involve students talking in class or, at worst, talking back to teachers. The worst discipline incident that occurred while I was at the school concerned a boy who set off a firecracker outside school—an action that cost him five days' suspension from school.

As you walk down the corridors during lessons, you don't hear teachers shouting or students clamoring for attention. It is not a common occurrence for students to be paddled. The general atmosphere is one of an efficient, perhaps unquestioning institution, where most people (administrators, faculty, and students) seem mostly concerned with getting on with their work.

Most teachers agree that the key problem is motivation. "In every class there are one or two (students), perhaps sometimes it's more, who just sit there, and whatever you do, however hard you try, it's just really difficult to reach them."

One of the guidance counselors sees the problem as being a general one:

> Motivation really is the big problem here. I don't understand why it is, but looking at it rationally, students in the northeast of the United States consistently score higher on tests of academic motivation than students in the South. Yet I am sure our students are just as able.

Motivation is an issue at the junior high school, too, though here it is more often expressed as a discipline or behavior problem. Where the assistant principal of the senior high school despairs of students' (Black and White) failing to capitalize on their abilities and opting for courses below their capabilities, the principal of the junior high school worries more about disorder and changing moral values.

Local perception has it that a particularly difficult year-group is presently going through the system. The teachers say that the current seventh grade has a generally low standard of attainment, lacks a core of highly able students, has more than its share of remedial cases, and is generally immature. The principal worries about a number of the girls who seem to him to be high-risk pregnancy cases. He sees this really as a problem beyond the school's control, but worries anyway. In Pine City, parents and neighbors often make such things seem the school's responsibility. It's not that teenage pregnancies are any more frequent than they ever were, the principal explains, but he seems at a loss to understand current attitudes toward such things, particularly the lack of guilt, concern, or even foresight that students seem to show.

How would you design a program so students would be motivated to study science? What would

you do, as a teacher, if you were going to have the "particularly difficult group" next year? These are some of the questions that you might think about since you may have to answer them yourself in the future.

We return to Mary Lee Smith's report from Fall River. The following summary is, perhaps, the most succinct answer to our question, "What is science teaching like?" We use this as a conclusion because it could have been written for any of the case study reports and probably for any school district.

A Conclusion about Science Teaching

Three statements conclude four months of watching the teachers of Fall River; probing their motives; listening to students, parents, and administrators; reading the records and studying the evidence.

Virtually nothing meaningful can be said about the Fall River "science program" in general. The district has developed a science curriculum packed with articulated objectives and brimming with specified content; yet there remain differences in content, method, and sense of purpose from one grade level to the next, among schools, among departments within schools, even from teacher to teacher. This diversity and complexity suggest why national efforts to reform the curriculum become transformed, attenuated, or lost entirely before they reach the classroom. The schools have lives of their own, existing as organisms exist, to "be on with it," perpetuating themselves and protecting against assault from without.

People in schools are conscientiously doing the jobs they have defined: tutor, scholar, but also at times counselor, steward, custodian, and social director.

Teachers must juggle the expectations of the invisible, distant, and mostly impersonal profession of science education and the local, powerful, and relentless demands of teaching. The two roles do not necessarily conflict, but the latter usually overpowers and preempts the former.[11]

Complete Activity 1–4, "Investigating Science Teaching: An Interview with a Science Teacher."

■ How Can I Become an Effective Science Teacher?

We assume that you have the normal concerns of beginning teachers. Alongside these fears we also assume that you are motivated to become an effective science teacher. Three things will help reduce these fears and increase effectiveness: time, experience, and preparation. Remember that this is only the be-

=== REFLECTING ON SCIENCE TEACHING ===

Why Is Science Important?

On a site visit for the Case Studies in Science Education Project, Beth Dawson asked the question in the title.[10] Here is the conversation:

VISITOR: Why is science important?
STUDENT: Because we need scientists to go to the moon and make important discoveries.
VISITOR: But not everyone will be a scientist, so why should all kids learn about science?
STUDENT: Because no one knows what he will be when he grows up and we have to be prepared. . . . Anyway, even if we're not scientists, lots of jobs need some science.
VISITOR: But what about people who don't work in a job that needs science? What about mothers who stay home with their children?
STUDENT: Well, they might want to go to work someday and then they might need science.

Though the above comments are from students, the science teachers expressed the same ideas, albeit in more sophisticated language. Science is important because we might need it someday. There was no reference to consumer need or, more importantly, no reference to needing science for today. Why? Why do you think science is important?

---

ginning of your career as a science teacher and you cannot accomplish everything you wish, learn everything you need, or do everything you would like during the science methods course or even during the first year of teaching. Becoming an effective science teacher, comfortable in your role, takes time.

The corollary to time is experience. There is no substitute for the actual experience of teaching science. It is the one sure way that will help you detect strengths and weaknesses in yourself as a teacher. You will learn more about yourself and science teaching in the first year than you can now imagine. It will not be easy, but it will be interesting and challenging. Every day will involve you in experiences which contribute to your effectiveness.

There is something concrete and immediate that can be done to help you reduce your concerns and develop your effectiveness. *Be prepared.* The message of these two words is important. Some teachers equate preparation with knowledge of their scientific discipline. Although this is important, there is much more implied by the words, "Be prepared." We have mentioned some ideas such as plans and procedures in the classroom, adequate relations with students, enthusiasm for teaching science, and strategies and models of science teaching. Since these are in fact the topics of this book, there is little need to develop them now. One thing we can do is turn to you and ask about your concerns, apprehensions, and needs concerning science teaching. We do this in the form of Activity 1–5, "Investigating Science Teaching: My Concerns," at the end of this chapter.

■ Becoming a Science Teacher: Some Closing Reflections

One of the premises of this chapter (and book) is that you do not have to be a bad science teacher to become a better science teacher. Students entering science teaching and those already in the profession are concerned about improving the quality of instruction in science. There is ample evidence for this statement. Your own concerns and activities in studying this book and taking the methods course have already demonstrated your willingness to learn more about science teaching. Once you obtain a teaching position there will be workshops, curriculum revision, and continuing education courses. Participation in all of these programs indicates a desire to become a better science teacher.

A second premise is that you are the one person who best knows what is necessary for you to become an effective teacher. This is the reason for the self-evaluation exercises. There will also be feedback from your college supervisor, methods professor, and perhaps classroom teachers. This feedback will help, especially when you combine it with your own insights and act on the information. That is, you have many personal choices in the process of becoming a science teacher.

Ultimately, the responsibility for becoming an effective science instructor is yours. There are many individuals and an abundance of programs to aid you. But you are the person who must combine all of the elements and facilitate the science education for your students.

=========================== **GUEST EDITORIAL** ===========================

The Personal Rewards of Science

C. Stuart Bowyer
Professor of Astronomy, University of California,
Berkeley, California

"Why is doing science so much fun?" I've asked that question, or variations of it, from my first high school general science class up to the present. In truth, some of the variations have included, "Given how miserable I feel right now, why am I in this game anyway?" While it's true that any career has its ups and downs and joys and sorrows, it's truly remarkable that most scientists really love their work, myself included. Why?

There are some standard answers; probably the reason they are standard is that there is some basic truth in them, at least for many scientists. But for me, the reasons have changed with time, or at least different shadings have become apparent as my career has evolved. Let me share some of my thoughts on this topic with you.

My first experience with science was through a four-year high school science sequence, general science through physics, all taught by Mr. Brown. I loved the courses, I loved Mr. Brown, and I almost never asked why. I took a standard interest test my junior year and it showed that I liked science. "So much for the insights available through modern psychological testing," I thought. But I did wonder *why* I liked science.

I should say that I found high school science easy. I mention this because I found the next level, college science, very difficult. Difficult enough, in fact, that I started questioning whether science really was fun and again, if so, why? I eventually worked my way into one of the standard answers that I referred to earlier: science was fun, or at least interesting, because it provided an understanding of why things are the way they are. Many of us have this kind of interest, as testified by the popularity of magazines like *Popular Mechanics* or, on another level, *Scientific American*. For a non-science corollary, ponder the nearly universal interest in the "news behind the news" which promises to tell us *why* things are the way they are, rather than just the way they are. Although my college reason for liking science was generally satisfying to me, there were several disquieting aspects to science as a career. First, science was difficult for me and I was acutely aware that it was not difficult for my better classmates. Second, I was only learning the facts of science, not *doing* science, and I was deeply concerned that doing science on a day-to-day basis would be like the worst aspects of my courses: problem sets for which I couldn't get right answers, laboratory experiments which wouldn't work out—I'd best stop the list now before I fill the rest of the page.

In graduate school I made several discoveries. First, learning science is difficult for everyone. Some may find it easier at one point or another, but everyone struggles with it. My better classmates who were sailing through the course work weren't all that better, they just studied harder and kept their moaning quiet. Once the course work was over and I began to do a research project for my thesis, I discovered that doing science on a day-to-day basis was nothing like I had imagined (and feared). Instead, science was an interactive, highly social thing, with discussions with colleagues on how to do specific tasks, the importance and ultimate significance of the experiment currently underway, and why we had to get it done soon or our competitors at State University might do it first and reap all the glory that could be ours.

And the greatest joy was unquestionably when, at the end of the successful experiment, we, our little research team, knew something that no one else in the world knew or had ever known. We, and we alone, were privy to one of Mother Nature's innermost secrets. At those moments it's hard to believe that other people have to work for a living. During the course of my career, I've been fortunate enough to have been involved with a discovery or two. While I still hope to uncover a few more secrets (providing my next experiments work out), I've discovered a few other joys which, while perhaps not as intense as the joy of discovery, are personally satisfying. One is talking to my graduate students who are walking around on the ceiling because they have just made their own first discovery of one of Mother Nature's secrets. Another is the feeling that the world is just a little richer, that mankind's knowledge is just a little deeper, because of the work I have been involved with. Perhaps not much richer, mind you. But enough.

We can suggest several goals that are related to the process of becoming a science teacher.

Becoming a science teacher means continually:

1. Demonstrating an adequate understanding of scientific knowledge. This goal includes an indepth understanding of specific disciplines as well as a broad understanding of science in general. It also includes a comprehension of the role of science in our society and in the world.
2. Demonstrating an adequate understanding of the methods of science. Specifically, this understanding includes the attitudes and skills of inquiry and the application of scientific philosophies to classroom instruction.
3. Demonstrating an adequate awareness of educational foundations and the place of science education as a discipline in the larger framework of education.
4. Demonstrating an adequate understanding of teaching methods. This goal includes the ability to plan and organize activities for the classroom, to carry out standard classroom procedures, to use a variety of techniques and equipment in teaching science lessons, and to evaluate student progress.
5. Demonstrating adequate interpersonal relations and an enthusiasm for working with secondary-level students.
6. Demonstrating the synthesis of these five goals into the actual practice of teaching science in the secondary school.

■ Summary

The experience of becoming a science teacher is identifiable through the questions one asks. Here we have asked, "Am I qualified to teach science?" While it is impossible to answer the question, several activities were presented, each allowing you to inquire into some aspect of the question. We also described some of the attributes essential for science teaching: understanding science, understanding students, organizing materials for science instruction, personalizing your interaction with students, recognizing personal meaning as a part of learning, and, very importantly, realizing your own role as decision maker in the science classroom.

After discussing the first question, we turned to a second: "What is science teaching like?" To answer the question, we used a series of vignettes drawn from case studies of schools from all over the country. They represented a variety of schools and science programs.

Next we turned to the question of becoming an effective science teacher. The question seems to be a part of the natural sequence of questions asked by students as they enter teaching. Once the initial anxiety of becoming a science teacher has been overcome, individuals turn to the problem of becoming a better teacher. Time, experience, and preparation contribute to the increasing effectiveness of the beginning teacher. One way of helping to overcome apprehension is to identify concerns and act on reducing them. In this case the investigation of science teaching is a self-examination and a personal response to the question, "What are my concerns?"

The chapter ends with some goals related to the process of becoming a science teacher. The goals are summarized as demonstrating an understanding of scientific knowledge and methods, of science education as a discipline, and of teaching methods; adequate interpersonal relations with students; and a synthesis of these goals into actual teaching of science in the secondary school.

■ References

1. Joseph D. Novak, "Learning Science and the Science of Learning," *Studies in Science Education* 15 (1988): 77–101.
2. David Ausubel, *The Psychology of Meaningful Verbal Learning* (New York: Grune and Stratton, 1963).
3. Arthur W. Combs, Donald L. Avila, and William W. Purkey, *Helping Relationships: Basic Concepts for the Helping Professions* (Boston: Allyn and Bacon, 1978).
4. The project, titled "Case Studies in Science Education," was directed by Robert Stake and Jack Easley at the Center for Instructional Research and Curriculum Evaluation at the University of Illinois at Urbana-Champaign.
5. Rodolfo G. Serrano, *The Status of Science, Mathematics, and Social Science in Western City, U.S.A.,* *Case Studies in Science Education, Booklet 7* (Urbana-Champaign: University of Illinois, June 1977), pp. 10–13.
6. Mary Lee Smith, *Teaching and Science Education in Fall River, Case Studies in Science Education, Booklet 2* (Urbana-Champaign: University of Illinois, May 1977), pp. 5–9.
7. Wayne Welch, *Science Eduation in Urbanville: A Case Study, Case Studies in Science Education, Booklet 5* (Urbana-Champaign: University of Illinois, April 1977), pp. 4–5.
8. This figure is obtained by dividing the total biology enrollment by the number of sophomores. Some juniors and seniors, however, take biology and some sophomores take other sciences.
9. Rob Walker, *Case Studies in Science Education: Boston, Booklet 11* (Urbana-Champaign: University of Illinois, April 1977), pp. 6, 7, 15, 25.
10. Elizabeth K. Dawson, reported in Gordon Hoke, *Vortex as Harbenger, Case Studies in Science Education, Booklet 10* (Urbana-Champaign: University of Illinois, May 1977), p. 55.
11. Smith, *Fall River*, p. 23.

===== **INVESTIGATING SCIENCE TEACHING** =====

ACTIVITY 1–1

How I See Myself as a Science Teacher

The statements in this exercise allow you to examine your perceptions about yourself as a science teacher. The exercise is designed for your personal knowledge and need not be shared with others. Read the statement and decide if you strongly agree, moderately agree, agree, are neutral, slightly disagree, moderately disagree, or strongly disagree. Then place the appropriate number in the space to the left of the statement.

Strongly agree	Moderately agree	Slightly agree	Neutral	Slightly disagree	Moderately disagree	Strongly disagree
7	6	5	4	3	2	1

_____ 1. I am well informed about science and technology.

_____ 2. Students can generally take care of themselves.

_____ 3. I identify with people.

_____ 4. My task as a science teacher is one of assisting students to learn.

_____ 5. The meaning of science and technology for our society is more important than the facts and events of science and technology.

_____ 6. Science and technology are meaningful in my personal life.

_____ 7. For the most part, other people are friendly.

_____ 8. Basically, I am an adequate science teacher.

_____ 9. I see my purpose as concerned with larger issues of science, technology, and society.

_____ 10. I try to understand how my students perceive things.

_____ 11. I have a commitment to the field of science and technology.

_____ 12. Students have their own worth and integrity.

_____ 13. I am a dependable and reliable science teacher.

_____ 14. I usually do not conceal my personal feelings and shortcomings from students.

_____ 15. Teaching science is best done by encouraging personal development of students.

_____ 16. Science and technology are essential in our society.

_____ 17. People are basically trustworthy and dependable.

_____ 18. Students generally see me as personable and likable.

_____ 19. I am personally involved with my students.

_____ 20. I am accepting of individual differences in my students.

_____ 21. My understanding of science and technology is adequate.

_____ 22. Students are important sources of personal and professional satisfaction for me.

_____ 23. As a science teacher, I am worthy of respect.

_____ 24. The process of learning science is important for our culture.

_____ 25. My orientation is toward people more than things.

The items in this list are keyed to five important dimensions of science teaching as a helping profession. If you would like to see how you perceive yourself on these dimensions, complete the following section. Add your response for the items in the left column. Divide that number by five. The result should be a number between seven and one for each of the dimensions of science teaching listed. The numbers give some indication of your perceptions of yourself as related to the different categories.

Items		Average	Dimensions of Science Teaching
1, 6, 11, 16, 21	=	_____	Perceptions about science subject matter
2, 7, 12, 17, 22	=	_____	Perceptions of students
3, 8, 13, 18, 23	=	_____	Perceptions of yourself as a science teacher
4, 9, 14, 19, 24	=	_____	Perceptions of your purpose as a science teacher
5, 10, 15, 20, 25	=	_____	Perceptions of the teaching task

ACTIVITY 1–2

The What and How of Science Lessons

In this activity you are presented with a teaching situation on the left and asked to match a method from the right to achieve your teaching goal. In each case you should be able to give a rationale for your choice of method. Complete the activity alone. Then share your responses with several other students in the class.

What you want to accomplish—the goal	How you would accomplish your goal—the method	Methods of teaching
1. Introduce the concept of acids and bases.	_____	A. Bulletin board
		B. Demonstration
2. Clarify the effects of air pollution.	_____	C. Discussion
		D. Field trip
3. Summarize the effects of erosion.	_____	E. Film
		F. Film loop (single concept)
4. Show the interrelationships of organisms in a community.	_____	G. Filmstrip
		H. Guest speaker
		I. Laboratory investigation
5. Evaluate the students' understanding of pulleys.	_____	J. Library research
		K. Lecture
6. Differentiate the phylum Echinodermata from the phylum Chordata.	_____	L. Projects
		M. Questioning
		N. Quiz
7. Realize the ethical decisions involved in scientific research.	_____	O. Reading records
		P. Role playing
		Q. Slides (35mm.) presentation
8. Introduce the structure of DNA.	_____	R. Simulation game
		S. Television
9. Show the dynamic qualities of weather.	_____	T. Test
		U. Chalkboard
10. Expand the students' understanding of the systems concept.	_____	V. Computer
		W. Calculator (hand-held)
		X. Records
11. Review the concept of force.	_____	

12. Teach students to handle the microscope correctly.   _____

13. Outline safety procedures for the chemistry laboratory.   _____

14. Introduce students to careers in science.   _____

15. Help students understand the role of science and technology in society.   _____

ACTIVITY 1–3

A First Lesson

It is strongly recommended that you teach a short science lesson early in the methods course. Preferably, this lesson should be taught in a local science class; however, it may be taught for your peers in the methods class. An important objective of this lesson is to help you answer two questions: "Can I teach science?" and "What is science teaching like?" There is no better way to answer these questions than to actually teach a science lesson.

Here are some guidelines to help you prepare your first lesson.

1. Keep the lesson simple. Try to present a single concept, single process, or single skill.
2. What do you hope to accomplish by the end of the lesson? What should the students know or be able to do that they could not do before the lesson?
3. What experiences will best achieve the goals and be interesting and motivating for the students?
4. What is the most effective way to organize the materials or experiences of the lesson? What is its conceptual structure and instructional sequence?
5. Use the following format as the basis of your lesson plan.

Title of Lesson	
Goal of lesson (See item 2 above)	
Procedures (outline the progress and methods of the lesson)	
What do you want to teach?	*How* do you plan to teach it?
1.	1.
2.	2.
3.	3.
4.	4.
5.	5.
6.	6.

What is your plan for starting the lesson?

What is your plan for ending the lesson?

Materials needed for lesson:

Length of lesson in minutes:

Self-Critique of Your First Lesson

1. Rate the following:

	Poor	Fair	Good	Excellent	Comments
Voice quality and articulation	____	____	____	____	_____
Poise	____	____	____	____	_____
Adaptability and flexibility	____	____	____	____	_____
Use of English	____	____	____	____	_____
Procedure	____	____	____	____	_____
Enthusiasm	____	____	____	____	_____
Continuity	____	____	____	____	_____
Maintenance of good class control	____	____	____	____	_____
Provision for individual differences	____	____	____	____	_____
Ability to interest students	____	____	____	____	_____
Ability to involve students	____	____	____	____	_____
Ability to ask questions	____	____	____	____	_____
Ability to answer questions	____	____	____	____	_____
Use of instructional methods	____	____	____	____	_____
Provision of adequate summaries	____	____	____	____	_____
Budgeting of time	____	____	____	____	_____
Organization of the lesson	____	____	____	____	_____
Knowledge of subject	____	____	____	____	_____

2. Did you achieve your goals?

3. What were the strengths of the presentation?

4. What were the weaknesses of the presentation?

5. What would you change if you were to teach this lesson again?

6. Give your personal answer to the question, "Can I teach science?"

7. Overall, how well do you think you did on the lesson?

8. Based on this experience, answer the question, "What is science teaching like?"

ACTIVITY 1–4

An Interview with a Science Teacher

One way to find out what science teaching is like is to interview a science teacher. Tell the teacher the reason for the meeting and the general topics of discussion. If at all possible, make arrangements to observe a class period before the interview. This visit will give you some insights concerning the teacher's style and approach to science instruction. It will also provide some bases of discussion. You may wish to ask the following questions to get the conversation started.

1. *What is the science program in your school?*
   How many courses are offered?
   What is the enrollment in life science? Earth science? Physical science?
   What textbook is used?
   How does the science program in your school relate to the rest of the science program in the district?
   Do you offer any special science courses?
   Has the science program changed in the last five years?

2. *What do you see as the important trends and issues in science teaching?*
   Have enrollments in science increased? Decreased?
   Has the science budget increased? Decreased?
   How much do you use the laboratory in science teaching?
   Do you introduce any science-related social issues?

3. *What are your concerns as a science teacher?*
   Are your facilities adequate?
   Do you have materials for your program?
   Is student interest high? Low?
   Is maintaining discipline a problem?

4. *What are your greatest rewards as a science teacher?*
   Seeing students learn?
   Helping other people?
   Working with interesting and exciting colleagues?
   Contributing to the public's scientific literacy?

5. *Why is science important?*

ACTIVITY 1–5

My Concerns

Listed below are several statements that are commonly expressed by students entering teaching. Indicate your present concern about the problem by placing an X in a space provided on the continuum: Number 1 indicates little concern, whereas number 9 indicates a high degree of concern.

1. Developing short- and long-term purposes, goals, and objectives for science instruction

2. Understanding the scientific enterprise, the processes of science, and different philosophies of science

3. Motivating students to learn science

4. Designing programs to increase the learning of science

5. Recognizing and responding to different developmental levels of students

6. Understanding the dynamics of student groups

7. Adapting to the needs, interests, and abilities of pupils, including special and gifted students

8. Designing programs for the individual needs of students

9. Knowing about science-curriculum programs and instructional materials

10. Incorporating other disciplines, such as mathematics or social science, into the science program

11. Understanding and using different instructional strategies

12. Planning and organizing science activities

13. Evaluating student progress

14. Handling problems of classroom management, pupil control, and student misbehavior

15. Preparing for practice teaching

16. Budgeting time and judging the flow of science lessons

17. Handling routines such as making out reports, attendance, and keeping records

18. Lack of an adequate background in science

19. Lack of self-confidence to teach science

20. Presenting science demonstrations, questioning, and guiding student discussions

21. Adapting to the unique problems of school facilities, materials, and equipment

22. Understanding and using special school services such as counseling and testing

23. Knowing how to obtain a science teaching job

24. Understanding the place and importance of science education

25. Other concerns

(Each item is accompanied by a rating continuum marked: 1 2 3 4 5 6 7 8 9)

These statements constitute a personal inventory of concerns. Many of them are addressed in this book and will be included as part of the methods course. Identifying and clarifying your concerns will better enable you to direct your work, study, and activities during this preparation for science teaching.

CHAPTER 2

Beginning Your Instructional Theory

Teaching science requires continual decision making. Do the students understand the concept of equilibrium? The light burned out on the overhead projector—what should I do? Where should I use this new piece of software? Is this laboratory safe? Indeed, there are many variables for science teachers to consider from moment to moment and day to day. One characteristic of effective science teachers is the ability to act efficiently and respond constructively to numerous classroom situations. Before continuing in this chapter, you should complete "Activity 2–1, "Investigating Science Teaching: What Would You Do?" By considering different answers and reflecting on what you would do and why, you begin the process of constructing your instructional theory.

■ **Why Develop an Instructional Theory?**

One goal of science is to construct theories. Scientists use theories to guide them to new insights into the intricacies of nature. A theory is an effective intellectual tool that integrates many of the mind's processes. Through knowing relatively little—a theory—the individual actually knows a great deal. A theory has three fundamental attributes: it organizes observations and data, explains phenomena, and predicts events and therefore provides direction. It is through theoretical understanding that we can interpret and synthesize volumes of information.

As a science teacher, your effectiveness can be enhanced by your ability to organize observations of students, explain behaviors, and predict what will happen as a result of your activities and actions in the classroom. Although an instructional theory may

not have the power and utility of a scientific theory, it will certainly help you bring consistency to the variety of decisions you make in the process of teaching.

■ **What Are the Foundations of an Instructional Theory?**

There are several bases for an instructional theory in science education. Much of theory comes from the behavioral sciences. Principles of learning, motivation, development, and social psychology should be included, as well as attitudes and values of the scientific enterprise, curriculum materials, and instructional techniques. All of these elements must be combined in a way unique to the individual science teacher.

Think for a moment of the implications of knowing the theory of evolution. Given a stratum containing fossils, you can predict the types of fossils you may find above and below the layers of exploration. You can explain the processes of change. And, if you bring fossils up from different layers, you know how to organize your findings and put the fossils in the proper order. All of this activity would be very difficult without a theory.

■ **Characteristics of an Instructional Theory**

Some years ago Jerome Bruner outlined the characteristics of an instructional theory in a book entitled *Toward a Theory of Instruction.*[1] According to

=================== **GUEST EDITORIAL** ===================

Anticipating Student Teaching

Mary McMillan
Science Education Student—Geology, Carleton College,
Northfield, Minnesota

As I anticipate my student teaching placement in the fall, I am beginning to formulate my definition of a successful teacher. The ideal teacher is organized, energetic, and confident. He or she uses subject matter as a means of helping students to develop an appreciation of themselves, others, and society. During my student teaching placement, I hope to develop the skills of an "ideal" teacher. As I work toward my goal, student teaching will have a dual purpose for me. I want to help my students appreciate their own abilities and I hope to learn more about myself as a science teacher.

To recognize students' abilities, I will need to become acquainted with them and their interests. As I search for topics that interest them, I will hope for interesting moments and sparks of thoughtful questions. It will be necessary to appreciate diversity. Some students will have trouble with analytical skills, but they may demonstrate the ability to lead others, to communicate, or to be creative. To provide each student with the opportunity for success and enthusiasm, I will have to include a broad range of activities.

As I envision activities for students, I recognize one of the causes for my own enthusiasm. I believe that science classes provide a means of understanding the earth and its resources. Such an understanding is essential if we hope to protect and improve the environment. The science courses I most enjoyed were those that increased my awareness of the environment and my perceptions of change. As a teacher, the opportunity to select materials and topics will be very important to me. I hope to teach about general principles by providing a background of specific examples. I plan to infuse a good deal of environmental education in my classes and I hope that my enthusiasm for science will be shared.

As I try to share my interests and concerns with others, I will also be learning about myself. A cooperating teacher will probably provide both criticism and praise. Students' actions and reactions in the classroom will challenge my assumptions as well as my creativity. There will be times when I cannot select the exact subject matter I would like to teach. Unless I demonstrate my willingness to take risks and correct mistakes, however, I will not learn the ways in which I need to change. To succeed as a student teacher, I will need to be persistent, open, and energetic. I want to help others value their own abilities and, by doing so, I hope to become better acquainted with myself.

Bruner (1968), a theory of instruction is *prescriptive*. It gives direction and provides guidelines for effective instruction, and enables the teacher to evaluate teaching techniques and procedures. A theory of instruction is also *normative*; it is general rather than specific. For example, a theory of instruction would give some criteria for a chemistry lesson on acids and bases but would not give specific guidelines for the lesson.

What help does a theory of instruction provide? What questions will it answer? An instructional theory has four important characteristics. It should help the science teacher specify:

1. The experiences that will most effectively motivate the learner. An instructional theory helps you answer the question: What activities will encourage a predisposition toward learning?

2. The most effective way in which knowledge can be structured to enhance learning. An instructional theory helps you answer the question: What is the best way to structure the knowledge of biology? Of physical science? Of earth science?

3. The best sequence in which to present material. An instructional theory helps you answer the question: How do you present the structure of the discipline?

4. The feedback and evaluation process. An instructional theory helps you answer the questions: How and when should feedback be given? When should instruction be evaluated? How should instruction be modified?

One of the most important conditions for learning is *active participation by students*. Science teach-

=== REFLECTING ON SCIENCE TEACHING ===

A General Theory of Instruction

We close this section with a summary of a general theory of instruction provided by Paul Brandwein:

> In any specified act of instructed learning, a new environment is created; in responding to the altered environment by initiating activity involving the manipulation and transformation of concepts, values, or skills, an individual learner gains demonstrably in capacities not achieved through prior experiences but specified in the given act of instructed learning.[2]

1. How does this statement relate to the earlier criteria of optimal motivation, structure, sequence, and feedback?
2. How would you create a new environment to initiate learning activity?
3. Why do you think Brandwein used the phrase "instructed learning"?

---

ers often ask, "How can I motivate students?" You will slowly accumulate ideas and activities that encourage within your students a predisposition toward learning. Engaging the learner is difficult for even the most experienced science teacher. Recall your own response to the problems in Activity 2–1, "Investigating Science Teaching: What Would You Do?" Ideally, the problems engaged your interest. One response you could have made was the exploration of alternative solutions to the problem. Another was a curiosity concerning details of the situation. Both of these responses originated in the uncertainty and the ambiguity of the problems. But there is an optimal level of uncertainty and ambiguity. Too little, and the problem is easily resolved; too much, and there is confusion, anxiety, and lack of resolution. Part of your task as a science teacher is to help learners stay within the optimal range of their curiosity.

Once you have engaged the learner, he must continue to work on the problem. To stimulate continued interest, the rewards of the exploration must be greater than the risks. Was this true with your work on the problems in "What Would You Do?" Giving or receiving instruction should increase the rewards and decrease risks; if such is not the case, your instruction is not as effective as it should be.

Finally, you need a direction or goal. From the alternatives provided, you were asked to resolve the classroom problems in the best way that you could. The question, "What would you do?" helped define the direction and goal.

A second condition for effective instruction is the *optimal structure of the knowledge*. In most cases, this condition is provided by the science curriculum. The body of knowledge should be presented in a form simple enough to be understood by the learner. The fact that the material is in a textbook or curricular program does not guarantee this. You may

have to adapt the structure of knowledge to the needs of your students.

A third condition for learning is the *optimal sequence of knowledge*. As science instruction progresses, ideas, processes, and skills are presented and related. The sequence should increase the probability that at each step the learner understands, transforms, and applies the ideas, processes, and skills. Here again, you can encounter the problem of steps that are too small, resulting in boredom, or steps that are too large, resulting in frustration. In part, the purpose of your instructional theory is to help you bridge the gap between the structural and sequential logic of the curriculum and the social and psychological needs of the students.

A fourth condition essential to the earlier three is your ability to receive and respond to the *feedback in the teaching environment*. Motivating, structuring, and sequencing of instruction are contingent on your ability to receive and respond to cues from the students. Student feedback should in turn influence your instruction and your response to student achievement.

■ Some Ideas to Consider in Forming Your Instructional Theory

Some research findings are congruent with earlier stated postulates of an instructional theory and should be considered in your own theory.

For many years Arthur Combs and others[3] have investigated the characteristics of effective helping relationships, including teaching. Their research indicates that a teacher's perceptions of self, students, and the teaching task are critical to effective instruction. Of course, the effective teacher is well-informed about science in general. But there is also a commitment to the scientific enterprise,

TABLE 2–1
Science educators grand mean ranking compared with other populations' data reported by rank

Category	Science Educators N = 172	In-Service Teachers N = 76	Preservice Elementary Majors N = 58	High School Students Average N = 44	High School Students Disadvantaged N = 106	High School Students Advantaged N = 31	Elementary School Children Grade 6 N = 25	Elementary School Children Grades 4-5-6 N = 18
Knowledge of subject matter	4	4	4	3	4	3	3	3
Adequate personal relations with students	1	1	1	1	1	2	1	1
Adequate planning and organization	5	5	5	4	3	4	5	4
Enthusiasm in working with students	2	2	2	2	2	1	2	2
Adequate teaching methods and class procedures	3	3	3	5	5	5	4	5

and a belief that science is an important social institution.

Effective teachers perceive other people, particularly their students, as able, friendly, worthy, intrinsically motivated, dependable, and helpful. In the same manner, the effective teacher sees herself as a good teacher who is needed, trustworthy, and relates well to other people.

The purposes of teachers also play an important role in their effectiveness. Better teachers see themselves assisting and facilitating rather than coercing and controlling. They identify with larger issues, are personally involved with issues, problems, and other people, and view the whole process of education as more important than the achievement of specific goals. In addition, they tend to be altruistic and self-revealing. Effective teachers see their task as helping people rather than dealing with objects. And, generally, they try to understand the perceptions and experiential backgrounds of their students.

Why all this discussion of perceptions? Because the perceptions that you have of self, others, the task, purpose, and science influence your behavior and, subsequently, your science teaching.

Combs's studies delineated the perceptions of effective teachers. What about the students' perceptions of the science teacher? If the theory of perceptual psychology holds, these perceptions will influence student behavior. Bybee conducted research on the perceptions of the ideal science teacher.[4-6] The results of these studies are summarized in Table 2–1, which shows that adequate personal relations with students and enthusiasm in working with them consistently rank as the most important characteristics

for science teachers. With only one exception, these two categories were ranked first or second by all the groups studied.

Although this research indicates that personal qualities are perceived as important dimensions of science instruction, knowledge, personal relations, planning, enthusiasm, and methods are all important for effective instruction in science. An instructional theory should incorporate these elements, adapting them individually and in toto to the situation in the science classroom.

Lee Shulman of Stanford University reported the role and development of teachers' knowledge in relation to teaching.[7] Shulman identified three categories of content knowledge: (1) subject matter, (2) pedagogical, and (3) curricular.

Subject Matter

For science teachers, subject matter is more than information and facts about a discipline or disciplines. Content knowledge of a subject includes what Joseph Schwab called the "substantive and syntactic structures" of a discipline. That is, substantial knowledge is an understanding of the different ways the basic concepts and principles of a discipline are organized. Do you know the major conceptual schemes in your discipline? If you had to organize the information and facts of physics, chemistry, biology, or the earth sciences, what major ideas would you identify as basic structures of these disciplines? In biology, for example, one can use the organization of a molecular approach, studying biology from the smallest parti-

========= REFLECTING ON SCIENCE TEACHING =========
An Understanding of Subject Matter

Science teachers should be able to define for students the major conceptual schemes of their discipline and explain how new knowledge within the discipline is evaluated.

1. Can you identify the major conceptual schemes for your discipline?
2. Can you describe the processes scientists use to obtain and establish new knowledge in your discipline?

---

cles to larger domains, and explaining living processes in terms of molecular activities. One can also use an ecological approach in which the ecosystem is the basic level of study and individual activities are studied in terms of the systems in which they live and interact. Using either of these structures, you can develop basic conceptual schemes of biology, such as energetics, genetics, diversity, and evolution.

The syntax of a discipline is the set of ways scientists establish the truth or falsehood, validity or invalidity of new or existing claims. Science teachers' use of inquiry and discovery introduces students to the processes of obtaining new knowledge, such as observation, hypothesis, and experimentation. There is the additional understanding that knowledge must be evaluated. By what criteria do biologists, geologists, or astronomers evaluate the worth of different theories?

Pedagogical Content Knowledge

Pedagogical content knowledge describes the depth and breadth of knowledge a teacher has about teaching a particular subject. Examples of pedagogical knowledge include forms of representing concepts, use of analogies, examples, illustrations, and demonstrations. Pedagogical knowledge is the capacity to formulate and represent science in ways that make it comprehensible to learners. Effective science teachers have a variety of ways and means of representing ideas such as ionic bonding, density, recombination of DNA, or stellar evolution.

Another dimension of pedagogical knowledge is the understanding of what makes a concept easy or difficult for a learner to grasp. What misconceptions might students have about phenomena? What preconceptions do students have for objects and events in the natural world? The science teacher's instructional theory helps establish linkages between new concepts and the students' current understanding.

Curricular Knowledge

One goal of this book and your course is to introduce you to the many methods and materials used in science teaching. The science curriculum includes a full range of materials with which science teachers should be familiar. Materials are designed for a particular subject, at a particular level, to be used with particular students. Each discipline has its own textbooks, kinds of laboratory equipment and educational software, films, filmstrips, and demonstrations.

In addition to knowledge of curricular materials and how best to use them, curricular knowledge extends to science teachers' abilities to relate topics of study to the curricula their students may be studying in other disciplines. These include topics and issues that have been and will be studied in science. Curricular knowledge encompasses a horizontal and vertical understanding of both school and science curricula.

The discussion of teacher knowledge as it relates to content, pedagogy, and curriculum is obviously important, even essential, but you will need more than an adequate knowledge base for your instructional theory; you will also have to make decisions. David Berliner reviewed research on teaching and provided some valuable insights about these decisions, using the categories of preinstructional decisions, instructional decisions, and post-instructional decisions.[8]

Preinstructional Decisions

Before you begin teaching a science lesson, you should be aware of the effect of certain decisions on student achievement, attitudes, and behaviors. You must make *content decisions*. What is the content of your lesson? You must consider not only state and local guidelines but also your judgments about issues, such as the effort required to teach a subject and the problems that you perceive the students will have with the subject. Finally, you must take into account the subjects you enjoy teaching. Which are the areas within your discipline that you really like? Are you excited about introducing students to the processes of science? Do you think it most important to have students recognize science-related social issues?

Science teaching involves groups of students. *Grouping decisions* are part of your preparation for a lesson. What is the best size of a group? How much laboratory equipment do you have? Who should (or should not) work together? Should you use cooperative groups? What criteria do you have for forming a particular group? Whether you lecture to the entire class or work in the laboratory, you will usually make grouping decisions. Even when assigning individual work on projects, experiments, and tests, a group in some sense still exists.

Finally, you will have *decisions about activities*. Laboratory work, for example, has specific functions, that is, it is used to achieve certain goals. In a laboratory, students may learn to design an experiment and to manipulate equipment. Operations— the rules or norms of conduct for the activity—are also important. Is it okay to be out of one's seat? What type of conversation is acceptable? What rules *must* be followed for safety reasons?

The importance of these kinds of decisions cannot be overstated. We also should point out that science teachers do not list decisions to be made and check them off one by one—teaching is too complex for that. An instructional theory will help you to review these decisions. Just reading this section should make you aware of the many and varied decisions you must make *before you begin teaching even one lesson.*

Instructional Decisions

Once you begin teaching a lesson, numerous factors determine the amount your students learn. The amount of time students spend on a task—*engaged time*—is directly related to how much students will learn. Although this seems obvious, the amount of engaged time varies from class to class. You should be aware of the amount of time students are actually working. Engaged time is especially important for underachieving and low-ability students. These students will benefit most from time "on task," and they are also the students who are most likely to be "off task."

The *success rate* of students is related to continued achievement. Success in the early stages of learning new concepts or skills is especially impor-

tant for unsuccessful and low-ability students. If students do not experience some success in the early stages of lessons, their frustration and lack of understanding can contribute to the cycle of low achievement and failure.

Decisions you make about *questioning* will also influence your teaching effectiveness. Science teachers in particular should ask many questions—questions about the natural world are the foundation of science. The first thing to consider is the cognitive level of the question. Most teachers ask low-level questions: "What do the letters DNA stand for?" "What is the second law of thermodynamics?" or "What is a silicon oxygen tetrahedron?" Although questions of this nature have some benefit, you should remember that higher-level questions facilitate thinking and learning. Questions that require students to analyze and synthesize will produce higher levels of student achievement. You could, for example, provide data in graph form and ask the students to analyze the results. Or, you could provide information from two separate but related experiments and ask students for their predictions of possible outcomes. (See chapter 20, Evaluating Classroom Performance, for additional discussion.)

The second point about questioning concerns the importance of *waiting* after you have asked a question. Research by Mary Budd Rowe[9] confirms the importance of wait time. Longer waits (most teachers wait less than one second after asking a question) result in increases in the appropriateness, confidence, variety, and cognitive level of responses. A two- to three-second adjustment in your teaching style can result in a much higher return for you and your students.

Postinstructional Decisions

Now that the lesson unit or semester is over, how much did the students learn? Science teachers usually arrive at an answer through the tests, grades, and feedback given to students.

Testing is not the central issue. You should ask yourself how closely the test is correlated with your aims and the nature of the subject matter. Should you use a standardized test? How can you construct a test that accurately represents the content and skills that students had an opportunity to learn? You do not want to emphasize higher levels of cognitive thinking during instruction and then undermine that with lower-level questions, or vice versa.

Grades do motivate students to achieve. However, the overuse of grades or their use as coercion can have detrimental effects. Corrective *feedback*, if properly given (the earlier discussions of Arthur

Combs's research is important here), results in positive achievement and attitudes on the part of students. Your decisions to give praise for correct work, recognition for proper behavior, and personally neutral criticism (as opposed to sarcasm) for incorrect responses can all influence student learning.

By now you must be overwhelmed at the number of decisions that go into science teaching. Early introduction of these ideas is intended to prepare you for the topics and activities to come. For now, only an awareness of these decisions is necessary. Remember that you are just beginning to form your instructional theory.

Research on Effective Teaching

Research on good teaching provides some insights that may help you synthesize the ideas in this section. After reviewing the research on good teaching, Andrew Porter and Jere Brophy of the Institute for Research on Teaching at Michigan State University concluded that the concept of good teaching is changing.[10] In the past, teachers were sometimes viewed as technicians who had to apply "how to" lessons, or as "weak links" in the education system who had to be circumvented with a "teacher-proof" curriculum. Those approaches did not work. The current concept deals with empowering teachers rather than working around them. How are teachers empowered? A short-term answer is through the application of research on teaching, and a long-term answer is through the continuous development of an instructional theory. Our discussion assumes that student learning within science classes requires good teaching, and good teaching requires science teachers who

make appropriate decisions about how to educate students.

A contemporary image of the good teacher is that of a thoughtful professional who works purposefully toward educational goals. According to Porter and Brophy:

- Effective teachers are clear about their instructional goals. They inform their students of the instructional goals, and keep these goals in mind as they design lessons and communicate with students.
- Effective instruction provides students with strategies they can use for their own learning.
- Effective instruction creates learning situations in which students are expected to learn information, solve problems, and organize that information in new ways.
- Effective teachers continually monitor student understanding and adjust instruction accordingly.
- Effective teachers frequently integrate other subjects and skills into their lessons.
- Effective teachers design instruction so that what is learned can be used in the future.
- Effective teachers are thoughtful and reflective about their instruction.

Table 2–2 summarizes these points.

Science teachers have been depicted as individuals who can do almost everything or practically nothing. In reality, science teachers are continually developing and improving their approach to instruction—what we call an instructional theory. The feature that mediates between the instructional theory and teaching practice is decision-making as it applies to different teaching situations. In the next section, we introduce many of the teaching methods that you

---

TABLE 2–2
Highlights of research on good teaching

Good teaching is fundamental to effective schooling. From the studies of the Institute for Research on Teaching and from other studies conducted over the last 10 years, there is a picture of effective teachers as semi-autonomous professionals who

- Are clear about their instructional goals
- Are knowledgeable about lesson content and strategies for teaching it
- Communicate to their students what is expected of them—and why
- Make expert use of existing instructional materials in order to devote more time to practices that enrich and clarify lesson content
- Teach students meta-cognitive strategies and give them opportunities to master them
- Address higher- as well as lower-level cognitive objectives
- Monitor students' understanding by offering regular and appropriate feedback
- Integrate their instruction with that of other subject areas
- Accept responsibility for student outcomes
- Are thoughtful and reflective about their practice

Source: Andrew Porter and Jere Brophy, "Synthesis of Research on Good Teaching: Insights from the work of the Institute for Research on Teaching," *Educational Leadership* (May 1988), 75.

will apply in different classroom situations. We have provided background in research and theory for your consideration.

■ Some Methods to Consider in Forming Your Instructional Theory

When science teachers lecture, show a film, take a field trip, have students work in the laboratory, or guide a discussion, they are using instructional methods that will develop understanding, skills, or values relative to science and technology. The assumption underlying an instructional method is that it is the most effective and efficient means of presenting the material. A method should also be appropriate for the subject and students.

In this section, we introduce a variety of teaching methods. They are listed in alphabetical order along with a brief description and guides for effective use.

Chalkboard

Purpose: To illustrate, outline, or underscore ideas in written or graphic form.
Predominate Learning Mode: Visual
Group Size: Small to Large

Chalkboards are used extensively in science classrooms. Their uses vary, as does their effectiveness. Most science teachers use the chalkboard with some skill; here are a few helpful hints:

• Say what you are going to write before writing it. This allows the student to begin processing the information while you write and/or diagram.
• Use key words or concepts. Try to avoid extraneous material.
• Be aware of the relationship of ideas as expressed by their position and organization on the chalkboard.
• Write legibly and large enough to be easily read.
• Stand to the side of the material so the students can see the board and you can see the students.
• Erase the board before writing a new concept, idea, or diagram.

Debate

Purpose: To allow students to gain information and discuss different sides of an issue.
Predominate Learning Mode: Auditory
Group Size: Medium: 10–15 students

Debate is an effective way to introduce different sides of science-related social issues. While involved in the debate, students will have to understand some information concerning their position and develop the skills of analysis and evaluation concerning their opponent's position. Debate is an excellent method to encourage students to take a different perspective and engage in ethical discussion of issues. Here are some guidelines for using debate.

• Be sure the debate topic has clear pro/con sides.
• Use teams of 3 to 4 per side of an issue.
• Set clear time limits for opening statements, rebuttals, and closing statements.
• Make it clear that there are to be no interruptions while a speaker has the floor.
• Let the "audience" vote on the outcome.
• The debate can continue over several days and involve several teams in various aspects of a topic.

Demonstrations

Purpose: To provide students the opportunity to see a phenomenon or event that they otherwise would not observe
Predominate Learning Modes: Visual, Auditory
Group Size: Medium to Large

Demonstrations can be used to teach concepts or skills directly, or to prepare students for work in the laboratory. Demonstrations are often used due to danger or lack of equipment. The science teacher is the "sage on stage." The best demonstrations have a theatric quality and usually deal with something that is puzzling to the students. A few helpful hints:

• Be sure students can see and hear.
• Do the demonstration *before* trying it in front of students.
• Take any necessary safety precautions.
• Plan your demonstration so it clearly shows the intended concepts or skills.

Discussion

Purpose: To promote an exchange of information and ideas among members of a group or class.
Predominate Learning Mode: Auditory
Group Size: Small to Medium: 2–8 students

Discussions are one of the more frequent methods of science instruction. To be effective, discussions must be carefully designed and facilitated. The teacher must plan the discussion so information is accurate and students stay on the topic. Some suggestions:

- Think very carefully about the topic and initial questions.
- Have the students prepare for the discussion through reading, or a field or laboratory experience.
- Provide a sheet of topics and/or questions that help guide the discussion.
- As teacher you should facilitate discussion through planning, questioning, and summarizing. Avoid using the discussion method as a means of lecturing.

Educational Software

Purpose: To allow students the opportunity to review, record, model, and acquire concepts and skills.
Predominate Learning Modes: Visual and Auditory
Group Size: Individual to Small: 2–4 students

Educational software is being used in many science classrooms. Initial use centers on individual pieces of software that are predominately tutorial. Examples of this technology in the science classroom include word processing, computer-assisted instruction, microcomputer-based laboratories, HyperCard, simulations, and modeling. Suggestions for use of software:

- Select software aligned with the learning task.
- Use the software as part of the planned instruction (that is, not extra credit or "rainy day" activities).

Field Trip

Purpose: To provide a learning experience that is unique and cannot be accomplished in the classroom.
Predominate Learning Modes: Kinesthetic, Visual, Auditory
Group Size: Large

Field trips can be an exciting complement to the science program. They can also be a disaster. The difference between a learning experience and a disaster lies in the preparation for and appropriateness of the trip. As a science teacher you will have to decide the appropriateness of the timing, destination, and place of the trip in the instructional sequence. Concerning preparation, here are some guides:

- Take the trip yourself before making the trip with students.
- Prepare the students for the trip by informing them of the objectives, activities and required behaviors, class codes, and your general expectation.
- Make sure transportation arrangements have been made and are adequate.

- Confirm any prior arrangements for admission, guides, etc. at your destination.
- Obtain permission slips from parents.
- Arrange for additional adults (teachers and/or parents) to go on the trip.

Films

Purpose: To present information in an interesting and efficient manner.
Predominate Learning Modes: Auditory and Visual
Group Size: Small to Large

Most students are interested in films, so motivation is not a problem. Science teachers need to use films in a manner that will attain the established objectives. Placement of a film in the instructional sequence is critical. Too often teachers use films as "fillers." Doing so decreases the potency of film as an instructional method. Some recommendations for effective use of films:

- Preview the film before showing it to the class.
- Decide where the film can best fit in the instructional sequence.
- Outline some introductory remarks.
- You may wish to prepare questions and distribute them to the students.
- Generally, students should *not* take notes during the film. Have them concentrate on watching the film.
- You may wish to identify one or two places to stop the film and have a brief discussion. This is an effective technique if not overdone.
- Conduct a discussion after the film. You can evaluate the students' understanding of key concepts. Answer questions and make connections between the film and students' previous knowledge and/or future topics of study.

Games

Purpose: To give the students an opportunity to learn in an enjoyable, stimulating manner.
Predominate Learning Mode: Kinesthetic
Group Size: Small to Medium

Use of games can provide students with a variation on the usual classroom procedures. If used wisely, they can be valuable for developing concepts and ideas not generally conveyed by other methods. We have found that students tend to become involved and learn from games just as they do from other activities. That is to say, they do take seriously the lesson of the game. There are many commercial games available for science teaching. Here are some guides to the use of games:

- Be aware of the difficulty of the game.
- Consider the appropriateness of the game for your objectives.
- Provide clear rules for the game.
- Conduct pre- and postgame discussions.

Laboratory

Purpose: To give students experience in the actual use of equipment and materials as they resolve problems and develop knowledge, skills, and values related to science and technology.
Predominate Learning Mode: Kinesthetic
Group Size: Individual to Small

The laboratory has become an important aspect of science teaching. Methods related to use of the laboratory include problem solving, inquiry, and projects. Like other instructional methods, placement of the laboratory in the instructional sequence is an important consideration. For example, laboratory work can be used to introduce, illustrate, verify, or extend a concept. Some introductory guides:

- Select the laboratory that best illustrates the concepts or skills you have as objectives.
- Make any necessary changes in the physical arrangement of the room.
- Be sure materials are available and functional.
- Check any equipment to be sure it works.
- Give clear, succinct directions including safety precautions, how to handle equipment, where to obtain materials, assignment of groups, and your expectations of conduct and reporting.

Laboratory Report

Purpose: To have students formalize their laboratory experiences and make connections between prior and present knowledge.
Predominate Learning Mode: Visual
Group Size: Individual to Small

Laboratory reports can be valuable means to bring different ideas into focus, to have students consider the context of concepts and to reflect on the meaning of the laboratory experience. In order for the laboratory report to be effective we recommend the following:

- Provide a purpose for the report.
- Outline what you expect in terms of length, format, and thoroughness.

- Review the reports.
- Don't use laboratory reports as busy work.
- If reports are completed by groups, have all members sign the report, indicating they contributed.

Lecture

Purpose: To present a large body of information in an efficient manner.
Predominate Learning Mode: Auditory
Group Size: Large

Lecturing is one of the most frequently used methods of teaching science in secondary schools. Unfortunately it is used more often than is effective, especially for middle students. Some suggestions for effective lecturing:

- Be sure the lecture is organized; use an outline and either distribute it before the lecture or place it on the overhead projector.
- Supplement the lecture with slides, overheads, or charts to illustrate concepts and ideas.
- Monitor student attention and understanding.
- Talk clearly and in a manner that classifies key points and facilitates note taking.

Oral Reports

Purpose: To allow students to demonstrate their understanding of a subject.
Predominate Learning Mode: Auditory
Group Size: Individual to Small

Oral reports are the student equivalent of the teacher's lectures. Students, individually or in small groups, research information, organize material, and present a report. In effect, students teach other students. Helpful hints:

- Coordinate topics so there is an organized sequence of presentations that are aligned with the science program objectives.
- Allow students to report on topics of interest to them, or that they have selected from a list of topics.
- In order to give structure to the reports you might organize presentations as if they were to take place at a professional scientific meeting.
- Help students with any audiovisual aids they wish to use.
- Set clear time limits for the preparation and presentation of reports.
- Ten minutes and fifteen minutes are recommended times for middle school and high school students respectively.

• Have a formal evaluation form that the students know of in advance.

Problem Solving

Purpose: To give students experience in identifying and resolving a problem.
Predominate Learning Mode: Visual
Group Size: Individual to Small

Problem solving is a continuing objective of science teaching, but is not used as often as one would expect. Basically, the method is to place the students in a situation where they must take some action that is not immediately obvious. Since students usually have not had much experience in problem solving, it is helpful to do some of the following:

• Identify some general problems for study and resolution.
• Have the students narrow their study of the problem.
• Have the students give their own statement of the problem.
• Provide an opportunity to brainstorm possible solutions to the problem.
• Select reasonable solutions for the problem; try some of the solutions.
• Evaluate the tested solutions.
• Prepare a formal report using the protocol of professional papers.

Projects

Purpose: To give students knowledge, skills and understanding related to a unique problem.
Predominate Learning Mode: Kinesthetic
Group Size: Individual to Small

Many science teachers like to have students work on projects and participate in local or regional science fairs. We believe projects are a wonderful way to give students a real sense of science. If you are going to have students complete a project, here are some things to consider:

• Develop a list of project ideas from which they can select.
• Provide written guidelines concerning the purpose and nature of the project, the final product, time limits, and any special expectations you might have.
• Provide time and assistance as the students work on their projects, particularly in locating resources and designing experiments.

Questioning

Purpose: To stimulate thinking by engaging the learner.
Predominate Learning Mode: Auditory
Group Size: Individual, or Small, Medium and Large

Questioning is one of the primary means teachers use to engage learners. Asking questions can be one of the most effective and efficient means of stimulating students to think about the topic. Suggestions on questioning:

• Use a variety of questions, some convergent and some divergent.
• Provide time for students to think about the answer.
• Use questions that require thinking at different levels, that is, recall, comprehension, application, analysis, synthesis, and evaluation.

Reading

Purpose: To present information that is uniform and consistent.
Predominate Learning Mode: Visual
Group Size: Individual

Reading is central to effective instruction. Though reading should be used in science classes, it should not be the *exclusive* learning method; it should be balanced with other methods in the instructional sequence. We also encourage reading of materials other than the textbook. Guidelines:

• Use reading materials that are appropriate to the students' abilities and your program objectives.
• Assign a variety of readings (for example, textbook, science books, popular magazines, and articles or tracts of historical significance).
• Make available a variety of reading materials in the classroom.

Simulations

Purpose: To increase students' abilities to apply concepts, analyze situations, solve problems, and understand different points of view.
Predominate Learning Modes: Visual and Auditory
Group Size: Small to Medium: 5–15 students

Simulations are being used with increasing frequency in science classes. They are fun for students and provide teachers with a means of presenting situations, concepts, and issues in a condensed and simplified form. Simulations are especially useful for involving students in science-related social issues. Use of simulations can be enhanced through:

• Selection of a problem or issue of interest to the students with at least two different viewpoints.
• Be sure that key issues and concepts are included in a realistic way.
• Make the procedures clear, including expected behaviors, roles to be played, time limits, and guidelines for the simulation.
• Use lifelike materials and situations.
• The conclusion of the simulation is a good time to discuss different perceptions of the issue, how the students felt about the issue, how the conflict was resolved, and what actions might be taken in the future.

Tests

Purpose: To provide feedback to both the students and teacher about student understanding of concepts and ability to use skills.
Predominate Learning Mode: Visual; occasionally Kinesthetic
Group Size: Individual; occasionally Small

Tests and quizzes, used frequently in science classes, should be designed to provide accurate feedback concerning student progress. Appropriate and effective use of tests includes the following:

• Test what was taught.
• Use laboratory tests to evaluate the process skills.
• Be sure students receive feedback about their strengths and weaknesses.
• Use questions and situations that require thinking and problem solving at different cognitive levels, i.e., recall, comprehension, application, analysis, synthesis, and evaluation.

In comparison to earlier discussion, this section on methods was concrete and functional. Your instructional theory should incorporate both the abstract and structural and the concrete and functional. This description of methods is intentionally brief; complete chapters are devoted to some of them later in this book. You will use the methods described in this section in Activity 2–2, "Investigating Science Teaching: Applying the Best Method."

■ Building Your Instructional Theory

As you read about different theories of psychology, philosophies of science, curriculum programs, and teaching methods, you will undoubtedly find ideas and activities that you would like to include in your teaching. A teacher seldom finds one approach that fits all educational occasions.

Building your own instructional theory is a process of synthesizing the strong points of different theories, ideas, and methods. In addition, you must identify your own preferences and styles as a science teacher. The final theory will, of course, be your own, but it should be a combination of the best that you and others have to offer, tempered by your understanding of the students, school, and science. Here are some guidelines to help you continue building your instructional theory.

Clarifying Your Aims and Preferences as a Science Teacher

Take a few minutes and think about your own aims and preferences as a science teacher. Complete the questions in Activity 2–3, "Investigating Science Teaching: My Aims and Preferences," at the end of this chapter.

The objective of this step is to have you formulate, as clearly as possible at this time, your perceptions of yourself as a science teacher.

■ Understanding the Theories and Methods of Teaching Science

Study the different psychological theories, teaching methods, and philosophical ideas thoroughly. As you begin to develop your own theory of instruction, it is essential that you have a clear understanding of the ideas you are considering. We encourage you to make notes on ideas you would like to incorporate into your science teaching. Ask yourself, "What kinds of teaching situations are most applicable for the theories?" "How can I translate this theory into practice?" "What problems may emerge that cannot be resolved by this theory?" "What constitutes a consistent application of this theory or method?" Many teachers do not apply psychological, methodological, or philosophical principles consistently.

■ Analyzing the Similarities and Differences among Theories and Methods

As your study of theories and methods continues, you will find areas of agreement and disagreement. Find examples of classroom situations and see how two theories explain the same phenomenon. Can the same science concepts be taught using different methods? What are the advantages and disadvantages of different theories? Methods? The task of analysis is crucial because one theory or method is seldom appropriate for all instructional situations. Knowing the differences, strengths, and weaknesses will help you make the best decision for your situation. But analysis is not enough; there must be a synthesis of ideas.

■ Synthesizing Your Goals and Preferences with Appropriate Theories and Methods

By this stage you should have an idea of your own preferences and perceptions as a science teacher and some understanding of the theories and methods suggested by other people. The first step of formulating your instructional theory is finding areas of agreement between your goals and the ideas of others. As you begin to form a coherent system, keep in mind that you want to have a theory that (a) agrees with your personal goals and preferences, (b) gives direction and helps predict the outcome of instruction, (c) explains the largest range of occurrences in the classroom, and (d) organizes your observations about what has happened in the instructional program.

Exercise caution in the synthesizing process. First, be sure to include the essential elements of personal goals and theories. Excluding important components weakens your instructional theory and produces inconsistency. Second, your goals should be congruent with the theories and methods you incorporate into teaching science. Lack of congruence will result in a feeling that you are doing someone else's task and not being yourself as a science teacher. Third, your instructional theory should be compatible with other variables, such as the budget, curriculum, students, administrators, facilities, and the community. Failure to consider such factors can result in a sense of isolation and frustration or conflicts with other teachers, administrators, and parents.

Developing your personal instructional theory will be one of the most helpful and rewarding accomplishments of your preparation for science teaching. The result will be consistency in your teaching and the ability to transcend the minor day-to-day difficulties that are major problems for some teachers. The preceding process will help you build your instructional theory and improve your effectiveness.

■ A Final Note

Education has fractionated, divided, and isolated many of the important components of successful teaching. Unfortunately, many teacher preparation programs emphasize these as ad hoc components: "If you are well planned . . . ," "If you use this curric-

ulum . . . ," "If you understand the child's cognitive stages . . . ," and "If you know your subject." Planning, classroom procedures, methods, and subject matter are obviously important but they are means, not ends. This educational view has shifted the emphasis of programs away from the primary and crucial variable in the classroom—the teacher as a person. Science teachers with an adequate instructional theory have knowledge, plans, methods, and curricular materials. In addition, they have larger goals for their interaction with students and the added dimension of a personalized approach to education.

When the goals, theories, techniques, plans, and materials are combined you are ready to interact with students. The *way* in which science teachers combine these elements and build a helping relationship with students is crucial. An instructional theory will help provide the needed direction. Science teaching is characterized by situations that require the teacher to react immediately. The creative, insightful, perceptive, and prepared science teacher will effectively respond to the instantaneous needs of the students and school.

■ Summary

An instructional theory will help the science teacher make predictions, explain, and organize instruction. It increases instructional effectiveness by prescribing motivation, structure, sequence, and feedback.

Research indicates that knowledge of subject matter, pedagogical content knowledge, and curricular knowledge are all important to effective teaching. This knowledge can be applied to specific decisions relative to preinstruction (content, time allocation, pacing, grouping activities), instruction (engaged time, success rate, questioning), and postinstruction (tests, grades, feedback). All of these ideas contribute to the goal of good teaching. Characteristics of good teachers include the following:

- Clarity of instructional goals
- Knowledge of content and strategies to teach it
- Adequate communication with students
- Expert use of extant materials
- Knowledge of student needs and development
- Development of lower and higher order thinking in students
- Monitoring of student learning with appropriate feedback
- Integration of science instruction with other disciplines
- Thought and reflection about their teaching

=========================   **GUEST EDITORIAL**   =========================

Teaching Science

Caryl E. Buchwald
Professor of Geology and Director of the Arboretum,
Carleton College, Northfield, Minnesota

Science is important to all of us. The world is in desperate need of more and better science precisely because it has been one of the dominant forces in our lives and the life of the world for several hundred years. Science and its derivative, technology, have increased the life expectancy and material well-being of Western people but at the same time have led us to the brink of disaster through ecological catastrophe or nuclear war. Science raises the hope that we can truly progress to a higher understanding of ourselves and our interrelationships with nature.

There can scarcely be a higher calling or more honorable occupation than teaching science to young people. It is important because, when well taught, science leads us to discover two characteristics that are important not only to our own lives but to the future of humanity. Science should help us to discover humility on one hand and the ability to affect our own futures on the other.

Humility comes from studying science, for the obvious reason that we learn about our own place in nature. That we are miniscule in the universe, but domineering in the biosphere, is a position not always easy to grasp. That we are a part of the very biosphere that we dominate should lead us to realize that we cannot deny the integration of our own lives with nature.

Science is often portrayed as possessing facts and laws. Yet, when we attempt explanation in our own research, most of the time we discover that facts are contextual in time and place. Because science is really explanation and not discovery, the explanations change as we learn more or see causal relations that were previously unsuspected. When reflecting on my own career as a teacher, I am constantly amazed by how the so-called facts have changed. What has not changed is the search for data and their meaning, the use of logic, the need for verification, and the consequences of knowledge.

The consequences of knowing are important. They lead us to moral dilemmas time and time again. Atomic research has given us improved medical treatment, but also nuclear bombs. Better medical treatment has eased human suffering, extended our lifetimes, and contributed to the population explosion. It is hard to do one thing at a time. The reality remains; knowledge requires action.

What can we do with and for our students to improve their understanding of science? It seems to me that the best teachers possess two essential attributes: enthusiasm and patience. Enthusiasm stems from a love of what is being done, a belief that science is importatnt and worth doing. Patience is needed because science is a process that must be internalized. Science is not a set of operating procedures that goes one, two, three . . . conclusions. Often it is difficult to figure out the steps that were actually taken in framing a question and seeking an explanation. To require a lock-step progression from data gathering through hypothesis to conclusion not only denies the reality of scientific activity but is likely to make students seek preconceived answers rather than to invent their own explanations.

Patience means letting students seek the relationships and explanations that fit their experience. If we insist that they hunt for the right answers we end up teaching them the wrong thing; that is, that science is discovering the hidden. We want to teach them that science is a way to perceive nature. Seeking right answers also leads to the conclusion that science has answers entrusted to an elite, and that is counter to the democratic ideal.

So, we must be enthusiastic. That enthusiasm will flow from belief in what we are doing and our confidence with our subject. We must be patient because science is a complex way of thinking and it takes time for it to develop and mature.

Science teachers should consider their perceptions of themselves, students, the teaching task, and the subject before starting an instructional theory. Once this is done they can begin to formulate such a theory by clarifying goals and preferences, understanding the theories and methods of science teaching, analyzing similarities and differences of theories and methods, and synthesizing their goals and preferences with appropriate theories and methods. And, above all, the science teacher should realize that she is the most important variable in the instructional theory.

■ References

1. Jerome S. Bruner, *Toward A Theory of Instruction* (New York: W. W. Norton, 1968).
2. Paul Brandwein, "A General Theory of Instruction," *Science Education* 63(3) (1979):291.
3. Arthur Combs, Donald Avila, and William Parkey, *Helping Relationships: Basic Concepts for the Helping Profession* (Boston: Allyn and Bacon, 1978).
4. Rodger Bybee, "The Teacher I Like Best: Perceptions of Advantaged, Average, and Disadvantaged Science Students," *School Science and Mathematics* 73(5) May 1973:384–390.
5. Rodger Bybee, "The Ideal Elementary Science Teacher: Perceptions of Children, Pre-service and In-service Elementary Science Teachers," *School Science and Mathematics* 75(3) March 1975:229–235.
6. Rodger Bybee, "Science Educators' Perceptions of the Ideal Science Teacher," *School Science and Mathematics* 78(1) January 1978:13–22.
7. Lee S. Shulman, "Those Who Understand: Knowledge Growth in Teaching," *Educational Researcher* 15(2) February 1986:4–14.
8. David Berliner, "The Half-full Glass: A Review of Research on Teaching," in *Using What We Know About Teaching*, ed. Philip Hosford (Alexandria, Va: Association for Supervision and Curriculum Development, 1984).
9. Mary Budd Rowe, "Wait Time and Rewards as Instructional Variables: Their Influence on Language, Logic, and Fate Control. Part One, Wait Time," *Journal of Research in Science Teaching* 11 (1974):81–94.
10. Andrew Porter and Jere Brophy, "Synthesis of Research on Good Teaching: Insights from the Work of the Institute for Research on Teaching," *Educational Leadership* (May 1988):74–85.

═════════════════   **INVESTIGATING SCIENCE TEACHING**   ═════════════════

ACTIVITY 2–1

What Would You Do?

When you become a science teacher, you will continually be required to make decisions. An instructional theory helps you to make those decisions. This investigation directs your attention to sample situations that require decisions.

It is Monday morning. You have planned a lesson examining life in pond water. Over the weekend, the heating system failed and there is no life in your pond. *What would you do?* (Select the answer closest to what you think you would do. Then prepare a brief justification of your answer.)

1. Omit the section on "life in a pond."
2. Tell the students to read the section in their text entitled "life in a pond."
3. Have the students find other life to examine.
4. Say nothing, ask the students to find life in the water and, when they discover that there is none, have them determine what could have happened.

Justification:

As part of an environmental-studies unit the class is to examine the possibility that a local mining operation is polluting the environment. The next day a group of parents asks you to describe your science program at the next PTA meeting. Their primary concern is that you are going to cause trouble for the community's major economic support. *What would you do?* (Select the answer closest to what you think you would do. Then prepare a brief justification of your answer.)

1. Decline the invitation.
2. Accept the invitation, take samples of the lesson, data sheets, and questions the students will be answering, and be prepared to explain your goals.
3. Accept the invitation on the condition that the parents come to class and complete the lesson *with* their sons and daughters.
4. Accept the invitation and plan the lesson in cooperation with the PTA.

Justification:

You are in the middle of a class discussion. You have noticed that for 20 minutes, one student has not only paid no attention, but he has also been creating a disturbance. You reprimand him. The student merely looks at you, then continues to talk and disturb the class. *What would you do?* (Select the answer closest to what you think you would do. Then prepare a brief justification for your answer.)

1. Demand that the student stop talking.
2. Request that the student conform to the class rules.
3. Tell the other students that you cannot expect much more from such a person (hoping that public ridicule will terminate the disruptive behavior).

4. Tell the student that "we have a problem" and we will have to work it out. Then, ask the student to leave the room temporarily.

Justification:

All of the materials are ready for your first lesson in physical science. The lesson is on density. As you explain the procedures you notice that the students are sending nonverbal messages of "Oh, no—boring!" Then, several students say, "We did this same lesson last year—the answer is $D = m/v$." *What would you do?* (Select the answer closest to what you think you would do. Then prepare a brief justification of your answer.)

1. Have the students describe what they did in the experiment last year.
2. Skip this lesson and go on to the next, where students apply the concepts of density.
3. Do the activity as planned and try to extend each student's understanding of density through personal discussion.
4. At the end of the investigation, have the students answer questions to see if they understand density.

Justification:

ACTIVITY 2–2

Applying the Best Method

When planning a lesson, it is important to have in mind a variety of teaching methods to complement the many classroom situations you might encounter. In this activity you meet various situations, suggest a teaching method to accomplish your goal, and provide a short justification for the method you select. Your teacher may assign different situations to individuals or groups. The line to the left of the number is provided for you to indicate the suggested teaching method. The methods described in this chapter are listed below. Even if your teacher does not assign these, we recommend that you complete at least one situation in each category.

A. Chalkboards
B. Debate
C. Demonstrations
D. Discussion
E. Educational Software
F. Field Trip

G. Films
H. Games
I. Laboratory
J. Laboratory Report
K. Lecture
L. Oral Report

M. Problem Solving
N. Projects
O. Questioning
P. Reading
Q. Simulations
R. Tests

Situation	Method	Justification

Applications

_____ 1. A student has brought to class a newspaper clipping of a current scientific event.

_____ 2. You wish to use an everyday application as a review.

Situation	Method	Justification

_____ 3. You wish to make your course particularly functional by relating it to a "do-it-yourself" experience.

Appreciations

_____ 4. You wish to bring about the realization that we have not exhausted the unsolved problems in science. On the contrary, the more we know the more we realize how much is still to be learned.

_____ 5. You wish to develop an appreciation for the work of scientists in the past.

_____ 6. You wish to apply scientific concepts just acquired to the home situation with particular emphasis on how lack of knowledge often leads to inadequate solutions.

_____ 7. You wish to relate scientific knowledge developed in class to intelligent consumer buying.

_____ 8. You decide to try to develop an appreciation for a truly unusual scientific phenomenon.

_____ 9. You decide to try to orient the group to an appreciation for the rapid advances of scientific knowledge through consideration of what new things the text might contain for students taking the course ten years from now.

Attitudes

_____10. You wish to develop the proper attitude toward thorough observation and proper interpretation of what is observed.

_____11. You wish to guide the group in developing a sensible attitude toward those scientific problems or situations for which there is not, as yet, a definite answer.

Demonstrations

_____12. A demonstration experiment has just failed to produce the desired scientific results.

_____13. You wish to teach the proper method to use a scientific device.

_____14. You wish to demonstrate how the proper problem-solving approach can be used to answer a "why does it work" type of question.

Situation	Method	Justification

_____15. You wish to make the teaching of a scientific principle more functional by demonstrating several everyday applications.

_____16. You wish to demonstrate a new scientific principle in a simple manner which the students themselves can try out at home.

Individual Differences

_____17. You wish to make a genuine effort in adjusting to differences by teaching one concept so that the slowest person will understand it and the most capable one will not be bored.

_____18. You wish to familiarize students with new vocabulary at the beginning of a unit and convince them of the need for correct knowledge of new words.

_____19. You wish to emphasize the opportunities available in science careers in a manner that will appeal to students.

Knowledge

_____20. You wish to orient the students to the first unit of the course.

_____21. You wish to correct a prevalent misconception.

_____22. You wish to place a complex concept in a more concrete setting.

_____23. You wish to develop an understanding that our idea of what is "true" changes as we gain more knowledge.

_____24. You wish to bring about the realization that, through functional knowledge of a principle, we can group together many everyday applications.

Methods

_____25. You wish to emphasize the dangers of making quick decisions without enough supporting evidence.

_____26. You wish to use the inductive approach to teach a scientific principle.

Situation	Method	Justification

Review

_____27. You wish to conduct a drill experience but at the same time use a technique that will be enjoyable for the students.

_____28. You wish to use an instructional game as a means of developing new learning or review, or to lend variety to the class instruction.

_____29. You wish to give a demonstration using "common gadgets" as a means of reviewing material previously taught.**

You may wish to share your responses with other members of the class. These situations form a good basis for discussion.

**The original list of situations was provided courtesy of Lawrence Counrey, "Instructional Techniques," unpublished work, University of Michigan, Ann Arbor, Mi.

ACTIVITY 2–3

My Aims and Preferences

1. What do you wish to accomplish as a science teacher?
2. Which goals do you see as important outcomes of science instruction? Rank the following in order of importance.
   _____ Develop an understanding of fundamental knowledge of science.
   _____ Develop an understanding of and an ability to use the methods of science.
   _____ Prepare students to make responsible decisions concerning science-related social issues.
   _____ Fulfill the personal needs and development of students.
   _____ Inform students about careers in science.
3. What do you think is important for effective instruction in science? Rank the following in order of importance.
   _____ Knowledge of subject matter.
   _____ Adequacy of personal relations with students.
   _____ Planning and organization of classroom procedures.
   _____ Enthusiasm in working with students.
   _____ Adequacy of teaching methods and strategies.

CHAPTER 3

Understanding Science and Technology

For a society to make rational decisions about scientific and technological endeavors, the members of that society must be aware of the relationships between science, technology, and the society. Moreover, the society should have an accurate awareness of the scientific enterprise, and this awareness should lead to a realistic assessment of the potential and the limitations of science and technology for resolving (or creating) serious problems. The society should provide public support for promising scientific and technological developments.

The public's science education is the primary means by which it develops an awareness of the assumptions, methods, values, and procedures of the scientific enterprise. For the most part, the public's understanding of science is established by its experiences in science classrooms. In turn, what is presented and experienced in the science classroom is based on the teacher's own understanding of science.

How well do you understand the scientific enterprise? Before reading this chapter, you should complete Activity 3–1, "Investigating Science Teaching: Understanding Science and Technology," at the end of this chapter. It is best done as part of a class period.

■ Students' Understanding of Science

National evaluations of students' understanding of science occur periodically. The National Assessment of Educational Progress (NAEP) completed evaluations in 1969–70, 1972–73, and 1976–77.[1] In 1982–83 a national assessment in science was completed

by the Science Assessment and Research Project at the University of Minnesota. Results from that assessment were published in *Images of Science*[2] and elsewhere.[3] The most recent assessment was completed in 1986 and is reported in *The Science Report Card: Elements of Risk and Recovery.*[4]

The NAEP survey questions are written by experts and reviewed by science educators, representatives of the general public, and individuals trained in testing and measurement procedures. The questions are then administered to samples of students. In the specific case of this discussion, the questions were administered to 9-, 13-, and 17-year-olds representing the national population of students at these age levels.

The NAEP uses five levels of science proficiency to present its results. Those levels of proficiency are presented below and are described in greater detail in Figure 3–1.

Level 150–Knows Everyday Science Facts
Level 200–Understands Simple Scientific Principles
Level 250–Applies Basic Scientific Information
Level 300–Analyzes Scientific Procedures and Data
Level 350–Integrates Specialized Scientific Information

Higher levels can be characterized as interactions of increasing complexity between knowing about science and developing the ability to "do" science. Additionally, the levels represent students' abilities to use scientific information, to infer relationships, and to draw conclusions. Figure 3–2 displays the national trends for ages 9, 13, and 17. The results span the years 1969 to 1986.

Levels of Science Proficiency

Level 150–Knows Everyday Science Facts

Students at this level know some general scientific facts of the type that could be learned from everyday experiences. They can read simple graphs, match the distinguishing characteristics of animals, and predict the operation of familiar apparatus that work according to mechanical principles.

Level 200–Understands Simple Scientific Principles

Students at this level are developing some understanding of simple scientific principles, particularly in the Life Sciences. For example, they exhibit some rudimentary knowledge of the structure and function of plants and animals.

Level 250–Applies Basic Scientific Information

Students at this level can interpret data from simple tables and make inferences about the outcomes of experimental procedures. They exhibit knowledge and understanding of the Life Sciences, including a familiarity with some aspects of animal behavior and ecological relationships. These students also demonstrate some knowledge of basic information from the Physical Sciences.

Level 300–Analyzes Scientific Procedures and Data

Students at this level can evaluate the appropriateness of the design of an experiment. They have more detailed scientific knowledge, and the skill to apply their knowledge in interpreting information from text and graphs. These students also exhibit a growing understanding of principles from the Physical Sciences.

Level 350–Integrates Specialized Scientific Information

Students at this level can infer relationships and draw conclusions using detailed scientific knowledge from the Physical Sciences, particularly Chemistry. They also can apply basic principles of genetics and interpret the societal implications of research in this field.

FIGURE 3–1
Levels of science proficiency used by the National Assessment of Educational Progress (NAEP).

Nine-Year-Olds

In the 16-year period of NAEP science assessments, the performance of 9-year-olds declined slightly in the early 1970s, remained stable until the late 1970s, and then improved on the 1982 and 1986 assessments. Improvements in the last two assessments brought the average proficiency of 9-year-olds in 1986 to that of the first assessment in 1970.

Thirteen-Year-Olds

Trends for 13-year-olds are quite similar to those for 9-year-olds—a period of initial decline was followed by improvement. However, the initial decline was greater and the recovery smaller than for 9-year-olds. The average proficiency for 13-year-olds in 1986 was below that of 1970.

Seventeen-Year-Olds

Performance for 17-year-olds dropped dramatically from 1969 to 1982 and then improved significantly from 1982 to 1986. Although these results are encouraging, performance in 1986 was still below that of the first national assessment of science in 1969.

International Comparisons

The good news of steady increases in performance on NAEP assessments is offset by the bad news of low scores on an international assessment—*Science Achievement In Seventeen Countries.*[5] The scores of students from the United States—particularly those completing high school—are among the lowest of all participating countries.

- At age 5, United States students ranked in the middle relative to 14 other countries.
- At age 9, United States students ranked next to last.
- At the high school level, United States "advanced students" ranked last in biology and behind the majority of other countries in chemistry and physics.

These assessments display a disturbing trend. As students progress in school, their performance in

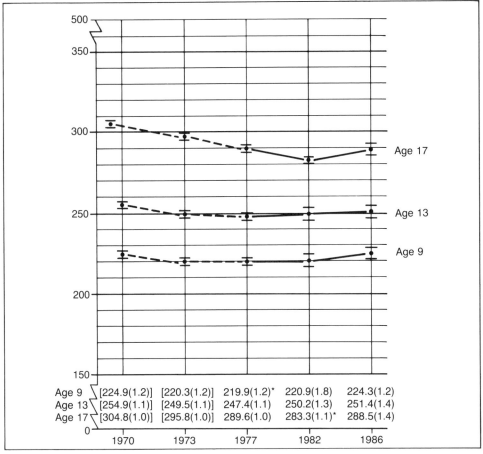

Age 9   [224.9(1.2)]   [220.3(1.2)]   219.9(1.2)*   220.9(1.8)   224.3(1.2)
Age 13   [254.9(1.1)]   [249.5(1.1)]   247.4(1.1)   250.2(1.3)   251.4(1.4)
Age 17   [304.8(1.0)]   [295.8(1.0)]   289.6(1.0)   283.3(1.1)*   288.5(1.4)

[- - -] Extrapolations based on previous NAEP analyses.

* Statistically significant difference from 1986 at the .05 level.
Jackknifed standard errors are presented in parentheses.

Note: While 9- and 13-year-olds were assessed in the spring of 1970,
17-year-olds were assessed in the spring of 1969.

 95% Confidence Interval

THE NATION'S
REPORT
CARD

FIGURE 3–2
National trends in average science proficiency, ages 9, 13, and 17, 1969–70 to 1986†

science declines. One explanation is that the curriculum and instruction is weak in the elementary years, and the early deficits of learning are increased as the students continue to middle and high school. The burden of improvement, however, falls upon science teachers at all levels within the system.

Science Achievement for Demographic Subgroups

The recent NAEP report showed improvements in average performance at all ages assessed (see Figure 3–2). Improvements for subgroups varied. The largest gains were reported for Black and Hispanic students, those often considered to be at the greatest risk for educational problems. These improvements have narrowed differences in performance, but substantial differences still remain. Figures 3–3 and 3–4 display the results for groups defined by race/ethnicity and gender.

Both white and Black students showed steady declines between 1969–70 and 1973. This trend generally continued until 1977; the exception was Black 13-year-olds, whose performance improved between 1973 and 1977. (Data are not available for Hispanic students from 1970 to 1973.)

Between 1977 and 1986, Black and Hispanic students at ages 9 and 13 showed large gains, while white students showed slight gains. For all 17-year-olds, the negative trends in achievement continued until 1982. All three subgroups improved between 1982 and 1986; but only Black students showed significant gains during the period 1977–1986. Note that the larger gains by Black and Hispanic students are encouraging, but a significant disparity still exists between those groups and white students. Minority students perform about four years behind their ma-

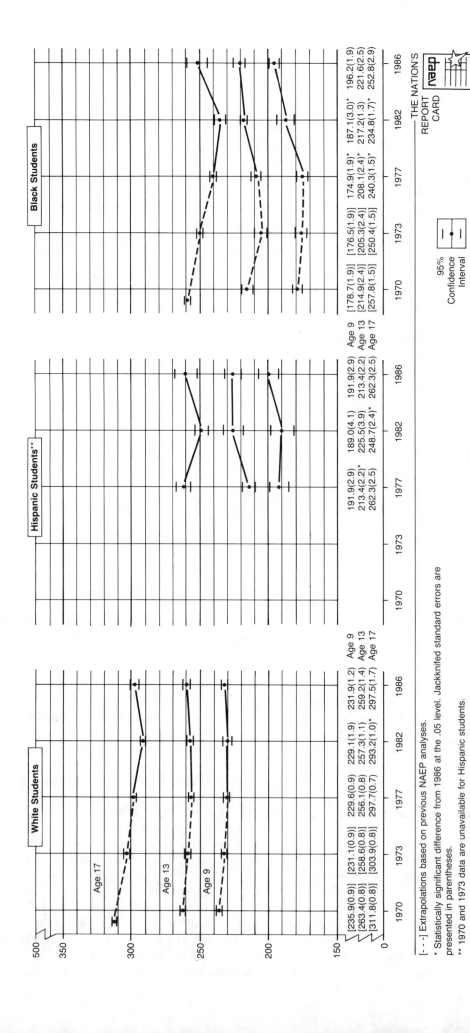

FIGURE 3–3
Ages 9, 13, and 17: trends in average science proficiency by race/ethnicity, 1969–70 to 1986†

[- - -] Extrapolations based on previous NAEP analyses.

* Statistically significant difference from 1986 at the .05 level. Jackknifed standard errors are presented in parentheses.

** 1970 and 1973 data are unavailable for Hispanic students.

Note: While 9- and 13-year-olds were assessed in the spring of 1970, 17-year-olds were assessed in the spring of 1969.

46

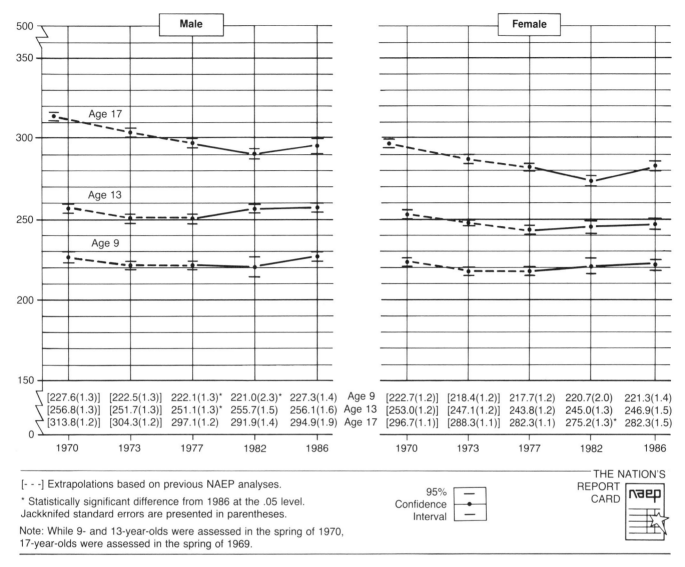

FIGURE 3-4
Ages 9, 13, and 17: trends in average science proficiency by gender, 1969-70 to 1986†

jority cohorts. This disparity in performance is a serious concern for all science teachers, and it presents a significant challenge for those entering the profession.

Figure 3-4 displays trends in science performance by gender. Science proficiency for females has been below that of males since the 1967-70 assessment. These differences were still evident in 1986. Trends in average performance have varied for males and females. Across time, however, the performance gap for 9-year-old males and females has increased. For 13-year-olds, the performance gap between males and females has more than doubled. Similar trends of decline continued for 17-year-olds from 1969 to 1982, followed by improvements for both groups between 1982 and 1986. Because females' improvement was statistically significant and males' improvement

was not, the gap between 17-year-old females and males was reduced slightly between 1969 and 1986.

In general, these trends are encouraging, but they must continue. The gaps between subgroups of race/ethnicity and gender, in particular, must be decreased.

■ Science and Technology

Throughout history, individuals have pondered the natural world. We still hear these questions: Why is the sky blue? Where do the colors in rainbows come from? Where did I come from? Why do objects fall? For a long time, people relied on answers from authorities such as Aristotle. They never sought answers through actual obervations until science emerged in the 16th and 17th centuries when individuals began comparing authoritative explanations to actual observations. The means used to develop explanations about the world—observing, reasoning, experimenting, and verifying—differentiate scientific knowledge from other knowledge, such as philosophy, art, and religion.

Science as a Way of Knowing

The phrase *science as a way of knowing* concisely presents what students should understand about the nature of science. The phrase suggests that science is *a* way of knowing, and not *the* way of knowing. The word *way* can be interpreted as meaning courses of action, habits of mind, sets of procedures, or inclinations to certain behaviors. There are evident connections to the "processes of science" and "inquiry methods." Likewise, implied attitudes and values inform an individual's actions in the conduct of inquiry.

The phrase "way of knowing" conveys the idea that science is an ongoing process that focuses on developing and organizing knowledge. A simple, yet dynamic quality to the phrase conveys much more than the traditional definition of science as both product and process.

Scientific knowledge is in a continuous state of change. In recent decades, the change has occurred at increasing rates and in varied directions. Scientific knowledge is revised, expanded, and elaborated based on new observations, better instrumentation, or experimental evidence. New theories may replace extant theories as a result of crucial observations, experiments, and new insights.

Change in scientific knowledge is governed by the values of science and the methods and processes scientists use in their work. The nature of science is represented as a dynamic relationship among three factors—the extant body of scientific knowledge, the values of science, and the methods and processes of science.

The product of the scientific enterprise is a generally confirmed body of knowledge consisting of descriptions and interpretations of the natural world on which the scientific community agrees. The tentative nature of the extant body of knowledge is a basic tenet of the community.

The procedures and standards of science are a reflection of values shared by the community of scientists. Those values include honesty, precision, verifiability, and parsimony.

The methods of science are difficult to describe outside the context of specific investigations. There is no *one* scientific method, nor a fixed set of steps that scientists always follow. Methods differ among the science disciplines depending on the type and stage of scientific investigation and whether the problem requires a descriptive or a theoretical approach. Among the methods of science common to scientists are observation, measurement, hypothesis formulation and testing, data collection, experimental investigation, and prediction. In the next sections we discuss in greater detail the nature of scientific knowledge, the values of science, and the methods of science.

Nature of Scientific Knowledge

Scientists share common beliefs about the world. They believe, for example, that the world is knowable and understandable. The universe is not capricious, and patterns in nature reflect on underlying order in the universe. They also believe that through systematic study, and application of instruments and the intellect, we can discover more about the world.

Scientists also assume that the universe is a single system containing numerous subsystems. The basic rules for one time and geographic location on the earth apply at other times and locations. For example, the law of gravitation applied in the past at various locations and also applies now. Another assumption is that knowledge gained from studying one portion of the universe is applicable to other parts of the universe. Again, the laws of gravity are the same for earth as for other planets. We have chosen five factors from a list of many to illustrate the nature of scientific knowledge.

Scientific Knowledge Is Both Tentative and Stable

The processes of science produce knowledge. Inevitably, any scientific knowledge is subject to change because new observations and experiments will result in knowledge that challenges extant explanations. So, the knowledge of science is neither absolute nor complete. Science does not prove anything once and for all time; scientific knowledge enables one to make probabilistic predictions and temporary explanations.

Although scientific knowledge is tentative, it is also durable. The processes of science often result in modification and reconstruction of ideas rather than outright rejection. Powerful explanations tend to survive and develop while less powerful explanations are discarded.

Scientific Knowledge Is Public

One assumption of science is that others can eventually arrive at the same explanations if they have access to similar experiences and evidence. Therefore, scientists are required to make public new knowledge and the methods used to discover that knowledge. What is commonly referred to as "the scientific method" is actually the protocol for scientific articles and presentations. Presentation of the protocol as the actual procedure is usually a misrepresentation of scientific inquiry. (See this chapter's guest editorial, "Data in Search of a Concept.")

Scientific Knowledge Is Empirical

Observation and experimentation are the basis for scientific knowledge. The validation or refutation of scientific knowledge is based in the physical world. Knowledge claims are tested through empirical validation.

Scientific Knowledge Is Replicable

Scientists working in different places at different times should be able to repeat another scientist's observations and experiments and derive the same evidence.

Scientific Knowledge Is Historic

Scientific knowledge is cumulative. Knowledge from the past is the basis for present scientific knowledge, which is the subsequent basis for future knowledge. Historical knowledge must be examined in the context of the period rather than evaluated in light of contemporary understanding. Similarly, contemporary scientific knowledge should be understood in social, technological, and political contexts.

Values of the Scientific Enterprise

Students should understand the principles, standards, or values that govern scientific work. By implication, these values of science are considered to be worthy characteristics of the scientifically literate person. Although understanding is a first step, one goal of science education should be to develop inclinations to apply the values of science when interacting with the natural and technological worlds. The five values of science listed below are based on the seven listed in the 1966 report, *Education and the Spirit of Science,* published by the National Education Association.[6]

Knowledge Is Valued

Knowledge and understanding are the outcomes of science. Scientists consider the investment of time and resources worthwhile in the search for knowledge.

Questioning Is Essential

Development of scientific knowledge is based on questioning current knowledge. All things are subject to question, and, based on new knowledge, subject to revision. Authoritative statements, beliefs, and self-evident truths need not be accepted as good reason to change scientific explanations. Questioning leads to inquiries and subsequently to empirical assessment; new knowledge eventually results.

Data Are Fundamental

Statements of fact, not arguments of belief or appeals to authority, are the basis for resolving scientific disputes. The basis for scientific knowledge is data. Acquisition and ordering of data are fundamental to the construction of theories.

Verification Is Demanded

The validity and accuracy of findings are open to review. Scientists should honor requests for their data, respect experimental observations made by others, facilitate replications of original experiments, and complete crucial empirical tests.

Logic Is Respected

Scientists respect the patterns of reasoning that connect empirical findings to construct scientific knowledge.

Methods and Processes of Science

Scientists use a variety of methods and processes in their work. The aim here is to present some of the methods and processes as part of the description of the nature of science. We have selected five categories to represent the domain of methods and processes of science. Our list is drawn from the NAEP report *Learning by Doing,*[7] the "processes of science" outlined in 1964 by the Commission on Science Education for the American Association for the Advancement of Science (AAAS),[8] and the report *Science for All Americans.*[9]

Observing, Classifying, and Inferring

Observation—use of senses to obtain information about the world—is the basic process of scientific inquiry. Because numerous objects and events can be observed, scientists need to impose a system of organization on these objects and events. This is the process of classifying. Inferring is the construction of explanations, or drawing conclusions based on observations and a system of classification.

Formulating Hypotheses

A *hypothesis,* an explanation for a number of objects or events, is subject to empirical testing, validation, and possible refutation.

Interpreting Data

Finding patterns and meaning in a collection of data is an important scientific process. Interpreting data

=========== **GUEST EDITORIAL** ===========

Data in Search of a Concept

François Haas
Director, Institute of Rehabilitation,
New York University Medical College,
New York, New York

At a scientific meeting I presented a study on the respiratory effects of altered upper-body position. My presentation followed the classic research protocol, i.e., the scientific method.

Hypothesis: The forward-tilted upper-body position adopted by runners aids breathing.
Method: Respiratory function was tested in both the erect and running upper-body postures.
Results: Test results improved in the running position.
Discussion: This respiratory improvement could be attributed to improved action of the muscles of the upper chest wall and neck and to changes in the geometry of the airways.
Conclusion: Runners tend, without thinking, to use an upper-body position that optimizes their respiration.
Speculation: Since people with severe chronic pulmonary diseases tend to hold the upper body in a forward-tilted position, is the consequence of this postural alteration adaptive, i.e., does it aid respiration?

Pick any professional research journal off the library shelf and open it at random. The sequence of activities in the investigation under your thumb will also follow the classic research protocol. Most people—including scientists—would call these examples typical of scientific investigation and scientific thought. Each study followed the logical sequence of activities prescribed by the scientific method. The scientist presented his hypothesis, then the results of testing it in the laboratory, then he studied his results to see if they proved or disproved his initial hypothesis, and finally he speculated a bit on what it all means.

Does the scientific method mean that science is primarily a way of doing things, the use of a particular methodology to study a point that interests or puzzles you? Is a scientist a scientist by virtue of his consistent use of the scientific method, or do certain critical qualities of science appear only between the lines of the finished product?

My research study appears to be the result of a meticulously thought out approach to studying the runner's characteristic posture. It wasn't that at all. It evolved from a combination of logic, chance, and serendipity, sparked by the capacity to integrate nonscientific interests and experience with my professional work. Its beginnings had nothing to do with runners.

Several years before, I had taught a class on pulmonary physiology and function to master's degree students in a physical therapy program. One of my students asked me to supervise his thesis project. He was interested in the effects of the upper-body posture that characterizes patients with advanced emphysema and chronic bronchitis, the two most common pulmonary diseases. Such a patient uses his neck muscles excessively in respiration.

Because the experiment would have to be conducted after working hours, it would be virtually impossible to find patients to participate. To me a master's thesis is basically a learning exercise in conceiving and implementing a research project, so I didn't view this constraint as a problem. I suggested instead that we study healthy subjects in two neck positions, the normal and one mimicking the patients he was interested in.

---

leads to development of hypotheses and the formulation of generalizations, or explanations of phenomena.

Designing Experiments
This process includes planning the methods and procedures for gathering data in order to answer a question, confirm a hypothesis, or challenge a theory.

Conducting Inquiries
Conducting inquiries synthesizes the methods and processes of science, the values of science, and the skills of the scientist in actual discovery of scientific knowledge. In addition to topics described above, conducting inquiries includes such processes and skills as communicating results (making findings public), controlling variables, defining terms, and formulating models.

Data in Search of a Concept—cont'd

Although some of the data were contrary to findings reported in the literature, we were handicapped in attempting to explain or reconcile this disparity. Previous investigators had not described their experimental neck positions sufficiently for us to know whether we had duplicated them or not. My student wrote his thesis, explaining his results as best he could. His learning experience was complete and we both forgot the project.

That fall I began running to condition myself for a winter vacation of cross-country skiing. Because I live in a large city, the area where I run is densely populated with fellow runners. I began to notice, with growing interest, that most ran with the torso tilted slightly forward and the neck stretched forward. The neck position was very similar to the one that my student and I had used in simulating a patient with severe pulmonary disease. The first time that I browsed through a collection of running publications I was struck by the photographs of world-class runners. They all ran in this posture. I dug the student's thesis out of my file and reread it. I realized that we had ignored the torso, focusing solely on neck position. I replicated our original experiment on myself. It immediately became obvious to me that altering only the neck from the normal erect posture brought antagonistic muscles into play, thereby impeding respiration. My former student and I collaborated on a repetition of the entire study, adding the "running" posture to the two neck positions we had previously used. This time our findings agreed with the existing literature.

Our next step was to document the runners' posture, which we did by randomly photographing runners during a marathon. Then we realized that these photographs also held the key to discovering the cause behind the respiratory benefits of this posture. As we studied our collection of

photographs, it became clear that the upper-chest-wall musculature shifted into a more advantageous position, improving leverage during inspiration. The interpretation of our data raised a sequence of fundamental questions:

1. Is the characteristic runner-like posture, adapted by the pulmonary patient, an adaptive one in terms of respiration?
2. If it is, can the exhausted runner fighting for breath serve as a model for the pulmonary patient struggling for air when at rest?
3. If it is a useful model, would it mean that there is a continuum of respiratory function along which the bedridden patient, the "normal" person, and the elite marathon runner all fall, or are there qualitatively different conditions?
4. If there is such a continuum, can the methods for training marathon runners be adapted for rehabilitating the pulmonary patient?

We ended up where we began, studying the posture of the pulmonary patient, but look at the ground we covered in between and the perspective and direction our travels gave us. The dead-ended master's thesis would have gathered dust in my file cabinet if I left science behind me when I locked the laboratory door at the end of my working day. The final results of our work were translated into the classic methodological structure strictly for the purpose of professional communication.

Sometimes productive research projects really do follow these neat classical lines of development. More often they don't. Science is not just a way of doing. It is a way of seeing, a way of thinking. The scientist's curiosity is a way of life. All of the scientist's experiences are potential sources for observations. All of his observations are potential sources for progress and insight in the laboratory.

Technology as a Way of Adapting

Technology is as old as the human species. The development and use of tools is characteristic only of humans. The primary goal of those who develop technologies is adaptation. Other expressions of this goal include extending the senses, improving the quality of life, and bettering the human condition.

The phrase "technology as a way of adapting"

has the same qualities and characteristics as the phrase "science as a way of knowing," simultaneously conveying a sense of process and product. The phrase *"way of adapting"* broadens the meaning of technology, which is more than computers and space shuttles. Through analysis, one can evaluate why a particular technology was designed and measure the effectiveness of various devices in achieving those purposes.

Technology originates with a problem of human adaptation. The devices and processes used to resolve the problem are constrained by information, physical laws, and the properties of materials. A number of other factors are involved, including societal values, aesthetics, costs, risks, and benefits. One of the essential underlying values of the process of developing technologies is efficiency: getting the best device that has the greatest benefit, the lowest cost, and the least amount of risk.

Technology Involves Control

The goal of human adaptation with its attendant technological systems involves control. Comparison of what is happening with what *ought* to be happening within a system, and making appropriate adjustments, is the essence of technological control. Thermostats, automobiles, and airplanes are all examples of systems where there is input to the system, adjustment, ouput that results in further input, and so on. Control of heat, combustion rate, and speed, respectively, are controlled in the examples just cited.

Technologies Have Unintentional Effects

Technologies are neither entirely beneficial nor totally detrimental. Work can be made more efficient by a technology, but workers may suffer from its effects. It is very difficult to predict all the outcomes of a new technology, which is the reason that engineers include risk/benefit analysis and the government requires impact statements, evaluation of new drugs, and assessment of safety for new products.

Technologies Eventually Fail

There is an easy way to express this idea: *things break.* Just as scientific explanations are not enduring, so technological solutions are not permanent. Materials wear, systems malfunction, and parts break, resulting in eventual failure of technological systems.

Relationships Between Science and Technology

Modern science and technology are closely linked in their processes and their products. Technology contributes to the advancement of science, and likewise, scientific understanding facilitates technological innovations. Technological advances have allowed scientists to "see" larger portions of space and smaller portions of cells. Measurement, data collection, treatment of samples, and analysis of data are all greatly enhanced by technology. At the same time, scientific knowledge aids technology. For example, scientific knowledge helps engineers estimate the strength and durability of materials.

Figure 3–5 illustrates the relationship between science and technology and their relationship to educational goals. Note that science originates from questions about the natural world while technology originates from problems of human adaptation. Both science and technology apply certain methods to answer the questions and solve the problems, and many of those methods are similar. These processes result in proposed explanations and solutions for science and technology, respectively. Those explanations and solutions in turn pose new questions and problems, and so the processes continue. Connections to society and to individuals are primarily a result of using the scientific explanations and technological solutions.

■ Science and Philosophy

The 16th and 17th centuries marked the birth of empirical science. Prior to this time the philosophy of science was influenced by Platonism and by Aristotle's deductive method. The search for truth was centered in the analysis of universal ideas, and there was little interest in verification through experience. The exposition of logical inconsistencies or an appeal to the authority of Plato's and Aristotle's writing were used to solve arguments.

Francis Bacon and Rene Descartes both developed empirical methods. They maintained that there was little need to appeal to authority, for each person could find truth either through careful observation or through the power of the intellect. Descartes criticized the appeal to the authority of others. Since he could not find one person whose opinions seemed authoritative, he formed his own methods of obtaining knowledge.[10]

Bacon and Descartes encouraged individuals to think for themselves and described methods for discovering truths. For Bacon, the "authority" concerning the solution to problems was sensual perception and for Descartes it was the intellect.

For Descartes, the foundation of knowledge rested on clear and distinct ideas. The method for arriving at these ideas is paraphrased from his *Discourse on the Methods of Rightly Conducting the Reason and Seeking for Truth in the Sciences.*[11]

1. Accept nothing as true which is not clearly recognized to be true. Avoid prejudice in judgments and accept nothing more than is presented to the mind so clearly and distinctly that there is no doubt about the statement's truth.
2. Divide the problems into parts for further resolution.
3. Study the objects that are simplest and easiest to understand, later raising by degrees to an order

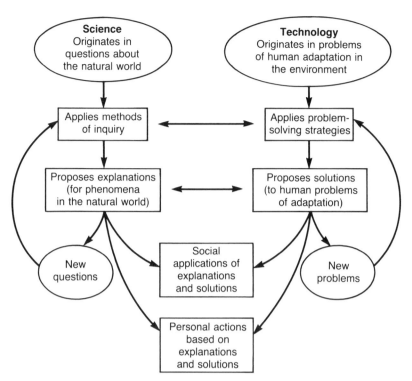

FIGURE 3–5
The relationship between science and technology and their connection to educational goals

of more complex knowledge those observations which do not follow the natural sequence.

4. Make observations so complete and reviews so general that nothing is omitted.

These statements represent the initial methodology of rationalism, a philosophy that emphasizes the exercise of reason and thought as a valid basis for knowledge. Descartes' rational method centers on the scientist's mind which, through insight and induction, combined with systematic doubt, results in new knowledge. This method has been criticized by empiricists because of Descartes' metaphysical assumptions of preexisting knowledge in the mind of the scientist.

■ A Model of Scientific Induction

Francis Bacon's method for discovering knowledge started the empiricist tradition. Bacon criticized Descartes' method in *Anticipation of the Mind* and *Interpretation of Nature*.[12] In these works, Bacon described two empirical methods and stated that the interpretation of nature without subjective input by the scientist is the correct scientific approach.

Unlike Descartes, Bacon's method did not involve a prior reasoning that resulted in obvious and unquestionable knowledge; rather, Bacon's method was empirical. The scientist starts with observations and forms wider and wider generalizations about the

physical world. The generalizations are then checked by experiment.

The goal of Bacon's method was to discover knowledge in the physical world of nature, not the psychological world of the scientist's mind. He claimed that if his methods were followed, the truth would be discovered.

Bacon's Methods

Observation of things and events was the first step in the Baconian method. Then, he moved inductively from specific observations to generalizations, being careful not to make this jump directly. He proposed experiments to guard against any "anticipation of the mind" in these observations.

At this point in Bacon's method the scientist would deduce from a generalization, conduct an experiment, and look for confirming or refuting instances of the generalization.

> Now experiments of this kind have one admirable property and condition; they never miss or fail. For since they are applied, not for the purpose of producing any particular effect, but only of discovering the natural cause of some effect, they answer the end equally well whichever may they turn out; for they settle the question.[13]

Pointing out the importance of a negative instance of an experiment is a significant contribution of the Baconian method to scientific investigation. If a negative instance occurs during an experiment, the basic principle must be modified to include the discrepant event. Through the process of experimentation, the lesser principles develop to middle principles, and, finally, to the most general principle.

Bacon espoused the inductive method, in which facts are accumulated and slowly guide the individual to knowledge. Knowledge grows steadily from observations to axioms of increasing importance and generalization, with periodic experiments which result in verification or modification of the principle. If an experiment fails to verify the principle, the principle is changed to account for the results. The inductive procedure, if it is correctly done, reveals natural truths or major generalizations.

Bacon pursued answers to the question "How can one guard against and eliminate error in finding new knowledge?" or "Which method will produce verifiable knowledge?" According to Bacon, if the correct method is used and erroneous knowledge is found, the fault is with the scientist because truth exists; it doesn't change and Bacon's is the correct method for finding it. This argument leaves the observer at fault for either incorrectly using the method or allowing prejudice and bias to enter into the observations. In science classrooms this argument is simply translated to "You made a mistake in the procedures" or "You did not record what actually happened."

There are several historical examples that seem to exemplify the position of a classical Baconian method: the generalizations of planetary laws described by Johann Kepler after long and tedious review of Tycho Brahe's accumulated records; Charles Darwin's accumulation of numerous observations and the slow development of his theories on evolution; and, in the realm of psychology, Sigmund Freud's long and slow production of his psychoanalytic theory based on extensive clinical observation.

The Role of the Scientist in the Baconian Method

For Bacon, knowledge existed in natural phenomena. Knowledge is real and can be observed in natural events; therefore, the role of the scientist is to find and record it. Truth is revealed with the aid of a pure mind and correct method. Assuming proper method, error results only from prejudice and/or ignorance and bias by the observer. Bacon felt that the scientist must purge his mind of anticipation, conjectures, or interpretations; scientists are not to imagine or suppose but to discover what exists in nature.

The Logical Problem in Bacon's Method

Human factors, such as misinterpretation of the facts and unreliable observations, are continuing prob-

lems for Baconian methodology. A much more serious problem in his philosophy is that of logic. The logical problem was described by David Hume in 1748. Hume was concerned with the question, "What is the nature of reasoning as related to matters of fact?" He said that "cause and effect" was the answer. He continued by asking, "What is the foundation of reasonings and conclusions concerning cause and effect?" Experience was his answer. Finally, and most importantly, he asked, "What is the foundation of the conclusions from experience?" At this point he discovered the logical problems of the Baconian methodology.[14]

Hume's criticism of the Baconian method was the logical fallacy committed in the progression from observable facts to general principles. For instance, I have observed that the sun rises every morning and, therefore, it can be generalized that the sun will rise every morning in the future. Or, all swans that I have observed are white. Therefore, I make the generalization that all swans are white. The crucial point of the logical fallacy is the induction from the facts, observed in the past, to the untested generalizations concerning the future. The sun may not rise every morning; in fact, it probably will not, albeit millions of years from now.

And, we have not observed *all* swans; there may be living swans that have not been observed and there are swans yet unborn that may not be white. Logically, one cannot observe a few and generalize to all. Hume's critique is contained in *An Enquiry Concerning Human Understanding.*

> As to past *Experience,* it can be allowed to give direct and certain information of those precise objects only, and that precise period of time, which fell under its cognizance: but why this experience should be extended to future times, and to other objects, which for aught we know may be only in appearance similar; this is the main question on which I would insist. . . .At least, it must be acknowledged that there is a certain step taken; a process of thought, and an inference, which wants to be explained.[15]

Hume's criticism influenced the philosophy of science by attempting to overcome the logical fallacy committed through the induction from specific observations to generalizations.

So, what did Hume suggest that scientists do to overcome these problems? Here is his proposition. First consult experience, combine the facts of experience into effects, and then deduce causes from the effects. The major shift from the Baconian to Hume's method is in the interpretation of what is observed. In the Baconian method, experiences are specific instances of causes; they are grouped into axioms from which experiments are used to check the accuracy of the induction from the particular facts. On confirmation or modification of the experience the general principles are inductively deduced.[16]

■ A Model of Scientific Deduction

The orientation in the empiricist methods of scientific inquiry is that theories must be submitted to the test of experience to be valid. Hume and other British empiricists such as John Locke and George Berkeley influenced the development of 19th century forms of empiricism, of which logical positivism has had an important influence on the philosophy of science.

Logical Positivism

As indicated earlier, the empiricists find fault with any metaphysical arguments concerning knowledge. Scientific methods cannot admit theories which cannot be tested directly by experience. The problems of science, for the logical positivists, should be confined to descriptive generalizations which can, either immediately or in the future, be directly verified by experience. There is disagreement among positivists concerning the degree to which scientific theories must be capable of observation and verification but, in general, a positivist is skeptical about scientific theories or assumptions which apparently cannot be reduced to direct experience and observation.

The Method of Logical Positivism

The first step in the method of logical positivism is the collection of data, that is, observed instances (effects) of something (cause). These data are in and of themselves meaningless until they are combined with other observations.

Next is the formulation of an operational definition. The observable conditions (general data, i.e., effects) are stated so that the definition can be empirically observed as either true or false, for example, "Do the words (definition) correspond to actual things or behavior?" These new observations constitute fact; they are instances of operationally defined concepts. This step establishes the concept as having meaning.

As the operational definitions are combined they produce generalizations or universal statements. Since the generalizations assert more than has been observed, they may prove to be inaccurate. The role of experimentation enters here. Experimental testing of the generalizations verifies their accuracy. The effects have been described, grouped, and generalized; now they are to be checked with the causes by deduction from the generalization to a specific experiment. A positive result verifies or confirms the generalization. A negative result weakens the generalization or logically refutes it. The generalization can be preserved by modifying it or by adopting new concepts.

In *Language, Truth and Logic*, A. J. Ayer, a noted empiricist, discussed the principle of verification.

> The principal of verification is supposed to furnish a criterion by which it can be determined whether or not a sentence is literally meaningful. A simple way to formulate it would be to say that a sentence had literal meaning if and only if the proposition it expressed was either analytic or empirically verifiable.[17]

Ayer also asked the rhetorical question. " What is the criterion by which we test the validity of an empirical proposition?"

> The answer is that we test the validity of an empirical hypothesis by seeing whether it actually fulfills the function which it is designed to fulfill. And we have seen that the function of an empirical hypothesis is to enable us to anticipate experience. Accordingly, if an observation to which a given proposition is relevant conforms to our expectations, the truth of that proposition is confirmed. One cannot say that the proposition has been proved absolutely valid, because it is still possible that a future observation will discredit it. But one can say that its probability has been increased. If the observation is contrary to our expectations, then the status of the proposition is jeopardized. We may preserve it by adopting or abandoning other hypotheses; or we may consider it to have been confuted.[18]

Ayer's statements briefly describe the problem of verification or confirmation of a proposition or hypothesis. The strength of support for a hypothesis depends on various characteristics of the observed evidence. Variables such as quantity of supporting evidence, absence of unfavorable evidence, the variety and diversity of evidence, and the precision of the experiments all contribute to the strength and validity of the initial propositions.[19] It should be pointed out that the logic of the confirmation process is still not fully understood by philosophers.[20]

The positivist method is not a set of rules for discovery, as described by Bacon, but, rather, a set of rules and procedures for stating scientific ideas. In science teaching this procedure has taken the form of the "scientific method," which includes:

1. Stating the problem
2. Formulating a hypothesis
3. Designing an experiment
4. Making observations

5. Recording data from the experiment
6. Confirming the hypothesis
7. Forming conclusions

These steps are the ways in which scientific information is to be reported. They are based on the logical positivist's approach to science.

The role of the scientist in the positivist system is to record the facts without bias or psychological projections, then transform them into carefully written operational definitions. These definitions are then combined to form larger generalizations and, finally, theories. There is a deduction from the generalization and a confirmation by experiment. The positivist method attempts to be valueless and neutral; its strengths are in the logical construction and the clear language used to describe nature.

The objectivity of science is defended by the empiricist for three reasons. First, science starts from publicly observable data that are described in language free of theoretical assumptions. Second, the generalizations or theories of science can be confirmed or refuted by comparison with experimental data. Third, the choice between theories can thus be rational, objective, and based on specifiable data. In the late 1950s and early 1960s the ideas of empiricism were strongly criticized by other philosophers. In general, these criticisms were: (1) all data are value-laden and have theoretical assumptions; (2) theories are not confirmed or falsified through single experiments: (3) there are no value-free criteria for choice between theories.[20,21]

The Collection of Data

One of the first tenets of positivism to be criticized was the contention that data could be collected and described in a neutral observational language, independent of theory. This contention omitted the role of the scientist's creative imagination in the development of theories. One of the philosophers who criticized the positivist conception of theory construction was Michael Polanyi. Polanyi clearly states his position, and that of strict empiricists, concerning the collection of data in *The Study of Man:*

> Natural science has been taught to regard itself as a mere description of experience, a description which can be said to explain the facts of nature only in so far as it represents individual events as instances of general features. And since such representation of the facts is supposed to be guided merely by an urge to simplify our account of them, rival explanations are professed to be merely competing descriptions between which we choose the most convenient.[22]

Actually, two criticisms are contained in this statement by Polanyi, the collection of data and the concept of valueless choice between rival theories. Polanyi criticized strict empiricism for eliminating the human experience as a part of the scientific enterprise, and argued that elimination of the scientist's mind weakens the structure of science.

Concerning the role of the scientist in the collection of data, Polanyi centered on the mind of the scientist and argued that his creative imagination should be accepted as an important element in the growth of knowledge. He advocated a change in the ideal of knowledge. The participation of the scientist, the knower, in shaping knowledge has not recognized the true power of our cognitive abilities.[23] Polanyi also advanced the idea that there are two kinds of knowledge, both important to science: explicit and tacit knowledge.[24] The tacit dimension of human knowledge is an internal, preconscious, or nonrational conception based on the idea that we can know more than we can communicate.

Values and Science

In *Science and Human Values,*[25] Jacob Bronowski discussed the values inherent in the scientific enterprise. Bronowski's discussion is a step beyond the scientist's simple, individual testing of what is true or false. The growth of knowledge relies on other people; the endeavor of scientists is not a unilateral effort. The growth of knowledge is a collateral enterprise. Bronowski agrees with Polanyi concerning the tacit dimension of human understanding; however, Bronowski carries the idea a step further by asserting that our descriptions of nature are veiled by uncertainty.[26,27] Bronowski differentiates between the facts of science and the activity of science. Since there are values inherent in the sciences, Bronowski argues that the activity of science is not neutral.[28] Based on the value of truth as the goal of science, he derives other important values such as independence, freedom, and the right to dissent.

> This is why the values of science turn out to be recognizably the human values: because scientists must be men, must be fallible, and yet as men must be willing and as a society must be organized to correct their errors.[29]

It is this type of reasoning that led us to include "the person" as a third part of our definition of science.

Commitment to Paradigms

Thomas Kuhn's book, *The Structure of Scientific Revolution*,[30] has been influential in the controversy among philosophers of science concerning the relation of observations, experiments, and theories. Kuhn's ideas were particularly influential as a counter argument to the positivist's position that theories are confirmed or falsified through single experiments and that the selection of theories is rational and objective.

The first theme of Kuhn's book is that paradigms dominate the scientific enterprise. In *The Structure of Scientific Revolution* there are two important uses for the term paradigm. First, a paradigm is a "universally recognized scientific achievement that for a time provides model problems and solutions to a community of practitioners."[31] In this context, paradigms provide broad conceptual and methodological orientations that are founded in the "shared examples" through which individuals learn about dominating theories within scientific disciplines. The types of research questions, the metaphysical assumptions, and the types of acceptable results for working (normal) scientists are implicitly defined by the dominating scientific paradigm.

The second use of the term has a distinctly socio-psychological orientation. In a postscript written in 1969, Kuhn discussed the socio-psychological dimensions of a paradigm as a "shared commitment." He says that a paradigm "stands for the entire constellation of beliefs, values, techniques, and so on, shared by members of a given community."[32]

"Normal" science continues when a paradigm is not in revolution. There are three types of inquiry that occur during periods of normal science: investigations into important revealing aspects of the paradigm, articulation of its various components, and verification of its theoretical predictions. Research in normal science is guided by the paradigms, that is, the scientific attempt to shape nature into forms predicted by the paradigm.

The second theme of Kuhn's book is that scientific revolutions are major shifts from an existing paradigm to a new one. During the period of normal science, experiments often do not verify or confirm the paradigm; thus, there are anomalous results. At first the anomalies are set aside or accommodated through ad hoc modifications of basic assumptions. As these anomalies increase, the structure of the old paradigm is rejected and replaced by the new one. This shift amounts to a scientific revolution. Kuhn also points out that the choice between two different paradigms is not determined by the normally conceived rational, objective criteria. There is much personal resistance by scientists to the new paradigms

and Kuhn writes about the older generation of scientists being "converted" to the new paradigm. According to Kuhn, the paradigm shift or revolution is much more subjective than is usually presented by philosophers and scientists. This statement refers to the criticism made against the logical positivists that choices between two theories are not value-free.

There are two other themes that have been briefly mentioned: (1) observations and experiments by scientists are paradigm-dependent, and (2) there is no neutral observation language. All the data observed and recorded are theory-laden, that is, they are dependent on the paradigm within which the scientist is working.

■ A Model of Scientific Conjecture and Refutation

For positivists the principle of verification seemed simple and straightforward. The only meaningful statements are operational definitions and empirical propositions verifiable by sense experience. However, one cannot verify a theory by showing that conclusions deduced from it agree with an experiment, since future experiments may conflict with the theory and other theories may also explain the present evidence. In short, verification is induction in reverse; thus, a logical fallacy is committed when universal generalizations are stated. This problem was pointed out by Karl Popper, who described a method of conjecture and refutation in science.

The inductive and deductive approaches attempt to establish valid and verifiable knowledge through correct use of a scientific method. Their basic assumption is that knowledge exists in nature; they then assume that if it is discovered through right procedures and methods, it is valid and reliable. Thus the body of knowledge is increased. The questions asked by the earlier philosophers were, "What is the best method for obtaining knowledge?" and "How do we justify our knowledge claims?" Attempts to answer these questions are found in the various methods described earlier. Popper changes the question; he is primarily interested in the growth of knowledge. His question is, "How can we hope to detect and eliminate error as we accumulate knowledge?"[33]

Truth is still the goal of Popper's approach to scientific inquiry; however, it is a much more abstract conception than that of the other systems. For Popper, truth is beyond the scientist's reach. Science must try to approach this ideal and must also realize that accumulated knowledge is short of this highest goal.

Karl Popper's Method

Popper starts with the problem concerning the growth of knowledge. Whereas other were concerned with sources of knowledge, Popper asserts:

> Never mind the source, or the sources, from which it may spring. There are many possible sources, and I may not be aware of half of them; the origins or pedigrees have in any case little bearing on the truth.[34]

All sources of knowledge are welcome. The problem of a scientist then is to try to determine the degree of fallibility of the knowledge. Neither observation nor intuition is reliable. Since knowledge advances mainly through modification of earlier knowledge, attempts must be made to refute the assertions. Through criticism and attempts to find error, science will continue to grow with a minimum of erroneous knowledge.

Repeated observations and experiments are tests; they are attempts to refute the original conjectures. If the results are positive, they have affirmed the hypothesis, but in Popper's method the assertion is that they have failed to refute the hypothesis, so the conjecture is tentatively accepted. This assertion avoids the logical problems indicated earlier. A negative instance refutes the conjectures and provides new sources for them.

Theories are universal but not absolute explanations; they are conjectures, tentative and subject to logical and empirical criticism.[35] Some critics of Popper's philosophy have asked, "Is a theory not a universal statement and therefore in violation of the rules of logic?" Popper's method is not to produce theories; it is to eliminate false theories.[36]

> Without waiting, passively, for repetitions to impress or impose regularities upon us, we actively try to impose regularities upon the world. We try to discover similarities in it, and to interpret it in terms of laws invented by us. Without waiting for premises we jump to conclusions. These may have to be discarded later, should observation show that they are wrong. . . .This was a theory of trial and error—of conjecture and refutation.[37]

■ Summary

Understanding science is essential in today's society. The public's understanding of science is largely influenced by its experiences in science classrooms. It is therefore important that science teachers understand science and give an accurate representation of it in their classrooms.

According to NAEP data, science proficiency of 9-, 13-, and 17-year-olds has increased since 1982. Still, the achievement level is lower than 1970 achievement levels. Although these trends are an improvement, international comparison indicates that U.S. students are among the lowest in performance of all participating countries. Achievement of demographic subgroups—Hispanic, Black, and females—has improved in recent assessments. Still, achievement of these groups is lower than among their age cohorts who are male and white.

Science originates from questions about the natural world, and technology originates from problems of human adaptation. Science and technology answer questions and solve problems using identifiable procedures. New knowledge and techniques create new questions and problems that continue the scientific and technologic processes. Unique bodies of knowledge, values, and methods are used in both science and technology.

■ References

1. National Assessment of Educational Progress. Three National Assessments of Science: Changes in Achievement 1969-77, NAEP Science Report No. 08-5-00 (Denver, CO Education Commission of the States, June 1978).
2. Stacey, J. Hueftle, Steven J. Rakow, and Wayne W. Welch, *Images of Science* (Minneapolis: Science Assessment Research Project, University of Minnesota, June 1983).
3. Steven J. Rakow, Wayne W. Welch, and Stacey J. Hueftle, "Student Achievement in Science: A Comparison of National Assessment Results," *Science Education* 68 (5) (1984): 571–578.
4. Ina V. Mullis and Lynn B. Jenkins, *The Science Report Card: Elements of Risk and Recovery* (Princeton, N.J.: Educational Testing Service, September 1988).
5. International Association for the Evaluation of Educational Achievement (IEA), *Science Achievement in Seventeen Countries* (New York: Pergamon Press, 1988).
6. Educational Policies Commission, *Education and the Spirit of Science* (Washington, D.C.: National Education Association, 1966).
7. National Assessment of Educational Progress, *Learning by Doing* (Princeton, N.J.: Educational Testing Service, May 1987).
8. Arthur Livermore, "The Process Approach of the AAAS Commission on Science Education," *Journal of Research in Science Teaching*, 1964.
9. National Council on Science and Technology Education, *Science for All Americans* (Washington, D.C.: American Association for the Advancement of Science, 1989).
10. Rene Descartes, "Discourse on the Method of Rightly Conducting Reason," in *The Philosophical Works of*

Descartes, ed. Elizabeth Haldone and G.R.T. Ross (New York: Cambridge University Press, 1970) p. 91.

11. Descartes, "Discourse on Reason," p. 92.
12. A. J. Ayer, *Language, Truth and Logic* (New York: Dover Publications, 1952), pp. 134-138.
13. Francis Bacon, "The Importance of the Experiment," in *Exploring the Universe*, ed. Louis B. Young (New York: McGraw-Hill, 1963), p. 143.
14. Francis Bacon, *The New Organon* (New York: Bobbs-Merrill, 1960), p. 96.
15. David Hume, "An Enquiry Concerning Human Understanding," in *Hume: Selections*, ed. Charles W. Hendel, (New York: Charles Scribner's & Sons, 1955), p. 123.
16. Hume, "Human Understanding," p. 125.
17. Ayer, *Language, Truth and Logic*, p. 5.
18. Ayer, *Language, Truth and Logic*, p. 99.
19. Carl G. Hempel, *Philosophy of Natural Science* (Englewood Cliffs, N.J.: Prentice Hall, 1966), pp. 33-46.
20. Wesley C. Salmon, "Confirmation," *Scientific American*, May 1973, pp. 75-83.
21. Ian G. Barbour, *Myths, Models and Paradigms* (New York: Harper & Row, 1974), pp. 92-93.
22. Michael Polanyi, *The Study of Man* (Chicago: University of Chicago Press, 1959), p. 20.
23. Michael Polanyi, *Personal Knowledge:Toward a Post-Critical Philosophy* (New York: Harper & Row, 1964).
24. Michael Polanyi, *The Tacit Dimension* (Garden City, N.Y.: Anchor Books, 1967).
25. Jacob Bronowski, *Science and Human Values* (New York: Harper & Row, 1965).
26. Jacob Bronowski, *The Identity of Man* (Garden City, N.Y.: Doubleday/Natural History Press, 1966), p. 84.
27. Jacob Bronowski, "The Principle of Tolerance," *The Atlantic Monthly*, December 1973, pp. 60-66.
28. Jacob Bronowski, "The Values of Science," in Abraham Maslow (ed). *New Knowledge in Human Values* (Chicago: Henry Regnery Company, 1959), p. 55.
29. Jacob Bronowski, *Science and Human Values* (New York: Harper & Row, 1975).
30. Thomas Kuhn, *The Structure of Scientific Revolution* (Chicago: University of Chicago Press, 1970).
31. Kuhn, *Structure of Scientific Revolution*, p. viii.
32. Kuhn, *Structure of Scientific Revolution*, p. 175.
33. Karl Popper, *Conjectures and Refutations:The Growth of Scientific Knowledge* (New York: Harper & Row, 1965), p. 25.
34. Popper, *Conjectures and Refutations*, p. 27.
35. Karl R. Popper, *The Logic of Scientific Discovery* (New York: Harper & Row, 1968), p. 27.
36. Popper, *Conjectures and Refutations*, p. 25.
37. Popper, *Conjectures and Refutations*, p. 46.

===== **INVESTIGATING SCIENCE TEACHING** =====

ACTIVITY 3–1

Understanding Science and Technology

Directions
1. In the blank provided in front of the statements about the scientific enterprise, you should indicate whether you agree (A), partially agree (PA), disagree, (D), don't know (DK), or have no opinion (NO) concerning the statement.
2. Review and discuss your individual responses in a small group of three or four persons. At this step you should add new statements, combine, modify, or omit statements. Your group should reach agreement on the statements.
3. Compile the statements from the small groups into a class set.
4. As you read the chapter and have further class discussions you should expand, modify, and/or correct the original class set of statements about the scientific enterprise.

_____ 1. The goal of science is knowledge. The knowledge may originate from experiments, spiritual revelation, mystical experiences, or creative insights.

_____ 2. Unexpected observations can play an important role in solving technological problems.

_____ 3. Observing, classifying, predicting, and hypothesizing are examples of important skills used by scientists and engineers.

_____ 4. Sometimes technologists do not find solutions to their problems.

_____ 5. Observations of nature are sources of scientific information.

_____ 6. Scientists believe that some unexplained events do not have causes.

_____ 7. There are often several different methods of solving a single technological problem.

_____ 8. If a conflict exists between matters of empirical evidence and matters of tradition, authority and power are usually accepted.

_____ 9. Some of today's scientific theories will be inadequate in the future.

_____ 10. The simplest theory that accounts for the most phenomena is the best.

_____ 11. Scientists try to improve their explanations of natural phenomena.

_____ 12. The fundamental values of science do not apply to technology since it is an application of science to human situations and must, of necessity, have either different values or no values.

_____ 13. Even though incomplete, theories are useful.

_____ 14. A basic tenet of scientific inquiry is that the universe is knowable.

_____ 15. An important result of technology is a new gadget.

_____ 16. Of all the goals of science, truth is the greatest.

_____ 17. Predicting and controlling future events are important uses of scientific theory.

_____ 18. Scientists should report exactly what they observe.

_____ 19. Scientists should neither question nor criticize the work of another scientist.

_____ 20. Technology is a part of the society in which it exists. The goals and values of a society directly influence the existence and development of technology.

_____ 21. New knowledge is more a result of skepticism, criticism, and questioning of present knowledge than it is of verifying, confirming, and strengthening present knowledge.

_____ 22. If a scientist reports his/her results precisely and truthfully, other scientists should accept the finding without skepticism.

_____ 23. Science is concerned with the formulation of general principles, theories, and laws. Processes such as hypothesizing, experimenting, and classifying are means to these ends.

_____ 24. The scientific method, i.e., stating a problem, formulating a hypothesis, designing an experiment, and drawing conclusions, is central to the whole scientific enterprise. It is the exact process that scientists use in their daily work because it ensures objectivity.

_____ 25. Once a good scientific paradigm has been developed, scientists usually stick together and discourage others from finding anomalies in the paradigm.

_____ 26. The universe is ordered and it is the job of science to discover the order and specify the relationships between events.

_____ 27. Science has neither the methods nor the capability of explaining _all_ of the physical world and human experience. Therefore, it should not try to do so.

_____ 28. The processes and products of science and technology must be evaluated apart from the needs and goals of society.

_____ 29. There is nothing beyond the limits of scientific study. Therefore, sicentists (and science teachers) should refrain from negative responses to the prospect of studying phenomena, no matter how weird or unusual the study.

_____ 30. Scientists should change their explanations based on new information.

_____ 31. Science is neither moral nor immoral but scientists are, so they should not speak out on controversial issues.

_____ 32. Scientists often give diverse explanations about the same observations.

_____ 33. Science starts with publicly observable data that should be described atheoretically.

_____ 34. Scientific theories are confirmed by comparison with experimental data.

_____ 35. When scientists choose between two theories, both of which explain the same natural phenomena, the choice between theories is rational, objective, and based on specifiable data.

CHAPTER 4

The Psychology of Motivation and Learning

Individuals are complex psychosocial systems. Students are simultaneously motivated, learn, develop, and are influenced by their peers. To help you understand student behavior, we discuss motivation and learning in this chapter and development and social psychology in the next.

Motivation is usually thought of in one of two ways: as influenced by external objects, events, or organisms; or as originating from within the individual. The different perspectives are often revealed through questions such as, "How can I motivate students?" and "How can the motivations of students be explained?" Asking and answering questions about motivation are material to the science teacher. The next two sections discuss the external and internal dimensions of motivation.

■ Motivation: The External Dimension

One assumption made about science curriculum materials and teaching techniques is that they should motivate individuals to learn. Student behavior is subsequently judged on the basis of this assumption. So, for instance, when students do not pay attention to a laboratory science teachers often blame the materials or themselves. Occasionally, they attribute the lack of motivation to some quality of the students. This is the topic of the next section. We return to the question cited above—"How can I motivate these students?" Note that this question assumes that motivation results from external factors. All of us know that there are numerous factors motivating students, and many of them are beyond a teacher's control. One's family, peers, and previous experience with science are but three examples of influences beyond

a science teacher's control. As a science teacher wishing to motivate students you are best served by looking at, and using, those factors over which you do have control. In *Mastery Teaching*[1] Dr. Madeline Hunter has described several very practical ways to increase student motivation. Throughout the section on motivation Dr. Hunter underscores the fact that these controllable factors work together in concert, to increase student motivation. You might begin by deliberately manipulating two (or three) of these factors in your first classes.

Level of Concern

Science teachers can affect how much students care about learning. Think of it for a moment in terms of this book and the science education course you are taking. If you had no concern about teaching science, there would be little motivation to read this book or take the course. At the other extreme, if your concern were so high it was acute anxiety the book and course would do little good. The answer? A moderate level of student concern will probably motivate student learning. Effective science teachers raise and lower the level of concern as appropriate to the educational situation.

Feeling Tone

How students feel in a situation affects learning. Feeling tone can be thought of as a continuum ranging from pleasant through unpleasant. Both pleasant and unpleasant atmospheres can motivate learning. For example, desirable consequences for finishing an assignment and undesirable consequences for not finishing an assignment can both serve to motivate students. For the most part we recommend not using undesirable feeling tones because it can result in unwanted side effects such as poor attitude toward science, science class, and the science teacher. If you do create an unpleasant feeling, we recommend returning to the pleasant atmosphere as soon as possible.

Success

Few things will motivate students like success. To use success as a motivator you must design activities where students will have to expend an effort in an uncertain situation. Success is felt when one has a challenging goal and achieves it. Again, think of it in terms of teaching science. If it requires little or no effort, there is little or no feeling of success. If the teaching challenge is beyond achievement, the potential for success quickly becomes frustrating. Science teachers can adjust the level of difficulty and their teaching techniques to bring about success and, subsequently, continually motivated students.

Interest

Interest in the learning task increases students' intention to learn. There are two ways that Dr. Hunter recommends to increase interest. Utilize the students' interest in themselves. Almost any science lesson can be related to some facet of the students' lives. Emphasize the novel and unique in teaching a lesson. Also, such simple factors as changing your voice or position in the room can affect student interest. From time to time change, and use a variety of teaching methods and materials.

Knowledge of Results

All of us appreciate feedback relative to our achievement. The amount, specificity, and immediacy of feedback can improve student motivation. The three factors—amount, specificity and immediacy—are critical. Providing students with the right amount of feedback is important. Be specific; tell them exactly what the feedback is for. "That's a good report," is often too general. "The discussion section of your laboratory report was very good," is more precise. It also conveys the message that you have read and recall the paper. Finally, give feedback as soon as

possible. Knowing how one did on a quiz taken two months ago provides little incentive to learn or relearn the material.

It seems these factors—level of concern, feeling tone, success, interest, and knowledge of results—are so simple that one need not state them. But they are often overlooked as teachers search for ways to motivate students.

Implications

We shall list some implications for each of the factors discussed.

1. The *level* of student concern can be increased by:
   - Standing near "unmotivated" students.
   - Indicating material will be on a quiz or test.
   - Giving a test.
   - Announcing that material will need their effort, because it is difficult.
2. The *feeling tone* of students can be increased by:
   - Indicating the consequences of certain behavior, and then following through with the consequences.
   - Designing pleasant consequences for tasks students are not motivated to do such as listening and cleaning the room.
   - Use statements such as:
     "In spite of the difficulty you have in science, you are doing well."
     "This is our first introduction to these ideas, do your best to understand them, but don't worry if you feel confused."
3. *Success* can be used to motivate students by:
   - Designing activities so all students will succeed.
   - Adjusting your questions to students' abilities.
   - Changing your teaching methods so all students can succeed in your class.
4. *Interest* can be increased by:
   - Using activities relevant to adolescents.
   - Using the laboratory.
   - Varying methods, techniques, and activities in the science classroom.
5. *Knowledge of results* or *feedback* can be used to motivate students if:
   - It is immediate.
   - It is specific.
   - It is appropriate to the student and task.
   - There is an adequate amount.

External motivation is associated with behavioral psychology. Incentives and reinforcements, from outside the student, are important sources of motivation. In a science classroom such extrinsic motivation might include concern, classroom climate, interest, teacher approval, grades, and other rewards.

Motivation can also be discussed from the students' point of view by asking yourself such questions as "What motivated the behavior of the adolescents?" in the activity "Investigating Science Teaching: Motivational Needs" at the end of this chapter. It is probable that many factors such as level of maturation, past experience, and external stimulation were involved in motivating the students' behavior. Although these factors are important, science teachers should also recognize the power and range of personal needs on motivation. One way to describe individual motivation is in the context of Abraham Maslow's theory, which posits a hierarchy of motivational needs that influence behavior.[2,3,4] This hierarchy is a continuum including physiological, physical, and psychological needs and, at the highest level, needs that are creative, ethical, intellectual, and esthetic.

■ The Hierarchy of Needs

Assumptions

Motivational needs are common to all people and are part of the individual's biological essence. At the physiological and physical levels the motivation toward fulfillment of these needs is very strong; the strength of motivation, however, diminishes at the higher levels, given equal deprivation of all needs. Maslow used the term "instinctoid" to differentiate the hierarchy of needs from the stronger, biological "instincts." According to Maslow, these instinctoid needs bridge the gap between genetically programmed changes and changes consciously made by individuals. As such, instinctoid needs are weak and easily repressed. Repressing these weak motivations to continue developing one's potentials is one of the basic problems with which individuals constantly struggle. Social forces can easily influence the repression of personal needs. To provide further clarification, some general characteristics of the basic needs will be discussed.

Characteristics

The relation among motivational needs is one of order, strength, and priority. Maslow uses the term "prepotency" to indicate the strength of one need over another. For example, hunger is prepotent to self-esteem; that is, hunger is stronger and more pressing if both are deficient.

There is flexibility in the hierarchy; it is not a rigid and fixed order of progression. Rather, it has a more holistic-dynamic quality. The hierarchy is not an invariant sequence, although it generally predicts an order of progression. There are some individuals who seem to have "lost" or reduced their needs. The hungry, poorly sheltered artist is a stereotypical example.

Satisfaction of the needs is relative, not absolute. A need does not have to be completely satisfied at one level before others emerge at the next level. Further, the emergence of the next level is not guaranteed, simply because a need has been satisfied, and it is quite possible for the level of motivation to regress, given deprivation of a lesser need. These are a few of the important characteristics of Maslow's theory of motivation; next is a discussion of the hierarchy.

The Levels of the Hierarchy

Physiological

Physiological needs—food, water, air, and sleep—have the greatest motivational force in the hierarchy. An individual's motivation, if total deprivation is chronic, would be toward fulfillment of physiological needs, and higher-level needs would have only a marginal influence on behavior.

Of greater importance to the science teacher is student motivation at the physiological level. In the activity, "Investigating Science Teaching: Motivational Needs," there are examples of a restless girl, Mary, and a sleeping boy, Robert. Later that morning Mary was seen to be eating something, and it was learned that Robert had an early-morning paper route. It became apparent that these students' behaviors were at least partially motivated by physiological needs. When physiological needs no longer dominate behavior, new needs at the safety and security level may emerge and influence motivation.

Safety and Security

This level is described by a need for order, structure, stability, dependency, security, and freedom from chaos and fear. Students generally prefer an undisrupted routine. They perceive their environment as secure when it has regular patterns and when people are persistent and dependable. In short, students need an orderly world.

For example, students should not perceive the science laboratory or field work as chaotic, unmanageable, and unorganized.

Belongingness

The frustrations associated with belongingness needs are characterized by many words implying existentialism: alienation, loneliness, aloneness, and rejection. The specific striving of the student is to give and receive affection, to have a friend, to belong to a group, and to find a place with people and a community.

Most teachers are aware of students who feel rejected because they do not belong to groups, who need affection and positive regard from the teacher, and who are generally frustrated in the fulfillment of belongingness needs. Belongingness and esteem, the next level, are important motivational needs in contemporary society. Many problems with students occur because these needs are not fulfilled. The implications for you as a science teacher are clear—students should have a sense of belonging in your classroom and a feeling that you care about each of them.

Self-Esteem

The fourth level of needs includes motivation toward a stable, firmly based, positive perception of self. The need for personal esteem is divided into mastery needs and prestige needs.

Mastery is the individual's need for achievement, competence, and confidence in carrying out duties and obligations. Prestige is more social-psychological in nature. It is the need for others to show a respectful attitude toward the individual. Status, recognition, importance, and dignity are defining characteristics of need fulfillment at the prestige level.

Frustration of self-esteem needs produces insecurity, inferiority, and anxiety about personal worth. For the student, these unfulfilled needs can lead to compensatory behavior and, for the teacher, they can cause discipline problems depending on the degree of frustration and the ability of fulfillment through acceptable means. Two students in "Investigating Science Teaching: Motivational Needs," Karen and Martin, were probably motivated by self-esteem needs. Karen was fulfilled in both the mastery and prestige needs, whereas Martin probably only fulfilled the need for prestige from his peer group, not the teacher. Martin is an example of negatively achieved self-esteem, something science teachers encounter daily.

Fulfillment of esteem needs results in feelings of personal adequacy, individual integrity, and self-worth. Healthy self-esteem is based on mastery and prestige that are deserved and earned rather than on unwarranted adulation. Self-esteem fulfilled through an individual's distorted perceptions of herself or through false imposition of perceptions from others can cause immense personal difficulty, since maintaining such false esteem in the face of reality is a consuming exercise that can lead directly to personality disorders.

Self-Actualization

Motivation through the various levels of the hierarchy is toward the full development of an individual's potential. When the more fundamental needs are largely fulfilled, there emerges the need to develop and use one's capabilities, talents, and potentialities. The ways in which persons continue to develop are largely unique to the individual. Some will direct their unique talents toward science and some toward other careers and hobbies. Maslow's concept of self-actualization is a way of saying that individuals need to continue developing in their own unique ways.

From his studies of healthy people, Maslow synthesized characteristics of individual self-actualization. They include: creativeness; a clear perception of reality; a continuing freshness of appreciation; a quality of detachment and need for privacy; acceptance of self, others, and nature; a problem-centered attitude; a philosophical, unhostile sense of humor; a democratic character structure; and identification with all humanity and personal values that transcend the culture.

The concept of full self-actualization is a goal, although few people achieve it, except in rare moments of heightened awareness and insight. During these experiences, individuals glimpse their own self-actualization. People reporting these experiences often use terms associated with values such as justice, truth, beauty, goodness, and so forth. This experience is the heart of Maslow's argument for human values as a part of basic human nature.

Structure

Living organisms have systems that fulfill two basic functions, that is, maintenance and change. Maslow's hierarchy has this type of structure, although the structure originates biologically and operates on a continuum to the social-psychological. Fundamentally, fulfilling the lesser, deficiency needs results in physical or psychological maintenance of the individual, whereas fulfilling the higher, growth needs results in continued changes and growth. Figure 4.1 is a graphic presentation of Maslow's hierarchy. Central to the presentation is personal development, the result of fulfilling both lesser and higher needs.

Equalization is the process by which the lesser needs are fulfilled. Motivations for food are fulfilled by external factors and the level of need returns to a relatively stable, balanced state. The fact that another

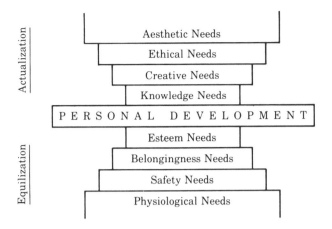

FIGURE 4–1
Motivational needs and personal development

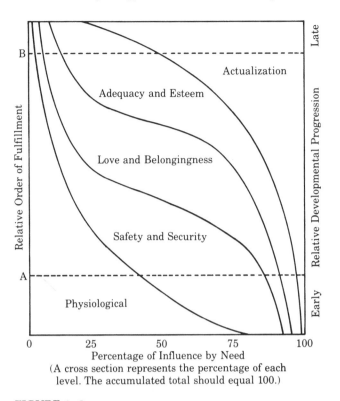

FIGURE 4–2
A phase diagram of Abraham Maslow's hierarchy of motivational needs

set of motivational needs can then influence the person points out the dynamic quality of Maslow's system.

Actualization, the upper portion of Figure 4.1, represents the needs that influence the individual toward continuing change and growth. These needs are not easily fulfilled; they do not return to a state of equilibrium. Rather, they seem to push the individual toward further growth and development of individual capacities. The dual process of equalization and actualization contributes to continued personal development of the individual.

Function

Individual needs tend to be viewed as the sole motivational determiners. It is better to view the motivational needs as different percentages that influence behavior. Figure 4.2 is a way of viewing the hierarchy based on a phase diagram such as geologists use for describing the mineral composition of rocks. The dotted line labeled *A* could represent a student's motivational needs. The major need is for safety and security; it is clear that other needs are also present, though in lesser degree. Likewise, a person at level *B* is primarily motivated by self-actualizing needs but is also influenced by lower needs.

Implications

The major implication of Maslow's theory is related to the broad goal of encouraging the personal development of students. The full development of an individual's potential includes the traditional goals of acquiring knowledge and evolving attitudes. With development as the aim of science teaching, Maslow's theory adds a new dimension to others such

as Jean Piaget's theory of cognitive development and Lawrence Kohlberg's theory of moral development.

Maslow did not stress development of the affective at the expense of the cognitive. Science teachers should recognize the influence of the affective domain on learning and behavior. In Maslow's theory, learning, behavior, and development are influenced by the motivational needs. Cognitive needs and conative needs are synergistic, not antagonistic.

According to Maslow, knowledge is gained through personal experience. He speaks of two types of experiences. One is rational, conscious, cognitive, and primarily about the physical world and the other is nonrational, preconscious, conative, and primarily about the self. The first type of knowledge has been, and will continue to be, emphasized in science teaching; the second is gradually being recognized as important.

There are some specific implications concerning the motivational needs of students. As a science teacher you can infer the spirit of the implication and then, based on your understanding of Maslow's theory, your school, your students, and yourself, decide about the educational application.

1. Recognize the physiological and physical needs of students. Factors such as hunger, thirst, room temperature, and need for rest all contribute to

a student's motivation. There are often overt behaviors that indicate needs at this level; try to be aware of these behaviors and respond as best you can within the school environment.

2. Maintain a physically and psychologically safe classroom. For example, help students with their "little" problems, avoid situations that are threatening or frightening to the students, avoid using humiliation and embarrassment as motivators for learning, and, if routines are changed or a different approach is implemented, inform the students of the change and try to make the transition gradually.

3. Show the students that you are interested in teaching them and that they "belong" in your room. Addressing them by name, recognizing their achievements both in and out of your classroom, talking with them about topics of common interest, and listening to some of their ideas can all contribute to a feeling of acceptance and belongingness in your classroom.

4. Arrange learning experiences so all students will gain some esteem in your class. Give acknowledgement and praise when appropriate and avoid harsh criticism; rather, help students with difficult problems, concepts, and choices.

5. Provide opportunities for individuals to experience success, both individually and in a group. This means teaching in terms of an individual student's educational needs and not the demands of a text, lesson plan, or curriculum project. It also means that you encourage cooperation among students on tasks and projects, rather than continuous competition among them.

6. Discuss and clarify personal values as a part of the educational program. Techniques such as class meetings, decision-making, and value clarification are helpful in achieving this goal.

7. Arrange experiences that will enhance the choices for personal growth by the students. Sometimes this enhancement can be achieved through ambiguous, though directed, assignments. When necessary, suggest a possible activity that is challenging but attainable for individual students.

8. Provide times when students are allowed to make choices and learn in their own individual ways. The accurate interpretation of this implication is freedom with limits, not unlimited freedom.

If fulfilling needs motivates individuals to interact with their surroundings, what happens during the interaction? The answer is, of course, that many things happen. The one that we will focus on is learning. The next sections discuss various aspects of learning that are important for science teachers. As

the discussion progresses, you will note that the section is designed so that it moves toward increasing complexity: from the external to internal and, finally, the interpersonal.

■ Learning: The External Dimension

This section emphasizes behaviorism. The behaviorist school maintains that observable behavior is the essential study in psychology. Behaviorism stresses the importance of environmental influences on behavior.

What do the behaviorists mean by learning? Learning encompasses observable changes in behavior due to environmental experiences. Learned behavior is relatively permanent and consistent. This qualification differentiates learned behavior from performance or motivated behavior. According to this definition, personal thoughts, feelings, and desires are not usually considered learned.

Classical Conditioning

Classical conditioning refers to the ideas of Ivan Pavlov, a Russian physiologist who, in 1904, received a Nobel prize in medicine for his studies of digestion. Pavlov's theory of conditioning was originally based on studies with dogs.[5] When he gave them food, the reflexive behavior was salivation. This is an unconditioned response (UCR); in this case the food is called an unconditioned stimulus (UCS). Let us say that another stimulus, a small bell, is presented at the same time as the food. Initially the bell would not cause the dog to salivate. However, if a bell is rung repeatedly as food is presented, the dog eventually will respond by salivating when the bell is rung without the presence of food. The bell is then a conditioned stimulus (CS). The dog's salivation to the bell's sound (CS) is referred to as a conditioned response (CR). The dog has learned to respond to the bell. Classical conditioning is summarized in Figure 4.3.

Associationism

Edward L. Thorndike, the father of educational psychology, further developed Pavlov's ideas.[6] In one experiment, Thorndike put a hungry cat in a box that would open if the cat activated a release mechanism. Initially, the cat simply jumped around until it accidentally hit the release mechanism. Eventually, through a process of trial and success, the cat learned to release itself from the cage. Thorndike developed

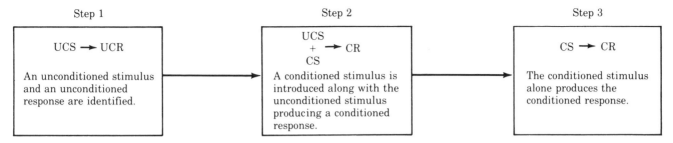

Step 1		Step 2		Step 3

UCS → UCR

An unconditioned stimulus and an unconditioned response are identified.

UCS + CS → CR

A conditioned stimulus is introduced along with the unconditioned stimulus producing a conditioned response.

CS → CR

The conditioned stimulus alone produces the conditioned response.

FIGURE 4–3
The process of classical conditioning

the idea that it was the association between the stimulus and the response that was important. Repetition of the correct response was essential to learning because it strengthened the association. Experiments such as this were the basis for Thorndike's famous "law of effect." Stated simply, Thorndike's principle is that *successful behavior is likely to reoccur in similar situations.*

Operant Conditioning

Operant conditioning is a form of behaviorism in which the environmental consequence or reinforcement is paired with a behavior. The positive or negative results of the behavior influence the likelihood of that particular behavior reoccuring. B.F. Skinner is the psychologist associated with operant conditioning.[7,8] The term operant indicates that the organism operates on the environment to receive reinforcement. We can set up an experiment to see how learning occurs through operant conditioning.

Imagine a small box about one meter square. At one end there is a small door with a bar that, when pushed, opens the door and releases a morsel of food. Now we place a hungry rat in the cage. After a while the rat pushes the bar and is fed. Soon the rat learns that pressing the bar releases food. After this behavior is learned, food pellets could be supplied only under certain conditions. Suppose we want the rat to push the bar when we sound a bell. Soon the rat would learn to push the bar at the sound of a bell, more rapidly when the bell was rung, then decreasing when the bell stopped ringing.

Several important concepts of behaviorism are demonstrated in this experiment. The rat learned a specific behavior due to *reinforcement.* When the behavior was not reinforced, extinction occurred; that is, the likelihood of the behavior occuring decreased. At first there was a *generalized* response, in that the rat pushed the lever as much when there was no bell as it did when there was a bell sound. However, with time the rat *discriminated* among stimuli and pushed the bar more often with the sound of a bell.

Several important ideas for learning science are worth noting. First, rewarded behavior increases the *probability* of that behavior reoccurring. However, this does not mean that the behavior will always occur. Second, *extinction* can occur if the behavior is not continually reinforced. Third, it *takes time* for individuals to learn behaviors even though they have been reinforced. We will examine reinforcements closely because they are very important to this theory of learning.

Reinforcement and Punishment
Reinforcement increases the probability that a behavior will reoccur. There are two types of reinforcement—positive and negative. Positive reinforcement is the presentation of a pleasant stimulus after a behavior. For example, a science teacher may smile at a student who answers a question correctly or praise completion of a laboratory activity. Negative reinforcement is the removal of an aversive stimulus after a desired behavior. For example, a student may constantly look around rather than pay attention. The teacher continually frowns and reprimands the student. On appropriate classroom behavior, such as listening and responding, the teacher discontinues the unpleasant looks and smiles and praises the behavior. Both negative and positive reinforcement are combined. First the teacher stopped frowning and then praised and smiled, giving positive reinforcement.

Punishment is often confused with negative reinforcement. The two processes differ and have different results. Punishment decreases the probability of a behavior occurring, whereas reinforcement (both positive and negative) increases such probability. Punishment results when an aversive stimulus is presented to an individual, such as spanking for not cleaning one's room, or withholding a pleasant stimulus such as not getting an allowance because one's room was not cleaned. Figure 4.4 is a convenient way

Psychologist B. F. Skinner discusses his theory of operant conditioning with science teachers. (National Science Teachers Association)

	Present Stimulus	Remove Stimulus
Pleasant Stimulus	Positive reinforcement and increase in behavior	Punishment and decrease in behavior
Aversive Stimulus	Punishment and decrease in behavior	Negative reinforcement and increase in behavior

FIGURE 4–4
Reinforcement and punishment

to remember the difference between reinforcement and punishment.

Reinforcers must be important for the student whose behavior one wishes to modify. David Premack's method of identifying a reinforcer is to use any natural behavior that occurs relatively often to reinforce another behavior that occurs less often.[9] "You must pick up materials and clean your laboratory area before recess." This statement is a simple example of the Premack principle. To apply this principle, the teacher should observe the types of activities preferred by the students. We realize that this idea has been applied by teachers, parents, and grandparents probably since teaching and parenting began. But it is often done without conscious observation and deliberation concerning the behaviors and reinforcers. We encourage the thoughtful use of these ideas in the science classroom.

Scheduling Reinforcements

Rewards and punishments are given in classrooms every day. However, usually rewards for productive behavior are distributed randomly, whereas punishment is aligned with disruptive behavior. Also, some things that teachers consider to be reinforcers may not be so for the student; conversely many things that are very good reinforcers are seldom used. Science teachers can use a much more organized and consistent approach to reinforcement. There are two basic schedules of reinforcement: ratio and interval. In ratio schedules, reinforcement is given after a number of responses. The number can be fixed, let us say at every five problems: fifth, tenth, fifteenth, and so on. Or the reinforcement can be variable; that is, the number of required responses varies around a number. On the average, every five problems completed would be rewarded but it may be the sixth, the eighth, and the fifteenth problems.

Interval schedules require that a specified amount of time elapse before the next reward is given. Again, there can be fixed interval schedules in which the first response after a given time is reinforced; for example, reinforcement is every five minutes. Like the variable-ratio or the variable-interval schedules, rewards are dispensed around an average amount of time; for example, on the average, a reward is given every five minutes but the rewards may be at two, six, and sixteen minutes.

Understanding reinforcement schedules is important because of the behavior patterns that continue when reinforcement ceases and extinction begins. When reinforcement ceases, organisms on fixed-interval schedules will continue responding for the shortest time, then those on variable-interval, fixed-ratio, and, finally, variable-ratio schedules.

Reinforcement schedules provide for consistent rewarding of desired behavior and help the science teacher who is trying to change disruptive behavior. If the teacher provides intermittent reinforcement to disruptive behavior, the behavior will continue longer than if reinforcement has been constant and then ceases. Consider this example. There is a student who talks incessantly and you wish to change this behavior. Usually the student receives occasional attention, from his teacher and peers, for talking. This is intermittent reinforcement for talking and results in the most difficult behavior pattern to change.

Most teachers use punishment or negative reinforcement as they try to change behavior. Since these methods are used, it is important that teachers know their negative consequences. There is the possibility of unintended emotional responses. For example, a student who is punished in science class may be conditioned to fear doing whatever he/she did, but also to fear other aspects of the science classroom. Another result is avoidance of situations which produce the pain or anxiety associated with punishment. So, a student may skip school or not go to science class. Finally, it must also be noted that one student's punishment may be another's reinforcement. If a student's need is attention, receiving punishment is one way of getting attention, albeit a painful way. Punishment can result in emotional re-

=== REFLECTING ON SCIENCE TEACHING ===
Behavioral Psychology

1. List several ways that you could reinforce behavior in a science classroom.
2. How does Skinner's operant conditioning differ from Pavlov's respondant conditioning?
3. What are some applications of the Premack principle for the science classroom?
4. Why is it important to schedule reinforcements?
5. Suppose you had a student who would not complete laboratory reports. How could you apply behavioral psychology to change this behavior?

---

sponses that are more enduring than the immediate aversive stimuli. We recommend using positive reinforcement for desired behavior and combining positive/negative reinforcement to increase desired and reduce undesired behavior.

Implications

What do you do when trying to apply the ideas of behaviorism in classroom situations? There are simple procedures that science teachers can use.

1. Identify the problem behaviors. What are the specific behaviors that you wish to change? This step is especially important if you wish to change unnecessary or disruptive behaviors. (If you are only concerned with teaching science, this step may not be applicable.)
2. Clarify the behaviors you desire. Your expectation should be specific and describe a behavior: "I want the student to pay attention." One recommendation is to use behavioral objectives. In this case, the terminal behavior is defined: "The student should be able to sit in her seat." "The student should be able to finish her work."
3. Identify the available reinforcers. Do not presume that candy or a smile is a reinforcer for the student. Spend some time identifying things that are reinforcing for each student. Use the Premack principle if possible.
4. Determine the most effective reinforcement schedule. As situations and behaviors vary, so should schedules of reinforcement. If you have a student who is very disruptive, you should select (1) reinforcers that are important to the student, (2) schedules that allow for immediate reinforcement of desired behaviors, and (3) continuous reinforcment of behavior. Different schedules can be used in less extreme situations, such as having students work on lessons which involve learning science concepts or having them clean the laboratory.
5. Establish a baseline of behaviors. Once you have

identified behaviors you wish to change, take a few days and observe how often these behaviors actually do or do not occur. Graph these observations. It is important to have a standard of comparison so that you will know how your reinforcement program is working.
6. Determine successive approximations of the behavior. In most cases the desired behavior is more than can be achieved by the student; however, a reinforcement should not be given until the behavior is demonstrated. You will have to *shape* the desired behavior by establishing successive approximations of the final behavior and then reinforcing those approximations until the full behavior pattern is established.

Reinforcement works. There is reinforcement in every classroom, so it is not a question of whether or not it occurs. The question is one of consistency and direction. Are you consistent in reinforcement? Do you have goals and objectives that indicate a direction of improvement for student behaviors? Affirmative answers to these questions and a systematic application of the ideas presented in this section can decrease problems and increase learning in your science class. The easiest dimension to change is the external. Attention to the external aspects of learning will increase your effectiveness as a science teacher. But science teaching is more than reinforcements; there is also mental change that occurs in the learning process. This change we will discuss as the internal dimension.

■ Learning: The Internal Dimension Gestalt

Imagine that a chimpanzee is placed in a large cage with several objects for his entertainment. Before long, the chimpanzee discovers that he can use a stick to pull things toward him instead of walking across the cage. One day a long stick and a banana are left outside the cage. The chimpanzee discovers that he has a problem when he tries to rake in the banana with the stick from the cage. He wants the banana but he cannot reach it. The frustration upsets the chimp and he retires to one corner of the cage and sits brooding about his problem. Suddenly he jumps up, runs across the cage, and seizes the short stick. He uses the stick to rake in the longer stick and then uses the long stick to rake the banana into the cage. He has discovered a solution to his problem.

This famous experiment was done in the 1920s by Wolfgang Kohler, a Gestalt psychologist.[10] In this experiment, the chimpanzee (Sultan) was first presented with a problem. To solve the problem several old patterns of thought and behavior had to be combined into a new pattern.

How does this approach to learning differ from the theory of reinforcement and operant conditioning? Kohler did not specifically condition or reinforce Sultan for any of his activities. It might be argued that Sultan was indeed conditioned to rake things and reinforced for this activity, even though the rewards were not scheduled. However, the situation, problem, and solution seem unique enough to suggest that old behaviors could not have been generalized to the new patterns necessary to solve the problem. Rather, it seems that the essence of learning in this case was the coordination of thought patterns into a new organization. See Figure 4.5 for a summary of the problem-solving process. The basis for this learning was a problem situation; to solve the problem Sultan had to reorganize patterns of thought. Insight was discovering the pattern that would solve the problem. Finally, the insight was applied and the problem solved. Since this pattern occurs within the individual, it is discussed as the internal dimension of learning.

Constructivism

In the early twentieth century Jean Piaget proposed a major theory of development. The developmental theory is presented in the next chapter. Part of Piaget's theory relates directly to learning theory and the constructivist position referred to in earlier chapters. Piaget underscores the fact that, when students think, they must adapt to the immediate experience and reconstruct modes of thought in light of that experience. The result is a new, more inclusive mode of thought.

As students interact with the environment, they naturally encounter situations and objects with which they are unfamiliar. These situations result in some puzzlement or query by the individual. Piaget termed this puzzlement *cognitive disequilibrium*.[11] To resolve the pending situation the child must change her way of thinking. Or, to use Piaget's term, the student must mentally adapt.

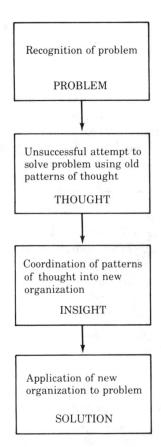

FIGURE 4–5
Learning through discovery

Adaptation is divided into assimilation and accommodation. Assimilation is the taking in of environmental experiences and incorporating them into existing ways of thinking. Play is an example of assimilation. Accommodation is the modification of existing ways of thinking so that a new experience can be incorporated into the cognitive structure. Imitation is an example of accommodation.

The processes of assimilation and accomodation usually occur together. Think of a young child who first throws a ball. The child has undoubtedly thrown other objects prior to the ball. There exists the concept (and behavior) of throwing, but throwing the ball is new and must be assimilated. The child must also accommodate to the size and hardness of the ball if it is to be thrown. As the child is confronted with this new "throwing the ball" problem, there must be adaptation to the present situation. The new and somewhat augmented ways of thinking about both throwing and balls is then integrated and *coordinated* or organized into the child's cognitive structure. In this example, the child has learned about throwing a ball.

Learning through adaptation and organization requires mental activity by the student, which certainly supports active involvement by students in the science classroom. There is the added dimension of problem solving, that is, providing situations that will engage the learner. The next steps will then be easy since the student will try to solve the problem.

Implications

Problem solving as an instructional approach is the direct result of the theories discussed in this section. Here are some general steps in the process of problem solving.

1. *Recognition of the problem.* Science problems can be very complex and involved, so much so that some individuals may not recognize them as problems. You can think of this as a "readiness" for problem solving. You need to know simple mathematics before you can recognize or solve calculus problems.

2. *Motivation to solve the problem.* Presenting a problem in science class may or may not result in the student's being motivated to solve the problem. If the problem has meaning for the student because it is of interest and/or because materials related to the problem are physically present, motivation is enhanced. The problem should present a challenge but one that is within the student's abilities. It should be neither too simple nor too complex. Students should work in an atmosphere which is conducive to exploration of problems.

3. *Time to solve the problem.* Once you have engaged learners in a problem, they should have time to work on the solution. At first they will put forth a concentrated effort to resolve the problem using old ideas, habits, and bits of knowledge. This is the logical and analytical phase. However, for many problems, this approach fails to produce results. You can tell when students are near the end of this phase because they show frustration, tension, and discomfort. They are at the end when they give up in apparent failure. But this is when the next phase begins. During this intuitive, nonrational, creative phase, new perceptions and new orientations emerge. Students may suddenly "see" the solution. The end of this phase is signaled by the excitement and exhiliration of this insight.

4. *Modification and elaboration of the solution.* When a tentative solution is reached, you should encourage the students to test their ideas. Does it work? How does it stand up to the test of reality? With this step there can be some modification and then elaboration of the solution.

5. *Communication of the solution.* Without communication, solutions may have personal value but they lack social import. Have the students write up their results. They should be able to present their solution clearly and logically, both orally and in writing.

Problem solving as pedagogy brings together many aspects of psychology. For science teachers especially, it shows the importance of both logical and creative thinking. Problem solving integrates the unique functions of both right and left hemispheres of the brain. We are now recognizing the importance of creativity in the problem-solving process and its place in the science classroom. Teaching techniques such as methods and materials that actively involve students, the use of counter-intuitive problems, and thought-provoking questions are all supported by the theories presented in this section.

■ Learning: The Interpersonal Dimension

Psychologists and educators have identified different "domains" of learning. Such divisions are important, even essential, for clarifying and discussing different aspects of learning and for educational research. However, students enter our science classes as more than "cognitive domains," "affective responses," "psychomotor structures," or "problem solvers." Their behavior is a combination of intellectual, emotional, physical, and social variables. Student behavior, whether directed toward learning science concepts or creating classroom chaos, is a result of numerous personal and environmental variables. Science teachers often forget these simple ideas and the fact that categories such as "cognitive domain" and "problem solving" are created for study, communication, and evaluation. Students are more than the categories we have created. And learning is more than presenting problems and applying reinforcements. The term *humanistic* reminds us that our students are, after all, human beings. The implication is that science teachers should recognize the importance of personal qualities of students and interpersonal dynamics in classrooms as they relate to students' ability to learn science.

Education in science contributes to the student's development in ways unique to the discipline; that is, the knowledge, methods and values of science are central to science teaching. At the same time, we cannot ignore the personal development of the student in other areas nor the interpersonal skills essential to learning science. The personal, humanistic dimension of teaching is inevitable if one is to be an effective science teacher.

In the next pages we will look at the interpersonal dimensions of learning. The theories of Carl R.

Laboratory activities
enhance learning through
personal involvement.
(Photo by Lloyd
Lemmerman.)

Rogers, as expressed in his book, *Freedom to Learn,*
are the central focus of discussion.[12]

Personal Meaning and Learning

Carl Rogers defined two types of learning. There is
learning that is important, significant, and meaningful *to the individual,* and there is learning that is
unimportant, insignificant, and meaningless. The *individual* is the final authority on the appropriateness
and importance of the learning experience. Rogers
described the components of significant learning;
they are similar to earlier discussions of problem
solving. *The learning is initiated by the individual.*
The motivation to learn, to engage in an activity,
originates in part from within the individual, not
solely in the environment. The second aspect of significant learning is *personal involvement.* The
learner is actually involved with activities, materials,
and environments that lead to new understandings
about the physical world. Self-initiation and personal involvement do not necessarily mean that students should be left to learn on their own, although
they often do so. Teachers have the crucial role of
designing a learning environment that will maximize
the opportunities for learning and for facilitating the
process of learning once it begins.

Learning is summarized as: LEARNING =
COGNITION + MEANING. Cognition, as used here,
has the usual definitiion: the process of acquiring
knowledge or that which comes to be known. Note
that the amount of learning is equal to cognition *plus*
the meaning of that cognition for the individual. The
meaning of any particular knowledge is a result of
the individual's perceptions of the importance of the
knowledge. In this view a reinforcement, let us say
food, a smile, or a grade, may or may not have meaning; it depends on the individual's perception.

Personal meaning is a result of psychological
closeness; that is, self-initiation, motivation, and/or
physical closeness such as involvement of the individual with actual materials. Let us say that a student has a question about the different, colored
"things" (minerals) in rocks. Ideally the science
teacher would let the student examine and describe
the "things," discuss properties, and see if the same
"things" can be found in different rocks. In this example, learning was self-initiated and then there was
personal involvement with the actual materials. The
reverse is also possible. Students can engage in activities and with materials that originally have meaning due to their physical closeness. If the materials
are interesting, the next step is predictable: students
will ask why, how, what, and when; that is, they will
initiate their own learning. So the critical component

REFLECTING ON SCIENCE TEACHING
A Synthesis

Try to make one statement to your peers that would synthesize the internal, external, and interpersonal dimensions of science teaching.

1. Which dimensions are easiest to use? Hardest?
2. Is one dimension more important than another for problem solving? Inquiry teaching? Teaching effectiveness?

---

of personal meaning can work either way, from self-initiation to involvement or from physical involvement to interest and questions. But personal meaning must be present. The greater the degree of personal meaning, the greater the learning that occurs.

The science teacher's goal is facilitating learning by the student as opposed to presenting concepts. The key words are facilitating, that is, assisting, making easy, directing, presenting, introducing, offering, and displaying. Both presenting and facilitating are critical for learning. Emphasizing the facilitation of learning directs the science teacher toward the more personal aspects of teaching and meaningful learning. Facilitating learning includes the traditional goals of understanding science concepts and methods and places these ideas in a context of personal meaning and social usefulness for the student.

Being a Facilitator of Learning

Being an effective facilitator requires an understanding of scientific knowledge and the ability to plan lessons, organize classroom procedures, and use a variety of teaching methods. In addition there is the essential fact of all teaching—personal interaction with your students in the learning process. Following are some ideas essential to facilitating learning in the science classroom.

1. *Effective facilitators are, first and foremost, themselves.* They teach without facade, distortion, or artificiality. They exhibit the quality of being real, genuine, and natural. Being authentic includes expressing emotions such as anger, disappointment, or personal inadequacy. It also includes being happy, excited, and proud.
2. *Effective facilitators care for the learner.* The caring is directed toward students simply because they are persons. Caring is not based on qualities, actions, or expectations of the other. Although teachers admit that they can't love all their students, they are encouraged to strive toward a goal of respecting and caring for them.

3. *Effective facilitators accept students as they are.* This concept is closely related to caring. Accepting means starting with individuals where they are, not setting up expectations that must be met before acceptance is shown. Accepting the students does not mean condoning. For example, science teachers can accept and respect individuals but not condone their disruptive behavior.
4. *Effective facilitators develop an empathy toward students.* This attribute refers to the ability to understand students from their frame of reference, to see problems as students see them, and to feel the same things that students do. Frustration at not getting a problem, uneasiness about a question, or anxiety about scientific ideas are three examples in which empathy will help the teacher-student interaction and, as a consequence, perhaps overcome the problem and facilitate learning.

Implications

The ideas in this section provide valuable insights concerning the dynamics a science teacher should use to gain an accurate understanding of the student's perceptions. Then, based on this understanding, the teacher can provide challenges and opportunities that will further learning and development.

1. *Develop rapport.* Developing rapport with students communicates a desire to help and nurtures the reciprocal process, the desire to be helped. Initially, the burden for establishing and developing a helping relationship is on the science teacher. With time, the student should also communicate the desire to be helped.
2. *Attend to the student.* Observing and listening to the learner communicates the desire to understand and the active process of trying to comprehend just how the student views the situation. Active attending is per-

================= **GUEST EDITORIAL** =================

Neuroscience: The Brain and Behavior

Nathaniel G. Pitts, Ph.D.
Program Director, Integrative Neural Systems

Have you ever wondered how you remember your best friend's telephone number, or what allows you to learn the words to a song and then repeat them when you hear the proper melody? Learning and memory are two behaviors in which humans excel and which make us very unique in the animal kingdom.

Did you ever want to know why you experience different tastes or various smells, and how you hear different tones, and why you see in color, not just black and white? Have you ever thought about how your skin tells your brain a touch is soothing and not painful? Our sensory systems are superb and actually gather more information than we consciously use.

Have you ever considered the difference between left-handers and right-handers? Have you ever wondered why a person who has a spinal cord injury is forever crippled? Nerves don't grow and develop at the same rate throughout life and this has a big impact when the brain or spinal cord is injured after a person is past the infant stage.

If you have answered yes to any of the above questions you are interested in the same line of basic research as thousands of brain researchers or neuroscientists. We are all interested in knowing how the brain and nervous system work. Brain research is a large scientific frontier with many unanswered questions. We need pioneers in this field who have daring approaches to questions regarding brain function and malfunction.

When I was younger my favorite academic subjects were biology and math. Of course, I once wanted to be a professional athlete, but soon discovered that precious few can succeed at that endeavor. When I went to college, I took classes in psychology that introduced me to the idea of the brain as the controller of human behavior. My curiosity made me pursue this subject, and led me to combine all my interests and do basic research on what I would call the biological bases of behavior.

In studying the nervous system we are studying one of the most complex systems known to humans. The sensing devices—the eye, ear, nose, and skin—are extremely effective and efficient. The brain acts as the central information processor or computer. Its ability to integrate and sort the massive amounts of information that the senses feed into it is unsurpassed. The brain's ability to be logical, to be artistic, to produce emotions, and to cause actions makes it a very unique system in this universe. We need creative minds to supply ideas to answer many of our unsolved problems, and we invite you to join us as we try to answer questions about the brain and behavior.

---

sonal involvement in the learner's perception of the problem, concept, or activity.

3. *Respond to the student.* The next important part of understanding the learner is communicating your perceptions of the situation. Reflecting and clarifying what the student has expressed establishes better communication and gives the student insights and a feeling of being understood. Importantly, this communication gives you a clearer view of the student's understanding of science.

4. *Question for understanding.* Your questions can be a key to further understanding. After

you ask questions, it is often helpful to ask students to justify their answers. "How did you come to this conclusion?" "Can you tell me why your decision is the best one?" After you have asked the question—wait. When the student answers—listen.

5. *Facilitate the student's learning.* The next step is suggesting or initiating activities, projects, readings, and so on that will enable the student to move a step further in her learning. By this time you should have a clear understanding of the student, some idea of her goals and what she understands in science; then it is up to you to assist,

TABLE 4–1
Some principles of motivation and learning applied to science teaching

Active Participation—Engage the learner's mind through the use of laboratory materials, scientific equipment and audio-visuals. Active participation includes overt ("hands-on") and covert ("minds-on") activities.

Anticipatory Set—Connects previous learning in science with present lesson, provides a focus, context and connection for the present lesson and past lessons. Science teachers should
- use past science experiences,
- focus attention on learning task, and
- involve the learner

Motivation—Personal needs, reinforcement, interest, activity and questions are used to capture, maintain and enhance the learner's attention in the science lesson. Extrinsic motivations include
- classroom atmosphere,
- personal interest,
- feedback on responses,
- affective level, and
- success at task.

Intrinsic motivations include
- basic needs,
- growth needs, and
- personal development.

Meaning—Content of science lesson is related to the learner's past, present or future experience. A rationale, understanding, memory aid, underlying structure or interesting point may be provided for the material to be learned. Science teachers can provide meaning by
- relating to past, present, or future needs of students,
- establishing use or value of learning to the student, and

- connecting affective and cognitive aspects of the science lesson.

Modeling—Critical skills, knowledge and understandings of science are demonstrated and communicated to the learners by the teacher. For example the science teacher could
- demonstrate the use of scientific knowledge and attitudes and
- apply scientific approaches to present personal and social issues.

Reinforcement—Productive behavior is encouraged and non-productive behavior is discouraged through the use of positive and/or negative reinforcement, or extinction. Science teachers should know:
- positive or negative consequences increase behaviors,
- extinction eliminates behaviors, and
- punishment decreases behaviors.

Practice—Proficiency in many scientific skills is achieved through repetition of a task. Practice can be either as a group at the initial stages of learning, or individualized and included throughout the learning sequence or at the end of a learning sequence. Important aspects of skills development include:
- repetition of important skills and
- correction of deficient skills.

Closure—Learners summarize skills, knowledge or understanding of science at the conclusion of a learning experience. Important points include:
- summary by learner of science knowledge, skills and attitudes, and
- relate to objectives of science lessons.

direct, and guide her toward the next steps in the learning process.

The central theme of this section has been on the personal ingredients that must be present for learning to occur. Although the interpersonal dimensions are difficult, they are no less essential than the external and internal dimensions for teaching science.

■ Summary

Motivation is discussed using an external and internal distinction. The external dimension includes many factors in the environment over which science teachers have control. External elements that can increase student motivation to learn include level of concern, feeling tone, success, interest, and knowledge of results, or feedback.

Maslow's motivational theory is based on a hierarchy that can be summarized as physiological, physical, and psychological. The higher levels, that

is, motivation toward self-actualization, form, to use Maslow's phrase, "the farther reaches of human nature." The structure and function of the hierarchy should be viewed holistically. All needs influence motivation to some degree, although certain needs tend to be more dominant. Fulfilling motivational needs ensures maintenance and survival as well as continued development of the person. Ideally, there is a gradual transformation from lower to higher needs. Progression or regression within the hierarchy can occur; this aspect of motivational needs is self-regulatory. The hierarchy is a dynamic system that functions simultaneously to maintain and change the individual, and it is structured in a way that ensures continued personal development. Table 4.1 summarizes this system as it applies to science teaching.

Maslow's theory has two general implications for science teachers: You should be aware of the influence of unfulfilled lower needs on behavior and you should encourage growth and personal development toward a goal of self-actualization.

Behaviorists emphasize the external dimensions of learning. Stimuli and reinforcements exist in the environment and influence learning. The organized use of reinforcements can greatly increase the effectiveness of instruction and thus produce greater learning. Science teachers have the greatest control over the external environment, making this dimension crucial to teaching. The primary implications of behaviorism are to specify the behaviors you wish to change or achieve, identify available reinforcers, and use consistent reinforcements.

Science teachers are concerned with the perceptions, motivations, and thought patterns that influence behavior; that is, the internal dimension of learning. Learning amounts to reconstructing old thought patterns into new ones. The behaviorist determines which behaviors are desired, changes the environment, and reinforces the desired behaviors. In this sense the behaviorist controls behavior through changes in the environment. The other theorists also change the environment to encourage learning. But these theories state that individuals learn through problem situations that result in new perceptions of unique relationships among objects and events.

When these theories about external and internal dimensions of learning are applied to science teaching, different methods and techniques are implied. The primary methods of the S-R approach are those of carefully organized, programmed learning, i.e., the use of teaching machines and class monitoring of student behavior. The problem-solving approach is the closest application of theories stressing the internal dimension. In the discovery approach, you would design problem situations that would result in new insights by your students. As the teacher you would present the problems and provide the means and opportunities for students to solve them. Your role would include questioning, assisting, giving clues or hints at possible solutions, or new directions for solving the problem.

Interpersonal dimensions of learning were presented in the final section. The science teacher's role is to facilitate learning through opportunities to study materials and solve problems which have personal meaning for the student. Qualities of a good facilitator include authenticity, caring, acceptance, and empathy. The interpersonal is, in many ways, the dimension that pulls the external and internal together.

■ References

1. Madeline Hunter, *Mastery Teaching* (El Segundo, CA: TIP Publications, 1982).
2. Abraham Maslow, *Motivation and Personality* (New York: Harper & Row, 1970).
3. Abraham Maslow, *Toward a Psychology of Being* (New York: Van Nostrand Reinhold, 1968).
4. Abraham Maslow, *The Farther Reaches of Human Nature* (New York: Viking Press, 1971).
5. Ivan Pavlov, *Conditioned Reflexes* (New York: Dover Publications, 1960).
6. Edward L. Thorndike, *The Fundamentals of Learning* (New York: Teachers College Press, Columbia University, 1932).
7. B. F. Skinner, *Science and Human Behaviour* (New York: MacMillan, 1953).
8. B. F. Skinner, *Beyond Freedom and Dignity* (New York: Knopf, 1968).
9. David Premack, "Reinforcement Theory," in *Nebraska Symposium on Motivation*, ed. D. Levine (Lincoln, NE: University of Nebraska Press, 1965).
10. Wolfgang Kohler, *The Mentality of Apes* (New York: Harcourt, Brace and World, 1925).
11. Jean Piaget, *The Development of Thought: Equilibration of Cognitive Structures* (New York: Viking Press, 1977).
12. Carl R. Rogers, *Freedom to Learn* (Columbus, OH: Charles E. Merrill, 1969). See also Rogers, *Freedom to Learn for the '80s* (Columbus, OH: Charles E. Merrill, 1983).

══════════════════   INVESTIGATING SCIENCE TEACHING   ══════════════════

ACTIVITY 4–1

Student Motivation

This activity is to be completed during an observation period in a science classroom. First, identify three students of differing motivational levels—one highly motivated, the second about average, and the third an "unmotivated" student. You may have to ask the science teacher for recommendations. Second, observe these students for 15 minutes each. During this time note the behaviors that you think reveal their level of motivation. Finally, indicate what you would recommend to *increase* their motivation.

	Observations	Recommendations
Highly Motivated Student		
Student of Average Motivation		
Unmotivated Student		

1. How would you modify the science class to increase student motivation?

2. What role do the curriculum materials play in student motivation?

3. What role do instructional methods play in student motivation?

ACTIVITY 4–2

"How Can I Motivate Students to Learn?"

This activity is based on the discussion of external motivation. You are to spend a period of time (at least one class period and preferably two or three) observing a science teacher. During this observation period you are to note examples of the factors Madeline Hunter suggests will increase student motivation. (See the text of her book, *Mastery Teaching*.)

Factors	Examples	Effect on Students
Level of Concern		
Feeling Tone		
Success		
Interest		
Knowledge of Results		

How do these factors interact?

Provide your own examples of the way you would implement these factors.

1.

2.

3.

ACTIVITY 4–3

Motivational Needs

Imagine that you observed these behaviors in a tenth-grade biology class.

Mary was restless and fidgeting during the lesson; something seemed to be competing for her attention. The science teacher ignored her. Two desks away Robert sat quietly, head on his desk, sleeping. The teacher awakened Robert and firmly suggested that he pay attention. Karen paid close attention to the teacher. She was careful to record the important points of the lesson and then started her assignment. After completing her work and handing it to the teacher, she was given recognition that was earned and deserved. Martin came into the class and immediately started clowning around, climbing on desks and causing a commotion. He was also given recognition—it was also earned and deserved; however, the teacher had to make a great effort to get him to behave in an appropriate manner.

1. What do you think might be motivating these behaviors?

2. How could you find out more about the motivations of these students?

3. How would you respond to the students in a different way?

ACTIVITY 4–4

Rewards and Punishments

In connection with learning about psychology as it is applied in education, you should plan to spend several hours in observation of a science class. Your task is to determine the reinforcements and punishments that are given. Use the following guide, which is similar to Figure 4.4 in this chapter, to help systematize your observations. Review the definitions involved and then make a check each time you observe a reinforcement or punishment.

	Present Stimulus	Remove Stimulus
Pleasant Stimulus		
Aversive Stimulus		

1. Which did the teacher use most—reinforcement or punishment?

2. What types of reinforcers and punishments were used?

3. Did any particular method seem effective? Ineffective?

4. What did you learn about the use of reinforcement and punishment in the science classroom?

CHAPTER 5

The Psychology of Development and Groups

In this chapter we discuss developmental and social psychology. Emphasis is placed on cognitive development since this is an important concern of science teaching. A brief discussion of ethical development is also included. Social psychology is discussed in the second section of the chapter.

■ Cognitive Development

For over fifty years, the late Dr. Jean Piaget and his coworkers at the Genetic and Epistemology Institute in Geneva, Switzerland, have studied cognitive development. Table 5.1 describes some basic ideas of Piaget's theory.

Piaget believes there are four stages of mental development from birth to adolescence.[1] From the earliest interactions with the environment, individuals continuously construct a system of cognitive structures. The four stages are identifiable steps in the construction, with each developmental stage explaining the next. To understand later stages, it is necessary to first understand the earlier ones. So, we shall discuss all four stages, but emphasis will be placed on the concrete and formal stages since these stages, and particularly the transitions from one to the other, generally occur during the years of secondary school. A summary of development across the four stages appears in Table 5.2.

The Active Child
Sensorimotor Stage (0-2 Years)

During this stage the child begins to construct the cognitive and affective structures that will be continually expanded. Language is absent and the child has not yet formed means of symbolic function. Cognitive development occurs through the sensory responses and physical movements.

TABLE 5-1
Concepts of cognitive structure, function, and stage

Intelligence is the ability to *organize* and *adapt* to the environment.

Cognitive functions of organization and adaptation contribute to the development of the cognitive structure.

Cognitive functions do *not* vary with development.

Cognitive structures *do* vary with development.

A set of cognitive structures at relative equilibrium is a stage.

Each stage integrates the cognitive structures from previous stages into a new higher order structure.

Source: This table as well as substantial portions of this chapter first appeared in Rodger W. Bybee and Robert B. Sund, *Piaget for Educators*, 2nd ed. (Columbus, O.: Charles E. Merrill, 1982, 1976). Used with permission.

TABLE 5-2
Four stages of mental development

The Active Child	0–2	Sensorimotor
The Intuitive Student	2–7	Preoperational
The Practical Student	7–11	Concrete Operational
The Reflective Student	11–14	Formal Operational

Child Is Stimulus-Bound

During the sensorimotor stage the child interacts with the environment primarily by using her senses and muscles and is directed by external sensations. The ability to perceive, touch, and react is developed at this time. Most body motions are, in a sense, an experiment with the environment. As the child interacts with her surroundings, she slowly learns to deal with the physical environment. For example, she eventually perceives depth, whereas in the early part of the stage she sees things as flat only.

Order and Organization Begin

As a child develops, she is faced with challenging experiences to which she must adapt. These experiences are then organized so that later the child will be able to call on them as needed. A child, therefore, obtains several kinds of experience. One kind, perceiving phenomena and interacting with objects and materials, is mainly physical. Another kind of activity is mainly mental. For example, when a child mentally acts on information, she classifies objects in the environment. She then acquires mental experience, which is also essential for development.

During the sensorimotor stage, the child is exposed to a wealth of experiences which help her to develop the foundation of cognitive skill so important for the later stages of development. She begins to form rudiments of cognitive activity, which are organized into more elaborate schemes as development progresses. Innate reflexes are adapted to the objects around the child, advancing by coordinating the various actions that are possible on each object, thus identifying the object's properties. She touches, feels, pushes, and slides the objects, learning, as a result, that they have certain properties.

The Child Does Not Coordinate Mental Operations with Physical Experience

In the sensorimotor stage the child cannot imagine objects or acts. What is not in sight is not in mind. The child cannot add, subtract, or even classify unless acting on real objects. Even the most rudimentary sense of direction and purpose does not develop until the child is well into this stage.

Labeling Ability Develops

At the end of this period the child is able to imagine. She can call to mind certain people, animals, objects, and activities. By age two, she has "names" for many things and activities, enabling her to elaborate concepts. Space is limited to the area in which she acts, and time is limited to the duration of actions. Progress develops as the child becomes more involved with activities concerning space and time.

The sensorimotor child spans a tremendous cognitive distance in two years. The infant grows from a reflex dominated creature to a dynamic, reacting, and sometimes exasperating little rascal. The active child has adapted and learned how to obtain satisfaction, thereby demonstrating to some degree intelligent behavior. The active child has advanced from being able to make slight discriminations to identifying objects, places, and people. The sensorimotor child has slowly evolved to some understanding of causality by knowing objects can be removed and replaced. Object permanence has been attained. There has been movement from a gurgling infant to one using verbal means of communicating. The active child has left the crib to become involved and experiment in play by acting out roles and in imitation. Because the infant has developed these and other mental abilities, she is capable of moving into the preoperational stage.

The Intuitive Student Preoperational Stage (2-7 Years)

The second stage of cognitive development (ages 2-7) is called preoperational because the child is not yet capable of mental operations. An operation is defined as an interiorized action which modifies an object of knowledge. To classify an object is to mentally operate on it so that it may be included in the classification system. Piaget's examples of mental operations include those listed in Table 5.3.

TABLE 5-3

LOGICAL OPERATIONS		
Adding	$+$	Combining
Subtracting	$-$	Taking Away
Multiplying	$\times$	Repeating Addition
Dividing	$\div$	Repeating Subtraction
Correspondence	$\sim$	Aligning one Row with Another Row
Placing in Order	$><$	This Is Greater Than or This Is Less Than
Substituting	$=$	Replacing Something with Another Entity
Reversibility	$\rightleftarrows$	Subclasses Belong to a Class – A Class Has Subclasses

Preoperational children widen their perceptions of the environment and demonstrate the gradual evolution of structures, providing the base for operational thinking that emerges in the next stage of cognitive development. Due to the absence of logical reasoning patterns, students often resolve problems intuitively. Representational thought has increased, contributing to the acceleration of language development. They now speak using fairly complex sentence structures but still seldom use connectives in their language. Although preoperational children are still relatively egocentric, they are losing this egocentricity, as indicated by their increasing ability to play games and follow rules. They still, however, have difficulty differentiating among truth, fantasy, and realism in their explanations. Semilogic, using logical patterns of thinking but only in one direction, and transductive thinking have developed. Toward the end of the period these children begin developing the various types of conservation, starting with conserving substance. Their conceptualizations of space and time have broadened considerably from those of the sensorimotor period.

Child Is Stimulus-Limited

The child's thinking in this stage is limited to what has been experienced. She functions on a plane of representation and can use language. However, during this period she may use images that are not logical. In the early part of this stage, for example, a child may call all men "Daddy." The preoperational stage is said to be intuitive because as the child develops she begins to sense mentally the difference between such things as an individual item and its class, singular and plural, some and many, man and men, and "Daddy" and other men.

Attention Is Centered on Striking Aspect of Problem

The preoperational child centers attention on striking aspects of a problem. For example, if you take a ball of putty and roll it out, the child will notice that it is longer; attention is centered only on length. The child will not notice that the putty is also thinner;

attention has not included the simultaneous compensation of length and width. If you ask the child whether the rolled-out putty weighs more, less, or the same as the ball of putty from which it was made, the usual response is that the rolled out putty weighs more even though you may reroll it into a ball in front of him (Figure 5.1).

Child Focuses on States, Not Transformations

A preoperational child cannot combine a series of events to show how they are unified by the changes they have undergone. For example, a child is shown a series of pictures of a pencil falling and asked to order them in the sequence in which the pencil fell. As a result, the child focuses on the state of the pencil before and after it has fallen and will probably place the first and last picture in order but be confused about the others (Figure 5.2).

Thought Processes Are Not Reversible

A child at this stage doesn't reverse thought processes. If asked: "What is a chicken?" the child will say, "It is a bird." Then, if asked: "What would happen if all the birds were killed? Would there be any chickens left?" The child would probably reply, "Yes." If you force some other answer you will usually get an irrational one such as, "There are chickens left because they ran." The child doesn't realize that the subclass chicken belongs to the class bird. If the class is destroyed, the subclass is also destroyed. To grasp this point the child must have a good idea of class and subclass plus be able to reverse his mental process to go from class to subclass as well as from subclass to class.

Child Is Egocentric

It is difficult for a child of this period to understand views other than her own. For example, she talks even though she pays little attention to whether she is being understood or even listened to. The child thinks that the way she sees things is the way all

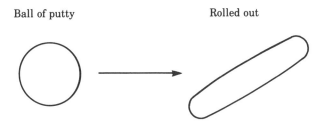

FIGURE 5–1
Child centers on length and thinks rolled out piece weighs more

FIGURE 5–2
Child centers on end states and does not perceive the sequence of transformation

people view them. This egocentricity changes in time largely by confrontation in social interaction with other individuals' ideas.

Time and Space Concept Now Expanded

Impressions of time have changed during this stage from thinking only in the present to being able to think of future and past time. The child's understanding of time, however, does not extend very far beyond the present. The concept of space has enlarged to include an understanding of the nearby environment, e.g., home, neighborhood, and school.

Science teachers should be aware of the developmental levels of students and structure the learning sequence in such ways as to facilitate the development of logical operations by the students. Science teachers can engage the intuitive student in problems that establish the cognitive structures that are fundamental to more developed patterns of thought. Suggestions include such things as the following skills of scientific investigation:

- Observation: Looking at objects and events critically.
- Measurement: Establishing the length, height, width, volume of objects using a standard unit.
- Quantity: Identifying how much there is of something.
- Time: Describing events as present, past, or future.
- Seriation: Putting objects in order by following a pattern or property to construct the series.
- Classification: Grouping according to similarities, partitioning a group into subgroups based on some property, and arranging these in a hierarchy.

The Practical Student
Concrete Operational Stage (7-11 Years)

The concrete operational period begins for most students around age seven and terminates at age eleven. It is called concrete because students' thought is mainly restricted to what they encounter in direct experience. So you have practical students. They think about the properties of existing objects. They also think of the actions or the things they actually can do with them. The period is operational because children during the span of these years slowly develop mental operations which appear as logical reasoning patterns and the ability to mentally reverse a series of changes.

The practical student increasingly uses mental representation for physical action. With time mental representation takes the place of physical action. Through the elementary school years this representation and action are tied to experience. In this period

semilogic, thinking in only one direction, turns into logic. The practical student thinks about objects, their properties, and the possible actions that can be performed on them. Using the mind to perform such operations characterizes students in this period and provides the foundation for more sophisticated patterns of thought.

Conservation, classification, and seriation are all possible for the practical student. The student realizes that the quantity of a substance remains the same if nothing is added or subtracted from it. And this is so even if the substance undergoes a complex series of changes. The student can classify objects based on observable properties. The student can order objects according to an observable property. Knowing these patterns of thought are possible and, as we have seen, related to other educational components such as number and, clearly, language, is an important step in the application of Piaget's theory.

The practical student's conceptual understanding of space and time has broadened to include some notions of geographical space and historical time. She can think of the area of city, state, and she has some notions of different cities and places. She can become fascinated with some historical episodes and has some ideas of their place in time.

At this stage the child moves from the earlier physical actions to the use of mental operations. To know an object is to act on the object. And, in the process of acting or operating on the object, it is modified. Take, for example, a pencil. If you grouped it with other objects, such as yellow objects, objects of more than one material, or objects used for writing, you would be mentally operating on the pencil and modifying it by your classification.

Thoughts Are Related to Actual Objects

During the concrete operational stage a child slowly becomes proficient in developing the ability to perform all of the preceding logical and infralogical operations. Thought is mainly limited to physical objects and not mental propositions. However, students at this stage can be influenced by a book or other aid to think of places and times with which they have had no experience.

Class and Relation Concepts Are Devised

One of the main results of this stage of development is that the student constructs class and relation concepts, which enable her to more effectively order objects and events in the environment. The major cognitive structures include time and space, cause and effect, and conservation. Each new encounter with nature does not require extensive examination but can be classified according to structure and function. The child can go beyond things and think of groups. Since the concrete operational person can do reversible thinking, she is able, late in this stage, to classify things in an ascending as well as descending manner. This ability to form classes and groups enables the child to expand her mental activity.

Limited Hypotheses Are Possible

A child of this period can think of what happens when the volume of a container is altered; that is, what happens to a container receiving liquid as well as to one being depleted of it. However, the child is usually limited to making a single hypothesis involving only one variable, and she is better able to do this if the containers are visible.

Action Representation Occurs

Mental action takes the place of performing some real act on an object. For example, if you add water from a wide flat jar to a slender jar, the water level in the slender jar will be higher. The concrete operational child, when asked if there is more or less water in the slender jar than in the wide jar, will reply that it is the same. If you ask her why she thinks this is true, the reply will probably be, "If you returned the water to the wide jar, you will have the same volume as before." The child mentally performs the action of refilling the wide jar with water.

Students in Transition

Discussions of Piaget's theory tend to stress ages and stages. Educators have thus tended to try and identify the characteristic products of development aligned with particular stages. In reality most students are in transition. Even if you can absolutely identify a student's thought as concrete operational, what then is your educational task? Certainly your task must be more than announcing the student's level—"She is beyond the preoperational period and cannot yet complete formal operational problems." It is still important to encourage further development, to get the student to continue along the developmental path. Thinking of development as a process leads the science teacher to ask about transitions from one major period to another.

There are three identifiable levels of transition in the development of operational thought. The first level is one of direct physical action on objects without mental representation of the actions. Reasoning strategies (if they could be called this) are overt handling without conceptualization of the problem or an organized approach to solving the problem. Given a seriation problem of order blocks the student would be unable to establish any order. The task would be completed by placing the blocks in an arbitrary order.

At the second level (ages five to six) children are able to mentally represent aspects of the problem but cannot conceptualize the entire problem; they are not able to work with a definite approach. Rather, students are greatly influenced by perceptually dominating aspects of the problem and they use an intuitive, trial-and-success (or error) approach to the problem. Once the student starts a seriation sequence or makes a mistake in the sequence, she has difficulty correcting the problem. This is true even if only one block is out of place.

At the third level, by about age seven or eight, the student is able to conceptualize the entire problem and demonstrates a reasoning strategy as long as she actually has the materials or objects of the problem. However, students may not complete a similar problem when it is presented orally and requires completion without the use of concrete aids. Likewise, if students are given long and detailed problems, they may make mistakes. That is, they may have the basic idea, but make minor errors. The lack of correct response is explained by the child's inability to conceptualize all the relevant components and remember the components as the reasoning strategies are applied; thus, partially correct responses are given to complex problems.

Finally, students are able to conceptualize problems and apply reasoning strategies that are logical.

The Practical Student: A Summary of Achievements

Based on the review of this period, it seems we can summarize a few important educational achievements for the practical student.

1. Uses logical patterns of reasoning on concrete problems.
2. Understands part-whole relationships.
3. Demonstrates conservation of mass, weight, and volume.
4. Recognizes the properties of numbers.
5. Organizes events, objects, and situations in space and time.
6. Reverses thinking to justify changes of objects and events.
7. Completes mathematical operations requiring reversibility.
8. Establishes an order among objects, events, situations, using a common, but asymmetrical, property.

The Reflective Student
Formal Operational Stage (12-15 Years)

By attaining formal thought, the student passes through the intellectual gateway to adulthood. In doing reflective, hypothetical-deductive, and propositional thinking, the adolescent is able to better use her mind to interact more effectively with both the physical and social environment.

The formal operational period begins around age twelve and continues into adulthood. The over-riding characteristic of the period is the student's development of abstract reasoning. An individual at the formal operational level need not refer to concrete objects in order to think about them. Logical and mathematical relationships are used in relation to objects and events. Accordingly, we describe the reflective student. There are several broad characteristics of adolescent thought patterns. Possibilities become real rather than reality determining what is possible. This is one way of expressing the fact that formal thought transcends the concrete situation. Another characteristic of the reflective student is the possibility to generate and consider all possible combinations for a given situation. Reflective students can reason inductively and deductively. They can begin with a set of facts and provide a generalization, thus demonstrating inductive reasoning. They can also begin with a major generalization and deduce a specific conclusion, thus demonstrating deductive reasoning.

The understanding of time and space increases significantly for the reflective student. The adolescent thinks of distant places and larger and larger units of space. She also thinks more of imagining long periods of time. The formal operational thinker also grasps the meaning of infinity, historical time, global geography, and interplanetary space. She can conceive of both present and future problems caused by changes in today's world.

Student Reasons Theoretically

Students have the ability to apply theoretical constructs to objects and events that are not immediately and concretely observable. Making inferences, completing "if-then" propositions, serial ordering, and multiple classification are all possible for these students.

Reflective Thinking Processes Occur

One of the main characteristics of the stage is the student's ability to do reflective thinking. The student is able to think back on a series of mental operations, that is, reflect on them. In other words, students can think about their thinking. They can also represent mental operations by symbols. In science, for example, when a student finishes an experiment, she can be asked how it could be improved if she were going to do it again. To determine an improved approach, the student would have to reflect and evaluate everything she had done.

Probability and Combinatorial Reasoning Occur

The formal operational student thinks in terms of many possibilities rather than being limited to the immediate facts. Numerous combinations are conceivable at this stage.

Student Can Control Variables

If given an experimental problem, students who reason formally will recognize the need to control all variables except the one under investigation. They will be able to systematically change variables in a problem so that their causes and effects may be determined.

We suggest that you complete some of the interviews in the activity "Teaching Science Activities: Problems for Cognitive Development." Doing so will provide valuable insights into the reasoning patterns of adolescents.

Students in Transition

Most students should attain the formal operation stage in the middle school years. The difficulty for science teachers is that the age at which individual students develop formal reasoning patterns varies. Substantial numbers of adolescents do not use formal reasoning patterns. As a science teacher, it is probably safe for you to assume that the majority of your students will be in a transition from concrete to formal reasoning patterns.

Because of the significant advances in operational ability during this period, formal thinkers are capable of understanding, constructing, and applying abstract theories. Theoretical reasoning enables the individual to interact more effectively with the environment. However, adolescents vary considerably in their thinking. Many adolescents avoid thinking critically. They appear to avoid cognitive challenge and tend to remain in the comparative comfort of the concrete stage. Others, presumably because of more success in school, maturity, and environmental differences, confront formal tasks with great tenacity. This is not to say that it is easy for them. It usually isn't. Present a problem requiring propositional or hypothetical-deductive thought and watch their "body language." Many of them fidget, grimace, or frown as they force their mind to perform the operations required. The result of such discomfort is a broadened intellect. Science teachers should realize that adolescents do not automatically employ formal patterns of thought. Most students in secondary schools are *capable* of formal thought, but most students do not *demonstrate* this level of thought. Any number of factors can influence adolescent performance; for instance, motivation, self-esteem, and peers. With this caution, science teachers are advised to view formal reasoning as optimum patterns of thought.

Science teachers should realize that adolescents (and many adults) use formal operations in situations where they have interest, concern, and expertise. This observation points to the importance of knowledge, the content of thought, as it relates to the level of mental functioning.

Most science teachers in middle and senior high schools will encounter students demonstrating patterns of reasoning that have both concrete and formal elements. As a matter of fact, educators can expect most students to demonstrate varied reasoning patterns. Understanding the difference between concrete and formal patterns is important for educators since this understanding provides direction as teachers attempt to help students achieve higher levels of thought. (See Table 5.4.)

There is another point worth mentioning. By early adolescence, behavior is multidimensional and multidetermined. Considering a student's response in class or answer to a task must include more than an analysis of the cognitive content. While Piaget perceives this period as the pinnacle of development, other theorists remind educators that the adolescent period is one of physical, social, and personal turmoil. The transition that occurs during adolescence is more than cognitive. Multiple factors should be reviewed in the evaluation of cognitive achievement.

Science teachers are confronted with the task of facilitating development from concrete to formal levels of thought. To do so requires educators to understand the major differences between the two stages. (See Table 5.4.) Since both concrete and for-

mal periods are concerned with logical thought, what are some basic differences between the periods? There are two primary differences. First, in the formal operational period mental action no longer requires actual objects, events, or situations. For concrete students the realm of the real is possible. For formal students the realm of the possible is real.

The second difference between the two periods is that in the formal operational period there is a more complete coordination of mental operations, particularly the reversibility of thought. The logical operations of inversion and reciprocity become coordinated into a single structure. The difference between the coordination of these operations at concrete and formal levels can be illustrated by referring to the conservation of matter task. When a ball of putty is transformed into a hot dog shape, concrete operational students will conserve matter across the changes. (See Figure 5.1.) And they justify their answer by indicating the changes could be reversed. This is an example of inversion. The student may also indicate that the changes in one dimension (e.g., width) have compensated for changes in another dimension (e.g., height). This is an example of reciprocity. Concrete operational students can use either of these individually, but not in coordination. The formal operational student would use both inversion and reciprocity in justifying her response.

The Science Student's Construction of Knowledge

Psychological research on the process of concept development has made progress in recent years. Still, however, there are three different views of this process and they are all applied to classroom instruction. In the first view there are forces and pressures in the external environment that impress themselves on the student's mind. Knowledge has an exterior origin. Learning is a copy of reality. The second view emphasizes the growth and development of internal structures. Knowledge has an innate origin. Learning is an unfolding of these structures. The third view is that the development of concepts is a construction of knowledge which results from an interaction between the intellectual structure (but it is not innate) and the environment. Knowledge is a continuous and spontaneous construction. Learning is an adaptation and organization of experience. Equilibration is the process that explains the simultaneous maintenance and change of the intellectual structure. Maintenance and change occur through organization and adaptation respectively.

How can one simultaneously *maintain* the in-

TABLE 5–4
A comparison of concrete and formal reasoning

Concrete	Formal
Reference to objects, events, or actions are needed for logical reasoning.	Reasoning occurs conceptionally. Theories, hypothetical propositions, axioms, and indirect relationships are the bases for reasoning.
Conservation, class inclusion, serial ordering, and reversibility dominate patterns of logical reasoning.	Theoretical, combinatorial, propositional, functional, and proportional reasoning extend the concrete patterns.
The student is unaware of inconsistencies in her own thought patterns.	The student is aware of inconsistences due to the ability to "think about one's thinking."

TABLE 5–5
The student's developing understanding of the world: a summary

Content	Sensorimotor Period Beginning Characteristics	Preoperational Period End/Beginning Characteristics	Concrete Operational Period End/Beginning Characteristics	Formal Operational Period End/Beginning Characteristics	Continuing Characteristics
Action	Reflexive physical actions	Representational thought	Prelogical thought—Can reason in one direction	Logical-reversible thinking related to concrete experience	Combinatorial/propositional logic INRC group
Objects	Not permanent	Permanent objects	Conservation of identity	Conservation of quality, quantity classification, seriation, and number	Combinatorial logic, propositional logic
Space	No concept of space	Conceptualizes immediate space	Broadens concept of space	Understands relations with objects—elementary geometry	Understands relative space
Time	No concept of time	Conceptualizes short sequences and durations of time	Aware of past, present and future	Coordination of temporal order and duration	Understands relative time
Causality	No concept of cause/effect	Conceptualizes simple cause/effect relationships	Animistic	Understands cause/effect in concrete problems	Separation and control of variables in complex problems
Play	Repetition of reflexes	First symbolic play	Representative play	Practical play	Reflective abstraction and hypothetical thought
Imitation	Repetition of reflexes	First deferred imitation	Representative imitation	Practical imitation	Reflective abstraction and hypothetical thought
Self	No concept of self	First concept of self/not self	Egocentrism	Reduced egocentrism	Ideal self
Language	No language	First language	Egocentric language	Practical language	Abstract language

tegrity of the cognitive structure and *change* the cognitive structure? To resolve this problem, Piaget appeals to the biological principles of organization and adaptation. Only here, they are applied as metaphors for cognitive functioning. Organization and adaptation are complementary functions. We shall look at each briefly. *Organization* can be thought of as a basic inherited tendency of organisms. This is true biologically and for Piaget psychologically. Organization is the tendency to systematize and integrate actions—either motoric or cognitive—into coherent structures of a higher order. So, two experiences that may originate separately (e.g., looking at an object and grasp-

ing an object) may be eventually integrated into a higher level action of simultaneously looking and grasping. This higher level action does not eliminate the original actions. They are still available for use separately. Organization accounts for a continuity of the cognitive structure across time and development. It also accounts for the increasingly higher levels of complexity of the cognitive structure; that is, the patterns of action and thought associated with the major periods of development.

The cognitive structure changes through adaptation. *Adaptation* is the basic tendency of the organism to adjust to the environment. The central idea here is that experience has an effect on the cognitive structure. Development results from continuous adaptations to the environment. Adaptation is a process with two equally important components: assimilation and accommodation.

Assimilation of motoric or cognitive actions is based on an underlying cognitive structure. The individual "interprets" environmental situations in terms of existing cognitive structures. This is what is meant by the modification of reality to fit existing explanations as individuals attempt to "interpret" reality in ways that presently make sense to them. In other words, the individual attempts to adapt to her environment through assimilation.

Accommodation is the other component of the adaptive process. Here, the cognitive structure is changed to fit incoming information. This is a modification of an existing explanation to fit reality. In the process of accommodating to the environment, the cognitive structures are expanded, broadened, or generalized as they incorporate increasingly larger aspects of the world. There are definite limits on the adaptive process. This point is very important for educators to remember. For Piaget, assimilation and accommodation are two sides of the adaptive coin. They can be separated for discussion, but they are inseparable in the student's interactions with their world.

Implications

Following are some suggestions for applying what you have learned about cognitive development to teaching science.

1. Attempt to determine which students in your class are concrete or formal in their thinking. You can ask students, individually, to hypothesize about some scientific problem which is not visible to them or to do reflective thinking, i.e., ask, "If you were going to do an experiment again, how would you do it better?" Present a problem with which a scientist was concerned and ask them how they would solve it. If students do not do well on these tasks, it is indicative that they are concrete operational or in a state of transition from one stage to another. Therefore, teaching should rely less on verbal instruction and more on actions using materials and concrete activities.

2. If students are in the formal operational stage, require that they analyze their procedures, data, etc., and suggest ways of improving the experimental design. The students in transition from concrete to formal reasoning may be able to do some of these activities and those who are formal in their thinking should experience little difficulty.

3. Ask students to design an investigation. Rather than first telling them how to perform an experiment, ask students how they would set up an experiment to find the answer to the problem under discussion.

4. Provide them with several things and let them establish a classification scheme.

5. Give students as much freedom as they can handle in creating, inquiring, and discovering. This freedom allows for more cognitive involvement, contributing to their thinking ability.

6. Involve students in group projects requiring the solving of problems. Try to constitute the groups so that there will be opposing views, requiring an interchange of ideas. Social interaction is one of the factors forcing cognitive growth. Certainly an intellectual argument requires logical thinking and analysis of positions, facts, and variables.

7. The adolescent mind becomes relatively capable of determining and synthesizing general properties. Adolescents, therefore, should have many opportunities to use reasoning to discover general laws and principles of science.

8. Formal students are able to make correlations and deal with proportionality. Science teachers should provide the necessary guidance to help students comprehend problems of this nature. Many students, however, may have considerable difficulty in accommodating these ideas until they have had several experiences with them.

9. Students should be encouraged to make hypotheses, think propositionally, evaluate data, and originate their own problems. Ask questions such as: "What hypotheses would you make?" "If you were going to do an experiment to find out, what would you do?" "What other problems or experiments do you suggest?"

Applying the developmental approach in the science classroom requires the teacher to understand the student's level of development. Then, the teacher can expose the student to problem situations that are slightly beyond this level. In doing so, the student will experience conflict and dissonance while applying the current level of cognitive structures to problematic situations at a higher level; thus, disequilibrium and equilibration. The student's construction of knowledge is a result of psychological *and* physical activity on the external environment. This is a process of equilibration between the cognitive structure and the environment. Historically, classroom science instruction has emphasized, changed, and reorganized curriculum and materials more than focusing on the internal processes of the student.

Science teaching for the student's construction of knowledge requires two things: (1) an instructional style that emphasizes the student's level of development and (2) an understanding that the student's construction of knowledge occurs when the intellectual structure is modified through confronting problems and conflicting situations. It is important to remember that development explains learning; that is, the student has a cognitive structure that will be applied and modified in the learning situation. So, educators contemplating teaching with a recognition of Piaget's theory of equilibration should provide challenging situations that are within the students' parameters of intellectual adaptation. The challenges may be described by terms such as appropriate discrepancy, optimal discord, moderate novelty, tolerable mismatch, or reasonably problematic.

Above all, allow students as many opportunities as possible to think and use their reasoning abilities. They may organize their approach to a task, motivate other students to work with them on a project, interact with other students about a problem, collect and interpret data, decide on a class presentation, or create something for the class. Examples of various problem types are found in the "Investigating Science Activities," at the end of this chapter.

The fact that some students are not formal thinkers probably acts as a discriminating influence against them in taking certain courses. In research with junior high and high school students, Ball and Sayre found that only one physics student out of fifty-seven interviewed was reasoning at a concrete level and he was in serious scholastic difficulty (see Tables 5.6 and 5.7).[2] Students undoubtedly get the "word" that physics is difficult and that they cannot do it. Many, therefore, do not enroll in the course. This fact is particularly depressing since physics, if taught with an understanding of how students actively construct concepts, could be instrumental in helping these students become formal thinkers. The application of Piaget's theory to physics instruction has been discussed by several prominent science educators. We recommend that future physics teachers review the articles of John Renner and Tony Lawson.[3,4]

In the past, science teachers have largely assumed that the materials they used were aligned with the developmental level of their students. Research findings based on Piaget's theory indicate that this assumption is not accurate. Students vary widely in their cognitive abilities and, at best, curriculum materials and textbooks are designed for an average level of development. In the classroom the science teacher

TABLE 5-6

Comparison of junior high school students' grades with their overall performance on the Piagetian task instrument

Scholastic Grade	No. of Students Receiving	Formal Performance	Nonformal Performance	Percent Formal	Percent Nonformal
A	19	8	11	42.1	57.4
B	74	13	61	17.6	82.4
C	78	1	77	1.3	98.7
D–F	43	1	42	2.3	97.7

Source: Daniel W. Ball and Steve A. Sayre, "Relationships Between Student Piagetian Cognitive Development and Achievement in Science" (Ph.D. dissertation, University of Northern Colorado, 1972).

TABLE 5-7

Comparison of senior high school students' grades with their overall performance on the Piagetian task instrument

Scholastic Grade	No. of Students Receiving	Formal Performance	Nonformal Performance	Percent Formal	Percent Nonformal
A	51	45	6	88.2	11.8
B	78	49	29	62.8	37.2
C	55	20	35	36.4	63.6
D–F	21	4	17	19.0	81.0

Source: Daniel W. Ball and Steve A. Sayre, "Relationships Between Student Piagetian Cognitive Development and Achievement in Science" (Ph.D. dissertation, University of Northern Colorado, 1972).

has the crucial role of mediating, adjusting, and matching the materials to the students. To do so, the science teacher will rely on Piaget's stages of development as the student constructs meaning of the educational experiences.

■ Moral Development: *The Ethical Student*

Many science teachers have recently become interested in the ethical development of students. As it turns out, Jean Piaget also studied the ethical development of children.[5] In recent years, Piaget's original ideas were developed by the late Lawrence Kohlberg.[6] We should note here that Kohlberg's ideas have been criticized.[7,8] However, they still offer a good introduction to ethical development.

Lawrence Kohlberg used Piaget's research on moral development as the foundation for advancing further investigation into this area. Kohlberg carried on numerous studies in the United States and other countries striving to better define moral development. One of his main works, started in 1958, involved a longitudinal study of boys at ages ten and sixteen, and followed their development past the ages of twenty-four and thirty. Kohlberg also made several cross-cultural investigations.

Kohlberg's research has further substantiated Piaget's belief that moral development is hierarchical in character. Kohlberg believes it consists of three levels, each containing identifiable stages. The three levels are (1) preconventional, or premoral, (2) conventional, or conforming, and (3) postconventional, or self-accepting, moral principles.

Preconventional Level

At the preconventional level, the child is responsive to such rules and labels as good and bad, right and wrong. He interprets these labels to purely physical or hedonistic terms—if he is bad, he is punished; if he is good, he is rewarded. He also interprets labels in terms of the physical power of those who enunciate them. The preconventional level comprises two stages.

Stage One: Punishment Avoidance and Obedience Orientation
The *physical consequences* of an action determine its goodness or badness regardless of the human meaning of value of these consequences. Avoidance of punishment and unquestioning deference to power are valued in their own right, not in terms of respect for an underlying moral order supported by punishment and authority. Briefly, moral decisions are based on the avoidance of aversive consequences. Behavior is simply obedience to authority. "I'll do what you say in order to avoid a spanking" characterizes moral judgements at this stage.

Stage Two: Seeking Rewards
In this stage the child agrees to rules or does things because they benefit her. Right action consists of that which instrumentally satisfies one's own needs and occasionally the needs of others. "Taking care of number one" is foremost in moral decisions. Human relations are viewed in terms similar to those of the marketplace. Elements of fairness, reciprocity, and equal sharing are present, but they are always interpreted in a pragmatic way. Reciprocity is a matter of "you scratch my back and I'll scratch yours," not of loyalty, gratitude, or justice. Successful ends can justify questionable means.

Conventional Level

Expectations of the individual's family, group, or nation are perceived as valuable in their own right, regardless of immediate and obvious consequences. The attitude is one not only of conformity to the social order but of loyalty to it; of actively maintaining, supporting, and justifying the order; and of identifying with the persons or group involved in it. The level comprises the following two stages.

Stage Three: Social Approval Orientation
Good behavior is that which pleases others and is approved by them. There is conformity to stereotypical images of what is majority behavior. Behavior is frequently judged by intention. "He means well" becomes important. One earns approval by being nice. You don't do things because you might "lose face." Moral decisions and actions are based on what "pleases others." "Everyone was doing it" is a common justification for this stage.

Stage Four: "Law and Order" Orientation
Authority, fixed rules, and the maintenance of the social order are valued. Right behavior consists of doing one's duty, showing respect for authority, and maintaining the social order for its own sake. Concern is for the larger community. A larger social orientation is the basis of deciding right from wrong. Social authorities (e.g., principals, presidents, and teachers) must be obeyed for the maintenance of social order. Rules and laws are viewed as static.

Postconventional Level

At this level there is a clear effort to teach to others a personal definition of moral values—to define principles that have validity and application apart from the authority of groups or persons and apart from the individual's own identification with these groups. (Late in his life, Kohlberg indicated that due to difficulty in differentiating Stages Five and Six, they should be thought of as one stage. We have decided to include discussions of Stage Six.)

Stage Five: Social-Contract Legalistic Orientation

This stage has utilitarian overtones. Right action tends to be defined in terms of individual rights and the standards that have been agreed upon by the whole society. There is a clear awareness of the importance of personal values and opinions and a corresponding emphasis on procedural rules for resolving conflicts. Other than that which is constitutionally and democratically agreed upon, right is a matter of personal values and opinion. The result is an emphasis both upon the legal point of view and upon the possibility of making rational and socially desirable changes in the law through cooperative negotiation. Outside the legal realm, free agreement is the binding element of obligation.

Stage Six: Universal Ethical-Principle Orientation

Right is defined by the conscience in accord with self-chosen principles, which in turn are based on logical comprehensiveness, universality, and consistency. These principles are abstract and ethical, for example, the golden rule, Kant's categorical imperative (i.e., act only as you would have others act in the same situation). They are not concrete moral rules like the Ten Commandments. At heart, these are universal principles of justice, of the reciprocity and equality of human rights, and of respect for the dignity of human beings as individual persons. These six stages are summarized in Table 5.8.

Designing Ethical Dilemmas for the Science Classroom

1. Identify the conflict and theme for the dilemma (e.g., life, liberty, justice, truth, etc.).
2. Introduce the scientific or technological problem.
3. Clarify the conflict.
4. Be sure there is a dilemma (i.e., a choice between two equally unfavorable alternatives). Should the person be maintained on life-support systems or allowed to die? Should justice be done for the individual or the group, concerning air quality?
5. Describe the situation and dilemma to the students in understandable terms.
6. Delineate the decision made by the main characters in the dilemma.
7. Review the moral dilemma and describe what you perceive to be the pro/con positions for each stage.
8. Ask for a definitive decision with reference to

TABLE 5–8
Kohlberg's levels of moral development

	Stages	Motivation
Stage One:	Avoiding Punishment	Ethical decisions are made to avoid punishment. Self-gratification is important. Morality occurs mainly because of fear of punishment.
Stage Two:	Seeking Reward	Desire for personal reward and benefit. What is in it for me? What are the consequences?
Stage Three:	Social Approval	Anticipation of social disapproval or self-guilt. Has stereotypes of good and bad people.
Stage Four:	Law and Order	Anticipation of dishonor. Afraid of losing face or gaining dishonor. Follows social rules. Believes in rule maintaining. Exceptions cannot be made because everyone would start disobeying rules.
Stage Five:	Social Contract	Concern about self-respect or being irrational and inconsistent. Right actions are constitutional and democratically derived. Free agreement and contract binding between individuals. The way the American government operates.
Stage Six:	Universal Ethics	Concern about condemnation, about violating a person's principles, and about maintaining principles as a way of life. Sacredness of life; compassion for fellow humans, universal principle of justice.

the dilemma (e.g., what should Mary do—stand up for her rights or allow the person to die?).
9. A good dilemma is simple, straightforward, and relevant to students.
10. Be sure to ask for a justification for the response.

After introducing the dilemma, the science teacher should guide the discussion making sure the students stay on the topic. The teacher can point out inconsistencies in reasoning, and more adequate resolutions to the dilemma. Be sure to let the students answer the dilemma *and justify their positions.*

■ Social Psychology and Science Teaching

So far our discussion of psychology has reviewed motivation, learning, and development of individuals. Although they are unquestionably important, it is also true that most of the time science teachers are teaching *groups* of students. Anyone who has taught can tell you that teaching a group of thirty is different than teaching an individual. We should give some attention to the social influences on behavior. Individual behavior is influenced by the real or imagined presence of other human beings. Therefore, it is easy to see why some understanding of social psychology is important for science teachers.

Within the last decade, educational social psychology has been recognized as an important dimension of effective teaching. To gain a better understanding of students and to become a better science teacher, it is crucial to recognize the social psychology of individual behavior, the factors influencing classroom groups, the leadership role of the science teacher, and the effect of the classroom "climate" on the group.

Social Behavior

Social psychology is the study of the influence of other persons on an individual's thoughts, feelings, and behavior. The presence of other persons can be real or imagined. The definition of social psychology considers the fact that individuals can be engaging in social behavior even when they are alone. Consider a seventh-grade boy walking down a school hallway. He has not finished his assignment for science, so he is imagining a conversation with his science teacher. "What should I say?" "How will she respond if I tell her my baby sister tore up the paper?" "What about 'The dog chewed the assignment?'" "How about 'My mother threw it out with some other junk when she was cleaning my room?'" As he is walking, he meets two girls from his class, one of whom is his "first love." Meeting the smiling and bashfully interested girls, he stammers for something to say, "Ah, ah—ah, hi, Jane—oh and—Rita. What are you doing here?" "We go to school here, silly." "Oh yah. Ah—well—nice to see you—bye—I've got to go now—ah—see you later." Here, the boy's behavior was clearly influenced by the girls. When he reaches science class, the boy quietly goes to his seat and listens to the teacher give instructions for a laboratory activity. When she finishes, he and three other students work cooperatively on the assignment, talking about biology (and other important things). This example includes several situations where the boy's thoughts, feelings, and behavior were clearly influenced by the actual and imagined presence of others. It shows how behavior is almost always influenced to some degree by the social environment.

The Science Class as a Group

A group consists of two or more persons who interact and influence one another. With this definition in mind we wish to point out that students are placed in classrooms based on criteria such as age, ability, or scheduling compatibility. That is, students in your science classroom will not necessarily be a group. We can look at two educational situations to clarify the concept of a group. In the first situation, the science class is individualized. Student tests and aptitude scores are forwarded to the science teacher who, in turn, designs a totally individualized program. This program consists of reading the science textbook, doing selected units of programmed instruction, completing designated laboratory activities, and taking tests. All of this is done individually with an occasional meeting with the teacher. In contrast, a second approach to science teaching involves some teacher presentation to the entire class, laboratory work involving two, three, or four students working together, individual study time, discussions with the teacher, and discussions among the students themselves.

The first situation may in fact be good educational practice, but from the teacher's and student's points of view there is probably not a classroom group. On the other hand, the second situation has some immediately recognizable properties of groups including observable characteristics such as interaction, structure, goals and norms, and cohesiveness.

Interaction
Interaction is an important property of groups. Simply put, students affect one another through various types of communication. The interaction among individuals in the science class contributes to the development of other characteristics of groups such as

GUEST EDITORIAL

A Message to Teachers on Structuring Student Interactions in the Classroom

Roger Johnson
Professor of Science Education,
University of Minnesota, Minneapolis, Minnesota
David Johnson
Professor of Social Psychology, University of Minnesota,
Minneapolis, Minnesota

There are instances where traditional practice in schools has gone one way, while empirical research indicated that another course was more productive and desirable. Such is the case with the use of cooperative, competitive, and individualistic student-student interaction patterns for instruction. In the past forty years, competition among students has been emphasized in most American schools. In the past fifteen years, individualistic efforts toward achieving learning goals have been increasingly emphasized. The research indicates, however, that cooperative interaction among students would be more productive on a wide range of cognitive and affective instructional outcomes than either competitive or individualistic interaction patterns.

Perhaps the major reason for this discrepancy between educational practice and research is the fact that how students interact with one another has not been emphasized in the development of curriculum and in teacher preparation. The spotlight has been on the ways that students interact with materials and the role of the teacher; however, how students interact with each other during instruction has powerful and important effects on their learning and socialization.

There are three basic choices for student-student interaction patterns: competitive, individualistic, or cooperative. A competitive interaction pattern exists when students see that they can obtain their goals if and only if the other students with whom they are linked fail to obtain their goals. An example would be a spelling bee where students spell against each other to find the best speller in the class. Norm-referenced evaluation systems, such as rank-ordering students from best to worst or grading "on a curve," set up competitive interaction between students. An individualistic interaction pattern exists when the achievement of students' learning goals are unrelated to the goal achievement of other students. An example of this "we're all in this alone" situation would be a spelling class where each student has his own set of words to learn and a criterion for measuring individual success, so that the achievement of one student has no effect on the achievement of another. A cooperative interaction pattern exists when the students perceive that they can obtain their goal if and only if the other students with whom they are linked obtain their goals. An example of this "sink or swim together" situation is a group of students working together as a spelling group, preparing each other to take the spelling test individually on Friday. Each student's score is the number of words his group spells correctly. In competition, there is a negative interdependence in terms of goal attainment, in the individualistic situation there is independence between goal attainment, and in cooperation there is a positive interdependence in terms of goal attainment.

There are many research studies which have compared cognitive and affective results for students working cooperatively, competitively, and individualistically. The results indicate that, in comparison to competition and working individually, cooperation produces:

cohesiveness, structure, goals, and behavioral norms. Several factors can affect group interaction in science classrooms.

1. The science teacher facilitates the type of interaction.

2. Frequent interaction increases students' attitudes toward the class.
3. Seating arrangements should be conducive to the desired type of interaction.
4. Status and authority of the teacher and students can affect interaction.

1. Higher achievement and longer retention of the material learned,
2. More positive attitudes about the subject matter and the teacher,
3. Higher self-esteem,
4. More effective use of social skills, and
5. More positive feelings about each other. (This "positive cathexis" works regardless of differences between students and has implications for the integration of different ethnic groups, main-streaming of handicapped students into regular classroom settings, and managing the heterogeneity present in every classroom.)

These results represent only a few of the many which have been researched, but they emphasize the powerful nature of cooperative learning. Furthermore, the importance of cooperative learning experiences goes beyond improving instruction and making teaching more satisfying and productive for teachers, although these are worthwhile goals. The ability of all students to cooperate with others is the keystone to building and maintaining friendships, stable families, career success, neighborhood and community membership, and contributions to a society. Knowledge and skills are of no use if the students cannot apply them in cooperative interaction with other people.

With strong empirical support for cooperative learning and the fact that it makes sense for students growing up in a society, we must be careful not to overgeneralize. The research into cooperative learning does not say that having students work together cooperatively is a magic wand that will solve all classroom problems. It does say that those problems probably have a better chance of being solved in a cooperative than in a competitive or an individualistic setting, but it is not reasonable to expect hyperactive students to suddenly become calm or low mathematics students to suddenly master all the material. It does give the teacher a powerful edge, to go to work on the problems of orchestrating effective instruction for students. We recommend that all three interaction patterns be used in a classroom setting. Students must learn how to compete appropriately and enjoy the competition, win or lose; they must learn how to work independently and take responsibility for following through on a task; and they must learn how to work with one another effectively in cooperative relationships. Each of these interaction patterns must be used appropriately and integrated effectively within instruction, realizing that cooperation is the most powerful of the three.

There is little doubt that teachers who master the strategies needed to set up appropriate interaction patterns, maximizing the use of cooperation, will have a powerful and positive effect on their classroom learning environment. This addition to the teacher's repertoire does not mean a new curriculum. It takes only a few minutes to make clear to students the kind of student-student interaction that is expected, with some additional time needed at first to teach the appropriate interaction skills to the students.

The initial effort on the teacher's part and the time needed to carefully structure student-student interaction are effort and time well spent. It would be exciting to see the gap between the research findings and traditional classroom practice disappear so the students would say, "School is a place where we work together to learn and share our ideas, argue our point of view, and help each other find the most appropriate answers and understand the materials. Sometimes we have a fun competition and sometimes we work individually, but most of the time we learn together."

5. Guiding interactions in large groups is important.

Structure

As groups develop, a structure emerges. Some students will be perceived differently than other members of the group. For example, some students will be leaders, others followers. Structure within a group can be influenced by the physical setting of the classroom, the neighborhood environment, and other factors such as race, sex, and socioeconomic status. Needless to say, there are some structures that facilitate groups and others that debilitate them. The science teacher must often guard against group structures that are detrimental to others. Sometimes it is good to randomly assign students to working groups and, on other occasions, students can work with friends.

Goals

Goals are an important property. Several types of goals can coexist in a group, e.g., student goals, teacher goals, educational goals, and so on. Discussion, laboratory activity, projects, and field trips are group activities that would involve different goals. Groups that help formulate or clarify their own goals tend to have more interaction, a clearer structure, and greater cohesiveness.

Norms

What should individual students do in certain situations? What is expected of individuals in the group? When may they talk and when do they listen? There are unwritten rules in influencing student behavior, and it will contribute immensely to your effectiveness to be aware of the norms. When a science teacher assigns a laboratory activity and groups begin to work, norms of behavior are often clearly seen in student comments such as, "Let's work together," or "If we each do our share, we should be able to get this laboratory work done."

Cohesiveness

Cohesiveness is the degree of attachment which members of a group have for one another. Cohesiveness can be expressed as the number of friendships within the group, the degree to which group members function together effectively, the bonds that bind members to the group, or the degree of similarity among ideas and behaviors. For science, a test of cohesiveness is the degree to which students speak of *our* science project, *our* group assignment, *our* results.

Cooperative Learning

As you have seen, educational social psychology includes dimensions of learning, motivation and development not accentuated in traditional educational psychology. Some have criticized social psychology for generating a great deal of knowledge that was either self-evident or insignificant. Is there a place where social psychology has produced new understandings that will help the classroom science teacher? The answer is yes. And the understanding is related to such critical factors as achievement, socialization, critical thinking and higher levels of rea-

soning, attitudes toward the subject, self-esteem, and positive attitudes toward other students, including minorities and the handicapped.[9-12]

For over a decade David and Roger Johnson and their colleagues have worked at developing a substantial empirical base relative to cooperative, competitive and individualistic learning situations in classrooms. They began with the assumption, different from other theories of educational psychology, that the heart of socialization and development is the quality of the relationships children and adolescents have with others, particularly peers. (You might stop here and read the guest editorial in this chapter by Roger and David Johnson.) The implications of their research are significant for science teachers since many aspects of science teaching lend themselves to group work. Some implications include:

1. Cooperative learning can be used with any type of academic task. The efficacy of cooperation increases along a continuum from lesser to greater conceptual difficulty.
2. Cooperative learning can be used with controversial topics.
3. Students can keep each other on the assigned task and material in ways that facilitate higher levels of learning.
4. Students can support each others' efforts, regulate work, provide feedback, and ensure involvement of all members in the learning process.
5. Cooperative groups should generally contain low, medium, and high ability students.

By now you are probably asking "What is cooperative learning?" "How does one set up cooperative learning situations?" and "How do students learn the skills of cooperation?" We shall discuss these questions briefly. In doing this we will note that the model of cooperative learning is described in much more detail in Chapter 18, "Models for Effective Science Teaching." Also we will mention the book *Circles of Learning*[13] in which the cooperative learning model is presented in very practical terms.

Cooperative learning is a classroom technique requiring students to work together to achieve an academic task and simultaneously learn effective, positive interpersonal skills. During a science lesson using the cooperative model, small groups of students might be seen designing experiments, discussing results, explaining concepts and, in general, learning together. In the process, students also are practicing social skills such as working effectively with others, establishing positive friendships and maintaining healthy relationships with other adults.

There are four essential elements of cooperative learning. First, students share the view that they are in the learning situation together, and together they will "sink or swim." In short, there is a *positive interdependence* among individuals. Second, each student must learn the assigned material and assist the other group members to learn. There is *individual accountability*. Third, individuals have a close working relationship with each other. Groups are structured for *face-to-face* interaction. Finally, students must be taught the social skills needed for collaboration and maintenance of effective relationships within the group. Cooperative learning requires students to learn and use *interpersonal and small group skills*.

Cooperative learning is set up through the science teacher's use of five strategies.

1. Specifying the lesson's objectives.
2. Deciding on placement of students in groups.
3. Explaining the task, goal structure, and learning activity.
4. Monitoring group work and intervening to assist with the assigned academic work or to facilitate students' interpersonal and group skills.
5. Evaluating academic achievement and helping students discuss their collaborative skills.

Finally, there is the question of how students develop the skills of cooperation. In general, they progress through a hierarchy of four levels of skills.

1. Forming the skills needed to establish a cooperative group.
2. Maintaining the skills needed to manage a cooperative group.
3. Encouraging the skills needed to develop higher levels of understanding, stimulating higher reasoning strategies, and maximizing learning as material.
4. Challenging the skills and conceptualizations through constructive conflict, use of discussion, search for information, and the statement of a justification for one's conclusions.

Science teachers wishing to incorporate cooperative skills should be sure that students:

1. Understand the need for cooperative skills;
2. Understand what cooperative skills are and when they should be used;
3. Practice cooperative skills;
4. Discuss and receive feedback on their use of cooperative skills; and
5. Persevere in practicing cooperative skills until they are a natural part of group interactions.

Leadership in the Science Classroom

Leadership can be thought of as the influence of a person or persons on a relationship with one or more other persons. Leadership qualities are sometimes attributed to individuals because of personality; we say they have charisma. In other cases, persons are leaders because they have unique abilities which qualify them to lead. Finally, there are persons who are leaders because they are in positions of power and authority. It would be nice if, as a summary, we could say that science teachers were leaders because they had all these qualities: charisma, competence, and control. Unfortunately, few teachers possess all of them. Teachers do have some power and control because of their position and, hopefully, they are competent in their scientific knowledge, teaching methods, planning skills, and classroom organization and management. Finally, they may or may not have the enthusiasm and personality that contribute to charismatic leadership.

We will concentrate on the first, leadership due to the teacher's position. Fulfilling the second qualification is certainly one of our goals, so your methods course and this textbook should contribute to leadership due to your competence as a science teacher. Finally, we encourage charismatic qualities, but as yet psychologists have not clearly defined the traits contributing to charisma, and psychosurgery is not advanced enough to transplant the traits even if we could identify them.

Leadership in the science classroom involves developing a climate that sustains efficient and effective work by the classroom group while fulfilling personal needs and educational goals. In other words, leadership requires management of the total classroom—science content, the physical environment, individual student needs, and the students as a group. However, it would be misleading to leave the impression that leadership is solely a function of the teacher. One has only to recall the last organized bookdrop or the pleasant surprises that await substitute teachers to realize that leadership can originate from the ranks of students. In less extreme examples, leadership is commonly seen when students work in small groups on science activities. Mary Bany and Lois Johnson[14] described the two major functions of classroom leadership as *facilitation* and *maintenance*.

Facilitation

Facilitative tasks that contribute to effective leadership include:

1. Developing unity and cooperation among students,
2. Establishing policies and standards for the classroom,
3. Coordinating work procedures among students and groups,
4. Improving the classroom climate through cooperative problem solving, and
5. Modifying physical conditions in the classroom.

As a facilitative leader, the science teacher neither coerces nor persuades; rather she facilitates classroom unity by setting policies, procedures, and conditions through cooperative interaction with the student group. Facilitative tasks contribute to social cooperation among students. This cooperation has tremendous positive influence on individual behavior. When the classroom group has the ability to resolve problems and make decisions, many of the everyday problems of organization and management are avoided.

Maintenance

Even though the classroom group is working together and continuing to fulfill the needs of the group and goals of the teacher, there are, inevitably, times when management problems will arise. Schedule changes, all-school activities, and unplanned custodial work can all cause changes in the physical environment, classroom climate, or group composition. Often such situations require fast action by the teacher to maintain the classroom group. Some classroom maintenance functions are:

1. Sustaining morale,
2. Resolving conflicts,
3. Restructuring groups changed due to outside factors,
4. Reducing anxiety and fear.

Maintaining the classroom group in the face of changing and sometimes adverse conditions requires flexibility and adaptibility by the science teacher.

Leadership Styles

For our discussion, three styles of leadership can be described, based on teachers' consistent use of power. Consider three examples of a science class.

1. The students enter class and go immediately to their seats. The teacher tells the students exactly how to set up and complete the science activity, providing worksheets with specific step-by-step instructions. The teacher assigns student groups, indicates who should obtain the materials, how long each section of the activity should take, and when the written report is due. The students work in this structure, closely following directions for the remainder of the period; the report is due at class time the next day.
2. The students enter class and go to their seats. The teacher tells them that they will try to solve a problem. The problem is described and the teacher asks the students how it might be solved. Several suggestions are offered. The suggestions are summarized and developed into a science activity. The teacher clarifies different aspects of the activity and informs the students of the available materials. They are then told to form groups, obtain materials, set up, and complete the activity. The students work for the remainder of the period. The next day there is some time to finish laboratory work, time for group discussion, and time to complete the report and have a postactivity class discussion.
3. The students enter the class and start examining various science books, displays, and journals. The teacher calls the students to attention and they proceed to their seats. She presents a problem. The students are directed to solve the problem any way they can. They are informed about the location of materials and when the results of the problem are due.

Three similar situations have been used to describe three leadership styles—directive, participative, and permissive. Although it is true that a science teacher uses all three approaches at one time or another, one style tends to represent a particular individual's consistent style of leadership.

Science teachers must be directive some of the time, but we caution against carrying this style to an extreme. Power is used exclusively by the teacher. In this case, leadership is a result of the teacher's use of power and authority to control the students and their work.

The participative style of leadership allows students some input to the structuring of work, problem solving, or decision making, as in the second example. The participative teacher guided but did not control. Control came from the groups and their approach to resolving the problem. Here, the power and authority of leadership are derived from the students and are shared by them.

The third example was of permissive leadership. Here the science teacher made minimum use of the power and authority of her position. Power and authority were in fact largely given over to the

REFLECTING ON SCIENCE TEACHING

The Classroom Climate

The climate of the science classroom is a synthesis of many factors and recommendations outlined in this and earlier sections.

There is *respect* for students and teachers. All persons are treated with dignity, even when there are problems. Resolving classroom conflicts can be done with respect for the rights and dignity of the students and teachers. How will you plan to show respect for your students?

Trust in others is evident. Students feel that teachers are on their side and will not let them down. There is confidence that all members of the classroom group can be counted on to contribute their share, are dependable, and are honest. How would you facilitate and maintain this attitude in a science classroom?

Students and teachers have a high *morale* about what happens. They feel good about being in a science program. Is it possible to *feel good* about science and still meet educational goals? What factors contribute to positive feelings about a class? a teacher? other persons?

Appropriate *input* and *decision-making* opportunities are available for the students. How does this recommendation relate to leadership style? In what ways can the students also contribute to the formulation of rules for the science classroom?

There are *opportunities for students and teachers to have a voice* in the science program and classroom activities. What would you do if this goal were to be implemented in your science classroom? When, where, and how could you provide opportunities for student input to the program and activities?

A *cohesiveness exists* between members of the science class. Students want to be in the science class, they feel that they belong and are part of the group. How would you design a science lesson for the first day that would help develop group cohesiveness? How could you include other important aspects of group development, such as interaction, structure, norms, and goals?

Each student feels that some other student and the teacher *care* for him. All the students know that their health and welfare are to some degree a concern of the other students and especially of the teacher. They know that being or not being in science class makes a difference to other students and to the teacher. What can you say and do to show students you care for them? How can you resolve classroom conflicts and still show students you care for them?

---

students, although the position of leadership was maintained. This position is a precarious one for the science teacher. In this example the groups are left to their own means of resolving the problem. Experience has shown that most groups of students have difficulty fulfilling their needs and achieving educational goals without some degree of direction and/or participatory leadership by the teacher.

Although you may have read the examples and have determined that one is best, we caution against such a conclusion. Although each person has a preferred style of leadership, experience has shown that, in any science classroom, teachers must use different leadership styles at different times. The effective leader has the insight and flexibility to know when to direct, when to participate, and when to permit.

The Climate of the Science Classroom

How would you describe a positive climate for a science classroom? What factors are involved in a classroom climate? What about the physical condition of the classroom? What about the science program? What about the types of interaction between students and the teacher? There are certainly some tangible factors that come to mind, i.e., a good program, activities, involvement, and a warm, comfortable room. There are also some other, less tangible factors, such as good interpersonal relationships, respect, trust, and caring among students and between the students and teacher. The interaction among these factors and others contributes to a climate in the science classroom.

Implications

1. Until recently, social psychology was, unfortunately, omitted from teacher preparation programs. We strongly encourage you to understand and apply some of the basic principles concerning group dynamics in your own science classroom.

2. Do not assume that your class will naturally form the cohesiveness, structure, goals, norms, and

interaction characteristics of a good group. Include activities specifically designed to develop your class as a positive and productive group.

3. Develop your leadership qualities as a teacher in the science classroom. You can begin by identifying the different tasks of group facilitation and group maintenance that are important for your school and your students.

4. Be aware of the problems that occur during times of transition. For example, in going from a laboratory activity to seat work, a few minutes are required for the transition from one group structure to another.

5. Establish the rules and procedures for the classroom by using democratic procedures. Be sure all students know the rules.

6. Maintain a positive and productive classroom climate through respect, trust, democratic decision-making, and caring about students. These are some of the "details" of science teaching that are sometimes neglected in our enthusiasm for presenting a new formula or concept. More often than not, when teachers experience the difficulties of disruptive behavior, they are due to social and psychological factors.

■ Summary

Central to Piaget's theory are the concepts of cognitive structure, cognitive functions, and cognitive content. The cognitive structure refers, in the most general way, to the stages of development. Cognitive structures are identifiable patterns of physical or mental action that underlie specific acts of intelligence. For example, some patterns of action are more logical than others if one considers a specific act such as separating and controlling variables.

There are four distinct patterns of intelligent action in Piaget's theory: the sensorimotor stage, the preoperational stage, the concrete operational stage, and the formal operational stage.

The sensorimotor period is characterized by the fact that intelligent action is motoric. Internalized thought is largely not evident during the first two years of life. The cognitive structure develops through the overt behavior and action by the infant, hence the label "the active child."

At the preoperational period the child's cognitive structure manifests some internalized thought processes. The thought processes are based on the original sensorimotor processes developed in the prior stage. Though children show signs of "thought," it is not logical. Compared to later stages the thought is intuitive, so you have the "intuitive student."

The cognitive structure during the concrete operational period is logical. By operational Piaget means that the individual can establish a mental image of an object or event, change the object or event, and then return the image to its original form. Still, the concrete operational student does not show the most sophisticated level of cognitive structures because she depends on concrete information, objects, events, and so on before thinking is logical. If the situation is too abstract, the student may reason illogically; in this case teachers can identify "the practical student."

The most complete manifestation of the cognitive structure is the period of formal operations. Thinking is abstract, rigorous, and logical. Mental operations, or acts of thought, are completed on situations and information that have not, or may not, ever occur. At this level of development there are logical patterns of thought about ideas that may only exist as thoughts. Conceptual modeling and hypothetical reasoning are examples of thinking at this level. According to Piaget, this is the final and most complete development of cognitive structures. Teachers may observe the "reflective student."

The development of reasoning patterns requires disequilibrium and the student's active construction of concepts. Being engaged by the ideas and arguments of higher levels is the way development occurs naturally. As the student hears other ideas, he cannot quite understand the position. The result is a disequilibrium of cognitive structures. As the student resolves the cognitive disequilibrium, new, higher levels of reasoning patterns are constructed. Educators can facilitate the process of development by (1) helping students understand explanations by asking them what they do and do not understand; (2) providing information they understand; (3) encouraging them to try new patterns of reasoning; (4) allowing time for new patterns of reasoning to emerge.

Educators often tend to emphasize only the cognitive aspects of student development, but research by Jean Piaget and Lawrence Kohlberg has clarified ethical aspects of development as well. There are patterns of moral reasoning that identify the ethical student. Piaget has suggested that the ethical student is first a moral realist. Rules are derived from those in authority; they are rigid and static. Judgments are informed by the objective situation. Greater harm is determined by the amount of harm done; intentions of the actor are not considered. In early adolescence there is a passage from this heteronomous approach to rules to an autonomous approach. At this time the student is a moral relativist in that intentions and situations are evaluted in the process of making moral judgments.

Lawrence Kohlberg has described stages of ethical development. At the preconventional level the ethical student first has a punishment/obedience orientation (Stage One). He then becomes an instrumental relativist who makes moral decisions in terms of rewards (Stage Two). The conventional level is characterized first by social approval or being a good girl or boy (Stage Three) and then law and order (Stage Four). A few students develop patterns of moral reasoning that are postconventional. There is a social-contract (Stage Five) and a universal ethical (Stage Six) level of development.

Social psychology has important implications for science teachers since most of the time they are working with *groups* of students. A group consists of two or more persons who interact and influence each other. Some important properties of groups are interaction, structure, goals, norms, and cohesiveness.

One useful application of social psychology in science classrooms is the cooperative learning model. This model helps students develop interpersonal skills while mastering the assigned material. There are specific strategies for setting up the model, teaching students the skills of cooperation and incorporating the cooperative model into science classrooms.

Finally, the science teacher has an influence on the students. She is a leader of the classroom group. As a leader the teacher is responsible for facilitating and maintaining learning in a positive classroom climate. Being an effective leader requires the insight and flexibility to know when to direct, when to participate and when to permit students to work on their own.

■ References

1. Jean Piaget and Barbel Inhelder, *The Psychology of the Child* (New York: Basic Books, 1969).
2. Daniel W. Ball and Steve A. Sayre, "Relationships Between Student Piagetian Cognitive Development and Achievement in Science" (Ph.D. dissertation, University of Northern Colorado, 1972).
3. John W. Renner and Anton E. Lawson, "Piagetian Theory and Instruction in Physics," *The Physics Teacher* 11, no. 3 (March 1973), pp. 165-169.
4. John W. Renner and Anton E. Lawson, "Promoting Intellectual Development Through Science Teaching," *The Physics Teacher* 11, no. 5 (May 1973), pp. 273-276.
5. Jean Piaget, *The Moral Judgment of the Child* (New York: The Free Press, 1965).
6. Lawrence Kohlberg, "The Cognitive-Developmental Approach To Moral Education," *Phi Delta Kappan* (June, 1977), pp. 670-77.
7. Carol Gilligan, "In A Different Voice: Women's Conception of Self and Morality," *Harvard Educational Review*, 47 (November, 1977), pp. 481-517.
8. John Gibbs, "Kohlberg's Stages of Moral Judgment: A Constructive Critique," *Harvard Educational Review*, 47 (February, 1977), pp. 43-61.
9. David Johnson and Roger Johnson, "The Socialization and Achievement Crisis; Are Cooperative Learning Experiences the Solution?" in L. Bickman (ed.) *Applied Social Psychology Annual 4* (Beverly Hills, CA: Sage Publications, 1983).
10. David Johnson, Roger Johnson, and Geoffrey Maruyoma, "Interdependence and Interpersonal Attraction Among Heterogeneous and Homogeneous Individuals: A Theoretical Formulation and a Meta-Analysis of the Research," *Review of Educational Research*, 5, no. 1 (Spring 1983), pp. 5-54.
11. David Johnson, et al., "Effects of Cooperative, Competitive, and Individualistic Goal Structures on Achievement: A Meta-Analysis," *Psychological Bulletin*, 89, no. 1 (1981), pp. 47-62.
12. Roger Johnson, et al. "Integrating Severely Adaptively Handicapped Seventh-Grade Students into Constructive Relations with Non-Handicapped Peers in Science Class," *American Journal of Mental Deficiency*, 87, no. 6 (1983), pp. 611-618.
13. David Johnson, Roger Johnson, Edythe Johnson Holubec, and Patricia Roy, *Circles of Learning* (Alexandria, VA: Association for Supervision and Curriculum Development, 1984).
14. Mary Bany and Lois Johnson, *Educational Social Psychology* (New York: Macmillan, 1975).

========================= INVESTIGATING SCIENCE TEACHING =========================

ACTIVITY 5–1

Assessing Cognitive Development: Concrete Operations

The administration of tasks outlined in this section should provide you with insights into the cognitive abilities of middle school students. You should have little trouble administering the tasks. It will require making arrangements for the interview session and preparing the required materials. Interpreting the results may present problems. For this reason, some discussion is provided on how tasks can be interpreted. The experiences of questioning students about their reasoning will provide valuable insights into the stages of cognitive development.

Here are some specific suggestions for administering the tasks. Also, a suggested interview form is provided.

Each of the tasks to be administered outlines a basic structure for the interview. Certain specific suggestions for giving the tasks should be followed:

1. *Establish rapport.* It is important that the person giving the interview establish good rapport with the child before administering the tasks (i.e., ask her name, age, etc., as suggested on the interview form which follows). Tell her you have some games to play, and all answers are acceptable.
   Try to make the tasks fun to do, smile while the child does them, and do what you can to lessen the child's feeling that the interview is a threatening experience.
2. *Do not give answers.* Do not tell the child she is wrong or right, just accept her answer and either your or an assistant record them on the interview form.
3. *Ask for justification.* Always ask for the justification of an answer. In the interview we are interested in determining how the child thinks (i.e., Is she really conserving or is she just giving a correct answer?).
4. *Hypothesize about the child's thinking.* Formulate in your mind certain hypotheses about how the child is thinking. Ask the child questions to test your hypotheses to determine whether or not they are correct.
5. *Use the "another child told me" approach.* In asking the child to justify an answer, you may ask her why she thinks it is correct. Experience shows that some children will not respond to why questions. Generally, however, if you restructure your questions giving an episode like the following, they will respond: "The other day a boy told me that the rolled out clay in the form of a hot dog weighed just as much as the clay before it was changed. What would you say to him?"
6. *Allow for wait-time.* Remember that most tasks require some form of logical-mathematical reasoning. Thinking takes time. Therefore, do not rush the child in your interview. Allow her time to think; five or more seconds time allowance is not too much.
7. *Have fun.* Most of all, have fun giving the tasks and try to see that children have similar experiences.

Outlined below is an interview form to be used to note the task achievement of the student. It will probably be best for you to record the responses while you interview. The interview form needs some clarification. In each session you should *plan on giving six or seven tasks.* The time for administering these will vary from twenty to forty minutes, depending on the age and cognitive level of the child. Place a description of each task in the left-hand column. Check in the appropriate column whether the child achieved or did not achieve the task. In the column provided for the level of cognition, write the period the student demonstrated. With many students you will not get a clear demarcation of stage. They might perform preoperationally on three tasks and concrete operationally on four. You probably would indicate the transitional stage on the basis of your limited interviewing measures.

Piagetian Interview Form: Concrete Operational Period

Name of Child_____Interviewer's Name_____Location_____

Age_____Grade_____Sex_____

Activity description (e.g., conservation of substance, class inclusion)	Achievement: + Task achieved − Not achieved	Indication of cognitive level (e.g., operational). Note: If child doesn't achieve level of task, it is assumed he is at a lower level.	Other comments about the student's behavior or statements	Justification (child's reason for responding as he did)
1.				
2.				
3.				
4.				
5.				
6.				
7.				
8.				
9.				
10.				

How many tasks were achieved?

How would you classify this student's level of development? Transitional? Concrete operational?

How would you justify this classification?

How could you confirm this level?

What are the educational implications of your interview?

Piagetian Interview Activities

Time and distance.   Tell the child two persons are walking the same speed and distance, except one is walking on a straight path and one is walking on a crooked path. Ask, "Which one reaches his house first? Why?" Use two strings of equal length to represent the paths.

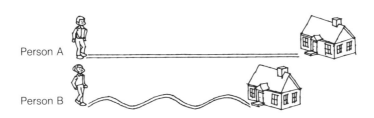

Person A

Person B

Discussion: Up to age nine, children usually have difficulty comparing the time taken and distance covered of two moving persons or objects. They believe going farther (in direction) takes more time. They do not compensate by increasing or decreasing the speed. For this reason, preoperational and early concrete operational children believe Person A will take more time.

Seriation. Prepare ten cards of stickmen, dolls, flowers, or some animal so that they progressively increase in size. Place the first and last of the series on a table and tell the child to place the rest of them in order.

Discussion: During the concrete operational period, a child develops her ordering ability. This ability usually occurs during ages seven and eight. Many children, however, even in the third grade, cannot do the task. If they cannot do it, they probably also have difficulty with number because ordering is basic to understanding mathematics.

Ordering. Show children, ages six through eight, stages of a developing moth, including the egg, larva, pupa, and adult. Discuss how the moth develops through these stages. Let the children look at the various stages of the organism and have them draw the stages in order of development.

Next, show them a picture of one of the stages and ask, "What would be the next stage? What was the stage before this? Why do you think so?"

Discussion: If the children can do this and give reasons for their placement of the stages, they probably are able to order. Many young children will not be able to do this. The activity is still valuable because it helps children grasp some concepts of development although they may not be able yet to interrelate them. If they do not order correctly, they probably do not see the stages as a continuum of an organism slowly progressing to maturity. Children unable to do this probably reason by transduction.

Speed. Obtain two toy cars of different colors. Draw on a piece of paper a line to indicate the end of a race. Place one of the cars behind the other at the start. Move both of these cars with each of your hands so that they come to the finish line at the same time. Ask, "Which of the cars was going faster, or did they both move the same? How do you know? How about the distance traveled? Did one cover a greater distance? When was one car ahead of the other? Why? Which one moved faster?"

Discussion: Young children believe if the cars finish the race together, they must be moving at the same speed. This is because they believe order, being in front or together, indicates speed. Usually at age nine or ten children take into consideration where an object started and stopped, distance traveled, and the time it took. If the child does not grasp this realization, he will have difficulty doing mathematical speed problems. This may occur even into the fifth and sixth grades. If a child cannot do such problems, use toy cars and other objects to help him discover the relationships of speed to time and distance so that he eventually will understand that speed = distance/time.

Conservation of substance. Show a child a diagram of a kernel of popcorn and then draw a picture of it after it has popped. Ask, "Is there more corn after it is popped than before it is popped? Why has the volume changed?"

Discussion: Preoperational children, being perception bound, believe there is more corn to eat after it is popped. Concrete children know that altering the corn's state does not change its amount.

Reversibility. Have children grow bean seeds or show them plants in various stages of development. After they have raised some plants, have them draw how they grew. Their drawings should be similar to the ones shown here. Give the children a diagram of a young plant and ask them to draw how it would look in stages before and after this picture. Next, have the children draw several pictures showing the stages of development of plants in reverse order. Ask, "Why do you think your pictures are true?"

Discussion: If the children can reverse properly and give you reasons why they are drawing the plants in this order, they have probably achieved reversibility in their thinking. Checking for reversibility can be easily done whenever the children have prepared and learned something in one order and are then asked to reverse the order.

Reverse seriation.   Obtain twenty straws. The straws should be cut so that you have two series of ten straws each that progress in length. Set up one series from short to long and then ask the children to take the other set and place them in reverse order.

Discussion: This task identifies whether or not children can reverse the order of a series of objects. Children of seven can usually seriate, but many children ages eight through nine have difficulty in reversing the order.

Classification—Ascending and descending hierarchy. Prepare a number of cards, some labeled *birds* with pictures of birds on them, some labeled *ducks* with pictures of ducks on them, and some labeled *animals* with pictures of various animals on them. Show these to a group of eight- to ten-year-old children. Ask them to arrange the cards in groups according to each of the three labels. Next, place the "bird" pile on the "duck" pile and ask, "Is the bird label, now on top, still appropriate? Why?" Now place the "animal" pile on the others. Ask, "Is this appropriate? Why? Do all the cards belong in this pile? Are birds animals? Are ducks animals? If all the animals in the world died, would there be any ducks? Why or why not?"

Discussion: This activity determines whether a child understands class inclusion: that is, ducks are not only ducks but also birds (an ascending hierarchy). Ducks are a subgroup belonging to birds, a higher major group. Asking if ducks would remain if all the animals are killed determines whether the child can also descend a hierarchy (go from animals, a major group, to ducks, a subgroup).

Conservation of area.   Obtain eight cubes of sugar. Stack four together so that they appear as shown in diagram A below. Then, arrange the other four so they appear as in diagram B. Or prepare and show the child diagrams of the two situations. Ask, "Is the distance around (perimeter) A the same as that around B? Why?" Tell the child, "The other day a girl told me they were not the same perimeter, or distance around. What would you tell her? How would you prove it?"

Discussion: By this age, children will usually conserve area. But they think that if the area is the same, the perimeter must be the same too. If each square were two centimeters wide, the perimeter of A would be sixteen centimeters and of B, 20 centimeters. If the child does not come up with correct responses, have her count the sides of each of the diagrams and then ask, "What do you think about the perimeters?"

Conservation. Rip a newspaper in half. Ask, "Do I have more, less, or the same amount of newspaper as I had before?" (conservation of substance). Ask, "Do the combined pieces of newspaper weigh more, less, or the same as the paper did before it was torn? Why?" (conservation of weight). Ask, "If I put these torn pieces of newspaper in a large tank of water, would they occupy more, less, or the same amount of space as when the paper was whole? Why?" (conservation of volume).

Discussion: Children do not develop conservation usually until after age six. In other words, they do not realize that physically altering one property of matter does not necessarily change its amount, weight, or the volume it will occupy. Conservation of substance and weight usually develop by age eight, while conservation of volume occurs later.

Number. Obtain ten straws. If the child can count, have her count them one through ten. Point to a middle straw and ask, "If the last straw is ten, what is the number of this straw?" Place the straws together and have the child count them. Move the straws apart. Ask, "Do I have more, less, or the same number of straws now as before?"

Discussion: Preoperational children often can count but do not know number. To fully comprehend number children must understand the following:

1. *Classification*—realize that the straws, although they may not look alike, are still straws.
2. *Cardination*—realize that no matter how you arrange objects in a set, you still have the same number.
3. *Ordination*—place the straws in order and realize that where the object is in the order determines its number.

Class Inclusion. Show the children some fruit (e.g., ten raisins and two pears). Ask, "In what ways are these alike? What do you call them? Are there more raisins than fruit? If I took the fruit and you took the raisins, would I have more, or would you have more? How would you be able to prove who had more?"

Discussion: This activity tests again for class inclusion. Does the child realize that the subclass *raisins* is included in the major class *fruit*? Is the child overcome by the perception of a large number of raisins?

ACTIVITY 5–2

Assessing Cognitive Development: Formal Operations

Valuable insights concerning patterns of reasoning can be gained from interviewing students and asking them to respond to simple tasks. The tasks in this activity are designed for assessment of formal operations. You may wish to include some tasks from Activity 5-1, "Assessing Cognitive Development: Concrete Operations." You should also review the suggestions for interviewing in that activity.

Piagetian Interview Tasks: Formal Operational Period	
Name_____	School_____
Class or Subject_____	Teacher_____
Sex_____	Level_____
Age_____(yrs.)_____(months)	General Demeanor_____
Date_____	Other_____

Proportional Reasoning

This task assesses the student's ability to apply the concept of ratio and proportion. The student is given an 8½ × 11-inch card. Stickmen are drawn on each side of the card, one being two-thirds the height of the other. The small and large stickmen should be constructed to measure four and six jumbo paper clips, respectively. Ask the student to measure the height of each of the stickmen with a set of eight connected jumbo paper clips. After the student has measured and recorded the heights of the two stickmen, the jumbo clips are replaced with a set of small paper clips. Ask the student to measure only the short stickman with the new set of clips. Remove the stickman. Then ask, "How tall is the large stickman in terms of the small paper clips?"

Task 1—Proportional Reasoning Responses

1. Predicted height of tall stickman:_____

2. Justification for prediction:_____

_____

3. Key statements indicating cognitive level:_____

_____

4. Classification of performance:_____

5. Suggestions for teaching:_____

Discussion: The measurement of the tall stickman should be six jumbo clips and nine small clips in length, and the small stickman should measure four jumbo clips and six small clips. The criterion for success on this task is the ability of the student to accurately predict the height of the tall stickman in terms of small clips (i.e., nine clips). The student's justification must include a reference to direct ratio or proportion. The student may just guess and give you a number. If the child does, he is not demonstrating the use of formal thought. If, however, he tries to figure it on paper or reasons in a rational way, indicating that the situation is a simple proportion, he is demonstrating formal thought:

Small Stickman		Large Stickman
4 clips	=	6 clips
6 clips	=	x clips

Separation and Control of Variables

This task utilizes a simple pendulum consisting of a length of string about 80 cm. long and a set of varying weights. Ask the student to determine which variable or variables affect the frequency of oscillation of the pendulum (the number of swings per unit of time, e.g., second). (Note: Since the length of the string is the only relevant variable, the problem is to isolate it from the others. Only in this way can the student solve the problem and explain the frequency of oscillations.)

Task 2—Separation and Control of Variables Responses

1. Question: Which variable or variables affect the frequency of oscillation of this pendulum?

   Response:_____

   _____

2. Question: Can you design an experiment to prove that your choice is correct?

   Response:_____

   _____

3. Key statements indicating cognitive level:_____

   _____

4. Classification of cognitive level:_____

   _____

5. Suggestions for teaching:_____

   _____

Discussion: The criterion for success on this task is the student's ability to identify the one variable (length of string) that affects the oscillation of the pendulum. The student's justification must indicate that he *held all variables constant while manipulating only one variable* in reaching his conclusion. The student should initially indicate that variables involved in the problem could be weight, length of string, or height at which the pendulum is dropped. He may initially think a combination of these may affect the frequency. He may then describe a set of hypotheses and test these. However, before finishing he should *design an experiment controlling one variable at a time*, such as length of string, to find out whether his hypothesis is correct. In this way he should systematically eliminate the irrelevant variables. The ability to plan experiments to separate and control, or manipulate, *one variable at a time*, observe it accurately, and make proper conclusions characterizes formal thought.

Proportional Reasoning

The student is presented with a balanced scale consisting of a wooden rod with equally spaced numbered positions. Weights are attached as indicated in the diagram. Begin by using equal weights (ten grams) equidistant from the fulcrum (pivoting point). Remove one. Maintain equilibrium of the balance by holding the force arm. Ask, "Using any of the weights in front of you, how could you get the scale to balance?" After the student responds ask, "What other ways are there to balance the scale besides the one you chose?" Remove the weight from the scale. Place another weight nearer the fulcrum and maintain equilibrium by holding the force arm. Ask, "How may the scale be balanced by using the weights? How do you justify your responses?"

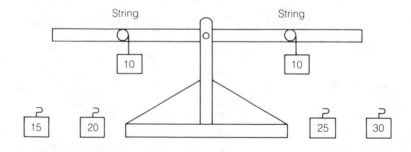

Task 3—Proportional Reasoning Responses
1. Question: Using any of the weights presented here, how could you get the scale to balance?

   Response:_____

   _____

2. Question (Justification): How did you arrive at this answer?

   Response:_____

   _____

3. Key statements indicating cognitive level:_____

   _____

4. Classification of cognitive level:_____

   _____

5. Suggestions for teaching:_____

   _____

Discussion: The criterion for success on this task is the student's ability to equate length times weight on one arm of the fulcrum with length times weight on the other arm or to figure out the problem by using proportions. In order for the student to balance the scale, he must apply the principle of levers.

Combinatorial Logic

Obtain five medicine droppers, baby food or other jars, and ten clear plastic cups. Prepare stock solutions of the following:
1. Dilute sulfuric acid (H_2SO_1)—10 ml concentrated H_2SO_4 to 100 ml H_2O
2. Distilled H_2O
3. Hydrogen Peroxide—3 parts of H_2O_2 added to 97 parts H_2O
4. Sodium Thiosulfate—10 grams sodium thiosulfate to 1 liter of H_2O
5. Potassium Iodide—5 g to 1 liter H_2O

Pour the stock solutions into the baby jars as follows: jar 1, dilute sulfuric acid; jar 2, water; jar 3, hydrogen peroxide; jar 4, sodium thiosulfate; and jar 5, potassium iodide, labeled g. The student is then given the four jars containing colorless, odorless liquids which are perceptually identical. Then present him with two glasses, one containing solutions 1 + 3, the other containing solution 2. The contents of the glasses are *not* revealed to the student. Several drops from jar g are poured into each of the two glasses. The student is asked to notice the reactions. (The container containing 1 + 3 turns yellow, the other remains unchanged.) The student is told that the two samples were prepared from the jars and that each contains g.

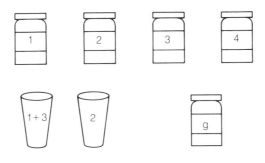

Ask, "Can you reproduce the color?" Ten plastic cups are made available, and the student is allowed to attempt to reproduce the color. Record the student's procedure. If the color is successfully reproduced, ask questions to determine if he can identify the functions of each liquid. (The child should indicate that jar 2 does not alter the reaction one way or the other and jar 4 eliminates the color.)

Task 4—Combinatorial Logical Responses
Record the procedure the student takes in solving the problem.

_____

_____

_____

1. Analysis of procedure. Check which one(s) of the following the student was able to do.

   a. Made the color in one way._____

   b. Made the color in two ways._____

   c. Knew that all of 1, 3, and g were necessary._____

   d. Knew that 2 had no effect, or did not help or produce the color._____

   e. Knew that 4 removed or prevented the color._____

2. Key statements indicating cognitive level:_____

_____

3. Classification of cognitive level:_____

_____

4. Suggestions for teaching:_____

_____

Discussion: The main criterion for determining whether the student is a formal operational thinker is whether he establishes a _systematic procedure_ for the role played by each of the solutions. Does he use, for example, a process of elimination? Does he realize that by combining 1, 3, and g the yellow solution occurs? If he cannot state these facts, but just goes about the activity by trial and error and does not indicate he understands the role of all the combinations, he is not a formal thinker.

Hypothetical Reasoning

Show a student the following diagram of the top of a pool table. Ask him to trace how he would hit ball _y_ so that it would collide with ball _x_, in each of the positions shown, to make _x_ go into one of the corner pockets. After he has drawn several ways he could hit the _y_ ball, ask him to describe any rule that could be used in the future. You might have to help the student construct a rule. Ask, "If you hit the ball straight on, how will it move? If you hit it on a 45° angle, how will it move?" (You have to diagram a 45° angle to ensure that he understands what you mean.) Ask, "Can you compare the reaction of a ball bouncing off a wall with _y_'s reaction to _x_?"

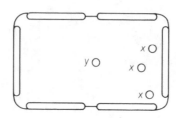

Task 6—Hypothetical Reasoning Response

1. Student's description of rule:_____

2. Justification for the rule:_____

3. Key statements indicating cognitive level:_____

_____

4. Classification of cognitive level:_____

_____

5. Suggestions for teaching:_____

_____

Discussion: The student should, in his own words, state that the angle of incidence equals the angle of reflection. If the student does state this rule, he should explain the meaning to be sure he has not memorized it. He need not use the above words, as long as he can explain the law or state some rule.

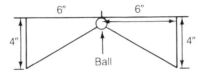

ACTIVITY 5–3

Group Structure

You will need to spend at least one class period observing a secondary science class. During the class, try to direct your attention to the students *as a group*.

To gain insights into group structure in a science class, you should answer the following questions. Use the one to seven continuum to indicate the degree to which the group characteristic is present. These questions are based on the earlier discussion of the defining characteristics of groups.

	Low		Medium			High	
1. To what degree do the students have a *solidarity* of opinion, purpose, and interests when they work in this class?	1	2	3	4	5	6	7
2. To what degree are the students *satisfied* with the class?	1	2	3	4	5	6	7
3. To what degree are members of other classes *attracted* to this class?	1	2	3	4	5	6	7
4. To what degree do students in the class group feel they are *wanted* and *belong* in the class?	1	2	3	4	5	6	7
5. To what degree (both quality and quantity) do students *interact* through various types of communication?	1	2	3	4	5	6	7
6. To what degree is the group *structure* beneficial to achieving goals?	1	2	3	4	5	6	7
7. To what degree are the *norms* of behavior adhered to by group members?	1	2	3	4	5	6	7

What behaviors did you observe that allowed you to make these decisions? How can you identify these properties of groups? After each of the words listed below place two or three behaviors that you think support your judgment.

Solidarity of groups:

Satisfaction with group:

Attraction of group:

Interaction of group:

Structure of group:

Norms of group:

## CHAPTER 6

All Students Are Special: Individual Differences in the Classroom

A great diversity of students come to science classes; they come from urban, suburban, and rural environments; they come from poor, middle class, and affluent homes. Some can read, others cannot; some are interested in science, others are not. Some are gifted, some are slow, and many are average. The list could go on. In fact, if we started a classification system, it could go on until we described each individual in each school. To state that each student is an individual is to state the obvious. And few teachers disagree, in principle, with the logical educational implication of such a statement, namely, students need individual attention.

■ Special Students in Education: A Rationale

Of the many issues that educators will have to face during the 1990s, perhaps one of the most encompassing is that of a "right to education" for all students. In the late 1970s attention was focused on the educational rights of students who were traditionally placed in restricted special education programs. One result of this movement is the recognition of individual differences and the conclusion that has been clear to many teachers for a long time—*all students are special.*

We all stand to gain from having special students in the regular science classroom. Although it is only natural to expect some initial hesitation, frustration, or fear on the part of students and teachers alike, once these feelings pass the gains are clear: Special students encounter a whole new range of educational opportunities; regular students learn that in terms of basic human needs and wants, special students are not very different from themselves; and teachers become more sensitive to the realities of different learning styles, subtleties of instruction, and of modifying curricula to meet students' personal needs. In the end, we all find out more about what it means to be human.

The points made in the preceding paragraph are important reasons for having special students in science classrooms. There is another reason; it is the just thing for science teachers to do. We have a responsibility to provide the best science program for *all* our students. Science teachers know that students have unique needs that are not fulfilled by curriculum materials alone. The task for science teachers is to accommodate our programs and teaching to the needs of students, not to make students adapt to our science programs and teaching strategies.

■ Special Students in Science Programs: The Law

Appeals to personal and professional benefit and to justice have not completely convinced teachers of the need to include special students in the science classroom. The most immediate and forceful argument seems to be the law. We have a *legal responsibility* to include special students in the mainstream of school programs.

One of the first laws that included protection of the rights of special students was the Rehabilitation Act of 1973, Public Law 93–112, Section 504 of which states:

> No otherwise qualified handicapped individual in the United States . . . shall, solely by reason of

his handicap, be excluded from participation in, be denied the benefits of, or be subjected to discrimination under any program or activity receiving federal financial assistance.

Since most, if not all, school systems receive federal financial assistance under this law, special students must be allowed to participate in, receive the benefits of, and have open access to educational programs.

Another piece of federal legislation that included safeguards concerning the rights of special students was Public Law 93–380, the Education Amendments of 1974. This law mandated due process procedures at the state and local levels for the placement of special students, assured placement of special students in the least restrictive environment and set a goal of providing full educational opportunities for all handicapped students within each state. Public Law 94–142, the Education for All Handicapped Children Act of 1975, the regulation with which most U.S. school personnel are probably familiar, requires that special students be integrated into regular classrooms whenever possible:

> It is the purpose of this Act to assure that all handicapped children have available to them . . . a free appropriate public education which emphasizes special education and related services designed to meet their unique needs, to assure that the rights of handicapped children and their parents or guardians are protected, to assist states and localities to provide for the education of all handicapped children, and to assess and assure the effectiveness of efforts to educate handicapped children.

Specifically, P.L. 94–142 requires the following of school personnel:

1. *Zero Rejection.* No student may be rejected from a free public education and related services. Court cases such as *Pennsylvania Association for Retarded Children v. Commonwealth of Pennsylvania*, 334 F. Supp. 1257 (E. D. PA 1971) and *Mills v. Board of Education of the District of Columbia*, 348 F. Supp. 886 (D.D.C., 1972) have resulted in a legal commitment to the public schools for the education of all school-age students. That all students have a "right to education, regardless of their present level of functioning" results in a principle of zero rejection. It should also be noted that education is defined as the development of students from their present level to the next appropriate level. In brief, the assumption is *all* students are educable.
2. *Classification and Placement.* Evaluation of students shall be nondiscriminatory. Diagnostic and assessment procedures are to be established by each state to ensure that cultural and racial bias are not evident in the system used for identifying special students. Tests shall be a fair evaluation of the student's strengths and weaknesses.
3. *Appropriate Education.* This stipulation is a requirement for an Individualized Education Program (IEP). An IEP should have statements concerning the student's present level of performance, how he will participate in the regular educational program, the type of special services needed, the date special services were initiated, and the expected length of services. In addition, the IEP should set short- and long-term minimum standards, measures of achievement, and an evaluation of educational progress which includes a conference between school personnel, parents, and the special student.
4. *Least Restrictive Placement.* To the maximum extent possible, handicapped students will be educated with nonhandicapped students. "Least restrictive placement" means that handicapped students should be educated in the "mainstream," the regular educational environment. They can be educated in special programs when the nature or severity of their handicap requires such treatment.
5. *Due Process.* The handicapped student (usually through parents or a guardian) has a right to question testing and placement. That is, special students are guaranteed procedural safeguards in the placement and provision of special services.
6. *Parental Participation.* Parents of the handicapped student have the right to be present for their child's evaluation, placement, and development of an IEP.

Public Laws 93–112, 93–380, and 94–142 are based on fundamental principles guaranteed in the Constitution. The handicapped have been systematically excluded from educational programs, which, in essence, has been a violation of the constitutional rights of approximately 35 million Americans. The Fourteenth Amendment guarantees equal protection under the law for all Americans. Recall that the *Brown v. Board of Education of Topeka*, 347 U.S. 483 (1954) overturned the earlier "separate but equal" ruling of *Plessy v. Ferguson*, 163, U.S. 537 (1896). It is instructive to read the *Brown v. Board* decision and make appropriate changes in the wording, such as handicapped for Negro or race, and classroom for school. Separate educational facilities for some students are, by definition, unequal; thus, the handicapped have been deprived of the equal protection of the laws guaranteed by the Fourteenth Amendment of our Constitution.

Of the three laws, P.L. 94–142 was probably the most significant piece of educational legislation of the 1970s, and its effect will be felt throughout the 1990s. There are several reasons for this fact. First, P.L. 94–142 incorporates parts of the other laws and clarifies the fundamental right of all students to an education. Second, because it is a federal law, it establishes the "right to education" as a national priority. Third, P.L. 94–142 commits us to the recognition of individual differences and to appropriate educational programs for special students because it is permanent legislation with *no* expiration date. This fact demonstrates the gravity with which Congress approached the legislation.

■ Handicapped Students in Science Class: Some Guidelines

Teachers' concerns are not in understanding why special students ought to be in science classrooms but rather in dealing with the fact that they are in our classrooms. And so the problems may be stated, "What can be done to provide the best science education program possible?" "What are the first steps?" "What should I do now?" The next sections are addressed to these questions. The ideas about teaching special students have been synthesized from many sources and should give the science teacher some information, some confidence, and some direction in working with special students.

There are some simple, straightforward things that science teachers can do that will enable them to better understand and help most special students. Certainly there are unique problems in integrating any special student into the science classroom. You

can anticipate some personal tension and educational problems during the period of adjustment. And, understandably, we cannot provide suggestions that will cover all situations. Nevertheless, there are some approaches that have proved helpful with most special students.

General Guidelines for Helping Handicapped Students

1. Obtain and read all the background information available on the student.
2. Spend time educating yourself on the physical and/or psychological nature of the handicap and how it affects the student's potential for learning.
3. Determine whether or not special help can be made available to you through the resources of a "special education" expert.
4. Determine any special equipment needed by the student.
5. Talk with the student about limitations due to his or her handicap and about particular needs in the science class.
6. Use resource teachers and aides to assist you.
7. Establish a team of fellow teachers (including resource teachers and aides) to share information and ideas about the special students. A team approach is helpful in overcoming initial fears and the sense of isolation in dealing with the situation. You may need to take responsibility for contacting appropriate school personnel and establishing the team; if so, take courage and do it.
8. Other students are often willing to help special students. Encourage them to do so.
9. Be aware of barriers, both physical and psychological, to the fullest possible functioning of the special student.

Many concepts can be learned from games. (June Albrandt, Biological Sciences Curriculum Study)

10. Consider how to modify or adapt curriculum materials and teaching strategies for the special student without sacrificing content, processes, or activities.
11. Do not underestimate the capabilities of the special student. Teachers' perceptions of a student's abilities have a way of becoming self-fulfilling prophecies. If these perceptions are negative, they may detrimentally affect the student and your ability to create new options for him or her.
12. Use the same standards of grading and discipline for the special student as you do for the rest of the class.
13. Develop a trusting relationship with the special student.
14. Educate the other students about handicaps in general, as well as specific handicaps of students in their class.

Hearing-Impaired Students

From an early age most children learn through listening. And there is every indication that most teaching is telling. Hearing impairment is defined as an auditory problem adversely affecting the student's educational performance. Students with hearing impairments often have developmental delays in speech and language. These delays have obvious effects on the ability to communicate. Hearing-impaired students will not necessarily have problems acquiring science concepts, although they may have difficulty learning the written or oral language to communicate their understanding.

Helping Hearing-Impaired Students
1. The hearing-impaired depend heavily on visual perception. Therefore, seat the student for optimal viewing.
2. Determine whether an interpreter will be needed and the nature of the student's speech/language problems.
3. Learn the student's most effective way of communicating.
4. Find the student a "listening helper."

Visually Impaired Students

Like the hearing-impaired, the visually impaired are those students whose vision is limited enough to require educational adaptions. Students who can read material with the use of magnifying devices and/or enlarged print are classified as partially seeing. Students who require braille or taped materials are classified as educationally blind.

Helping Visually Impaired Students
1. Visually impaired students learn through sensory channels other than vision, primarily hearing. Therefore, seat students for optimal listening.
2. Determine from the student what constitutes the best lighting.
3. Change the room arrangement whenever necessary but always make a special effort, formally and informally, to reorient the student.
4. Allow the student to manipulate tangible materials, models, and, when possible, "real" objects. Do not unduly "protect" students from materials.
5. Speak aloud what you have written on the board and charts.
6. Use the student's name; otherwise, the student may not know when he or she is being addressed.
7. Since smiles and facial gestures might not be seen, touching is the most effective means of reinforcing the student's work.
8. Be aware of student eye fatigue. This fatigue can be overcome by varying activities, using good lighting, and providing close visual work.
9. Have the student use his/her visual capacity when possible (unless otherwise directed).

Physically Impaired Students

Students with physical and health impairment represent a diverse group of special needs, for this category includes students with allergies, asthma, arthritis, amputations, diabetes, epilepsy, cerebral palsy, spina bifida, and muscular dystrophy. Some are mobile and others are confined to wheelchairs; some have good use of their limbs and others do not. Some have a single crippling condition and some are multihandicapped. The range of needs is such that some can work in the regular science classroom with little or no problem, whereas others require fulltime education in special classes.

Helping Physically Impaired Students
1. Eliminate architectural barriers.
2. Become familiar with the basic mechanics and maintenance of braces, prostheses, and wheelchairs.
3. Understand the effects of medication on students and know the prescribed dosage.
4. Obtain special devices such as pencil holders or reading aids for students who need them.
5. Learn about the symptoms of special health problems and appropriate responses.

Speech- and Language-Impaired Students

Until recently, classroom teachers had more contact with speech- and language-impaired students than any others with handicapping conditions. This situation may still be true in most schools, but learning disabilities programs are growing rapidly. Speech and language handicaps that you might encounter are articulation (the most common problem), dyslexia, delayed speech, voice problems, and stuttering. In addition, students with other handicaps such as cleft palate, cerebral palsy, and hearing loss may have speech and language problems.

Helping Speech- and Language-Impaired Students
1. Help the student become aware of his or her problem; students must be able to hear their own errors.
2. Incorporate and draw attention to newly learned sounds in familiar words.
3. Know what to listen for and match appropriate remedial exercises with the student's problem.
4. Be sure your speech is articulate; students often develop speech and language patterns through modeling.

Learning-Disabled and Mildly Mentally Impaired Students

There is a distinction between learning disabilities and mild mental handicaps. The difference is much too long and technical to summarize. Students with mild mental handicaps should be identified only through the use of multiple criteria. Classroom teachers may observe indications of mental handicaps in a student's social interaction, general intelligence, emotional maturity, and academic achievement. In contrast, students with learning disabilities show a significant discrepancy between their achievements and the apparent ability to achieve. The problem is manifest as a disorder of learning and not mental ability. Science teachers may observe learning disabilities in the areas of arithmetic, listening, reading, spelling, logical thinking, speaking, and writing.

Helping Learning-Disabled and Mentally Impaired Students
1. Listen closely so you can understand the student's perception and understanding of concepts and procedures.
2. Use an individualized approach based on the student's learning style, level of understanding, and readiness.
3. Use multisensory approaches to learning: visual, auditory, kinesthetic, and tactile.

4. Find and use the student's most refined sensory mode to aid in development of mental capacities.
5. Make use of the student's strengths and work on diminishing his or her deficiencies.
6. Reduce or control interruptions since many special students have short attention spans.
7. Stay within the student's limits of frustration. Rely on your judgment, not the level of curriculum materials.
8. Start conceptual development at a sensory-motor or concrete level and work toward more abstract levels.
9. Work on speech and language development.
10. Help special students to develop self-esteem; a good, firmly grounded self-concept is essential to their continued development.

Emotionally Impaired Students

These students probably cause the greatest concern and frustration for science teachers. As it turns out, they are also the ones who have been in science classrooms all along! Emotionally impaired and disruptive students show behavior that ranges from mild, attention-getting "pranks" to violent assault. They may also be mildly withdrawn to clinically depressed and suicidal. Other examples of behavior that teachers might identify as disturbed or disruptive include: regression, fears and phobias, chronic complaints of pains and illness, aggressiveness, overdependence, social isolation, perfectionism, excessive dieting, obesity, chemical dependency, defiance, and vandalism.

The student's behavior may be a result of forces within or from the environment. The first may be either physiological or psychological in origin. Environmental factors might include violence in the home, school pressures, and/or social problems. In many cases, schools and teachers have contributed to the development of disruptive behaviors. How so? Extreme emphasis on grades, teacher comments, harsh and punitive treatment, unwarranted social comparison, unrealistic physical and academic requirements, and teacher conversations about student behavior that in turn become fulfilled prophecies when other teachers have the same student are but a few things teachers have done, often inadvertently, that pushed students to extreme patterns of behavior.

Helping Emotionally Impaired Students
1. Spend time with the student when he is not being disruptive.
2. Make rules reasonable and clear.
3. Provide realistic, reasonable, and appropriate consequences if rules are broken.

GUEST EDITORIAL

Science and Special Students

Elizabeth Karplus
Special Education, Campolindo High School, Moraga,
California

Every science teacher is familiar with the case of Albert Einstein who failed mathematics as a young student because he could not memorize and had a nonverbal style of thinking. Or they have heard of Thomas Edison who was declared mentally retarded and whose mother taught him at home because she did not believe he was stupid.

Einstein and Edison are not just special isolated cases. I remember Alan, a very tall, skinny, slightly stooped, dark-haired student. In high school, he carried all of his books and papers in total disarray in a large backpack. As a child he had been diagnosed as dyslexic, dysgraphic, and dyscalculic at the California State Diagnostic School for the Neurologically Handicapped. This diagnosis was based on his profound problems with orientation in time and space and mild cerebral palsy evidenced in shaking hands, poor coordination and poor throat-muscle control and, therefore, poor speech. He was very distracted by the sensory stimuli around him and unable to attend selectively because he could not decide which signal of many was *the* important one for the current task. After diagnosis he was placed in a self-contained class for the learning disabled, where remedial mathematics and reading were begun by a large, loving woman. He ran away from school. The drill on symbols and phonics frustrated him because he was unable to get meaning from them in isolation. What he needed was an awareness that the events in the world, including symbols, were consistent and made sense and that the symbols were only useful in helping to describe that sense. He needed hands-on experiences where he could observe what

happened. He needed contact with ideas and with other bright students who could discuss those ideas, since reading about them was so difficult. Alan needed to learn to sequence his symbols (writing 73, not 37, when he meant seven tens and three units) and sequence directions according to the *meaning* or the expected result rather than trying to remember them in detail step-by-step since his memory was so poor. He needed taped textbooks so that he could listen to them to get information. He needed to ask "Why" and "What." He needed the encouragement of accepting teachers who weren't dismayed by his poor writing or his unusual approaches to problems. Those teachers, in turn, often needed to reword their explanations as class work became increasingly abstract, because words never carried quite the same meaning for him that they did for most of the class.

It was in the science classes that he had the greatest successes and it was the activities in these classes that provided the best environment for him to learn from his mistakes and to monitor his own learning, developing a style of learning he could apply to other subject areas. He is currently majoring in physics at a California state university—a modern success story.

Learning-disabled students, like Alan, need science or other activity courses (shop, home economics, arts, crafts) as much or more than the normal students. In science classes the students themselves can control variables, change conditions, observe results, and learn to discriminate between variables which affect the outcome of the experiment and those that do not.

---

4. Disruptive behavior ranges from low levels at which a student may merely be looking for attention or recognition through a spectrum that ends in rage, tantrums, or complete withdrawal. Try always to be alert to behaviors that, though minimally disruptive, could become more serious problems.

5. Avoid personal confrontations or situations that provoke troubled students.

6. Make directions for assignments, classwork, and laboratory procedures direct, clear, and complete.

7. Be aware of and prepare for transitional times in the classroom.

8. Provide troubled students with success experiences.

9. Resolve conflicts by talking about specific behaviors, reasoning, and involving the student in

The science classes can provide exposure to new equipment and ideas in a "hands-on" setting. New learning can be firmly embedded in a situational context so that it is easier to remember and reapply. Old learning can be applied in new situations, so that concepts are refined. Language usage itself can be refined and vocabulary increased. Science activities are filled with opportunities to measure along, around, through, diagonally, up, and down. The student can easily distinguish among thin, narrow, short, light, and weak and learn when each is an appropriate replacement for "little." Position and direction are encoded in the prepositions in, out, among, under, over, between, by, and up as well as in adjectives like contiguous or nouns such as circuit, test tube, or breaker. In science classes, instructions make sense and are usually monitored by the progress of the experiment, not by remembering an a priori order. You cannot filter a precipitate before the two interacting solutions have been mixed. If you haven't connected the battery, the bulb will not light. Most important, the student learns that failures do not represent disaster but are useful as sources of new information. The creative teacher can use each failure of an experiment, each mismeasurement to help the student to a new understanding of the phenomenon.

However, there are two cautions the science teacher of the learning-disabled student must observe. You must take special pains to recognize the learning-disabled student's preferred sensory channels (visual-reading; auditory-listening; kinesthetic-demonstration) for information input and his preferred channels for output or reporting his understandings to you (visual-writing or diagrams; auditory-oral speech; kinesthetic-demonstration). You may also need to change your preferred methods of presentation to match the student's methods; otherwise he may not be able to understand the lesson or you may not be able to discover how much he has actually learned. In my classes, we often read test questions or put laboratory instructions and text on cassette tapes so that the student may listen and understand rather than read and misunderstand.

Sometimes it is necessary to change laboratory setups to make them more usable for the students, particularly the physically handicapped whose movements may be jerky or ill-defined. Equipment can be clamped tightly to the desk or otherwise anchored. Special laboratory measuring devices are available for the blind or deaf and they are often very useful to the learning-disabled student, who can then use more than one sense and thus monitor his own collecting of accurate information.

Science classes are for everyone, including the learning-handicapped student. Learning science involves attention, reasoning, and questioning skills which are of constant value throughout life. Learning science can bring great satisfaction to the learning-disabled high school student because it is an important academic discipline and because he can develop skills in these classes which he needs for self-esteem. We owe these students their chance to learn how to learn—a skill most easily taught through well-designed science experiments.

the problem-solving process. Once a course toward aggressive or uncontrolled behavior is started, it is hard to stop.

10. Convey your intention to help resolve the problem mutually: "We have a problem here and *we* are going to resolve it."

11. If behavior problems escalate, try to talk about the process while providing solutions to the problem. For example, "We are both getting angry; can't we settle this calmly?" or "I see you are upset; let's try to solve the problem."

12. Avoid using comparison, embarrassment, ridicule, and unwarranted threats to change behavior.

13. Never use physical punishment for rule violation.

Academically Unsuccessful Students

These students have normal abilities and do not have any *significant* physical or psychological disabilities, yet they are below their expected level of achievement. Their handicap may be caused by such things as extreme poverty, a home environment that does not encourage learning, poor reading abilities, diminished self-concept, negative attitudes toward school, and language problems due to a first language other than English. In the past, these students were labelled "culturally deprived, slow learners, economically disadvantaged, and underachievers." We have used the words academically unsuccessful to suggest that the science teacher's attention should be directed toward the educational problems and their remediation or resolution, not to the student's culture, home, or economic condition. The role of the science teacher is to help these students overcome their educational problems and continue their development. It is *not* to identify a cause for the problem nor to excuse oneself from the important educational goal.

Helping Unsuccessful Students
1. Identify the educational problem, e.g., reading, and concentrate on resolving this problem.
2. Convey your expectations for achievement within a realm possible for the student.
3. See that physiological, physical, and psychological needs are fulfilled.
4. Use concrete learning experiences, such as the laboratory.
5. Provide experiences where the student will succeed.
6. Eliminate educational approaches that have *not* worked and try something new.
7. Give recognition to talents the student does have.
8. Approach the educational impairment with an attitude of, "When you are in science, *we* are going to work on this."
9. Provide time, materials, and experiences within the learning capabilities of the student.
10. Adapt instruction and the curriculum to the student, not the reverse.

■ Gifted Students in Science Class: Perspective and Resources

If you had a serious illness, you would want the best physician. If you had economic problems, you would want the best financial advisor. Everybody recognizes the need for unusual gifts and talents, yet this is a much neglected area in education. During the 1990s this problem will have increasing recognition and may be remedied. The mandate is clear and science teachers are a part of the problem's resolution.

Definitions of giftedness vary. Most, however, are paraphrased from the congressional report submitted by past Commissioner of Education Sidney Marland in *Education of the Gifted and Talented*.[1] Gifted and talented students are those identified by professionals who, by virtue of their abilities, are capable of high achievement. These students require educational programs beyond those normally provided, to fulfill their personal potentials and encourage their contribution to society. In a less cumbersome definition: gifted students have superior academic abilities. Talented students have special aptitudes in specific areas. The difference between giftedness and talents is not distinct, since most gifted students have talents and most talented students are gifted in some areas. Gifted and talented students may have demonstrated abilities in any of the following areas: academics (general or specific), leadership, visual and performing arts, music, creativity, mechanics, and athletics.

As a science teacher you should be interested in the characteristics of giftedness that you may encounter in the classroom.

Characteristics of the Gifted and Talented in Science Class
1. Enjoys solving scientific problems.
2. Solves problems easily and logically.
3. Demonstrates advanced ethical, cognitive, and aesthetic development.
4. Learns science faster than other students.
5. Understands scientific concepts quickly.
6. Asks many questions about science.
7. Shows an awareness of science far beyond that of other students.
8. Is motivated to read and study science.
9. Demonstrates unique abilities in designing laboratory equipment to solve problems.
10. Is highly creative.
11. Shows normal social adjustment.

In addition, there are a few negative behaviors such as boredom, frustration, and complaints that you may observe. This list gives a subjective and preliminary means of identifying gifted and talented students. If you think you have such a student, it is best to consult the school counselor so she can administer appropriate tests to confirm your initial impressions.

Adapting school programs for the gifted can be achieved in many ways. Businesses, industries, colleges, and universities often have programs for students showing special abilities. There are special honors classes, programs, and schools. Gifted students can work on advanced placement courses, accelerated schedules, take extra classes, enter college early, and work part-time and/or summers in projects where they can develop their talents. You can easily

===== REFLECTING ON SCIENCE TEACHING =====
Resistance to Change

Teachers, although mindful of individual differences, traditionally have done little to adjust instruction other than to give extra reading assignments to the more advanced students. Teaching to challenge the individual potential of students generally has not been done, for several reasons:

1. Traditional ways of instruction have been the primary barriers to such a change, e.g., the argument, "We have always done it this way and it seems to work."
2. There have been logistics problems. If students can progress at their own rate, more courses, materials, and equipment must be added. The class period may have to be lengthened, particularly in a laboratory-oriented situation. Adopting a scheduling system that allows variations of time spans, depending on the activity or class assignment of the student, presents fantastic logistics problems, particularly in the larger schools.
3. Group instruction is easy to direct and control. Because teachers have been trained for group instruction, they often feel insecure when confronted with the idea that not all students in a class will be performing tasks at the same time.
4. When a group of students progresses through a curriculum at varying rates and directions, according to their ability and interests, there must be more resources and equipment for them to use.
5. Facilities for individualized instruction are more costly because they require more space.

What is your position? Either alone or in a discussion group, review the arguments against teaching science to recognize individual differences. Design counterarguments for those listed.

---

find many options for the gifted students in your school.

Although resources are available, probably the crucial question you are asking is, "What can I do to help the gifted and talented student in science class?"

Helping Gifted and Talented Students
1. Use questions, problems, and projects that will facilitate higher levels of cognitive, affective, and psychomotor development.
2. Develop independent study programs.
3. Have special "honors seminars."
4. Initiate extracurricular science activities such as science fairs or helping teach an elementary science club.
5. Assign special projects.
6. Use inquiry and problem-solving.
7. Emphasize scientific methods.
8. Individualize a program based on the student's interests.

■ Teaching Science for Individual Differences

After reading the previous sections it should be clear that, as a science teacher, you will encounter a broad range of students. Even normal students have individual differences that should be recognized in the

science classroom. With increased recognition of individual problems and because of the laws cited earlier, more and more school systems are modifying their instructional programs so that greater attention is given to individual differences. Psychological research indicates that there are human differences which have implications for teaching. This research indicates that

1. Individuals come to the classroom with different conceptions of natural phenomena.
2. Individuals vary in the rate at which they learn concepts.
3. Individuals have different levels of motivation toward learning.
4. Individuals have different levels of psychomotor skills.
5. Individuals have different attitudes, values, and concepts in regard to science.

There are many more such statements that could be made concerning individual differences among students in the science classroom. Common sense and observation confirm the statements as much as research evidence. Yet there has been reluctance on the part of teachers to modify instruction. In this section we will describe several ways you can individualize instruction in your science classroom.

Individualized instruction is a process of adapting curriculum materials and instructional procedures to the student's needs. The aim of individualization is to maximize student development. Many schools have used grouping as a way of reducing instructional differences in a classroom or grade level. However, grouping alone cannot meet the needs of all students. So, other approaches are important.

There are some variations on individualized instruction in science. The entire science program may be individualized for all students, or only for students with exceptional needs. Individualized instruction may be based on any or all of the following: rate of learning (e.g., accelerated, extra time), direction of learning (e.g., independent study, student-selected projects), different methods (e.g., alone, small group, teacher-directed), different materials (e.g., reading, laboratory activities), and levels of achievement (e.g., tests, projects completed). So you see that there are many variations available to science teachers. These approaches only describe things you can do in the classroom and do not include approaches requiring administrative or school-wide reorganization. The following sections are brief descriptions of different approaches to teaching science for individual differences.

■ Approaches to Individualized Science Teaching

Grouping

In one plan, the students are grouped according to ability. They are assigned units of work to complete and, when they finish this work, they may be moved at the end of the semester to another group of higher ability and achievement. Sometimes teachers group within a classroom, so that there might be high, middle, and low groups in a class of 30. This system allows the teacher to adjust instruction to the different levels. It is usually not a good idea to maintain these groups on a permanent basis because that defines a "class" structure that may have disadvantages that outweigh the advantages.

Continuous Progress

A second approach is called the continuous-progress plan. It allows students to progress from subject to subject with no time restriction. If a student finishes biology in six weeks and passes an examination, he then moves into chemistry. This approach is linear, that is, it progresses through the regular sequence of science courses.

Enrichment Programs

Enrichment programs provide extra opportunities for students who complete the regular program and the extra time needed for others to complete the chapter or unit. Here, the faster students have the opportunity to work in depth and breadth within the science course. Using an enrichment program may require extra materials and a resource center.

Team Teaching

Another attempt to give greater attention to individual differences is to use some large-group instruction in a team-teaching situation on certain days, with small-group and individualized instruction on other days. This method is a compromise between having traditional group instruction and completely individualized instruction. This approach has the advantage of releasing teachers during the large-group instruction so that they may prepare and organize materials. When this method is used, there is no reason why the students cannot be taught on an individualized basis when the group is broken down into smaller sections.

■ Honors Classes, Special Seminars, and Second-Level Courses

Some schools have honors classes for science-talented students. Students in these classes are encouraged to work in laboratories on their own. They usually consult with the science teacher on a special problem or topic of study. The students are assigned laboratory space and have access to the materials needed for their work. Monthly reports of their progress are often required, as are seminars where they report on their research. In addition, the students may visit local scientific industries and/or have scientists visit and discuss the students' work and research.

Science teachers may have special seminars on selected topics. These seminars are similar to regular classes in that students may meet daily, weekly, or monthly to discuss a book or movie or interact with a visiting scientist. Students and/or teachers can select topics of study. All students are studying the same topic but the seminar gives them an opportunity to work beyond the regular science curriculum.

Second-level science courses are another alternative for meeting individual differences. The courses can be in physics, chemistry, biology, or earth sciences. These courses vary widely. Some simply use college-level texts and laboratory manuals.

Others have used materials of the Biological Sciences Curriculum Study (BSCS), such as the laboratory blocks, supplemented by outside reading.

Some junior high schools have offered high school biology for the gifted on the ninth-grade level. This innovation has been successful.

Special Science Courses

Some schools have instituted courses for those students who, for whatever reason, do not do well in the regular science program. They can be designed as special courses, which are taught like a seminar and use different materials designed for students with lower reading levels. Although there are clear advantages to these courses, it is also possible that they may become known as "science for dummies" or referred to by some other derogatory phrase. One way to avoid this problem is to let the students select the courses they wish, look over the texts, and discuss their career plans, motivation, and past achievement in science with you or their advisors. Nothing need be said about students for whom the course is designed; it is simply an option within the science sequence.

Small schools are seldom able to offer special classes. They have, however, encouraged students to do course work more or less on their own. The procedure is usually to have one or two students study a science film series or read the text and do laboratory experiments. The students may not have direct supervision, although a science instructor meets with them from time to time to discuss their work and assignments. This plan has the advantage of developing more self-direction and responsibility on the part of the students. Gifted students usually respond well to this type of operation; others may need more individual attention and help. Still, with a little thought and planning you should be able to use some of these ideas in setting up special science courses for individual students.

The approaches discussed thus far require varying degrees of administrative reorganization and support. The next section outlines an approach that requires only time and effort on your part.

Mastery Learning

Learning for mastery was first formally described by John Carroll.[2] In recent years the idea has been researched and developed by Benjamin Bloom.[3,4] The assumption underlying traditional science teaching is that if students are normally distributed with respect to aptitude for science and they are all taught the same material in the same amount of time, then the expected result with respect to achievement will be a normal distribution. The assumption underlying mastery learning in science is that all students are normally distributed with respect to aptitude for science *but* the quality of instruction, and particularly the amount of time available for learning science, is designed to meet the characteristics and needs of each individual student. When this is the approach to teaching, the majority (about 80 percent) of students can be expected to master the material. The primary variable is *time* to master the learning task.

The approach used by Bloom and his colleagues has been to supplement regular classroom instruction by using diagnostic evaluations and prescribing alternative materials and teaching methods. There are three main components to Bloom's strategy: preconditions, operating procedures, and outcomes. Below we have listed some operational elements of these components.

Preconditions—Defining the goals
- Specification of objectives
- Specification of content

Operating procedures—Use of formative evaluation
- Divide unit of study into smaller units of learning
- Use mastery test for each unit of learning
- Use of alternative learning resources on a prescribed basis

Outcomes—Use of summative evaluation
- Final examination of material
- Consideration of outcomes, e.g., cognitive, affective, psychomotor, self-esteem

To summarize, mastery learning provides for individual differences within the regular classroom. There are testing and feedback processes plus extra time for students who need it. Supplementing regular instruction with feedback and time allows for all (or almost all) students to master the material for a particular unit. The assumption is that if students have time they can learn, especially if they have corrective feedback on what to learn and how they are progressing. Many teachers like the mastery learning approach because it is an adaptation of regular classroom instruction. Listed below are steps in the mastery learning strategy. Again, they have been slightly modified for junior or senior high school science.

Steps in the Mastery Learning Approach
  1. Divide the science course into units of one or two weeks. These units may be chapters in your text or combinations of chapters and other learning activities.
  2. Specify objectives for each unit. The objectives

=== **GUEST EDITORIAL** ===

Women in Science

Jane Bowyer
Professor of Education, Mills College, Oakland,
California

There is no doubt that women in this country have made enormous strides in obtaining equal educational opportunities. Public schools began in Boston about 350 years ago and for the first 150 years admitted only boys. Colleges were even more reluctant to accept females. Harvard opened its doors in 1663 but it was 200 years before the first college allowed female students in bachelor-degree programs.

Since men and women today have equal access to schooling, it is easy to think that the two sexes enjoy identical educational experiences. Such, however, is not the case. In a random sampling of freshmen admitted to the University of California, Berkeley, 51 percent of the boys had taken four full years of mathematics in high school (including the trigonometry-solid geometry sequence) compared with 8 percent of the girls. This four-year sequence is required for admission to Math 1A at Berkeley, which in turn is required for majoring in *every* field at the University except for the traditionally female fields such as humanities, social sciences, librarianship, social welfare, and education.

The career filtering that occurs when students don't take high school math is especially critical for women. For all practical purposes, access to science-related jobs for most girls is eliminated before they begin college. Salaries are also negatively affected when women don't take math. Women who work in professions requiring math earn one-third more than women in other professions. In general, the average woman today with four or more years of college who works full-time earns less than the average male high school dropout, according to the Department of Labor.

This picture is beginning to change, however. Women are entering the labor force in record numbers and many are assuming more stereotypical male career goals and values. In fact, between 1970 and 1980 there was a 10 percent increase in the number of women managers, double the number of lawyers and judges, and a 3 percent increase in the number of female physicians. What about women in science-related careers? In spite of overall increased professional opportunities and the passage of federal legislation supporting women and work, there has actually been a slight decline in the last ten years in the number of women interested in pursuing science careers!

Stereotypical, sex-appropriate behaviors appear very early in our lives. Maleness and femaleness begin to be understood at about age two and are among the earliest concepts learned. Girls tend to receive a double reinforcement of approval for sex-appropriate behaviors, first as young children learning the female role from their parents, later in learning appropriate elementary school behavior. Studies show that girls are socialized early toward obedience, approval-seeking behavior, neatness, order, punctuality, and performance of detailed tasks. These behaviors are valued in the feminine personality and by the predominately female elementary classroom teachers.

Boys appear to learn very early to exist as nonconformists in the elementary classroom. While girls are gaining teacher approval by being quiet and obedient, boys are receiving a disproportionate amount of the teacher's active attention, both positive and negative. In fact, research studies indicate that boys are the most interesting students for both male and female teachers and, as such, receive more individual teaching time than girls, more skill work, and are rewarded three times as often for creativity.

Junior and senior high school presents a whole new challenge for students. No longer is school a "feminine" environment. Teachers, predominately male, often have quite different expectations regarding appropriate classroom behavior, the value of particular subjects, and criteria for quality school work. For example, math and science are seen as a male domain by most teachers and students. Boys are valued for thinking logically, independently, with self-confidence, and an appropriate degree of risk-taking. Girls are valued for their emotional expressiveness, sensitivity to others, dependency, and subjective thinking.

My interest in the question of female participation in school science began five years ago when I realized, quite by accident, that there were interesting implications on this topic in some of my research data from the study of a particular elementary science curriculum (SCIS). The unique feature of the SCIS was that students had no textbooks but rather learned about science concepts from their own experiments. I found that children who had used this curriculum from first through sixth grade were better able to understand and think logically about science problems. The unexpected finding was that the girls did as well as the boys. This was a surprise because reports from a nationwide assessment of school children's knowledge during the last decade have repeatedly shown that girls all over the United States are less knowledgeable than boys in science. If particular curriculum experiences can significantly modify girls' knowledge of science in elementary school, then taking high school science courses becomes a more realistic possibility for women.

Studies show that girls of all ages are consistently less positive than boys in their attitudes and feelings toward science. But my studies showed that girls' attitudes regarding science and the scientists can, in fact, be positively affected by special curriculum experiences. Interestingly, the boys' attitudes in the study were also positively changed, so that the differences between the girls' and boys' attitudes were identical to those of the control group. Innovative curricula might be able to modify attitudes but male-female differences still persist. Appropriate curriculum experiences appear to be necessary but insufficient for changing deeply held societal values toward science and women.

Teacher behavior appears to have a positive effect on female participation in science at both the elementary and secondary levels. Whether a teacher is male or female, if the following cluster of behaviors exists, girls participate more fully and positively in school science: (1) a responsive, flexible teaching style, (2) a positive attitude towards science, (3) an interest in science, and (4) a belief in the ability of all students to learn from their own science experiments.

In addition to particular curriculum and teacher effects, another approach that has been successful for increasing girls' performance in science is relying on older girls to counsel, encourage, and tutor younger ones. Modifying sexually stereotypical textbook materials is also extremely useful in counteracting prevailing popular public attitudes toward science and the scientist.

Schools are socializing agencies that have the potential for modifying student attitudes and knowledge when it is important to do so. However, schools cannot accomplish important changes, such as the democratization of opportunity, unless social reforms accompany the educational effort. When cultural values mediate against boys' and girls' achievement, as they do in science, disproportionate amounts of academic support are necessary to overcome their effects.

Science teachers are in a unique position to provide professional support for the 50 percent of our population who are conspicuously in need of more attention if women are to contribute fully to the scientific and technological achievements in our society.

should represent a wide range of cognitive, affective, and psychomotor results for the unit.

3. The science units are taught using regular group instruction, laboratory activities, demonstration, films, and so on.

4. Progress tests are administered at the end of a science unit.

5. Test results are used to diagnose learning errors of those who failed to master the material at a predetermined level, usually 85 percent. The tests provide positive reinforcement for those who master the unit.

6. The science teacher uses the test results to prescribe procedures for those students who did not master the unit. Based on the test, the teacher may suggest rereading the text, redoing laboratory work, using programmed materials, having private tutorials, or reviewing audiovisual aids. Additional time is provided for the student to master the material.

7. A test is administered at the end of the course. The test score is used to determine the student's grade. Grades should be predetermined levels of mastery; for example, 90 percent is an A, 80 percent is a B, and so on. These tests are criterion-, not norm-referenced. They should represent absolute levels of mastery.

8. Results from the final examination, unit tests, student responses, and effectiveness of materials and instruction are used by the science teacher to improve units for the next term or year.

The mastery learning approach emphasizes the achievement of all students for a given science unit and eventually the science program. Testing is used to identify learning difficulties and correct them through specific recommendations. Additional time is provided for students to learn material they missed or did not learn the first time through the unit. Student achievement is determined by an absolute level of mastery on each unit, not a performance relative to all other students in the class. The mastery learning approach makes a great deal of educational sense. As science teachers we want all students to understand science. This goal is accomplished through varying the learning time and designing the program for uniform mastery of science concepts, skills, and processes. In contrast, we usually hold time constant and accept a wide range of achievement from students.

■ **Individualizing Your Science Program**

Most science teachers prefer to individualize their programs. By doing so they can take into consider-

ation their interests, time, and facilities; the students' motivation and achievement; and administrative support. There are other obvious advantages, such as the availability of materials and other resources in and around the school.

In this section we give some guides for preparing your own individualized program. Recall that one of the requirements of P.L. 94–142, the law requiring mainstreaming of special students in regular classrooms, was that special students have an Individualized Education Program (IEP). The IEP requires the following: the student's present level of performance, short- and long-term objectives, how the student will participate in the regular program, what special services will be provided, measures of achievement, and progress. In outlining a general approach to individualizing science instruction, we have attempted to incorporate the primary requirements of an IEP for special students. Should you be required to complete an IEP, you can use this outline as a basis of your plans.

Typically, individualized programs should include: title, purpose, objectives, pretest, required activities, special services and resources, posttest, and enrichment activities.

Taking time to construct the individualized guide so that it is simple, clear, and direct will result in reduced procedural guidance and increased instructional time. You can expect the students to experience some confusion during the early stages of implementation, more so at the middle school than at the senior high levels. Bear with them, answer their questions, and refer them to the syllabus for direction and by the second or third unit they will understand the program.

Outline for an Individualized Science Program

Title
The title may be the textbook chapter or one that you have selected. It should be short, simple, and convey the theme of the unit. For example, "Science, Technology, and Society."

Purpose
The nature of the unit and the reason for studying it should be contained in this brief statement. Complex, longer, and uncommon topics may require longer statements of purpose. But, in general, it is best to keep the statement short. For example,

The purpose of this unit is to help you understand the relationship between science and society. Science and technology are basic to our society; they have contributed to healthier lives and more efficient work. They also hold promise of resolving some problems such as pollution and the population explosion. For these and other reasons, it is useful to know about science and society.

Objectives

The learning guide should contain short- and long-term objectives or, if you prefer, major goals for the unit and more specific objectives derived from the goals. The number of goals and objectives will depend on the length and complexity of the unit. Objectives should be specific enough to be used as test items. They should give you an indication of the student's performance and understanding of the material. An example of the objectives for a Science, Technology, and Society unit might be:

> After completing the unit on Science, Technology, and Society you should be able to

1. Differentiate between basic and applied research.
2. Identify four science-related social problems.
3. Give arguments for and against scientific study of controversial topics.

Stating your objectives as clearly and specifically as possible will help in the selection of materials and direct the student's activities. They will also provide the foundation for test items.

Pretest

In most units the pretest should contain eight to ten items that are related to the objectives. Such short tests can be included in the guide. If you do not wish to include the test in the guide, students should be given directions on how to obtain the test and procedures for completing and scoring it. The pretest may show that the student already understands the material. If he does, he can pursue an independent study or complete enrichment activities. In most cases the pretest will indicate parts of the unit that need close study by the student. There are several options concerning your use of the pretest. It can be administered individually or to the group, it can be used as a student self-evaluation, or for your diagnostic and prescriptive purposes. Sample pretest items that are based on two of the earlier objectives for a Science, Technology, and Society unit are shown here.

A Pretest for Science, Technology, and Society

Directions:
1. Answer the following questions.
2. Obtain the answer key from the teacher.

3. Score the pretest.
4. Determine the areas of study in which you need assistance.
5. Talk to the teacher about the specific items and any other assistance you may need for the unit.

Sample Questions:
1. Indicate which of the following refers to a basic research (B) topic and which refers to an applied research topic (A). Fill in DK if you don't know.
   ___a. The mechanics of continental drift
   ___b. Prediction and prevention of earthquakes
   ___c. Studying nuclear particles
   ___d. Solutions to the energy problem
   ___e. Long-term climatic changes
   ___f. Methods of reducing air pollution
   ___g. Migration and mating habits of fish
   ___h. Methods of farming the oceans
2. Which of the following social problems is least related to science? Check the correct answer.
   ___a. Reducing population growth
   ___b. Resolving foreign-relations problems
   ___c. Controlling communicable disease
   ___d. Increasing food supplies
   ___e. Reducing water and air pollution

Required Activities

This section should list the learning activities to be completed by the students. It may include such things as reading specific pages in the textbook, reading other sources, viewing movies, listening to tapes, doing laboratory activities, and completing projects. There are different formats for listing the required activities. Examples include learning hierarchies and sequential studies as related to the textbook. Specifying a date for beginning and completing activities is a good idea, especially for those activities, such as laboratory investigations, that may be done as a group. Listed in the example are several suggested required activities.

Required Activities

Directions:
1. You should complete the following by ___(date)___.
2. The laboratory will be done as a class on ___(date)___.
3. We will have a class discussion based on the unit on ___(date)___.
4. The unit examination is on Chapter(s) _____ in textbook on ___(date)___.

Sample Activities:
1. Do laboratory investigation 3 in Chapter _____ of textbook.
2. Read the magazine article "Science, Technology, and Society."
3. View filmstrip entitled "Science, Technology, and Society."

4. Answer the questions on page _____ of textbook.
5. Make arrangements with three other students to complete the simulation game "Science, Technology, and Society."
6. Complete the self-test.

Special Services and Resources

The orientation of this section is suggested by the IEP requirements for special students. In addition, it is a good idea to list any special services or resources that may be of interest or assistance to students, such as times when you are available for individual help, guest speakers, films, or exhibits.

Special Services and Resources
- There will be a guest scientist on __(date)__ and an interpreter will be available.
- A video recording of the pamphlet "Science, Technology, and Society" is available in the resource center.
- I will be available for questions and assistance each day at 10:00 A.M.–10:45 A.M. and 2:15 P.M.–3:00 P.M., and after school on M, W, Th from 3:30 P.M.–4:00 P.M.
- The film "Science, Technology, and Society" will be available for review in the learning center on __(date)__. Try to see the film on your free period.
- A tutor is available on request; see me if you would like some help.

Posttest

The posttest is an alternate form of the pretest. Its purpose is to measure the student's level of mastery of the unit. Questions should be directly related to the objectives as stated at the beginning of the unit. In general, a mastery of 85 percent is the suggested level of achievement. If this level is not achieved, the test results and a private conference should indicate the learning that is required. See the pretest for an example.

Enrichment Activities

Your individualized guide should include suggestions of activities that students can complete for enrichment. Usually they would select from among the activities listed, giving them a fine opportunity to pursue their interests and ideas. It is a good idea to set the time limits of the unit so that most, if not all, students will have an opportunity to complete some enrichment activities. This limit will also provide the time needed for slower students to master the basic material of the unit. Provide a wide range of activities from which the students can choose; there should be opportunities for in-depth study, practice or application of ideas, pursuit of new interests, and other things such as games or films related to the topic. Rather than listing enrichment specifically related to our continuous example of science, technology, and society, we have listed examples of different opportunities that may be provided as enrichment activities.

Enrichment Activities
- Read other books on the unit topic.
- Read newspaper articles.
- Read magazine articles.
- Read articles from professional journals.
- View films and filmstrips.
- Watch special television programs.
- Use programmed materials.
- Listen to tapes of lectures.
- Do special projects (individually or with a group).
- Conduct surveys.
- Play simulation games.
- Take field trips to parks, museums, and other areas related to the unit.
- Form discussion groups with other students.
- Build models.
- Do questions and problems in the textbook.
- Prepare and teach elementary school children a similar unit.
- Do independent study.

Individualizing Science Instruction: Advantages and Disadvantages

Now that you have some information about what is possible, it is appropriate to review some of the advantages and disadvantages in teaching science for individual differences. Individualized approaches endeavor to respond to the overwhelming evidence about individual variation. They are efforts to respect the "person." Science teachers who have gone from group-centered to more individualized instruction often state that they didn't realize how futile it was in the traditional approach to try to have all students learn particularly difficult material at the same rate. The fact that the slower academic student is not demeaned and frustrated because he doesn't learn rapidly or the gifted student is not held back until his classmates catch up is perhaps the major advantage of this approach.

There is, furthermore, a shift in emphasis from extrinsic to intrinsic rewards. A student doing an assignment at his own rate gains self-confidence and a sense of competence which may not manifest themselves so easily in group instruction. The real joy of learning in this manner comes in the student's completing the task on his own initiative, not simply because of grades given by the teacher.

Although an individualized approach ideally

has many practical advantages, there are also several disadvantages. A science teacher considering taking a position in a school or seriously thinking about the implementation of such a system should be aware of these disadvantages before she makes the pertinent decisions. Generally, the problems involve facilities, scheduling, materials, and cost.

Facilities

Schools implementing student-centered instruction seldom completely individualize their courses, for to do so means that there must be facilities available for large and small groups as well as individualized learning. To design and provide facilities to accommodate these various modes of teaching, architects must know in advance how many of each type are required, to ensure maximum utilization of the plant.

Scheduling

Because of the diversity of the program and this type of instruction, scheduling can become a problem. For example, if there is one large group-instructional room, it must be scheduled and used by several departments to ensure maximum utilization. Obviously, this use by various departments limits the flexibility for any one program because the instructors will be able to use the room only when they are scheduled to do so.

Staff

Individualizing a science program means that the faculty must operate as teams. Instructors must be well prepared in several subjects because they may be supervising a large laboratory containing students working on units spread over several areas in different subjects. Because students are often working on different units within each of these subjects, a teacher cannot read a chapter ahead of the students the night before and be prepared. Individualized teachers must know the subjects and curriculum well to interact appropriately with each student's needs.

Acting as a member of a fully functioning team is often difficult because of the differences in how members view their functions as teachers and what they think are appropriate requirements for the learners. For example, if some teachers believe that students should be directed to cover a lot of material and others think they should be given considerable freedom to become autonomous investigators, there are bound to be conflicts among the faculty team members.

Materials

Individualized science instruction demands more reading matter and audiovisual aids than does conventional teaching, since multilevel learning aids must be available so as to adjust the materials to the academic abilities of the students. For example, the intellectually gifted may read a college-level book or listen to a "teacher-prepared taped talk" about the subject topic. Educationally impaired may need materials emphasizing laboratory activities.

Cost

Because of the need for multilevel, multi-learning aids for varied student abilities, individualized instruction is more costly than traditional approaches, particularly because students wear out filmstrips, 35-mm slides, educational software, and tapes more rapidly than when they are used solely for group instruction. The problems of maintenance of these materials and the audiovisual machines require that a resource center be staffed by technically competent people, increasing the need for financial support.

■ Summary

Science teaching in the 1990s will, due to legal mandates, include greater recognition of the unique handicaps, gifts, and talents of students. Handicapped students will be mainstreamed in regular classrooms, and the gifted will also receive special attention. Although each special student, whether handicapped or gifted, presents a unique case, there are some guides and suggestions that can help the science teacher meet the unique needs of students.

Education has recognized the needs of students at either end of a continuum—handicapped to gifted. The process has clarified individual differences in general and it emphasizes the theme of the chapter— *all* students are special.

Students come to the science classroom with varied backgrounds and experiences. They vary in cognitive, affective, and psychomotor development and in the development of all of their human talents. Schools ordinarily have not taught for individual differences because of traditional philosophy and practices, problems of scheduling, poor teacher preparation, instructional costs, poor facilities, and poor equipment. In spite of these problems, many schools are now endeavoring to change the traditional pattern of instruction. This change has also been "encouraged" by laws requiring individualized programs for special students who are being taught in the regular classroom. Individualized grouping, continuous progress, enrichment programs, team teaching, honors classes, seminars, second-level science courses, and special science classes have been successful.

There are predesigned approaches to individualizing, such as individually prescribed instruction or mastery learning. In general, however, most science teachers like to design their own individualized program. When setting up a program, the following should be included as a part of the guide: title, purpose, objectives, pretest, required activities, special services, posttest, and enrichment activities.

Although there are advantages and disadvantages to teaching science for individual differences, on balance the advantages outweigh the disadvantages.

■ References

1. Sidney Marland, *Education of the Gifted and Talented* (Washington, D.C.: U.S. Government Printing Office, 1972).
2. John Carroll, "A Model of School Learning," *Teachers College Record*, 63 (1963) pp. 723-33.
3. Benjamin Bloom, *Human Chracteristics and School Learning* (New York: McGraw-Hill Book Company, 1976).
4. Benjamin Bloom, *All Our Children Learning* (New York: McGraw-Hill Book Company, 1981).

CHAPTER 7

The Goals of Science Teaching

You will begin this chapter by completing an activity concerning the goals of science teaching. Do the exercise, "Investigating Science Teaching: Goals of Science Teaching," at the end of this chapter.

Science teachers continuously reexamine the goals and objectives of their programs. "Which units shall I teach this year?" "What new topics shall I introduce?" Questions such as these, and the answers, are the bases of new goals and change in science programs. Only the individual science teacher knows the variables that must be evaluated in the decision-making process. "What is my budget?" "What are the abilities and attitudes of my students?" "What are my interests?" "What was the students' response to last year's units?" "What new ideas did I get from the National Science Teachers Association convention?" There are, of course, other questions, but these examples illustrate how goals are revised by the individual science teacher.

In the next two chapters we are not using the terms *goals* and *objectives* synonymously. There is a clear distinction. Goals are broad statements that give a general direction to a science curriculum or classroom instruction. Because they are broad, they have the advantage of relating to many aspects of science, society, and education and, simultaneously, of giving some direction to planning and instruction in the science classroom. The disadvantage of goals is precisely that they are too broad for specific direction concerning grade levels, science subjects, and personal aims and preferences of science teachers. So it is necessary to reformulate goals into objectives that are appropriate for the individual science teacher. Although goals and objectives differ, they are logically related in that objectives are derived from goals.

■ Basic Goals of Science Education

As you found in the introductory activity, there are many goals of science teaching. But by using the simple criteria listed below, most goals can be summarized into a few categories.

1. The goals should be comprehensive enough to include the generally accepted aims and objectives of science teaching.
2. The goals should be understandable for other teachers, administrators, and parents.
3. The goals should be neutral; that is, free of bias and not oriented toward any particular view of science teaching.
4. The goals should be few in number.
5. The goals should differ conceptually from each other.
6. The goals should be easily applicable to instructional and learning objectives.

Using these criteria the following goals of science education have been identified: scientific knowledge, scientific methods, social issues, personal needs, and career awareness. You probably recognize many of the goals in the introductory activity as relating to these categories. This was our intention. Certainly many objectives can be deduced from these goals and, at any one time, they are not equally important. Still, they have been the goals underlying science curriculum and instruction.

1. *Scientific Knowledge.* There is a body of knowledge concerning biological and physical systems. For over 200 years our programs have aimed toward informing students about these

natural systems. This goal has been and will no doubt continue to be one of great importance for science teachers. Stated formally this goal is: *Science education should develop a fundamental understanding of natural systems.*

2. *Scientific Methods.* A second goal has been the use and understanding of the methods of scientific investigation. Descriptions of the goal have changed; for example, the terms inquiry and discovery have been used to describe scientific methods but the goal itself has remained unchanged. The goal can be stated as: *Science education should develop a fundamental understanding of, and ability to use, the methods of scientific investigation.*

3. *Societal Issues.* Science education exists in society and should contribute to the maintenance and development of the culture. This goal is especially important when there are social issues that are directly related to science. This goal is: *Science education should prepare citizens to make responsible decisions concerning science-related social issues.*

4. *Personal Needs.* All individuals have needs that are related to their own biological/psychological systems. Briefly stated this goal is: *Science education should contribute to an understanding and fulfillment of personal needs, thus contributing to personal development.*

5. *Career Awareness.* Scientific research, development, and application continue through the work of individuals within science and technology and through the support of those not directly involved in scientific work. Therefore, one important goal has been: *Science education should inform students about careers in the sciences.*

■ Science Programs: Prelude to Reform

In the late 1970s three national surveys were conducted in an attempt to assess the status of science education: *The Status of Pre-College Science, Mathematics, and Social Science Education: 1955-1975, Volume 1: Science Education,*[1] *Report of the 1977 National Survey of Science, Mathematics, and Social Studies Education*[2] and *Case Studies in Science Education.*[3] The following discussion is based on an extensive review of these studies.[4] In addition, Paul DeHart Hurd's review, "The Golden Age of Biological Education: 1960-1975," in *Biology Teachers Handbook* (3rd Edition)[5] and the *1976-1977 National Assessment of Education Progress—Science*[6,7] were used.

We think this review of goals is especially important since it is a landmark in the history of science education. These studies present the first major national assessment of science education. We shall first describe a general review of science education and then discuss the specific goals outlined earlier.[8]

An Overview of Science Education

Between 1955 and 1975, the goals of science teaching changed very little but they are now in transition. Science curriculum programs developed during this 20-year period were based on two important goals: the conceptual structure of scientific disciplines and the processes of inquiry. Throughout the period of curriculum reform (1955-1975) the literature on science education included several reports emphasizing the importance of a broader perspective for science teaching. These goals included teaching about societal and cultural aspects of science, the interrelationship of science and technology, personal and humanistic goals, and decision-making skills. However, these goals were not widely implemented.

In the late 1970s and 1980s there was increased emphasis on goals related to basic skills, vocabulary, and study habits, i.e., "back to the basics" movement. In the science classroom, specific course objectives, such as knowing the parts of the frog, were used instead of general scientific goals, such as understanding the nature of scientific inquiry. Goals such as the latter were found primarily in district objectives. There is little evidence that the general goals of science education are clearly translated into classroom practice, but it is apparent that science teachers often use such ideas as justification for methods of science instruction. The many stated goals of science curricula include: understanding self, appreciating technology, preparing for college, advancing today's culture, and understanding local issues. New objectives indicate that the science curriculum is moving toward an emphasis on similar goals. The change in goals is supported by statements such as, "The purpose of science is to make better citizens, to study issues in society, and to identify scientific issues in politics," and by the fact that enrollments have increased in courses with goals oriented toward societal-scientific and technological concerns. Although courses in biology, chemistry, and physics still predominate, courses such as ecology, marine science, environmental education, environmental problems, science and society, and integrated science are increasing.

Generally, teachers showed little enthusiasm for teaching science as inquiry. Science teaching directed students to the "right" conclusion and little attention was paid to developing an appetite for submitting beliefs to empirical tests. The curriculum was the textbook and the goals were, by default, also those of the science texts. The textbook was usually seen as the authority on knowledge, and 50 percent of the science teachers used only one. Individual teachers or groups of science teachers were involved in selecting the textbook used in 98 percent of the school districts. It is probable then that science teachers do, to some extent, consider goals as a part of the textbook selection process. However, in spite of common texts and goals, there is a great difference in content from teacher to teacher, grade to grade, course to course, and school to school.

We can get another understanding of the status of science education by examining the longstanding goals described earlier: scientific knowledge, scientific methods, societal issues, personal needs, and career awareness.

Scientific Knowledge

Science programs are primarily oriented toward knowledge of the academic disciplines. In the classroom, knowledge goals become the scientific facts, concepts, and principles which reflect the structure of science. Science teachers report that they want their students to understand the subject matter of science. For example, they want the students to know scientific concepts and definitions of scientific words, and to develop problem-solving and critical thinking skills. Understanding science is generally interpreted as passing a test. Science teachers feel that the present emphasis on facts and knowledge is about right. Fundamental knowledge has been an important goal for two hundred years of American science education.

Scientific Method

There is little effort by science teachers to realize the methods goal. For example, BSCS laboratory guides are likely to be stored, rather than used, and science teachers do not use questioning techniques or instructional procedures that facilitate systematic inquiry.

There is positive evidence indicating that students attain an understanding of scientific inquiry as a process, develop essential inquiry skills, or can use these skills to improve their ability to think critically about science-related problems.

There are several influencing factors preventing widespread success in attaining the scientific methods goal. First, science teachers are neither "model inquirers" for their students nor have they been ed-

ucated in methodologies of scientific research. Second, most science teachers lecture for more than 75 percent of the class time, leaving students few opportunities to ask questions. Third, inquiry as a goal of science teaching is generally not seen as productive and is not accepted by most science teachers. Fourth, teachers who are aware of scientific methods as a goal of teaching feel that only bright, highly motivated students can profit from inquiry teaching. Fifth, inquiry teaching is seen by teachers as time-consuming, thus reducing the time available for "the basics." "Basics" is interpreted as learning facts and getting "right answers."

Societal Issues

Increasing interest in societal goals is evident in science programs. Science teachers are including these goals to make science relevant to the concerns of all students, not just to those who are talented and college-bound.

The goals for teaching science are in transition, with increasing emphasis on environmental concepts, world problems, decision making, and interdisciplinary studies, all areas related to the goal of teaching students how to deal with societal issues. State departments of education are influencing changes in goals through their legislative and regulatory powers. For example, there are specific requirements to include energy conservation, environmental problems, health, alcohol and drugs, nature study, and outdoor education in educational programs. Societal goals are usually met by electives in "popular science" courses. Examples include environmental education, ecological studies, and marine biology.

Contemporary societal issues are influencing science programs. For the most part, science teachers are developing new courses to meet this goal rather than incorporating societal issues into basic courses. An interpretation for this situation could be the conflict between the perceptions of the science teachers within a discipline and the interdisciplinary nature of contemporary problems.

Personal Needs

There is much rhetoric by school personnel and parents about meeting the personal needs of students through science education. This rhetoric takes the form of "life and work" skills related to science, the "preparation ethic," and vocational or career education. In response, science courses often emphasize "things that will be useful in everyday living." It appears, however, that the goal of fulfilling personal needs is not met for several reasons: there is no clear definition of the needs of young people, there is increasing emphasis on "the basics" and thus few concrete ways of dealing with personal needs, and science teachers see other goals as more important.

Attempts to meet personal needs are made primarily through health or advanced placement courses. Some of the other goals, such as career awareness, overlap with these courses. Sometimes personal needs are met as a secondary effect of another goal. For example, a socially relevant course on environmental education may provide fundamental knowledge that stimulates students to "examine the life worth living."

The goal of meeting personal needs has always been subordinate in science education programs, especially when compared to goals such as knowledge. In the past ten years, the goal of fulfilling students' personal needs has become increasingly important. This goal is closely related to both career and societal goals.

Career Awareness

One of the currently important goals of science education is to provide information and training that will be useful in future employment. Recent increased emphasis on this goal is due in part to public opinion. The career-awareness goal was found to be constant across science programs, although not the primary goal of science education. What mattered most were the scientific knowledge needed for the next course and whether all the courses were eventually related to one's future job.

> This vocational orientation of science education is consistent with several ideologies. First, science in secondary school is often seen as an elitist program intended not only for being the best in scholarship but the best in professional endeavor, e.g., engineering, medicine, actuarial science. Second, it reflects a pragmatic American culture, valuing what is essential for making a living, keeping one's possessions in good repair, etc. And another view links science with vocational preparation through an analytic epistemology, breaking down knowledge into its pieces; the facts, skills, procedures and components.[9] The elitist, pragmatic, and analytic somehow join forces to authenticate the study of science in the American schools as a proper vocational effort.[10]

There is some resistance to implementing the career goal in science education. There are several issues that emerge. Teachers and communities have questioned whether the school should serve labor needs; that is, whether the school should help prepare for work. They have questioned the apparent conflict between work of the school and the world of work. Science teachers are unwilling to sacrifice the scholastic program to help the young prepare for jobs. Furthermore, when teachers, parents, and science coordinators were asked about vocational goals of science courses, they all agreed that these goals should be included; however, the majority selected general education goals over vocational goals.

The inclusion of career goals in science programs has been increasingly important over the last decade, undoubtedly because of the continuing economic instability and the associated realities of unemployment and underemployment. Resistance to this goal can be interpreted as science teachers' perceptions that their task is to teach "pure" science, not applied science or vocational training. Still, science textbooks clearly show that some information on scientific careers is being included in science programs. Although the career goal has been emphasized and is important, the preceding criticism indicates that it probably will not become a primary goal of science education.

■ The Goals of Science Education: A New Reform Movement

The 1980s witnessed a flurry of reports calling for reform in American education.[11] Though varied in approach and recommendations, the national reports on education in the United States consistently identified science and technology as a vital area with a pressing need for reform. What brought about this national concern over science and technology education was a number of disturbing trends, including declines in the following:

- science enrollments in secondary schools,
- science education in elementary schools,
- achievement test scores,
- students entering science and engineering careers,
- qualified science teachers,
- public attitudes toward science education,
- the quality and quantity of American science education compared to that of other countries.[12–14]

As soon as discussions of reform in science education began, so did talk of rethinking goals. Obviously the direction of reform had to be guided by new goals. Anna Harrison called attention to the inadequacy of science education goals in an editorial in *Science*.[15] And Ronald Anderson asked the rhetorical question, "Are Yesterday's Goals Adequate For Tomorrow?"[16] He, too, called attention to the inadequacy of contemporary goals. These are only two instances of people who began directing science educators toward the reform of goals for science teaching.

Others began addressing the need and substance for new goals in more detail. In a short monograph entitled *Reforming Science Education: The Search for a New Vision*, Paul DeHart Hurd summarized the emerging vision of goals.

> *The rationale and goals are derived from a consideration of how science and technology influenced social well-being and human affairs. The goals for teaching science are based on scientific and technological systems in social, cultural, and individual contexts.* (Italics in original)[17]

A major report issued by the National Science Board in 1983 was titled *Educating Americans For The 21st Century*.[18] This report was quite comprehensive, including a section on goals for science and technology education. The list of general outcomes recommended by this report were:

- Ability to formulate questions about nature and seek answers from observation and interpretation of natural phenomena;
- Development of students' capacities for problem-solving and critical thinking in all areas of learning;
- Development of particular talents for innovative and creative thinking;
- Awareness of the nature and scope of a wide variety of science- and technology-related careers open to students of varying aptitudes and interests;
- The basic academic knowledge necessary for advanced study by students who are likely to pursue science professionally;
- Scientific and technical knowledge needed to fulfill civic responsibilities, improve the student's own health and life and ability to cope with an increasingly technological world;
- Means for judging the worth of articles presenting scientific conclusions.

The report continues by saying that materials to achieve these outcomes must be developed and tests must be devised to measure the degree to which these goals are met. The section then concludes with a summary statement of the goals.

> In summary, students who have progressed through the Nation's school systems should be able to use both the knowledge and products of science, mathematics and technology in their thinking, their lives and their work. They should be able to make informed choices regarding their own health and lifestyles based on evidence and reasonable personal

preferences, after taking into consideration short- and long-term risks and benefits of different decisions. They should also be prepared to make similarly informed choices in the social and political arenas. (p. 45)

The goal statement is finally extended to the curriculum.

> New science curricula that incorporate appropriate scientific and technological knowledge and are oriented toward practical issues are needed. They also will provide an excellent way of fostering traditional basic skills. The introduction of practical problems which require the collection of data, the communication of results and ideas and the formulation and testing of solutions or improvements would: (1) improve the use and understanding of calculation and mathematical analysis; (2) sharpen the student's ability to communicate verbally and to write precisely; (3) develop problem-solving skills; (4) impart scientific concepts and facts that can be related to practical applications; (5) develop a respect for science and technology and more generally for quantitative observation and thinking; and (6) stimulate an interest in many to enter scientific, engineering and technical careers. (p. 45)

Developing a new reform for goals is based on the notion that education in science and technology should be grounded on recent advances in scientific and technologic disciplines, needs and aspirations of society, and the interrelationship of science, technology and society.

First and foremost is the need to develop a contemporary perspective of goals for science and technology education. While there have been tremendous advances in science, changes in social needs, and newly recognized interactions between science and society, these changes have not been recognized in the goals of science and technology education. A new reform should include the following emphasis:

- Scientific knowledge that will enable students to deal with personal and social problems intelligently. Concepts fundamental to scientific disciplines presented *in the context* of personal and social issues.
- Scientific inquiry will include basic skills such as observing, measuring, classifying, predicting, describing and inferring. Additionally, students will need skills to generate, categorize, quantify and interpret information. And, once information is gained, there is an increasing need to *use* the information to solve problems and make decisions.
- Social issues will be one focal point of science programs. Students will have to have knowledge

and use inquiry skills about social issues and personal needs.

- Personal needs will be another focal point of science programs at the middle/junior high school.
- Career awareness will include opportunities to interact with scientists, technicians, health care professionals and others in science and engineering-related fields. Illustrations of careers will be provided by persons of different lifestyles, ethnicity, sex, and disabilities. In order to make responsible career choices students should have an accurate view of requirements and experiences needed *prior to* college or vocational schools.

■ Summary

Five enduring goals of science education were identified: scientific knowledge, scientific methods, societal issues, personal needs, and career awareness. The status of these goals can be reviewed through three national studies and other current reports.

The goals of science education are in transition. Some educational factors, such as the basics movement, are having an impact; but more importantly, the potential for a revision of goals of lasting importance seems to be emerging from areas related to social and personal concerns, namely, ecology, energy, and the environment. Textbooks are the curriculum. Any review of the major science texts reveals that they have goals such as "the structure of a discipline" that are related to older goals, in this case, scientific knowledge. Few texts have substantial goals related to contemporary social issues.

The curriculum reform movement of the 1960s advocated teaching science as a process of inquiry. Class and laboratory curriculum materials were designed to actively engage students in procedures used by scientists to establish reliable information. However, the goal of scientific methods is apparently not implemented by science teachers, who are more inclined to view sciences as a body of information to be learned as dogma and accepted on faith.

There is also a slight shift toward personal, career, and societal goals. The federal projects of the 1950s, 1960s, and early 1970s were developed using Jerome Bruner's concept of "the structure of the discipline." This structure includes the knowledge and skills important for a discipline such as biology, physics, chemistry, or geology. In the 1970s, 1980s, and 1990s the focus has been on life and work skills, ecological problems, and the impact of science and technology on society.

Historically, scientific knowledge has been the important goal of science teaching, that is, "the structure of a discipline." The knowledge goals were presented as facts and concepts. Now science teachers are including knowledge related to personal needs, societal issues, and careers.

Science subject matter and instructional materials are used for socialization, that is, the inculcation of values. This use of the knowledge goal is subtle and pervasive, although not stated in terms of science goals, which may be one of the reasons for the rejection of inquiry strategies and experimental materials. It may also be the reason for resisting the personal, societal, and career goals. When socialization is combined with the elitism of science issues, there is particularly compelling evidence that setting a new direction for science education will not be easy. Still, it seems clear that there is a need for reform and, to some small degree, the search for new directions has begun. Science teachers will have to continue the search and development of new directions through their formulation of teaching goals.

■ References

1. Stanley L. Helgeson, Patricia E. Blosser, and Robert W. Howe, *The Status of Pre-College Science, Mathematics, and Social Science Education: 1955-1975, Vol. 1, Science Education* (SE 78-73 Vol. 1, Center for Science and Mathematics Education, Ohio State University, NSF Contract C762067) (Washington, D.C.: U.S. Government Printing Office, 1977).

2. Iris R. Weiss, *Report of the 1977 National Survey of Science, Mathematics, and Social Studies Education* (SE78-72, Center for Educational Research and Evaluation, Research Triangle Institute, NSF Contract C7619848) (Washington, D.C.: U.S. Government Printing Office, 1978).

3. Robert E. Stake and Jack Easley, et al., *Case Studies in Science Education, Vol. 1: The Case Reports and Vol. 2: Design, Overview and General Findings* (SE 78-74 Vol. 1. and SE 78-74 Vol. 2, Center for Instructional Research and Curriculum Evaluation, University of Illinois at Urbana-Champaign, NSF Contract C7621134) (Washington, D.C.: U.S. Government Printing Office, 1978).

4. Work on this review was completed as part of one author's (Rodger W. Bybee) participation on the National Science Foundation's "Project Synthesis." Dr. Norris Harms, Director. Dr. Paul DeHart Hurd, Dr. Jane Kahle, and Dr. Robert Yager also worked on the project. We wish to thank them for their comments, criticism, and discussion.

5. Paul DeHart Hurd, "The Golden Age of Biological Education: 1960-1975," in *Biology Teachers Handbook* (3rd ed.), ed. William Mayer (New York: Wiley & Sons, 1978).

6. National Assessment of Educational Progress, *Science Achievement in the Schools, A Summary of Results from the 1976-1977 National Assessment of Science*

(Science Report No. 08-01) (Denver, CO: Education Commission of the States, 1978).

7. National Assessment of Educational Progress, *Three National Assessments of Science: Changes in Achievement, 1969-1977* (Denver, CO: Education Commission of the States, 1978).

8. We have not footnoted each statement, fact, and statistic in this discussion, so that reading the summary is easier. All material is supported by the studies and reviews cited at the beginning of the section.

9. One argument is that if knowledge is treated as a collection of pieces, rather than as ideas or models or metaphors, then the vocational relevance of courses can be controlled, with the irrelevant pieces trimmed away or never acquired in the first place (Stake and Easley, 1978, 12:22).

10. Stake and Easley, *Case Studies in Science Education*, 12:22.

11. See The National Commission on Excellence in Education, *A Nation At Risk* (Washington, D.C.: U.S. Department of Education, April, 1983); Task Force on Education for Economic Growth, *Action For Excellence* (Denver, CO: Education Commission of the States, June, 1983); John Goodlad, *A Place Called School* (New York: McGraw-Hill, 1984); Mortimer Adler, *The Paideia Proposal* (New York: Macmillan, 1982); Ernest Boyer, *High School* (New York: Harper and Row, 1983); and Theodore Sizer, *Horace's Compromise* (Boston: Houghton Mifflin Co., 1984).

12. Bill Aldridge and Karen Johnston, "Trends and Issues in Science Education," in *Redesigning Science and Technology Education*, 1984 NSTA Yearbook, eds. Rodger Bybee, Janet Carlson, and Alan McCormack (Washington, D.C.: National Science Teachers Association, 1984).

13. Paul DeHart Hurd, "State of Precollege Education in Mathematics and Science," *Science Education*, 67, no. 1 (January 1983), pp. 57-67.

14. Marjorie Gardner and Robert Yager, "How Does the U.S. Stack Up?" *The Science Teacher* (October, 1983), pp. 22-25.

15. Anna Harrison, "Goals of Science Education," *Science*, 217, no. 4555 (July 1982), p. 109.

16. Ronald Anderson, "Are Yesterday's Goals Adequate For Tomorrow?" *Science Education*, 67, no. 2 (1983), pp. 171-176.

17. Paul DeHart Hurd, *Reforming Science Education: The Search For A New Vision* (Washington, D.C.: Council for Basic Education, 1984), p. 17.

18. The National Science Board Commission on Precollege Education in Mathematics, Science and Technology, *Educating Americans for the 21st Century* (Washington, D.C.: National Science Board, 1983).

================ **INVESTIGATING SCIENCE TEACHING** ================

ACTIVITY 7–1

Goals of Science Teaching

Directions:

1. In the blank in front of the goal statements, you should indicate whether you agree (A) or disagree (D) with the goal or have no opinion (NO).
2. Review and discuss your individual responses in a group of three or four persons. At this step you can add new goals, combine, modify, or omit goals. As a group you should agree on the goal statements.
3. Compile the goals from the small groups into a class set of goals for science teaching.

Goals:

Science teaching should:

_____ 1. Make students aware of good health practices
_____ 2. Include contemporary social problems and solutions for those problems
_____ 3. Emphasize analytic skills more than the skills of synthesis
_____ 4. Prepare students for careers in science-related fields
_____ 5. Help individuals cope with their environment
_____ 6. Provide students with an understanding of the crucial role of science and technology in our society
_____ 7. Provide students with the ability to form a hypothesis and plan an experiment to test the hypothesis
_____ 8. Be more concerned with scientific facts than with broad generalizations since students cannot comprehend the generalizations
_____ 9. Develop skills basic to technical occupations and professions
_____ 10. Be related to and clarify individual beliefs, attitudes, and values
_____ 11. Make students aware of the fact that science is the only answer to our many social problems
_____ 12. Help students organize concepts into broad conceptual schemes
_____ 13. Make students aware of science-related careers
_____ 14. Enable students to use the scientific method to solve daily problems
_____ 15. Present fundamental knowledge and not contemporary, relevant information. If students understand the fundamentals, they can deal responsibly with personal and social issues
_____ 16. Be future-oriented; the past and present should receive marginal emphasis
_____ 17. Place more emphasis on the methods and processes of scientific investigation
_____ 18. Train the intuitive, inventive, creative talents more than the rational, logical, and methodological. The former more than the latter talents are responsible for new knowledge
_____ 19. Actually involve students in science activities
_____ 20. Develop the following abilities: creative thinking, effective communication, and decision-making
_____ 21. Demonstrate the aesthetic and ethical values of science
_____ 22. Place great emphasis on recognizing the moral obligation of science and technology to the individual and to society
_____ 23. Deal with broad, encompassing knowledge, since it is impossible to determine the best specific knowledge that most students will need
_____ 24. Focus on the nature of scientific inquiry since this is the one aspect of the scientific enterprise that does not change
_____ 25. Help students differentiate between facts and opinion and determine which is the best information available concerning problems

ACTIVITY 7–2

The Status of Goals and Programs

The National Science Foundation studies on the status of science education (circa 1978) certainly point out some interesting facts about the goals of science teaching. As you enter this profession, it is important to reflect on your goals of science teaching in comparison with our best estimate of what is actually happening in "the field." To assist you in this process you might answer the following questions.

1. Why did the goals of science teaching remain unchanged for approximately 20 years (1955–1975), then go into a period of transition?

2. What do you see as the direction of transition in goals for science teaching?

3. What is your position on teaching science by inquiry?

4. Why have science teachers shown little enthusiasm for teaching science by inquiry?

5. What do you think are the important goals of science teaching?

6. What is the best way of achieving those goals?

7. Do you think "socialization" should be a goal of science teaching? How would you justify your answer?

8. What is your reaction to the reported widespread socialization in science classrooms?

9. What is your reaction to the teaching of science as "a body of information to be learned as dogma and accepted on faith"?

10. What can you do about this situation in your own classroom?

ACTIVITY 7–3

Goals of Science Textbooks

You have seen that the goals of textbooks are, essentially, the goals for science programs. In this activity you will first compare the goals of three textbooks or curriculum programs in your discipline. In the second part of the activity you will observe a science class for several days to see if goals are recognizable aspects of daily science teaching.

First, select three textbooks in your discipline (e.g., physics, chemistry, biology, or earth science) and the level at which you plan to teach (e.g., junior high, middle, or high school). Next, examine the textbooks and teacher guides carefully and identify the goals of the program. Are they stated clearly? Did you have to derive the goals from the text materials? Complete the following information about goals

	Text 1	Text 2	Text 3
1. Which goals were present and recognizable? (Y = yes, N = no, or M = marginal)			
Scientific knowledge	____	____	____
Scientific methods	____	____	____
Societal issues	____	____	____
Personal needs	____	____	____
Career awareness	____	____	____
2. Rank the importance of goals presented in the text. (1 = very important, 2 = important, 3 = somewhat important, 4 = marginally important, 5 = not important)			
Scientific knowledge	____	____	____
Scientific methods	____	____	____
Societal issues	____	____	____
Personal needs	____	____	____
Career awareness	____	____	____
3. Were the goals: (Y = yes, N = no, M = marginal):			
Comprehensive enough to include the generally accepted objectives of science teaching?	____	____	____
Understandable to other teachers, administrators, and parents?	____	____	____
Free of bias toward a particular philosophy of science teaching?	____	____	____
Few in number?	____	____	____
Conceptually different?	____	____	____
Applicable to teaching and learning objectives?	____	____	____

Now that you have reviewed the goals of three texts:

1. Which text do you prefer?

2. How does the text reflect your own goals for science teaching?

3. What did you learn about the transfer of goals to the science classroom?

ACTIVITY 7–4

Reforming Goals

The initial task of redesigning science programs is to identify what it is about science and technology that has significance for students. This statement applies to national curriculum reform or the local development of a science program. Why don't you take a few minutes and answer the following questions.

1. What knowledge, values, skills and sensibilities relative to science and technology are important for citizens in the last decades of the twentieth century? (This question is the basis for articles by one of the authors.* You may wish to look up the articles and discuss the different views.)

2. What scientific and technologic *knowledge* do you think is important? Why?

3. What values of science and technology would you emphasize? Why?

4. What skills are important? Why?

5. What are the sensibilities required of citizens?

*Rodger W. Bybee, "The Restoration of Confidence in Science and Technology Education," *School Science and Mathematics*, Vol. 85 No. 2, February, 1985, p. 95–108, and "The Sisyphean Question In Science Education: What Should a Scientifically and Technologically Literate Person Know, Value and Do—As A Citizen?" in Rodger Bybee (Ed.) *Science-Technology-Society*, 1985 NSTA Yearbook (Washington D.C., National Science Teachers Association, 1985.)

## CHAPTER 8

The Objectives of Science Teaching

One of the best ways to learn is to be actively involved in and with the material to be studied. To apply this principle, start by completing the exercise "Investigating Science Teaching: Objectives of Science Teaching," at the end of this chapter.

Suppose you were going on a trip from New York City to a specific street and address in San Francisco, California. You have a goal and a road map of the United States which provides you with enough direction to get you to San Francisco. When you arrive in the San Francisco Bay area, you would probably need another map with more specific directions, so you could reach your destination. Some maps are better for your purposes than others; a topographic map may be interesting, but it would be of little help in locating San Francisco streets and addresses. What you need is a more detailed map of the area.

By now you have probably made the connection between the map analogy and goals and objectives for science teaching. In the last chapter we described some of the larger purposes and directions of science education; now we will discuss some of the specific objectives for science teaching. Several points should be made about the analogy. General goals are related to specific objectives and both should be related to your purposes as a science teacher. Be sure you have the most appropriate objectives for your purposes.

■ Selecting Objectives for Science Teaching

There are many objectives for science teaching, as you probably discovered during the introductory activity. Rather than giving our answers to your questions about objectives, we will clarify different types of science objectives and then discuss the preparation of objectives for science teaching. First, we examine six criteria that will help differentiate objectives from goals and give you a guide to selecting objectives for science teaching.

1. Science objectives should be general enough to be identifiably related to science goals and specific enough to give clear direction for planning and evaluating science instruction.
2. Science objectives should be understandable for students, teachers, administrators, and parents.
3. Science objectives should be few in number but comprehensive for any lesson, unit, or program.
4. Science objectives should be challenging yet attainable for your students.
5. Science objectives should differ conceptually from each other.
6. Science objectives should be appropriate for the subject you are teaching.

Types of Objectives for Science Teaching

Objectives can be stated in terms of instructional or learning results. In the first the emphasis is on what the teacher does; in the second it is on what the student does. Here are examples: which is the teaching objective and which is the learning objective?

To demonstrate to students how to use a barometer.

To describe the steps in the proper use of a barometer.

The advantage of stating objectives as instructional results is that it gives you direction. The disadvantage is that you may not be clear as to whether the students learned anything. In general, we suggest that you concentrate on learning results when forming objectives. Doing so will help define the instruction sequence and set the stage for evaluation.

Objectives can be classified as either behavioral or nonbehavioral. Behavioral objectives state how the student will behave as a result of instruction. The behaviors are an observable indication that learning has occurred. Examples of behavioral objectives are:

The student should be able to:
• Identify symbols on a weather map
• Describe predator and prey relationships
• Define the term energy

For contrast, here are some nonbehavioral objectives:

The student should:
• Learn scientific names for common animals
• Comprehend the concept of work
• Know how to use the scientific method

All six of these examples could be objectives for science lessons and they are all stated in terms of learning results for students. In the first set the specific behaviors have been stated: if the student can identify . . . , describe . . . , and define . . . , then she has learned. The second set is a little less clear as to how you will know whether or not the student has learned . . . , does comprehend . . . , or does know. Are behavioral objectives better than nonbehavioral? Here are some advantages and disadvantages of behavioral objectives.

Some of the advantages of behavioral objectives are:

1. They help the science teacher become more precise in her teaching.
2. They clarify exactly what is expected.
3. The teacher plans more carefully because she knows what performance the students should display after finishing a science lesson, unit, or course of study.
4. The teacher knows what materials are needed and is able to give more specific help to students in directing them to outside sources of information.
5. They provide performance criteria for student achievement and accountability for the teacher.
6. The science teacher who prepares behavioral objectives finds them very helpful in evaluation. When preparing paper and pencil tests, the ques-

A student teacher and her supervisor review objectives for science lessons.

tions can be matched to the objectives and, by deciding on certain criteria of performance, questions can be phrased in such a way that the teacher has precise knowledge of the ability of the student to perform certain tasks.

Some disadvantages of behavioral objectives are:

1. They may tend toward an emphasis on trivial behaviors and ignore important objectives that are too difficult to define behaviorally.
2. They may inhibit the teacher's spontaneity and flexibility.
3. They may provide a precise measurement of less important behaviors, leaving more important outcomes unevaluated.
4. They may be used against teachers who are held accountable for the performance of students who do not learn.
5. They tend to focus the teacher's attention on the small, less significant aspects of teaching, leaving the "whole picture" unattended.
6. They represent only one particular psychology and philosophy of education.

■ Domains of Objectives for Science Teaching

It is customary to think of objectives in three aspects: cognitive, affective, and psychomotor. These terms come from the work of Benjamin Bloom and others who developed taxonomies of educational objectives.[1-3] Cognitive objectives deal with intellectual

======= REFLECTING ON SCIENCE TEACHING =======
Behavioral Objectives: Pro and Con

You have read some of the advantages and disadvantages of behavioral objectives. What is your resolution of the problem?

1. Should you state your science objectives in behavioral terms?
2. Can you resolve the differences and find an appropriate position concerning the statement of objectives? What is your position?

---

results, knowledge, concepts, and understanding. Affective objectives include the feelings, interests, attitudes, and appreciations that may result from science instruction. The psychomotor domain includes objectives that stress motor development, muscular coordination, and physical skills. Traditionally, cognitive objectives have received far more attention over the years than affective or psychomotor objectives. With increased attention to behavioral objectives and performance competencies, the cognitive area becomes fertile ground for writing objectives that stress performance in science knowledge and conceptual understanding. Still, science teachers should not omit important learning results in the affective and psychomotor domains.

Your understanding of the three domains will be one of the most helpful aids in formulating objectives for science teaching. We have used categories from the cognitive, affective, and psychomotor domains as the basis for tables summarizing instructional objectives in science (see Tables 8.1 through 8.7). The tables are based on the original work of Bloom et al., Krathwohl et al., and Gronlund.[4] The domains are arranged in a hierarchical order, from simple to complex learning results.

The cognitive domain starts with acquiring simple knowledge about science and proceeds through increasingly more difficult levels—comprehension, application, analysis, synthesis, and evaluation. The categories are inclusive in that higher-level results

TABLE 8–1
Cognitive domain for science teaching

Knowing
Knowledge represents the lowest level of science objectives. The definition of knowledge for this level is remembering previously learned scientific material. The requirement is to simply recall, i.e., bring to mind appropriate information. The range of information may vary from simple facts to complex theories, but all that is required is to remember the information.

Comprehending
Comprehension is the first step beyond simple recall. It is the first level, demonstrating and understanding of scientific information. It is the ability to apprehend, grasp, and understand the meaning of scientific material. Comprehension is shown in three ways: (1) translation of scientific knowledge into other forms, (2) interpretation of science knowledge by reordering and showing interrelationships and summarizing material, and (3) extrapolation and interpolation of science knowledge. Here the students can estimate or predict future trends or infer consequences between two points or items of data.

Applying
Application is the ability to show the pertinence of scientific principles to different situations. At this level stu-

dents may apply scientific concepts, methods, laws, or theories to actual concrete problems.

Analyzing
Analysis requires more than knowledge, comprehension, and application. It also requires an understanding of the underlying structure of the material. Analysis is the ability to break down material to its fundamental elements for better understanding of the organization. Analysis may include identifying parts, clarifying relationships among parts, and recognizing organizational principles of scientific systems.

Synthesizing
Synthesis requires the formulation of new understandings of scientific systems. If analysis stresses the parts, synthesis stresses the whole. Components of scientific systems may be reorganized into new patterns and new wholes. A bringing together of scientific ideas to form a unique idea, place, or pattern could be a learning result at this level.

Evaluating
Evaluation is the highest level of learning results in the hierarchy. It includes all the other levels plus the ability to make value judgments based on internal evidence and consistency and/or clearly defined external criteria.

===== **GUEST EDITORIAL** =====

Environmental Education and Science Teaching

Jeff Mow
Science Education Student, Environmental Education
Carleton College, Northfield, Minnesota

As a junior at Carleton College, I am just beginning my career in science education. Originally a Geology major, later I changed to Environmental Education. As I completed a science methods course, I realized that the informal teaching and educational opportunities found outdoors have the most meaning for me. I would like to be an outdoor educator or perhaps a visiting teacher and curriculum developer. One reason for this choice is that I have a strong interest in geology and would like to explore the career opportunities in that field. Another reason is that I have been teaching and developing curriculum materials for the U.S. Geological Survey. Because of this opportunity, I have already been exposed to some novel approaches to environmental education. This experience, in conjunction with my own personal education and teacher training, have made me think about issues in environmental education.

The first question I have is, "What is environmental education?" A common conception of environmental education is that it is recreationally oriented. Also, environmental programs often offer such a different subject-matter focus that students are unable to relate the environmental activity to an everyday experience such as going to school. This lack of integration often results in an ineffective environmental program. Is environmental education a hike in the woods, viewing a film on pollution, or hugging a tree? Or is environmental education calculating the rate of erosion on a poorly managed farm field or making physical measurements of the forest regeneration process? I think that environmental education should take the latter form, as it allows students to integrate concepts learned in the classroom with an actual life experience. I also

think that it is important that the outdoor experience can and should be used as a laboratory, that is, a classroom without walls. I have developed and taught a map unit of the U.S. Geological Survey in which I have secondary students make detailed maps of their local environment. When I first taught this course, many of the students took the opportunity to run off. Since then, I have learned that, for the exercise to be successful, I have to lay down some initial ground rules. The result of outlining my expectations of them is that I am able to focus the students' activity despite the loss of the classroom's physical constraints. I have found that the environmental activities I have taught have been successful, and I would hope that you might also try this approach.

A much larger issue is the role of science education in our society. My own education and what I have seen in the schools indicate a distinct gap or void between the science taught in the classroom and that encountered in life. As a future science educator, how can I help bridge this gap? For example, in your high school physics course how much exposure did you have to daily scientific issues such as nuclear technology and electronic technology? A poll of my peers has revealed that these issues were not dealt with and that, in hindsight, they wished that they had been. I believe it is important that, as a future science teacher, I try to relate classroom material to everyday science applications. I think that it is clear that science and technology will be an important factor in solving many of our world's problems and that, as a science teacher, I have the responsibility of creating an increased awareness of the importance of science in our society.

---

incorporate the lower levels. For example, students must *know* a science concept before they can *apply* it. Science teachers have usually concentrated on the cognitive domain and the lower levels of learning within the domain. Understanding the hierarchical nature of this and other domains will increase your awareness of higher levels of science objectives and

subsequently higher levels of student achievement. (See Tables 8.1 and 8.5 for a summary of the cognitive domain and examples of general and specific instructional objectives in science.)

Affective objectives deal with feelings, interests, and attitudes. Science teachers are becoming increasingly concerned with this area in our schools

TABLE 8–2
Affective domain for science teaching

Receiving

Receiving or attending to stimuli related to science is the lowest level of learning result in the affective domain. Receiving means that students are aware of the existence of and willing to attend to scientific phenomena. When students are paying attention in science class, they are probably behaving at this level. There are three levels of receiving: (1) awareness that science-related topics and issues exist, (2) willingness to receive information about science, and (3) selective attention to science topics.

Responding

Responding means that the learner does something with or about scientific phenomena. The student not only attends but reacts to science-related materials. Learning results can have three levels of responses: (1) acquiescence, meaning that the student does what is assigned or required, (2) willingness, meaning that the student does science study above and beyond requirements, and (3) satisfaction, meaning that the student studies science for pleasure and enjoyment.

Valuing

Valuing refers to consistent behavior which indicates the student's preference for science. The valuing level is based on internalized values related to science. Again there are three levels: (1) acceptance of scientific values, (2) preference for scientific values, and (3) commitment to scientific values. Instructional objectives related to attitudes and appreciation would be included at this level of the affective hierarchy.

Organizing

Organizing means that the student brings together different scientific values and builds a consistent value system. Learning results include the conceptualization of scientific values and the organization of a personal value system based on science. The student is organizing a philosophy of life based on scientific values.

Characterizing

Characterizing means that, in effect, the individual has developed a life style based on the preferred value system, in this case science. The individual's behavior is consistently and predictably related to scientific values. Learning results related to general patterns of behavior would be aligned with this level.

---

today. It seems that neglect or lack of attention to attitudes has produced some unexpected results. Students are often losing interest in science at a time when scientific advances are unparalleled in the history of mankind. More and more students and adults are questioning science, perhaps because of a poor understanding of its role in society or because of confusion over the relationships between science and technology.

Writing affective objectives is usually more difficult than writing those in the cognitive area. It requires more care to formulate criteria for feelings, interests, and attitudes. It is impossible to peer inside the student's head and determine what attitudes lie there. However, certain behaviors are indicative of one's attitudes or interests. Also, students have attitudes and values toward the scientific enterprise. And, of course, scientific enterprise is valuable in itself.

As science teachers we are as much obligated to present scientific attitudes and values as scientific facts and concepts. What are some of these attitudes and values? In Chapter 3 we described some scientific values. Others are curiosity, openness to different ideas, objectivity, precision, accuracy in reporting, perseverance in work, and questioning of ideas. Tables 8.2 and 8.6 should further clarify science objectives for the affective domain.

■ Writing Affective Objectives

Behaviorizing the student objectives in the affective domain requires attention to the use of action verbs that describe behavioral changes in such things as interest development, changes in attitudes, appreciations, and development of values. These are all legitimate objectives and important in the growth of understanding the essence of science and technology in society today.

Because the observation and evaluation of behavioral changes among students in the affective areas is somewhat more difficult than in cognitive and psychomotor domains, it is important to design objectives that are carefully thought out and stated with precision. Many affective changes in behavior can be observed by the teacher during the course of instruction. These might be called overt behavioral changes. Others, more subtle, may not be directly observable and, therefore, can be called covert.

Here are some examples of overt and covert behavioral objectives in the affective domain.

Overt: "The student should be able to give evidence of behavioral change in the development of interest in the study of crystals by voluntarily selecting three or more books from the library and reading them for his own understanding of crystals."

Note that in the statement of this behavioral

TABLE 8–3
Psychomotor domain for science teaching

Moving

The first level is generally referred to as gross body movements. It involves the coordination of physical actions or movements. In its most basic form, moving is a muscular reponse to sensory stimuli. There are movements of either upper or lower limbs and coordination of movements involving two or more large parts (limbs, head, torso) of the body. Learning results include physical coordination and smooth movements while in the science classroom.

Manipulating

Manipulating can include movement but adds fine body movements. Here, the activity includes coordinated patterns of movements involving body parts such as eyes, ears, hands, and fingers. Again there are movements of body parts such as hands, feet, fingers; coordination of movements involving two or more body parts, for example, hand-finger, hand-eye, ear-eye-hand; and finally, there is the combination of coordinated sequences of actions involving both moving and manipulating. Learning results include setting up laboratory equipment and handling and adjusting microscopes.

Communicating

Communicating is activity that makes ideas and feelings known to other persons or, conversely, makes the need for information known. This level is based on movement and manipulation and extends these levels in that something that is known, felt, or needed as a result of movement or manipulation is communicated to others. At the most basic level there are signals involving nonverbal messages through facial expression, gestures, or body movements; speech, the verbal communication, starting with sounds and progressing to word-gesture coordinations; and finally, symbolic communication through the use of pantomime, writing, pictures, and other abstract forms. Science teachers are usually interested in learning results at this level.

Creating

Creating is the process and performance that results in new ideas. Creative products in science or the arts usually require some combination of moving, manipulating, and communicating in the generation of new and unique products. Here the cognitive, affective, and psychomotor are coordinated in efforts to solve problems and create new ideas.

---

objective, the word "voluntarily" is included. This is important because evidence of behavioral change in interest development can only be credible if the student shows a voluntary response. If it is in the form of a teacher assignment, extra credit, or some other structured request, one is in doubt whether the response represents a true behavioral change.

Covert: "The student will give evidence of behavioral change in development of a set of values in classroom demeanor by voluntarily self-reporting that he plans to assist another student to improve his skills of sharing with other classmates."

In this statement, one notes the addition of the words "self-reporting." This is important because in a covert objective, there can be no outward sign of the behavioral change, although such change may have taken place in the student. Therefore, one must rely on the student's own statement of intent. While this may not insure complete validity, it is an improvement over complete lack of evidence observable to the teacher. Many covert objectives involving feelings, likes and dislikes, and valuing fall into this category.

In science, psychomotor objectives concern learning results which involve physical manipulation of apparatus, skill development, and proficiency in using tools, such as scientific instruments and devices. Many of these desired behaviors are not ends in themselves but are means for cognitive and affective learning. This observation points out the interrelation of the three domains and stresses the im-

portance of total learning by the individual. Since one of the goals of education is to produce fully competent individuals who are self-reliant and capable of pursuing learning on their own throughout their lives, the psychomotor objectives occupy an important place in the overall educational endeavor. Although psychomotor objectives play a major role in physical activities, their importance in science classes should not be overlooked, especially since much of science instruction involves laboratory work which requires the physical handling and manipulation of materials.

The taxonomy of psychomotor objectives is not as well organized as the cognitive and affective domains. In Tables 8.3 and 8.7 we have relied on our own experience and understanding of psychomotor skills required for learning science.

The cognitive, affective, and psychomotor domains have been outlined for your use in preparing instructional objectives for science teaching. Each domain has a hierarchical order that goes from simple to complex learning results. As you prepare objectives for science teaching, we suggest that you use Tables 8.1 to 8.7 as guides to the levels of learning and the formulation of general and specific objectives. The tables should help you:

1. Clarify objectives for an instructional unit.
2. Identify appropriate levels for instructional objectives.
3. Define objectives in meaningful terms.

TABLE 8–4
Alternative view of psychomotor domain for science teaching

Simple

This initial state of psychomotor behavior is one which confirms positive readiness and mental set for the learner's further development in this skill area. It is not to be viewed as an objective in "performance" terms. Learner objectives need not be written at this level. However, if the teacher is keenly observing the learner's imitative activity, and reads the learner's need accurately, she can, at this point, identify appropriate learner objective(s) to move him through the succeeding stages (manipulation, etc.).

Imitation

Perceptual readiness (eyes, touch, muscle sense, etc.) When the learner is exposed to an observable action, he begins to make covert imitation of that action. Such covert behavior appears to be the starting point in the growth of psychomotor skill. This is then followed by overt performance of an act and capacity to repeat it. The performance, however, lacks neuromuscular coordination or control and hence is generally in a crude and imperfect form. This level is characterized by impulse, crude reproduction, and repetition. There is a low degree of learner control, accuracy and confidence.

Manipulation

Emphasizes the development of skill in following directions, performing selected actions, and fixation of performance through necessary practice. At this level the learner is capable of performing an act according to instruction rather than just on the basis of observation as is the case at the level of imitation. He is able to follow directions, give attention to form, and begin to integrate his motor responses.

Precision

The proficiency of performance reaches a higher level of refinement in reproducing a given act. Here, accuracy, proportion and exactness in performance become significant. The actions are characterized by minimal errors, higher degree of control and increased self-confidence.

Articulation

Emphasizes the coordination of a series of acts by establishing appropriate sequence and accomplishing harmony or internal consistency among different acts. There is accurate, controlled performance which incorporates elements of speed and time. The learner's responses become habitual, yet are capable of being modified.

Naturalization

A high level of proficiency in the skill or performance of a single act is required. The behavior is performed with the least expenditure of psychic energy. At this level, the performance is smooth and natural. It is routinized, automatic and spontaneous, and performed with a high degree of learner confidence.

---

4. Prepare comprehensive lists of objectives for instruction.
5. Integrate the cognitive, affective, and psychomotor domains in your teaching.
6. Communicate intentions, levels, and nature of learning, relative to your instructional unit.

Don't be a slave to the classification systems. You may have some objectives that do not fit in any domains and others that fit all three. Be less concerned about classifying your objectives and more concerned about how they will contribute to making you more effective as a science teacher so that your students will become better learners.

■ Preparing Objectives for Science Teaching

The task of writing objectives can be simplified by following these steps.

1. *Have your overall instructional objectives in mind.* What are your general objectives for the lesson or unit you are going to teach? Is it improvement of a skill? Developing the understanding of a concept? Stimulating interest in a new area of science? A combination of these objectives? Are your objectives cognitive? affective? psychomotor? Is there a congruence between the levels of objectives and your instructional aims? For example, your instructional objective may be: To teach problem solving.

2. *Select the content desired to achieve the objectives of the unit.* In many teaching situations, unit goals may depend on the sequence of topics found in a science textbook or curriculum guide. However, the presence of a topical outline should not influence your teaching objectives. After all, you are trying to achieve certain objectives for a unique group of students. The topics chosen should be vehicles to achieve these objectives. Usually, several subject-matter topics can be used to accomplish the task. Select those that are appropriate in terms of student interests and needs, your interest, suitability to the background of the students, and other factors. If you live in a mountainous area, use mountain terrain and topography to teach about variations of weather in different locations. Adapt your teach-

TABLE 8–5
Examples of general objectives, behavioral objectives, and terms for specifying objectives for science instruction in the cognitive domain

	General Objectives	Behavioral Objectives	Terms for Objectives
Knowing	Knows scientific facts Knows scientific methods Knows basic principles of earth science, biology, chemistry, physics Knows the conceptual schemes of science	To label the parts of a frog To list the steps in the scientific method To state the second law of thermodynamics	Define, describe, identify, label, list, name, select, state
Comprehending	Understands scientific facts Interprets scientific principles Translates formulas to verbal statements Estimates the consequences of data Justifies procedures of scientific investigation	To distinguish between scientific facts and theories To explain Newton's laws To give examples of density To infer the results of continued population growth To defend procedures in problem solving	Convert, defend, interpolate, estimate, explain, extrapolate, generalize, infer, predict, summarize
Applying	Applies scientific concepts to new situations Applies theories to practical events Constructs graphs from data Uses scientific procedures correctly	To apply the theory of natural selection to new data To predict the results of fossil fuel depletion To prepare a graph of temperature changes of ascending and descending air masses	Apply, compute, discover, modify, operate, predict, prepare, relate, show, use
Analyzing	Identifies stated and unstated assumptions of a scientific theory Recognizes logical fallacies in arguments Differentiates between facts and inferences Evaluates the appropriateness of data Analyzes the structure of a scientific inquiry	To identify the assumptions of Newtonian physics To point out logical connections in the reasoning of scientific principles applied to practice To distinguish fact from assertion To select relevant data for the solution of a problem	Analyze, diagram, differentiate, discriminate, divide, identify, illustrate, infer, relate, select
Synthesizing	Gives an organized account of two theories applied to a problem Proposes procedures for solving a problem Integrates principles from meteorology, biology, and chemistry in a discussion of pollution Formulates a scheme for resolving an interdisciplinary problem	To combine the second law of thermodynamics and principles of supply and demand in discussing energy To solve an original scientific problem To relate different scientific principles To design procedures for classifying unrelated objects	Arrange, combine, compile, compose, construct, devise, design, generate, organize, plan, relate, reorganize, summarize, synthesize
Evaluating	Judges the adequacy of a theory to explain actual phenomena Judges the value of a solution by use of internal and external criteria	To criticize the theory of continental drift To evaluate the Green Revolution as a solution to world food problems	Appraise, compare, conclude, contrast, discriminate, explain, evaluate, interpret, relate, summarize

ing to local situations. If brachiopods and trilobites can be found in a local limestone quarry, use that resource to teach about fossils rather than discussing forms that can be found only as pictures in books or in exotic collections from laboratory supply houses. Selection of content is very important. Try to find content that is both appropriate to your objectives and personally meaningful to your students. An example related to the first step could be: Each student has a predator-prey problem.

3. *Write general statements describing how the student should perform.* Begin these statements with a verb (knows, defines, responds, calibrates, etc.) and then state what it is you intend to accomplish. It is helpful to write these statements in terms of learning results for the students. Be sure you have stated only one learning result per objective. Three or four general objectives should be sufficient for any lesson and six to eight for sets of lessons or units. When the general objectives are completed, you should be able to relate them to the general goals of science education and to identify an instructional plan or sequence for your lesson. (See the first column of Tables 8.5, 8.6 and 8.7.) Following is another example: Understands the process of scientific inquiry.

4. *Write specific objectives under the general statements.* Again, the objective should start with a verb and state a learning result that is related to the general objective. Usually two or three spe-

TABLE 8–6
Examples of general objectives, behavioral objectives, and terms for specifying objectives for science instruction in the affective domain

	General Objectives	Behavioral Objectives	Terms for Objectives
Receiving	Attention to activities in science Awareness of the importance of science Sensitivity toward science-related social issues	To listen during chemistry class To ask questions about physics To select a book on geology to read	Ask, attend, choose, follow, identify, listen, locate, look, select, tell
Responding	Completes assignments in science Participates in science class Discusses science Shows an interest in science Helps other students with science	To respond to questions related to photosynthesis To complete a report on glaciers To discuss the limitations and potential of science in social issues	Answer, assist, complete, discuss, do, help, perform, practice, read, recite, report, select, tell, watch, write
Valuing	Demonstrates confidence in science and technology Appreciates the role of science and technology Demonstrates the values of scientific problem-solving Prefers science over other subjects	To initiate further study in ecology To work on community projects relating to recycling To complete a science project To accept leadership in the science club	Accept, argue, complete, commit, describe, do, explain, follow, initiate, invite, join, prefer, propose, read, report, study, work
Organizing	Recognizes the responsibility of science and technology to society Develops a rationale for the place of science in society Bases judgments on evidence Accepts scientific values as personal values	To present scientific values as one's own To defend the right of scientists to do research To argue using fact, evidence, and data	Adhere, alter, argue, combine, defend, explain, integrate, modify, organize, synthesize
Characterizing	Uses problem solving for daily problems in work Displays scientific values Shows a consistent philosophy of life based on scientific values	To solve problems objectively To verify knowledge To display scientific attitudes	Act, confirm, display, influence, perform, practice, propose, question, refute, serve, solve, use, verify

TABLE 8–7
Examples of general objectives, behavioral objectives, and terms for specifying objectives for science instruction in the psychomotor domain

	General Objectives	Behavioral Objectives	Terms for Objectives
Moving	Walking smoothly in science class Moving around the science class without problems Keeping up with the class on science field trips	To clean and replace science materials To carry a microscope properly To obtain and carry materials for laboratory activities	Adjust, carry, clean, follow, locate, move, obtain, store, walk
Manipulating	Manipulating science materials without damaging them Coordinating several activities during laboratory periods Performing skillfully in the science laboratory Operating science equipment safely	To set up science laboratory equipment quickly To adjust a microscope so that the image is clear To dissect with precision To operate scientific instruments correctly To assemble science apparatus To pour chemicals safely	Adjust, assemble, build, calibrate, change, clean, connect, construct, dismantle, fasten, handle, heat, make, mix, repair, set, stir, weigh
Communicating	Informing the teacher of problems Communicating results of science activities Drawing accurate reproductions of microscopic images Talking and writing clearly and logically Explaining science information clearly	To communicate problems in handling equipment To ask questions about problems To listen to other students To write legibly To report data accurately To graph data accurately	Ask, analyze, describe, discuss, compose, draw, explain, graph, label, listen, record, sketch, write
Creating	Creating new scientific apparatus for solving problems Designing new scientific devices Inventing different techniques	To create different ways of solving problems To combine different pieces of equipment to form a new science instrument or device To plan ways to solve problems	Analyze, construct, create, design, invent, plan, synthesize

cific objectives will be sufficient to describe the specific learning results. You may wish to change general and/or specific objectives after the closer analysis provided by this step. (See the second and third columns of Tables 8.5, 8.6, and 8.7.) Following is an example using the general objective stated in step 3.

Understands the process of scientific inquiry:
1. Applies the process to her own problem.
2. Summarizes the process in her own words.
3. Identifies correct and incorrect problem-solving procedures in the work of others.

Note that the conditions for good objectives are clear in the example; that is, both the general and specific objectives are clear, since they use a verb and they define observable learning results. Sat-

isfactory performance of the task can be shown by the student's ability to apply the inquiry process to her own problem, to summarize the process, and to identify correct and incorrect procedures in the work of other students. Certainly there could be other learning results for this problem, but this one should serve as an example.

5. *Review and evaluate objectives in terms of their comprehensiveness, coherence, and contribution to the science lesson unit or program.* The evaluation should identify any imbalance between levels of objectives or domains. Are all your objectives at the lower levels of the cognitive domain? We hope not. (Use Tables 8.5, 8.6, and 8.7 to help in the review.)

■ Summary

It is important to have good objectives for science teaching. Without objectives, teaching becomes a confused and directionless experience, frustrating to the teacher and ineffective for the students.

Recent years have seen increased attention to stating objectives in performance terms. Good objectives include a statement using "action verbs," signifying learning results in observable or measurable terms, the conditions under which the performance can be expected, and the level of attainment needed to satisfy the objective. Objectives are often divided into cognitive, affective, and psychomotor types. The first pertains to conceptual understandings or knowledge objectives. The second refers to attitudes, feelings, interests, and appreciations. Psychomotor objectives refer to skills and competencies that involve manipulation, muscular coordination, or sensory achievements.

The steps in preparing objectives are: (1) review your general intentions; (2) select the content; (3) write general objectives; (4) write specific objectives; (5) review your objectives for comprehensiveness, coherence, and contribution to the lesson.

The use of clearly stated objectives in science teaching is significant. Although critics have cited certain pitfalls to be avoided, the overall effect of good objectives appears to be beneficial. Science teachers are more conscious of the performance they expect from their students. Evaluation becomes more precise. Progress toward the attainment of goals is more easily measurable. Science teaching assumes a quality that is more satisfying and defensible.

■ References

1. Benjamin Bloom et al., *A Taxonomy of Educational Objectives: Handbook, 1, The Cognitive Domain* (New York: David McKay, 1950).
2. David Krathwohl et al., *Taxonomy of Educational Objectives: Handbook 2, Affective Domain* (New York: David McKay, 1965).
3. R. Kibler et al., *Behavioral Objective and Instruction* (Boston: Allyn and Bacon, 1970).
4. Norman Gronlund, *Stating Behavioral Objectives for Classroom Instruction* (New York: Macmillan, 1970).

====== **INVESTIGATING SCIENCE TEACHING** ======

ACTIVITY 8–1

Objectives of Science Teaching

Directions:

1. In the blank provided before each statement of objectives, indicate your evaluation of each. Is it excellent (E), good (G), fair (F), poor (P), or not an objective (NO)? Complete this portion individually.
2. Review your individual responses in a small group of three or four persons. At this stage you should discuss why you evaluated the objectives the way you did.
3. As a class, review the strengths and weaknesses of the objectives as you presently understand them.

Objectives:

_____ 1. Describe the relationship between pressure and volume of an enclosed gas and predict either variable when the other is changed independently.

_____ 2. Demonstrate skill in setting up science laboratory materials.

_____ 3. Know science.

_____ 4. Appreciate the nature of scientific inquiry.

_____ 5. Teach students the concept of density.

_____ 6. Enjoy interacting with friends in science class.

_____ 7. Given a scientific problem, will define variables, formulate hypotheses, and test the hypotheses.

_____ 8. Handle a microscope properly.

_____ 9. Record data appropriately.

_____ 10. At the completion of the lesson, prepare a growth curve showing the relationship of the age of a bacterial culture to the density of organisms and predict the results of continued growth.

_____ 11. Really show curiosity.

_____ 12. Show scientific attitudes, e.g., openness, reality testing, risk-taking, objectivity, precision, perseverance.

_____ 13. Perform skillfully while working in the laboratory.

_____ 14. Judge the logical consistency of a scientific theory.

_____ 15. Display habits of safety.

_____ 16. Know common scientific terms.

_____ 17. To demonstrate to the students different geologic processes.

_____ 18. Having fun in science.

_____ 19. To identify energy chains in a community.

_____ 20. Is able, upon completion of the lesson, to draw, label, and explain it.

_____ 21. Science teaching should make students aware of the relationship between the scientific enterprise and society.

_____ 22. At the completion of this lesson the student should understand the meaning of science as it relates to the good life.

_____ 23. Operational definition of scientific truth.

_____ 24. The student shows the scientific attitude of perseverance by pursuing a problem to its solution.

_____ 25. Understands the basic principle of density.
   a. States the principle in his or her own words.
   b. Give an example of the principle from life, physical and earth science.
   c. Distinguish between correct and incorrect applications of the principle.

ACTIVITY 8–2

Objectives of Science Textbooks

The object of this investigation is to evaluate the objectives of three science programs or textbooks. In the second part of the activity, you observe a science class for several days to see if objectives are clearly evident as part of instruction and of learning.

Select three textbooks or programs in your discipline and at the same grade level. Examine them and identify the objectives for the chapters, units, or lessons. How do objectives for the three programs compare? To assist your evaluation, answer the following questions by placing Y for yes, N for no, or M for marginal.

Were the objectives:	Text 1	Text 2	Text 3
1. Identifiably related to one of the major goals of science teaching?	___	___	___
2. Specific enough to give clear direction for planning and evaluating science instruction?	___	___	___
3. Understandable for students, teachers, administrators, and parents?	___	___	___
4. Adequate for the lesson, unit, or chapter?	___	___	___
5. Challenging yet attainable for the students?	___	___	___
6. Conceptually different?	___	___	___
7. Clearly aligned with the subject?	___	___	___
8. Did you find the statement of objectives helpful in understanding the presentation of lessons or units?	___	___	___

Observe a secondary science class for several days. While in the classroom you should talk to the teacher about objectives and review the textbook objectives.

1. What objectives were you able to observe?

2. What do the objectives look like in the context of a science class?

3. Do the students understand the class objectives?

## CHAPTER 9

Science, Mathematics, and Other Disciplines

Science teachers frequently operate in an isolated environment. It is as if they sometimes feel that science is an "island" in the curriculum, with few if any connections to other subject disciplines. As the world of the child becomes increasingly complex, this point of view is no longer satisfactory. The problem is addressed in an article by Hans Anderson where, in quoting Charles Slicter, he makes the point:[1]

> It is not important to teach interesting things as the quacks proclaim, but to make interesting those things that ought to be taught.[2]

Anderson feels that it is increasingly important for our children to become well educated. Many argue that it is our moral duty to educate each child to his or her greatest potential.

Other authors feel that fewer children are interested in science courses because of economic reasons. Students do not see job possibilities in science, so they pursue other studies. Another reason, according to Anderson, is that students often think science is dull, particularly when the only science they encounter is that presented in textbooks. According to this method of teaching, science becomes a reductionistic exercise.

According to Anderson, what is needed in our world is the ability to synthesize information. This ability implies an integrated view of science, that is, integration not only between science disciplines but also among other areas of educational and intellectual growth. He recommends the holistic method of teaching science. By holistic, he refers to science as a discipline with many dimensions: esthetic, empir-

ical, futuristic, historical, philosophical, and technological.

James Meyer describes an interdisciplinary, humanistic program high school that incorporates science, along with English, social studies, speech, dramatic arts, music, and art.[3] Several needs are identified in this article, including: (1) the need to do something positive about humanizing people, (2) the need to broaden educational horizons and general education beyond the traditional English and social studies in the junior and senior years, (3) the need to improve communications within the high school by breaking down departmental barriers, through an interdisciplinary project, (4) the need to expand opportunities for individualizing instruction, and (5) the need to encourage more students to try new experiences, even though they may not feel particularly talented in certain areas.

Six significant characteristics stand out in the description of this interdisciplinary course. The key descriptors are interdisciplinary, thematic, individualized, affective, exploratory, and creative. The title of the course was "Major Values and Concerns of Man" and it was divided into a total of six units with three units each semester. The titles of the units were (1) Man and Society, (2) Freedom and Justice, (3) Values, Harmony, and Discord, (4) Man and the Environment, (5) War and Peace, and (6) Change and the Future of Man.

William Romey expresses the need for an integrated approach to learning by stating:

> The young are likely to approach questions from a problem-centered view. This viewpoint automatically integrates. If I set out to solve a problem

=================== **GUEST EDITORIAL** ===================

There's More to Science Teaching Than Facts, Concepts, and Memorizing

Marie Del Toro
Earth Science Teacher, Fountain Valley School,
Colorado Springs, Colorado

Whether one has been teaching science for ten years or ten months, in a public or private school, or to a classroom of fifty or five, there is the common belief that teaching is a demanding but very rewarding profession. As a new teacher I have had my share of good and bad experiences, all of which proved very worthwhile. The purpose of this editorial is to relate some of my experiences and how they have helped me grow as a science teacher.

Fountain Valley is a small college preparatory school located in Colorado Springs, Colorado. Its 220 students come from 28 states and 8 foreign countries. As a result, there is a great diversity in student interests, values, and levels of academic performance. Although Fountain Valley encourages individualism, it also strives to further a community spirit. That spirit is exemplified in the following ways: students are assigned advisers to oversee their progress both academically and socially, students and faculty eat family-style dinners twice a week, and finally, faculty live on campus, thus providing personal interaction between students and faculty.

Although the school is small, it offers many science courses. Obviously, every student in science will not choose science as a career. The school is sensitive to that fact. As a result, Fountain Valley has developed a broad curriculum ranging from traditional one-year courses in biology and chemistry to one- and two-term electives in oceanography, geology, and anthropology. The assumption is that something will appeal to every student through a diversity of offerings.

Teaching in a boarding school requires a great deal of time and effort. It is not enough to teach a student the basics in math or science for, as teachers in a boarding school, we are obligated to a much larger commitment. In effect, we are serving as the student's parents, and so our teaching should encourage growth in all phases of a student's cognitive, affective, and psychomotor learning.

If a student is to develop into a caring, sensitive, and intellectual person, the classroom atmosphere should be conducive to attaining those goals. Like any other subject, science could be five lectures a week. However, it seems that the essence of science, learning through discovery, is lost if this method is used. As a result, the best approach to science I have found is an integration of methods such as experimentation, problem solving, reading and questions, student speeches, and field trips.

Two of my most interesting and rewarding experiences have been associated with field trips. One occurred very early in the fall during interim week. The purpose of this week is to provide students opportunities to expand their intellectual, cultural, social, and vocational horizons. I was fortunate enough to accompany another teacher and thirteen students to the Oregon coast to study marine biology, rain-forest ecology, and coastal geology. Before the trip, I knew few of the students but after spending a week living, eating, and talking with them, I developed a very special relationship with some students which could not have been kindled in any other environment. They have seen me in a situation outside the classroom and they know how I can act. This additional contact with students helps them realize that a

and have real permission from my teacher to pursue it, I'll try to apply all possible kinds of resources to study—physical, chemical, biological, geological, mathematical, social, psychological, as well as esthetic, philosophical, and historical. I see no reason why we should not move toward a totally integrated schooling experience. The best school is most likely the real world. This is already being done in many open public and private schools now being developed in various parts of the United States.[4]

Curriculum developers throughout the world have recognized the need to integrate and unify science disciplines for general education. The Center

teacher is a person too and not just someone whose job it is to give A's and F's.

The other very rewarding experience occurred during a field trip with my geology class. After spending the afternoon driving around Colorado Springs looking at various geologic oddities, two of my students told me that they had become highly motivated about geology due to my influence. They also expressed an interest in pursuing geology in college, which is ironic considering their lack of confidence at the start of the course.

A few days later, one of these students asked me if I would help with her senior independent project which, surprisingly, dealt with geology. Reflecting on the fall term, I must say that those students advanced in their understanding of geology and, more importantly, in their outlook toward science and in their newly acquired confidence.

Experiences such as these certainly make teaching worthwhile. However, it is not always that way. That is where the true challenge begins. The good student will learn regardless of the teacher and the poor student may or may not learn with the most exciting, motivating teacher.

As a first-year teacher, my duties include teaching four courses, coaching two sports, supervising the girls' dorm one night a week and every sixth weekend, co-sponsoring the rock-climbing club, and chaperoning various trips to the school's mountain campus located in the Colorado mountains. With this spectrum of duties, I see many students other than those in my classes and this contact is good. The hard part is in assuming so many roles: teacher, coach, disciplinarian, friend, and surrogate mother, father, brother, or sister. It must be exceedingly frustrating for a student not to know how I will react or, more importantly, how I will act in any given situation. A student rarely sees me perform all of these roles.

Coaching allows me to see students in an environment outside the classroom. It is great to watch students enjoy a sport whether or not they are highly motivated in an academic situation. Sometimes students feel teachers judge them by their level of academic achievement, and so underachievers may tend to shy away from certain teachers. This attitude is rather unfortunate for there are certain traits, just as important in life as math or science formulas, which can be instilled only in competitive sports. A student who works hard at a sport is learning a great deal about patience, sportsmanship, teamwork, and modesty, all of which are valuable and are not limited to athletics but hopefully will carry over to the classroom.

Teaching is both demanding and rewarding. It is a profession which will take as much as you are willing to give. There are always days when nothing seems to be going right but then there are days when your students excel. If I had to start again, I would make a concerted effort to listen more intently to various students' needs and excuses, keep my expectations high, for students need to strive for more than they think they can attain; and, finally, I would make it a point to be consistent in my treatment of various classroom activities. At present, teaching is proving to be a very satisfying and exciting experience.

---

for Unified Science, established in 1972, gave its attention to this problem in its first newsletter.[5]

■ What Is Unified Science Education?

It would seem that such a direct and concise question should have an equally direct and concise response. However, such is not the case. Unified science education means different things to different people, especially to those who are involved in developing unified science programs. There are simply no two unified science programs that are alike. There is general agreement that unified science education is an approach to science curriculum development in which the organization is based on something different from traditional specialized sciences. Science is viewed as a kind of human endeavor in which certain pervasive characteristics transcend the traditional compartmentalized areas of the specialized sciences.

This holistic philosophy does not deny that the specialized sciences are convenient, probably necessary, divisions to facilitate the work of many scientists. However, a unified science philosophy asserts that the whole of science is potentially more meaningful and valuable as an educational base to every individual than is some small selection from a few of the specialized sciences.

The unified science approach thus leads to courses that dissolve or minimize the arbitrary compartments of the specialized sciences. However, the same philosophical approach leads to different course structures. In some cases, a first step is combining two previously separate courses of study into one—as physics and chemistry. In other cases, all science, including the social sciences, is taken as the base from which subject matter is selected and organized using less traditional themes. Examples of the latter are courses based on the persistent problem "pollution" or on the permeating concept "systems."

Additional support for a unified approach to education in science at the secondary level was given in a progress report of the Panel on Educational Research and Development.[6]

> The division of science, at the high school level, into biology, chemistry, and physics is both unreasonable and uneconomical. Ideally, a three-year course that covered all three disciplines would be far more suitable than a sequence of courses which pretends to treat them as distinct.

■ Mathematics and Science

The discipline most closely aligned with science in the secondary schools is mathematics, which has been an integral part of the advance of science through the years. No scientific discipline has become truly respectable until bolstered by data compiled and analyzed by mathematical methods. The evidence provided by natural phenomena, experimentally tested in the laboratory or in the field and subjected to intensive scrutiny by mathematics forms the foundation on which science rests. The data collected by Tycho Brahe did not contribute substantially to the understanding of astronomy until the mathematical genius of Kepler put it into order and formulated certain laws of planetary motion. The hypothesis, developed by Jonas Salk, of polio inoculation by weakened virus did not gain public acceptance until it was tested by statistical methods on a large scale.

The science teacher in the junior and senior high school has an obligation to convey to her students an understanding of the role of mathematics in science. Every opportunity should be used to show the integral nature of mathematics courses in grades seven through twelve, although little crossover between these disciplines is currently afforded. Students are led to believe that science and mathematics are unrelated entities. This attitude is often perpetuated by the teachers of both subjects, perhaps because they are unfamiliar with possible common objectives and applications.

In practice, the difficulty of incorporating mathematics into science classes is compounded by extreme variations in mathematical ability among students. At any grade level, students in the science classes have mathematics competencies which range several grade levels above and below the average for the particular grade. Some students may have real difficulties with simple addition and subtraction operations. Others may have good understandings of ratio and proportion, percentage, and use of science notation.

It is important for the science teacher to realize this great variation and to plan her science activities accordingly. The mathematical requirements for any given activity or experiment are also extremely varied. By suitably individualizing the instruction, students can be challenged at their level and in the process helped to gain competence in the particular mathematical skill. See, for example, the "Teaching Science Activities" on pages 444-446.

Mrs. Phelps planned to have her general-science class do a half-life determination using the radio-activity demonstrator. The radioisotope for this experiment was obtained from the Atomic Energy Commission. It was iodine 131, which has a suitably short half-life for classroom purposes.

Certain members of the class, whose mathematical abilities were weak, were assigned the task of recording the counts per minute registered by the scalar. Simple averaging of three successive readings taken 30 seconds apart was required for each scheduled observation time. Readings were taken every five minutes during each class period for a week. The task was distributed among several students throughout the week.

At the end of a week, the data were plotted on semilog paper. Several of the students needed help on this phase of the experiment. Others were able to handle it with ease.

A discussion period was scheduled to calculate the half-life of the sample. Questions of the following nature were discussed:

1. What happened to the counts-per-minute rate?
2. What caused this?
3. After what period of time will the count rate be half of the initial rate?
4. What is the half-life?
5. Why were the data plotted on semilog paper?
6. What would the curve look like if plotted on regular coordinate paper?
7. What will the count rate be at the end of two half-life periods? Three half-lives? Ten?

This experiment provided several opportunities for development of mathematical skills at varying levels. Counting, recording data, averaging, plotting a graph, analysis of a graph, predicting an outcome, etc. were used at various stages. These skills covered a broad range of difficulty. The teacher could fit the skill difficulties to individuals within the class and also stimulate growth in previously unlearned skills.

The inquiry approach to science teaching requires increased use of mathematics skills. There are many opportunities to apply these skills in solving sentence problems. These problems are presented or arise normally during laboratory experiments. Junior and senior high school students have increasing experience in the laboratory. Solutions of laboratory problems require data. Collection and analysis of data implies mathematical operations.

Mathematics Taught in the Secondary School

Analysis of the mathematics courses in junior high school reveals the following types of skill operations presently being taught or reviewed:

1. Addition and subtraction
2. Multiplication and division
3. Proper and improper facts
4. Percentage
5. Ratio and proportion
6. Simple graphing (histograms, line graphs, and bar graphs)
7. Recognition and use of simple geometric figures
8. Area and volume problems
9. Use of units
10. Scientific notation
11. Metric system (mass, length, area, volume)
12. Basic algebra
13. Basic theory of sets
14. Number systems and bases
15. Other introductory topics

At the senior high level, a student is given further experience in all of those operations taught in the junior high school, by way of brief reviews and usage. In addition, the following topics are introduced:

1. Advanced algebra, i.e., series and power functions
2. Trigonometric functions
3. Logarithms
4. Coordinate systems in two and three dimensions
5. Use of the calculator
6. Dimensional analysis
7. Advanced graphing techniques (log and semilog, reciprocal, reciprocal powers, etc.)
8. Simple statistics (mean, median, standard deviation, quartiles, etc.)
9. Significant figures and standards of accuracy
10. Analysis of error
11. Elements of basic calculus

For these students in their junior and senior years who are preparing for college, the following competencies are frequently added to the mathematics programs:

1. Solid geometry
2. Analytic geometry
3. Differential and integral calculus
4. Statistical techniques

Development of these skills in mathematics classes should be accompanied by application in science classes. Frequent opportunities for using these mathematics skills should be provided. Such opportunities should arise in connection with the solution of laboratory problems and exercises, as well as in connection with word problems assigned from the textbooks.

Relating Science to Concurrent Mathematics Courses

Occasional joint planning between the mathematics and science teachers can bring about improved conditions, in both areas, for relating mathematics and science. If the mathematics teacher is aware of the uses of mathematics in the science classes at particular grade levels, she may point out the possible applications to her students. In assigning homework problems, she may use currently significant examples from science. Mathematics textbooks can be improved significantly on this point. The scientist is concerned with proper use of units and measurement. Attaching appropriate units to the figures given in word problems in mathematics can develop skills in usage, recognition, and manipulation of units by

Hand-held calculators have changed the way mathematics is taught.

the students. The problems will take on increased meaning and show the applications of mathematics to science.

Team-teaching arrangements between science and mathematics teachers can afford many opportunities for interrelating the two disciplines. Many teachers are trained equally well in both areas and have teaching responsibilities in both. In this case, maximum effectiveness should be achieved.

■ Mathematics and Its Bridges to Other Subjects

Too often the mathematics learned by secondary school science students seems to have little relevance to the mathematics used in their science courses. There needs to be increased cooperation and planning between mathematics and science teachers to bridge the gap that now exists, to make the mathematics revelant to the science being studied.

For example, developments in the teaching of biology at all levels reveals the need for students to have a mathematical background and an ability to bring mathematical experience and skills to bear on practical problems of measurement, classification, observation, and recording. It is equally clear that in studying biology meaningful, relevant situations can

provide a springboard and motivation for learning and applying mathematics.

The authors of biology textbooks assume that students understand the mathematics of measurement. The student may be asked to use a hand lens and to place the object being examined at the focal length of the lens, which is perhaps 6 centimeters (cm). Understanding of the metric system is required here. Reference may be made to the size of a human cell, which may be measured in micrometers and is frequently expressed using exponential notation. This also requires the student to be familiar with the metric system as well as the use of powers-of-ten notation.

Ratio and proportion are other important mathematical concepts frequently used in biology. The ratio of length to width of plant leaves and the proportion of biomass to nutrition provided for plant growth are two concepts that require these mathematical understandings.

Statistical understanding is needed because frequently such things as the mean, median, and mode are expressed when talking about population and growth. When frequency tables are used, the knowledge of collecting a sample in order to make a statistical count is needed. It is also important for students to understand the idea of using discrete and continuous data in graphing notations.

═══════════════ REFLECTING ON SCIENCE TEACHING ═══════════════

Integrating Science and Mathematics

1. Plan a laboratory assignment in which students are given maximum opportunity to practice mathematics skills with which they are currently familiar from their mathematics classes.
2. Obtain a mathematics textbook of the type usually used in the eighth grade. Select an appropriate chapter and rewrite all the problems at the end of a section or chapter in such a manner as to emphasize the interrelatedness of science and mathematics.
3. Interview a teacher of mathematics to discover the types of mathematics skills students are expected to learn by the time they have completed her course.
4. Write a two- or three-paragraph essay on how you would implement the teaching of needed mathematics skills in your science class.
5. Write a one-page position paper expressing your point of view on holistic education in the secondary school.

Calculating relationships between two sets of unit measurements such as Fahrenheit and Celsius temperature scales requires mathematical understanding. To be able to make conversions from one temperature scale to another is a skill required not only in biology but in many other sciences.

The concept of very small and very large numbers is another mathematical tool frequently used in biology. For example, giving students a problem involving bacteria growth where the number of bacteria doubles every 25 minutes provides a beautiful opportunity for them to calculate exponentially.

Another concept of immense importance is the idea of scaling and scaling factors. An interesting exercise is for students to determine the food requirements of a small mammal, such as a mole, and of a very large animal, such as an elephant. Does the food requirement alter with respect to size, volume, mass, or other factors? This concept can also be applied to heat loss and the necessary rate of metabolism to maintain life. All of these are mathematical concepts that are needed in biology and when practically applied will enable students to gain a better understanding of the use of mathematics in science.

Mathematics concepts used in chemistry at a more sophisticated level are those of ratio and proportion. Concepts of pressure, volume, and temperature change, and the use of the general gas laws give many opportunities for students to apply these mathematical operations. Manipulations of equations and formulas also require mathematics. Calculations need to be made in balancing equations. A chemical equation is similar to a mathematical formula in its application.

It is evident that mathematics has much to offer to chemistry, biology and other science subjects. Conversely, mathematics can also gain greatly from these subjects if the teachers of mathematics and the sciences make an effort to plan and to standardize the notation systems they use. If the mathematics teachers in their applications will use science examples and if the science teachers will apply the mathematics at every opportunity in working science problems, students will understand that mathematics and science are inseparable entities and are both highly important aspects of the scientific endeavor.

Simple Statistics

An aspect of mathematics in science that needs greater attention is the use of simple statistical techniques. Opportunities should be provided for students to assemble data, construct frequency distributions, and calculate certain measures of central tendency such as the mode, median, and mean, and certain measures of dispersion such as the range, average deviation, and standard deviation. Exercises requiring these operations will help students see the intimate relationships between science and mathematics. Certain experiments lend themselves well to statistical computations, particularly those dealing with biological populations or probability problems. Another source of useful data to give practice in statistical methods is the class scores on tests and exercises. Students will profit from the opportunity to work out class averages, range of scores, and standard deviations. If the teacher uses statistical methods in determining grades, the students have an opportunity to see for themselves the application of statistics to a very real and personal situation.

■ Summary

Increasingly, science teachers recognize the need to associate science with other disciplines. The ability to synthesize information, to view world problems

========================= **GUEST EDITORIAL** =========================

Earthquakes: Reducing Death and Damage

William A. Anderson, Ph.D.
Program Director, Earthquake Hazard Mitigation
Program, Division of Critical Engineering System

On September 19, 1985, a large earthquake rocked Mexico City, left thousands of people dead, and caused millions of dollars in property damage. Some years before, on March 27, 1964, an earthquake in Alaska killed over a hundred people and caused millions of dollars in property damage. I studied the social and economic impact of the Alaskan earthquake as a graduate student in sociology. As a result of my work I realized that many parts of the world are threatened by earthquakes such as these—in the United States alone, 39 states are subject to earthquakes.

Because earthquake hazards touch many countries, a global community of researchers study the phenomena. When appropriate, the United States has joined in establishing cooperative international programs for joint research and the sharing of vital information. I have worked with researchers from Japan, China, and Mexico. In particular I have been active in a program, which was established with Mexico following the great 1985 Mexico City earthquake, that has taught us many lessons on how to reduce earthquake hazards.

Many people in different scientific and technical disciplines are required to extend our understanding of earthquakes. Some of the researchers I work with include seismologists, geologists, engineers, and sociologists like myself.

Through their investigations, seismologists and geologists are developing a basic understanding of what causes earthquakes. Their goal is to understand seismic events well enough to predict earthquakes, thereby giving the public time to prepare. Engineers are completing equally important work in the design and development of buildings that can withstand the enormous structural strains and stresses caused by earthquakes. More earthquake casualties result from collapsed and damaged buildings than from any other cause, so improved buildings would save many lives.

Sociologists are also contributing to our growing knowledge about the effects of earthquakes. As a sociologist, I study the actions that people and organizations must take to prepare for and respond to earthquakes; some of these actions include finding effective ways to educate the public about the earthquake hazard, reducing the exposure of populations to earthquakes through land-use planning, and organizing such emergency actions as medical response, and search and rescue. The common goal of the researchers who study earthquakes is to reduce the property damage and loss of life that result from these disasters. I personally find it satisfying to work with those who are exploring this frontier of science.

---

holistically, and to look at the many interrelated dimensions of problems that affect human life is becoming more important. Interdisciplinary programs and unified approaches to studying science appear to be growing.

There is a need for greater emphasis on relating mathematics and secondary school sciences. Students of mathematics should have opportunities to apply their mathematical skills to the solution of scientific problems; applications should be called to their attention.

The use of inquiry methods in science teaching provides many opportunities for incorporating mathematics. In this way, mathematics is seen as a tool of science for quantifying and testing hypotheses.

Students practice, on a realistic and meaningful level, the skills learned in their mathematics classes. In addition to practice in the usual skills of addition, subtraction, scientific notation, logarithms, use of calculators, etc., students in modern science learn to evaluate measurements, express precision of data and results, work with significant figures, and apply statistical tests to their data. These skills are practiced at all levels of junior and senior high school science. Advanced students use calculus and other higher-level mathematics in some of their science classes.

Modern curricula in science and mathematics have changed the traditional patterns of teaching these subjects. The interrelatedness of the two dis-

====================== **GUEST EDITORIAL** ======================

Astronomy: Exploring Beyond the Earth

Laura P. Bautz, Ph.D.
Division Director, Division of Astronomical Sciences

In late February 1987, the explosion of a star 170,000 light years away became visible in the Southern Hemisphere. It immediately stimulated research all over the world as astronomers raced to observe and analyze this spectacular event. Press coverage of this occurrence attested to the public's interest in the phenomenon by which a star, many times more massive than our own sun, blew itself apart in the last stages of its life.

Events such as the 1987 supernova are not the only ones in astronomy to capture the imagination. Astronomy is the science that leads to understanding conditions found on other planets, how stars form and evolve, what happened to shape the present universe, and other questions. On an immediate level, astronomy assists in measuring time, in explaining tides and seasons, and in enhancing pleasure at viewing the night sky.

Professional astronomers gather and analyze information that comes from distant celestial objects. Most of this information comes to earth as light, which we view through telescopes, or radio waves, which we collect through enormous antennae. We then process our data in computers.

One does not need sophisticated equipment to view the skies, however. A pair of binoculars is sufficient to reveal craters on the moon, and if there are no city lights to interfere, one can see clouds of stars, bright gas among some stars, and the rich diversity of astronomical objects. These can all be seen in more depth at planetariums, observatories, and science museums.

Astronomy is a physical science, and one that requires an initial effort to master the basic principles. Students who want to become astronomers should keep their options open, and study mathematics and basic science courses.

---

ciplines is being emphasized with beneficial results to both. Students involved in modern programs are well equipped to absorb the skills and concepts required of scientists, engineers, and mathematicians of this technological age.

■ References

1. Hans O. Anderson, "The Holistic Approach to Science Education," *The Science Teacher* (January 1978), p.27.
2. Charles Slicter, *Science in a Tavern* (Madison: University of Wisconsin Press, 1968).
3. James H. Meyer, "An Interdisciplinary Humanities Program for a Wide Range of High School Students," *The Science Teacher* (December, 1974).
4. William D. Romey, "Integrating Science and Social Science," *The Science Teacher* (February 1973), p.29.
5. Center for Unified Science Education, *PRISM II*, vol. 1, no. 1 (Autumn 1972).
6. *Progress report of the Panel on Educational Research and Development to the U.S. Commissioner of Education Director of NSE and the Special Assistant to the President for Science and Technology* (March, 1964).

CHAPTER 10

Computers in Science Classes

The burgeoning growth of computer technology has been with us more than two decades. The use of microcomputers in our schools continues to expand at a rapid rate. Has this new technology succeeded in improving education in the sciences?

This chapter will look at some of the uses of computers in the schools, discuss some of the potential effects, and make some recommendations about improving their effectiveness.

The history of education is replete with examples of various teaching aids that have been produced over the years. Some of these, such as the reliable chalkboard, have stood the test of time and still form the mainstay of most instruction. Wherever teachers are educating students, they strive to make the teaching more effective by using innovative teaching styles as well as devices that impact on a variety of the senses. Since all learning takes place through the senses, it is logical that as many as possible should be stimulated for the most effective instruction. Other teaching aids that continue to be effective are various types of film projectors, films, overhead projectors, and slide projectors.

Certain types of teaching aids, such as teaching machines and programmed instruction, were popularized for a short period but did not live up to their promise. While many of these devices contributed to a better understanding of the learning process and were effective in certain special situations, lack of general adoption in schools and particularly in science education indicated they did not reach their potential. Historically, many of these technological devices were ineffectual in education because they were capable of only a few very basic instructional functions, such as drill and practice, visual projection, or presentation of teacher-controlled information. These teaching aids failed because they were not cost-effective; student achievement was meager in proportion to the input of time, energy, and other resources. Many early aids were difficult for students to master, and did not adapt easily to changing instructional requirements. The net result was that their popularity waned and the devices gathered dust on schoolroom shelves.

Recently the microcomputer has made its appearance. Will this promising new innovation follow a similar pattern of introduction, unusual promise, meteoric rise in popularity, and gradual fadeout in the next decades? Its present status seems to give every indication of excellent staying power. One of the dominant features of microcomputer use in the classroom—the trend toward interactive programs and personalized instruction—is already becoming an important aspect of contemporary education.

■ Computer Literacy

The computer may best be examined as a new medium of communication and learning. Considerable attention has been given in recent years to the concept of "computer literacy." With the rapid advancements in science and technology, becoming a computer-literate person today involves not only being able to write and speak programming languages but also requires familiarity with the technological devices that make learning possible and increasingly effective. As yet no standards for computer literacy have been set up. What currently separates the computer-literate person from the illiterate is little more than hands-on exposure to computers. People who have become reasonably productive on one or two prewritten software products are well on the way to becoming computer literate and may well have the knowledge or experience to adapt to virtually any future machine or applications software. Excellent prewritten software is becoming available in the area of science and it is not necessary to master a programming language to produce your own software programs. The National Council of Teachers of Mathematics has said that "computer literacy is an essential outcome of contemporary education." Each student should acquire an understanding of the versatility and limitations of the computer through firsthand experience in a variety of fields.

An operational definition of computer literacy states, "A computer literate person is one who has some knowledge of how to operate a computer and some knowledge of programming techniques."

Several state agencies have attempted to define computer literacy and to develop guidelines for computer-oriented curriculum development. As one example of such an effort, the Texas Education Agency has described several "essential elements" that comprise computer literacy. These elements plus the respective descriptors for various secondary school grade levels are given below:[1]

1. Computer-related terminology and use
   7th grade   Identify computer terms
               List uses of computers in a variety of situations
   8th grade   Understand the uses and limitations of computers
               List computer attributes
   9th grade   Classify types of computers
               List advantages and disadvantages of using specific types of computers for various applications
2. History and development of computers
   7th grade   Identify generations of computers
   8th grade   Discuss inventors who have made significant contributions to computing
   9th grade   Investigate the development of various computing devices
3. Use of the computer as a tool
   7th grade   Use a computer keyboard
               Load software from an external storage medium
   8th grade   Use software packages in a variety of applications
               Learn editing procedures in the context of data entry or other applications
   9th grade   Review and evaluate software
               Determine which software is most

appropriate for various applications
Practice data entry and error checking
4. Communicating instructions to the computer
   7th grade   Follow and give step-by-step instructions
               Use and develop flowcharts
               Develop problem-solving skills
   8th grade   Learn the syntax of a higher level computer language
               Apply the syntax of a computer language to problem-solving situations
               Write reasonably structured programs
   9th grade   Interpret error messages
               Find and correct program errors
               Predict output of given programs
5. Computer-related careers
   7th grade   List various computer-related occupations and careers
   8th grade   Identify training requirements for computer-related careers
   9th grade   Learn editing procedures in the context of data entry, or other applications

The computer is seen as a powerful new teaching implement that can do what no educational technology has ever done before: it can be genuinely interactive. This means students are able to question the computer and receive partial answers or guiding questions that lead to further steps, and also have access to resources upon which to make and base decisions.

Teachers of such subjects as science and mathematics have found that computers are helpful in a variety of teaching problems, including motivation, diagnosing student achievement, tutoring, and problem simulations. Computers can also be used to integrate class test data and synthesize computer-stored instructional activities for individuals and groups. Based on the classroom test results, different assignments can be devised for each group in a classroom. Computers make effective student review of subject matter possible. Their word processing capabilities assist students and teachers alike in organizing logical writing patterns.

■ Objectives for Computer Use in Science Teaching

Computers often play a dual role in the science classroom in addition to assisting in the delivery of instruction in such modes as tutoring, drill and practice, and simulation. The following objectives relate to this role and reflect the tasks and responsibilities of science teachers using computers in their classrooms.[2] Teachers should:

1. Demonstrate knowledge of sources of software to assist in the delivery of science instruction.
2. Describe appropriate uses for computers in teaching science such as simulations, computer-based instrumentation, problem solving, calculation, and other tool uses.
3. Demonstrate skills in using the computer as a dynamic blackboard or demonstration apparatus.
4. Demonstrate skills in the evaluation of science software.
5. Demonstrate skills in the integration of computer-assisted instruction and tool use applications within the existing science curriculum.
6. Demonstrate skill in using a simple database to collect and analyze laboratory data.
7. Demonstrate skills in using computer analysis of data such as graphing.
8. Demonstrate sufficient skills in programming to allow generation of problem-solving programs in the science classroom.
9. Demonstrate skills in using the computer for student calculations and numerical analysis.
10. Demonstrate the ability to write programs that aid students in calculation, to modify existing programs, and to generate simple CAI lessons.
11. Demonstrate knowledge of the computers' use in science-related careers.
12. Demonstrate knowledge of appropriate instructional arrangements for computer-based learning experiences in the science classroom (physical arrangements, grouping, and management).
13. Demonstrate knowledge of scientific modelling with the computer.
14. Demonstrate skills in using the computer for statistical analysis of laboratory data.
15. Demonstrate skills in using management software to help in recordkeeping functions, such as automated inventory and reference systems.

Following is a descriptive classification of the educational uses of computers in public schools. In most cases, computer software will exhibit qualities of more than one of the distinctions named.

Drill and Practice

Computers are perhaps most frequently used for drill and practice. Giving students the opportunity to work many examples repeatedly, the computer also provides feedback that tells them when mistakes have been made and gives examples of how to complete the work correctly. Computers can generate a large number of problems, keep records, determine success levels of students, and provide references to noncomputer sources of assistance. An important auxiliary to drill and practice material is the computer's ability to provide remediation based upon the learner's difficulties.

Testing

Evaluating student progress is one of the responsibilities of all teachers, and it is usually among the least enjoyed. The computer can relieve the teacher of many of the onerous tasks relating to evaluation, such as generating and administering tests, and grading, reporting, and summarizing the results. Properly programmed data can provide individual tests or quizzes that are unique to the students and to the subject matter. Interactive quizzes can also be developed that give immediate diagnostic aid to the students.

Tutorial/Dialogue

In a tutorial, there is a dialogue between the learner and the designer of the computer program. Information, techniques, and attitudes are developed in an environment in which the learner is invited and encouraged to play an active rather than a merely passive role, such as when listening to a lecture or reading source material. Usually guiding questions are provided that lead the learner along successive steps that culminate in successfully solving the problem.

Simulation

The computer's versatility is demonstrated in its ability to generate rich, creative, and manipulative environments for the learner, which may attempt to duplicate reality or may go beyond the real world into impossible environments. In a laboratory simulation, the user gathers data rapidly in a variety of situations, and may be permitted to perform experiments that cannot normally be done in lab. In the world of the computer, the learner is in complete control and can change variables, study situations, and acquire more basic knowledge and better understanding.

=========================== **GUEST EDITORIAL** ===========================

How to Choose Software for Science Teaching

Dr. David Trowbridge
Visiting Assistant Professor, Department of Physics,
FM 15, University of Washington, Seattle, WA 98195

As microcomputers migrate into our school science and math classrooms, we as teachers need to be increasingly knowledgeable and discriminating about instructional software. The range of quality of available software is considerable; we must learn to separate the wheat from the chaff.

Generally, it is a good idea to maintain a certain amount of skepticism about computers. We need to keep in mind that computers are no more a panacea for education than any technology ever was. When selecting instructional software for our students, the following six questions are worth asking:

1. What educational purpose is served?
2. Is the computer suitable for this purpose?
3. Is the program well designed pedagogically?
4. Is the program well designed visually?
5. Is it easy for students to use the program?
6. Shall I try to write the program I need myself?

Educational Purpose

First we should ask whether the program addresses a real educational need. Is the program capable of doing what it purports to do? How does the program fit into the instructional goals of the curriculum? The publisher of the software may have specified some educational objectives, but do these match our own objectives? It is important to examine the running program oneself. Most reputable publishers will provide a preview copy of educational software that one can see before deciding whether to buy it.

Suitability

When thinking about the educational purpose, it is important to ask whether the computer is the most effective medium for that purpose. If the computer screen is being used mainly to display text, then the computer medium may not be suitable. A book or other form of printed matter may be more appropriate. On widely available microcomputers, text is still generally less readable than in a book, and usually less conducive to skimming, browsing and reviewing.

Similarly, if the program attempts to display realistic pictures, then the computer screen, with its limited display capabilities, may not be appropriate. Of course, there are many things that a computer can do that are impossible to do with books or television. The program should capitalize on these special capabilities.

One of the most exciting applications of computers in the schools is the connection between the computer and various laboratory probe devices. Students can make simple measurements and see their data displayed graphically on the computer screen as they take it. Newer programs are enabling students to analyze their data as well and generate models to explain their observations.

Pedagogical Design

The uniqueness of the computer medium lies in its interactivity and flexibility, not its ability to display text or visuals. Unlike books, slides, films or television, the computer can take in, analyze and respond to user input.

In examining a piece of educational software, we must think about whether the program is well-designed pedagogically. As any teacher knows, the student who is most actively involved in the learning process is the one who benefits most from instruction. The more a student's mind is engaged in a task, the more he or she will learn from that task.

High quality educational software is highly interactive. That is, it requires the student to do things; it asks questions, presents learning tasks and poses problems to solve. In order to proceed through such a program, the student must make lots of choices, reach many decisions and formulate lots of answers—in short, the student must think. The more frequent the interaction, the better.

In addition, the well designed program is robust; it accepts and responds in a reasonable way to alternative phrasing. It does not stop running when the student presses unexpected keys or complain when the student uses an alternative format to enter what should be considered an acceptable answer. A good program accepts a wide range of possible correct answers to questions.

Visual Design

One should ask whether the program is well designed visually. Visual design is an important component of educational software, just as it is in other educational media. The organization of information on the screen affects its intelligibility. The effective use of graphics can reduce the amount of reading required and present information in a succinct form that is easily remembered.

The layout of text can aid readability and comprehension. Unlike the page of a book, the computer screen is a dynamic medium, capable of changing with time. Good software is designed so that at any given time, the user knows how to proceed and what options are available.

Ease of Use

It is important that the software be easy to use. It should be easy to start the program running. It should be easy to exit the program and to move about freely in it. Well written programs make it easy to start over or to go back to any point for review. Some programs use a pointing device such as a mouse for input, which alleviates the need for typing commands. Modern user interfaces, such as that popularized on the Apple® Macintosh®, use the mouse extensively to simplify the operation of the computer. The design of the user interface of interactive computer programs is important, but difficult to do right. Only recently has this area been receiving the attention it needs.

Well designed software can be used immediately, without consulting user manuals or receiving special instruction. There are a few examples of educational software that can be used effectively without extra explanatory materials, but there need to be more.

Writing Programs Yourself

In the early days, writing educational software that had reasonable performance on microcomputers was exceedingly difficult; only highly skilled programmers were able to create new applications. Today, software tools are much more powerful and enable developers to create better applications in a shorter time. In addition, they make authoring accessible to a much wider population. Authoring environments now available make it possible for teachers with relatively little programming experience to create their own programs for students to use. Among the options available today are Apple's HyperCard™, (bundled with the Macintosh), Course of Action™ from Authorware, Inc. (for the Macintosh and IBM® PC), and cT℠ from Carnegie Mellon University (Macintosh, IBM PC and IBM PS/2).

Emerging Technologies

Microcomputers have come a long way since the introduction of the Apple II in 1977. The *minimum* configuration of personal computers today contain about *twenty times* as much memory as the early micros and *five times* as many graphics display elements. We are seeing wider use of color, sound and speech. These newer capabilities have given us two major opportunities. First, the enterprise of creating programs is becoming accessible to a much wider group of people, including teachers who don't have much time outside of their teaching responsibilities. Second, applications development is becoming a multi-media activity. Connection to videodisks and other optical storage devices is making it possible to create learning environments that appeal to our senses in many ways simultaneously.

Computers have a great potential for aiding teachers' effectiveness and making their jobs easier. If this potential is ever to be realized, teachers must be able to evaluate critically, to select wisely, and eventually, to participate directly in the development of high quality educational software.

TABLE 10–1
Rankings of computer literacy competencies

Percentage of Respondents Rating Competency as Very Important or Important	Computer Literacy Competencies for Science Teachers

Essential Competencies

92	1.	Use the computer as a tool in the science classroom. This would include knowledge of available software and peripherals interfaced with laboratory apparatus for direct collection of laboratory data, simple data bases for storage of laboratory data, graphing programs for analysis, and use of the computer as a "Dynamic Blackboard" or demonstration apparatus.
90	2.	Demonstrate ways to integrate the use of computer-related materials with noncomputer materials, including textbooks.
90	3.	Describe appropriate uses for computers in teaching science, such as: • computer-assisted instruction (simulation, tutorial, drill, and practice) • computer-managed instruction • computer-based instrumentation • computer-assisted testing • problem solving • word processing • materials generation and management • information utilization
90	4.	Respond appropriately to common error messages when using software.
88	5.	Use computer courseware to individualize instruction and to increase student learning.
88	6.	Load and run a variety of computer software packages.
87	7.	Understand *thoroughly* that a computer only does what the program instructs it to do.
87	8.	Assist in the selection, acquisition, and use of computers in a science department.
86	9.	Plan for effective pre- and post-computer interaction activities for students (for example, debriefing after a science simulation).
85	10.	Plan appropriate scheduling of student computer activities.
84	11.	Apply and evaluate the general capabilities of the computer as a tool for instruction.
84	12.	Plan methods to integrate computer awareness and literacy into the existing curriculum.
83	13.	Display personal satisfaction with and confidence in using computers.
82	14.	Locate commercial and public domain software for a specific topic and application.
82	15.	Respond appropriately to changes in curriculum and teaching methodology caused by new technological developments.
81	16.	Value the benefits of computerization in education and society for such contributions as: • efficient and effective information processing • automation of routine tasks • increasing communication and availability of information • improving student attitude and productivity • improving instructional opportunities
80	17.	Locate and use at least one evaluative process to appraise and determine the instructional worth of a variety of computer software.
79	18.	Demonstrate awareness of such major applications of the computer as information storage and retrieval, simulation and modeling, process control and decision making, computation, and data processing.
78	19.	Communicate effectively about computers by understanding and using appropriate terminology.
78	20.	Describe the ways the computer can be used to learn about computers, to learn through computers, and to learn with computers.
76	21.	Recognize that an aspect of problem solving involves a series of logical steps and that programming is translating those steps into instructions for the computer.
76	22.	Demonstrate awareness of computer usage and assistance in fields such as: • health • science • engineering • education • business and industry • transportation • communications • military
75	23.	Voluntarily choose to use the computer for educational purposes.
75	24.	Demonstrate appropriate uses of computer technology for basic skills instruction.

TABLE 10–1
Continued

Percentage of Respondents Rating Competency as Very Important or Important	Computer Literacy Competencies for Science Teachers

	Secondary Competencies
74	25. Identify, describe, and demonstrate the function and operation of various components of computers and related peripheral devices (for example, keyboards, printers, modems, graphics tablets, etc.).
74	26. Know by example, particularly in using computers in education, some types of problems that *are* and some general types of problems that *are not* currently amenable to computer solution.
73	27. Assemble or connect computer systems typically used in instructional situations.
72	28. Make authorized copies of computer software.
69	29. Describe ways computers can assist in decision making.
68	30. Describe the impact that technological developments have on various career options.
66	31. Use various diagnostic strategies to find the cause of a malfunction and to determine if the problem is related to hardware or software.
66	32. Define major computer system components such as input, memory, CPU, control, and output.
66	33. Describe appropriate instructional arrangements for computer-based learning experiences, such as physical arrangements and student groupings.
66	34. Read, understand, and modify simple programs.
65	35. Identify, evaluate, and use a variety of sources of current information regarding computer uses in education.
62	36. Locate and use a variety of evaluations of software.
61	37. Relate the logic of elementary computer programs to thinking and problem-solving skills taught in the regular K–6 curricula.
61	38. Discuss irresponsible behavior that may be associated with computer technology, such as computer crimes, violation of copyright laws, and unauthorized use of information.
60	39. Evaluate various hardware configurations that might be used in instructional applications, based on software availability and instructional requirements.
59	40. Describe factors limiting the successful educational use of computers, such as quality of software, quantity of software, cost, hardware limitations, and human factors.
58	41. Describe unique characteristics of computers that can facilitate learning (for example, nonthreatening feedback, learner control, adaptability, and accessibility).
58	42. Determine whether they have written a reasonably efficient and well-organized program.
57	43. Define the elements of a district plan for computer-based instruction, and define the role of the individual instructor supporting that plan.
57	44. Discuss some of the positive and negative consequences of computer use in today's society, for example: • machine dependence vs. machine independence • depersonalization vs. personalization • increase vs. decrease in job availability
56	45. Use a high-level language such as BASIC, PASCAL, LOGO, or PILOT to read and write simple programs that work correctly.

	Low-Rated Competencies
53	46. Use and teach the unique nomenclature of computing.
52	47. Assist students in making informed decisions about choosing careers in digital electronics.

Problem Solving or Inquiry

Courseware emphasizing problem solving seeks to develop organizational, deductive, and inductive skills. The emphasis is on developing problem-solving skills rather than accumulating content knowledge.

As an Intellectual Tool

In this role the computer may be used as a sophisticated calculator or a laboratory instrument for collecting, graphing, storing, retrieving, and analyzing information. (See, for example, the "Teaching Science Activity: Using Microcomputers in Interdisciplinary Problems," on page 446.)

Data Management

The use of the computer for data storage, manipulation, analysis, and retrieval adds to the efficiency and effectiveness of the classroom environment. Word processing programs and simple database programs can make the student's and teacher's work far easier and more productive.

■ Computer Simulations

Computer simulation is now regarded as one of the most powerful tools available to the science teacher. Learners using simulations can ask numerous "What if" kinds of questions, can make low-risk decisions, and can receive immediate feedback in the form of simulated consequences. For a sample problem, see "Teaching Science Activity: Using the Microcomputer to Model Solutions to Problems," p. 447.

"We shall define computer simulation as a representation of the behavior of a real situation or system."[3] In simulations, the computer models some event or condition in the real world. It is able to generate creative, perhaps even impossible environments. It may permit time compression by condensing a great amount of data into a very short time frame or it may expand the time base to allow a minute look at changes within a short time frame. It can produce graphic displays of processes at work. Computer simulations have been called "dynamic blackboards" by some teachers because the kinds of information that they normally must laboriously handwrite on blackboards can be presented on video monitors in a dynamic flow that can display the simultaneous effects of various factors and treat them as operator-dependent variables.

Simulations allow the effects of changes to be seen in a model before irrevocable changes are made in the real system. In this sense, minor or hypothetical risks can be taken without the cost or danger of carrying out the experiment in real life. Students using simulations are forced to make decisions on the basis of incomplete data, and the results of these decisions can be seen quickly. This is excellent practice for the real world, in which profound decisions frequently need to be made on the basis of meager information.

It has been found that simulations can increase students' enthusiasm and motivation because of the immediacy of the problems and the instant feedback that permits them to see the results of their decisions in a matter of seconds or minutes.

In general, though, simulations should complement, not replace hands-on experience. Exceptions to this include situations such as the following:

1. Very complex experimental techniques that would require expensive equipment, inordinate amounts of time, and/or extremely long, complex processes.
2. Experiments involving very long or very short durations. Biological and environmental problems are frequently of this nature. It is often impossible in real life for students to carry out long-range experiments because of the extreme slowness of a given reaction time. In a computer simulation these can be reduced to manageable period lengths. Similarly, very rapid events can be slowed down to allow students to analyze them in detail.
3. When certain dangers are involved, such as the use of toxic chemicals, rapid or explosive chemical reactions, or other natural processes that would be far too dangerous to be carried out in a typical chemistry laboratory.

It has been found that "simulations teach processes and concepts by letting the students manipulate and test out the elements of processes until real learning and real understanding occurs."[4] Programs are designed to help students learn such subjects as physics and mathematics by manipulating data and observing the results of their manipulations.

Because of the difficulty of teaching abstract concepts in the typical secondary school situation, students can sometimes give correct answers but still not understand the concept or process involved in getting them. Computer simulation allows them to repeatedly study the problem, or drill and practice, until complete understanding occurs.

The following analogy illustrates how simulation specifically enhances concept learning:

> For example, think about the concept of gravity. We tell the students that gravity is what makes things fall and is the force that holds Americans and Australians alike close to the earth. Students are given some rules about how gravity relates to such things as velocity and acceleration and then tested on how well they play back the definitions and rules they have been given. They can do well on the test without having real world understanding of the concepts of gravity.
>
> Using computer simulations, however, the student observes the rules in action. The student sees and hears a heavier block accelerating the same as a light one on a frictionless surface. The student observes that a rough surface decreases the acceleration because of friction. Thus the student learns about the concept of gravity and how it relates to acceleration and velocity by actually varying the conditions and observing the results. At each knowledge gap the student can test out further ideas to either jump the gap or run around it.[5]

It has also been found that students should work together, not in isolation, and that social interaction contributes to concept learning. Students work together to arrive at common understandings. Students also need to interact because school is still the area in which children learn to get along with others and develop their social skills. Intensive one-on-one interaction with a microcomputer does not contribute much to social learning.

In a study involving researching the effectiveness of using computer-simulated experiments on junior high school students' understandings of the concepts of volume displacement, it was found that computer-simulated experiences were as effective as hands-on laboratory experiences, and also that males performed better on a posttest after having hands-on laboratory experiences than did females in the same situation. However there were no significant differences found between males and females using the computer simulations on the volume displacement task. The study also showed that there were no significant differences in retention levels when scores of the computer simulation groups were compared with those that had had hands-on laboratory experiences (Choi and Gennaro, 1987).[6]

This study may give some confidence that the microcomputer can provide a useful teaching aid in some situations where hands-on experiences are not available or where teachers prefer to use the technology available.

■ Daily Use of Microcomputers in Science Labs

Because many traditional science labs are cookbookish, requiring students to follow prepared instructions, gather routine data, and answer cut-and-dried questions, frequently the result is to obscure the true nature of investigation and to decrease interest in science. Microcomputers can restore the excitement

of inquiry and speed up certain aspects of the investigative process to provide a more rounded picture of the nature of science. These instruments have the ability to measure directly such quantities as temperature, light intensity, force, velocity, acceleration, pressure, short time intervals and many other physical measurements.

A useful guide for putting into action many desirable microcomputer measurement labs is provided by Tinker, (1985).[7] Detailed information on how to obtain light information using a phototransistor and an APPLE IIe microcomputer is given. Suggested software such as Light Meter and Distance by APPLE are described. Others are Bank Street Lab (Holt, Rinehart and Winston) and Light Lab (Hayden). (See Tinker, 1985.) Other types of measurements such as speed, timing, heart rate, temperature, cooling curves, heats of neutralization, and sound are also described.

■ Interfacing

One exciting area under consideration as a use for microcomputers in secondary schools is *interfacing*, the ability of computers to be connected to reading devices associated with experiments and to collect and analyze data directly. Many experiments require hundreds of observations, the tedium of which discourages secondary students from taking such observations in the usual manner and recording them manually on tabulation sheets. Using the microcomputer through the interfacing mechanism permits more experiments to be done more accurately, efficiently, and meaningfully. The data are received directly from the sensing instruments and are stored, graphed, and analyzed. More samples can be done during a given laboratory period, there can be a wider

Learning about computers can be a cooperative program. Photo by David Strickler.

variety of experiments, and the computer can be used to make extrapolations beyond the data collected. Relationships between theory and reality can be explored more fully, as students are freed from time-consuming data collection.

As a teacher, you need to ask yourself several basic questions when considering using the computer for interfacing. Are you able to devise your own computer programs or would you prefer to purchase modules that can be used in a standard, routine manner? Can you develop an experiment or do you prefer to buy a laboratory package? Does the kind of microcomputer you have accommodate additional hardware easily, so that the logistics of various experiments can be satisfied? Is there adequate money in the budget to purchase the necessary hardware and connecting units? A minimum of $500 is thought necessary for this. Finally, are you familiar with the various types of experiments with which you wish to use the interfacing capability?

Basically, interfacing requires a *transducer*, which is an instrument that converts physical or chemical measurements into electrical signals. These can be fed directly into the computer. The second instrument needed is an *analog/digital converter*, which converts the electrical signals into the proper form for use by the computer. (See Fig. 10-1.)

When you are selecting an interfacing alternative, be sure to match your requirements with the capabilities of the method you are considering. Several criteria should be considered. First is *resolution*, which depends upon the capacity of the converter. Second is *timing*. Can you use your computer for timing and will it be accurate enough? The answer depends partly on the number of samples per second you wish to take. Third is *convenience*. Do you want to devise and construct your own transducer and signal circuitry or will you depend upon a package deal? Fourth is *speed*. How many samples per second do you want to take? The overall speed is only as fast as the slowest component. Fifth is *diagnostics*. How will you determine what is wrong if the experiment doesn't work? This is very important because it is necessary in an educational setting to identify the sources of error. A further question you should

ask yourself is whether laboratory interfacing is appropriate for your classroom. If students no longer collect their own information but depend entirely upon the interfacing mechanisms to gather original data, will they learn what is actually happening in the experiment? This is a judgmental question, and its answer depends upon your objectives.[8]

■ Characteristics of Good Software for Computer-Assisted Instruction

Because the usefulness of the microcomputer in the science classroom depends entirely on the software component, it is necessary to make sure the software purchased serves the objectives of the class for which it is intended. Some of the identified characteristics of good software are listed here.[9]

1. It should not be necessary for the student or teacher to have any knowledge of programming to use the software. The materials should be self-contained, with simple instructions, and capable of being used directly on the microcomputer without prior training.
2. Prompts should be used liberally so that students can negotiate through the program with the least amount of effort and confusion. Prompts consist of instructions on which keys to push or what steps to follow to successfully negotiate the program.
3. A well-written instructional program should be reasonably user-proof. It should be possible to follow the routines and the subroutines according to the instructions and find that the program will identify incorrect responses in a user-friendly manner so that the program can be used effectively.
4. In problem-solving situations, the program should display the correct methods of solving the problem for students who may encounter difficulty. This should be presented using step-by-step procedures that the student is asked to work through. For those who are unable to succeed the correct solution should be presented.

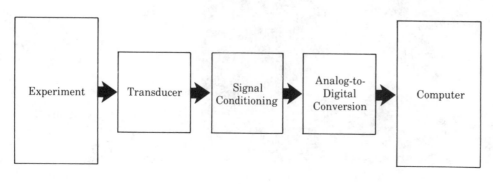

FIGURE 10–1
Interfacing hardware flowchart

5. The software should take advantage of the unique capabilities of various microcomputers. When color is available, programs should be able to make use of it for maximum educational impact.

6. Readability of the video display is important. This does not refer to the size of the screen, which is beyond the control of the software program, but refers to the density of materials, or jamming too many instructions into a small space.

7. The educational objectives of the program should be defined and the materials should reasonably and adequately meet those objectives. This feature should be designed for students as well as teachers.

8. Each program should be accompanied by a readable, detailed manual of instructions so that little time is wasted in putting the program to use.

■ Selection Guidelines for Microcomputers

Equally important for effective use in the classroom is the selection of hardware to be used. Since the initial financial investment is frequently quite high, it is important to make the best possible choice in advance. Also the input of time and energy in learning how to use the microcomputer and to adapt the proper software to it is quite substantial and it is therefore necessary to make an educated choice. Some guidelines to follow in this regard are as follows.[10]

1. Of primary importance is the availability of software written for the system. While there are many varieties of microcomputers on the market, there is a great variation in the amount and quality of software in the sciences available for use. This point should be checked before the computer is purchased, because its effectiveness in the classroom depends entirely upon one's ability to obtain useable material for it.

2. The memory size is important. Most commercial science software requires at least 48 K of memory.

3. The choice of disk drive as the data storage and retrieval system is an important consideration. While disk drives are expensive, they are fast at loading and retrieving programs or segments of programs for immediate use.

4. It should be possible to expand the system's memory if needed. Another consideration is whether peripheral attachments can be added to enable the system to function as a laboratory in-

strument. Can other drives or monitors be added as required?

5. Does the system have the capability to handle graphics and is this an important consideration for your classes? It has been found that most teachers wish to eventually have this capability available to them.

6. The availability of service and maintenance should be of prime consideration. It should be possible to obtain service quickly and inexpensively. Service contracts, warranties, and insurance policies should be looked into at the time of purchase.

7. The general feel of the system is an important matter. Most users will have some degree of typing skill; this facilitates the use of the microcomputer if its keyboard resembles a standard typewriter. Also the color of the monitor screen and its usefulness in varying levels of light in the classroom are important considerations.

8. The compatibility of the computer with other school systems is important, especially if using a modem to transmit information from school to school by telephone is desired.

Hardware and software available today for educational computing has changed dramatically in the past ten years. Also the perceptions of what educational computers can and should do in the classroom have evolved to more highly significant levels. Expectations of adequate graphics capabilities are commonplace. Levels of memory and speed of handling data have grown by factors of ten or more. Expectations for even greater advances in the future make the problems of hardware and software selection even more challenging.

Four questions might be considered essential as educators look to their future needs in the use of computers in the classroom. They are (1) What should be considered the minimum hardware acceptable for educational computing? (2) What expectations do we have for the ease-of-use of educational software? (3) What levels of functionality do we expect? and (4) What would we like to see in the future?[11]

Early microcomputers in schools lacked satisfactory graphics capabilities. This capability is central to the development of educational applications today. It is related to the size of memory in the microcomputer. Table 10.2 illustrates how the size of memory in microcomputers has increased over the past decade.[12]

The screen resolution has also increased significantly over the past few years. The number of dots that can be displayed on a screen determines the amount of visual information that can be con-

TABLE 10–2
Microcomputer memory

RAM (kilobytes)	1976	1978	1980	1982	1984	1986
48		Apple II				
64		Apple II+	--IIe--	IIc--		Commodore 64
128			IBM PC		Macintosh 128	
256				IBM PC XT		
512					Macintosh 512	
640		(DOS limit)			IBM PC AT	Atari 520ST
						Amiga
1024		(UNIX)				Atari 1040ST
2048						IBM RT
				Sun2		
4096						Sun3

TABLE 10–3
Microcomputer graphics

Number of Pixels (in kilopixels)	1976	1978	1980	1982	1984	1986
54		Apple II				
64				Commodore 64		
128				IBM PC CGA		
224					Macintosh IBM PC EGA	
256						Atari 520ST Amiga
1024					Sun	IBM RT

veyed. Table 10.3 shows how the graphics capabilities of microcomputers have increased on monochrome displays alone.[13]

■ Use of Computers with Special Students

One of the exciting potentials of the microcomputer in the classroom is its possible uses for children with special difficulties or needs. There has developed over the years a whole series of elaborate communication devices for nonspeaking, blind, deaf, or palsied children. These devices are now being replaced or supplemented by microcomputers with special input or output peripherals that the child can control at a comfortable rate.

Some examples of types of handicaps for which special-purpose computer programs have been devised are those individuals with mobile impairment, motor impairment, visual disabilities, hearing impairment, vocal impairment, educable mental retardation, emotional disturbances, psychological and social problems, autism, learning disabilities such as dyslexia, multiple handicaps, and long term illness.[14]

The remedies being proposed that involve computers range from speech synthesis, computerized musical compositions, voice-controlled computers, and the use of light pens and graphics tablets, to the control of mobility through computerized activation by the use of head sticks or air pressure mechanisms.

Access to enormous amounts of information through the use of the auxiliary equipment just described makes it possible for handicapped children to retrieve information from other computers and external sources such as videodisks and enables them to make contact with libraries, large data banks, schools, and other sources of information. Even young children can begin to use the computer effectively. Researchers are finding that both on the psychological and cognitive levels, the computer is able to give quiet and retiring students as well as children with special needs a chance to find experience many of them have never had in their previous school work. An additional advantage is that children enjoy computers. They are relatively uninhibited, unconstrained by the fear of technology that often strikes adults. They learn to use computers quickly and often cannot be drawn away from them. From the standpoint of academic motivation, nothing else in school seems to maintain as high a level of student interest. The microcomputer may finally place children with special needs on a par with average children and bring true meaning to the concept of mainstreaming in the schools of today.

■ Survey of Microcomputer Use in Schools

In an early national survey it was found that the majority of schools had microcomputers.[15] By January, 1983, 53 percent of all schools in the United States had obtained at least one microcomputer for purposes of instruction; secondary schools were likely to have more than one. Eighty-five percent of all high schools, 77 percent of all junior-senior combinations, and 68 percent of all middle or junior high schools had one or more microcomputers. The percentage was somewhat lower for elementary schools but was rising rapidly. Many elementary schools use cassette-based microcomputers rather than those with disk drives. The least likely owners in this field were small parochial elementary schools and public schools in poorer districts.

Numbers of computers in schools grew beyond all expectations. It was reported by Bork in 1984 that there were nearly one million computers in public schools enrolling 40 million students—an average of one microcomputer per 40 students. This number has undoubtedly increased significantly since then. Many of these microcomputers are now obsolete in terms of the new expectations and computing tasks envisioned for students in elementary and secondary schools of today.

According to Quality Education Data (Hayes, 1986),[16] over 75,000 or 90 percent of all U.S. schools were using microcomputers for instruction in 1986. This number jumped from 14,000 or 16 percent in 1981. Of those, 57 percent were APPLE IIs or compatibles, 8 percent were IBMs or compatibles, and 35 percent were other brands.

Survey questions on how schools primarily use their microcomputers brought forth the information that at the secondary level, 85 percent used the computer to introduce children to the concept of the device and 76 percent used them for some type of programming instruction. On the lower end of the scale, only 31 pecent used them for drill and practice, and 29 percent used them for solving problems. The least usage came in the areas of administrative use, making of teacher tests and worksheets, and word processing.[17]

It was also found that schools with more microcomputer experience leaned toward programming uses as opposed to instructional uses or drill and practice. When teachers were asked how they view microcomputers, most elementary teachers reported that they were primarily a tool to help teach basic skills. At the secondary level, teachers reported that they felt the computer was used as a resource for students to learn more about computing and electronic communication.

This information indicated a fairly rapid movement toward the acquisition and use of microcomputers in classrooms. As the costs of software and hardware are reduced over the years, it is quite likely that all schools will have one or more microcomputers, and in many cases multiple units will be available for a variety of instructional, administrative, and programming uses. Some projections indicate substantial growth of the computer's use in the next two decades. Nakhleh predicted:

(1) that 90 percent of all university students will be computer literate by 1990,
(2) 50 percent of all university faculties will be computer literate by 1990 with a significant increase to 90 percent by the year 2000,
(3) 90 percent of high school computer literacy will be achieved by the year 2000,
(4) 50 percent of the general public will have achieved computer literacy by the year 2000,
(5) 50 percent of all college students will have a computer terminal in their dormitory rooms by 2000, and
(6) 25 percent of all courses will use computer teaching of some sort as an alternative to traditional techniques by the year 2000.[18]

Along with the growth of computer usage comes the need for greater computer literacy. No standard definition of computer literacy yet exists but all current versions include a general feeling of confidence in the use of the computer and the ability to put it to practical use in the classroom. Knowledge of various kinds of hardware and software is also a necessary component of computer literacy.

To meet the needs of computer education, many states have developed guidelines for curriculum development in the field of computer science. Such activity portends significant changes in secondary school curriculums of the future through addition of computer education courses and interweaving of computer functions into existing courses.

Some of the functions of instruction to which computers can contribute significantly are drill and practice, testing, tutoring, simulation, problem solving, and data management. An additional new technique that shows promise for laboratory sciences is interfacing, which refers to the ability of computers to be connected to direct reading devices to collect data during experiments. The level of precision and general sophistication of experiments can be improved by such methods.

Guidelines for selection of hardware and software have been prepared by various groups, including the National Science Teachers Association. (The NSTA's 1983 "Computer Software Evaluation Instrument" is included at the end of this chapter for reference.) Use of these guidelines can assist the teacher in making intelligent choices when opportunities for purchasing computer materials arise.

Children with special needs can benefit from computer technology in the classroom. As mainstreaming of handicapped children in the schools becomes an accepted fact, teachers will rely more heavily on the computer as a communicator, motivator, and data gatherer for children with special needs.

With these changes coming about, teacher training programs will need to accommodate the new technology in a more complete and systematic approach than has been used in the past. The effective use of the computer in the instructional program will depend on well-qualified teachers who can not only function comfortably with computers but also lead the way in creating better instructional materials and devising better ways to use the new medium of instruction.

■ What Research Shows about Children's Learning from Computers

A number of studies have attempted to show what, if anything, children learn from use of microcomputers in the classrooms. Obviously the concern is that microcomputer usage demonstrate measureable gains in knowlege, skills, understanding of the nature of science, and attitudes toward science learning.

In a study to learn how students look at science data, especially that presented by computer, it was found that when looking at graphs, students rarely questioned the relationships displayed there, although they frequently misinterpreted them.[19] Results from the 1981-82 National Assessment in Science demonstrated that students are impressed by the infallibility of computers. For example, only 21 percent of 17-year-olds felt that measurement errors could occur when using computers.[20] These results highlight the importance of emphasizing critical evaluation of scientific data, especially that presented by graphical means.

In another study involving graphing, microcomputer-based laboratories showed promise for learning science concepts and graphing skills.[21] Significant gains were shown in a single class period in the ability to move between verbal and graphic descriptions of motion phenomena. The key feature appeared to be real-time graphing which allowed the students to process information about a physical event and its graph simultaneously rather than in a serial fashion.

Computer simulations proved to be useful strategies of instruction using microcomputers in beginning biological science classes. The unit objectives were met at least as well as in the control classes using traditional methods, and in the case of measuring scientific thought processes and using critical thinking, the experimental groups surpassed the control groups' performance.[22]

In commenting on ways to improve research on use of computers in the classroom it was argued that

> We must find or create software that enables students to manipulate variables and to observe effects on dependent variables in meaningful and interesting ways . . . all instructional software should provide information or feedback that is meaningful to students who are at a range of levels of development and conceptual understanding. . . . Computer assisted instruction should enable science teachers and their students to perform activities that complement, not simply replace, elements of traditional instruction.[23]

Thus, it appears that research supports the use of microcomputers in science classrooms, particularly in areas where traditional methods may provide insufficient opportunities for critical thinking, or where information is presented graphically.

■ Some Current Problems of Computer Acceptance

Despite the high hopes for a revolution in teaching through the use of computers, there are some negative factors that seem to be hindering their full acceptance. "The biggest stumbling block has been the shortage of computers in the schools. While 96 percent of all U.S. public schools have computers, most of them simply put 10 to 20 of the machines in a single computer laboratory, which various classes share. Because of the limited number of machines, even the minority of science and mathematics classes that used computers averaged less than 15 minutes of daily use for each student, according to a Research

TABLE 10–4

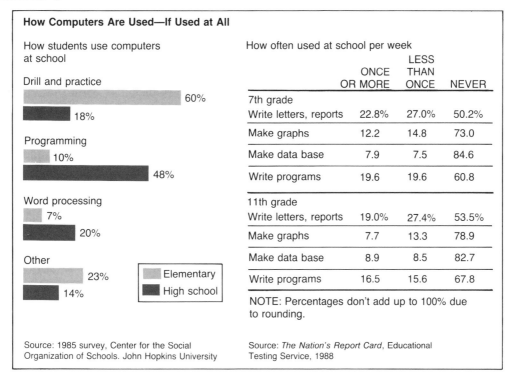

How Computers Are Used—If Used at All

How students use computers at school

Drill and practice
- 60%
- 18%

Programming
- 10%
- 48%

Word processing
- 7%
- 20%

Other
- 23%
- 14%

Elementary
High school

How often used at school per week

	ONCE OR MORE	LESS THAN ONCE	NEVER
7th grade			
Write letters, reports	22.8%	27.0%	50.2%
Make graphs	12.2	14.8	73.0
Make data base	7.9	7.5	84.6
Write programs	19.6	19.6	60.8
11th grade			
Write letters, reports	19.0%	27.4%	53.5%
Make graphs	7.7	13.3	78.9
Make data base	8.9	8.5	82.7
Write programs	16.5	15.6	67.8

NOTE: Percentages don't add up to 100% due to rounding.

Source: 1985 survey, Center for the Social Organization of Schools. John Hopkins University

Source: *The Nation's Report Card*, Educational Testing Service, 1988

Triangle Institute study for National Science Foundation; most other subjects used computers even less."[24]

Other hurdles were lack of suitable software and less-than-effective computer training, which emphasizes mere computer familiarity, rather than actual hands-on usage of the machines in the classroom.

Table 10.4 shows how computers were used in the schools in 1985 according to a survey by the Center for the Social Organization of Schools at Johns Hopkins University.[25]

■ Summary

The technology of microcomputers promises to be one of the most effective learning devices in a long line of technological aids to education over the past decades. However, its full potential is far from being realized as a superior instructional tool. The reasons for this lie in a number of factors, such as cost, lack of standardization of hardware, frequent poor quality of software, and reluctance on the part of sufficient teachers to incorporate microcomputers into their daily classwork.

In addition, it has not yet become clear what role or roles the microcomputer should play in instruction. Such necessary learning tasks as drill, tutoring, testing, simulation of events and experiments, problem-solving, data gathering and analysis are pos-

sible roles to play. Where these functions can best fit into daily instruction has not yet been fully exploited.

Despite these uncertainties, computer usage is increasing rapidly, having grown approximately tenfold in the past decade. Hardware and software capabilities have improved dramatically. In hardware alone, the memory capacity has increased nearly a hundredfold in a dozen years. The use of graphics, which is related to memory and available screen resolution has pointed the direction for the future of microcomputer use in a much more sophisticated fashion than heretofore. Rapid obsolescence of aging microcomputers poses still another problem for schools considering expanding their usage in classes.

Developing good software is a perennial problem. Much shoddy material has appeared on the market and has turned away some potential users. The National Science Teachers Association has produced an excellent software evaluation instrument for use by teachers and administrators as they consider purchases for the future.

Research continues to show superior instructional gains in classes using microcomputers when compared with classes undergoing traditional instruction. Graphing skills of data-display and analysis were prime beneficiaries of these methods of instruction. The key concepts to be judged in all microcomputer learning are the degree to which pupils have opportunities to interact with the information presented, questions asked, and results obtained in the exercises demanded of them. Such interactions

This instrument should help you and your colleagues in examining and discussing the merits of a microcomputer software package intended to be used in science instruction. The instrument provides a sensible process and basic criteria for judging science software packages. It also lets you add criteria which educators in your particular school situation need to consider.

We are interested in evaluating the entire software package, which includes:

(a) the computer program,
(b) any attendant student instructional materials which are not on the computer, and
(c) teacher's guide materials and/or program documentation.

The back page of the instrument has a space where you can describe the components of the package you are examining, its science content and other characteristics.

The four sections of this instrument call attention to four important aspects of evaluating microcomputer software packages: Policy Issues, Science Subject Matter Standards, Instructional Quality, and Technical Quality. Each aspect should be rated separately, and the four section ratings can then be listed to give a profile for the software package. (A box for the profile is on the back page.)

Leopold Klopfer et al. "Microcomputer Software Evaluation Instrument," *The Journal of College Science Teaching* 13, No. 4, Feb. 3, 1984. © 1984 National Science Teachers Association. Used with permission.

Under each section of the instrument is a set of descriptive criteria pertaining to that aspect of evaluating software packages. Bipolar scales (with + and − values) are used to obtain the rating in each section, so the section ratings of a software package you are evaluating may turn out to be negative, zero, or positive. We (the Task Force members) think that an acceptable package should never have any negative rating in its profile. Probably you and the other educators at your school will want a software package to show strong positive ratings in its profile before you would accept it to be used in science instruction. The exact standard you set for acceptability of software packages should be decided on the basis of your local conditions and your educational good sense.

Policy Issues

This section deals with the most difficult (and, we think, most important) questions that must be answered when any software package is being considered. These questions have to do with the appropriateness, compatibility, cost effectiveness (in both time and money), and instructional effectiveness of the software.

They include such concerns as these: Are the computer's special capabilities utilized to provide a learning experience not easily obtainable through other media? Does the computer program make good use of the student's time on the computer? Is the software package compatible with the goals and theoretical base of the school's instructional program? Does the computer encourage interaction among students while they are using it? What evidence is available that students attain the learning objectives of the software package? If you have other concerns of similar importance in your local situation, they should be added to the criteria of the Policy Issues Section.

Some people have suggested that, if a software package is seriously deficient on the criteria in the Policy Issues section, then it need not be given much further consideration. You should decide about this for your local evaluation process.

Science Subject-Matter Standards

Good science instruction must present good science. To assure that science software packages meet this expectation, this section is concerned with the accuracy of science content, the sound application of science processes, the absence of stereotyping, and other issues related to the honest representation of science in instruction.

There is ample space in the section for adding (if you want to) subject matter criteria that are important in particular science areas.

Instructional Quality

This section is concerned with matters of effective pedagogy, application of good instructional design principles, adaptability of the software to students' individual differences, assessment of students' learning, and the role envisioned for the students using the software package. You should add any omitted criteria that you think are particularly important for good instruction.

Technical Quality

The focus of this section is the technical quality of both the computer program and the other components of the software package. We are concerned with how well the computer program runs, how carefully its operational features are designed, and how well-designed the accompanying student and teacher materials are. Additional criteria may be needed here if you have particular computer hardware requirements or other expectations for a reliable software package.

■ Making Your Ratings

Each section of this instrument contains a set of bipolar scales. (Any criteria you add should be constructed with similar scales.) You should carefully consider the descriptions at both ends of each scale and then assign a value on the -3 to $+3$ scale according to how well the left or right description applies to the software package you are judging. Mark only one point on each scale. (If you cannot make a decision about a particular scale, mark the zero point for the scale.) To obtain the rating for each section, find the arithmetic sum of the values you assigned to all the scales in the section. You can enter the section ratings in the Software Package Profile box on the back page. The lower portion of the profile box should list the minimum standard you have determined for acceptability in each section. A comparison of the obtained ratings with the minimums can lead to a recommendation concerning the suitability of the software package.

■ Policy Issues

	LEFT DESCRIPTION IS				RIGHT DESCRIPTION IS		
	Definitely True −3	Partly True −2	Slightly True −1	Neither Description Applies 0	Slightly True +1	Partly True +2	Definitely True +3

Left Description	Right Description
The program makes the computer act as little more than a page turner or workbook.	The program exploits the computer's special capabilities (e.g., graphic animation, simulation) to provide a learning experience not easily possible through other media.
The program is wasteful of the limited time available for students to use the computer.	The program makes good use of the student's limited time on the computer.
The purpose and learning objectives of the software package are vague.	The purpose and intended outcomes of the software package are clearly defined.
The software package is in conflict with or irrelevant to the goals of the school's instructional program.	The software package is compatible with the goals and theoretical base of the school's instructional program.
The program expects one student to work on the computer and not to interact with anyone.	Two or more students are encouraged to interact with one another while using the computer program.
There is little or no evidence that students attain the learning objectives of the software package.	The evidence that students attain the software package's learning objectives is convincing.
The software package is incompatible with the learning objectives and instructional materials of a current course.	The software package fits in well with other instructional materials already being used in particular courses or classes.
This software package's cost is exorbitant for what it delivers.	The total cost of this package is reasonable compared to its instructional value.

■ Science Subject-Matter Standards

LEFT DESCRIPTION IS						RIGHT DESCRIPTION IS	
	Definitely True −3	Partly True −2	Slightly True −1	Neither Description Applies 0	Slightly True +1	Partly True +2	Definitely True +3

Left Description	Right Description
The package presents topics which are irrelevant to the educational needs of the intended students.	The topics included in the package are very significant in the education of the intended students.
The science content is very inaccurate.	The science content is free from errors.
Racial, ethnic, or sex-role stereotypes are displayed.	The presentation is free of any objectionable stereotyping.
Biased or distorted information is paraded as factual information.	Well-balanced and representative information is presented.
The package includes science information which is greatly outdated.	The science content presented in the package represents current knowledge.
The presentation of the science content is confusing.	The science content is very clearly presented.
The package gives no attention to the processes of scientific inquiry.	Science inquiry processes are well-integrated into this software package.

■ Instructional Quality

LEFT DESCRIPTION IS					RIGHT DESCRIPTION IS		
Definitely True −3	Partly True −2	Slightly True −1	Neither Description Applies 0	Slightly True +1	Partly True +2	Definitely True +3	

Left descriptions:

The student is given very few choices that control how he/she works in the computer program's environment.

The student using the program is passive and does little more than punch keys occasionally.

The instructional strategies used in the computer program do not take pertinent research results into account.

The program cannot easily adapt to differences in students' ability, prior knowledge, or learning style.

The software package fails to inform students about its learning objectives or the available activities.

The software package's instructional strategies and evaluation procedures ignore pertinent pedagogical principles.

The software package expects that all students will attain the same level of achievement.

The software package makes no provision for managing various instructional resources in a classroom.

Right descriptions:

The program offers the student several options about the content to work on, the level of difficulty, and the rate of presentation.

The student is actively involved in interacting with the computer's program.

The program's instructional strategies are based on relevant educational or psychological research findings.

The program has options which allow it to accommodate students' individual differences.

Directions in the software package tell students where they will be going (objectives) and what they will be doing (activities).

The instruction used in the software package incorporates good sequences, motivating features, and evaluation procedures.

Students using the software package can experience success in attaining learning objectives at several levels of sophistication or difficulty.

The software package incorporates a management scheme for deploying available instructional resources.

■ Technical Quality

LEFT DESCRIPTION IS				RIGHT DESCRIPTION IS		
Definitely True −3	Partly True −2	Slightly True −1	Neither Description Applies 0	Slightly True +1	Partly True +2	Definitely True +3

Left Description	Right Description
Students require an unacceptable amount of guidance by teachers to successfully operate the program.	Students can easily and independently operate the program after a modest period of orientation.
Feedback given by the program to student responses is inappropriate and confusing.	The program's feedback to student responses is appropriate, informative, and timely.
The program's graphics displays are crude and cluttered.	Graphics displays are crisp and clear.
The program's stance is callous and insulting.	The program is "user-sensitive."
The program has uncorrected "bugs" which cause it to behave inconsistently under certain circumstances or to "crash."	All possible combinations of user input and variable ranges are anticipated by the program, making its operation predictable and reliable.
Program documentation is incomplete, confusing, and inconsistent with the observed behavior of the program.	Program documentation is comprehensive, clear, and consistent with observed program behavior.
Student instructional materials other than the computer program are poorly organized, unattractive, and inappropriate.	Instructional materials other than the computer program are well-designed and appropriate for the students who will use them.
Teacher's materials in the software package are shabby, incomplete, and written in "hacker's" vernacular.	Teacher's guide materials are attractive, comprehensive, and suitable for the teacher-user who has little technical computer knowledge
The software package is physically flimsy and easily sabotaged.	The package's components are designed to survive classroom conditions.

189

Title of Software Package: _____

Publisher or Distributor: _____

Evaluators: _____

SOFTWARE PACKAGE PROFILE

	P	S	I	T
Ratings				
Minimum Standards				

Section P — POLICY ISSUES
Section S — SCIENCE SUBJECT-MATTER STANDARDS
Section I — INSTRUCTIONAL QUALITY
Section T — TECHNICAL QUALITY

Comments and Recommendations:

Software Package Description:
(Topics, program type, grade level, print materials for students, teacher guide)

Hardware Requirements:

The 1983 Version of this instrument was developed by our task force after more than a year of deliberation and discussion. The first draft was prepared by J.L. Fox and L. E. Klopfer, Learning Research and Development Center, University of Pittsburgh. The 1983 Version is our best current draft, which we expect to revise as computer technology and available software change.

We ask your help in preparing the next version. Information about your experience in using the instrument would be most helpful. Please send your comments and suggestions to:

Task Force on Assessing Computer-Augmented Science
Instructional Materials
National Science Teachers Association
1742 Connecticut Avenue, NW
Washington, D.C. 20009

Additional copies of Microcomputer Software Evaluation Instrument are available from NSTA Publications.

will capitalize on the better aspects of traditional teaching and may succeed in reaching larger numbers of children in shorter periods of time than otherwise. Optimistically, one can hope that this new technological innovation will display staying power as well as demonstrate improvements in the teaching/learning process.

■ REFERENCES

1. Bryan Cole, "Report of Task Force on Technology in Teacher Education," Report of Texas Education Agency, Austin, Texas, 1983.
2. Gary H. Marks, "Computer Simulations in Science Teaching: An Introduction," *Journal of Computers in Mathematics and Science Teaching* (Summer 1982), p. 18.
3. John Hollifield, "Let the Young Einstein Shine: Conceptual Software Lets Students Explore Physics and Math," *The Journal of Computers in Mathematics and Science Teaching*, 2, no. 1, (Fall 1982).
4. Hollifield, "Let the Young Einstein Shine."
5. Hollifield, "Let the Young Einstein Shine."
6. Byung-Soon Choi and Eugene Gennaro, "The Effectiveness of Using Computer-Simulated Experiments in Junior High Students' Understanding of the Volume Displacement Concept," *Journal of Research in Science Teaching*, 24, no. 6,(1987), pp. 539-552.
7. Robert Tinker, *Microcomputer-Based Laboratories—a Resource Guide*, Apple Education Affairs, 20505 Mariani Ave., Cupertino, CA 95014, 1985.
8. Jean L. Graef, "The Computer Connection: Four Approaches to Microcomputer Laboratory Interfacing," *The Science Teacher*, 50, no. 4, (April 1983), pp. 42-47. Reprinted with permission from *The Science Teacher*, a publication of the National Science Teachers Association, 1742 Connecticut Ave. NW, Washington, D.C. 20009.
9. Mary B. Nakhleh, "An Overview of Microcomputers in the Secondary Science Curriculum," *The Journal of Computers in Mathematics and Science Teaching*, 3, no. 1, (Fall 1983), pp. 13-21.
10. Nakhleh, "An Overview of Microcomputers," pp. 13-21.
11. David Trowbridge, "A Look at Educational Computing in 1987," Unpublished paper submitted to BSCS study of elementary school science, May, 1987, p. 4.
12. Trowbridge, "A Look at Educational Computing," p. 4.
13. Trowbridge, "A Look at Educational Computing," p. 4.
14. Adeline Naiman, "Computers and Children with Special Needs," *PTA Today*, 8, (April 1983), p. 21.
15. The figures given are from Henry J. Becker, "School's Uses of Microcomputers: Report # 1 from a National Survey," *The Journal of Computers in Mathematics and Science Teaching*, 3, no. 1, (Fall 1983), pp. 29-33.
16. J. Hayes, Quality Education Data, Inc., 1580 Logan St., Denver, CO, memo of January 20, 1986.
17. Nakhleh, "An Overview of Microcomputers," pp. 13-21.
18. Nakhleh, "An Overview of Microcomputers," pp. 13-21.
19. Rafi Nachmias and Marcia C. Linn, "Evaluations of Science Laboratory Data: The Role of Computer Presented Information," *Journal of Research in Science Teaching*, 24, no. 5,(1987), pp. 491-506.
20. S. J. Hueftle, S. J. Rakow and W. W. Welch, "Images of Science: A Summary of Results from the 1981-82 National Assessment in Science," University of Minnesota, 1983.
21. Heather Brasell, "The Effect of Real-Time Laboratory Graphing on Learning Graphic Representations of Distance and Velocity," *Journal of Research in Science Teaching*, 24, no. 4, (1987), pp. 385-395.
22. Robert H. Rivers and Edward Vockell, "Computer Simulations to Stimulate Scientific Problem Solving," *Journal of Research in Science Teaching*, 24, no. 5, (1987), pp. 403-415.
23. Joseph S. Kracjik, Patricia E. Simmons, and Vincent Lunetta, "Improving Research on Computers in Science Learning," *Journal of Research in Science Teaching*, 23, no. 5, (1986), pp. 465-470.
24. *Wall Street Journal*, June 6, 1988, p.23.
25. Ibid.

CHAPTER 11

Questioning and Inquiry Teaching

■ The Nature of Inquiry Teaching

The essence of inquiry teaching is arranging the learning environment to facilitate student-centered instruction and giving sufficient guidance to ensure direction and success in discovering scientific concepts and principles. One way in which a teacher helps a student to obtain a sense of direction and to use his mind is through questioning. The art of being a good conversationalist requires listening and insightful questions. A good inquiry-oriented teacher is an excellent conversationalist. She listens well and asks appropriate questions, assisting individuals in organizing their thoughts and gaining insights.

An inquiry-oriented teacher seldom tells but often questions because by asking questions the teacher assists the student in using his mind. A properly given question is a hint. For example, a student is studying a pendulum but hasn't discovered that its frequency is related to its length. The instructor moves about the class and notices that the student seems to be having difficulty. She goes to him and asks a series of questions. Listed below on the left are the questions she asked. On the right is an analysis of what the instructor is doing.

An Inquiry Discussion

1. What have you found out about the pendulum?

This is a good question because it is very divergent. It allows for a number of responses. The student will have found out something and being able to tell it to the instructor will help clarify any problems. This is a more convergent question. It helps the student center on frequency. He may not have thought of this before. The student replied that he didn't know.

2. What seems to affect the frequency, the number of times it swings a second?

The teacher then leaves and moves on to another student requiring some assistance. Later the teacher returns.

3. Try some things to find out.

Here again the instructor is asking a relatively divergent question since the student may have done many things. The student replied that he has used different weights.

4. What have you done to find out about the frequency?

The instructor is asking the student to interpret data. The student, however, still hasn't discovered that the length of the string affects the frequency.

5. How did the use of different weights affect the frequency?

This question is fairly directive-convergent.

6. What do you think the length of the string

193

would have to do with the frequency?	The instructor is helping the student to center on a particular variable.
7. How would you determine this?	This question asks the student to devise an experimental procedure.

Notice that the instructor aided the student, through artful questions, to make his own discoveries and to use his mind. The teacher did not steal the thrill of discovery from the student but she did facilitate it. Proper questioning is a sophisticated teaching art. To practice it, a teacher must know where the student's throughts are. To do so, the instructor must switch from the classical concept of teaching-telling to listening and questioning and being open to the students' thoughts. Consequently, the emphasis changes from teaching to student learning. After perceiving the student's difficulty, she must formulate a question which will be a challenge yet give guidance to the student. To do so, the instructor must know what she is trying to teach in a conceptual way and adapt the question so that it is appropriate to the student. As the teacher moves about the class, she must constantly adapt this procedure from student to student. This process requires unusual awareness and ability on her part. No wonder so many teachers fall back into the classical mode of teaching. But to move about a classroom in this manner is to truly individualize instruction, teach for the "person" and, if done constantly in a positive setting, humanize instruction.

Good questioning practices are involved in all

By moving about the class, the teacher can question and listen to students individually.

areas of science instruction, as indicated in the following list:

Where is questioning involved in science?

1. Discussion	7. Field trips
2. Laboratory exercises	8. Projects
3. Demonstrations	9. Games
4. Student worksheets	10. Lectures
5. Audio-visual aids	11. Simulations
6. Evaluations	12. Computing

For an example of how questioning can involve several of these aspects simultaneously, see the "Teaching Science Activity: How Can You Use Questions to Solve Problems?" on page 448.

■ Types of Questions

Questions may be planned before class or may arise spontaneously because of student interaction. It is always wise to plan a series of questions before entering an inquiry-oriented class. The mere fact that you have done so contributes to your questioning ability. Having thought about the questions gives you direction and a sense of security, thus furthering your ability to carry on a discussion.

An inquiry-oriented teacher must remain constantly flexible. Even though she has planned a series of questions, she must be willing to deviate from them and formulate new ones as she interacts with students. These unplanned, spontaneous questions may be difficult to create at first, but through attempting to develop good questioning techniques, an instructor becomes more sophisticated at devising them and is more likely to interact appropriately with students.

Before you devise your questions you should decide the following:

1. What talents are you going to try to develop?
2. What critical thinking processes will you try to nurture?
3. What subject-matter objectives do you want to develop?
4. What types of answers will you accept?
5. What skills do you wish to develop?
6. What attitudes and values do you wish to emphasize?

Educational Objectives and Questions

Just as objectives can be classified by this taxonomy, so can questions. Refer back to the preceding questions and classify them, on the left, according to the taxonomy. Then list five of the best questions and decide why you believe they are good. Bloom's abbreviated taxonomy is repeated to help you. An example of how you might use it is shown as a guide.

Bloom's Taxonomy

Cognitive domain	**Affective domain**
Evaluation	Generalized set
Synthesis	Organization
Analysis	Valuing
Application	Responding
Comprehension	Receiving
Knowledge	

Questions requiring responses from the higher levels of the hierarchy are more desirable because answering them involves more critical and creative thinking and indicates a better understanding of the concepts.

Using Bloom's Taxonomy to Classify Questions

Classification	**Sample Question**
Knowledge	1. How many legs has an insect?
Synthesis	2. What hypotheses would you make about this problem?
Application	3. Knowing what you do about heat, how would you get a tightly fitted lid off a jar?
Analysis	4. What things do birds and lizards have in common?
Comprehension	5. Operationally define a magnet.
Evaluation	6. If you were going to repeat the experiment, how would you do it better?
Valuing	7. What is your interest in earth science now compared to when you began the course?
Valuing	8. What do you value about this film?
Receiving	9. Do you watch science shows on television?
Responding	10. Do you talk to your friends about science?

Processes of Science and Questions

Another way to classify questions is to use the processes of science. This approach ensures that the basic structure of science and critical thinking is taught. Shown below is a guide of how you might classify questions using science processes.

Science Processes

1. Hypothesizing
2. Inferring
3. Measuring
4. Designing and experimenting
5. Observing
6. Setting up equipment
7. Graphing
8. Reducing experimental error

Classifying Using Science Processes

Classification	**Sample Question**
Observing	1. What do you observe about the landscape?
Hypothesizing	2. What do you think will happen to the solution when I heat it?
Designing an experiment	3. How would you determine the absorption of the different wavelengths of light in water?
Graphing	4. How would you graph these data?
Setting up equipment	5. Obtain the following equipment and set it up as directed.
Reducing experimental error	6. How many measurements should be made to report accurate data?
Inferring	7. What conclusions can you make from the data?

Convergent and Divergent Questions

Another way to classify questions is to determine whether they encourage many answers or just a few. Questions allowing for a limited number of responses and moving toward closure or a conclusion are called convergent. Questions allowing for a number of answers are called divergent; they provide for wider responses plus more creative, critically considered answers. In an inquiry discussion, it is generally desirable to start with very divergent questions and move toward more convergent ones if the students appear to be having difficulties.

Generally speaking, convergent questions, particularly those requiring only a yes or no answer, should be avoided because they allow for fewer responses, thereby giving students little opportunity to think critically. The fundamental purpose in using the inquiry approach is to stimulate and develop critical thinking, creative behavior, and multiple talents. Convergent questions certainly do little to achieve this end. Remember that, in an inquiry investigation, it is important that the student has a chance to use his mind. Learning to think rationally and creatively does much to increase a person's self-concept. Many teachers are so concerned with getting the right answer that they prevent students from using their minds. Even though a student may come up with wrong conclusions, he still has had a mental experience in thinking about the problem. Having this experience is probably more important than a right answer. We as teachers would, of course, like for a student to use his mind and obtain the correct answer as well. However, recall for a moment a mathematics teacher who only accepts the correct answer to a problem, ignoring the procedures used in obtaining it. The student may have used very good thinking processes to obtain the answer yet misplaced the decimal point. Is the teacher justified in saying that the student hasn't learned because he hasn't the right answer? The student will probably never have that problem again but he undoubtedly will have many situations requiring him to use similar logical strategies. It is the thinking that is most important! The teacher who doesn't reward thinking may stifle students.

Teleological and Anthropomorphic Questions

Teleological (Greek—*teleos*—an end) questions are those which imply that natural phenomena have an end or purpose. The word anthropomorphic comes from two Greek words: *anthropos*, meaning man, and *morphos*, meaning form. An anthropomorphic question implies that some natural phenomenon has the characteristics of man. For example, such a question might state that some natural phenomenon has a "want" or "wish"—rocks fall because they "want" to.

Why do you think these questions should be avoided? What do they do as far as developing critical thinking, leading to further investigation, and how do they contribute to misconceptions? The answers

to these questions should be obvious to you and need no discussion here.

Talent-Oriented Questions

Although the procedures thus far have mainly emphasized the importance of cognitive questions, other types are also important. Teachers should spend a considerable amount of time formulating talent-oriented questions to help them know their students.

We believe that you should not only determine talent but help to manifest it by rewarding students for all types of talent. Some teachers and administrators may argue that the only function of a science teacher is to develop scientific awareness. It is our view that this awareness will occur to a higher degree if a student has opportunities to manifest his best talents, thereby building his self-concept and developing more positive feelings about science. Some examples of talent-oriented questions are listed below.

Questioning to Discover Talent

Talent	*Question*
Artistic	1. What important ideas should be put on a mural to be hung in our laboratory?
Organizing	2. How should we organize the field trip?
Communicating	3. What should be included in a short article for the school paper about the science fair?
Creative	4. In what ways can we convey to the rest of the school how exciting biology, earth science, chemistry, and physics are?
Social	5. What shall be the social activities for the science picnic?
Planning	6. How shall we plan our investigations of the pond community throughout the year?

Teachers should also ask questions to find out students' interests. What "turns them on?" Determining these interests helps the instructor in planning more relevant lessons. Questioning individuals personally about their likes also helps convey to the students your interest in them as people and not as sponges to soak up scientific information.

Piaget pointed out that proper questioning gives

=============== GUEST EDITORIAL ===============

Medical Research: Science Lurches On

Carol Wilson,
Research Associate
Division of Biological Sciences and the Pritzker School
of Medicine, University of Chicago
Chicago, Illinois

Many distributions found in scientific study, in nature and in the laboratory, follow regular, predictable patterns. Examples include the bell-shaped normal curve of probability and the s-shaped or sigmoid population-growth curve. In a research laboratory, the actual process of gathering data is much more irregular and unpredictable. Scientific research rarely progresses smoothly; rather, it may vary greatly from day to day, with experimental failures outnumbering successes. This unpredictable quality prompted one research group to adopt the slogan, "Science Lurches On."

The "lurch" effect of research progress is particularly evident in a leukemia research laboratory. Here, most experiments focus on the study of leukemic white blood cells from sick patients. Thus, the workload is largely dependent on when patients become ill or when they schedule clinic appointments. If an experiment on cells from Patient 26 flops, the laboratory may have to wait as long as twelve months before she returns to the clinic so that the study can be repeated. In addition, one day could bring seven patient cases to study at once (each case requiring at least two hours of study time) and then there may be no more patients for two weeks! The laboratory must be prepared at all times to accommodate any kind and number of cases.

A research project begins with the definition of a question. This laboratory focuses on the study of hairy-cell leukemia, a rare lymphoproliferative disorder, and related diseases. Questions are asked about the origin and function of the malignant hairy cell. Defining the research problem, the direction of the project, is the easy task. The challenge begins with the development of experimental techniques that will lead to definite answers; in many instances, finding the right methods requires more time than the actual performance of experiments. For example, our laboratory was seeking to identify the different phospholipid components of the hairy-cell

membrane using one-dimensional, thin-layer chromatography. First, a literature search revealed thin-layer chromatography methods which appeared to be applicable to our system. Adaptation and expansion of the methods to accommodate our system required nine full months of trial and error experiments before a set of procedures that worked was defined. The actual data collection took only five months before answers to the problem began to fall in place.

Another facet of work in an active medical research laboratory is the coordination of the many projects which are conducted simultaneously. Researchers who work independently on separate problems must be prepared to overlap when an unscheduled case unexpectedly appears from the clinic or the emergency room.

Overall, perhaps the most exciting aspect of working in a medical setting is the interaction with several spheres of the hospital environment. A researcher may work with physicians and patients for part of a day, reviewing the symptoms and development of a disorder. The focus then shifts from patient to laboratory, where the cellular material is isolated, stored, cultured, extracted, and studied in various ways. Through our laboratory, for example, one blood sample may be analyzed by eight to ten different research groups, including the study of surface and cytoplasmic immunologic markers, transmission and scanning electron microscopy, cell-surface hormone receptors, chromosome abnormalities, and biochemical composition (proteins and lipids). Although each laboratory investigation is fascinating in itself, no research would be as interesting or rewarding without "putting it all together" to study overall patterns and interpret the meaning of the data. It is this interaction, along with development of applications that can improve and expand human life, that makes research so intriguing and worthwhile.

====================   REFLECTING ON SCIENCE TEACHING   ====================
Developing Constructive Questions

List as many words as possible which, when used as the first word of a sentence, would require only yes or no answers.

---

insights into a student's thought patterns. To do so, the instructor must hypothesize how the student is thinking, then pose questions to see if she is correct. When the student responds, the hypothesis may be confirmed or may need further investigation. She may have to formulate a new hypothesis and construct questions to determine its validity. This type of questioning is particularly necessary when the student seems to be having difficulty in discovering or conceptualizing. Excellent teachers in mathematics, physics, chemistry, and other courses often use this approach to diagnose students' thinking-process difficulties and help them resolve problems.

■ Questioning Procedures
Wait-Time Affects Quality of Responses

Mary Budd Rowe and her coworkers have done an extensive study of the questioning behavior of teachers.[1] In their analysis of taped classroom discussions, they discovered that teachers, on an average, wait less than a second for students to reply to their questions. Further investigations revealed that some instructors waited on an average of three seconds for students to answer questions. An analysis of student responses revealed that teachers with longer wait-times (three seconds or more) obtained greater speculation, conversation, and argument than those with shorter wait-times.

Dr. Rowe found further that when teachers were trained to wait five seconds, on the average, before responding the following occurred:

1. Students gave longer and more complete answers instead of short phrases.
2. There was an increase in speculative, creative thinking.
3. The number of suggested questions and experiments increased.
4. "Slow" students increased their participation.
5. Teachers became more flexible in their responses to students.
6. Teachers asked fewer questions, but the ones they asked required more reflection.

7. Students gave a greater number of qualified inferences.
8. Teacher expectations for student performance changed; they were less likely to expect only the brighter students to reply.

Dr. Rowe believes that the expectancy levels of students are more likely to change positively if they are given a longer time to respond. She has also found that the typical pattern of discussion: teacher–student–teacher can be altered by training instructors to get student–student–teacher reponses. This pattern will occur particularly well when students are involved in some controversy, e.g., the best design for an experiment or what conclusion can be drawn from data.

For inquiry teaching to occur, it seems reasonable that most instructors should attempt to increase their wait-time tolerance so that students may have more opportunities to think and create.

Good Discussions Are Student-Centered

Most teachers, when they are involved in a class discussion, dominate it to a considerable extent; an inquiry class should be student-centered, which means that the teacher's talking should be at a minimum. Note the two diagrams of discussion interaction in a class in Figure 11.1.

It is not easy to develop techniques so that the second type of interaction operates. How would you as a teacher get the second pattern to operate in your classes?

■ Some Precautions in Questioning

It has long been thought that the practice of questioning promotes student thinking and participation, and in most cases it does. However, sometimes certain questioning techniques have the reverse effect, actually shutting off student thinking. Frequently what the teacher actually does is initiate a question-and-answer practice that does not evolve into true classroom discussion and does not promote expres-

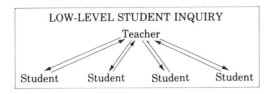

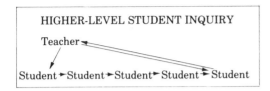

FIGURE 11–1

siveness, active participation, or independent thinking. Instead the process may encourage student passivity and dependency.

A few precautions are given to alert teachers to practices that may hinder using questions to initiate discussion. Sometimes this simply results in a back-and-forth interchange between teacher and students in which the teacher is the questioner and the student is the responder. To avoid this, you might hold back from asking questions at the start, and thus give the students the impression that they must take some responsibility for carrying on the discussion rather than simply being targets of teacher questions.

Second, questions are sometimes used to make a point in which a particular piece of information or idea is underscored. Sometimes this practice is counterproductive because the same information can be put forth more effectively as a declarative statement.

Third, questions are often asked to help students who pause or falter in their responses. We sometimes condition students to speak in short bursts in answer to direct questions from the teacher and not to expect to do anything further. True discussion, however, requires thoughtful, sustained expressions by the students. It requires more time to express complex thoughts or interpretations. If the teacher pushes in with a question too quickly, the effect is to halt student thought processes and substitute the teachers' thoughts.

Fourth, questions are sometimes used to elicit predetermined answers. In this case the teacher has a particular answer in mind and phrases questions so that that answer is brought forth from the student. This again shuts off speculative, thoughtful responses from the students.

Fifth, teachers sometimes ask questions in reply to a student's question. This is sometimes recommended as a way of promoting inquiry. However, it may convey the idea that only the teacher gets to ask the questions and that whenever students ask ques-

tions all they get is a redirected question to them or to someone else in the class.

Sixth, questions are sometimes used to draw out the nonparticipating students. This assumes that every student is in the frame of mind to respond equally with every other student. The practice may instead intimidate some students and cause others to become wary of future questions. They may thus be preparing answers in advance and failing to listen to the argument of the discussion. Such practices may cause students to withdraw even more rather than drawing them out.

Seventh, to use questions to probe the students' personal feelings and experiences is a risky practice. This may make the individual fearful and resentful. Such questions ought to be saved for more private contacts in which the teacher and the student can confer on a more intimate basis.

Alternatives to these practices can avoid the pitfalls described above. For example, the teacher could make a declarative statement rather than asking a question. This can still present the problem or issue to the students and open up avenues for further discussion.

A second alternative to questioning would be to restate the speaker's words. Try to make a statement that interprets what the student has said, thus giving the class an opportunity to reconsider the information that has been presented.

Third, declare your perplexity when you are confused as to what the student has said. Simply state, "I am confused about what you are saying."

Fourth, invite elaboration. Use a statement such as, "I'd like to hear more of your views on that."

Fifth, encourage class questions. In a discussion, it should be possible for students to ask other students questions or to direct their questions at the person who is speaking whether it is the teacher or another student.

Sixth, let the speaker pause and ask a question. This promotes discussion, indicates the speculative nature of the statements that are being made, and gives the student an opportunity to obtain feedback.

Seventh, simply maintain silence. Use a longer wait-time to indicate to the student that you are conducting a leisurely practice and you want to provide opportunities for reflection, introspection, and thoughtful answers.[2]

■ Using Questioning in a Competitive Learning Strategy

A useful technique which employs classroom questioning by the teacher has been described by a group of high school teachers in a Colorado school (Baker, et al, 1988).[3] This is in the form of oral quizzing which normally takes place once a week, usually during a Wednesday class period.

The rules for the oral quizzing are given below. The numbers on the seating chart represent the average numerical grade the student currently holds. Each student has an equal opportunity to move upward from the C section to the B section to the A section by successfully answering teacher questions on the day of the oral quiz. The strategy has superior motivating potential as well as serving as an excellent mechanism for classroom control.

Advance planning of questions by the teacher is necessary to insure that questions give proper attention to higher levels of cognition. Teachers who have used this questioning strategy have reported excellent results and recommend its use to others. It is important to recognize that the competitive spirit is emphasized in this strategy, a fact which may cause some teachers to seek alternatives to its use.

ORAL QUIZZING

WHEN: Any day

SEATING:

76	83	88	94	100
75	82	87	93	99
74	81	86	92	98
73	80	85	91	97
72	79	84	90	96
71	78	83	89	95

RULES:

1. Students in A or B seats cannot use notes or text during quizzing.
2. Students in C seats can use notes and text.
3. The student to whom the question is being directed must answer quickly. When the instructor calls for the next person his turn is over.
4. By design the questioning must start at the top A with the first question.
5. For missed questions the first student with the correct answer moves to where the question started. All the students in between move back one seat.
6. Tardy students or those who have been absent *for any reason* must move to the last seat in the last row.
7. Inappropriate behavior will also send a student to the last seat.
8. Each student must keep track of where his or her earned seat is. If there is a dispute or someone

forgets where to sit, he or she must move to the last seat in the last row.

9. Questions will *only be asked once*. Some questions may be clarified with the student asking "What do you mean by _____?"

GRADING:

1. Grades for earned seats will be recorded on Wednesday at the end of the period.
2. Oral quizzing grade will be used to replace the lowest test grade each quarter.

■ Research on Questioning in the Classroom

Questioning remains one of the most influential teaching behaviors in the classroom because of its potential in stimulating thinking and learning. The first major systematic research on questioning was conducted by Stevens at Columbia University in 1912. Almost all the research conducted from that time until the 1950s primarily focused on describing teacher questioning behavior. Results uniformly supported the finding that questions stimulating memory and recall were the type being emphasized in classrooms.

Around 1970 a new spurt of activity on teacher questioning began. The emphasis in this research was on identifying specific questioning levels and skills that have an impact on pupil growth.

A major concern today is the impact of teachers' questions on pupil learning as measured by achievement tests. Rosenshine in 1979 found no significant relationship between the frequency of higher-level questions and achievement. Although the frequency of such questions appears to be unrelated to achievement, verbalized higher-level questions were found to lead to greater achievement than low-level questions in several studies. Using seventh and eighth grade general science teachers and pupils in a study in 1965, Kleinman found the pupils of teachers who asked higher level, critical-thinking questions performed better on a science achievement test than pupils of teachers who asked questions requiring only information recall.

Also using junior high school science teachers and pupils in a ninth grade class, Ladd in 1969 found that teachers who used a greater proportion of higher-inquiry questions caused greater change in pupils' achievement as indicated on a posttest composed of high and low inquiry questions.

Other studies conducted more recently have

produced mixed conclusions relating to the influence of higher level questioning on achievement. But despite the mixed research findings, questioning is still regarded as an essential and influential instructional behavior. It is the most basic approach teachers use to stimulate thinking and learning in the classroom. Higher level questions produce situations of such complexity that their relative influence has not yet clearly been sorted out.

Fully functioning teachers almost certainly have educational objectives not only at the fact level but also at the concept level and even at the personal meaning and values levels. This necessitates asking higher-order questions of students. Teachers then need not determine whether to ask higher-level questions but rather how to find an appropriate balance of lower and higher order questions to achieve the instructional goals.

There has been much research on the use of questions as a learning strategy. Questions in textual material have been defended on the basis that they provide "advance organizers" for the material to be learned. The use of questions of the higher levels of cognition such as application, analysis, synthesis, and evaluation has been shown to have a significant positive effect on student learning. Questions placed within the text material appear to produce better understanding and retention than text material without questions.

In a study on presentation style (Leonard, 1987), groups of students reading material with questions at the beginnings of paragraphs scored higher on an immediate posttest than did groups reading without questions.

As a result of the research over the past 75 years several tentative conclusions can be drawn concerning questioning in the classroom.

1. Teachers appear to persist in asking questions that require students primarily to recall knowledge and information. It is important to consider stressing higher-level questions and to devise a variety of instructional objectives that balance low-level memory questions with preplanned higher convergent and divergent questions.
2. Teachers can be effectively trained to raise the cognitive emphasis of their questions.
3. There is a tendency for the cognitive levels of questions asked by teachers and responses from pupils to be positively related.
4. The extent of wait-time teachers use after asking questions dramatically influences the quantity and quality of pupil responses. Teacher educators need to provide training opportunities for teachers to practice increasing their wait-time to a minimum of three seconds.

5. At the primary level there is a tendency for the use of lower cognitive level questions to be related to pupil achievement. Teachers need to stress the importance of balancing low and high cognitive level questions to stimulate productive thinking at all grade levels.[4]

■ Summary

The ability of the teacher to ask questions to stimulate creative and critical thinking and to manifest multiple talents is basic to inquiry teaching. Inquiry types of questions may be involved in all areas of science teaching such as discussion, laboratory demonstrations, student worksheets, visual aids, and evaluations. An instructor should plan her questions before class but remain flexible and adapt her instruction as dictated by student interaction. Before outlining the question, a teacher should decide what talents, critical thinking processes, and subject-matter objectives she hopes to develop and the answers she will accept.

Questions may be classified as convergent or divergent according to Bloom's Taxonomy, by the science processes, and/or by the multiple talents they are trying to develop. Divergent types of questions and those requiring more cognitive sophistication should be stressed. Teleological questions, anthropomorphic questions, and those that could be answered by yes or no responses should be avoided.

The time a teacher waits for a response, called "wait-time," is very important. Most teachers wait, on an average, less than one second. A five-second average wait-time results in more responses by slow learners, more creative answers, more complete-sentence answers, more questions, and more suggestion for experiments.

The chapter suggests questioning techniques to involve students in investigations and to stimulate creativity.

Research indicates that teachers trained in questioning techniques do change their questioning behavior in the classroom, asking questions requiring greater cognitive ability. Teachers who do emphasize higher-level types of questions are more likely to have their students do better on national tests, which tend to test for all cognitive levels.

■ References

1. Mary Budd Rowe, "Wait-Time and Rewards as Instructional Variables: Influence on Inquiry and Sense of Fate Control," *New Science in the Inner City* (New York: Teachers College, Columbia University, September 1970). Unpublished paper prepared for the symposium at Kiel, Germany.

2. J.T. Diller, "Do Your Questions Promote or Prevent Thinking?" *Learning*, 11 (October 1982), pp. 56-57.

3. Boyce Baker, et al., Conversations with Baker and other teachers at Grand Junction High School, Grand Junction, Colorado, 1988.

4. William Wilen, "Implications of Research on Questioning for the Teacher Educator," *Journal of Research and Development in Education*, no. 2, 1984.

================= INVESTIGATING SCIENCE TEACHING =================

ACTIVITY 11-1

Recognizing Good Questions, Part 1

Read the following questions and mark them according to whether they are poor (P), fair (F), good (G), or excellent (E).

_____ 1. Why do roots thirst for water?
_____ 2. Why does water seek its own level?
_____ 3. Are all big trees the same size, shape, and age?
_____ 4. How does a siphon work?
_____ 5. How do seeds sprout?
_____ 6. How does soap clean?
_____ 7. What will happen if clothes are soaked with a bleach before instead of after washing?
_____ 8. How can the bleaching action be accelerated?
_____ 9. If ethylene glycol prevents avalanches, what other chemicals do you suspect might also prevent them?
_____ 10. If you were going to repeat the experiment with yeast, how would you improve it?
_____ 11. How would you design an experiment to_____?
_____ 12. If you have a straight-line graph indicating a relationship between population growth and time but the period ends at two days, what could you say about the population at four days?
_____ 13. How would you define a magnet operationally?
_____ 14. How could you be more certain about the conclusions you made from the data?
_____ 15. What do you think will happen to a potted geranium plant if it is placed near a window?
_____ 16. What evidence does the process of diffusion contribute to the molecular theory?
_____ 17. Look at the culture plates and describe what you see.
_____ 18. Place the organisms into any two groups you wish.
_____ 19. If the distance is doubled between two masses in Newton's gravitational formula, what will happen to the force?

Now provide an explanation for your responses. Why do you think some questions are poor, fair, good, or excellent?

ACTIVITY 11-2

Recognizing Good Questions, Part 2

Below are several questions related to the preceding activity. Read each question and attempt to answer it. Record your answers in the space provided and refer to them again after completing this chapter to see how well you did.

_____ 1. Of the preceding questions, which three are the best?
_____ 2. Which are teleological or anthropomorphic questions?
_____ 3. Which questions require the student to analyze?
_____ 4. Which questions require the student to synthesize?
_____ 5. Which questions require the student to evaluate?
_____ 6. Which questions are convergent?
_____ 7. Which questions are divergent?

_____ 8. Which questions require the student to demonstrate in his response the processes of science?

_____ 9. Which questions require students to reason quantitatively and what are they required to do?

_____ 10. Which questions require creative responses?

_____ 11. Which questions require the student to formulate an operational definition?

_____ 12. Which questions require a student mainly to observe?

_____ 13. Which questions require a student mainly to classify?

_____ 14. Which questions require a student to demonstrate experimental procedure?

_____ 15. Which questions require a student to formulate's model?

_____ 16. Which questions require a student to hypothesize?

_____ 17. Which question would an authoritarian personality most likely guess as if he didn't know the answer?

_____ 18. Which of the following two types of questions suggest a test?
   a. How do seeds sprout?
   b. What is needed for seeds to sprout?

_____ 19. It has been said that "how" questions do not lead to experimentation. Comment on this statement.

After you have answered these questions, compare and discuss your answers with other students in the class.

ACTIVITY 11–3

Classifying Questions in Normal Conversation

Observe normal conversation and classify the questions asked according to one of the classification systems suggested in this chapter.

ACTIVITY 11–4

Classifying Questions Using Bloom's Taxonomy

Write some discussion questions to be used in a class discussion and classify them according to Bloom's Taxonomy and science processes.

ACTIVITY 11–5

Classifying Questions: Divergent or Convergent?

In the blank in front of each question, place a *D* if you think the question is divergent, a *C* if you think it is convergent.

_____ 1. What do you think I am going to do with this apparatus?
_____ 2. What conclusions can you make from the data?
_____ 3. Can anything else be done to improve the growth of the plants?
_____ 4. Is heat an important factor in the experiment?
_____ 5. Do you think the salt precipitated because the solution was cooled?
_____ 6. Which of these three rocks is harder?
_____ 7. What can you tell me about the geology of this area from the picture?
_____ 8. Would you say you have sufficient data?
_____ 9. In what ways can you make the lights burn with the wire, switch, and power supply?
_____ 10. What things can you tell me about the biological make-up of this earthworm from your observations?

Which questions are the most convergent? What answers are possible for these questions? What words start these sentences? How would you change the sentences to make them more divergent?

ACTIVITY 11–6

Classifying Questions: Teleological or Anthropomorphic?

In the blank before each question, indicate whether the question is teleological (T) or anthropomorphic (A).

_____ 1. How do you think bacteria feel when ultraviolet light is shined on them?
_____ 2. Why does water seek its own level?
_____ 3. Why do plants seek the light?
_____ 4. Why will a body in motion want to stay in motion?
_____ 5. Why is the end of evolution to become increasingly more complex?

ACTIVITY 11–7

Leading a Discussion

1. Read the booklet *Creative Questioning and Sensitive Listening Techniques, A Self-Concept Approach.* Arthur Carin and Robert B. Sund (Columbus, Ohio: Charles E. Merrill Publishing Co., 1978).
2. Lead a small discussion and have someone check your wait-time and how well you get students to talk to students instead of students to teacher to student.

ACTIVITY 11–8

Self-Evaluation Instrument for Rating Your Questioning Ability

Lead a discussion and use a cassette tape recorder to record it. Read through the following questions. Then listen to the tape. Put a check mark in the blank preceding the statement for each time the action described in the statement occurred.

_____ 1. You asked what students knew about the topic before starting the discussion.

_____ 2. You asked a convergent question.

_____ 3. You developed student-student rather than teacher-student interaction.

_____ 4. You asked an affective question.

_____ 5. You reinforced an answer without saying that the response was correct.

_____ 6. You did not stop discussing a point when the right answer was given but asked students if there were other answers or further discussion.

_____ 7. You asked a question requiring science-process thinking (e.g., hypothesizing, designing an experiment, inferring).

_____ 8. You interrupted a student without giving him time to complete his thought.

_____ 9. You paraphrased a student's statement to clarify or focus for others on the topics.

_____ 10. Measure how many seconds on the average you waited for a response.

_____ 11. Measure how much class time (in seconds) you devoted to routine (e.g., roll taking, announcements), student activity and teacher talk.

_____ Routine:

_____ Student activity

_____ Teacher talk:

_____ 12. Rate yourself as a listener:

1 2 3 4 5 6 7 8 9 10

Poor listener   Average   Good listener

_____ 13. Rate yourself as a questioner:

1 2 3 4 5 6 7 8 9 10

Poor listener   Average   Good listener

Evaluate your responses and list those things you most want to change in your teaching. Record and rate yourself again at a later date or have a student or aide do it and note your improvement.

CHAPTER 12

Inquiry and Investigation

As a student, at this point you may be wondering what is important about inquiry teaching. How is it different from other teaching methods? To bring out some of its major ideas, we shall quote several writers' statements concerning inquiry teaching's importance in science education.

Pinchas Tamir states that, "The notion of inquiry has been central to science education for the last twenty years."[1] In studying science education literature, Tamir recognized that inquiry has been central to the learning process in secondary school science.

In 1966, Dr. Richard Suchman at the University of Illinois did research on inquiry teaching. He said, "Inquiry is the fundamental means of human learning."[2] This is a very important statement, because much of our science teaching is not done by inquiry.

In 1980–81, a large research project was done in the United States that examined science teaching methods being used at that time. The authors of that research project stated, "Beause the development of inquiry skills is one of the goals for science education, it is a natural focal topic for the study of science education carried out by a group of scholars under the auspices of "Project Synthesis."[3]

The position statement of the National Science Teachers Association, the largest science teachers organization in the world, states, "The major goal of science teaching is the development of scientific literacy for all people. Incorporated within the concept of scientific literacy is both the understanding of key principles in science and the understanding of how scientific ideas are developed."[4]

Another author stated, "A major emphasis for education for scientific literacy must be placed on the processes of scientific inquiry."[5]

Thus there are several authors who have declared inquiry to be an important and fundamental method of learning, and one that is particularly useful in science.

■ Development of Inquiry Teaching in the Schools

Scientific inquiry and investigation as we presently understand it did not enter our schools, nor even the practice of science in any important way, until the mid-nineteenth century. "Instead, faith was at least as important as empirical data and in many instances it dominated the practice of science. This faith was often a complex mixture of Christian theology, idealism, and entrenched traditions. It also was a condition that had its roots in many centuries of disagreements between the Church and the practices of science."[6]

Changes in the way science was studied—and taught—may be observed more clearly by looking at the innovations produced by individual scientists and teachers, rather than through any organized curricular movements. Examples are the methods of Louis Agassiz at the Lawrence Scientific School at Harvard, in which he "invited students to visit his lab, study specimens firsthand and thereby gain direct knowledge. He directed field trips to the countryside and seashore, encouraged students to make their own collections, and conducted instruction by correspondence with specimen collectors around the country."[7]

During the late 1800s and early 1900s, inquiry teaching was generally a rarity in science classrooms. Pestalozzi's "Object method" of the early 1900s may have had the germs of inquiry embedded in it but it was many decades before firsthand study of objects and phenomena in science became an accepted practice in science classrooms. Even today, many teachers avoid inquiry teaching because of several perceived problems with this method of instruction. Among these include the necessity for a slower pace, more time consumption, the need for large quantities of materials, a more active and perhaps chaotic classroom, the urgency to "cover" material to prepare for the next grade level, high emphasis of most tests on factual memorization, and other factors. Along with this is the normal inertia and resistance to changes in methods of instruction which many teachers hold. The burdensome problems facing teachers today leave little time for probing into new methods of teaching.

■ Defining Inquiry

Wayne Welch et al. define inquiry as, "a general process by which human beings seek information or understanding. Broadly conceived, inquiry is a way of thought. Scientific inquiry, a subset of general inquiry, is concerned with the natural world and is guided by certain beliefs and assumptions."[8] J. T. Wilson defines inquiry in the following terms:

> Inquiry is a process model of instruction based upon learning theory and behavior. Too often it is confused with open-ended, undirected activity which is assumed to simulate scientific activity. This is not the case. Inquiry results wherever and whenever stimuli challenge the existing expectations of the participant. The situation may occur in a well-equipped laboratory, but it may also occur in a well-planned and produced lecture, a stimulating reading assignment, or a simple novel situation. The emphasis of inquiry is not the mere acquisition of science knowledge or the production of scientists. It is rather an emphasis upon how humans process information in order to make intellectual decisions of all sorts.[9]

Some authors writing on the subject of inquiry make a distinction between general and scientific inquiry. Specifically, scientific inquiry is defined in the following terms:

> Scientific inquiry is defined as a systematic and investigative activity with the purpose of uncovering and describing relationships among objects and events. It is characterized by the use of orderly, repeatable processes, reduction of the object of investigation to its most simple scale and form, and the use of logical frameworks for explanation and pre-

diction. The operations of inquiry include observing, questioning, experimenting, comparing, inferring, generalizing, communicating, applying and others.[10]

Scientific inquiry has also been defined as "a systematic investigative performance ability which incorporates unrestrained inductive thinking capabilities after a person has acquired a broad and critical knowledge of particular subject matter through formal learning processes."[11]

Some authors believe that, in the secondary schools particularly, inquiry teaching is a way of developing the mental processes of curiosity and investigation so that students learn how information is obtained. Other authors believe teachers should not use scientific inquiry in the classrooms of the secondary school. They believe that it is a mistake to lead students to think that they are acting like scientists when in fact they may only be exhibiting general inquiry characteristics. They also believe that true scientific inquiry cannot be done until one knows the subject very well in advance, which would limit it to graduate students and laboratory researchers. The authors believe that it is necessary to introduce children in the secondary schools, and perhaps even earlier, to the ideas of inquiry and investigation, even though they may not know much science before they have this instruction. See the "Teaching Science Activities," on pp. 450–452, for examples of classroom exercises designed for students with minimal science backgrounds.

■ Discovery and Inquiry Strategies Distinguished

Over the last twenty-five years, most of the programs funded by the United States Government for developing modern instruction for the elementary and secondary schools have stressed student involvement in discovery- or inquiry-oriented activities. Millions of dollars have gone into constructing science and mathematics studies and curricula for this purpose.

What is discovery or inquiry? Many educators use these terms interchangeably whereas others prefer to differentiate their meanings. In our terminology, *discovery occurs when an individual is mainly involved in using his mental processes to mediate (or discover) some concept or principle.*

For a student to make discoveries he must perform certain mental processes such as observing, classifying, measuring, predicting, describing, inferring, etc. Many modern elementary school curriculum-project materials are mainly designed to involve children in discovery activities.

Making measurements helps develop skills of quantification.

Discovery

Discovery is the mental process of assimilating concepts and principles. Discovery processes include:

Observing
Classifying
Measuring
Predicting
Describing
Inferring

Starting in the middle school and becoming increasingly more sophisticated as students progress through high school, materials are designed to stress inquiry. Inquiry teaching, however, is built on and includes discovery, because a student must use his discovery capabilities plus many more. *In true inquiry the individual tends to act more like a maturing adult.* An adult behaves in a number of ways to unravel the hidden relationships relative to a problem. He defines problems, formulates hypotheses, designs experiments, etc. He performs certain relatively sophisticated mental processes, as indicated in the following chart.

A secondary student may be asked to choose and investigate an organism and report research he

has done on it. If he defines his own problem, designs experiments, collects data, etc., he is behaving in an inquiry manner. Refer to the charts on discovery and inquiry. How do their processes differ? How would you design a discovery-oriented lesson in your subject field? How would you design an inquiry lesson?

Inquiry

Inquiry is the process of defining and investigating problems, formulating hypotheses, designing experiments, gathering data, and drawing conclusions about problems. Inquiry processes include:

Originating problems
Formulating hypotheses
Designing investigative approaches
Testing out ideas (e.g., conducting experiments)
Synthesizing knowledge
Developing certain attitudes (e.g., objective, curious, open-minded, desires and respects theoretical models, responsible, suspends judgment until sufficient data is obtained, checks his results).

Because secondary teachers often do not clearly distinguish between discovery and inquiry, they tend to overemphasize discovery activities. Piaget indicated that adolescents are in the process of developing formal thought and should, therefore, have opportunities to use a higher level of thinking. Hypothetical-deductive and reflexive thinking are two characteristics of this period. Formulating hypotheses, designing investigations, evaluating data, and looking over an investigation to determine how it can be improved requires these mental operations. Middle and secondary instruction should, therefore, not only include discovery but an increasing number of inquiry activities.

Clearly, one develops discovery and inquiry thinking abilities only by being involved in activities requiring the performance of these mental tasks. Since an individual never really masters any of them completely, there is only a degree to which one becomes proficient in learning how to discover and inquire. Even the most sophisticated Nobel Prize scientist, author, painter, mathematician, or sociologist is still moving forward in developing these skills. The task of the school system is to construct its curriculum so students manifest these human investigative abilities.

■ Advantages of Discovery and Inquiry Teaching

You are probably beginning to see some of the reasons that discovery and inquiry teaching are used in the schools. Jerome Bruner, an eminent psychology professor, has been instrumental in leading the movement toward discovery teaching. He outlined four reasons for using this approach:

1. Intellectual potency
2. Intrinsic rather than extrinsic motives
3. Learning the heuristics of discovery
4. Conservation of memory

By intellectual potency, Bruner means that an individual learns and develops her mind only by using it to think. His second point means that, as a consequence of succeeding at discovery, the student receives a satisfying intellectual thrill—an intrinsic reward. Teachers often given extrinsic rewards (A's, for example), but if they want students to learn for the fun of it, they must devise instructional systems which enable students to obtain intrinsic satisfaction. In Bruner's third point, he emphasizes that the only way a person learns the techniques of making discoveries is to have opportunities to discover. Through discovering, a student slowly learns how to organize and conduct investigations. Bruner argues in his fourth point that one of the greatest benefits of the discovery approach is that it aids in better

memory retention. Think for a moment of some scientific idea you have thought out yourself and compare it with information you were given in a freshman course. The material you reasoned and came to some conclusion about is probably still in your mind, even though you may have learned it years ago. On the other hand, concepts you were told often escape recall.

Although these four justifications have been outlined for discovery teaching, they also have relevance for inquiry. The teaching strategies for the two approaches are similar in that they stress the importance of the students' using their cognitive mental processes to work out the meaning of things they encounter in their environment.

Although Bruner has suggested the salient justifications for modern teaching, there are at least six additional reasons for using student investigative approaches.

Instruction Becomes Student-Centered

One of the basic psychological principles of learning implies that the greater the student involvement, the greater the learning. Usually when teachers think about learning, they have in mind that the student is assimilating some information. This view of learning is very limited. Learning involves those aspects that contribute to the individual becoming a fully functioning person. For example, in inquiry situations students learn not only concepts and principles, but self-direction, responsibility, social communication, etc. In teacher-centered instruction, however, many of the opportunities for developing these talents are denied to the student by the instructor. She provides the self-direction and retains the responsibility. If you look at instruction as enabling a "person" to improve in all the facets that make up a human being, it is difficult to justify a teacher-centered learning environment.

Inquiry Learning Builds the "Self-Concept" of the Student

Each of us has a self-concept. If it is good, we feel psychologically secure, are open to new experiences, willing to take chances and explore, tolerate minor failures relatively well, are more creative, generally have good mental health, and eventually become fully functioning individuals. Part of the task of becoming a better person is to build one's self-concept. We can do this only by *being involved in learning* because through involvement we manifest our potential and gain insights into "self." Inquiry teach-

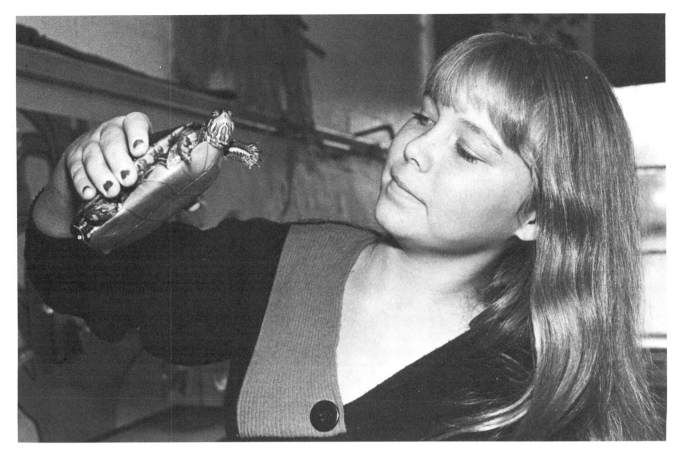

Involvement is a basic principle of learning.

ing provides opportunities for greater involvement, thereby giving students more chances to gain insights and better develop their self-concepts.

Expectancy Level Increases

Part of a person's self-concept is his expectancy level, which means that the student believes or expects that he can accomplish a task on his own. He has learned from previous discovery and inquiry experiences that he can "think autonomously." In other words, from having had many successful experiences in using his investigative talents, he learned, "I can solve a problem on my own without the help of a teacher, parent, or anyone else." As a consequence, he learns "I-can"-ness.

Inquiry Learning Develops Talent

Humans possess more than 120 talents. Academic talent is related to only a few of them. The more freedom we have to use these academic talents, the more opportunities we have to develop others, such as creative, social, organizing, and planning talents.

Inquiry Methods Avoid Learning Only at the Verbal Level

When you learned the definitions for words such as osmosis, photosynthesis, logarithm, and others, did you play memorization games or did you work out the meaning in your mind and really understand what you were learning? Could you define these terms operationally or could you give memorized definitions only? Inquiry teaching, since it involves students working out the meaning of their work, tends to avoid learning only at the verbal level.

Inquiry Learning Permits Time for Students to Mentally Assimilate and Accommodate Information

Teachers often rush learning, which results in students playing recall games. Students need time to think and use their minds to reason out and gain insights into the concepts, principles, and investigative techniques they are involved in. It takes time for such information to become a meaningful part of the mind. Dr. Jean Piaget believes that there is no true learning unless the student mentally acts on information and, in the process, assimilates or accommodates what he encounters in his environment. Unless this assimilation occurs, the teacher and student are involved only in pseudo-learning, which is retained for a short time only.

■ Guided Versus Free Inquiry

How much structure should be provided in inquiry situations? There should be enough to ensure that the student is successful in understanding the important implications of his studies.

If students have not had experience in learning through inquiry, initially they should be given considerable structure in their lessons. After they have gained some experience on how to conduct an investigation, the structure should then be lessened. In this text a general term *investigative* is used to include both discovery and inquiry teaching approaches. The term *guided discovery and inquiry* is used where there is considerable structure given and *free discovery and inquiry* indicates that there is little guidance provided by the instructor. Below is an example of a portion of a guided-inquiry lesson. Note that much of the planning is outlined by the teacher. The students, for example, do not originate the problem and considerable guidance is provided on how to set up and record the data. In a free-type lesson, the students may originate the problem and determine how to resolve it.

Guided Inquiry

In a guided inquiry approach the instructor provides the problem and encourages students to work out the procedures to resolve it. Examples of problems teachers might give to involve students in this type of process are:

1. How is algebra used in our community?
2. Given the story up to this point, how would you end it?
3. How would you write a poem to indicate your feeling about seeing the ocean?
4. What do you think about intermarriage?
5. How could you make a better salad dressing?
6. Here are some snails. Find out as much as possible about them.
7. Here is a pond and some apparatus. Find out as much as possible about how this pond changes over a year.
8. How could we make poetry more popular in our school?
9. A new highway is built through the jungles of Brazil and passes by an Indian village that has had little contact with modern civilization. What will happen?
10. Here is some apparatus for studying motion. Set it up in any way you choose to study the movement of an object.
11. How does using a different language change a person's perceptions of other cultures?
12. Here is some apparatus for studying circuits. Use it to find out as much as possible about circuits.
13. Do whatever you wish with this salt to determine its physical and chemical properties.
14. What should be done to improve the environment of our school?
15. Here is some water that is supposed to be polluted. How will you prove that it is?
16. If you were going to produce a piece of art to show contentment, what would you do and why?

In a guided inquiry plan students are encouraged to resolve problems similar to the preceding, either on their own or in groups. The teacher is available as a resource person, giving only enough aid to ensure that the students do not become too frustrated or experience failure. The assistance the teacher gives, however, should be in the form of questions he asks to help students think about possible investigative procedures. Ask students questions, giving them direction rather than telling them what to do. Good questions, given at the right time, may provide just the needed stimulus to cause the students to become more involved in creative investigation. Contrast this method with that of a teacher who says, "Study groups and tell how they are different." In the second instance the teacher has robbed the students of many opportunities for thought and creativeness.

Free Inquiry

After students have studied and learned how to attack a problem, gained sufficient knowledge about the subject, and performed modified inquiry, the instructor might invite them to become involved in free inquiry. This method differs from the modified approach in that the students identify what it is they would like to study. The following questions are suggested as a basis for this type of class activity:

1. If you were the teacher of this class and you were going to select the most exciting things to investigate this term, what would they be?
2. What are some problems related to our community that you would like to study?

1. What are the advantages and disadvantages of investigative types of teaching?
2. How can the investigative approach contribute to building students' self-concept?
3. What are "expectancy levels" and how might they be changed?

---

3. Now that you have studied, for example, salts, algae, light, heat, radiation, animal behaviors, etc., what problems can you come up with that you would like to investigate individually or in teams?

4. Now that you have finished this experiment, for example in population, what other experiments can you think of and which of them would you like to do?

5. When you see problems in the community, such as pollution, or some problem related to science that you would like to discuss, bring it to the class's attention.

6. What types of mathematical investigations would you like to conduct (e.g., determining the acceleration of a skier or a race-car driver)?

7. What authors would you like to read?

8. What biographies would you like to write or read?

9. What kind of play would you like to write, read, or produce?

■ Conditions for Inquiry Teaching

Suchman lists four conditions for good inquiry teaching.[12]

The first one he calls the "condition of freedom," meaning the freedom of learners to seek out desired information. They must be free to try out ideas and invent ways of accounting for what they see. This is the essence of the inquiry approach, that there is freedom to seek out the necessary information.

The second condition is the "condition of the responsive environment." A responsive environment is a classroom, a laboratory, or the outdoors on a field trip—anywhere that provides many opportunities for inquiry. It cannot be a sterile classroom or lecture hall. Teachers must have books, apparatus, experiments, aquaria, and many other things for students to work with. Inquiry can take place only in a responsive environment. The teacher must provide the information the students seek or she must provide the sources for that information. The teacher must make available a wide range of materials and facts from which the students can choose to meet their needs of the moment. This is the second important condition for inquiry teaching.

The third condition listed by Suchman is "the condition of focus." Inquiry is a purposeful activity, a search for greater meaning in some event, object, or condition that raises questions in the inquirer's mind. It is directed toward one goal, toward the solution of a problem. It is not scattered, the energies are not dissipated. This is what is meant by the condition of focus.

Suchman's fourth condition is "the condition of low pressure." Students will gain their reinforcement directly from the success of their own ideas in adding meaning to the environment or to their understanding of it. The teacher must respond positively to the student but neutrally to the product of the student's thinking. The teacher must recognize that not all students learn at the same rate. The condition of low pressure provides for students with different rates of learning to progress in the same classroom. Contemporary education sometimes defeats that purpose by putting too much emphasis on the class being 50 minutes long. The bell rings and the students must move to another class, which emphasizes educational uniformity. There is very little opportunity for teachers to provide for different rates of learning.

When you teach by inquiry, there are several important elements of an inquiry lesson that need to be followed. The basic elements of such a plan are described below:

- *The Problem:* This is the basic requirement and meets the "condition of focus" described by Suchman. If at all possible, the problem should be real, meaningful, and capable of study. If the problem can be elicited from the class, so much the better. A practical substitute, however, is one identified by the teacher and elaborated for the class.

- *The Background Information:* Some means must be found to provide the necessary information to put the class on a fairly common level of understanding. This may be in the form of a brief class discussion, some common reading matter, a textbook, or a preliminary experiment to give general understanding to all members of the class.

- *The Materials:* This refers to Suchman's "condition of a responsive environment." Provisions must be made to have adequate quantities of materials at hand, opportunities for individual work with the materials, and a chance for students to choose the materials they will need to solve the problem.

- *The Guiding Questions:* This consists of an anticipated list of questions to be asked by the teacher to direct the thought processes of the students. Prepare a skeleton outline of these but allow for ample deviation from the basic list in order to provide for student input.

- *The Hypotheses:* These should be formulated as a result of the discussions and the guiding questions. Permit a "condition of freedom" so as not to inhibit discussion.

- *The Data Gathering and Analysis:* This is the hands-on, experimental part of the inquiry lesson. Permit a "condition of low pressure" here to allow for mistakes and repeats. Emphasize record-keeping and a systematic approach to the problem.

- *The Conclusion:* This refers to the closure and should culminate in some final result based on the experimentation and discussion. Group conclusions are acceptable.

■ Research Findings about Using Investigative Teaching Approaches

Although the research findings still need further investigation, particularly concerning how students vary in feelings about the different approaches (affectivity) and the development of more than just subject-matter achievement differences, i.e., "multi-talents," "self-concept," etc., they do indicate that investigative approaches have been successful. Dr. Shulman, as a result of a Conference on Learning by Discovery, summarizes the research in discovery as follows: "In the published studies, guided discovery treatments generally have done well both at the level of immediate learning and later transfer."[13]

An early study of inquiry teaching was a three-year longitudinal one to determine the differences this type of teaching made on the learning behavior of students. Investigators at Carnegie-Mellon University found that an inquiry-oriented social studies curriculum significantly increased students' abilities to inquire about human affairs, compared to those studying noninquiry materials.[14] This study is important because it shows that inquiry teaching over a prolonged period (three years) can help individuals become better investigators. When teachers first begin to use this approach, they often become frustrated

and think they are not making sufficient progress. These instructors suffer from a "covering" compulsion; they feel better as teachers if they cover something because they have a mistaken idea of the function of teaching. They are surprised to learn that often students do not assimilate material covered by lecture (see Figure 12.1).

Highly significant research concerning inquiry teaching has been completed using meta-analysis (the analysis of previous analytical studies using a common statistical framework).[15] This meta-research involved a careful study of 25 years of research comparing student performance in "new" science curricula (post-Sputnik) to student performance in traditional courses.

Five measures were used in the comparison—achievement, attitudes, process, analytic abilities, and related skills. On a composite basis across all junior high and senior high school curricula in science, the average student in the new science curricula exceeded the performance of 64 percent of the students in traditional courses. This consistent pattern of positive effects clearly established the superiority of the new curricula over traditional courses.

Students' achievement scores were effectively raised 9–14 percentile points when the students were placed in a classroom using a new program.

Although inquiry teaching should receive a major emphasis in science teaching, not everything can or should be taught by inquiry. For example, for students to learn the names of chemical compounds, they must memorize them. If you want students to learn how to handle and use a microscope, you will probably have to show them. If there are safety precautions to be aware of, the instructor must tell the students about them.

You, as a teacher, will have to establish a value system and use it as a guide in determining when you will or will not teach something by inquiry. The preceding section should give you some assistance in evolving your philosophy in this respect.

■ Summary

Many of the modern curriculum materials for the middle and secondary school are discovery- and inquiry-oriented. In discovery teaching, a student uses his mind to gain insights into some concept or principle. In the process of discovering, an individual performs such mental operations as measuring, predicting, observing, inferring, classifying, etc. In inquiry, an individual may use all of the discovery mental processes plus those characterizing a mature adult such as formulating problems, hypothesizing, designing experiments, synthesizing knowledge, and

Non-Inquiry	Inquiry
Teacher covers more BUT Less is retained	Teacher covers less BUT More is retained

Teacher Orientation	Teacher Orientation
Views students as a reservoir of knowledge, subject-centered. Teachers have covering compulsion. The more they cover, the better they think they are.	More holistic view of the learner, student-centered. Teachers more interested in cognitive and creative growth. Teach for the development of multi-talents in helping students develop their self-concepts.

FIGURE 12–1
Differences between inquiry and noninquiry teaching

demonstrating such attitudes as objectivity, curiosity, open-mindedness, and respect for theoretical models, values, and attitudes. Discovery and inquiry teaching may vary from a relatively structured approach where considerable guidance is provided by the instructor to free investigation where the students originate problems.

Why use these investigative approaches? The philosophical and psychological advantages appear to be many. These methods increase intellectual potency; cause a shift from extrinsic to intrinsic rewards; help students learn how to investigate; increase memory retention; make instruction student-centered, thereby contributing to a person's "self-concept"; increase expectancy levels; develop multiple, not just academic talents; avoid learning only on the verbal level; and allow more time for students to assimilate and accommodate information.

Although there is a need to further assess the value of these approaches, particularly relative to attitudes, values, and self-concept attainment, there is much evidence that students taught by these methods perform significantly better on cognitive tasks involving critical thinking than those taught by traditional instruction.

Teachers often suffer from a covering syndrome. If they cover the material, they feel that their responsibility as teachers has been met. Because a teacher covers something is little assurance that students learned it. Student-centered instruction, because it often requires more time, results in less covering than does traditional teaching. The retention and critical-thinking ability of students in investi-gative-oriented classes, however, has been found to be greater.

■ References

1. Pinchas Tamir, "Inquiry and the Science Teacher," *Science Education*, 67, no. 5, (1983), pp. 657–672.
2. Richard Suchman, *Developing Inquiry* (Chicago: Science Research Associates, 1966).
3. Norris Harms and Robert Yager, "Project Synthesis," *What Research Says to the Science Teacher*, NSTA, 3, (1981), pp. 53–72.
4. *Science Education for the 80s*, 1, (Washington, D.C.: NSTA, 1979).
5. Leopold Klopfer, "The Teaching of Science and the History of Science," *Journal of Research in Science Teaching*, no. 6, (1969).
6. Carlton H. Stedman, "Fortuitous Strategies on Inquiry in the Good Ole Days," *Science Education*, 71, no. 5 (1987), pp. 657–665.
7. Stedman, "Fortuitous Strategies," pp. 657–665.
8. Wayne Welch, Leopold Klopfer, Glen Aikenhead, and J.T. Robinson, "The Role of Inquiry in Science Education: Analysis and Recommendations," *Science Education*, 65, no. 1 (1981), pp. 33–50.
9. J.T. Wilson, "Processes of Scientific Inquiry: A Model for Teaching and Learning Science," *Science Education*, 58, no. 1 (1974).
10. K.D. Peterson, "Scientific Inquiry for High School Students," *Journal of Research in Science Teaching*, 15, no. 2 (1978), pp. 153–59.
11. William Kyle, Jr. "The Distinction Between Inquiry and Scientific Inquiry and Why High School Students Should be Cognizant of the Distinction," *Journal of Research in Science Teaching*, 17, no. 2 (1980), pp. 123–30.

12. Suchman, *Developing Inquiry.*
13. Lee S. Shulman, "Psychological Controversies in the Teaching of Science and Mathematics," *Science Teacher* (September 1968), p. 90.
14. John M. Good, John U. Forley, and Edwin Featon, "Developing Inquiry Skills With an Experimental Social Studies Curriculum," *Journal of Educational Research,* 63, no. 1, (September 1969), p. 35.
15. James A. Shymansky, William C. Kyle, Jr., and Jennifer M. Alport, "The Effects of New Science Curricula on Student Performance," *Journal of Research in Science Teaching,* 20, no. 5 (1983), pp. 387–404.

====== **INVESTIGATING SCIENCE TEACHING** ======

ACTIVITY 12–1

Am I an Inquiry Teacher?

In the space provided indicate the degree to which you do what is described in the statement. Use the numbers 4 (regularly), 3 (frequently), 2 (sometimes), and 1 (seldom) to make your response.

_____   1. I focus on lessons involving exploration of significant problems that can be investigated at many levels of sophistication.

_____   2. I prepare for a broad range of alternative ideas and values which the students may raise, related to a central topic.

_____   3. I select materials and learning experiences to stimulate student curiosity and support student investigation.

_____   4. I make available a wide variety of resources and material for student use.

_____   5. Skill building exercises are tied directly to ongoing learning where they can be utilized and applied.

_____   6. My introductory lessons present some problem, question, contradiction, or unknown element that will maximize student thinking.

_____   7. My aim is for students to react freely to the introductory stimulus with little direction from me.

_____   8. I encourage many different responses to a given introductory stimulus and am prepared to deal with alternative patterns of exploration.

_____   9. The students talk more than I do.

_____ 10. Students are free to discuss and interchange their ideas.

_____ 11. When I talk, I "question," I do not "tell."

_____ 12. I consciously use the ideas students have raised and base my statements and questions on their ideas.

_____ 13. I redirect student questions in such a way that students are encouraged to arrive at their own answers.

_____ 14. My questions are intended to lead the pupils to explore, explain, support, and evaluate their ideas.

_____ 15. I encourage the students to evaluate the adequacy of grounds provided for statements made by them or by others.

_____ 16. My students gain understanding and practice in logical and scientific processes of acquiring, validating, and using knowledge.

_____ 17. My questions lead the students to test the validity of their ideas in a broad context of experience.

_____ 18. I encourage students to move from examination of particular cases to more generalized concepts and understandings.

_____ 19. I emphasize learning and the use of ideas, rather than managerial functions, such as discipline and recordkeeping.

_____ 20. I allow for flexible seating, student movement, and maximum student use of materials and resources.

_____ 21. Class dialogue is conducted in an orderly fashion that emphasizes courtesy and willingness to listen to each person's ideas.

_____ 22. Students are actively involved in the planning and maintenance of the total classroom environments.

_____ 23. I foster balanced participation by encouraging the more reticent students to take an active role in classroom activities.

_____ 24. I encourage and reward the free exchange and testing of ideas.

_____ 25. I avoid criticizing or judging ideas offered by students.

_____ 26. Each student's contribution is considered legitimate and important.

_____ 27. I evaluate students on growth in many aspects of the learning experience, rather than simply on the basis of facts required.

_____ 28. I emphasize that concepts, social issues, policy decisions, attitudes, and values are legitimate areas for discussion.

_____ 29. All topics are critically examined, not "taught" as closed issues with a single "right" solution.

_____ 30. Use of unfounded, emotionally charged language is minimized in discussing attitudes and values.

_____ 31. I encourage students to explore the implications of holding alternative values and policy positions.

_____ 32. I make the students aware of personal and social bases for diversity in attitudes, values, and policies.

_____ 33. I encourage the students to arrive at value and policy positions of their own that they understand and defend.

To find your score, total the numbers at the heads of the columns over each item you checked. A total of 50 or less means lots of room for improvement; 51–84, you're coming along; 86–110, you're better than most; 111–136, you've mastered inquiry techniques.

CHAPTER 13

Discussion as a Means of Inquiry

An excellent model for leading a discussion is a clever talk show host. What is it that such a person does to stimulate the interesting, even exciting discussions that frequently are held on radio and television programs?

A number of clues can be found in the manner in which the host conducts the show—both in preparation and during the show itself. While each is different, certain common elements can be seen. A good talk show host:

1. studies the topic before the show
2. presents an interesting background analysis before eliciting comments from the participants
3. relaxes his guests
4. avoids embarrassing anyone
5. keeps the discussion moving at a good pace
6. rewords any comments that might be misunderstood
7. prevents anyone from monopolizing the discussion or going off on a tangent
8. encourages the participants to speak about their feelings
9. uses humor to reduce tension
10. asks good questions of a divergent variety[1]

With these guidelines, a teacher can conduct a similarly interesting discussion that will stimulate students to open up and participate. There is no dearth of interesting topics in science to bring up for discussion, particularly now that the interrelationships of science to technology and society are fair game for discussion in science classes.

■ Advantages of Discussion

Students become more interested because they are involved. Discussion is a more desirable approach for class procedures. Since an objective of modern science instruction is to teach science as a process with emphasis on the cognitive development of the individual, students must have time and opportunities to think. Thinking is something one does! A student can't think unless he is given opportunities to do so. The presentation of problems in a discussion requires students to think before they can formulate answers. A teacher who tells students all about a subject offers no problem to the student but boredom. In addition, the students have been robbed of an opportunity to use their minds. All they have to do is soak up information and memorize it.

Discussion is more likely to develop inquiry behavior. A discussion leader interested in developing inquiring behavior seldom gives answers but asks questions instead. In answering questions, students learn to evaluate, analyze, and synthesize knowledge. They are often thrilled to discover fundamental ideas for themselves.

The teacher receives feedback. A discussion gives feedback to the teacher. An astute discussion leader learns quickly from the student comments how much they comprehend of the topic. She then guides the discussion, moving it rapidly when students understand the information and slowing it down when they have difficulty. A lecture-oriented teacher seldom knows what students are comprehending. She may concentrate on a point that the class understands or speed through information that few understand. One of the greatest mistakes a beginning teacher can make is to assume that the lecture method will work well in a secondary school.

■ How to Lead a Discussion

Leading a discussion is an art that is not easily learned. There is nothing more exciting than to see a master teacher conducting an interesting and exciting discussion. How can you bring students to this point? Excellent class discussions do not just happen. The inexperienced instructor may think she will walk into a class and talk about a subject "off the top of her head." After all, doesn't she know more about the subject than the students? It's true she may know about the material, but she is faced with the problem of helping students discover it and develop their talents. This process requires as much preparation as any other class procedure. The first step in preparing for a discussion is to determine what it is you wish to accomplish, i.e., your objectives. Next, outline questions you think may help students to reach these objectives. A good discussion leader uses the "What do you think?" approach to learning. She asks questions such as were suggested in the chapter on questioning. For example she might ask:

1. Why did you do this experiment?
2. What did the data show?
3. Why did you use this approach?
4. How would you go about finding answers to this problem?
5. How else could you find the answer?
6. What good is this answer for your daily life?
7. What mental steps did you make in solving the problem?
8. How many variables were involved in the experiment?
9. How do you feel about science?

Spend Time Analyzing Thought Processes

Every discussion should stimulate critical and creative thinking. You should spend time analyzing the types of questions you will ask in a discussion to ensure that they require the exercise of these abilities. In this way you will indicate to your students a belief in their *becoming* more exciting persons and will contribute positively to their expectancy level about critical thinking. Showing students that they are performing relatively sophisticated mental operations, i.e. inferring, hypothesizing, evaluating data, etc., will encourage them to accept the idea that they can use their minds to derive answers to relatively sophisticated problems. We come to believe that we are good thinkers only being successful in thinking and by receiving feedback about our thinking abilities from others. Futhermore, a teacher builds positive student self-concepts when she involves students in tasks requiring thinking and shows them how they are developing their minds. An actual inquiry discussion might follow these steps.

Present a problem such as, "What is the lifetime of a burning candle?" Encourage students to formulate hypotheses or give evidence for answers to the questions. For example, say an apparatus is set up as follows: a burning candle is placed upright in a pan in which there is some water, and the candle is then covered with a glass container. Show how the experiment is set up by projecting a transparency of it on a screen. Some types of questions to ask are: What will happen to the candle when it is covered? What else will happen to the apparatus as this is done? What would happen if the candle were lengthened, the size of the jar above it were increased, or the amount of water in the container holding the candle were decreased? How would you find out?

After the students have progressed this far, have some student reflect back on what has been said and summarize the good points of the discussion. As a discussion leader, you might at times have to assist a student in doing this by repeating: "What was the problem?" Review the cognitive processes they used in solving the problem. Ask: "What hypotheses were made?" "What was the best hypothesis and why?" "How were the conclusions reached?" "On what are they based?" "What is required to make better conclusions?"

Questions Must Be Directed at the Students' Level

A neophyte discussion leader often starts a discussion with too difficult a question. If there is no response to a question, the teacher should rephrase it to make it simpler or less complex. This procedure may have to be followed several times before there is a response. A question implies an answer. If the question is too vague the students may not respond; rephrasing a question may give them some insight. Leading a discussion by questioning without giving answers is a skill which brings great satisfaction, but to be an astute questioner requires practice and a keen awareness of the students' comprehension. By her questions, the sophisticated discussion leader can guide students toward understanding the concepts and principles involved in the lesson or experiment. The questions must be deep enough to re-

=========== **GUEST EDITORIAL** ===========

Thoughts on Science Teaching

Beth Schwarzman
Geologist and Director--Minority Participation in Earth
Science
U.S. Geological Survey
Menlo Park, California

Teaching can be fun and tremendously rewarding—if you like it. If you don't like it, be a computer programmer; there's lots more money in it. Students are very aware of your attitude, and if you are enthusiastic about what you are doing, eventually the enthusiasm will spread.

When I teach, I try to do three things with the students in the class:

1. I try to let them find out that science is something they can do. In approaching a subject with the frightening aura of "science," it is very important that the students do not feel overwhelmed or inadequate. I try to set up the lesson so that they can succeed and feel successful. I think it is of particular importance that they learn to feel comfortable with the processes of observation, comparison, and drawing conclusions.

2. I always give them things to handle, things to look at closely, and things to deal with on their own. Lectures work well at times, but if students don't have a chance to see and experience scientific principles for themselves, they will find them less interesting and understand them less well. It is somewhat harder to set up a lesson this way but very worthwhile.

3. As often as I can, especially with younger students, I have them take home something which is relevant to the subject under study, on the proviso that they tell someone (a little brother, a grandmother, a friend, or anyone they can get to listen) what it is they have brought home and why it is important.

Until schools teach them that other pursuits are more fun, learning is what children do for a living. Even if they have been turned off to learning things in school, children are hungry to learn about the world around them which, after all, is science. By science, I do not mean concepts such as Cambrian, Ordovician, and Silurian or vertebrates and invertebrates, useful as these mental constructs can be to organize our knowledge, but rather the real answers to children's questions, such as why earthquakes happen and how the leopard got his spots. The real hows and whys are what got you and me interested in science and they hold the same appeal for students in school today.

I was reminded that students are turned on to science when I was crossing a schoolyard recently and a couple of students came up to me, wanting to know if I was the science lady. I answered that I was and was immediately challenged with, "Okay, give us some science." What could I do? I'm a geologist and I was standing in the middle of a paved playground and I didn't even have any rocks in my pocket! It seemed important to respond to their request: I felt as though I were representing SCIENCE to them and didn't dare fail. So I grabbed at a straw and asked if they had ever really seen their fingerprints. We talked about the similarities and differences among our fingerprints and they found out that they could learn something about the world just by looking.

I teach in many classrooms every year as a resource person. I have made teaching a part of my job with the U.S. Geological Survey because I really like teaching science. That is one of my major pieces of advice to potential teachers: do it only if you like it.

I enjoy teaching science, at least in part because the students enjoy it too. I believe that any teacher who gives children something real to learn and who has an enthusiasm for teaching will find that students will enjoy learning.

---

quire critical thinking rather than a simple yes or no answer.

Eye contact is an important aspect in leading a discussion. A teacher's eyes should sweep a class, constantly looking for boredom, a student with an answer or a question, or one with a puzzled look. Eye contact gives the instructor feedback and motivates students to think and participate in the discussion. It also shows that you are more interested in the students than in the information being covered.

A Discussion Started in a Novel Way Gains Attention

A motivational technique useful in beginning a discussion is to start it with an interesting demonstration. For example, a vial of blood placed on a demonstration desk can stimulate questions, leading to a discussion of blood or the circulatory system. Burning a candle can lead to a discussion of several scientific concepts and principles. A good rule to follow is to start a discussion with a percept or observation whenever possible. Not all discussions will lend themselves to this procedure but those that involve the discovery of a concept almost always do. (See, for example, the "Teaching Science Activity: Using a Demonstration to Initiate Discussion—The Rubber Band Wheel," p. 453–454.)

Use Overhead Projectors When Appropriate

The use of overhead projection with transparencies helps concentrate the class's attention on clarifying a problem. For example, focusing students' attention on some of the approaches to devising a classification scheme can be done easily with an overhead projection. Use different-colored acetate cut to various sizes and shapes and ask students how they would group the materials. A discussion can arise from the demonstration of such cognitive processes as analysis, discrimination, and ordering. Another demonstration using the overhead projector might include a discussion of magnetism and magnetic lines of force; using a magnet and iron fillings sprinkled on top of transparent plastic sets the stage for a discussion of the properties of magnetism.

■ General Rules for Leading a Large Group Discussion

Some general rules to follow in using discussions are:

1. Create an atmosphere in the class in which questions are not only welcomed but *expected*. Be warm, open, and receptive.
2. As much as possible, include students' interests.
3. When you give reinforcement, do it positively as often as you can. Use very little negative feedback. Say: "That's a good answer." "That's right,

you have the idea." "Good, you're thinking; keep it up." "You have something there." "Who would like to react to this answer?" Do not ignore the students; always give some recognition to their answers. No response by the teacher should be a form of negative feedback. If students have the wrong answer, do not say: "That's wrong," "No, that answer is no good." But rather say: "Well, that is not quite right." "You may have something there but I am not sure I understand the point," or "Good, you are thinking; but that is not what I was leading up to."
4. When you encourage a student to think, evaluate the product on the basis of his level of comprehension. Even when you, with a more extensive background, are aware that the idea given is either incomplete or incorrect, accept it or even praise it if it indicates that the student has made effective use of the information he was expected to know at that stage of the course.
5. Praise a student for being a good listener when he calls attention to a mistake you have made.
6. When leading a discussion, try to remember previous comments and interrelate them. If at all possible, give recognition by referring to the name of the student who made the comment. For example, a teacher in responding to the idea of a student says, "Joan believes that there are other factors besides temperature determining the rate of expansion of a metal. George has just suggested that possibly humidity and air pressure may have a minor effect." The teacher has acted as a summarizer for two students' views and has given them recognition by using their names.
7. Maintain a positive and accepting attitude. Your attitude in leading a discussion does much to determine the quality of that discussion. If you walk into a class feeling and looking very glum and with the weight of the discussion on your shoulders, the students' response will be mild. However, if you start a discussion with the attitude that you and the students are going to have fun wrestling with ideas, the response is more likely to be impressive. In leading a discussion with adolescents, you must be able to laugh at yourself; discreet use of humor captures interest and gains participation.
8. When questions arise for which science does not yet provide an adequate explanation, state that, as yet, there is no answer. This gives students insight into avenues of research which we still need to explore.
9. When necessary, restate a student's answer before going on to your next remarks. Doing so often gives other students time to think about their answers.

=== REFLECTING ON SCIENCE TEACHING ===

Discussions

1. What are the advantages of discussion over lecture?
2. How can a discussion be used as an approach to inquiry?
3. How can you motivate students during a discussion?
4. Choose some topic and outline how you would present it in a discussion.

---

10. Call on both students who are willing to answer and those who are not.
11. Do not rush discussions. Remember that the major reason for having them is to give students time to think. When there is silence during a discussion, this may be the period where most of the thinking is going on. Remember that a desirable wait-time averages five seconds.

Breaking the class into smaller groups can also provide variety. A sample design for this type of discussion is found in the "Teaching Science Activity: Small Group Problem Solving," on page 454.

■ Special Precautions in Leading a Discussion

At times the following suggestions are proper, but the teacher should give serious consideration to their potential disadvantages as well:

1. Toss a question back to a class when it is asked of you. Have another student repeat the question in its entirety. Ask a student to speak up so that the entire class can hear. Ask a student to research an answer to the question on his own.
2. Encourage the entire class to take notes.
3. Avoid the appearance of carrying on a private conversation with the person who asked the question.
4. Deliberately let your eyes roam over the entire class while giving the answer.
5. Use questions requiring hypothesis formation.
6. Avoid sarcasm.
7. Encourage students to seek recognition before answering or have them be courteous of another and wait until that person finishes before they respond.
8. Do not let students make derogatory remarks about another student's question or answer, since this is demeaning to the person.
9. Suggest an individual conference with the student when:

a. The degree of difficulty in answering is greater than that expected of the class as a whole.
b. The subject matter involved bears little relation to the key ideas being stressed.
c. The answer is both detailed and lengthy.
d. The time spent in answering the question may destroy the sequence of thought being developed.

■ Special Discussion Techniques

Invitations to Inquiry

In its *Biology Teacher's Handbook*, the Biology Science Curriculum Study gives forty-four class-discussion outlines under the title "Invitations to Inquiry." The main purpose of these outlines is to involve students in the strategies of solving scientific problems—not to teach science subject matter. The invitations engage students in the process of solving problems in the way that scientists are engaged. A typical outline for an invitation is given below.

Format for an Invitation

1. Present a problem to the students.
2. Ask how they would go about solving it.
3. Describe the actual experimental design used by the scientist.
4. Ask the students what they would hypothesize about the experimental results.
5. Give the students the data the scientists collected.
6. Ask: "What conclusions can you make about these data?"
7. Ask: "If you were the scientist, what would be your next problem and why?"

BSCS authors state, in regard to invitations, "The primary aim is an understanding of enquiry. It is mainly for the sake of this aim that the active participation of the student is invoked. Both practical experience and experimental study indicate that con-

---

REFLECTING ON SCIENCE TEACHING

Evaluating Discussions

1. How does an inquiry discussion differ from one used to summarize?
2. What are some things that tend to stifle discussion?
3. What does your attitude have to do with setting the stage for a good discussion?
4. Why do students sometimes test your judgment while you are leading a discussion?
5. How can you indicate that you have good judgment?
6. What should you do when you don't know the answer to a problem?

---

cepts are understood best and retained longest when the student contributes to his own understanding."[2]

You can easily make your own "invitations." The steps are as follows:

1. Decide what your science processes and subject-matter objectives are.
2. State a problem related to your objectives. The idea for problems can come from actual scientific research reported in journals.
3. Devise questions which give students opportunities to set up experiments, make hypotheses, analyze and synthesize, and record data. Stress the understanding of science as a process and the cognitive skills involved.
4. Write the invitation as a series of steps. In different sections, insert additional information to help the student progress in depth into the topic or methods of research.
5. Evaluate your invitation, comparing it with the science-process list on page 000 and rewrite it to include more of these processes.

Invitations to inquiry can be written for various levels of learning. As much as possible, they should stress the development of the students' cognitive abilities. In addition to the science processes, students should also learn the necessity for having a control, understand cause-and-effect relationships, learn when to use quantitative data and how to interpret it, learn the role of argument and inference in the design of experiments, and so on.

Write an invitation! Your first invitation probably won't be very sophisticated, but in the process of writing it you will gain insight into how to construct them plus a better understanding of how to involve students in understanding science as a process.

Pictorial Riddles

Another technique for developing motivation and interest in a discussion is to use pictorial riddles, that is, pictures or drawings made by the teacher to elicit student response. A riddle is drawn on the chalkboard or on poster board or is projected from a transparency, and the teacher asks a question about the picture.

Pictorial riddles are relatively easy to devise. They can be as simple or as complex as a teacher desires. In devising a riddle, an instructor should go through the following steps:

1. Select some concept or principle he wishes to teach or emphasize.
2. Draw a picture or show an illustration that demonstrates the concept.
3. An alternate procedure is to change something in a picture and ask students to find out what is wrong in the picture. An example might be a picture of a large child being held up on a seesaw by a small child. Ask, "How is this possible?" Or show a farming community in which all of the ecological principles are misapplied and ask what is wrong with what has been done in the community.
4. Devise a series of questions, related to the picture, which will help students gain insights into the principles involved.

There are two general types of pictorial riddles. The first type shows an actual situation. The instuctor asks why the situation occurred. Figure 13.1 is of this type. In the second type the teacher manipulates something in a drawing or a series of drawings and then asks what is wrong with the di-

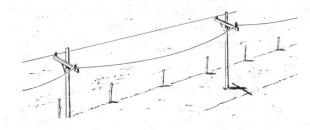

FIGURE 13–1
Pictorial riddle (physical science)

agram. Figure 13.2 is an example of this type. Some questions that might be asked about each riddle follow each picture.

1. What do you notice about the things in this picture?
2. What is similar in the picture?
3. Why do the fence and the telephone line appear to be similar?
4. Why would you expect the two telephone lines to be the same?
5. What do you think is the season of the year for each line and why?
6. What does temperature have to do with the appearance of the telephone lines and why?
7. At what time of year would you expect to see the sagging telephone line and why?

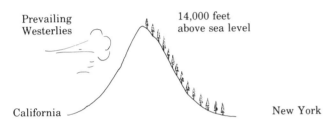

FIGURE 13–2
Pictorial riddle (biology)

1. What questions can you ask about this riddle?
2. What is wrong with this diagram?
3. Where do pine trees grow?
4. Why do they grow where they do?
5. If you were going to change the riddle to make it more accurate, what would you do and why?
6. What does the wind have to do with the ecology of the area?
7. Where would you expect to find the most and the least amount of vegetation on the mountain? Why?
8. How could you change this riddle to teach some additional science concepts?

A format for a riddle which lends itself particularly well to overhead projection is the before-and-after type of riddle. Students are shown a diagram or picture, some factor is then altered, and the students are shown another picture of the same situation after modification. The student is to hypothesize what happened in the before situation to reach the modification shown in the after diagram. Figure 13.3 shows some examples of before-and-after riddles.

The riddle in Figure 13.4 is constructed like the face of a clock. The arms are turned to different or-

ganisms and the class is asked what the ecological relationships are between them.

Riddles may be prepared from many types of materials, such as photographs and Polaroid 35 mm slides, magazine pictures, diagrams, cartoons, greeting cards, and objects.

Other Techniques to Motivate Discussion

Case Histories
Another technique to motivate discussion is to use case histories in science. These histories tell stories about the development of some science concepts. The instructor may tell the students part of what was done and then ask what they think was the next step. Case histories can be constructed from a classic experiment in the history of science.

Covers of Science Magazines
An activity to supplement a science lesson can be constructed around magazine covers depicting various aspects of science. *Science*, the journal of the American Association for the Advancement of Science, has some very interesting covers which lend themselves well to this approach. The instructor holds the cover picture up and asks questions to give students hints about the topic represented.

The Magic Circle as a Facilitator of Discussion
The magic circle is another means of stimulating discussions in the science classroom. The magic circle is simply a teaching technique designed to develop listening and communication skills, an awareness of self-worth, and an interest in and respect for other peoples' ideas.

To promote these objectives it is necessary to:

1. Ask questions about which students will have personal feelings. For example, ask humanistic questions ("How do you feel about . . .").
2. Ask divergent questions so that a variety of responses can be made.
3. You, the teacher, must positively reinforce statements made by the students so that they will feel that their contribution is worthwhile and that they, as people, are valuable and able to achieve success.
4. The other students should be encouraged to listen to the speaker. Students should also reinforce what the speaker has said with their own ideas and experiences so that the entire discussion is a sharing session.

Creativity
Teaching "creatively" is another means of stimulating discussion. Exactly what teaching creatively

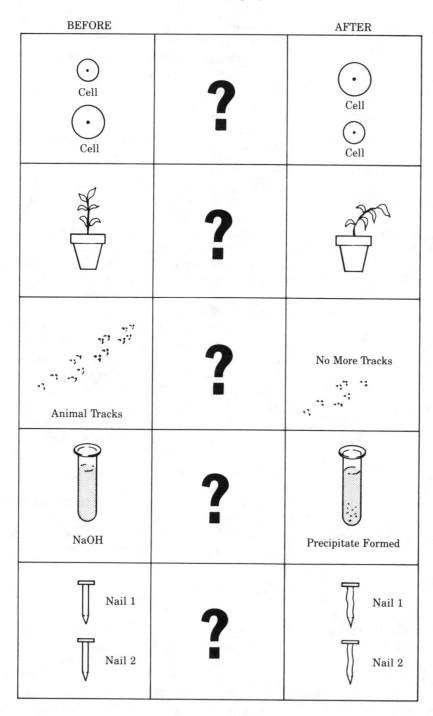

FIGURE 13–3
Sequential pictorial riddles.
Can you supply the missing form?

means is difficult to say. To get at the meaning and value of creative teaching, consider the following questions:

1. What is creativity?
2. Do you perceive of yourself as a creative individual? Why do you feel this way? How can you use creativity in the classroom?
3. When you have used creative teaching methods, what has been the response of your students?
4. How did they feel about their experience?
5. How did you feel about using creative teaching techniques in the classroom?
6. How might creative teaching be used in the science classroom?
7. How can we help the students to be more creative in their thinking?
8. What, if any, are the limitations of creative teaching?
9. What are the advantages and disadvantages of creative teaching?
10. If you had the choice of studying in a creative

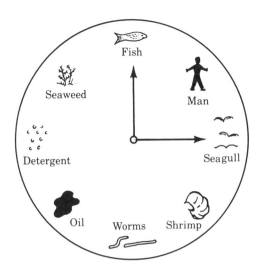

FIGURE 13–4
Riddles to show relationships

versus a noncreative classroom, which would you choose? Explain your answer.

11. Select any topic which you traditionally teach in your classroom. How could you make the teaching of that topic more creative?

12. What are some ideas for creative teaching techniques you have used in your classroom?

13. If a student teacher were to ask you about teaching creatively, what would your response be? Would you recommend trying some creative ideas?

14. If you believe creativity is important in education, how might you encourage a traditionalist to give this method a try?

Discussion as a Technique of Review

All of the preceding discussion techniques can be used to good advantage for class review. Discussion may also be used as an excellent review for laboratory work. After an instructor has had a class conduct several experiments in a unit, she should take time to discuss the conclusions that can be drawn from the laboratory work. Consideration should also be given as to how the information was obtained, what types of problem-solving and cognitive behaviors were involved in determining the answers, and what assurance the students have that their information is correct. A discussion of this type can do much to reinforce learning and divide the trivia from the really important aspects of learning.

The One-Word Type of Review
The one-word approach may be used to involve all the students in the review process. After students

have read, seen a film, performed a laboratory exercise, or been involved in other types of investigative work, ask them to write their impressions in one word. These words should then be passed to the front of the class and several of them should be written on the board. The students should then be asked to explain why they wrote their words. After they give their explanations, they should then be asked to take any three words and construct a sentence. This technique provides an excellent review of the material and involves all the students.

Learning to Lead a Good Discussion Never Ends
A teacher never quite perfects her ability as a discussion leader, but she should never stop trying to improve this ability. Excellence in discussion comes only with wisdom, not only in subject matter but in learning how to develop talents and self-concepts. For a dedicated teacher, there is probably no greater satisfaction than to walk out of class knowing that she has developed the students' mental abilities to the point where her presence is practically unneeded except as an organizer. To acquire this facility requires preparation and constant self-analysis, but it is one of the intellectual satisfactions that come only with good teaching.

■ Summary

The lecture method should play a relatively minor role in instruction in the secondary schools. Inquiry discussions motivate students and involve them more in cognitive processes than do lectures. There are definite techniques to be used in leading inquiry-oriented discussions. Primarily the instructor should question and give minimal information; the type of question asked by the teacher helps students discover the concept or principles involved in the learning situation. To lead a good discussion requires extensive preparation. The leader should know the objectives she wishes to attain, have a series of relevant questions outlined, and spend time at the end of the discussion analyzing how the conclusions were reached. Part of the discussion should be devoted to reflecting on the thought processes used in arriving at the conclusions. In this way, better understanding and development of the cognitive processes are ensured.

A discussion leader should give as much positive reinforcement as possible. She should compliment students on good ideas and suggestions and never deride or make sarcastic remarks about poor suggestions. Regardless of the answers given in a discussion, the teacher should try to react positively to the participants; ignoring a response is a poor procedure. Eye contact is important as a motivator and a means of receiving feedback. A good method of starting a discussion is to use a demonstration or overhead projection pertaining to a subject or topic of interest to the student. In leading the discussion, attempt to recall previous comments and interrelate the suggestions with the names of the individuals who made them. Remember that students will occasionally test your judgment to determine your competence as a teacher.

Some special techniques used in stimulating discussion are invitations to inquiry, a single-topic film, pictorial riddles, case histories in science, questions organized around covers of science magazines, and the magic circle technique. All of these methods can be used to suggest open-ended experiments if students are aware of the factors involved in experimentation. Discussion is also an excellent vehicle for review, both in class and laboratory work. The one-word approach may be used to involve all the students in the review process.

■ References

1. Jeff Passe, "Phil Donahue: An Excellent Model for Leading a Discussion" *Journal of Teacher Education*, 35, no. 1/43 (January/February, 1984).
2. Joseph J. Schwab et al., in *Biology Teachers' Handbook* 3d ed., ed. William U. Mayer (New York: Wiley & Sons, 1978), p. 47.

═════════════ **INVESTIGATING SCIENCE TEACHING** ═════════════

ACTIVITY 13–1

Invitations to Inquiry

1. Write an invitation to inquiry and classify the science processes you are requiring on the right.

2. How can an invitation to inquiry be used to suggest some open-ended experiments?

3. How is a single-topic film used as a method of inquiry? How does it differ from the traditional film?

ACTIVITY 13–2

Using Pictorial Riddles

1. Prepare a before and after type of riddle.

2. Prepare a riddle using a cartoon.

3. Describe an assignment where you would use the "one-word approach."

4. What are case histories and how may they be used?

5. What is the main role of an inquiry-discussion leader?

## CHAPTER 14

Demonstration and Laboratory Work

In the first-period general-science class, Mr. O'Brien took a candle out of a box and placed it on the demonstration desk. He told the class he would show them the difference between a physical and chemical change. He struck a match and placed the candle over the flame until the wick burned. Soon, some of the wax was melting, dripping, and then solidifying. He said, "This is an example of a physical change. The candle is partially burning and the wax is changed in the process of burning to carbon dioxide and water. This is a chemical change." The students watched the demonstration and some wrote notes in their notebooks.

Across the hall, Mr. Jackson was teaching the same unit. He also wanted to have students learn about physical and chemical changes. Mr. Jackson was not certain how he was going to do this. He asked Mr. O'Brien if he knew a good demonstration to show these changes. Mr. O'Brien suggested he burn a candle. Mr. Jackson, however, taught these concepts differently. After the bell rang and the students were seated, he took a candle and a match box out of his demonstration desk, placed them on top of the desk, and asked, "What am I going to do with the candle and match?"

Art answered, "You are going to light it."

Mr. Jackson replied, "That's right, but what will happen to the match and candle when I light them? How will they vary? What will happen to the candle when it burns? Will it drip?"

Several students raised their hands and suggested answers to his questions. He lit the candle and it started to drip. He asked, "Why does the candle drip? What will happen if we try to burn the dripped material? Where did the dripped material come from and how did it change while the candle was burning?"

George explained that the material merely melted and then solidified. Mr. Jackson asked the rest of the class what they thought of George's explanation, "What evidence was there for his suggestion?"

Several members of the class discussed the matter and agreed that this material had only changed form in the process of melting and resolidifying.

Mr. Jackson asked, "What is this type of change called?"

Two students raised their hands and suggested that it might be a physical change.

Mr. Jackson then asked what was happening to the candle as it burned. What caused it to get shorter and why would it eventually have to be replaced? The class discussed this matter and eventually discovered that the candle was also changing chemically.

■ Inquiry Through Demonstration

Which of these teaching methods do you think would be the more effective way to demonstrate physical and chemical changes and why? What did students learn from Mr. Jackson's approach that they might not have learned from Mr. O'Brien's? Which of the methods stressed the inquiry approach and why? Which method do you think took instructors more time to prepare? Which would be more inductive in its approach? Why do you think teachers have traditionally emphasized the deductive method in giving demonstrations? If you were going to teach this lesson, how would you do it better?

A demonstration has been defined as the process of showing something to another person or group. Clearly, there are several ways in which things can be shown. You can hold up an object such as a piece of sulfur and say, "This is sulfur," or you can state, "Sulfur burns; light some sulfur, and show that it burns." Showing in this way mainly involves observation or verification. Mr. O'Brien's use of demonstration was of this type.

A demonstration can also be given inductively by the instructor asking several questions but seldom giving answers. An inductive demonstration has the advantage of stressing inquiry, which encourages students to analyze and make hypotheses based on their knowledge. Their motivation is high because they like riddles, and in an inductive demonstration they are constantly confronted with riddles. The strength of this motivation becomes apparent if you consider the popularity of puzzles. Inviting students to inquire why something occurs taxes their minds and requires them to think. Thinking is an active mental process. The only way in which students learn to think is by having opportunities to do so. An inductive demonstration provides this opportunity because students' answers to the instructor's questions act as "feedback." The teacher has a better understanding of the student's comprehension of the demonstration. The feedback acts as a guide for further questioning until the students discover the concepts and principles involved in the demonstration and the teacher is sure that they know its meaning and purpose.

Demonstrations, in addition to serving as simple observations of material and verification of a process, may also be experimental in nature. A demonstration can become an experiment if it involves a problem for which the solution is not immediately apparent to the class. Students particularly like experimental demonstrations because they usually have more action. Students enjoy action, not words! They love to watch something happening before their eyes.

Demonstration Versus Individual Experimentation

Educators have stressed the importance of self-instruction and less reliance on large-group or class instruction. Education should be preparation for life and part of that preparation must be to ensure that the individual continues to learn long after formal education ends. It is important that the school reinforce habits and patterns of learning which will prepare the individual to continue his education many years after he leaves organized instruction. Laboratory work, because it involves the individual directly in the learning process, as well as imparting working skills, is thought to be superior to teaching by demonstration. A person working on a laboratory problem has learned far more than just the answer to the problem. He may learn to be efficient, self-reliant, and analytical; to observe, manipulate, measure, and reason; to use apparatus; and, most importantly, to learn on his own. Individual laboratory experimentation helps to attain these goals better than demonstrations do. For this reason demonstrations should play a lesser role in science instruction, with individual student investigation receiving top priority.

Demonstrations can be justified for the following reasons:

1. *Lower cost.* Less equipment and fewer materials are needed by an instructor doing a demonstration. It is, therefore, cheaper than having an entire class conduct experiments. However, cheaper education is not necessarily better education.
2. *Availability of equipment.* Certain demonstrations require equipment not available in sufficient numbers for all students to use. For example, not every student in a physics class needs to have an oscilloscope to study sound waves.
3. *Economy of time.* Often the time required to set up equipment for a laboratory exercise cannot be justified for the educational value received. A teacher can set up the demonstration and use the rest of the time for other instruction.
4. *Less hazard from dangerous materials.* A teacher may more safely handle dangerous chemicals or apparatus requiring sophisticated skills.
5. *Direction of the thinking process.* In a demonstration, a teacher has a better indication of the students' thinking processes and can do much to stimulate the students to be more analytical and synthetic in their reasoning.
6. *Show the use of equipment.* An instructor may want to show the students how to use and prevent damage to a microscope, balance, oscilloscope, etc.

Planning a Demonstration

To plan an efficient and effective demonstration requires extensive organization and consideration of the following points:

1. The first step is to identify the concept and principles you wish to teach. Direct the design of the entire demonstration to their attainment.
2. If the principle you wish to teach is complex, break it down into concepts and give several examples for each concept. For example, photosynthesis involves understanding concepts of radiant energy, chlorophyll, carbon dioxide,

glucose, water, temperature, a chemical change, and gases. A student's memorizing that green plants can make sugar in light with water results in little understanding if he does not know the meaning of these concepts.

3. Choose an activity that will show the concepts you wish to teach. Consult the sources at the end of this chapter for possible suggestions for activities.
4. Design the activity so that each student becomes as involved as possible.
5. Gather and assemble the necessary equipment.
6. Go through the demonstration at least once before class begins.
7. Outline the questions you will ask during the demonstration. This procedure is especially important in doing an inquiry-oriented demonstration.
8. Consider how you will use visual aids, especially the overhead projector, to supplement the demonstration.
9. Decide on the evaluation technique to use.

Written techniques
   a. Essay. Have students take notes and record data during the demonstration, and then have them write a summary of the demonstration.
   b. Quiz. Have students write answers to questions or prepare diagrams to see if they really understood the demonstration. Stress application of principles.

Verbal techniques
   a. Ask students to summarize the purpose of the demonstration.
   b. Give them problems in which they will have to apply these principles they have learned.

10. Consider the time a demonstration will take. Try to move it rapidly enough to keep students attentive. Prolonged or complicated demonstrations are generally undesirable because they don't hold the students' attention.
11. When you plan a demonstration, do it well, with the intention that you will probably use it for several years. It will then take less time to prepare in the future. Evaluate a demonstration immediately after giving it to determine its weaknesses and strengths. Add any questions which will contribute to the inquiry presentation when you use the demonstration again.

Giving a Demonstration

When giving a demonstration, keep the following guidelines in mind.

1. Make it easily visible. If you are working with small things, can you use an overhead projector to make them more visible?
2. Speak loudly enough to be heard in the back of the room. Do you speak loudly enough and modulate the tone and volume of your voice to avoid monotonous delivery? When a student responds, do you ask him to speak up so other students can hear? Do you repeat students' questions and answers for emphasis and audibility?
3. Do you display excitement in giving the demonstration? Do you make it come alive? A good demonstrator is somewhat of a "ham." He uses dramatic techniques to excite and involve his students. The way in which a teacher makes a demonstration come alive is as much an art as is reading Shakespeare well to an enraptured audience.
4. How do you stage the demonstration? How do you start it to involve everyone immediately? One suggestion is to place unique objects on a demonstration desk. For example, a transfusion container or a Van de Graff generator placed on a desk immediately motivates students' inquisitive minds. Before you even begin, you have the students with you, wondering what you are going to do.
   a. Teach inductively. Start your demonstration with a question. If you have interesting equipment, ask your students what they think you are going to do with it. Spend some time just questioning about the apparatus. In the construction of a transfusion container, for example, there are several scientific principles involved, such as partial vacuum, air pressure, sterile conditions, nutrient for the cells placed in the bottle, and anticoagulants to prevent clotting of the blood.
   b. Ask questions constantly about what you are going to do, what's happening, why they think it is happening, and what the demonstration is proving or illustrating.
   c. Know the purpose of what you are demonstrating. Use your questions as a guide only. The questions you have anticipated may be excellent, but also be ready to pick up suggestions from the questions students ask while they are observing the demonstration.
   d. Give positive reinforcement. Always recognize a reply: "Say, I think you have something there." "Good, you're thinking." "What do the rest of you think of John's remarks?" When a student gives a good explanation, compliment him. Seldom react negatively to a student's answer. Don't say, "That's wrong." Rather say, "It's good you're thinking, but your answer is not quite right."

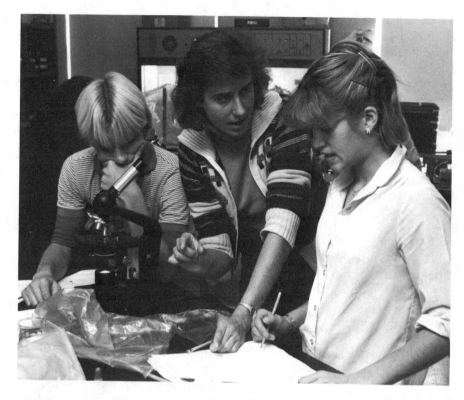

When giving a demonstration, ask questions constantly about what you're going to do, what's happening, and why.

5. Allow at least three seconds for students to reply to your questions. This wait-time is important so that the students may think and reason about the demonstration.
6. Use the blackboard to describe the purpose of the demonstration. Verbal explanations are seldom enough. Any picture or diagram you make on the board immediately attracts the students' attention. Remember that your students have lived in a TV-centered environment; as soon as they see a visual representation on the board, they are drawn to it. A beginning teacher often fails to realize or ever consider how the blackboard can complement the learning activity.
7. At the conclusion of the demonstration have a student summarize what has occurred and its purpose. This summation helps to fix the purpose of the demonstration in the minds of the students.
8. Evaluate your lesson—orally or in a written summary.

Ways to Present a Demonstration

Of the several ways in which a demonstration can be given, a teacher-centered demonstration is seldom the best way because it does not provide enough student involvement. When students participate actively in giving a demonstration, they are more interested and, consequently, learn more. Several types of student-participative demonstrations are shown in the "Teaching Science Activities", for this chapter, pp. 455–460. Here are five ways in which a demonstration can be presented.

1. *Teacher demonstration.* The teacher prepares and gives the demonstration by himself. This approach has the advantage usually of better organization and more sophisticated presentation.
2. *Teacher-student demonstration.* This is a team approach in which the student assists the teacher. This type of demonstration gives recognition to the student. The class may be more attentive because they like to watch one of their peers perform.
3. *Student-group demonstration.* This method can be used on occasion; it has the advantage that it more actively involves students in the presentation. The group approach can be used to advantage if students are allowed to select the members of their group. The teacher should evaluate the group as a whole and assign the group a grade which is the same for each of its members. The groups will form at first among friends. However, if some of the members are not productive, they will be rejected the next time groups are selected. The peer pressure to produce and become actively involved replaces the necessity for a teacher to encourage students to work. This group arrangement may also be effective in organizing laboratory work. The only

Demonstrations

1. Suppose that you wanted to teach the molecular theory of matter. How would you start your unit? What demonstrations would you do and why?
2. What does the word *demonstration* mean?
3. How does an experimental demonstration differ from a scientific verification?
4. What are the advantages and disadvantages in giving a demonstration?
5. How is the staging of a theatrical production similar to the staging of a demonstration? What considerations must be made in preparation for both?

---

problem is that the teacher must be patient until group pressure is brought to bear on the non-productive students in the class.

4. *Individual student demonstration.* This method can produce very effective demonstrations, especially if the student has status among her peers. An effective way to have individual student demonstrations is to have upperclassmen, from advanced science classes, demonstrate to the lowerclassmen. A freshman general-science class may become enthralled when a physics or chemistry senior comes into the class to give a demonstration. An upperclassman, excited about giving a demonstration, helps to convey that excitement to the students.

5. *Guest demonstration.* Guest demonstrators can do much to relieve a boring pattern of routine class activities. Other science teachers in the school may be called in to present a demonstration or activity in which they have some special competence. Professional scientists are often willing to give special demonstrations.

Silent Demonstration

Some authors have stressed the importance and desirability of the silent demonstration. In the passage below a verbal demonstration is compared with silent one.

The usual kind of demonstration by which science teachers give their students visual or auditory experiences is the teacher-talking demonstration. In this performance the teacher is actor and commentator. The pupils, who are supposed to be learning from the new experience how to attack a difficulty or develop a concept, are spectators. But they do not necessarily learn scientific facts or principles from a demonstration in which everything is done for them. Pupils really learn when they observe and react to what is presented.

There is a kind of demonstration that is likely to ensure, on the part of the student, careful observation, accurate recording of data, and practical application, later, of the ideas gained from the experience. This procedure is the silent demonstration. The following comparison of the two kinds of demonstrations shows how they differ.[1]

The silent demonstration, since it cannot be supplemented or strengthened by explanation, requires more careful planning than does the teacher-talking demonstration. (See Table 14–1.) In preparing the silent demonstration, the teacher may find this general procedure a good one.

1. Fix clearly in mind the object of the demonstration.
2. Select the apparatus and materials best suited for the demonstration.
3. Determine the beginning point of the demonstration. The beginning is based on what the teacher assumes that the pupils know.
4. Consider difficulties as learning steps. Perform the parts of the demonstration to explain these difficulties.
5. Perform the techniques so that they may be observed in all parts of the room. The steps should follow some order in relation to the learning steps.
6. Give pupils an outline of the steps to be used. Outlines may be mimeographed or put on the chalkboard.

Silent demonstrations should not be used frequently because there is no way for the teacher to determine if the students are achieving the objectives while the demonstration is being given. Silent demonstrations can, however, provide a welcome change in the routine activity of the class. They can be used effectively if an instructor accentuates his movements in the demonstration so that the students can see and have some hints about what is relevant. In a silent demonstration, *visibility* is extremely important and must be ensured; otherwise, the students

When a student assists the teacher in a demonstration, class interest may be heightened.

TABLE 14–1
Comparison of teacher-talking and silent demonstration

Teacher-Talking Demonstration	Silent Demonstration
Teacher states purposes of the demonstration.	Pupil must discover purpose as the demonstration progresses.
Teacher names pieces of apparatus and describes arrangement.	Teacher uses apparatus. Pupils observe equipment and arrangement.
Teacher is manipulator and technician, tells what is being done, points out and usually explains results.	Teacher performs experiment. Pupils observe what is being done and then describe results.
Teacher often points out the things which should have happened and accounts for unexpected results.	Pupils record results as observed. Teacher checks for accuracy and honesty in reporting. Teacher repeats the experiment if necessary.
Teacher summarizes the results and states the conclusion to be drawn. Pupils usually copy the conclusions as stated.	Pupils summarize data and draw their own conclusions based on what they observed. Teacher checks conclusions and repeats experiment if necessary.
Teacher explains the importance of the experiment and tells how it is applied in everyday life.	Pupils attempt to answer application questions related to the demonstration.

will quickly become frustrated, and eventually discipline problems will ensue.

Storage of Demonstration Equipment

Equipment made by you or your students can lend an added fascination to a science demonstration because students are often more impressed by homemade equipment. Parents, industrial companies, and students will often construct or provide apparatus for the school without cost. Having students build equipment involves them in improving the science instruction of the school. This personal investment helps to build student morale and to show the community that the science department is an active and dynamic part of their school.

Much thought should be given to storing equipment after use so that it may be found easily in the future and set up again with little effort. One way to do so is to establish a list of headings under which to store materials. For example, in physics, storage areas might be labeled: "electricity," "magnetism," "heat," "light," "sound," "atomic structure," etc. In biology, storage categories might be: "glassware," "chemicals," "slides," "preserved plant and animal specimens," etc. The next time you wish to find the equipment, it can be easily located under the proper storage title. Such a system also makes it easy for students to assist you in storing or obtaining equipment for use in demonstrations.

An efficient way to store small demonstration materials for future use is to obtain several shoe boxes. (See Figure 14.1.) Place all of the materials you need for a demonstration in the box and label the end. For example, a box might be labeled "electrostatic demonstration materials." You might also include in the box a sheet of paper describing the demonstration. This procedure helps lessen future preparation time for the same demonstration. A student laboratory assistant can get the box down, read the included sheet describing the demonstration, check to see if all of the equipment needed is present, and replenish needed supplies. The box then will be ready for use and you will require practically no preparation time. This storage procedure works particularly well with general-science and simple physical materials. A drawback is that when many materials and articles of equipment are stored in the boxes they are not then easily available for other demonstration work during the year.

Special Equipment

Free Sources of Equipment

Science courses often require special science equipment. Some of this specialized equipment may be available to the teacher without cost if he goes through the proper channels. In some areas of the country, there are companies which will donate materials to the schools when they receive a written request from the teacher. Consult with experienced

FIGURE 14–1
Storage box for demonstration equipment

teachers or professional scientists in your community to determine what is available.

Overhead Projector

Every science class should have an overhead projector with suitable transparency supplies. Such a projector can become a valuable teaching aid during a demonstration or discussion. For example, in biology a teacher may want to show how to make a wet-mount slide. This procedure cannot be demonstrated easily except by using an overhead projector. Many of the properties of magnetism can be demonstrated by the use of such a projector.

Microprojector, Videotape Recorder, and Amplifier

Another special piece of equipment of particular value to biology classes is the microprojector to project slide material. The advantage of this projector is that the teacher and the student view the material simultaneously. These microprojectors cost over $2,000 and are beyond the reach of most schools. An alternative to the use of the microprojector is a closed-circuit television camera adapted for use over a microscope; the students view the material on a television console. Amplifiers can be used to good advantage to study heartbeats of various animals and to let the class hear them. Some teachers have a small tape library which may contain information that can be used as an actual part of a demonstration. In the study of sound in general science or physics, tape recorders can be put to good use.

Stressing the Higher Levels of Learning

A demonstration should contribute to the objectives of the course and school. It should be used to stimulate critical thinking and offer opportunities for creativity. A demonstration may further be used to develop understanding of the philosophical basis of science. For example, the instructor may ask:

- How certain are we of our data?
- What evidence is there of certainty in science?
- How do scientists fractionate knowledge to find answers to bigger problems?

- How are the fractional bits of knowledge related to the whole?
- I have just produced a pollutant. What are the social implications of this act?
- How can a scientist be moral, immoral, or amoral?

Questions of this type can be used discriminately throughout a series of demonstrations to build a philosophical awareness of the foundations of modern science. The responsibility to impart knowledge of this sort offers great challenge to the teacher in formulating lessons.

A demonstration technique that embodies higher understanding, more students' individuality, and creative reactions is illustrated in the "Teaching Science Activity: Evaluation of Student Understanding of a Basic Physical Principle," on p. 456.

■ Inquiry through Laboratory Work

It has often been said that science is not really science unless it is accompanied by experimentation and laboratory work. In the secondary schools there continues to be interest in the laboratory as the focal point for the study of science. It is worth noting that this is not the first time in the history of science education in the United States that the laboratory has come into prominence. The late 1800s saw the construction of laboratories in secondary schools and colleges with a corresponding change in emphasis in the methods of instruction in the sciences. The recitation method and the catechetical approach for learning science principles were gradually replaced by "experiments" in laboratories with the expressed purpose of verifying the laws of physics and chemistry. It was believed that students would learn science best by repeating, in an abbreviated fashion, the classical experiments of Newton, Galileo, Hooke, Priestley, Boyle, and many others. Students would see principles of natural science at work, enabling them to understand the underlying science concepts. Laboratories and apparatus were designed to duplicate as nearly as possible the materials and equipment used in the original experiments, with "modern" refinements to ensure reasonable accuracy in the hands of science students.

The Inquiry Approach

Beginning in the late 1950s there was a definite shift in emphasis in high school science. The laboratory became the center of attention at all levels of secondary science, including the junior high school. The particular goals and methods used in the various new curriculum projects of the Physical Science Study

=========== REFLECTING ON SCIENCE TEACHING ===========
Evaluating Demonstrations

1. What can you do to determine if you are moving through a demonstration at the right rate?
2. What advantages are there to a student demonstration?
3. How would you give a silent demonstration?
4. What are the advantages and disadvantages of demonstrations compared to student laboratory work?
5. Explain how you would give a demonstration to ensure that higher levels of learning would be required.

Committee, the Biological Sciences Curriculum Study, the Chemical Education Materials Study, the Chemical Bond Approach Project, the Earth Science Curriculum Project, and others are discussed in detail in Chapter 16. Without exception, these projects emphasized and provided for inquiry methods, in which students themselves were the investigators and which gave many opportunities for creativity.

The inquiry method in the science laboratory can be promoted by several fairly simple but important changes. Paul Brandwein and Joseph Schwab, in describing the "inquiry curriculum" had this to say about inquiry methods:

> In general, conversion of the laboratory from the dogmatic to the inquiring mode is achieved by making two changes. First, a substantial part of the laboratory work is made to lead rather than lag the classroom phase of science teaching ... Second, the merely demonstrative function of the laboratory (which serves the purpose of the dogmatic curriculum) is subordinated to two other functions.
>
> One of these functions consists in a new service to the classroom phase of instruction. With classroom materials converted from a rhetoric of conclusions to an exhibition of the course of inquiry, conclusions alone will no longer be the major component. Instead, we will deal with units which consist of the statement of a scientific problem, a view of the data needed for its solution, an account of the interpretation of these data, and a statement of the conclusions forged by the interpretation. Such units as these will convey the wanted meta-lesson about the nature of inquiry. But they will appear exceedingly easy and simple, conveying little of the real flavor of scientific inquiries, unless the verbal statement of the problem situation and of the difficulties involved in the acquisition of data is given meaning by an exhibition of their real physical referents. ...
>
> The second function of the inquiring laboratory is to provide occasions for an invitation to the conduct of miniature but exemplary programs of inquiry. The manual for such a laboratory ceases to be a volume which tells the students what to do and what to expect.[2]

The inquiry mode of teaching, in addition to requiring a different philosophical approach by the teacher and students, also demands higher levels of proficiency in the use of the tools of inquiry. These tools consist of the skills needed to inquire into natural events and conditions. For example, one could not learn very much about how forces cause masses to accelerate unless he could make careful measurements of distance, time, force, and mass. To learn the interrelationships between all of these factors requires that the student refine his measurement skills. It is necessary to know how to use a meter stick or measuring tape, to read the units correctly, to read a stop watch, to operate a beam balance correctly, and to measure force with a spring scale or some other method. In the classroom, the student must have opportunities to practice the skills required for a particular inquiry situation; otherwise, the experience will probably be frustrating and the learning minimal.

Research on the Laboratory's Role in Science Teaching

Science educators over the years have examined the influence of the laboratory on achievement and other variables such as reasoning, critical thinking, understanding science, process skills, manipulative skills, interests, retention, and ability to do independent work, among others. Much of this research gave inconclusive results, but science teachers in general feel that the laboratory is a vital part of science teaching.

Some positive findings can be cited. Three studies done between 1969 and 1979 found that laboratory instruction increased student problem-solving abilities. Other researchers reported positive results when working with disadvantaged students in the laboratory to encourage cognitive development, introduce scientific ideas, give concrete examples, and learn how to manipulate materials.[3]

Data from a national survey in 1978 show that laboratory work and hands-on science activities are

=== REFLECTING ON SCIENCE TEACHING ===

Giving Demonstrations

1. How would you store demonstration equipment so that you would be able to use it with greater efficiency?
2. Two chemistry teachers were talking. One said, "I never answer questions." How could the teacher do this and still be a good teacher?
3. Do you now feel more competent to give a demonstration than before reading this chapter? Why?

---

not used optimally in science teaching. Many teachers say students are apathetic about laboratory work and that labs are difficult to stock, maintain, and control. However, it is not likely students will experience much of the nature, methods, and spirit of science without this important component of science teaching.

Skill Development in the Laboratory

The complaint has frequently been lodged against science teaching that students and teachers alike have difficulty in expressing exactly what the goals of science teaching should be.

In taking up this challenge, we will identify the types of skills which science students ought to "be able to do better" after having taken the courses in science in the junior and senior high schools. We have listed five categories of skills: acquisitive, organizational, creative, manipulative, and communicative. No attempt is made to rank these categories in order of importance, or even to imply that any one category may be more important than any other. Within each of the categories, however, specific skills are listed in order of increasing difficulty. In general, those skills that require only the use of one's own unaided senses are simpler than those that require use of instruments or higher orders of manual and mental dexterity.

Categories of Skills
A. Acquisitive skills
  1. Listening—being attentive, alert, questioning
  2. Observing—being accurate, alert, systematic
  3. Searching—locating sources, using several sources, being self-reliant, acquiring library skills
  4. Inquiring—asking, interviewing, corresponding
  5. Investigating—reading background information, formulating problems
  6. Gathering data—tabulating, organizing, classifying, recording

  7. Research—locating a problem, learning background, setting up experiments, analyzing data, drawing conclusions
B. Organizational skills
  1. Recording—tabulating, charting, working systematically, working regularly, recording completely
  2. Comparing—noticing how things are alike, looking for similarities, noticing identical features
  3. Contrasting—noticing how things differ, looking for dissimilarities, noticing unlike features
  4. Classifying—putting things into groups and subgroups, identifying categories, deciding between alternatives
  5. Organizing—putting items in order, establishing a system, filing, labeling, arranging
  6. Outlining—employing major headings and subheadings, using sequential, logical organization
  7. Reviewing—picking out important items, memorizing, associating
  8. Evaluating—recognizing good and poor features, knowing how to improve grades
  9. Analyzing—seeing implications and relationships, picking out causes and effects, locating new problems
C. Creative skills
  1. Planning ahead—seeing possible results and probable modes of attack, setting up hypotheses
  2. Designing a new problem, a new approach, a new device or system
  3. Inventing—creating a method, device, or technique
  4. Synthesizing—putting familiar things together in a new arrangement, hybridizing, drawing together
D. Manipulative skills
  1. Using an instrument—knowing the instrument's parts, how it works, how to adjust it, its proper use for a given task, its limitations
  2. Caring for an instrument—knowing how to store it, using proper settings, keeping it clean,

handling it properly, knowing its rate capacity, transporting it safely

3. Demonstration—setting up apparatus, making it work, describing parts and functions, illustrating scientific principles
4. Experimentation—recognizing a problem, planning a procedure, collecting data, recording data, analyzing data, drawing conclusions
5. Repair—repairing and maintaining equipment, instruments, etc.
6. Construction—making simple equipment for demonstration and experimentation
7. Calibration—learning the basic information about calibration, calibrating a thermometer, balance, timer, or other instrument

E. Communicative skills
1. Asking questions—learning to formulate good questions, to be selective in asking, to resort to own devices for finding answers whenever possible
2. Discussion—learning to contribute own ideas, listening to ideas of others, keeping on the topic, sharing available time equitably, arriving at conclusions
3. Explanation—describing to someone else clearly, clarifying major points, exhibiting patience, being willing to repeat
4. Reporting—orally reporting to a class or teacher in capsule form the significant material on a science topic
5. Writing—writing a report of an experiment or demonstration, not just filling in a blank but starting with a blank sheet of paper, describing the problem, the method of attack, the data collected, the methods of analysis, the conclusions drawn, and the implications for further work
6. Criticism—constructively criticizing or evaluating a piece of work, a scientific procedure or conclusion
7. Graphing—putting in graphical form the results of a study or experiment, being able to interpret the graph for someone else
8. Teaching—after becoming familiar with a topic or semiexpert in it, teaching the material to one's classmates in such a manner that it will not have to be retaught by the teacher

Is There a Need for Science Skill Development?

Courses in elementary and secondary schools emphasize the processes of science as much as the concepts and generalizations. Understanding a process involves skill competencies. Learning "how to learn" requires adequate learning tools. In addition, students need confidence in their ability to perform the tasks needed in self-learning. Skill competency strengthens self-reliance.

Can Skill Development Be Guided Through a Graded Sequence of Difficulty—From Simple to Complex?

This progression is possible because of certain characteristics of skills themselves, such as level of difficulty and complexity. For example, skills requiring the use of unaided senses are simpler than those requiring the use of instruments. It is easier for a student to use his unaided eyes to compare the colors of minerals than to operate a petrographic microscope to do the same thing at a higher level of sophistication. Also, groups of simple skills may be included in more difficult complex skills. Graphing, for example, requires competency in the simpler skills of counting, measuring, and using a ruler (instrument). In the same way, higher levels of learning, such as analysis, synthesis, and evaluation, require higher levels of skill proficiency.

Does Skill Development Enhance or Preclude Concept Development?

Growth in conceptual understanding is enhanced by expertise in skill usage. In teaching skills, concepts form the vehicle by which the skills are learned. One cannot learn a skill in a void—there must be substantive information on which to operate. The skill of comparing, for example, is useless unless there are things to compare. In the same context, a hierarchy of skills forms a framework to which concepts can be attached. As one learns increasingly sophisticated skills, the subject matter (concepts) can be adapted and changed as required.

Can Achievement of Skill Competencies Be Tested?

There is ample evidence that skill achievements can be structured in behavioral terms. Performance can be observed and evaluated. Various performance levels of individual skills can be graded on a continuum from minimum to maximum success. Not only is it possible for teachers to create testing situations using performance objectives, but it is equally possible to provide self-evaluation opportunities for students to gain knowledge of their own progress and levels of performance.

What are the Implications of the Skill-Development Approach in the Science Classroom?

Conditions necessary for success when emphasizing the skill or process goals are:

1. Time must be provided for practice and experience in the skills being developed. One does not become proficient without practice and drill.
2. Teachers must clearly understand the skill objective. Planning must revolve around these objectives rather than traditional content goals alone.
3. Ample materials must be available. There must be a "responsive environment" permitting students to operate with the "things of science."
4. A variety of conceptual materials may be selected to facilitate skill development. Most conceptual themes or topics provide ample opportunities for teaching varied skills. In planning for teaching, however, it is important to concentrate on a few skills in any particular lesson.
5. Evaluation emphasis must be placed on performance or behavioral terms, not mere factual memorization or recitation. The superficial coverage of content must be de-emphasized and performance and depth of understanding brought to the foreground.

Mere identification of skills to be taught is, of course, only a first step in the realization of a science objective. To aid in skill development and ultimate mastery of the desired skills, the teacher must devise suitable teaching plans and student activities. In this type of learning, "learning by doing" is an important maxim. Pupils must be given opportunities for activities which give repeated practice in the desired skills. The laboratory becomes an important facility at this point because most of the skills involve procedures which, to a greater or lesser extent, require materials and apparatus.

A sample lesson, oriented toward skill development, is given in the "Teaching Science Activity: Teaching Inquiry Skills," on p. 460.

Organizing Laboratory Work

Effectiveness of the laboratory experience is directly related to the amount of individual participation by students. *Individual participation* here means active involvement in the experiment with definite responsibilities for its progress and success. In theory, the ideal arrangement would be to have each student wholly responsible for conducting the experiment from start to finish. In this way, the preliminary planning, gathering materials, preparation of apparatus, designing the method, collecting data, analyzing results, and drawing conclusions are unmistakably the work of the individual student and the accompanying learning is at a maximum.

In reality, the maximum learning may be achieved, for certain students, by working in pairs or very small groups. With good cooperation and sharing of duties, the stimulation of pair or small-group activity may be beneficial. In group work, a shy student may be stimulated into action and thought processes of which he may be entirely incapable by himself. An extroverted student may assume directive and leadership qualities not developed in individual work. The science teacher must be aware of these possibilities and plan the methodology of laboratory work accordingly. There should be opportunities in the laboratory to provide experiences using both arrangements. Avoiding stereotyped and inflexible arrangements should be of concern to the teacher of laboratory sciences.

Experiments will vary greatly in complexity. Even in a typical laboratory science, such as chemistry, "experiments" may be no more than carrying out a preplanned exercise of observation and data gathering, or they may be as extensive and demanding as research on a problem whose solution is totally unknown. Arrangements for laboratory work must accommodate these extremes. A student of general science in the junior high school may need more of the "exercise" type of experiment to gain the skills needed for complex experiments. However, he should also be given opportunities to work on true experiments so that he might sense the joy of discovery in the same way as a practicing scientist.

The Use of Laboratory Assistants

Preparations for laboratory work require exorbitant amounts of time on the part of the conscientious science teacher. Ordering materials, providing for their storage, inventorying, repairing equipment, and preparing for laboratory experiments daily add up to a tremendous drain on the science teacher's time and energy. Some teachers have developed systems where student laboratory assistants are used to perform many of the tasks needed to carry on successful laboratory programs. One teacher has prepared a handbook for laboratory assistants included here to illustrate the organization of such a program.[4] Students are given credit for participation.

Handbook for Laboratory Assistants

Philosophy
Each laboratory assistant should constantly be working to make the Science Department more successful. There are definite responsibilities, duties, and dan-

═══════════ **GUEST EDITORIAL** ═══════════

The Laboratory in Science Teaching: Main Course or Dessert?

Robert Yager
Director—Science Education Center
The University of Iowa
Iowa City, Iowa

For many years the laboratory was thought to be an extra in science teaching in the secondary school, even though science educators have expounded on the values of laboratory teaching for many years. Seemingly, the laboratory was established as central to secondary science teaching with the advent of the national curriculum efforts of the 1960s. Before 1970, few would have thought that anyone would conceive of school science without students active in laboratory settings.

The 1980s brought disillusionment—with Vietnam, national goals, the promises of science, the polluted environment, and other societal problems. The decline in school enrollments, fragile economic conditions for schools, and the loss of "a place of honor" for science in school programs have brought clear questions of the importance of the laboratory for science instruction for the 1980s.

That the place of the laboratory in school science could be questioned is amazing. Apparently the centrality of the laboratory to the programs for the past two decades was not verified in practice, either for teachers or students. Again the laboratory appears to be the "dessert" for science teaching rather than the "main course." How could this be? Could it be related to

disagreement as to the features and functions of an ideal laboratory in science instruction?

A general classroom may be a place for students to learn *about* science but a laboratory is a place where students *do* science. Can a meaningful experience with science exist only in the "about" realm with no experience "with" science?

Science is a human enterprise where persons ask questions of nature in an effort to understand it better. To ask questions is an important first step but to seek answers to such questions is basic to science. The laboratory is the typical place where the seeking occurs. It does not have to be the traditional room with laboratory tables, test tubes, special electrical outlets, and the rest. However, to assume that science can be learned and/or experienced without a place to seek answers to questions about nature is much like assuming that one can learn auto mechanics without a shop, or music without instruments, or art without specific media, or physical education without a place to practice physical skills.

The problem with laboratories in a traditional sense is the fact that they are not treated as "laboratories" in the sense that science is done in such places. Too many so-called laboratories are

gers involved in the program for assistants. The department of science depends on you to a great extent. It is expected that each assistant is to be trusted and relied upon to perform his/or her duties properly without the necessity of close supervision.

Responsibilities and Duties

It is the purpose of the Laboratory Assistants Program to aid science teachers, help maintain and organize the equipment and supplies of the department, and to improve the science program.

Specifically this includes:

1. The care and organization of the stockroom.
2. The preparation of laboratory exercises and demonstrations for teachers.
3. The preparation of papers, information sheets, class lists and other clerical work for the teachers.
4. The inventorying of supplies.
5. The correction of papers for teachers.
6. The preparation of charts, posters, signs and labeling of shelves, etc.

Required Individual Project

In all classes you will have tests and homework but in the Laboratory Assistants Program an individual project is required instead. One project is required each semester, or a partially completed project will be accepted the first semester if the project is extremely complex and permission has been given in advance.

merely places for checking out what the teacher or the textbook says, or places where one goes to manipulate with approaches, or places where one goes to follow the directions in a manual or a so-called laboratory sheet. Such inappropriate labeling of a laboratory (or such inappropriate use of the laboratory) should not be used as a reason for abandoning real laboratories or the central role that laboratories must have for meaningful science learning.

Laboratories help correct the erroneous idea that scientific information exists only to be learned. Scientific information is valuable only if it is learned *and* used. A laboratory is a place where knowledge can be used; hence knowledge is exemplified as a means for action, not as an end in itself. Science laboratories should enable students to use information, to develop a general concept, to determine a new problem, to explain an observation or nonconformity in nature, or to make a decision. Laboratories are active places where the unknown is confronted. When laboratories are so defined and viewed, they do exemplify the essence of science. As such, they are indispensible.

If the laboratory is viewed as "dessert," it probably does not meet the criteria for a science laboratory. Classifying the laboratory as "dessert"

probably means that it is being used to test knowledge and/or it is being used as an interesting digression from the more important mastery of information which occurs in the regular classroom setting. When laboratories are viewed as "dessert," they do not meet the basic criteria for laboratories and hence are misnamed. Laboratories when properly defined must be the "main course" in science programs. They become the place where science is experienced!

There are several features of an effective laboratory for school science. Such laboratories are places of action where something is done to satisfy curiosity. They are not necessarily special rooms in schools. They are often interdisciplinary in nature, often open-ended; they are places where questions are raised, procedures defined, and tentative decisions reached. Actions in the laboratory often become the basis for discussion, for use of iteration, for practice with logic, for the formulation of new questions, for explaining observations. Laboratories in good science instruction cannot be "extra"; they cannot be the dessert after a meal. Laboratories should be the "meal"—the main course of student experiences with science.

Project proposal (plan). At the end of the first quarter a proposal should be submitted. If accepted by the science department, the student will then take data in the experiment.

The Project: The project should include a substantial report discussing the project, theories, procedure, data, etc. The report is due the last day of the semester.

Special Short Courses
Classes on special skills will be conducted at the weekly meetings to improve your abilities.

1. Handling glassware I (cleaning)
2. Handling glassware II (cutting, bending, and assembling)

3. Preparation of solutions (molarity, normality)
4. Safety in the laboratory
5. Analytical weighing
6. Setting up a biology lab
7. Setting up a chemistry lab

Grading
Grades will be determined and recorded objectively. A conscientious student should receive an A or B in science. However, it is possible to receive a lower grade for unsatisfactory performance. Grades will be based on the following items:

Required Projects: Each laboratory assistant will be required to complete one project each semester. This project may be in any area of science.

Special Projects: Each laboratory assistant

should be constantly working to make the Science Department better. Any ideas that you may have for improving the department will be considered a special project when organized and completed by the student. Projects of a student's own initiative must be cleared through a faculty member before starting.

Demonstrations: Teachers will assign demonstrations to the laboratory assistants whose responsibility it will be to find the equipment, set up demonstration and run it at least twice to make certain it works properly.

Laboratory Experiments: Teachers will assign experiments to be set up, and tried by the laboratory assistants. This will include Physics, Biology, Chemistry, Advanced Biology, Biological Science Laboratory Practicals, and Freshman Science. Students are required to clean up the laboratory after the experiments.

Sections: Each laboratory assistant will have an assigned section in the preparation room and will be responsible for organizing it, inventorying, and seeing to the cleanliness of the section. The section assignments will be rotated on a regular basis.

Attendance at Meetings: Failure to come to a meeting may drop your grade.

Daily Grades: Teachers will be evaluating the laboratory assistants at all times for cooperation, fulfillment of responsibilities, and adherence to rules and regulations.

Log Book: Keep a notebook to include daily accomplishments, notes of meetings and special classes, to be turned in at the end of each quarter.

Point System	Maximum Points
Section grade =	100 points/week
Preparation of laboratory experiments =	100 points/experiment prepared
Special projects =	200 points/special project
Demonstrations =	100 points/demonstration (if performed for a class)

Semester Grade: Determined from the average of the two quarter grades and the semester special science project.

Meetings

All laboratory assistants are required to attend all meetings since this is a credit course.

Meeting Schedule:

Noon meetings every other week on Monday. All students must be present at 12:00 noon. Bring your lunch.

Seventh period meetings on the week when there are no noon meetings (Tuesday, 7th period at 2:10 to 3:05). These meetings are for organizing sec-

tions, working on special projects, classes, and individual projects.

Procedure for Preparing a Chemistry Experiment

I. Obtain experiment number and approximate date it is to be ready.
II. Preparation
   a. Read experiment in laboratory manual.
   b. Read directions in teacher's manual.
      1. Equipment needed
      2. Precautions
      3. Laboratory hints
III. Setup
   a. Check all chemicals, etc. (Report anything not available in proper quantities.)
   b. Check to see if solutions are old.
   c. Make all necessary solutions in proper quantities.
   d. Make one set of chemicals per table (8). Label solutions with formula and concentration. Use the correct size bottles.
   e. If experiment has unknown, prepare a key to unknowns to be turned in.
IV. Perform experiment
   a. Make certain experiment is completely set up.
   b. Check to see if proper results were obtained.
   c. Record data.
V. Experiment report ready
VI. Clean up all glassware and put away all materials after experiment is completed.

Procedure for Preparation of Demonstrations

I. Find a demonstration to prepare.
   a. Use any source you can find.
   b. Consult with a science teacher.
   c. Use special demonstration books in science department.
II. Read demonstration carefully.
III. Organize, collect all material necessary.
IV. Try demonstration, *perfect it;* be certain that it works.
V. Find out when teachers could utilize demonstration.
VI. Store chemicals in a proper place for safekeeping, and clean up work area.
VII. Perform demonstration.
   a. Give demonstration for proper class, or
   b. Bring in all the material for demonstration (on a cart) for the teacher at the *proper* time.
   c. Don't leave demonstration or experiment lying around if you don't complete it in one period—always put material in proper place even if overnight.

Orienting Students for Laboratory Work

In general, students of the sciences look forward to a laboratory class with pleasant anticipation. Being pragmatic by nature, they sense that this is "truly science" and that an exciting experience awaits them. This attitude, most prevalent in the junior high school, must be carefully nurtured and guided as the student progresses to more rigorous disciplines. If laboratory work becomes a bore because of excessively rigid formality, unexciting exercises, "cook-book" techniques, or for whatever reason, the student will probably have been lost as a potential science participant. An atmosphere of excitement, curiosity, interest, and enthusiasm for science should be encouraged in the laboratory, tempered by care and restraint in use of apparatus and diligence in the tasks assigned. Obviously a hands-off policy regarding equipment cannot be adopted nor can a complete laissez-faire attitude be condoned. Respect for the problem, the materials, and the probable results of experimentation must be developed. The laboratory experience is but one vehicle by which the objectives of science teaching are developed. Suitably carried out, it can be one of the most effective methods of teaching and learning.

Orientation for laboratory work may involve creating a suitable frame of mind for investigating a problem. The problem must appear real to the student and worthy of study. He must have some knowledge of possible methods of attack. He should know what equipment or apparatus is needed and be familiar with its use. He must have time to work on the problem. In a given situation, the science teacher may need to give attention to one or more of these factors to begin students on their laboratory investigations.

The Place of Discussion in Laboratory Work

In recent years, there has been a trend toward placing laboratory work at the very beginning of a new unit of study. The laboratory guidebook or manual is designed to identify problems requiring observation and solution. The student performs the assigned tasks or devises procedures of his own to arrive at a solution to the problem. While doing so, he discovers the need for further information to explain his observations. He is motivated to read a textbook, search for information in a sourcebook or handbook, read supplementary material, or consult his teacher.

Laboratory work is followed by class discussion, short lectures, or question periods. During these activities, student questions are answered, observed phenomena are clarified, and certain misconceptions may be discussed. Other activities such as problem assignments, projects, extra reading, reports, tests, and demonstrations may follow in their proper context as part of the teaching and learning process.

In this method, it is likely that more than half of the total class time is spent in laboratory activities. The follow-up sessions become extremely important. The teacher usually must ascertain the accuracy of the learned concepts, correct misconceptions, and promote maximum learning more than he does in a conventional course. At the same time, the student is more directly involved in the task and may be more highly motivated than he would otherwise be.

Laboratory Work in the Junior High School

Extension of laboratory practices to the junior high school is occurring with greater frequency. Facilities for effective laboratory work are being built into modern junior high schools and youth of this age level are beginning to experience laboratory work on a regular, planned basis.

Junior high school students are enthusiastic participants in the laboratory method of teaching. Curiosity and a buoyant approach to learning make this group responsive to the laboratory approach, and proper guidance by the teacher can make this method a fruitful one for these students. Because junior high school science leads to more rigorous and laboratory-oriented sciences in the senior high school, it is worthwhile to consider its contributions to more effective learning when the student reaches biology, chemistry, or physics. It is reasonable to assume that certain attitudes, knowledge, and skills learned in the junior high school contribute to better and perhaps more rapid learning in the senior high school.

Following is a suggested list of basic knowledge and skills which might be developed in fifth- through ninth-grade science and which are considered desirable prerequisites for senior high science:

1. To understand the purposes of the laboratory in the study of science
2. To understand and be familiar with the simple tools of the laboratory
3. To understand and use the metric system in simple measurement and computation
4. To attain the understanding necessary to properly report observations of an experiment
5. To keep neat and accurate records of laboratory experiments
6. To understand the operation of simple ratios and proportions

7. To understand the construction and reading of simple graphs
8. To understand and use the simpler forms of exponential notation
9. To understand the proper use and operation of the Bunsen burner
10. To use the calculator for simple operations
11. To understand and demonstrate the use of a trip balance
12. To work with glass tubing in performing laboratory experiments
13. To keep glassware and equipment clean
14. To put together simple equipment in performing laboratory experiments
15. To measure accurately in linear, cubic, and weight units

Laboratory work in the junior high school can be broadened to include such features as out-of-doors observations, excursions, and certain types of project activities, as well as conventional experimentation in laboratory surroundings. Systematic nighttime observations of planets, constellations, meteors, the moon, and other astronomical objects may properly be considered laboratory work. Similarly, meteorological observations and experiments involving record keeping and correlations of data are included under this heading. Excursions for collecting purposes, observations of topographical features, studies of pond life, and ecological investigations are true laboratory work. The narrow connotation of *laboratory work* as something which takes place only in a specially designed room called a laboratory must be avoided in the junior high school sciences.

The range and variety of activities performed by students in the laboratory make it necessary to use many evaluation methods.

A teacher of science must be aware of these prerequisites and alert to new possibilities as well. Increasing emphasis on laboratory methods is almost certain to broaden, rather than narrow, the range of individual differences among students. Suitable means must be devised for evaluating the progress and achievement of these students in their laboratory experiences.

■ Safety Precautions in the Laboratory

An inevitable result of greater student participation in laboratory work is increased exposure to potentially dangerous apparatus and materials. Instead of viewing this fact as a deterrent to the laboratory method of teaching, the alert and dedicated science teacher will approach the problem realistically and will take the proper precautions to avoid accidents among students in the laboratory.

Accidents and injuries often occur because students lack knowledge of the proper techniques and procedures. These techniques can be taught in advance if the teacher plans properly. Certain minimum standards of acceptable procedures may be demanded of students before they are allowed to work in the laboratory. The motivation to engage in laboratory work is usually strong enough to overcome the student's reluctance to develop the requisite skills, particularly if he is convinced of the inherent dangers and the need for proper safety techniques.

According to the National Safety Council, about 32,000 school-related accidents occur each school year; about 5,000 of these are science-related. Junior high grades 7-9 experience the highest frequency of accidents while elementary grades report the lowest accident frequency. Another source estimates one major accident per 40 students per year in laboratory settings throughout the country.[5]

A 1970 study on high school science safety revealed the following:

- Advanced placement groups have the most accidents.
- *Class enrollment* and *laboratory space* have a significant relationship to laboratory accidents; the higher the classroom enrollment and the smaller the laboratory space, the higher the frequency of accidents.
- Fewer accidents occur when individual laboratory stations exist.
- The chemistry class is more prone than other classes to laboratory accidents.[6]

The prevention of accidents can be accomplished through a positive science safety educational program which places emphasis on teacher and student awareness of the potential dangers in science-related activities. "SAFETY FIRST" should be the basic motto for the school science program. However, safety considerations should seldom rule out a science lesson. Effective planning can sometimes be used to capitalize on safety problems. Developing and maintaining positive attitudes toward safety require continual efforts in safety education. Hopefully, safety training in the science program will instill in the student the importance of safety in all areas of work and play.[7]

Some general laboratory skills which will prepare the student to work safely are these:

1. Ability to handle glass tubing—cutting, bending, fire-polishing, drawing tubing into capillar-

ies, inserting tubing into rubber stoppers, and removing tubing from rubber stoppers

2. Ability to heat test tubes of chemicals—knowledge of proper rate of heating, direction, use of test tube racks, etc.

3. Ability to handle acids—pouring, proper use of stopper to avoid contamination, dilution in water, return of acid bottles to designated shelves, etc.

4. Ability to test for presence of noxious gases safely

5. Ability to treat acid spillage or burns from caustic solutions

6. Ability to operate fire extinguishers

7. Ability to set up gas generators properly

8. Ability to use standard carpenter's tools

9. Ability to use dissecting equipment, scalpels, etc.

An excellent publication dealing with safety in the secondary science classroom is published by the National Science Teachers Association.[8] In a section entitled "Suggestions for a Safe Science Program," the publication provides many excellent guidelines for teachers and students in science classes.

A survey of accidents in high school chemistry laboratories in California, reported by McComber, showed that accidents were usually caused by poor laboratory techniques. There were more serious accidents in large classes and accidents were more frequent when horseplay was involved. Forty percent of the accidents occurred among students who were above average in scientific inquisitiveness. The types of accidents which most frequently had serious results were explosions and burns from phosphorus; the easy availability of dangerous chemicals used occasionally in the normal chemistry course seemed to contribute to accidents as well.[9]

The following safety precautions to be observed in the chemistry laboratory may be put into effect in a school by discussing them with the students, supplying copies for the students' notebooks, and posting them in a prominent place in the laboratory:

A List of Safety Precautions in the Chemistry Laboratory
The work you do in the chemistry laboratory is a very important part of your chemistry course. Here you will learn to observe experiments and draw your own conclusions about your observations. The following is a list of safety rules to follow in making your laboratory work as safe and efficient as possible:

1. Observe all instructions given by the teacher. Ask for help when you need it.

2. In case of an accident, report to your teacher immediately.

3. Be careful in using flames. Keep clothing away from the flame and do not use flames near inflammable liquids.

4. Follow the directions carefully when handling all chemicals.

5. If acids or bases are spilled, wash immediately with plenty of water. Be sure you know where the neutralizing solution is located in the laboratory. Ask your teacher how to use it.

6. Read the labels on all reagents very carefully. Make a habit of reading each label twice on any reagent used in an experiment.

7. Dispose of waste materials in the proper receptacles. Solid materials should be placed in special crocks provided for the purpose.

8. Be sure you know the location and proper usage of the fire extinguishers and fire blankets provided in the laboratory.

9. Consider the laboratory a place for serious work. There is no excuse for horseplay or practical jokes in a science laboratory.

■ Safety and Law

The principal is responsible for the overall supervision of the safety program in the school. Likewise, the science teacher is responsible for the supervision of safety in the science class.

Individual teachers can be held liable for negligent acts resulting in personal injury to students. Some school boards have liability coverage which might support teachers if legal action is brought against them. Teachers should inquire about the nature of local board coverage and/or their own personal liability coverage. The extent of a teacher's liability is discussed in the NSTA publication, *Science Teaching and the Law*.[10]

■ Summary

A demonstration has been defined as showing something to a person or group. The techniques of planning a demonstration involve determining the concepts and principles to be taught, deciding on activities, gathering the materials, practicing the demonstration, outlining the questions to be asked, and deciding on the evaluational methods to be used.

Plan a demonstration with the intention of using it again. A teacher, in giving a demonstration, should be aware of visibility, audibility, and all the aspects which go with good staging. He should have

SUGGESTIONS FOR A SAFE SCIENCE PROJECT

**National Science
Teachers Association
Subcommittee on Safety**

To avoid accidents and injuries in the science classroom, both teachers and students should heed the following safety suggestions.

The teachers should be aware that:

1. It is the initial responsibility of teachers to prevent accidents and assure that the laboratory is as safe as possible.
2. Laboratory safety should be taught continuously. Safety rules should be posted in a conspicuous place in the laboratory.
3. Teachers should demonstrate where possible and instruct students on necessary safety procedures immediately before beginning laboratory work.
4. Teachers are responsible for following prescribed accident procedures if an injury or accident occurs.
5. In case of an emergency, the prompt and calm handling of an emergency situation is imperative if panic is to be avoided.
6. Teachers should receive certification from the American National Red Cross in First Aid.
7. Teachers should notify those in authority of the existence or development of any hazard that comes to their attention.
8. When using flammable volatile liquids, such as alcohol, in a demonstration experiment, care must be taken that all ignition sources are removed from the classroom.
9. Demonstrations involving explosive mixtures must be so arranged as to shield both pupils and teachers from the results of the explosion. Even when there is no likelihood of an explosion, pupils should be asked to evacuate seats directly in front of the demonstration table whenever there is any possibility of injury to them by the spattering of a chemical, an overturned burner, inhalation of fumes, etc.
10. Class conditions for lighting, ventilation, heating, and orderliness should be controlled by the teacher.
11. Readily accessible spill packages for cleaning spills and metal containers for the disposal of broken glass should be available.
12. The floor should be kept free of equipment, refuse, and spilled materials. Good housekeeping is essential to proper safety.
13. Reagent shelves should be equipped with a ledge or restraining wire to prevent slipping or sliding of bottles or glassware.
14. Teachers should know the location of and how to shut off utilities. Label and/or color code all master shut-offs clearly.
15. Ventilation hood escape outlets and fans should be checked periodically to assure proper operation.
16. All poisons and dangerous reactants should be locked when not being used.
17. Teachers should know the location and proper operation of fire extinguishers.
18. Sand, fire blanket, vermiculite, bicarbonate of soda, etc., should be kept on hand for fires and absorption of spilled reactants.
19. Safety shower and eye and face shower should be checked daily.
20. A well-supplied First Aid kit should be provided. A chart showing proper treatment for specific injuries should be prominently posted.
21. Teachers should dispose of dangerous waste chemicals and materials as prescribed by appropriate standards and the laws for your community. Provide separate waste receptacles for broken glass and waste paper.
22. Laboratories and storage facilities should be locked at all times when not under direct supervision of responsible person.
23. You should have a thorough understanding of the potential hazards of all the materials, processes, and equipment that will be in the school laboratory.
24. Students should not have indiscriminate access to the laboratory stockroom and should never be permitted to study, work, or experiment without competent supervision in the laboratory.
25. All reagent bottles should be prominently and accurately labeled with labeling materials not affected by the reagent.
26. Teachers set an example for their students. Follow all safety regulations and constantly remind students of hazards.
27. Teachers should guard against poisoning by:
    a. Providing adequate ventilation for students working with volatile substances.
    b. Instructing about the avoidance of the ingestion of chemicals.
    c. Identifying plants and animals that may cause poisoning by contact or by a bite.
    d. Setting up safeguards against exposure to radioactive substances.

28. Make accident reports promptly, accurately, and complete.

The student should be aware that:

1. All accidents should be reported to the teacher immediately, no matter how minor.
2. Only those laboratory activities where instructions and permission have been given by the teacher should be performed.
3. Only materials and equipment authorized by your instructor should be used.
4. Written and verbal instructions should be followed carefully.
5. Chemical goggles should be used when working with dangerous chemicals, hot liquids or solids, radioactive materials, and other potential sources of splashes, spills, or spattering.
6. Students should prepare for each laboratory activity by reading all instructions before they come to class. Follow all directions implicitly and intelligently. Make note of any deviations announced by your instructor.
7. Labels and equipment instructions should be read three times before using. Be sure that you are using the correct items and that you know how to use them.
8. No food, beverage, or smoking is permitted in any science laboratory.
9. Never taste or touch chemicals with the hands unless specifically instructed to do so.
10. While in the laboratory using solutions, specimens, equipment, or materials, hands should be kept away from the face, eyes, and body. Gloves should be worn when handling some reagents. Hands should be washed thoroughly with soap at the conclusion of each laboratory period.
11. Students should note the location of the emergency shower, eye and face wash fountain, fire blanket, and fire extinguishers and know how to use them.
12. Students should know the proper fire drill procedure.
13. Long sleeves should be rolled up above the wrist. Ties, coats, and sweaters should be removed. Long hair should be tied back during laboratory activity, especially when an open flame is nearby. (Use hairnets, if necessary.)
14. Student apparel should be appropriate for laboratory work. Long hanging necklaces, bulky jewelry, and excessive and bulky clothing should not be worn in the laboratory.

15. Work areas should be kept clean and tidy.
16. Students should always clean, and wipe dry, all desks, tables, or laboratory work areas at the conclusion of each laboratory activity.
17. Broken glass should be removed from work area or floor as soon as possible. Never handle broken glass with your bare hands. Use counter brush and dustpan and/or wet cotton wads held with forceps and dispose in proper containers.
18. All solid waste should be thrown in separate waste baskets, jars, or other designated receptacles. Do not discard any solids in the laboratory sinks, especially glass items such as tubing or cover glasses.
19. Matches should not be thrown into waste paper baskets. A metal container with sand should be provided for them.
20. Litmus paper, wooden splints, toothpicks, etc. should be disposed of in the same manner as matches.
21. Gas burners should be lighted only with a sparker in accordance with your teacher's instructions.
22. Extreme caution should be exercised when using a burner. Keep your head and clothing away from the flame and turn off when not in use.
23. Do not bring any substance into contact with a flame, unless specifically instructed to do so.
24. Only lab manuals and lab notebooks are permitted in the working area. Other books, purses, and such items should be placed in your desk or storage area.
25. Students are not permitted in laboratory storage rooms or teacher work rooms, unless directly instructed to do so.
26. Upon first entering the laboratory, students are not permitted to touch laboratory equipment until directed to do so.
27. Any science project or experiment that requires the use of dangerous drugs or chemicals that are caustic or poisonous, must be approved by the teacher in accordance with school policies.
28. Always twist, never push glass tubing into stopper holes. Lubricate stopper hole and glass tubing with water or glycerin to insert easily. Always use glass tubing with fire polished ends.
29. Students should be alert and proceed with caution at all times in the science laboratory. Take care not to bump another student and remain in your lab station while performing an experiment. An unattended experiment can produce an accident.

zest, present the demonstration inductively, ask inquiry-oriented questions, give positive techniques, summarize, and evaluate the demonstration. A demonstration may be conducted by the teacher, by the teacher and students together, by a group of students, by an individual student, or by a guest. More attention should be given to demonstrations other than those presented by the teacher, with accompanying comments. Silent demonstrations offer a different approach and emphasize observational techniques.

Equipment should be stored so that it is easily located for future demonstrations. Special equipment can often be secured from local industries without cost. The overhead projector and microprojector are excellent teaching aids for demonstrations.

Individual experimentation is usually a more desirable teaching technique than are demonstrations, but demonstrations have the advantage of economy of time and money, allow for greater direction by the teacher, and provide certain safety precautions. Demonstrations should contribute to the higher levels of learning—those requiring critical thinking and creativity.

Laboratory work in the junior and senior high school is constantly changing. From the emphasis on "verification" experiments in the traditional mode, the student is now invited to "inquire into" or "investigate" a problem. Laboratory experience becomes the initial experience with a new topic of subject matter, followed by discussion, reading, and further experimentation. The experiment may lead to new problems that warrant investigation.

The junior high school is becoming increasingly oriented toward a laboratory approach. Not only does this approach give students an early start in learning the methods of science, but certain skills are introduced and practiced that will have value in later sciences taken in the senior high school.

With more of the responsibility for learning in the laboratory being allocated to the student himself, the matter of safety becomes even more important. The science teacher must carefully train students in the use of laboratory apparatus and materials. This training may precede actual work in the laboratory or be an intrinsic part of the laboratory work early in the students' experience.

The promise of science for the future continues. A breakthrough has been achieved in which students at last have become participants in the search for knowledge, not mere recipients of facts and generalizations dispensed by authoritative teachers and textbooks. The laboratory is the key instrument in science teaching.

■ References

1. E. S. Obourn, *Aids for Teaching Science Observation—Basis for Effective Science Learning*, Office of Education Publication No. 29024 (Washington, D.C.: U.S. Government Printing Office, 1961).
2. Paul F. Brandwein and Joseph J. Schwab, *The Teaching of Science as Enquiry* (Cambridge: Harvard University Press, 1962), pp. 52-53.
3. Patricia Blosser, "The Role of the Laboratory in Science Teaching," *School Science and Mathematics* 83(2), February, 1983.
4. Clifford Hofwolt, *Laboratory Science Course Handbook for Laboratory Assistants*, Mimeographed (University of Northern Colorado, Greeley: Department of Science Education, 1968).
5. George J. O'Neill, Television Series Program #1, *Safety in the Science Laboratory* (Sponsored by the N. E. Tennessee Section of the American Chemical Society in cooperation with WSJK, Knoxville, TN, 1975).
6. John Wesley Brennan, "An Investigation of Factors Related to Safety in the High School Science Program," Ed.D dissertation, University of Denver, 1970. (ED 085 179).
7. *Safety First in Science Teaching*, Division of Science, North Carolina Dept. of Public Instruction, Raleigh, NC (1977).
8. NSTA, *Safety in the Secondary Science Classroom* (Washington, D.C.: NSTA Subcommittee on Safety, 1978).
9. Robert McComber, "Chemistry Accidents in High School," *Journal of Chemical Education* (July 1961) pp. 367–68.
10. *Safety First in Science Teaching.*

=====   INVESTIGATING SCIENCE TEACHING   =====

ACTIVITY 14–1

Doing Experiments for Skill Development

Design an experiment that students can do in the classroom or laboratory and which gives practice in the skills of science as discussed on page 211. Choose a particular grade level and select suitable apparatus and materials to achieve the "skill-development" objectives.

ACTIVITY 14–2

The Laboratory

1. Suggest a suitable format for a laboratory report in a high school science. Keep in mind that this is not to be a rigorous form but one that is kept flexible and open to student initiative.

2. Study the laboratory guides of several of the following curriculum projects: PSSC, BSCS, CHEM Study, CBAC, ESCP, IPS, and others. What similarities do you find? How do these laboratory guides differ from traditional laboratory manuals? Be prepared to discuss these differences in class.

CHAPTER 15

Materials and Facilities for Science Teaching

The science teacher is fortunate in having an abundance of teaching materials to draw on. Her problem is selecting the proper materials and techniques to accomplish this task. Recent years have seen a proliferation of teaching materials of every description; the display areas of any large convention of science teachers present an overwhelming variety of these materials.

With so many teaching aids available, it is well to consider the purposes they serve in the process of educating science students:

1. More of the students' senses are stimulated by teaching aids. They frequently activate the avenues of learning involving sight, sound, touch, smell, and taste. Combinations of senses are appealed to more often.
2. Teaching aids maintain interest. Students are likely to be in a receptive frame of mind for maximum learning.
3. Teaching becomes less fatiguing when a variety of methods and materials is used and the teacher's enthusiasm is maintained.
4. Individual differences are most adequately served by a variety of teaching aids. Students frequently learn better by one method than by another.
5. Teaching aids provide opportunities for frequent changes of pace, which is particularly useful in middle school teaching.
6. Specific materials designed for specific teaching tasks are more effective because of their refined nature. For example, a well-designed model of certain geological features may illustrate a point

better than a photograph or in some cases better than an actual field trip to the scene.

■ Using Science Learning Materials

Printed materials will continue to be important in science teaching. Textbooks are still a basic source of information in science classes, and when they are used judiciously and with realization of their limitations, textbooks contribute substantially to the teaching-learning situation.

A publication by the National Science Teachers Association provides some guidelines concerning science learning materials.[1] Their recommendations are intended to offer some guidance in determining the kind and quantity of such materials.

1. When needed for learning, individual textbooks and laboratory manuals should be available without cost to every student.
2. The science textbooks used by students at any time should be no more than four years past the date of the last major revision.
3. For each science course there should be an ample supply of diverse printed materials to supplement the textbook and laboratory manual.
4. The school science library should contain an adequate selection of books, periodicals, and pamphlets on the sciences, the applications of science, and the history, philosophy, and sociology of science.
5. An adequate supply of modern science equipment should be available for individual and

National Science Teachers Association

A wide variety of materials and apparatus is available to the science teacher.

small-group activities and experiments.

6. A diverse supply of audiovisual learning materials must be readily available for each science course.
7. Certain items of audiovisual equipment should be provided as permanent equipment for individual courses.

■ Use of Textbooks

The selection of science textbooks frequently reflects concerns for readability, topical content, recency or currency of information presented, and other factors that emphasize the practical and pragmatic matters associated with textbook adoption. Decisions based on what is best for particular students who will receive instruction from the textbooks sometimes are lacking in perspective.

An example of an attempt to use a sociological perspective in selecting science textbooks was reported by Lynn M. Mulkey at Hunter College in New York City.[2] The main research question was "Does selection of science textbooks deprive younger chil-

dren in working-class school districts the benefits of perspectives that will help make them 'participants' in science while simultaneously enriching the scientific preparation of older children in middle-class school districts?"

The findings indicated that the availability of (textbook) knowledge important for the development of a scientific role (career) was, on the average, the same for both middle- and working-class districts. However, social class had a distinctive effect on orientation to cognitive flexibility. The middle-class child is more likely to receive encouragement in developing cognitive flexibility (the privilege to be nonconforming). Textbooks appear to be written and selected for children who are perceived as prepared for cognitive flexibility and may have "an accumulated advantage which may or may not be attributable to differences in capacity."[3] The science teacher must place the textbook in its proper perspective in her classes. Students generally feel more comfortable with a textbook than without one. It serves to organize information, stress important concepts, direct activity, and set goals for the study of a particular science. All of these contributions are important. It must be remembered, however, that a textbook alone cannot achieve even a majority of the objectives of science teaching. It cannot provide laboratory experiences, develop true inquiry skills, or teach self-reliance in solving problems. These are objectives that are achieved best by other methods and materials. But, in collaboration with a variety of other materials, the textbook is an important contributor to these objectives.

Selecting a textbook for a given science class is frequently a haphazard affair. Textbooks are often chosen after superficial inspection. Color may influence one's choice more than content; photographs may carry more weight than organization of subject matter; advertising appeal may be more of a deciding factor than usefulness to students.

In selecting a textbook in science, criteria should be established against which competing books can be rated. These criteria include:

A. Factors which deal with the subject-matter content and organization
   1. Logical organization, sequence of difficulty, grouping of topics
   2. Emphasis on principles and concepts
   3. Accuracy of information
   4. Usefulness of information, applications, and functional nature of the material
   5. Recent information, modern concepts, theories, and applications
B. Factors which deal with development of noncontent objectives

1. Attention given to development of interests, appreciations, and attitudes
2. Attention given to problem-solving approach
3. Attention given to skills of science learning
4. Attention given to the role of science in society and to scientific literacy

C. Factors which deal with experiments, demonstrations, and activities
1. Inquiry or verification approach
2. Student participation, activity, and investigation
3. Use of simple materials, degree of structure in laboratories
4. Emphasis on drawing conclusions on the basis of observation and experimentation

D. Factors which deal with mechanical features of the textbook
1. Binding, size, durability, attractiveness
2. Size of type, level of reading difficulty, summaries, glossaries, index
3. Illustrations, maps, charts, graphs, captions
4. General ease in using the book

E. Factors which deal with authors of the textbook
1. Qualifications (experience, level of preparation)
2. Quality of writing, interest, and readability
3. References to purposes of the book and intended use

F. Factors which deal with prospective useful life of the textbook
1. Copyright date, revisions, and reprintings
2. Nature of material, rate of obsolescence, years of usability

It is suggested that these criteria be used with a rating scale for comparison with competing textbooks. A number scale like the one that follows might be used:

0	Book totally lacking in the characteristic
1	Occasional evidence of the characteristic
2	Greater evidence of the characteristic but below average
3	Reasonably frequent evidence of the characteristic
4	Excellent evidence of the characteristic
5	Superior in all aspects of the characteristic

Readability Analysis

Probably the most important consideration when analyzing textbooks for a science class is its readability. The reading level of students in any given class varies by several grade levels. To meet individual differences, to avoid discouraging students with low reading levels, and to avoid frustration, it is necessary to select a book that will meet the needs of a variety of students. Usually, these criteria result in the selection of books with reading levels at or slightly below the grade level for the class.

Just what is readability? Readability refers to reading difficulty of a book, paragraph, or prose passage. Many factors enter into readability, such as types of sentence construction, length of sentences, vocabulary, number of syllables in words, type of print, and concept density. There are at the present time several readability formulas which are frequently used in analyzing textbooks. Unfortunately, the results obtained by the various formulas do not agree. (See Activity 15-1, p. 270.)

■ Audiovisual Materials

Recent years have seen the development of many audiovisual aids for the science teacher. These materials have not always enjoyed the best possible usage because of certain limiting conditions. It is important for the science teacher to have a good working knowledge of several audiovisual devices and to be aware of their teaching possibilities.

In using an audiovisual aid, the teacher's most important consideration is, "Is this the most effective method at my disposal for teaching these concepts?" If the answer is yes, every effort should be made to incorporate the aid into classroom planning. Mental inertia or unwillingness to try a new device should not remain a deterrent to good teaching in science.

Films

Motion-picture films have been used with varying effectiveness for many years. Their limitations are:

1. Poor scheduling or inability to secure the film at the optimum time or place in the course.
2. Poor showing techniques, such as unfamiliarity with the equipment, inadequate room darkening, or general ineptness resulting in wasted time.
3. Poor choice of film. Films thirty minutes long may have only five minutes of appropriate learning material in them. The intellectual level of the film may not be appropriate for the class.
4. Indiscriminate use of films that do not contribute to attainment of the course objectives.
5. Cost of rental or purchase, which may be prohibitive for some school systems.

The advantages of motion-picture films are numerous. They include:

1. Close-up sequences, which may be superior to a live demonstration
2. Organization of content in succinct and in capsulized form
3. Showing of experiments not feasible in the average laboratory because of time and expense
4. Slow-motion or time-lapse photography, which demonstrates phenomena too rapid or too slow for first-hand observation
5. Showing of natural scientific phenomena from places not accessible for class visitation
6. Animated sequences that help to clarify difficult concepts
7. Creative sound and visual effects for dramatic reinforcement learning

Variations on the standard film techniques are becoming more common. Single-concept films are produced by several companies. These films are brief and develop a single important idea which can be further pursued in class discussion.

Teacher's guides for films are often provided. They give a resumé of the major film ideas, suggestions for use, questions raised in the film with possible answers, and a list of supplementary reading materials.

Eight-millimeter film loops are now available in a number of areas in biology, chemistry, physics, and general science. Fitted into a small cartridge with a specially designed silent-film projector, these film loops can be operated by individual students when necessary. Since they are usually less than ten minutes long, they can be run repetitively until the concepts are thoroughly understood.

Filmstrips and Slides

Filmstrips have several advantages for science teaching:

1. Relatively inexpensive and can be purchased by a library or science department for a permanent collection. The projectors are correspondingly less expensive than motion-picture projectors.
2. Can be stopped at a given frame for whatever time is needed to discuss the ideas presented.
3. Students may study these films individually with minimum disruption of other class work. They are noiseless and require only a moderately darkened area.
4. Frequently available at no cost from industry and government sources. They are usually accompanied by a printed narrative guide or lecture for use when showing the film.

There is no single rule for the best usage of films. The science teacher must be free to use films creatively and flexibly, as they can be fitted into his teaching objectives.

Slides present innumerable opportunities for good teaching. Their relatively low cost and flexibility in use are points in their favor. A science teacher may acquire a highly effective teaching aid by making a collection of his own photographs on colored slides. The purchase of a tripod and inexpensive close-up lens enables a teacher to make pictures of plant and animal life for use in the classroom. The slide collection acquired in this way becomes more valuable each year. Students frequently can produce their own slides for reports, projects, or classroom research activities.

Overhead Projection

Most science teachers are using overhead projection as an aid to teaching. The versatility of this instrument makes it an extremely useful tool for everyday classroom use. Some teachers consider it an indispensable piece of equipment.

An overhead projector costs relatively little, much less than a motion-picture projector, for example. The cost of transparencies, or the materials for making them, is likewise low. Only moderate darkening of the room is needed for satisfactory visibility. The instrument is as convenient to use as the chalkboard and is frequently used as a replacement for it.

Materials that can be used with the overhead projector in science teaching are contained in the Tested Overhead Projection Series (TOPS) produced by a project of the National Science Foundation.[4] In this series, several chemistry demonstrations were designed to be conducted on the overhead projector in full view of the entire chemistry class. There are other adaptations for physics and biology.[5] In many cases, demonstration apparatus is designed to be used with standard overhead projectors.

Television

Radio and television have not yet fulfilled their promise as teaching aids for the science teacher in the average classroom. Ordinary AM radio has occasional use, as special programs in science or science-related areas are broadcast, but they at best are of a general nature for lay consumption. A few educational FM stations have produced science programs, but the average science student has not benefited perceptibly from them. Probably the most direct benefit has been derived from on-the-spot news reports of scientific events such as space exploration, natural disasters, or scientific breakthroughs.

The dream of television as an effective teaching tool has still to be realized. However, news coverage of scientific events has become immeasurably more dramatic since the advent of television and probably has contributed to vastly improved understanding of these events. The opportunity to witness a space shuttle launch or a television program about planetary exploration is tremendously stimulating. It undoubtedly molds public opinion in regard to scientific problems and progress. In this respect, one of the objectives of science teaching, development of scientific attitudes, is being met by forces outside the control of the science teacher. It remains to be seen whether this will be beneficial. A false impression of science as a gimmick-filled world of spectacular advancements in technology may be created at the expense of a sound understanding of the role of science in society.

As a direct teaching tool, television has yet to come into common use. The technical problems and expense of installation and upkeep are formidable. Closed-circuit television may become the tool of the future, but it has not yet received wide acceptance; too few science teachers are trained to use it and explore its many possibilities. Furthermore, very few schools are equipped to make use of it on a planned and regular basis. For an example of television's educational use, see the "Teaching Science Activity: Weather: Air Masses and Fronts," on page 461-462.

A more feasible use of television results from the development of inexpensive portable videotape recorders. Many schools and teacher-training institutions are using this tool for instruction and micro-teaching experience. In many cases, one-half-inch tape units are completely satisfactory and introduce an element of versatility into the teacher's instructional plans. It is important that units be designed for compatibility so that tapes can be interchanged and recorded or played on several different models.

Some of the advantages that may be realized from television are:

1. Direct teaching to large numbers of students by a well-prepared master teacher with access to adequate demonstration equipment.
2. Opportunity for close-up viewing by the television camera, giving optimum visibility to all students.
3. Opportunity for on-the-spot viewing of scientific events.

4. Opportunity for training science students in television techniques and familiarizing them with its teaching and learning possibilities.

Desirable as these results are, it is important to realize that television has limitations as well. It cannot replace the science teacher. It cannot develop laboratory skills or replace the difficult, repetitive problem-solving practice necessary for mastery of certain science concepts and skills.

Tape Recorders

Tape recorders have become popular as teaching aids in science as well as in other subjects. In biology, for example, they might be used to record sounds of nature such as bird calls and other forest sounds. Classroom use of the tape recorder might include taping student reports, interviews with community resource people, or scientific programs on radio or television. The tape recorder is an instrument most science students take to readily. Their resourcefulness in its use may surprise the science teacher at times.

The advent of reliable cassette tape recorders has placed this teaching aid in the nearly indispensable class. Inexpensive units with almost maintenance-free care for years of satisfactory use, even when subjected to rough handling, make the cassette tape recorder an innovative tool for teaching.

Materials for the Laboratory

Science deals with the phenomena of nature. These phenomena cannot be studied effectively through abstract or theoretical discussion alone, although this may be necessary at times. Most science students find that actual objects, models, or living specimens make a phenomenon concrete enough to be understood. Science materials and apparatus—demonstration equipment as well as materials for experimentation—are designed to fulfill this function.

One of the major problems for the junior and senior high school science teacher is the procurement and maintenance of laboratory equipment. Questions of what and how much to order, how to use the apparatus most effectively, and how to store it conveniently for future use are difficult ones, especially for a beginning science teacher. Frequently, it is the teacher moving into a new position who faces these problems in their most acute form. If the preceding teacher has not kept careful records of apparatus and equipment and maintained them in good

Laboratory equipment such as microscopes can make a concept easily understandable to students.

working order, the job of inventorying can be overwhelming.

If possible, it is wise for a teacher beginning a new science position to plan on spending several days in advance of the regular opening of school to work on inventorying equipment, checking its condition, and preparing orders for needed supplies for the year. This preparation will contribute to more effective teaching throughout the year. Teaching plans may be built around certain materials that are available in sufficient quantities for classroom demonstrations and experiments. It is highly recommended that schools and science departments use their microcomputers to inventory their materials and equipment.

Ordering and Inventorying

Factors to be considered in purchasing equipment and laboratory materials are:

1. Is this the best available item for the teaching purpose intended? Because of the importance of the teaching task and the limitations of time, it is essential to have the best possible tools at hand. The equipment must be basically simple, be capable of illustrating the intended principles, and be engineered to work well.
2. Will the materials serve their intended purpose for a reasonable length of time? Classroom

| (Subject) |
| Inventory for _____ |
| Item _____ Catalog No._____ |
| Company _____ Cost_____ |
| Storage Code _____ |

Date No. Condition Reorder Date Cost

FIGURE 15–1
Inventory card

equipment and other materials receive hard use as successive classes work with them. They must be designed to withstand rough handling for several years. A poorly engineered and constructed apparatus, though possibly less expensive to purchase, is rarely economical in the long run.
3. Are the materials functional? Can they be stored easily without excessive disassembly? Do they lend themselves to student use? It is generally a mistake to purchase overly delicate apparatus or equipment with unnecessary precision capabilities for the secondary science class.
4. Is the cost reasonable for the quality of equipment purchased? Comparing catalog prices from several companies can result in savings. It is essential to check the specifications carefully on all apparatus ordered, to ensure that they meet the requirements of the situation.

New equipment and materials of the nonexpendable variety should be inventoried on receipt. A three-by-five card file system is a useful method to keep a record of new purchases and current stock of materials and apparatus. A suggested form for an inventory card is shown in Figure 15.1.

Each nonexpendable item in stock should be inventoried on a card of this type. Expendable items should be inventoried on a longer form of the checklist variety. With a well-kept inventory checklist, it should be possible to ascertain the amount and condition of expendable items at a glance. Since the preparation of such a list and the effort required to keep it current is quite time-consuming, this task should be assigned to student laboratory assistants if possible. An inventory checklist might look like the one shown in Figure 15.2.

■ Supplementary Teaching Aids

The sources of supplementary teaching materials are multiplying year by year. For the science teacher, a major problem in using them is proper selection.

Inventory of Expendables, Chemistry					
Date	Item	Condition	On Hand	Needed	Cost
4/81	Tubing, glass (4 mm.)	Ex.	10 lbs.	0	
4/81	Tubing, glass (5 mm.)	Ex.	10 lbs.	0	
4/81	Tubing, glass (10 mm.)	Ex.	0	5 lbs.	$.75/lb.
4/81	Tubing, rubber (4 mm.)	Good	50 ft.	0	
4/81	Tubing, rubber (5 mm.)	Good	10 ft.	40 ft.	$3.50/ 100 ft.

FIGURE 15–2
Inventory checklist

Educational departments of industrial companies have created or made available to teachers innumerable aids for science teaching. Many of these materials are free or can be obtained at minimal expense. Many kits and project materials for the use of junior and senior high school students are now available. Some of them are free if ordered in small quantities.

A very useful type of supplementary teaching aid is student science periodicals such as *Science News, Current Science, Science World*, and *Science and Math Weekly*. Subscription rates for students are nominal. In addition to highly informative articles on current science topics, these publications frequently contain suggested activities and experiments for students. A teacher's edition, containing suggestions on how to use the activities and other materials, is sometimes provided. The science teacher of today would be remiss if he failed to use these very teachable science materials.

Some activities require minimal materials, often very simple items the students can make themselves. For an example, see the "Teaching Science Activity: The Evolution Simulation Game," on page 463–466.

As with the standard equipment and materials discussed earlier, storage and availability for effective use are problems in the classroom. A storage file for printed materials, indexed by subject, is a necessary item, and periodic updating is required.

■ The Role of the Science Staff in Planning Facilities

Assisting in the planning of modern science complexes and the remodelling of old facilities to meet the demands of new instructional methods in science is the responsibility of the science teacher. It is a rare

Many industrial companies offer kits and project materials that can be rented, borrowed, or purchased at a low cost.

teacher who will not be involved in this type of activity during her professional career.

Planning a facility that will be educationally effective and efficient for thirty to forty years requires the best minds available. Several well-qualified persons should be involved in the planning, including science teachers with vast experience; science educators; and local, state, and national science supervisors. Building a structure which may cost millions certainly warrants expenditures for planning. It is desirable that some science teachers be hired during the summer so that they can devote their full time to this task.

A teacher's philosophy of education defines activities which suggest facilities. It is important that a teacher consider what he wishes to accomplish educationally and then what type of facilities will enable him to reach these objectives. A teacher must remember, however, that he will not be the only instructor to use the plan. It will undoubtedly be in use long after he has retired. It is paramount that he think to the future, to science teaching in the 1990s and the 2000s, and ask, "What can I help design today that will not hinder other teachers two or three decades from now?"

It is the responsibility of science teachers to outline the educational specifications for the archi-

Preparing for the First Year

Susan Stewart
Physical Science Teacher, Kenny C. Guinn Junior High
Las Vegas, Nevada

Are there really slot machines in the classrooms? Do cacti grow on the playground? Do most of the teachers lose their paychecks in the local casino once a week? These and similar questions were asked by the folks back home when I left my conservative Midwestern hometown to start an adventure as an eighth-grade science teacher in Las Vegas. Regardless of the different images people have of this city, I am certain that my experiences as a first-year teacher here are very much like those of my fellow graduates in other parts of the country. Adolescents are adolescents no matter where they live. The first year of teaching junior high is frustrating and exhausting. But as my colleagues assure me, it gets easier with experience, and I believe them.

Las Vegas is growing by leaps and bounds and consequently is one of the few places in this country crying for teachers. Kenny C. Guinn Junior High just opened this fall with 1,150 students drawn mainly from a rapidly expanding part of town. Most of the parents in this area are employed by the hotels on the Strip. Because of the growth of this town and the fact that in most cases both parents work, Clark County is a fairly wealthy district. Comprehensive special education programs, vocational-technical education, and career exploration are emphasized at all levels. Strong emphasis is placed on basics and comprehensive programs are offered in all schools for youngsters who need special help in reading and mathematics. The Clark County School District reflects all ethnic backgrounds in its student population, staff, and approach to learning. The ethnic distribution of students is 78 percent Caucasian, 15 percent Black, 5 percent Spanish-American, 0.4 percent American Indian, and 1.6 percent others.

With three new schools opening in September 1979, the district had 110 schools. It is a privilege to be a member of the staff which opened one of these new schools. It is exciting and challenging to participate in setting precedents and in creating new curricula for over 1,100 students. Other "thrills of opening a new school" (as my principal loves to say) include dealing with unfinished rooms and laboratory facilities, undelivered supplies and equipment, waiting for defective doors and pencil sharpeners to be repaired, and running a program that has never been tried before. These are times which call for the highest virtues a teacher can possess: flexibility, creativity, and patience.

This first year as a junior high science teacher is an eye-opening experience. There are so many things I am facing now for which no college course or textbook ever prepared me. Who could have taught me how to handle the politics within an administration or of a district school board? What course trained me to deal with the parents of different students? Was there a textbook recipe on how to deal with the normal day-to-day stress which confronts anyone who works with teenagers up to eight hours a day? I am very thankful for the preparation I did have in my undergraduate years. There, I developed very important organization skills. I learned how to express my creativity and my love for science through writing curricula. I was challenged to develop an educational philosophy and to learn how to apply it to practical and realistic objectives for the classroom.

My strength as a teacher lies in my enthusiasm for my subject and in my wholehearted conviction that it is valuable for every youngster. I also have a certain empathy for junior high

tect. The science teacher does not design the room. The design of the science area obviously must fit into the total scheme for the school. Designing the area for optimum fulfillment of the educational specifications is the responsibility of the architect.

The science staff has a role to play in site se-

lection. They should urge the administration, before the site is selected, that consideration be given to how the site can add to the instructional program of the school. Such a consideration is of particular importance in the area of biology, where field work does much to complement the class instruction. The final

students and a genuine concern for guiding them through "those difficult years." Supposedly, those qualities are enough to start the young teacher off with a smooth-running classroom. Well, if you do not discover it in student teaching, you soon find out on your first job how fragile all those idealistic goals and perceptions of education are; they shatter before your eyes within the first three months. It takes persistence and faith to piece together again a modified educational philosophy consistent with the classroom realities.

One of the major areas for which college courses have failed to prepare teachers in the past is discipline. As a first-year teacher, I did not anticipate spending 70 percent of the class time in teaching students that there are logical consequences to their actions. Genuine concern, conscientious hard work, and creative lesson plans are not enough. The prospective teacher needs to be *trained* in effective classroom control. I, like many other teachers, have learned classroom management by trial-and-error and have ended up using methods which just seem to work. For certain periods of time, my actions became mechanical and/or inconsistent; they were designed to eliminate my stress and they did not always consider the best interests of the child. To create a workable and consistent philosophy of discipline, the young teacher needs more background in adolescent psychology and more practical experience in the classroom with time to apply, evaluate, and revise this philosophy.

Teaching is not an eight-hour-a-day job; you are a teacher around the clock. The demands by the public for what a good teacher should be are increasing. The trend to make teachers accountable

for cranking out reading, writing, and calculating students is on the uprise. More and more guidelines and restrictions are being established as to what you can teach. College is the place to learn some self-preservation and sanity-saver techniques. Gather ideas for your future curricula. Learn how to express your creativity in concrete objectives. Spend as much time as you can in the classroom—observing, experimenting, and evaluating. Solidify what you believe about children, the role of the teacher, and the role of the school and start to observe how it works in practice.

There are still several things for which no text or course can prepare you. At times, as a first-year teacher, there will appear to be few rewards and even those few will not be immediately visible. You need to be aware of the potential morale problems you will face among your faculty. Although you confront disillusionment, you must resist being drawn into a negative attitude. Keep hold of those ideals; you may have to reconstruct them but do not ever abandon them. Budget cuts, crowded classrooms, and apathetic parents are other challenges which await you. It is part of the occupation, however, and your decision to stick with it boils down to your own conviction that you possess a potential power to make a dent in it all.

My personal conviction is strong enough that I know I want to make teaching my career. I plan to finish coursework for a Master's degree in geology or biology. With that, I would like to try teaching overseas for a few years. Environmental education also appeals to me and I may want to move into the position of a consultant. This first year is just the beginning, of course, and there are many possibilities ahead.

decision in this matter is the responsibility of the Board of Education and must be based on cost and other factors. For example, a site desirable because it offers a good natural area for science work may present a problem in transporting students to and from school.

■ Influences on Science Facilities

Trends in Science Instruction

To ensure that facilities will not be outdated, the science staff must be aware of the trends in science instruction. Science education has undergone a dynamic revolution in curriculum and in teaching methods and techniques. Modern technology and research in learning theory alter the present methods of instruction. To insure that facilities do not restrict new methods of instruction they should be designed so that they are flexible, easily modifiable, and take into account the trends in science education.

Teaching Methods

Two instructional approaches which are receiving attention are team teaching and individualized instruction. Team teaching involves some large-group instruction for 80 to 100 students, with smaller laboratory sections. Instruction for large lecture-demonstration classes is afforded by lecture complexes or by rooms divided by operable walls which open for large groups. Individualized instruction is designed to allow each student to progress at his own rate. This approach requires many individual work areas. Both group and individualized instruction require diverse facilities far removed from those of the traditional classroom.

A variation on this concept is that of differentiated staffing. In this concept, various groups of teachers serve different functions. There may be one or more master teachers in each subject-matter discipline. Other teachers serve in supporting roles, along with noncertified teacher aides, specialists, and other individuals. The differentiated concept is considered to be more efficient in the use of the school's time and allows more teacher-student interaction. It also provides a basis for differentiation of pay scales and the application of merit-pay concepts.

In recent years a different concept of education has been tried, namely, that of the open school (sometimes called free school). There are several examples of this type in the United States and in Europe. The open school may be completely ungraded, yet it may extend from ages four or five up through ages seventeen and eighteen, corresponding to the twelfth grade. Some of the innovations in the open school are the use of noncompulsory attendance, freedom of choice by the students for the classes they wish, and the use of teacher aides, parents, specialists, and individuals who can work through a broad spectrum of problems. To be effective, the open school must have a responsive and rich environment with ample materials available for students to work with. At the present time, most open schools are at the elementary level, but there are several exceptions which continue to ages seventeen and eighteen.

It appears that a developing trend throughout science education is the application of more humane methods of teaching. There is more concern about student attitudes and interests and other aspects of the affective domain. Teachers are beginning to make an effort to develop feelings of mutual trust between the students and themselves. They consider that each student has individual worth. Increasingly, teachers attempt to develop and maintain positive attitudes for education and schooling.

There is an increased use of audiovisual aids by small groups and individuals engaged in special work. Tape recorders are being used more often to enrich class instruction. Some of the new schools have multiple tape-recording outlets and a series of tapes so that individual students can listen to various tapes at the same time. This arrangement is similar, on a limited basis, to the type of activity that goes on in language laboratories. Provision must be made to ensure widened use of audiovisual material on both individual and group bases.

Another development is emphasis on more varied instruction. Not all students necessarily perform the same experiment in the same class period. In one class, students may be engaged in several different activities.

More space for both equipment and storage is being provided in many schools. This change includes the provision of more preparation areas.

Curriculum

Certain curriculum changes have become more and more evident in the past twenty years. Among them are the use of new curricula at the middle school, junior high, and senior high levels. Frequently the sequence in the junior high is "living sciences" in the seventh grade, "physical science" in the eighth grade, and "earth science" in the ninth grade. Some schools have developed mini-courses, which are one-semester courses on rather specialized topics and which are offered on an elective basis so that students may choose them to satisfy individual needs. In recent years, various courses in environmental sciences have been developed as part of the mini-course offerings.

A discernible change in the interpretation of the word *laboratory* seems to be evident in recent years. Rather than thinking of the laboratory as merely a room equipped with gas, water, and electricity, it now is thought of as a place where experiments can be conducted. This conception might include the outdoors as well as the indoors, and it might include observational experiments, particularly with respect to the life and earth sciences. Modern curricula emphasize laboratory approaches, which require more

=========== REFLECTING ON SCIENCE TEACHING ===========

Designing Facilities

1. Discuss what Churchill meant by the statement, "We shape our facilities; thereafter they shape us."
2. What relevance does the statement "form follows function" have for science teachers?
3. Who should be involved in the planning of science facilities and why?
4. Many schools are built with little or no consultation with school personnel. Why is this an undesirable practice?
5. What does a teacher's philosophy of education have to do with facilities?

---

laboratory space and supporting facilities, such as preparation rooms, live rooms, greenhouses, and student research and project areas.

Most of the modern curriculum developments emphasize inquiry. Facilities must be provided to allow for inquiring in several ways, such as reading, observation, experimentation, study of models, films (sixteen- and eight-millimeter), charts, preserved specimens, field work, slides, overhead projection, and film-strip projection. Information from a variety of sources is becoming more available to students, requiring greater flexibility in space utilization.

Some curriculum developers discern a recent trend in science classrooms toward a return to teacher demonstrations and seatwork.[6] This trend may reflect higher costs of laboratory equipment.

Some schools use the block approach to learning science. This method is most advanced in the BSCS biology course, in which students concentrate on laboratory work in depth for four to six weeks. This arrangement requires greater storage space, as do some other modern developments in science instruction.

Advanced science courses, such as science seminars or advanced placement, are frequently used and require more work areas.

Trends in Science Facilities

Flexibility of design is an important feature of science facilities. What does this mean? One definition frequently used is, "Flexibility is the capability of an internal space to be changed or defined *solely* by the user." This implies (1) the equipment used should have optimal functionality and mobility and (2) the degree of flexibility is determined by the number of usable changes; that is, the more usable changes, the greater the degree of flexibility. There should be the capacity for immediate change (changes which require only minutes to make) and long-range changeability (something which might take place over a weekend or during a vacation period).

The adaptation gaining popularity is the "service sandwich," a 36-inch space between floors in which are contained wiring, lighting fixtures, TV conduits, air ducts, plumbing, and other utilities. Access to these utilities may be through the ceiling at designated points, spaced so that rooms may be changed at will but utilities will be easily accessible. There is not much point in being able to change partitions around if one cannot also change the lighting arrangements, plumbing, controls for air conditioning, and other services. Grid troughs containing electrical conduits, ducts for hot and cold air and return ducts, fluorescent light tubes, telephone lines, electrical wiring conduits, switches, outlets, radio and TV circuitry, and intercom systems are designed into the service sandwich.

Between 1970 and 1972, exemplary science facilities were studied by the National Science Teachers Association.[7] Six task force members visited more than 140 schools in the United States. These schools had been nominated by individuals, state science groups, and the National Science Supervisors Association. The purpose of the study was to assess the status of science teaching facilities in the middle, junior high, senior high, and junior college levels.

Two characteristics of science facilities were considered necessary to earn the judgment of "exemplary." They were "flexibility" and provision for "individualization." Early in the study it was found that facilities themselves could not be studied separately or isolated from other characteristics of science teaching, including programs, curriculum materials, and instructional staff.

Two modes of science instruction, showing the trend toward greater emphasis on student-centered learning through the use of materials and facilities, are shown in Figure 15.3. In the first mode, the traditional teaching situation involves a teacher, resource materials, books, and other sources of information impinging on the student from many directions. The student himself has little control over what he receives. In the second emerging pattern of school instruction, the student finds himself at the

FIGURE 15–3
Contrasting modes of science instruction

center of learning with freedom and opportunities to select from a variety of teaching modes, including resource rooms, carrels, laboratories, resource persons, lectures, textbooks, and other materials. The difference between these two modes is based on the place at which the student is put in the learning pattern.

The evolving patterns in facilities and programs are shown in Figure 15.4. The arrows indicate the transition from rigid, traditional patterns near the bottom to flexible and optional modes at the top of each ladder.

Trends in School Buildings

One of these trends is that of the "open-concept" school. Schools designed along this line frequently do not have interior walls, or if they do have walls, they are minimal and frequently are not load-bearing. Movable partitions are used frequently. Bookcases and room dividers are used in place of the typical cinderblock wall. The environment in such schools is usually pleasant, particularly if the interior of the building has been acoustically treated. This treatment includes carpeting of the floors and walls, if possible, and the use of acoustical tile or varied ceilings to break up the sound patterns.

The open-concept schools give considerable freedom of movement and, when combined with flexible scheduling patterns, provide an atmosphere that is casual and aesthetically pleasing. Students move from area to area in small groups or individually and the typical clatter found in a traditional classroom when the bell indicates the end of a class period is usually absent in this type of school. To provide for freedom of movement, there must be flex-

ible furniture and ample work areas for small groups. Laboratories are often placed along the perimeter or are designed in some kind of movable fashion, which leads to some innovation in laboratory furniture. One innovation coming into the foreground is the use of "power islands" which include electricity, gas, and water as well as waste disposal units. For maximum flexibility there is access through the floor for connections to all the necessary utilities. Using such connections enables one to cover the floor access port completely, move the power island out of the way, and redesign the room as much as one wishes. Usually associated with the power island are movable laboratory tables which can be used to form work areas, extending from the power center.

A new innovation in laboratory furniture is a portable carrel. Such a carrel stands about six feet high and is about three feet wide and folds into a compact unit which may be locked. When a student wishes to use his carrel, he unlocks the combination, pulls out a door, and a seat appears with bookshelves and writing surfaces immediately available.

Other innovations, which are appearing in new schools and which are conducive to better science teaching, are computer terminals for using computer-assisted instruction facilities. A second innovation is the provision of a combined teacher-office work area to facilitate team planning. This area is particularly useful when curriculum planning is done by the individual teachers in the district or in team-teaching situations.

Other changes include the use of ramps to accommodate wheelchairs, use of color, and aesthetically pleasing work areas. Another innovation is the use of adjoining outdoor-environment centers to which students in the earth science and biology classes may have immediate access.

=== REFLECTING ON SCIENCE TEACHING ===

Trends and Facilities

1. What trends of science education have implications for facilities?
2. Can you think of other trends that have implications for science facilities?

As teachers remove themselves more and more from the position of primary information source, their role changes to that of director of learning or diagnostician. Consequently, the student has more control over the rate at which he proceeds and the sequence of information with which he interacts. Information from a wide variety of sources is becoming more available to the students, thus demanding greater flexibility in space utilization.

Large, open laboratories are becoming more common, as is the growth of technologically assisted study. Calculators and computer terminals are sometimes installed for individualized instruction. The open laboratories must be large enough for sufficient separation between groups. This space acts as a sound barrier and works adequately as long as the total number of students is not excessive. Other methods of breaking up the large open areas while retaining flexibility are to use book shelves as room dividers, movable self-supporting partitions, and varied furniture arrangements to give visual and aesthetic satisfaction.

Guidelines for Planning a Science Complex

When all of these trends are considered, it is clear that the science complex must contain more of everything and must be designed with an emphasis on flexibility. In planning science facilities, attention should be given to the following principles.[8]

Planning Facilities

1. Those who select the school site should consider the potential contributions of the surroundings to the teaching of science. The location of science rooms within the science complex in relation to supply, outdoor areas, and sunlight exposure needs consideration. For example, a biology classroom is best located on a ground floor with access to growing areas.
2. Planning of science rooms should incorporate the ideas of many qualified individuals who have had experience in planning science facilities, not just the architect's ideas.
3. The needs of science should be considered in

floor planning, illumination, ventilation, plumbing, and placement of sinks and water taps. Electric plugs for each student should be provided if necessary.
4. Consideration should be given to windowless classrooms, since they do have some advantages for storage, thermal control, and audiovisual programs.

Area and Space Resources

1. The amount of floor space provided should be thirty-five to forty-five square feet, or more, per student (fifty square feet if storage area is included).
2. The number of rooms and how much they will be used throughout the day should be carefully determined. If a room will not be filled with science students all day, what other classes will be in it?
3. There should be enough space for projects to remain assembled for varying periods of time.
4. Enough space should be provided for proper storage of all materials.
5. Space should be provided for displaying student-constructed projects and other products and devices.
6. Space should be provided for the science teacher to work in.
7. More aisle space must be provided in multipurpose laboratories, because of greater student movement.

Different Learning Activities

1. The science rooms should provide for a wide range of learning activities for individuals, small groups, and the entire class.
2. Facilities should permit students to experiment with many materials.
3. Areas should be provided where experiments and projects may be conducted for others to observe.
4. Facilities should be available for individual experimental work.
5. There should be provision for small-group or individual conferences with the science teacher.

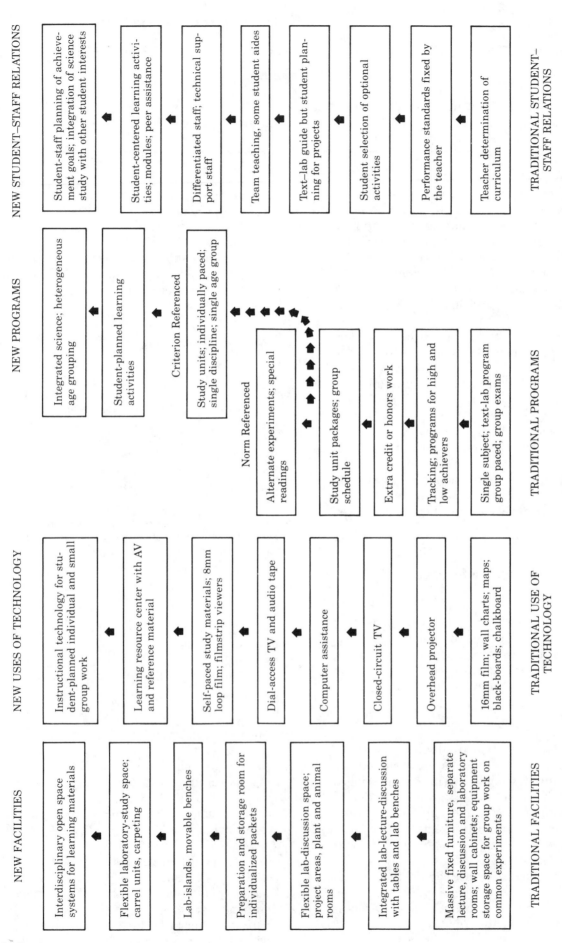

FIGURE 15–4
Evolving patterns in facilities, technology, programs, and student-staff relations in science teaching

Arrows show general trends from traditional (bottom of chart) to emerging characteristics (top), with descriptions ordered in approximately the sequence of development observed by the study team.

Furniture and Decor

1. Rooms should be pleasant and attractive. Using several colors in cabinets and display cabinets helps to give the room a pleasant appearance.
2. Rooms should be flexible, to accommodate a variety of uses. Furniture that is not permanently installed ensures greater flexibility, since it can be easily moved as conditions warrant.
3. Adaptable furniture should be provided.

Auxiliary Facilities

1. Planning science facilities should include consideration of the community resources that can be used to supplement the program (libraries, museums, parks, etc.).
2. There should be a facility for construction and repair of equipment.
3. Provisions should be made for published materials to be available.
4. Facilities should be provided for effective use of audiovisual aids.

In planning a science complex, careful consideration must be given to the study of space relationships. Where should the biology rooms be located in relation to the physics, chemistry, and other science rooms? What relationship should they have to the storage areas? Should there be a central storage area with access to all classrooms or should each classroom have a storage facility? The advantage of the former arrangement is that it requires less space and makes equipment available for multiple use. For example, a vacuum pump may be easily available to physics, chemistry, physical science, and general science classes. A central storage area, however, requires greater organization and agreement among the faculty involved on how the equipment will be used and returned to the storage area.

The National Science Teachers Association, through its Commission on Professional Standards and Practices, has prepared a document entitled "Conditions for Good Science Teaching."[9] In its recommendations, it has dealt with resources for learning, among which are science rooms and laboratories. A list of its recommendations follows:

Conditions for Good Science Teaching

1. There should be at least one separate laboratory for each kind of science course offered.
2. There must be enough laboratory rooms provided for each science course to accommodate all students who can profit from the course and wish to take it.
3. Each laboratory must be large enough to accommodate real experimentation.
4. Each laboratory should have ceilings that are at least 10 feet (3 meters) high.
5. Each laboratory should be appropriately furnished for each science.
6. Each laboratory should have conveniently located electric, gas, and water outlets.
7. Waste-disposal facilities must be provided in all laboratories.
8. For work efficiency and safety, laboratories should have lighting which takes into account the variations in working conditions common to science laboratories.
9. Reasonable considerations of comfort and health require that each laboratory have the capability of renewing the room air at a rate compatible with normal student occupancy and the potential uses of science laboratories, such as maintenance of animals, noxious gases, etc.
10. Fire blankets and fully operable fire extinguishers must be located where they are quickly accessible. Every laboratory should be protected by automatic overhead sprinklers.
11. Chemistry laboratories must contain an emergency shower, an eye-wash fountain, and safety goggles for all students.
12. Every science laboratory must have two unobstructed exits.
13. There should be an annual, verified safety check of each laboratory.
14. No more than twenty-four students should be assigned to a space intended for group discussion and activity (as distinct from large-group lecture).
15. A science classroom should have full audiovisual capability and facilities for conducting scientific demonstrations.
16. Specialized facilities are needed (plant growth facilities, animal room, darkroom, and science shop).
17. Individual project areas are needed for students working on special experiments.
18. Ample science-library space must be available.
19. Conference rooms are needed for teacher-student conferences.
20. Ample space is needed for the storage of supplies and equipment.
21. Every science teacher requires access to a preparation area free from students.
22. Every science teacher should have private office space.
23. The science department budget should appear as a separate account within the whole school budget and it should be subdivided functionally.
24. Supplies should be budgeted on a per capita ba-

sis with the amount varying according to the nature of the course and the consumables involved.

25. Budgets should provide leeway for items to be ordered during the school year for new projects, perishable materials, and unforeseen contingencies.

■ Handicapped Students and Science Facilities

In 1977, Joseph A. Califano, then Secretary of Health, Education, and Welfare, signed the regulations implementing Section 504 of the Rehabilitation Act of 1973. Section 504 provides that "no otherwise qualified handicapped individual . . . shall solely by reason of his handicap be excluded from the participation in, be denied the benefits of, or be subjected to discrimination under any program or activity receiving federal financial assistance."

In many cases, there have been dramatic changes in the actions and attitudes of institutions and individuals who are recipients of federal funds.

Some of the implications of the regulation are:

1. All new facilities must be barrier-free.
2. Programs or activities must be made accessible to the handicapped and/or structural changes must be made within a given time period.
3. Qualified handicapped persons may not, on the basis of a handicap, be denied admission or employment even if facilities have not been made barrier-free.
4. Colleges and universities must make reasonable modifications in academic requirements, where necessary, to ensure full educational opportunity for handicapped students.
5. Educational institutions must provide auxiliary aids, such as readers or interpreters for the deaf.

It is evident that the educational systems and the design professions, as well as material and product manufacturers, must determine the needs of the handicapped. In turn, this understanding must be translated into practical, economical ways of providing opportunities for the handicapped so that they may enjoy educational accomplishment.

In the past, architects and educators have been content to function with respect to the "average person." In many cases, they have been unaware of the many physically handicapped who are striving to function as productive citizens. This has been true not only in the design of buildings but also in the design of the science curricula.

Since, as much as possible, the handicapped should participate equally in campus activities with the nonhandicapped, it is imperative that the entire educational facility be considered. This consideration not only benefits the handicapped participant but also aids staff members and visitors who may be handicapped.

Various institutions have been modified so that accessibility for handicapped persons is available. Stairways are being supplemented with ramps and elevators. Braille letters and symbols are used for signs. The problem is not easily solved in laboratories, however. In many cases, spacing work areas in the laboratories requires complete remodeling. The standard laboratory table does not accommodate the wheelchair-bound person, so that many facilities are totally inadequate for compliance with the new laws.

A laboratory that has been modified to accommodate a wheelchair-bound person does not necessarily meet the needs of every handicapped individual. Problems involving manual dexterity require additional modifications, involving not only the station but also the specific items of equipment associated with that station.

The physical barriers present just one phase of the problem of accessibility for handicapped persons. Another aspect relates to the affective approach to the problem. For this reason, the overall environment for the student must be considered.

The new regulations may encourage more handicapped students to study science. One of the reasons that disabled individuals may have avoided the science field, or any other program requiring science courses, could be their inability to find appropriate means of completing laboratory requirements. For the first time, the handicapped may have the opportunity to satisfy the requirements for a particular major.

■ Summary

The science teacher in today's schools has almost unlimited choices of materials with which to enhance his teaching. Wise selection of appropriate materials is a major problem. In making these choices, it is important to recognize the basic reasons for using a variety of materials in science teaching. Individual differences among students demand variations in methods and materials. The psychology of learning supports the thesis that variety of materials promotes better learning. More of the senses are stimulated and more avenues of learning are activated. Availability of many materials gives opportunity for individual work and experimentation.

Published materials form a large segment of today's science-teaching arsenal. Textbooks continue to be essential tools, although their limitations are

=========== **REFLECTING ON SCIENCE TEACHING** ===========

Instructional Facilities

1. What five considerations do you think most important in facility design for science teaching?
2. Design a modern floor plan for a science complex. Justify your design.
3. How do the facility requirements for individualized instruction vary from those of group instruction?

---

better recognized. It is still important to select textbooks in science carefully and with understanding of their contribution to the learning situation. Many supplementary monographs and pamphlets are now available. These materials are usually written at a level suitable for junior and senior high school students. Authors of these publications have done an excellent job of communicating difficult concepts at the research frontiers as understandable science for the nontechnical reader. At the same time, they have demonstrated the processes of science admirably and conveyed realistic ideas of the role of science in society.

Audiovisual equipment and materials continue to gain in sophistication. Although radio and television have not yet realized their potential as teaching aids in the average classroom, increasing strides are being made in their use. New techniques with overhead projectors, film-loop projectors, and single-concept films are finding increasing popularity. Individual differences are being better served by these materials and individualized instruction is enhanced by more flexible audiovisual aids.

Science teaching depends greatly on laboratory work. Materials for the laboratory are increasing, both in variety and in abundance in science classrooms. The science teacher must become familiar with sources of laboratory apparatus and supplies. In choosing equipment, educational value must be considered above all. In addition, durability and usefulness are important considerations. Once purchased, equipment must be maintained in usable condition. An up-to-date inventory is necessary and an adequate budget for purchase of new materials must be available.

In this chapter we have not attempted to give an exhaustive treatment of the problems of facilities design. We have tried to show the teachers' responsibilities in ensuring that new facilities are an improvement over the old ones and to point out some considerations in providing modern facilities. Science teachers are the people most competent to know what facilities are needed for efficient and effective teaching. It is their responsibility to suggest that these facilities be provided.

In writing educational specifications, teachers must take care that the facilities will not be outdated in twenty or thirty years. This problem can be avoided if facilities are made flexible and if teachers understand trends in teaching that have implications for science instruction.

New federal requirements mandate that handicapped students be provided with suitable facilities, materials, and services to ensure full educational opportunities for this group. Substantial modification of laboratory space and facilities is required.

■ References

1. National Science Teachers Association, "Conditions for Good Science Teaching in Secondary Schools" (1970), p. 6.
2. Lynn M. Mulkey, "The Use of a Sociological Perspective in the Development of a Science Textbook Evaluation Instrument" *Science Education*, 71, no. 4 (1987), pp. 511-522.
3. Mulkey, "The Use of a Sociological Perspective," pp. 511-522.
4. Hubert N. Alyea, "Tested Overhead Projection Series," *Science Teacher* (March, April, September, October, November, December, 1962).
5. Walter Eppenstein, *The Overhead Projector in the Physics Lecture* (Troy, N.Y.: Rennselaer Polytechnic Institute, May, 1962).
6. Marjorie Gardner, "Ten Trends in Science Education," *The Science Teacher* (January, 1979), pp.30-32.
7. J.D. Novak, *Facilities for Secondary School Science Teaching: Evolving Patterns in Facilities and Programs* (Washington, D.C.: National Science Teachers Association, 1972).
8. This list has been modified from National Science Teachers Association, *Science Facilities for our Schools*, Publication K–12 (Washington, D.C., 1963).
9. "Conditions for Good Science Teaching in Secondary Schools," (Washington, D.C.: National Science Teachers Association, 1984).

==== INVESTIGATING SCIENCE TEACHING ====

ACTIVITY 15-1

Readability Analysis

For the busy teacher or review committee selecting textbooks, a primary consideration is ease of use. Fortunately, one of the readability formulas, the Fry Readability Graph, is a simple tool which can be used by the average classroom teacher in selecting textbooks. It is a good exercise to try your hand at determining the readability of a textbook that you might use for your particular subject, to familiarize yourself with the difficulty and usefulness of such a formula. Remember, however, that the results are only approximate and largely dependent on the technical nature of the material being analyzed. Many of the readability formulas do not take into adequate consideration the technical nature of many science subjects.

	Sentences per 100 words	Syllables per 100 words
100-word sample Page 6	4.5	138
100-word sample Page 90	3.1	150
100-word sample Page 171	5.3	162
	3 ⟍12.9	3 ⟍450
Average	4.3	150

FIGURE 15-5
Graph for estimating readability (Edward Fry, "A Readability Formula That Saves Time," *Journal of Reading* (November, 1968), pp. 513-516; 575-578.

Fry's Readability Graph. The Fry graph is used for narrative and expository writing only; do not use it for poetry, dialog, drama, or unusual styles of writing. The Fry graph assesses technical difficulty, not interest, style, or content.

Directions for Using the Readability Graph

1. Select three 100-word passages from near the beginning, middle, and end of the book. For anthologies, average nine samples (three samples from each of three stories or essays).
2. Avoid samples from the beginnings and ends of chapters.
3. Include proper nouns (except for common names like Dick or Sue) in your word count.
4. Count the total number of sentences in each 100-word passage (estimating to nearest tenth of a sentence). Average these three numbers.
5. Count the total number of syllables in each 100-word sample. There is a syllable for each vowel sound; for example: cat (1), blackbird (2), continental (4). Don't be fooled by word size; for example: polio (3), through (1). Endings such as -y, -ed, -el, or -le usually make a syllable; for example: ready (2), bottle (2). Average the total number of syllables for the three samples.
6. Count numbers in figures (1973) as one syllable. If the number is written out, count it in full syllables.
7. Plot on the graph the average number of sentences per hundred words and the average number of syllables per hundred words. The point where these plots coincide designates the grade level. If your computation places the estimated reading level in the shaded area on the graph, start over again with different samples. (Plot these two points on the Fry Graph in Figure 15.5. What is the approximate grade difficulty level of this material?) Most plot points fall near the heavy curved line. Perpendicular lines mark off approximately grade level areas.
8. Add one year to the estimated reading level if the material has been translated from another language.
9. Add one year to the estimated reading level if the material was written before 1900.
10. If great variability is encountered either in sentence length or in the syllable count for the three selections, randomly select several more passages and compute their average before plotting.

ACTIVITY 15–2

Evaluating Textbooks

Select three textbooks for secondary science teaching in your field of preparation or interest. Evaluate them using the criteria in this chapter. What are the major strengths and weaknesses of the books you have chosen?

Science Textbook Evaluation Form

Guidelines for Evaluation of Science Texts Scoring:
10 = Outstanding, 8 = Excellent, 5 = Good, 3 = Fair, 1 = Poor

Text A: _____

Publisher: _____ Copyright date: _____ Cost: _____

Text B: _____

Publisher: _____ Copyright date: _____ Cost: _____

Text C: _____

Publisher: _____ Copyright date: _____ Cost:_____

Grade level: _____

	Textbook A	B	C

I. *Content: (sample all units/chapters)*
   A. Most of the necessary topics/units for this level
   B. Historical development of science/scientists
   C. Present-day environment/energy/social/scientific issues
   D. Balance of life/physical/earth topics/units
   E. Appropriate level of mathematics/science content (i.e., Piaget)

II. *Presentation: (sample all units/chapters)*
   A. Balance of content vs. inductive laboratory skills/methods/inquiry
   B. Development of ideas prior to use of scientific vocabulary
   C. Interesting informal writing style
   D. Unfamiliar/important terms/principles in italics/boldface
   E. Problem solving and scientific methods are integrated

III. *Accuracy: (sample 5-10 of each item)*
   A. Indexed topics were scientifically correct
   B. Measures are only SI metric and technically correct
   C. Glossary is scientifically correct and understandable
   D. Directions for structured activities are precise and they work
   E. Appropriate safety is stressed at all times

IV. *Organization: (sample 2-3 units)*
   A. Unit introduction/abstract sets the stage for student involvement
   B. Sequential development of ideas/concepts/skills
   C. Investigations are integral, not just add on
   D. End of unit questions require thinking/application
   E. Well-indexed cross references

V. *Readability*
   A. Words per sentence = _____ (for grades 5-6, below 21 = outstanding)
   B. 60% of sentences are simple or compound (not complex)
   C. Reading level is .5 to 1.5 grade levels below text level
   D. 3-4 personal references per 100 words
   E. 1-2 examples/applications of abstract principles (low concept density)

VI. *Adaptability*
   A. Provisions for wide range of student skills/interests/learning styles
   B. Useable as a reference book
   C. Provides for a wide range of learning activities (not just verbal)
   D. Chapters/units can be omitted
   E. Includes appropriate controversial topics (i.e., evolution)

VII. *Teaching Aids*
   A. Annotated references for teachers
   B. Annotated references for students (books, periodicals, films, etc.)
   C. Publisher provides appropriate in-service
   D. Teacher's Guide includes wide variety of activities, methods, etc., besides answers
   E. Complete lists of permanent/consumable kit materials and sources

VIII. *Illustrations*
   A. Boy/girl and white/minority balance sex/minority stereotype
   B. Photos/art: large, clear, and appropriate (not too "arty")
   C. Illustrations integrated as direct references
   D. Adequate labels for all art/photos
   E. Modern art/photos, except for historical settings

IX. *Activities*

Textbook
A	B	C

A. At least ⅓ of activities are laboratory-oriented
B. Balance of large/small muscle, in/out seat activities
C. Wide range of difficulty = success for all levels
D. Balance of structured/inquiry activities
E. Activities stress understanding/application, not just memorization

X. *Appearance*

Textbook
A	B	C

A. Size/style/layout of print makes for easy reading
B. Appropriate pleasing page balance/placement of art/copy
C. Size/shape of book is appropriate for grade level
D. Durable, non-glare, opaque paper
E. Attractive/durable binding and cover

Total

ACTIVITY 15–3

Learning Materials

1. Begin a file of free and inexpensive materials related to your teaching area. Arrange an indexing system for easy access and location of items when needed.
2. Survey the current research in science education for information on the effectiveness of teaching by television. On the basis of your findings, what conclusions can you draw concerning the future of educational television in the field of science?

ACTIVITY 15–4

Designing the Science Facilities for a Small Middle-Senior High School

At some point in your teaching career, you may be called upon to participate on a committee to design or contribute plans for a science room, science wing of an existing building, or perhaps to help plan an entirely new structure, including science classrooms and laboratories. For practice in this, use the following information to design a science wing for a school of 600 pupils, grades 7–12. Assume there are 350 students in the sciences in a given year. The classes include 2–7th grade life science, 2–8th grade physical science, 2–9th grade earth science, three 10th grade biology classes (required), 2 classes of 11th grade chemistry (optional) and one 12th grade physics class, also optional.

After discussing this with your classmates and considering all the possibilities, draw the plans for the science wing giving attention to the following points:

1. Number and size of science classrooms required
2. Number of laboratories—either combined with classrooms or separate
3. Required storage space for equipment, chemicals, and projects
4. Plant growing room and animal facilities
5. Safety factors, traffic flow for students, gas, water and electrical services.
6. Site selection, facilities for science outdoors
7. Any other factors of importance.

Remember as you plan, you are building for at least 25 years into the future. Consider possible changes in enrollment patterns of growth or decline. Be able to justify your choices in class discussion. Remember a science facility should be built to accommodate a variety of teaching methods and should be planned with flexibility in mind.

CHAPTER 16

The Middle/Junior High School Science Curriculum

This chapter, and the next, are about the science curriculum. By now, you probably recognize that curriculum is really more than content. Your curriculum includes science content, manipulative skills, attitudes you wish to achieve, the context or environment of the classroom, and the means you use to assess student progress. There will be a difference between the science curriculum represented in your school district syllabus, what your textbook presents, what you emphasize, and what your students learn. Discussing the curriculum is more complex than it may seem. Rather than resolve all the issues surrounding the curriculum, we direct most attention in these two chapters to instructional materials representing different courses of study you may encounter.

Before discussing the curriculum, it is important to provide some background and context for later discussions. We begin with a brief overview of curriculum reform.

■ The Need for Curricular Change

A major reform in American science education began in the late 1950s.

The date most often referred to as marking the beginning of this reevaluation of our science programs is October 4, 1957, the launching date of Sputnik I, the first man-made satellite to orbit the earth. Russian scientists beat our own scientists by a mere four months, but the reverberations set off in education by the rumblings of the first Russian satellite booster were felt for many years.

The curriculum development projects in the United States, (sparked by this event), went on for more than 15 years. A host of new and exciting curricula came into being at all levels, from elementary grades through college. Although the "Golden Age" of curriculum development has now run its course, its impact on curriculum change will continue to be felt well into the future.

The late 1980s and early 1990s is another period of curriculum reform. The issue is not a race to space; instead, it is a need for a strong defense, a sound economy, and a stable environment that is shaping the new curriculum.[1] Why do reforms such as these occur? What happens to the science curriculum?

From time to time science programs, or aspects of them, become outdated. Though reasons for curricular obsolescence vary, they are relatively few. Briefly put, changes in society, new understandings about students and learning, and advances in science and technology result in the need for curricular reform. Let us look at the reform movement of the 1960s with these themes in mind.

Before the Sputnik spurred reform, science teaching had traditionally been concerned mainly with knowledge—the product of science. Textbooks in subjects such as physics, chemistry, biology, physical science, and general science were written predominantly by high school teachers, whose primary concern was accurately communicating scientific knowledge to the student. As teachers, they were rarely involved in actual scientific research; consequently, the methods of scientific research were given lip service, but students were not given experience using these methods.

As scientific knowledge compounded in the first half of the twentieth century, textbooks became larger, so that they might include the scientific advances and their technological applications. The science disciplines became, for the student, a compendium of knowledge to be memorized. Little attention was paid to the logic of thought development and to the basic cohesiveness of the scientific disciplines.

Recognition of the burgeoning knowledge in each of the sciences led curriculum planners to try new arrangements. However, the real problems caused by excessive attention to applications of scientific knowledge and an encyclopedic approach to the subject were not solved.

The advent of Sputnik 1 was another powerful force for educational reform. When a rival nation launched a satellite before the United States, our society demanded the educational system be severely overhauled and the science curricula received attention first. A new group of individuals took charge of the curriculum—scientists, not teachers, directed most of the major curriculum projects. Their emphasis was vastly different from traditional textbooks. The new emphasis was on the structure of knowledge that formed the scientific disciplines and the modes of inquiry used by scientists. The programs of the 1960s and 1970s were quite different from those of the 1940s and 1950s.

The new authors emphasized "big ideas" or conceptual schemes instead of information, and they made extensive use of the laboratory instead of lectures and demonstrations. The curriculum program of the 1960s also incorporated the most recent understanding of how students learn and develop. The works of theorists such as B.F. Skinner, Jean Piaget, and Jerome Brunner were central to the new programs.

To review, science courses remain relatively stable over the years. New courses enter the curriculum from time to time, but only after the character of the student population changes, new scientific and technologic advances are made, or national emergencies make their existence necessary. Courses that come into being often find permanent status. Changes in the science curriculum are gradual and reflect changing conditions such as industrial advancements, compulsory school laws, or national defense needs.

From the mid 1970s through the 1980s, there was a gradual shift in textbooks away from the models of the "Golden Age" of reform. Science textbooks became larger as more and more information was included; they reduced the emphasis on the laboratory and teachers and returned to an emphasis on lecture, discussion, and demonstrations.[2] For the reasons just cited, the late 1980s and 1990s are a new period of reform for middle/junior high and high school science programs.

■ Junior High and Middle Schools

Adolescence is a period of significant physical, intellectual, social, and emotional development. The fact that adolescence generally spans the years of secondary education makes understanding this period generally important, but of particular importance is the period of junior high or middle school. Education during the middle school years, generally from ages 10 to 14, must extend the experiences of elementary school; the goals, curriculum, and instruction for science should be conceptualized and implemented as unique and congruent with the particular needs of the developing adolescent. In recent years, educators have increasingly realized the crucial and singular role of education during adolescence. In the next section, we review the history of junior high and middle schools, then return to science programs for this level of secondary education.

History of the Junior High

Describing science education during early adolescent years is somewhat confused by the fact that there are apparently two different school systems for this age group; one is termed middle school, the other junior high school. This situation is clarified by a brief history.

In the latter part of the nineteenth century, most elementary schools included grades 1 through 8 while high schools included grades 9 through 12. By 1920, about 80 percent of students graduating from high school had experienced eight years of elementary and four years of high school. While the schools were actually structured in this eight-four plan, leading educators continually debated school organization for over three decades beginning in the 1890s. Junior high schools, or school systems with six years elementary, three years junior high, and three years of high school, had emerged in the early 1900s. Not until the 1918 Commission on the Reorganization of Secondary Education (CRSE) did the junior high become firmly established in the American education system. The 1918 CRSE report, *Cardinal Principles of Secondary Education*, stated

We, therefore, recommend a reorganization of the school system whereby the first six years shall be devoted to elementary education designed to meet the needs of pupils approximately 6 to 12 years of age, and the second six years to secondary education designed to meet the needs of pupils approximately 12 to 18 years of age. The six years to be devoted to secondary education may well be divided into two periods which may be designated as the junior and senior periods.[3]

The concept of junior high schools was established and their numbers grew. In 1920 there were an estimated 800 junior high schools in the United States. And by 1930 there were 1,787 separate junior high schools. While the numbers of junior high schools were increasing, so were criticisms of these schools. The reasons for the rapid increase of junior high schools were shortages of facilities and economic restraints placed on schools between World War I and World War II. Justifications for junior high programs cited the needs of adolescents, the transition to high school, the elimination of dropouts, and vocational preparation. By 1940 prominent educators had developed a rationale for the junior high school. Gruhn and Douglas summarize the essential functions of junior high schools as

- *Integration.* Basic skills, attitudes and understanding learned previously should be coordinated into effective behaviors.
- *Exploration.* Individuals should explore special interests, aptitudes, and abilities for educational opportunities, vocational decisions, and recreational choices.
- *Guidance.* Assistance should be provided for students making decisions regarding education, careers, and social adjustment.
- *Differentiation.* Educational opportunities and facilities should provide for varying backgrounds, interests, and needs of the students.
- *Socialization.* Education should prepare early adolescents for participation in a complex democratic society.
- *Articulation.* Orientation of the program should provide a gradual transition from preadolescent (elementary) education to a program suited to the needs of adolescents.[4]

The reality of the time, however, was that most teachers were trained for the high school and had little desire to teach at the junior high level. A junior high school teaching job was perceived as a stepping stone to a high school position. The important goals of education for early adolescents were forgotten or ignored and education in grades 7, 8, and 9 became scaled-down versions of grades 10, 11, and 12. Criticisms of junior high schools continued into the 1960s. Some of the criticisms were:

- a shortage of qualified professionals,
- lack of agreement on purpose,
- high dropout rates,

- programs (athletics, music, and social) that were inappropriate for early adolescents,
- ineffective discipline, and
- teachers who did not understand early adolescents.

Emergence of Middle Schools

During the 1960s several factors contributed to the emergence of the middle school as an alternative to junior high schools. Some of the factors included: general criticisms of the schools and a need to increase the quality of education; an emphasis on curriculum improvement in science, mathematics, and foreign language; renewed interest in preparation for college; recognition of Jean Piaget's work in developmental psychology; the need to eliminate de facto racial segregation; restructuring of schools due to overcrowding; and a general desire to improve education. These and other factors contributed to an increase from 100 middle schools in 1960 to over 5,000 in 1980. In 1988, there were 12,000 separate middle schools with an estimated enrollment of 8,000,000 students.

We think the middle school is an important conceptual and physical change in the education system. Some of the important characteristics of the middle school were described in a 1981 report, *The Status of Middle School and Junior High School Sciences.*[5]

- A program specifically designed for pre- and early adolescents
- A program that encourages exploration and personal development
- A positive and active learning environment
- A schedule that is flexible with respect to time and grouping
- A staff that recognizes students' needs, motivation, fears, and goals
- An instructional approach that is varied
- An emphasis on acquiring essential knowledge, skills, and attitudes in a sequential and individual manner
- An emphasis on developing decision-making and problem-solving skills
- Interdisciplinary learning and team teaching

Middle schools, in structure and function, have many advantages; several thought important are:

- The middle school has a unique status; the school and program are not "junior" to another program.
- Specific subjects, like science and mathematics, can be introduced at lower grades by specialists.
- Developing new middle schools provides the im-

petus for redesigning goals, curriculum and instruction for the early adolescent learner.
- Development of middle schools can facilitate changes in teacher certification standards and subsequently teacher education programs.
- Some discipline problems can be eliminated through different groupings of students, primarily the inclusion of younger students.
- Middle schools can be designed to provide greater guidance and counseling at the time it is needed.

Time will answer questions about the role of middle schools in American education. We believe their time has come, and they will be recorded as an important educational advance. The present period of reform should contribute substantially to their implementation, but in the interim we have both middle and junior high schools. Science programs and science teachers must be prepared for either, since student characteristics are not changed by the grade-level designation of the school.

■ Reform of Junior High School Science Programs

Science in the junior high school has been faced with perplexing problems since its inception. General science was the course offered in the ninth grade of 84 schools when the first junior high schools came into existence. Begun in the decade 1910-1920, the course was designed to satisfy the needs and interests of students in early adolescence. The first course was established through research and was designed to fill a perceived need.

Several difficulties were encountered in junior high school science. There was a shortage of well-trained general science teachers. Many teachers at this level were physics, chemistry, and biology teachers whose primary interest was not the problems of junior high school science. Also, teachers in other disciplines such as English, mathematics, and physical eduation were recruited to teach science. For these reasons, the general science texts for these grades were written in an effort to relieve this problem, but the variations in school organization such as six-three-three, eight-two-two, and eight-four necessitated much repetition of science topics to produce universally salable textbooks.

There were deficiencies in equipment and facilities for teaching science. Many science classes were taught in ordinary classrooms without water or gas outlets and without adequate facilities for demonstrations and experiments.

There was no clear knowledge of what junior high school science should actually accomplish. Ob-

jectives ranged from "preparation for the rigorous science courses in the senior high school" to "general education for good citizenship." Much thought was given to development of attitudes and interests. Some felt that general science should be exploratory in nature. Courses designed on this premise became rapid surveys of chemistry, physics, astronomy, meteorology, biology, and geology. Others believed that students should study the applications of science in the world around them. Courses of this kind dwelt on home appliances, transportation, communication, health problems, and natural resources.

Enrollments in general science grew to about 65 pecent of the ninth-grade classes by 1956, then declined as new courses began to permeate the ninth grade and as the seventh and eighth grades took over more of the general science offerings.[6]

Revision of junior high school science courses through national curriculum studies of the 1960s was delayed, while attention was centered on the senior high school courses. With time, attention turned to the junior high science curriculum.

Middle and junior high school science is usually organized in one of three patterns: (1) a one, two, or three year program called general science; (2) a three year program in which life, physical, and earth sciences are taught individually for a year each; (3) a one, two, or three year program of integrated or thematically organized science. One of the first two patterns is found in the majority of schools.[7] Before reviewing some programs developed during the "Golden Age" of science education we will note that the reform movement of the 1960s and 1970s made no effort to improve general science. In fact, the hope was that by implementing new life, earth, and physical science programs the traditional general science would eventually be replaced. As we shall see later, this has not occurred. Following is a review of some life, earth and physical science programs for the middle and junior high school.

Science Courses in the Junior High School

Earth Science

Early in 1963, the American Geological Institute was given a grant to support a curriculum development, called the Early Science Curriculum Project (ESCP) for the ninth grade. This course was interdisciplinary, involving geology, meteorology, astronomy, and oceanography. Its emphasis was on laboratory and field study, in which students actively participate in the process of scientific inquiry.

Materials of the ESCP included a textbook, *Investigating the Earth*; the laboratory was augmented by the text, teacher's guide, films, laboratory equipment and maps, and a pamphlet series. After three years of testing and preparation of materials, the course was published commercially.

The Table of Contents from the first edition (1967) included the following chapters.

1. The Changing Earth
2. Earth Materials
3. Earth Measurement
4. Earth Motions
5. Fields and Forces
6. Energy Flow
7. Energy and Air Motions
8. Water in the Air
9. Waters of the Land
10. Water in the Sea
11. Energy, Moisture, and Climate
12. The Land Wears Away
13. Sediments in the Sea
14. Mountains From the Sea
15. Rocks Within Mountains
16. Interior of the Earth
17. Time and Its Measurement
18. The Record in Rocks
19. Life—Present and Past
20. Development of a Continent
21. Evolution of Landscapes
22. The Moon: a Natural Satellite
23. The Solar System
24. Stars as Other Suns
25. Stellar Evolution and Galaxies
26. The Universe and Its Origin

The project continued its programs until 1969, when two offshoots, Environmental Studies (ES) and Earth Science Teacher Preparation Project (ESTPP), were initiated to deal specifically with the environmental problems and issues of teacher peparation in the earth sciences.

A serious problem faced by the ESCP was the preparation of persons qualified to teach the course, because of the increasing demand for earth science teachers. Recent efforts in teacher preparation have narrowed the gap between supply and demand. Many earth science teachers have been recruited from other disciplines. Still there is a problem concerning preparation of qualified earth science teachers. The advances made in the design and implementation of *Investigating the Earth* were commendable. The text design, integration of concepts from life and physical sciences and the careful presentation of knowledge, process, and skills were unprecedented. Subsequent revisions of the text have replaced many traditional topics and realigned the book with other standard earth science texts.

Physical Science

Another program developed for the junior high school was the Introductory Physical Science Program of Educational Services, Incorporated. This project was supported by the National Science Foundation. Its purpose was to develop a one-year course in physical science for use in junior high schools. Laboratory work is emphasized and equipment has been designed in such a way that students can perform the experiments in ordinary classrooms. The Table of Contents of the IPS course includes the following chapters:

1. Introduction
2. Quantity of Matter: Mass
3. Characteristic Properties
4. Solubility and Solvents
5. The Separation of Substances
6. Compounds and Elements
7. Radioactivity
8. The Atomic Model of Matter
9. Sizes and Masses of Atoms and Molecules
10. Molecular Motion
11. Heat

The Introductory Physical Science (IPS) course was tested in several centers throughout the United States and the materials, which included textbooks, teachers' guides, laboratory notebooks, and comprehensive apparatus kits, were eventually made available through commercial sources.

The attractiveness of the IPS course to better-than-average junior high school students was made clear in the results of a test survey of representative IPS students in the 1965-1966 school year. "In that year, 1,005 ninth-grade IPS students and 400 eighth-grade IPS students took the School and College Abilities Test (SCAT) Survey Form, a test of verbal and mathematical ability. The results made it clear that the IPS students were more scholastically able on the average than typical junior high school students in the nation."[8]

As the success of a new course depends on well-qualified teachers, the National Science Foundation supported a program to locate qualified science teachers and to prepare them to instruct other teachers in the use of IPS. The program was quite successful; in IPS workshops, teachers were trained by their peers in the local environment.

Integrated Science

Several other junior high school courses have appeared on the scene in recent years. Among them are the Intermediate Science Curriculum Study (ISCS) financed by the U.S. Office of Education and National Science Foundation and developed at Florida State

University. "The fundamental assumption underlying the ISCS plan is that science at the junior high school level serves essentially a general education function."[9] Three levels were prepared, corresponding to the junior high school grades seven, eight, and nine. Level I for seventh grade was tightly structured. Its title, *Energy, Its Forms and Characteristics*, permitted students to delve into physical-science principles by dealing with things of science in their environment. Level II puts the student more and more on her own in designing experiments and recording and interpreting her data. This level deals with *Matter and its Composition and Model Building*. Level III for the ninth grade deals with biological concepts and is designed to use laboratory blocks six to eight weeks long as its basic plan of operation. The student is expected to use the concepts and investigative skills acquired in the seventh and eighth grades. All of the class activity in the ISCS course is planned for individualized work. The teacher's main duty is assisting students to work on their own. No formal lectures or information-dispensing sessions are planned for the course, unless needed on a short-term basis by a small group of students.

An innovative feature of the ISCS course is the production of a complete course on Computer-Assisted Instruction (CAI). Using behavioral objectives and a system of computer feedback, it was possible to obtain detailed information on the progress and problems encountered by each student working in the system. This information was used to modify and revise the trial versions of the course.

There are other smaller-scale projects for revising junior high school science. Among them are the Interaction Science Curriculum Project (ISCP), Ideas and Investigations in Science (IIS), and a BSCS program titled *Patterns and Processes in Science*. Each has been extensively field-tested and certain elements of success have been claimed. It is safe to say that the field of science teaching in the junior high school has received an impetus similar to that enjoyed by senior high school teaching a few years earlier. Since the basic philosphy in the two areas was the same, it is likely that pupils fortunate enough to participate in these courses at both the junior and senior high school levels will be prepared in science more effectively than before.

The Junior High and Middle School Science Curriculum of the 1970s

A 1978 report by Iris Weiss provides some valuable insights concerning the science curriculum in middle and junior high schools, classes offered, and enrollments.[10] General science was offered in 70 per-

cent of all schools with only grades 7–9. This far surpasses the percentage of schools offering life science (21 percent), earth science (20 percent), and physical science (13 percent). The most commonly offered science course in grades 7–9 was general science; 30 percent of all science classes were general. Twenty-five percent of all classes in grades 7–9 were earth science, 16 percent life science, and 15 percent physical science.[11] In 1978, the largest science enrollment in junior high and middle schools was in general science, with approximately 5 million students. Another 2 million students in schools with grades 7–12 or 9–12 were also enrolled in general science. In all, approximately 7 million students were enrolled in general science in 1978. In comparison, life, earth, and physical enrollments for comparable schools had about 1.25 million students per discipline areas. The total enrollment in discipline-oriented science did not exceed that in general science. Enrollment in life, earth, and physical science courses was just over half (about 4 million) of the total number of students in general science in 1978. In 1986, life science, earth science, and physical science were the most commonly offered science courses in grades 7–9. This is a shift away from general science courses.

The Junior High and Middle School Science Curriculum of the 1980s

Curriculum programs at the middle/junior high school level take one of three forms: (1) a factually oriented textbook based on the premise that students must develop a background of information before concepts and inquiry can be used; (2) a "middle-of-the-road" textbook that has encyclopedic facts and vocabulary, a separate laboratory guide, and a separate guide for the "inquiry" teacher to use; and, (3) a program that presents science as active involvement by the student. Ninety percent of curriculum programs are represented by textbooks of types (1) and (2). The next paragraphs summarize programs of types (1) and (2), the present status for about 90 percent of the middle/junior high school science curriculum.

The goals are typically (1) to present the fundamental concepts representative of biological, physical, and earth science disciplines; (2) to acquaint students with scientific inquiry (the scientific method) such as by making observations, recording information, and reporting findings; (3) to acquire "scientific attitudes," such as curiosity, respect for valid and reliable information, critical thinking, willingness to be wrong, and appreciation of the cultural contributions of science; and (4) to acquire skills as-

=========== REFLECTING ON SCIENCE TEACHING ===========

Curriculum Change

Based on the statistics cited above, what conclusion do you reach about (a) science curriculum changes in middle and junior high school, (b) the role of the government in curriculum development, and (c) the role of science teachers in curriculum reform?

If you were going to reform the science curriculum in one middle school how would you approach the task?

---

sociated with inquiry development, such as recording observations in suitable ways (e.g., as tables, charts, and graphs) and doing experiments or designing investigations.

The goal dominating all of the textbooks is scientific knowledge. The major emphasis is upon acquiring information about the physical and biological world. Scientific knowledge is presented as knowing facts. In some textbooks an effort is made to have students organize their learning into concepts, for example, "living things are related to their environment," or "matter is neither created nor destroyed."

Scientific inquiry as represented in laboratory activities is usually distributed throughout textbooks. These activities require students to actually do something in the laboratory. In contrast to this type of "activity" there are occasional experiments or situations in which students have to answer questions or solve problems by gathering and interpreting information in an organized way. In experiments students are required to measure, count, or describe observations in some quantitative way. Only a few textbooks make a special effort to use laboratory activities as an integral part of the curriculum program.

What about the goals of social issues and personal needs? Social issues such as population growth, air quality, health and disease, land use, water resources, energy shortages, and environmental pollution are typically presented in a single chapter in the textbook. Science-related social issues are identified but are not explored or investigated in terms of the complexities of problems; the short- and long-term effects of the problems; appropriate, reasonable, and prudent actions that might be taken; or the role of personal, governmental, or industrial responsibilities. The goal of personal needs is really only recognized in life science programs. Topics such as health, nutrition, disease, and "drugs" are examples of this goal in middle and junior high school science programs.

Little effort is made in middle/junior high school programs to develop career awareness. There

are occasional photographs of famous scientists, engineers, or individuals working in health professions. The variety of career options within the sciences and engineering is usually not presented. However, the extent to which science teachers actually direct attention toward this goal is not known. Greater recognition should be given to this goal since adolescence is a time when attitudes about career options are formulated.

What about the NSF curriculum programs developed in the 1960s? In 1976–77, at least one federally funded science program was being used in 39 percent of the school districts. The programs being used in school districts and the percentage of districts using the materials were Earth Science Curriculum Project (ESCP)— 12 percent, Intermediate Science Curriculum Study (ISCS)—11 percent, Introductory Physical Science (IPS)—8.6 percent, and Outdoor Biology Instructional Strategies (OBIS)—3 percent. In the 1986 National Survey only one program, Introductory Physical Science (IPS), was used by more than 2 percent of teachers. Dominating the middle/junior high school market are commercial programs that were certainly influenced by, but not developed during, the "Golden Age" of reform.

In most ways, the middle and junior high school science curriculum is once again a reflection of high school programs. It is a "junior" version of senior high school science. Reading level is lower, vocabulary is defined more frequently and there is some recognition of the needs and interests of early adolescents. We think there is a vital need to redesign middle and junior high school science programs. Adolescence is a unique period of human development and the education program should reflect this uniqueness.

Table 16.1 shows selected science curricula. Some of the NSF programs developed during the "Golden Age" are presented, as well as some of the most frequently used programs.

The need for curricular change was evident. In the first years of the 1980s there were numerous committees, commissions, reports, and books pro-

TABLE 16–1
The middle/junior high school science curriculum: Selected programs

		Highly Structured	Moderately Structured	Loosely Structured
5th GRADE		SCIENCE—A PROCESS APPROACH (S—APA) Text Series e.g. *Accent on Science* (Merrill) *Concepts in Science* (Harcourt) *Heath Science Series* (Heath)	SCIENCE CURRICULUM IMPROVE-MENT STUDY (SCIS) LIFE-PHYSI-CAL SCIENCE SEQUENCE	ELEMENTARY SCIENCE STUDY (ESS) UNITS • Pond Water • Microgardening • Changes
6th GRADE		S—APA Text Series e.g. *Accent on Science* (Merrill) *Concepts in Science* (Harcourt)	SCIS—• Life Science • Physical Science	ESS UNITS • Small Things • Streamtables
7th GRADE		*Energy—Its Form and Characteristics* (ISCS) *Interaction of Man and Biosphere* (Rand) *Focus on Life Science* (Merrill) *Life Science* (Scott, Foresman)	*Modular Activities in Science* (Houghton-Mifflin) *You and the Environment* (Houghton-Mifflin)	ESS UNITS • Rocks & Charts • Mapping
8th GRADE		*Introductory Physical Science* (IPS) *Interaction of Matter and Energy* (Rand) *Principles of Science* (Merrill) *Focus on Physical Science* (Merrill)	*Matter and Its Composition and Model Buildings* (ISCS) *Ideas and Investigations in Science—Physical Science* (Prentice-Hall)	ESS UNITS • Kitchen Physics • Pendulums • Batteries and Bulbs II
9th GRADE		*Focus on Earth Science* (Merrill) *Investigating the Earth* (ESCP) *Physical Science II* (Prentice-Hall) *Modern Biology* (Holt) *Introductory Physical Science* (Prentice-Hall)	*Ideas and Investigations in Science—Earth Science* (Prentice-Hall)	*Probing the Natural World—Biology* (ISCS)

*These programs were selected on the basis of frequency of use, NSF development, and different organizational structure. Curriculum project or publisher is given in parenthesis.

claiming the need for reform in American education. These reports return to themes mentioned in an earlier section. Changes in society, new understandings about students, and advances in science and technology all underscore the need for change in the curriculum.

The 1980s was a period of transition and reform for middle/junior high school programs. In 1986, the National Science Teachers Association (NSTA) published a position statement entitled "Science Education for Middle and Junior High Students."

This position statement described the goals and orientation for curriculum and instruction.

> The primary function of science education at the middle and junior high level is to provide students with the opportunity to explore science in their lives and to become comfortable and personally involved with it. Certainly science curriculum at this level should reflect society's goals and scientific and technological literacy and emphasize the role of science for personal, social, and career use, as well as prepare students academically.[12]

This position statement continued with a specific discussion indicating that the science curriculum should fulfill the needs of the early adolescent and address both the personal needs of students and issues of a global society. Experience at this level should be concrete, manipulative, and physical. The position statement recommended the curricula should focus on the relationship of science to

• content from life, physical, earth sciences, and ecology with frequent interdisciplinary references;
• process skills, such as experimenting, observing, measuring, and inferring;
• personal use in everyday applications and in practical problem solving that allow open-ended exploration;
• social issues that involve individual responsibilities and call for decision making;
• all careers;
• limitations of science and the necessity of respecting differing, well-considered points of view;
• developing written and oral communication skills; and
• positive attitudes and personal success.[13]

The NSTA position statement is important for two reasons. First, the clear emphasis on the student differentiates this curriculum from high school programs. And second, there is a definite trend toward the middle school and away from the junior high school. Table 16.2 displays some characteristics of science curricula for middle schools and aligns those characteristics with middle school programs.

The Middle School Science Curriculum of the 1990s

In 1988, the National Science Foundation (NSF) issued a request for proposals to develop programs for

TABLE 16–2
Ideal middle schools and science programs

Characteristics of an Ideal Middle School	*Characteristics and/or Needs of a New Science Program*
• Teachers knowledgeable about and committed to the education of early adolescents	• Teacher education programs and staff development specifically for middle school science
• A balanced curriculum of academic goals and developmental needs of adolescents	• A balance of knowledge, inquiry, personal needs, social issues, and career awareness goals
• Different organizational arrangements for instruction, e.g., individual, small group, large group • A variety of instructional methods	• A mixture of instructional groupings, e.g., individual projects, group activities, and large group presentations • Use of traditional and new methods such as simulations, role modeling, debate and use of computers
• An active learning environment	• Use of problem-solving, laboratory investigations, field studies, and other activities
• Flexible scheduling	• Schedules designed for class presentations, field trips, individual projects, etc.
• Continuous progress	• A coordinated science program across the middle school years to provide a smooth transition from elementary to high school
• Students master skills of decision making and problem solving • Cooperative planning and coordinated teaching	• Emphasis on scientific processes, information processing, and decision making • Science, mathematics, and social studies teachers plan the S-T-S program and teach units in parallel or as a team
• Exploratory and enrichment studies	• Opportunities to meet and interact with a variety of individuals in the community whose careers are in science, technology, and mathematics
• Interdisciplinary learning • Emphasis on all three domains	• An integrated approach to science • Science programs that emphasize knowledge, attitudes, and skills related to science and technology integrated with personal needs and social issues

Source: The characteristics of an ideal middle school are based on several sources including *The Exemplary Middle School* by William Alexander and Paul George (1981), *The Essential Middle School* by G. Wiles and H. Bondi (1981), *This We Believe* by the National Middle School Association (1982), *The Middle School We Need* by Thomas Gatewood and Charles Dilg (1975), and a 1973 article entitled, "Do You Have a Middle School?" by Nicholas Georgiady and Louis Romano.

middle school science. The NSF solicitation contained descriptions of the orientation for middle school programs.

> In *middle school years*, they [students] should begin to develop a more disciplined approach to inquiry and experimentation—improving their ability to organize and articulate knowledge, and to approach problems systematically.[14]

Included in the solicitation were some characteristics of middle school materials. Those characteristics included the following:

• integration of science with other subjects,
• hands-on experiences,
• establish a coherent pattern of science topics,

• capitalize on the interests of students,
• use of recent research on teaching and learning, and
• identification of standards of student achievement.

In the early 1990s, the programs developed with these NSF grants will be available. You should be familiar with the orientation of the programs. What follows is a brief description of the programs developed in this reform of science education at the middle school.

Science and Technology: Investigating Human Dimensions (Rodger W. Bybee, Biological Sciences Curriculum Study)
This Biological Sciences Curriculum Study (BSCS) project is a three-year, activity-based, middle school

science and technology program for grades 5-9 with the following characteristics:

- a focus on the development of the early adolescent,
- strategies to encourage the participation of female, minority, and handicapped students,
- an emphasis on reasoning and critical thinking skills,
- cooperative learning as a key instructional strategy,
- an instructional model that enhances student learning,
- a conceptual approach to science and technology,
- an introduction to careers in science and technology fields,
- a continuation of the BSCS K–6 program,
- inclusion of science-technology-society (STS) themes, and
- a plan to enhance the implementation of the program.

Science and Technology: Investigating Human Dimensions will be a unique program for the middle school. Because the program is unique, both evaluation and implementation will be an integral aspect of the program.

The BSCS program will be published by Kendall/Hunt Publishing Company and the materials supplied by Science Kit & Boreal Laboratories.

Improving Urban Middle School Science (Judith Opert Sandler, Education Development Center)

Educational Development Center's proposed project is a multidisciplinary science program for the seventh and eighth grade that is targeted to the needs of early adolescents in urban environments. Modules integrate scientific concepts and understandings from the physical, human and health, life, and earth sciences within the context of science, society, and technology problems. This project will build on the conceptual framework and pedagogical strategies, school district partnerships, teacher training design, and assessment and publishing partnerships established through the NSF-funded Improving Urban Elementary Science Project currently under development at EDC and Sunburst Communications.

School districts and teachers in Boston, Cleveland, Los Angeles, San Francisco, Baltimore, and Montgomery County, Maryland will collaborate fully in the development effort and field-testing. Operation SMART, a research and development project of the Girls Clubs of America, will consult on informal science education strategies which are particularly responsive to urban youth and which will complement the curriculum. The materials will be reviewed for

scientific accuracy and pedagogical soundness by a distinguished advisory panel, while field-testing and evaluation will be conducted by the Boston College Center for the Study of Testing, Evaluation, and Educational Policy (CSTEEP). Sunburst Communications, Inc. will publish the final product and field test materials, contribute to a Teacher Development Fund, and provide technical assistance throughout the project to ensure marketability of the proposed modules.

Explorations in Middle School Science (Ruth Von Blum, Education Systems Corporation)

To address the special needs of our middle schools and junior high schools, Education Systems Corporation promises a computer-based program that will be developed by a highly qualified team of content experts, science educators, instructional designers, and marketers. Participants will include practicing scientists; teachers and other representatives from such professional organizations as the National Science Teachers Association and the National Association of Biology Teachers; seven major school districts; the California State Department of Education; Apple, Tandy, and IBM; and Education Systems Corporation, a successful developer and marketer of computer software for schools. And the University of California, Irvine, will be responsible for the evaluation and teacher training portions of the project.

Explorations in Middle School Science will provide a set of 90 computer lessons in Life, Earth, and Physical Science for grades 6–9. At the heart of each lesson will be a computer simulated laboratory to involve students in "doing" science and improving 1) understanding science concepts by applying critical thinking to solve problems; 2) skills in scientific processes and communication; and 3) attitudes about science.

These lessons will reflect specific science education objectives in state guidelines from across the country and realize the full power of computer technology to reach these objectives. Students will use a number of on-line tools (notebook, data base manager, calculator) to help them perform the simulated laboratory experiments, most of which would be too difficult, dangerous or time consuming to be done in a "live" laboratory. Suggested extension investigations will lead the students to experience nature first hand, away from the computer. Explorations in Middle School Science will be modular, flexible, and well documented. The lessons will be strongly curriculum based, and run on a networked, managed system of microcomputers with 16 colors, sound, mouse input, and excellent graphics.

Interactive Middle-Grades Science (George Dawson, Florida State University, Science Education Program)

The Interactive Middle Grades (IMS) Project will apply many of the latest recommendations for change in science education to the critical middle grades. Florida State University at Tallahassee and Houghton Mifflin Company will develop a science program for grades six through eight that will meet the diverse needs of today's teachers and students. IMS will integrate teachers, textbook and laboratory with applications of the microcomputer and the laser videodisc, producing a commercially marketable system for science instruction, classroom management and student evaluation. Science content, processes and skills focusing on appropriate problems of science, technology and society will be integral parts of the program. This joint effort will involve professional societies, distinguished science educators and will be consistent with guidelines offered by the National Science Teachers Association and National Association of Secondary School Principals.

Florida State University has built a reputation in curriculum development through the principal investigator in this project and other well-known staff members who will be available to assist in the development of the IMS program. The partners in this project, the School and Educational Software Divisions (ESD) of Houghton Mifflin Company, have designed and marketed high quality computer software for the elementary and secondary school market since 1966. The publisher will invest in excess of $14 million in this project during the three-years development phase and will contribute substantially to its continuance and teacher training.

■ Summary

Adolescence is a unique period of life. Over our educational history, we have seen changes in the science curriculum for this age group. The junior high school was created in the late 1800s. Then in the late 1900s, there emerged the middle school. Junior high schools were "junior" versions of high school programs. The middle school curriculum is uniquely designed for the early adolescent.

Although textbooks were significantly changed during the 1960s and 1970s, the 1980s and 1990s have witnessed a return to models similar to those prior to the 1960s. Contemporary reform will have an impact on middle/junior high school programs in the early to mid-1990s. Several new NSF programs serve as models for science education at the middle school level.

■ References

1. Audrey B. Champagne and Leslie E. Hornig, eds., *This Year in School Science: The Science Curriculum* (Washington, D.C.: American Association for the Advancement of Science, 1987).
2. Bonnie Brunkhorst and Michael Padilla, "Science Education for Middle and Junior High School Students: An NSTA Position Statement," *Science and Children*, 24, no. 3, (November/December, 1987), pp. 62-63.
3. Commission on the Reorganization of Secondary Education, *Cardinal Principles of Secondary Education*, Bulletin 1918, no. 35, (Washington, D.C.: U. S. Bureau of Education, 1918), pp. 12-13.
4. W. T. Gruhn and N. R. Douglas, *The Modern Junior High School*, 3rd ed. (New York: The Ronald Press, 1977), p. 133.
5. Paul DeHart Hurd, James T. Robinson, Mary McConnell, and Norris Ross, *The Status of Middle School and Junior High School Science* (Center for Educational Research and Evaluation. The Biological Sciences Curriculum Study, The Colorado College, Colorado Springs, CO, 1981), pp. 4-5.
6. Brown and Obourn, *Offerings and Enrollments* (Washington, D.C.: U. S. Government Printing Office, 1961).
7. Hurd, et al, *The Status of Middle School and Junior High School Science*, p. 15.
8. *Introductory Physical Science—Physical Science II: A Progress Report*, (Newton, MA: IPS Group, Educational Development Center, 1968), p.16.
9. David D. Redfield and Stewart P. Darrow, *The Physics Teacher*, 8 (April 1970), pp. 170-180.
10. Iris Weiss, *Report of the 1977 National Survey of Science, Mathematics, and Social Studies Education* (Washington, D.C.: U. S. Government Printing Office, March, 1977).
11. Iris Weiss, *Report of the 1985-86 National Survey of Science and Mathematics Education* (Research Triangle Park, NC: Research Triangle Institute, 1987).
12. Brunkhorst, "Science Education," p.62.
13. Brunkhorst, "Science Education," p.62.
14. National Science Foundation, "Program Solicitation: Programs for Middle School Science Instruction," (Washington, D.C.: National Science Foundation, 1988).

==================== **INVESTIGATING SCIENCE TEACHING** ====================

ACTIVITY 16–1

Evaluating Middle/Junior High School Textbooks

At some time in your career, you will select a new textbook. This activity introduces you to that process. The form you will complete is adapted from the American Association for the Advancement of Science publication *Science Books & Films*.

Select three textbooks from the discipline and grade level you intend to teach. Review the textbooks and complete the following chart. List the textbooks you compare by author(s), title, publisher, and copyright date.

Textbooks

1.

2.

3.

GENERAL EVALUATION	N/C	Poor	Fair	Adequate	Good	Excellent
Text						
Content accuracy						
Content currency						
Content scope						
Structure and methods of science						
Organization and coherence						
Comprehensibility						
Labs: in text/supplementals						
Comprehensibility						
Practicality of required apparatus						
Summary: text supplementals						
Teach the nature of scientific enterprise						
Encourage students to reason to testable conclusions						
Stimulate awareness of science, technology, and society						

1. Were the textbooks for middle school or junior high school?
2. How were the textbooks similar? Different?
3. Describe an outstanding feature of each textbook.
4. Describe the weakest feature of each textbook.
5. Which textbook would you select to use? Why?

CHAPTER 17

The High School Science Curriculum

The high school science curriculum has changed over history. The history of high school programs is examined in the first part of this chapter. The latter portion of the chapter is devoted to the process of designing a curriculum.

■ Reform of High School Science Programs

The high school science curriculum is subject to the same forces of reform that were discussed in the chapter on middle/junior high school programs. Changes in society, science, and education all influence the reform of curriculum. At the high school level, advances in science and technology have traditionally exerted the greatest influence on programs.

Each of the traditional courses—physics, chemistry, and biology—are discussed in this chapter.

Physics

Physics was first known as "natural philosophy" and appeared in the academies of the early 1700s. Content was organized into topics similar to those of our traditional courses today. Mechanics, fluids, heat, light, sound, magnetism, and electricity were the topics taught, mainly by recitation. The Civil War and the advent of land-grant colleges in the 1860s placed emphasis on military and vocational aspects of science, and the course became known as physics. Laboratory instruction was emphasized. A list of standard experiments, called *The Descriptive List*, was circulated by Harvard in 1886 for use by the high schools. Candidates for admission to Harvard, who offered physics as a prerequisite, were then tested by use of these experiments.

Physical Science Study Committee

In 1956, a group of university physicists at Cambridge, Massachusetts, looked at the secondary school physics curriculum and found that it did not present the content or spirit of modern physics. From this group, the Physical Science Study Committee (PSSC) was formed, with the objective of producing a new physics course for the high school.

In the four following years, this group developed a textbook, laboratory guide, teacher's guide, set of apparatus, monographs, and films. All of these aids were correlated closely with one another to produce an effective curriculum package. In addition, there were many summer institutes for upgrading teachers in physics and in the philosophy of the new course.

Some of the important differences between the PSSC physics course and traditional high school physics became apparent:

- fewer topics covered at greater depth,
- greater emphasis on laboratory work,
- more emphasis on basic physics,
- less attention to technological applications,
- development approach showing origins of basic ideas of physics, and
- increased difficulty and rigor of the course.

Teachers and administrators had conflicting opinions about the merits of the PSSC course. There was general agreement that it was a definite improvement over traditional courses, especially for better-than-average college-bound students. For average or below-average students, its greater merit was questionable.

In a 1971 study by Wasik, PSSC students showed significantly higher performance than non-PSSC students in the process skills of application and analysis.[1] On the other hand, non-PSSC students performed at a higher level on the taxonomic process measure of knowledge. It was concluded that the results essentially supported the position of new curriculum writers that the PSSC instructional materials were most effective in developing higher cognitive-process skills.

A 1983 analysis of the effects of new science curricula on student performance revealed that the physics curricula was second only to the biology curricula in terms of overall advances in student performances. Studies of achievement and analytic skills showed that students participating in the new physics courses gained at least a half-year more than students in traditional courses.[2] This result indicates that the new physics curricula was successful in achieving part of its stated goals. The goal generally not assessed was the students' perceptions of physics. This omission is unfortunate, because it could have given some insights to help slow the long and steady decline in physics enrollments that we are currently experiencing.

Project Physics

A second physics course was developed, designed for the average student. Project Physics, a course produced at Harvard University, attempted to treat physics as a lively and fundamental science, closely related to achievements both in and outside the discipline itself.[3]

Financial support for the project was provided by the Carnegie Corporation of New York, the Ford Foundation, the National Science Foundation, the Alfred P. Sloan Foundation, the United States Office of Education, and Harvard University. Several hundred participating schools throughout the United States used and tested the course as it went through several revisions.

The philosophy of this course is emphasized in eight points.[4]

1. Physics is for everyone.
2. A coherent selection within physics is possible.
3. Doing physics goes beyond physics.
4. Individuals require a flexible course.
5. A multimedia system stimulates better learning.
6. The time has come to teach science as one of the humanities.
7. A physics course should be rewarding to take.
8. A physics course should be rewarding to teach.

Materials of the Project Physics course include a textbook, teacher's guide, student guide, experiments, films, transparencies, tests, film loops, readers, and other items.

The chapter headings for the Project Physics course are:[5]

Unit 1. Concepts of Motion
Unit 2. Motion in the Heavens
Unit 3. The Triumph of Mechanics
Unit 4. Light and Electromagnetism
Unit 5. Models of the Atom
Unit 6. The Nucleus

Several studies attempted to find reasons for the decreasing enrollments in high school physics. In a questionnaire sent by Thompson to 1,382 high school physics teachers, 79 percent believed that students stayed away because the course was too difficult.[6] Of these students, 40 percent ascribed their reluctance to fear of jeopardizing their grade average and 16 percent attributed it to fear of mathematics.

In a study of 450 physics students enrolled in Project Physics in 1966–1967, Wayne Welch concluded that students receive lower grades in physics than in their other courses.[7] In the sample studied, the median I.Q. was at the 82nd percentile but the average grade received by these bright students was in the C+ to B- range. Thus the students were dissatisfied with their experience.

The course was extensively evaluated during its development. Results were encouraging, both with respect to the performance of Project Physics students on standard tests such as the College Board Examinations and with respect to attracting increasing numbers of high school students to elect physics in their junior or senior years. The percentage of girls taking the course also appeared to have increased over PSSC or traditional physics courses.

Chemistry

The teaching of high school chemistry began in the early 1800s in girls' academies. The Civil War years gave a stimulus to the course because of the military and industrial applications of the science. Laboratory work was increased during those years, and efforts were made to reproduce many of the classical experiments of early chemists such as Priestley and Lavoisier. As with physics, Harvard in 1886 placed chemistry on the optional list for college entrance but controlled the quality of entering students by publishing *The Pamphlet*, containing sixty experiments, on which the prospective enrollee was tested in the laboratory. Influence of *The Pamphlet* was profound and the high school chemistry course became highly standardized. Laboratory workbooks were developed, containing "experiments" that were mainly exercises in observation and manipulation of chemical reactions.

Chemical Bond Approach

In 1957, a summer conference of chemistry teachers at Reed College in Portland, Oregon, produced a plan for a new type of chemistry course and initiated the Chemical Bond Approach (CBA) Project. There followed a series of writing conferences, use by trial schools, and the production of a commercial textbook in 1963. The major theme of this course was the chemical bond, and particular attention was given to *mental models* (conceptual schemes) of structure, kinetic theory, and energy.

The laboratory program and textbook parallel and reinforce each other. No unusual chemicals or equipment are required and the cost of conducting the CBA chemistry course is not significantly different from that of conducting conventional courses.

Chemical Education Materials Study

A second course-improvement project in chemistry was initiated at Harvey Mudd College in Claremont, California, in 1959. Called the Chemical Education Materials Study (CHEM), the project developed a course that is strongly based on experiment and that includes the text and laboratory manual, a teacher's guide, a score of excellent films, and a series of wall charts.

Both the CBA and CHEM Study chemistry programs received grants from the National Science Foundation, which supported numerous inservice and summer institutes for teachers.

Enrollments in CBA and CHEM chemistry classes increased initially. In 1968, approximately 40 percent of high school chemistry taught in the United States was the CHEM study course.[8] Approximately 10 percent of the schools were using CBA.[9]

At that time, the CHEM project terminated its work and commercial publishers were invited to prepare courses based on the philosophy and materials of the CHEM study course. Several publishers produced high school chemistry textbooks influenced by the philosophies and pedagogies of the CHEM and CBA programs.

In a survey by Fornhoff in 1970, in which 2,395 students were queried, the most widely used high school chemistry textbook was *Modern Chemistry*; *Chemistry—An Experimental Science* was second and *Chemical Systems* was third.[10] The latter two texts are CHEM study and CBA chemistry, respec-

tively. Some other information obtained in the study showed that most chemistry classes met five times per week for 40 to 59 minutes and 13 percent reported students taking a college-level chemistry course in high school.

In a 1978 report it was estimated fewer than 25 percent of chemistry teachers were using either CHEM study, CBA approach, or a combination of the two.[11] The same study found that CHEM study was used in 15 percent of school districts; yet neither textbook appeared on the list of most commonly used textbooks. A 1983 report on the effects of new curricula found that the new chemistry curricula, both CBA and CHEM study, produced the least impact in terms of student cognitive achievement and process skills.[12]

Interdisciplinary Approaches to Chemistry

In March 1972, a new chemistry course was developed by the University of Maryland. This was the IAC (Interdisciplinary Approaches to Chemistry). The IAC course approached the teaching of chemistry somewhat differently, by using a group of modules dealing with special topics of an interdisciplinary nature. The titles of the modules were:

- Reactions and Reason (Introductory)
- Diversity and Periodicity (Inorganic)
- Form and Function (Organic)
- Molecules in Living Systems (Biochemistry),
- The Heart of the Matter (Nuclear),
- Earth and Its Neighbors (Geochemistry),
- The Delicate Balance (Environmental), and
- Communities of Molecules (Physical).

Among the goals of IAC was the "realization that a student's attitudes or feelings about chemistry are just as important in the long run as his acquisition of special chemical concepts. Thus in molding the IAC program, equal emphasis has been placed on providing the student with a sound background in those basic skills and concepts normally found in an introductory high school chemistry course as well as on developing the attitude that chemistry is not a dry, unrealistic science, but an exciting, relevant, human activity that can be enjoyable to study."[13]

There seem to be several characteristics that make IAC chemistry different from traditional chemistry or previous curriculum projects. An effort was made to make chemistry more relevant and successful for the student. The program is modular, instead of being a single structured text. Each module is devoted to a different aspect of chemistry, and its relationship to the other sciences and society is emphasized. This format allows for many degrees of flexibility within the program.

A module consists of chemistry content and laboratory experiments, integrated into a unified whole. The program includes suggested readings for students, problems and activities, safety precautions, and relevant chemical data such as periodic tables and charts. Each module deals with a specific area of chemistry as indicated in the titles, relating chemistry to other sciences and phenomena encountered in the natural world.

IAC was revised in 1979 to update its content and teaching techniques in concepts and in laboratory experiments. It has been well received by chemistry teachers who seem to enjoy the freedom to experiment with different modules in their classes and to rearrange content in accordance with student and teacher interests.

Research by Robert Stevenson in 1977–1978 on the use of IAC chemistry in high school indicated that age, sex, and attitude had no effect on the achievement level of students; that cognitive-reasoning ability and grade-point averages were highly correlated with achievement success; and that achievement success on the introductory module tests could be used to predict success on subsequent modules.[14]

Biology

Biology had its beginnings in botany, physiology, and zoology and was patterned after college courses in these subjects in the nineteenth century. A course of study in biology appeared in New York in 1905 and the College Entrance Examination Board prepared an examination for the course in 1913. Biology was placed in the ninth grade in schools of the six-three-three type of organization and in the tenth grade of eight-four schools.

Of all the high school sciences, biology had the largest enrollment, due to a combination of factors. Placement in the ninth or tenth grade where the effect of school dropouts is less pronounced, the effect of compulsory education laws, the nonmathematical nature of the course, and the general requirement of a minimum of one science course for graduation from high school combined to increase enrollments over the years. In 1958 approximately 68 percent of tenth-grade students enrolled in the biology course.[15]

Biological Sciences Curriculum Study

To modernize the secondary school biology course, the American Institute of Biological Science organized the Biological Sciences Curriculum Study (BSCS) at the University of Colorado in 1958; Arnold B. Grobman was appointed director. In discussing the design of the course developed by the BSCS, he said,

A realistic general biology program must take into account a wider range of student ability, interests, and potential than exists in other high school science courses. It must be a course that most tenth-grade students can handle and at the same time prove challenging to the above-average student. For these reasons the committee thought it undesirable to limit the course to a single design.[16]

Three courses were developed, based on a molecular approach, a cellular approach, and an ecological approach, respectively. Although the courses differ in emphasis, nine common themes run through them:

1. Change of living things through time-evolution
2. Diversity of type and unity of pattern of living things
3. Genetic continuity of life
4. Biological roots of behavior
5. Complementarity of organisms and environment
6. Complementarity of structure and function
7. Regulation and homeostasis: the maintenance of life in the face of change
8. Science as inquiry
9. Intellectual history of biological concepts[17]

A complete set of materials was provided for the course. Textbooks, laboratory guides, teacher's guides, supplementary readings, and tests are but a few of these materials. Innovations include the laboratory blocks, consisting of a series of interlocking and correlated experiments on a special topic of biology. Eleven "blocks" were developed, including, for example, "Plant Growth and Development," "Microbes: Their Growth and Interaction," and "Interdependence of Structure and Function."

A second-level course was prepared for advanced biology and a simpler course called *Patterns and Processes in Science* was designed for unsuccessful learners.

Other supplementary materials are excerpts from historical papers, BSCS Invitations to Inquiry, discussion outlines for the laboratory, films on laboratory techniques, the *Biology Teacher's Handbook*, the BSCS Pamphlet Series, and many other materials.

The BSCS biology courses received generally favorable response throughout the country. Two versions of the course are still available and it has been found that different versions are chosen in different regions. Several foreign countries are also using the course.

Much research has been done on the effects of

BSCS biology in the schools. In one study, Kenneth George found that students taking the Blue Version of the course scored significantly higher on critical thinking, as measured by the Watson Glaser Critical Thinking Appraisal Form ZM, than did students taking conventional biology.[18] Adams found that there was no difference in the retention of biological information between BSCS students and those taking traditional biology.[19] However, there were significant relationships between retention and intelligence, reading scores, and teacher grading, with the BSCS students generally scoring higher. Granger and Yager found no significant difference between students experiencing BSCS and non-BSCS backgrounds with respect to achievement in either high school or college-level biology. However, a significantly larger percentage of BSCS students felt their background was better in meeting individual needs, as well as preparing them for college-level biology.[20] Carter and Nakosteen, in a study with 8,500 college freshmen, found that BSCS students scored higher on inquiry and recall items on the BSCS Comprehensive Biology Tests than did students who had a non-BSCS course in high school.[21]

In a 1983 report, BSCS fared very well in the major review of new curricula cited earlier. Biology curricula showed the greatest effect on student performance, and it was particularly high in developing analytic skills.

In a 1984 report on the BSCS programs, James Shymansky had this to say:

> We found the new science programs to be consistently more effective than their traditional counterparts. Moreover, we found Biological Sciences Curriculum Study (BSCS) biology to be the most effective of all the new high school programs.[22]

■ Common Elements of Golden Age Courses

A survey of various course materials developed in secondary school science during the 1960s and 1970s shows close similarity in types of materials offered and in general objectives. The following common elements are discernible:

1. There was less emphasis on social and personal applications of science and technology than in the traditional courses.
2. There was more emphasis on abstractions, theory, and basic science—the structure of scientific disciplines.
3. There was increased emphasis on discovery— the modes of inquiry used by scientists.

4. Quantitative techniques were used frequently.
5. They presented newer concepts in their subject matter.
6. They required upgrading of teacher competency in both subject matter and pedagogical skills for successful teaching.
7. They were accompanied by various teaching aids, which were well integrated and designed to supplement the courses.
8. There was little emphasis on career awareness as a goal of science teaching.
9. The programs were primarily oriented toward college-bound students.
10. Both high school and junior high school programs were similar in emphasis and structure.

■ High School Science Curriculum in the 1990s

We have briefly reviewed the history and major programs developed during the "Golden Age" of science education. It may now be important to turn attention to the present situation since many of the "new curricula" have been in existence for over 25 years and have undergone several revisions.

We should first note that the high school science curriculum is largely determined at a local level— by science teachers, administrators, and school boards, using suggestions and guidelines from state departments of education. Even with significant autonomy, recent NSF studies have shown two things to be true: there is considerable uniformity of programs, and the curriculum has not changed significantly in recent history.

Typically, the senior high school science curriculum is biology at the 10th grade and chemistry and physics at the 11th and 12th grades respectively. General biology is offered to all students and enrolls three million students each year. About 80 percent of graduating seniors have taken high school biology. There is a note concerning this statistic that is of critical importance for biology teachers. *For 50 percent of high school students who graduate each year, biology is their last experience with any science course.*[23] The 1977 NSF survey by Iris Weiss cited earlier indicated approximately 1.2 million students took a physics course. High school chemistry and physics are generally perceived as college preparatory, as are the majority of other science courses offered in the average high school. The high school science curriculum is generally void of science courses appropriate for students other than the college-bound. The issue here is that only about 50 percent of all high school students go to college.

The nature of the science curriculum can be

determined by examining textbooks for the respective disciplines. Again, there is remarkable similarity among textbooks for a discipline and even between textbooks for different disciplines. Some of the characteristics include a significant number of facts presented in simple and condensed form, an emphasis on extensive vocabulary rather than a focus on fewer principles, and conceptual schemes. By nature of the emphasis on science facts and vocabulary, there is little attention to the espoused goals of scientific processes, investigation, and analytic thinking. While all the NSF materials developed during the "Golden Age" acclaimed these aims, recent changes in textbooks have slowly evolved in the direction just mentioned. A recent review of the inquiry goal in science teaching found that teachers gave little attention to the aim of inquiry and associated skills.[24] (See Table 17.1)

A related point is that, although familiarity with and knowledge of science and technology is increasingly important to students' everyday lives, the high school science curriculum gives little recognition of important goals related to personal needs, social concerns, and careers. One recent study by Faith Hickman suggested that only about 5 percent of the secondary science curriculum was devoted to topics of personal and social significance.[25]

Let us note that we are pointing out the present status of high school science curricula. If confronted with the central question about NSF programs and the "Golden Age"—Did we accomplish what we set out to do?—the answer would have to be "yes"; this answer is supported by research.[26] The main point of this discussion is that changes in science, technology, society, and our understanding of student learning all indicate we need to once again rethink the high school science curriculum.

In the early 1990's, the National Science Foundation (NSF) will probably issue solicitations for proposals to develop new programs for high school science. When you begin teaching science you can expect new and innovative materials in the early 1990s.

■ Designing Your Science Curriculum

Much of the discussion in this chapter has been directed toward the development of curriculum materials by national projects. These were large-scale projects requiring a team of scientists, science educators, and classroom teachers of science. With the help of major funding, primarily from government agencies such as The National Science Foundation, materials were developed, field-tested, revised, field-tested again, revised, and then published. The curricular changes were so large and sometimes new, as with earth science, that there was a need for substantial inservice education as the new programs were implemented. This is one approach to curriculum development, and it is the approach that dominates our thinking when it comes to curricular reform. This model of curricular reform can be characterized as (1) occurring at a national (or state) level,

TABLE 17–1

The high school science curriculum: Selected examples *

	Highly Structured	Moderately Structured
10th GRADE	Modern Biology (Holt) Biological Science: A Molecular Approach (Heath) Biology: Everyday Experiences (Merrill) Biology: Living Systems (Merrill)	Ideas and Investigations in Biology (Prentice Hall) Patterns and Processes (Kendall/Hunt)
11th GRADE	Modern Chemistry (Holt) Chemistry and Experimental Science (CHEM STUDY) Chemical Systems (CBA) Chemistry: An Investigative Approach (Houghton Mifflin) Chemistry: A Modern Course (Merrill) ChemCom (Kendall/Hunt)	Interdisciplinary Approaches to Chemistry (IAC)
12th GRADE	Modern Physics (Holt) Physics: Principles and Problems (Merrill) The Project Physics (PP) Physics (PSSC) Conceptual Physics (Addison Wesley)	

*These programs were selected on the basis of use, NSF development, and different organizational structure. Curriculum projects or publishers are given in parenthesis.

(2) being heavily funded, and (3) approached "from the top down"; that is, developed and published first and then implemented by classroom teachers.

A reform movement of the same type and magnitude such as science education experienced in the 1960s and 1970s is not likely in the foreseeable future. Though there is a need for reform, curriculum development in the near future will also be: (1) at the local or district level; (2) funded within the usual budgets of schools and school districts, perhaps with some assistance from state, federal or private agencies; and (3) approached from the "bottom up"; that is, initiated and developed by classroom teachers and then implemented within the school district. In some instances the programs may be "exported" to other districts through groups such as the National Diffusion Network and the National Science Teachers Association, particularly the Search for Excellence in Science Education, that has identified and described many excellent programs.

The second approach to curriculum development is a smaller-scale approach to change. Here, an individual science teacher or team of science teachers is appointed to initiate, develop, and implement a new science curriculum. The task could encompass anything from a minor revision of an existing course to development of a new K-12 science program for the school district.

The new demands for educational reform combined with the level of funding at the national level suggest that the burden for change will increasingly fall to the local school district and the science teaching personnel. As we increasingly become an "information society," curricular changes will also be more frequent, perhaps best thought of as continuous, and will require more than developing and implementing a few new lessons or units.

There is a third approach to curriculum development. Though usually not recognized as such, the adoption of new science textbooks represents the selection and implementation of a science curriculum. In most cases the textbook is the curriculum.

With the preceding paragraphs as background and rationale we will now direct our attention to a discussion that will be useful to either beginning or experienced teachers confronted with the task of designing a science curriculum. We begin by noting several resources that form the basis of our discussion, beginning with Ralph Tyler's classic 1949 book, *Basic Principles of Curriculum and Instruction.*[27] Approaching 40 years of age, its model has not lost its vitality as an important process for identifying curricular objectives and learning experiences. This model is applicable today because it does not suggest a program, it outlines procedures for developing a

curriculum. The utility and simplicity of Tyler's model is found in four basic questions.

- What educational purposes should the school seek to attain?
- How can learning experiences be selected that are likely to attain these objectives?
- How can learning experiences be effectively organized?
- How can we determine whether these purposes are being attained?[28]

Another resource for our discussion is the "discrepancy model" used in Project Synthesis and reported in the NSTA publication *What Research Says to the Science Teacher*, vol. III.[29] The point of this model is to first describe a "desired curriculum" and then your "present curriculum." By analyzing the discrepancies between such components as goals, materials, facilities, and so on, one can arrive at what is needed to develop and implement a new program. There is an added strength to this model; a realistic assessment of time, materials, and money is a part of the process.

Although this discussion is about curriculum development by individual teachers and local teams of teachers, the national projects do have some important processes and "advice." In 1987 Joseph McInerney, director of the Biological Sciences Curriculum Study, wrote about curriculum development at BSCS. McInerney outlined several criteria for the selection of content for a new program. Those criteria are paraphrased:

1. How well does the information being considered illustrate the basic, enduring principles of the scientific discipline?
2. Do other teachers, administrators and parents perceive the proposed materials as useful and important?
3. What is the relationship between the proposed curriculum materials and the prevailing context of general education?[30]

Asking and answering questions such as these will help with the difficult issue of deciding what content should be included, and assuring that the program is understandable and acceptable to the scientific and educational communities.

This section also incorporates suggestions from the Council of State Science Supervisors and from Jefferson County (Colorado) Public Schools. Table 17.2 summarizes several of these approaches to curriculum development. Finally, other valuable sources for individuals developing new programs are

TABLE 17–2
Some models for designing a science curriculum

Ralph Tyler's Approach to Curriculum Development

    I. Examination of Traditional Factors Influencing the Curriculum to Determine an Initial Set of Instructional Goals
- Examination of Student Interests and Characteristics
- Analyze Social Trends and Issues
- Synthesize Information from Disciplines

    II. Development of Preliminary Curriculum Program
- Synthesize Objectives from Step I into a Cohesive Program

    III. Reconsideration of Objectives in Terms of Philosophy and Psychology
- Review Program Objectives for Congruence with Curriculum Designer's Philosophy
- Review Program Objectives for Congruence with Current Learning Theories

    IV. Development of Curriculum Program
- Arrange Curriculum Objectives into an Organized Program

Project Synthesis

    I. Identify Primary Goal Clusters of Science Education
- Personal Needs
- Societal Issues
- Academic Preparation
- Career Awareness

    II. Setting the Perspective by Developing a "Desired State" (i.e. operational definitions of effective science education) using the categories:
- Goals
- Curriculum Programs
- Teacher Characteristics
- Teacher Education
- Facilities and Equipment
- Instructional Practices
- Student Characteristics, and
- Evaluation and Testing.

    III. Determining the Status
- Study and analyze data concerning the actual state in science education.
- Categories used in developing desired state are used again.

The Year in School Science 1986,[31] *The Year in School Science 1989,*[32] *The Science Curriculum,* and *Improving Indicators of the Quality of Science and Mathematics Education in Grades K-12.*[33]

The discussion that follows is our synthesis of these approaches and recommended steps for redesigning and implementing a science curriculum.

Step 1—Review Influences on the Science Curriculum

The first phase is to spend some time reading, thinking, and discussing three traditional influences on the curriculum—science, society, and students.

What are the recent advances in science and technology that are important for students to use in their personal lives and/or know as citizens? Obviously, all scientific knowledge and technologic advances cannot be incorporated into school science programs. Science teachers must decide "what knowledge is of most worth."

What are the trends, issues and problems in society that are related to science and technology? Reviewing some of these issues provides another goal component of the science program. Finally, an examination of student needs, interests, and characteristics is essential. Here you can include the unqiue needs of students in your school or district. After reviewing these three components a first set of gen-

TABLE 17–2
Continued

IV. Analyzing Discrepancies
- Compare the desired and actual states of science education for differences
- Identify aspects of goals, curriculum, instruction and evaluation which need improvement
- Locate factors which will impede changes and consider alternative means
- Locate factors which will facilitate change and consider how to utilize

V. Recommendations for Change

PHASES OF SCIENCE CURRICULUM DEVELOPMENT
Council of State Science Supervisors

I. Evaluate present program
- Determine the philosophy
- Study current trends
- Identify special needs—strengths and weaknesses of present program

II. Planning for curricular changes
- Organize a science curriculum advisory committee
- Review all available programs
- Select programs that are consistent with the philosophy and educational objectives of the local school district
- Pilot-test the programs
- Evaluate tested programs and select those best suited to the school situation.

III. Implementation of new programs
- Provide inservice education
- Provide additional time and pay for extra time needed to implement the program
- Provide consultants for periodic feedback and on-the-spot assistance
- Reevaluate and revise the program
- Continue inservice as new teachers are added to the program
- Provide funds for continued supply of necessary materials

PROGRAM DEVELOPMENT
Jefferson County (Colorado) Public Schools

I. Identification of student needs
II. Establishment of program goals and objectives
III. Development of curriculum units
IV. Pilot test of curriculum in selected schools
V. Field test of curriculum in additional schools
VI. Evaluation and revision of curriculum
VII. Implementation of curriculum in schools

eral objectives can be stated. This first step is presented graphically, in Figure 17.1.

Step 2—Synthesize Goals into a Proposed Science Curriculum

This phase consists of bringing the objectives identified in the first phase into a proposed program. At this point, no effort is made to evaluate or filter the objectives due to various constraints. Synthesize your objectives into a program that has a scope and sequence, as well as classroom facilities, materials, equipment, instructional approach, and evaluation

components. This can be a very exciting exercise, so use your creativity. Graphically, the development now appears as shown in Figure 17.2.

Step 3—Describe the Present Science Curriculum

One mistake often made in local curriculum development is the omission of any consideration of the present curriculum. What are the present goals? What is the textbook? What about the scope and sequence of the present program? Reviewing the present program also includes reviewing any special top-

=== **GUEST EDITORIAL** ===

Why a Crisis in Science Education?

Bill G. Aldridge
Executive Director
National Science Teachers Association
Washington, D.C.

There is overwhelming evidence that *we are producing a citizenry that is scientifically and technically illiterate.* The knowledge gap between scientists and engineers and the general public has widened most in this time when *the public has most needed knowledge to make important personal and societal decisions.* What are the most serious causes of this failure in our educational enterprises?

In an average American high school with a 1977–78 ninth-grade class of 1,000 students, there were 720 high school graduates in 1981. Of the 416 graduates who entered college, there were 96 declared science or engineering majors in 1983. From this group there will be 39 bachelor's degrees in science or engineering in 1985, 5 master's degrees in 1987, and 2 doctoral degrees in 1989. What high school science did we offer to the original 1,000 students? And was it appropriate?

The content of high school physics, chemistry, and biology is essentially what was produced by the curricular reforms of the early 1960s. It is science as seen by the pure scientist. The course material is carefully and logically developed, with abstractions, derivations, and other features that appeal to the interests of scientists working in fields of basic research.

The courses focus on pure science and are largely devoid of practical applications, technology, or the relevancy of science to society's problems, such as acid rain, nuclear wastes and disposal of hazardous materials, or improper nutrition. These courses do not prepare people to enter the myriad of nonscience occupations that require technological knowledge; nor do they open the way toward careers in math, science, and engineering for *all* those who have the intrinsic ability to succeed. High school science and math courses also duplicate content offered in college courses. They offer little more than preparation for that next course, which the vast majority of students will never take. Present proposals to increase high school graduation requirements in science and math will force a greater number of students either to take these inappropriate courses or drop out of school.

Not only are there these problems with course offerings, there are also problems of teacher qualifications and shortages of competent science teachers.

Some 20 states have already increased their requirements for science and math and 20 other states are in the process of doing so. As math and science requirements are increased, students are assigned to these courses, instead of being allowed to register for nonrequired electives in other

---

ics, units, or lessons that you develop. This phase of development is a "matter-of-fact" approach, outlining what exists in terms of materials, equipment, time, space, budget, and your competencies. Use the categories of goals, curriculum materials, teacher interests and competencies, classroom facilities and equipment, instructional methods, and evaluation. Note that the same organizing categories were suggested in development of the preliminary curriculum. This phase is represented in Figure 17.3.

Step 4—Analyze the Discrepancies Between the Proposed and Present Science Curriculum

Using the same categories, i.e., material resources, instructional methods, classroom facilities, and teacher interests and competencies provides a convenient way to identify the differences between where your

FIGURE 17–1
Curriculum review flowchart

Review Advances in Science and Technology	Review Social Trends and Issues Related to Science and Technology	Review Student Needs, Interests and Characteristics

subjects. As a result, teachers of those other subjects are made surplus and many of them are reassigned to teach science and math classes for which they are unqualified. There is evidence that this reassignment process has occurred and will continue to occur on a massive scale. Approximately 30 percent of all teachers currently teaching science and math in secondary school classrooms are now either completely unqualified or severely underqualified to teach those subjects. Yet the supply of science and math teachers has declined by a factor of four in the past decade. How can this be explained?

The secondary school student population has declined over the past several years, and this decline will continue until 1991, when the population will begin to rise again. Overall, there has been a surplus of secondary school teachers, and there will not be a shortage until 1991 when the student population begins to rise again. Large numbers of class sections in physical education, home economics, social sciences, and business have been eliminated, and the teachers of those classes have become surplus. Many of the surplus teachers in these other subjects have minimal qualifications in science or math. When science or math teaching slots open up, while the overall teaching force must be reduced, it is the surplus

teachers who are given these positions.

What is the National Science Teachers Association doing about the problems? We are working hard to implement recommendations of the various national commissions to broaden course objectives and content. We have developed four goals clusters which provide exactly what the various national commission reports recommend. *These goals focus on developing students' skills for living in a technological world, preparing students to make informal decisions about societal issues, providing a strong foundation in academic areas that allow students to pursue scientific careers if they choose, and presenting up-to-date career information that includes the wide variety of technology-based careers available.*

To improve the quality of science teachers, we have approved new certification standards (which have also been approved by NCATE). These standards meet or exceed the standards of almost every state. To help ensure that teachers meet our high standards, we are implementing a program of individual science-teacher certification. We hope to do this with the cooperation of several discipline-oriented science teacher organizations.

From *Education Week*, Nov. 14, 1984. Reprinted with permission of B. Aldridge. (Italics added.)

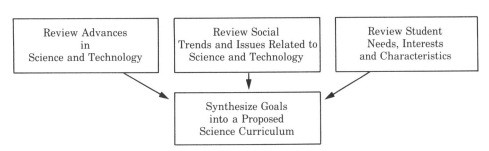

FIGURE 17–2
Curriculum synthesis flowchart

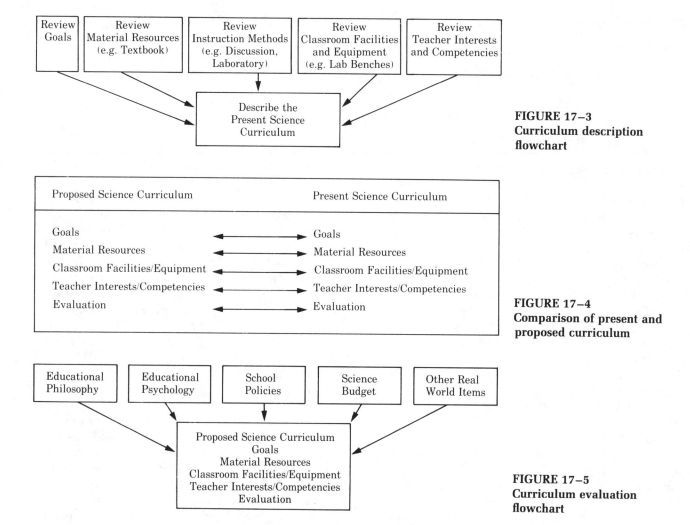

FIGURE 17–3
Curriculum description flowchart

FIGURE 17–4
Comparison of present and proposed curriculum

FIGURE 17–5
Curriculum evaluation flowchart

science curriculum is and where you want it to be. This phase is represented in Figure 17.4.

As a result of this stage you should have a good idea of what is needed in order to develop your science curriculum.

Step 5—Evaluate the Proposed Science Curriculum

This step is critical. Here is a place to reevaluate what you propose doing in terms of what is possible. The phase is infused with reality. Things such as educational philosophy, learning theory, time, budget, and any other "real world" items should be factored into the possible science curriculum. Screening everything at this point sets the stage for the review, purchase, development, or synthesis of materials, changes in goals, and suggestions for inservice appropriate to your proposed program. At the end of this phase you should have a realistic picture of what can be done, who is required to do what, and how long it will take, as presented in Figure 17.5.

Step 6—Development and Implementation of Your Science Curriculum

There are two things to remember at this point. You don't have to develop the program *de nova*. You can select new materials and adapt extant materials. The second point is that the new science curriculum does not have to be developed in a week, month, or even a year. As a result of your analysis and synthesis to this point you should have a long-range plan for your professional development; material acquisition; development of lessons, units, or modules; adoption of new textbooks, and so on. Implementation can occur slowly over a period of time.

Step 7—Evaluation of Your Science Curriculum

From time to time it will be necessary to reevaluate the ongoing program. Ideally, you would monitor and change the science curriculum continuously. Doing

TABLE 17–3
Designing a science curriculum

I. Review Influences on the Science Curriculum
  • Advances in Science and Technology that have personal and social utility for students
  • Social trends and issues related to science and technology
  • Student needs, interests and characteristics, including national concerns and local issues
  • Outline goals relative to the three areas reviewed
II. Synthesize Goals into a Proposed Science Curriculum
  • Curriculum Materials
  • Instructional Strategies
  • Facilities, materials, equipment
  • Teacher Competencies
  • Evaluation
III. Describe the Present Science Curriculum
  • Goals
  • Curriculum Materials
  • Instructional Strategies
  • Facilities, materials, equipment
  • Teacher interests and competencies
  • Evaluation
IV. Analyze Discrepancies Between Proposed and Present Program
  • Compare differences and identify priorities in terms of categories listed above
V. Reevaluate the Proposed Science Curriculum
  • Reevaluate proposed program in terms of priorities and possibilities, e.g., budget
  • Review proposed program in terms of educational philosophy and policies of district, school and/or science department
  • Revised proposed program incorporating contemporary educational psychology, e.g. development and learning theory
VI. Development and Implementation of the Science Curriculum
  • Review curriculum materials appropriate for the proposed program, e.g., textbooks, teaching modules
  • Consider adaptation of existing materials for proposed program
  • Develop curriculum materials, e.g., lessons, units, modules as necessary
  • Implement new materials in an organized fashion.
VII. Evaluation of the Science Curriculum
  • Monitor and adjust curriculum periodically
  • Repeat process of redesign of science curriculum

this would allow you to maintain those curricular components that are appropriate to the present state of science, society and students, while changing those aspects of the program that, for various reasons, have become outdated and outmoded. The seven steps we have outlined are summarized in Table 17.3.

The process of designing or redesigning the science program has, to this point, primarily focused on materials. The success of your curriculum develop-

ment will also depend on the awareness, interactions, and work of the people directly and indirectly involved in the process. The materials of the science curriculum are relatively easy to change, and while change of materials is necessary, it is not sufficient. Efforts to design a new science curriculum must also take into account the beliefs, attitudes, and perceptions that teachers, administrators, and the public have about science and technology education and the particular need to design a new program.

So, we also suggest the addition of some other components for a successful science curriculum development and implementation.

1. Establish the need to change the science education curriculum among the science faculty and with other teachers and administrators.
2. Describe the nature, direction and realities of change to those interested and concerned—especially administrators and the public.
3. Obtain endorsement and support from the principal, school board, and community.
4. Require and develop materials within the budget.
5. Establish a realistic timeline for development and implementation.
6. Provide for released time, inservice programs and summer time for personnel directly involved in the project.
7. Monitor and adjust the process of development and implementation.

■ Summary

The need for changes in high school science programs became increasingly evident midway through the twentieth century. A number of forces produced conditions that affected the curriculum. The rapid increase in scientific knowledge, the competitive nature of the race for space, technological advancements in teaching tools, a gradual dissatisfaction with the encylopedic approach to the teaching of science, and new understandings of student learning and development combined to encourage changes.

The first secondary science curriculum course to react to these pressures was physics, followed by chemistry, biology, and junior high science, in that order. New courses for all these subjects appeared, stimulated by massive financial support from the National Science Foundation and a few other agencies.

Students of the investigative sciences were given opportunities for increased laboratory work and application of inquiry methods for learning. They were directed to better understandings of how scientists work and how knowledge is obtained.

More attention was given to the processes of science. Apparatus and facilities promoted investigations of natural phenomena, while the teacher became more a director of learning than a dispenser of knowledge.

The impact of "Golden Age" curriculum changes will be felt for many years. It is doubtful whether as stable a pattern of science offerings as that characteristic of the first half of the twentieth century will again be achieved. Science of the future will need to be dynamic and changeable to meet the demands of a rapidly accelerating scientific and technologic age. The models set by the curriculum revisions helped science students gain the initial skills and knowledge necessary to successfully handle the problems of our changing society.

In the 1980s a new wave of educational reform was initiated. Numerous national reports on education in general and also on science education have stimulated new interest in the science curriculum. Aspects of the new emphasis can be summarized as follows:

- Presentation of knowledge in context of science and technology related social issues
- Inquiry and discovery methods will be expanded to include decision making
- Laboratory activities will include both holistic and reductive analysis of problems
- Science curricula will be largely determined by science teachers in local school districts
- Interrelationships and interdependence of science, technology, and society will be stressed
- An integration of disciplines to understand contemporary science and technology will be highlighted
- Science and technology literacy for personal, social, and civic understanding will be the primary emphasis of the secondary science curriculum

In order to design, develop, and implement your own science curriculum we outlined seven steps.

1. Review influences on the science curriculum.
2. Synthesize goals into a proposed science curriculum.
3. Describe the present science curriculum.
4. Analyze discrepancies between proposed and present programs.
5. Evaluate the proposed science curriculum.
6. Develop and implement the science curriculum.
7. Evaluate the science curriculum.

■ References

1. John L. Wasik, "A Comparison of Cognitive Performance of PSSC and non-PSSC Students," *Journal of Research in Science Teaching*, 8, no. 1 (1971), pp. 85–90.
2. James A. Shymansky, William Kyle, and Jennifer Alport, "The Effects of New Science Curricula on Student Performance," *Journal of Research in Science Teaching*, 20, no. 5 (1983), pp. 387-404.
3. Harvard Project Physics, Newsletter no. 1 (Cambridge: Harvard University Press).
4. Harvard Project Physics, Newsletter no 7. (Cambridge: Harvard University Press).
5. Harvard Project Physics, Newsletter no. 10 (Cambridge: Harvard University Press).
6. Raymond E. Thompson, "A Survey of the Teaching of Physics in Secondary Schools," *School and Society*, 98 (1970), pp. 243–244.
7. Wayne W. Welch, "Correlates of Courses Satisfaction in High School Physics," *Journal of Research in Science Teaching*, 6 (1969), pp. 54–58.
8. J. David Lockard, ed., *Seventh Report of the International Clearinghouse on Science and Mathematics Curricular Developments* (College Park: Science Teaching Center, University of Maryland, 1970), p. 305.
9. Gordon Cawelti, "Innovative Practices in High Schools: Who Does What—and Why—and How," *Nations Schools*, 79 (1968), pp. 36–41.
10. Frank J. Fornoff, "Survey of the Teaching of Chemistry in Secondary Schools," *School and Society*, 98 (1970), pp. 242–243.
11. Iris Weiss, *Report of the 1977 National Survey of Science, Mathematics and Social Studies Education* (Washington D.C.: U.S. Government Printing Office, March 1978).
12. Shymansky, et al., "The Effects of New Science Curricula," pp. 387–404.
13. IAC Newsletter (College Park: Chemistry Department, University of Maryland) 2, no. 1 (January, 1973), p. 3.
14. Robert Stephenson, "Relationships Between the Intellectual Level of the Learner and Student Achievement in High School Chemistry," (Ph.D. dissertation, University of Northern Colorado, 1978).
15. Kenneth Brown and Ellsworth Obourn, *Offerings and Enrollments in Science and Mathematics in Public High Schools, 1958* (Washington, D.C.: U.S. Government Printing Office, 1961).
16. Quoted in American Association for the Advancement of Science, *The New School Science: A Report to School Administrators on Regional Orientation Conferences in Science*, Publication no. 63–6, (Washington, D.C. 1963), p. 27.
17. The New School Science, p. 29.
18. Kenneth D. George, "The Effect of BSCS and Conventional Biology in Critical Thinking," *Journal of Research in Science Teaching*, 3 (1965), pp. 293–299.
19. B.J. Adams, "A Study of the Retention of Biological Information by BSCS Students and Traditional Biology Students," (Ed. D. dissertation, Colorado State College, 1968).
20. James Shymansky, "BSCS Programs: Just How Effective Were They?" *The American Biology Teacher*, 4, no. 4 (1984), pp. 54–57.
21. Jack L. Carter and Alan R. Nakosteen, "Summer: A

BSCS Evaluation Study," *The Biological Sciences Curriculum Study*, 42 (February, 1971).

22. Shymansky, et al., "The Effect of New Science Curricula," pp. 387–404.

23. Paul Hurd, Rodger Bybee, Jane Kahle, and Robert Yager, "Biology Education in Secondary Schools of the United States," *The American Biology Teacher*, 42, no. 7 (1980), pp. 380–410.

24. Wayne Welch, "Inquiry in School Science," in N. Harms and R. Yager, *What Research Says to the Science Teacher*, 3 (Washington, D.C.: National Science Teachers Association, 1981), pp. 53–58.

25. Faith Hickman, "Education for Citizenship: Issues of Science and Society," *The American Biology Teacher*, 44, no. 6 (1982), pp. 358–367.

26. Shymansky, et al., "The Effect of New Science Curricula," pp. 387–404.

27. Ralph W. Tyler, *Basic Principles of Curriculum and Instruction* (Chicago: University of Chicago Press, 1949).

28. Tyler, *Basic Principles of Curriculum and Instruction*, p. 1.

29. N. Harms and R. Yager, *What Research Says to the Science Teacher* (Washington, D.C.: National Science Teachers Association, 1981).

30. Joseph McInerney, "Curriculum Development at the Biological Sciences Curriculum Study," *Educational Leadership* (December 1986/January 1987), pp. 24–28.

31. Audrey Champagne, ed., *This Year in School Science: The Science Curriculum* (Washington, D.C.: American Association for the Advancement of Science, 1986).

32. Audrey Champagne, ed., *This Year in School Science: The Science Curriculum* (Washington, D.C.: American Association for the Advancement of Science, 1987).

33. Richard Murnane and Senta Raizen, eds., *Improving Indicators of the Quality of Science and Mathematics Education in Grades K-12* (Washington, D.C.: National Academy Press, 1988).

=============== INVESTIGATING SCIENCE TEACHING ===============

ACTIVITY 17–1

Evaluating High School Textbooks

Select three textbooks from the discipline and grade level you intend to teach. Review the textbooks and complete the following chart. List the textbooks you compared by author(s), title, publisher, and copyright date.

GENERAL EVALUATION	N/C	Poor	Fair	Adequate	Good	Excellent
Text						
Content accuracy						
Content currency						
Content scope						
Structure and methods of science						
Organization and coherence						
Comprehensibility						
Labs: in text/supplementals						
Comprehensibility						
Practicality of required apparatus						
Summary: text supplementals						
Teach the nature of scientific enterprise						
Encourage students to reason to testable conclusions						
Stimulate awareness of science, technology, and society						

## CHAPTER 18

Models for Effective Science Teaching

In this chapter we introduce models of effective instruction. Over the years research and curriculum development have shown that effective instruction is much more than the presentation of a concept, process, or skill.[1] In simplest terms, one must think carefully about the objectives; beginning, middle, and end of the lesson; and, very importantly, the use of materials to engage the learners and develop scientific concepts, processes, and skills. Kevin Wise and James Okey summarize the effects of various science teaching strategies on achievement as follows:

> The effective science classroom appears to be one in which students are kept aware of instructional objectives and receive feedback on their progress toward these objectives. Students get opportunities to physically interact with instructional materials and engage in varied kinds of activities. Alteration of instructional material or classroom procedure has occurred where it is thought that the change might be related to increased impact. The teacher bases a portion of the verbal interactions that occur on some plan, such as the cognitive level or positioning of questions asked during a lesson. The effective science classroom reflects considerable planning.[2]

Note that this summary underscores the importance of objectives, feedback, use of materials, and varied activities. We would also have you note that there are both planned and flexible components of instruction. The science teacher must know where she is going, and she must be able to detour in the areas of interest, motivation, and relevance or "impact."

The next section outlines models that will help you organize for effective instruction. These consti-

tute the planned sequence of instruction. The flexible component is something you will develop with experience in science teaching. The chapter concludes with a general instructional model that incorporates many elements of other models. This model is presented in detail and is recommended as a model that is both usable and effective for science teaching.

■ Designing Your Instructional Sequence

Using the textbook, facilitating learning, grouping students, and sequencing instruction are examples of factors you must consider in designing an instructional sequence. Teaching is probably more difficult than you imagined. The current reform in education includes emphasis on effective instruction. Many talented individuals have subsequently considered instructional strategies and sequences that you can use. This section reviews some of the prominent models for science teaching.

Using Textbooks Effectively

You may think it unusual to have a section on using textbooks but textbooks are central to science teaching. In spite of some common myths, textbooks in and of themselves are not bad, most good teachers use textbooks, and textbooks can be used to enhance learning.

The majority of teachers use textbooks. In a 1985 survey, Iris Weiss found that 93 percent of science teachers in grades 7–12 used a published textbook.[3] Interestingly, the majority of science teachers did not consider textbook quality to be a significant problem in their schools. The most highly rated aspects of science textbooks were their organization, clarity, and reading level. We should note here that a number of individuals and groups *do* see problems with the quality and usability of textbooks.[4,5,6,7]

Since the 1960s the prevailing wisdom in science education was that programs should be activity-based and not textbook dominated. Research shows that the opposite is the case—teachers are using fewer activities and relying more on the textbook.[8] Use of textbooks is necessitated by the need for science teachers to plan for several subjects, the reduction of budgets, and the scheduling of science classes in nonlaboratory rooms.

Our purpose in this section is to assist you in becoming an intelligent user of the textbook. That is, to help you recognize the potentials and limitations of textbooks, and to use them to enhance learning. The section relies heavily on the research and writing of Kathleen Roth and Charles Anderson[9] of the Institute on Research for Teaching and Learning, Michigan State University.

Science teachers use textbooks in several ways. Textbooks help teachers make decisions about the curriculum. Questions about topics, activities of coverage, depth, sequence, and emphasis are answered by reference to the textbook. Although the textbook helps teachers with the efficiency of decisions, they do not necessarily help make the best decisions for students. Teachers must carefully mediate those decisions.

Textbooks help teachers select teaching strategies. Again, this use of textbooks has both advantages and disadvantages. The clear advantage is efficiency. It takes considerable effort to manage an activity-based program. It is much easier to have students read the textbook. The disadvantage is that reading the textbook may not facilitate student learning. We will discuss this in greater detail later.

Textbooks provide scientific explanations. Descriptions of key concepts and information are usually straightforward and succinct in textbooks. Providing students with good descriptions of scientific ideas is difficult; it is especially difficult when teachers are teaching out of their discipline. So textbooks can be a useful resource for scientific explanations.

You can see that textbooks are quite helpful. Given the function of textbooks, it is easy to see why the majority of teachers rely on them. What do science teachers need to understand in order to use textbooks more effectively? First in importance is to understand how *students* use textbooks.

Several times we have pointed out that students have prior knowledge about science. Often this knowledge is inadequate or incomplete when com-

pared to scientific knowledge, thus the label misconceptions. Students' prior knowledge is important to understand when considering students' reading strategies. What happens when students are asked to read a text that has explanations about phenomena that are incompatible with their current explanations? Students seem to use several strategies to accommodate the difference between their conceptions and those presented in textbooks.[10] Here are the different strategies students use.

Reading for Conceptual Change

A few students use the text to change current conceptions to more appropriately scientific conceptions. As students confront concepts that conflict with their own ideas, they give up their concepts and assimilate those presented as formal scientific explanations in the textbook.

Overrelying on Prior Knowledge and Distorting Text to Make It Compatible with Prior Knowledge

Here students use elaborate strategies to link prior knowledge with text knowledge. These students genuinely try to make sense of the text and integrate text ideas with their own knowledge. Still, they just cannot give up their own strongly held ideas. Thus, the strategy of linking scientific with their own ideas.

Overrelying on Facts in the Text with an Additional Notion of Learning—Separating Prior Knowledge and Text Knowledge

These students focus on the memorization of vocabulary and facts. They do not relate the facts and vocabulary to each other or to their prior knowledge. Reading for conceptual change is not possible.

Overrelying on Details in the Text— Separation of Prior Knowledge and Text Knowledge

These students pay great attention to the text. They attend to the details, as opposed to concepts, and fail to attach any meaning to the details. The details, most often the specialized vocabulary of science, are isolated words that have no relationship to anything. These students think they understand science if they are able to decode the words and identify details in the textbook.

Overrelying on Prior Knowledge and Ignoring Text Knowledge

Some students rely on their own experiential knowledge to interpret the textbook . If asked about text knowledge, they equate textbook explanations with their own explanations, ones that have nothing to do

============ STEPS FOR DESIGNING LESSONS ============

Using Textbooks Effectively

1. Direct students' attention to important concepts.
2. Challenge students' thinking and misconceptions.
3. Ask students to construct explanations of everyday phenomena.
4. Probe student responses.
5. Provide accurate feedback to students.
6. Construct alternative representations of textbook explanations.
7. Make explicit the connections between textbook explanations and student misconceptions.
8. Select activities that create conceptual conflict and encourage conceptual understanding.

---

with scientific explanations. The text "makes sense" in terms of their prior knowledge.

What can teachers do? There are a few recommendations for effective use of science textbooks. The principles are based on studies of text-based science teaching[11] and understandings gained from studies of students' reading strategies.[12]

Directing Students' Attention to Important Concepts

Textbooks typically contain numerous ideas and vocabulary words. This situation causes students to memorize facts and lists of words rather than focus on strategies that will result in conceptual change. Focusing students on central issues that are problematic, keeping lessons related to the concepts, and keeping vocabulary to a minimum will contribute to conceptual change.

Challenging Students' Thinking and Misconceptions

Textbooks are written from a scientist's perspective. Seldom do textbook authors consider students' perspectives as they organize textbooks. Still, students will interpret text material in terms of their prior knowledge. Effective teachers identify the differences between students' concepts and those in the textbook. By asking questions and challenging students' thinking, teachers can initiate the process of conceptual change. The questions should be stated in relation to ideas in the textbooks or students may not make the connections.

Asking Students to Construct Explanations of Everyday Phenomena

Questions in textbooks seldom have students apply knowledge to real-world experiences. Encouraging students to compare, challenge, and debate each other's explanations are all methods that result in conceptual change.

Probing Student Responses

Listen for students' thinking rather than for right answers. Ask questions that will have students justify and clarify their responses.

Providing Accurate Feedback to Students

Teachers typically respond to student answers by praising correct answers and ignoring incorrect answers. The greatest concern is the latter. While teachers think this approach helps students, in actuality it does not. Giving positive feedback for any answer encourages students to maintain their current conceptions and to use ineffective strategies to find correct answers. Effective teachers give clear and accurate feedback about the strengths and limitations of student responses.

Constructing Alternative Representations of Textbook Explanations that Make Explicit the Relationships Between Scientific Explanations and Student Misconceptions

Give the students time to struggle with explanations in the textbook. Most textbooks are packed with explanations that are presented in one way, then the text moves to the next explanation. There is little time and variation that helps students construct new concepts. After students have time to grapple with concepts, the teacher should provide different representations of the ideas. The representations will be most effective if they clearly contrast the students' and scientific explanations.

Selecting Activities that Create Conceptual Conflict and Encourage Conceptual Understanding

In the move away from laboratory-based instruction, teachers and textbooks have included activities that do not necessarily encourage conceptual change. Selection of activities is based on criteria such as interest, a sense that it is important to do something in science, or the need to do activities that are easy to manage. Discrepant events are good examples of the types of activities that create conceptual change. In the end, doing activities is not as important as helping students make sense of their experiences.

The Learning Cycle

The *learning cycle* originated with the work of Robert Karplus and his colleagues during the development of the Science Curriculum Improvement Study (SCIS). Originally, the learning cycle was primarily based on the theoretical insights of Jean Piaget, but it is consistent with other theories of learning, such as those developed by David Ausubel.[13]

There are three phases to the learning cycle. Exploration, invention, and discovery were the first terms used in the SCIS program. Later these terms were modified to Exploration, Concept Introduction, and Concept Application. While other terms have been used for the three original phases, the goals and pedagogy of the phases have remained similar.

During the first, or *Exploration*, phase of the learning cycle students learn through their own involvement and action. New materials, ideas and relationships are introduced with minimal guidance by the teacher. The goal is to allow students to apply previous knowledge, develop interests, and initiate and maintain a curiosity toward the materials at hand. It is also the case that the materials should be carefully structured so involvement with them cannot help but engage concepts and ideas fundamental to the lesson's objectives. During the exploration teachers can also evaluate students' understanding and background relative to the lesson's objectives.

Introduction of the concept is the next phase. Various teaching strategies can be used to introduce the concept. For example, a demonstration, film, textbook, or lecture can be used. This phase should relate directly to the initial Exploration and clarify concepts central to the lesson. While the Exploration was minimally teacher-directed, this phase tends to be much more guided.

In the next phase, *Application*, students apply the newly learned concepts to other examples. The teaching goal is to have students generalize or transfer ideas to other examples used as illustration of the central concept. For some students the period of self-regulation, equilibration, or mental reorganization of concepts may take time. Having several activities where a concept is applied can provide the valuable time needed for learning. An excellent introduction and science teaching examples of the learning cycle have been developed by Howard Birnie,[14] and Robert Karplus and colleagues.[15]

John Renner and his colleagues examined the effectiveness of altering the sequence of the learning cycle. They found that the normal sequence (that described above) is the optimum sequence for achievement of content knowledge.[16,17]

Anton Lawson has made important connections between research on student misconceptions and use of the learning cycle. Lawson suggests that use of the learning cycle provides opportunities for students to reveal prior knowledge (misconceptions) and opportunities to argue and debate their ideas. This process can result in disequilibrium and the possibility of developing more adequate conceptions and patterns of reasoning.[18]

Lawson proposes three types of learning cycles: descriptive, empirical-inductive, and hypothetical-deductive. While the sequence is similar to that described above, the difference among the types of learning cycles is the degree to which students gather data in a descriptive manner or in a manner that explicitly tests alternative explanations. In descriptive learning cycles, students observe natural phenomena, identify patterns, and seek similar patterns elsewhere. According to Lawson, little or no disequilibrium occurs in descriptive learning cycles.

Empirical-inductive learning cycles require students to explain phenomena thus expressing any misconceptions and providing opportunities for dialogue and debate. Hypothetical-deductive learning cycles require students to make explicit statements of alternative explanations of phenomena. Higher order reasoning patterns are required in order to test alternative explanations.[19] Research conducted by Renner and his colleagues and recommendations made by Lawson are practical, useful, and insightful for science teachers.

Cooperative Learning

As a science teacher you will be in a position to structure lessons in several different ways. Most commonly lessons are structured so students compete with one another for recognition and grades. You might also design your lessons so students can follow an individual approach, or learn on their own. There is a third option that lends itself very well to science teaching, especially when the laboratory is a central part of instruction. That is a cooperative approach where students are arranged in pairs or small groups to help each other learn the assigned material. David Johnson, Roger Johnson, and their colleagues have developed a substantial research base for the use of a cooperative learning model.[20] Over the years the Johnsons have also developed the practical, instructional approach based on their model. The discus-

======================= STEPS FOR DESIGNING LESSONS =======================

Applying the Learning Cycle

Concept Exploration

1. Identify interesting objects, events or situations that students can observe. This experience can occur in the classroom, laboratory or field. Just about any instructional method can be used to explore a concept.
2. Allow the students time in which they explore the objects, events or situations. During this experience the students may establish relationships, observe patterns, identify variables, and question events as a result of their exploration. In this phase the unexpected can be used to your advantage. Students may have questions or experiences that motivate them to understand what they have observed.
3. The primary aim of the exploration is to mentally establish a concept that will later be introduced.

Concept Introduction

4. In this phase the teacher directs student attention to specific aspects of the exploration experience. Concepts are introduced in a direct and formal manner. Initially, the lesson should be clearly based on student explorations. In this phase the key is to present the concepts in a simple, clear, and direct manner.
5. The word *explanation* is being used in the general sense of an act or process in which concepts are made plain, comprehensible and clear. The process of explanation provides a common use of terms relative to the concept(s).

Concept Application

6. Identify different activities in which students extend the concepts in new and different situations. Several different activities will facilitate generalization of the concept by the students. Encourage the students to identify patterns, discover relationships among variables, and reason through new problems. During post laboratory discussions and individual and group questions be sure to point out the central concepts that are being applied in the different contexts.

---

sion in this section is based on their recent book *Circles of Learning: Cooperation in the Classroom.*[21] (We recommend that you go back to Chapter 5, pages 96–97, and reread the Guest Editorial by David and Roger Johnson, "A Message to Teachers on Structuring Student Interactions in the Classroom.")

There are four basic elements that must be included in cooperative learning models. To be truly cooperative small groups must be structured for positive interdependence, face-to-face interactions, individual accountability, and use of interpersonal and small group skills.

Positive interdependence is established when students perceive that they are in positive and interdependent relationships with other members of their group. There are several ways of achieving positive interdependence. You can establish mutual goals for the group; a division of labor for a mutual task; dividing materials, resources, or information so group members will have to cooperate to achieve their task; assign students different roles such as recorder, researcher, organizer, etc.; or joint rewards for the group can be given.

Face-to-face interactions among students is a central aspect of cooperative learning. Cooperative work and verbal exchanges among students form the learning experience.

Though they work in groups, students must still be individually accountable for learning the assigned materials. Cooperative learning is not having one person do a report for two or three others. The aim is for all students to learn the material. In order to accomplish this it is necessary to determine the level of mastery of students and then assign groups to maximize achievement.

Finally, students have to learn to use interpersonal and small group skills. Students are not naturally skilled at cooperative learning. They must be taught the social skills of collaboration, they must be given time and experience in collaboration, and they must be taught to analyze the group process to see if effective working relationships have been maintained.

Science teachers will have to teach students the skills of cooperation. This statement leads to the obvious questions, "What skills need to be taught?" and "How does one teach these skills?" We refer again to *Circles of Learning: Cooperation in the Classroom.*[22] Answering the first question, there are four levels of cooperative skills. First there are *forming* skills. That is, the basic skills needed to *organize* a group and establish norms of behavior for cooperative interaction. Here are some suggestions to help the initial formation of cooperative groups.

Applying the Cooperative Learning Model

Objectives:

1. *Objectives for the lesson should be clearly specified.* The teacher should make clear the two types of objectives: academic and collaborative skills. The former are those used in most lessons. The latter provides students with the specific skills used for cooperative learning during the lesson.

Decisions:

2. *Deciding on group size.* This decision may be influenced by time, materials, equipment, and facilities. A general recommendation for beginning science teachers is to use pairs or groups of three.
3. *Deciding on who is in the groups.* Generally, the recommendation is to have heterogeneous groups randomly assigned by the science teacher. Other alternatives include homogeneous grouping and "select your own group."
4. *Deciding on the room arrangement.* Again, this decision may be influenced by facilities and equipment. For optimum cooperative learning, group members should sit in a circle and be close enough for effective communication. Be sure you have easy access to each group.
5. *Deciding on the instructional materials to promote interdependence.* In early stages of developing cooperative learning groups attention should be paid to the ways materials are used to facilitate interdependence. Three ways are suggested: *materials interdependence,* e.g., one set of materials for the group; *information interdependence,* e.g., each group member has a resource needed by the group; and *interdependence with other groups,* e.g., intergroup competition.
6. *Deciding on roles to ensure interdependence.* You can assign roles such as summarizer, researcher, recorder, observer, etc. that will encourage cooperation among group members.

Explaining:

7. *Explain the assignment.* Be sure students are clear about the academic task. Connections should be made to past experience, concepts, and lessons. Define any relevant concepts and explain procedures and safety precautions. Check on students' understanding of the assignment.
8. *Explain the collaborative goal.* It is of critical importance that students understand that they are responsible for doing the assignment and learning the material, and that all group members learn the material and successfully complete the assignment.

- Move into groups without undue noise and unnecessary interaction with other students.
- Students should stay in their group.
- Students should speak softly.
- Students should encourage each other to participate.
- Use names and look at each other during discussions.
- Avoid sarcastic remarks or "put downs" of other people.

Group functioning is the second skill level that will need to be developed. Here, the lessons involve those skills that will *maintain* the group and facilitate effective working relationships. Some important skills of group maintenance are:

- Students should understand the purpose, time allotment, and most effective procedures to complete their work.

- Support for each other's ideas and work should be expressed.
- Students should feel free to ask for help, information, or clarification from other group members or the science teacher.
- Students might learn how to paraphrase and/or summarize another student's ideas.
- As appropriate, students should learn how to express their feelings about the assignment and/or group process.

The next phase described by Johnson et al. is that of *formulating understanding* of the concepts, processes, and skills of the assigned lesson. The skills are designed to *maximize* each student's learning. Here are some suggestions:

- Each student should summarize—aloud—the important ideas contained in the material assigned.

9. *Explain individual accountability.* Each individual should understand that he/she is responsible for learning; and that you will assess learning at the individual level.
10. *Explain intergroup cooperation.* Sometimes you may want to extend the cooperative group idea to include the entire class. If so, the method and criteria of access should be clear.
11. *Explain the criteria for success.* In the cooperative learning model evaluation is based on successful completion of the assignment. So it is important to explain the criteria by which work will be evaluated.
12. *Explain the specific cooperative behaviors.* Students may not understand what is meant by cooperative work, so it is important to give specific examples of your expectations of their behaviors. For instance, "stay as a group," "talk quietly," "each person should explain how he/she got the answer," "listen to other group members," and "criticize ideas, not people" are all suggested behaviors.

Monitoring and Intervening:

13. *Monitor student work.* Once the students begin work your task is to observe the various groups and help solve any problems that emerge.
14. *Provide task assistance.* As needed, you may wish to clarify the assignment, introduce concepts, review material, model a skill, answer questions, and redirect discussions.
15. *Teaching collaborative skills.* Because collaboration is new, it may be important to intervene in groups and help them learn the skills of collaboration.
16. *Provide closure for the lesson.* At the end of the lesson it may be important for you to intervene and bring closure. Summarize what has been presented, review concepts and skills, and reinforce their work.

Evaluation:

17. *Evaluate the quality and quantity of student learning.* Evaluate the previously decided upon product, e.g., report.

Processing:

18. *Assess how well the groups functioned.* If group collaboration is truly a goal, then some time should be spent on this. Point out how the groups could improve next time.

- Other students should correct and clarify summaries.
- Students should elaborate on each other's summary.
- Students can give hints about ways to remember ideas.
- Ask all group members to participate in the discussion.

The last stage is that of *fermenting*. The point here is to have students develop skills that will help *reconceptualize* and *extend* ideas. At this level there is already a firmly developed group structure, so it is possible to introduce challenges, conflict, and controversy. Because of the skills already developed, situations that challenge have the possibility of bringing about deeper thinking, more synthesis of ideas, gathering of more information, and constructive arguments about conclusions, decisions, and solutions. In this case the science teacher may be the person

who brings about the extension of ideas. It is possible, even desirable, for students to function at this level. The teacher will have to decide about the degree of group development and level of interaction as this level is reached. Skills that facilitate this stage include:

- Criticize ideas, not other students.
- Clarify disagreements within the group.
- Synthesize different ideas into a single statement.
- Ask other students to justify their conclusions.
- Ask probing, clarifying questions.
- Generate several answers or conclusions and select the best for the given situation.

We now turn to the second question, "How does one teach these skills?" As a science teacher interested in cooperative learning it will be critical to identify students who have not developed the group skills discussed earlier. There are several ways that

STEPS FOR DESIGNING LESSONS

Applying the Hunter Model

Before designing a daily lesson you should complete the following evaluation.

Pre-Lesson Evaluation

1. Determine the continuing strand or theme of science concepts and processes.
2. Identify a major objective in the strand or theme of science concepts and processes. Then locate the students' understanding relative to the major objective.
3. Select specific objectives for daily lessons based on this evaluation.

Lesson Planning & Lesson Sequencing

For each teaching sequence you should consider the following steps to determine if and how they are appropriate for your objectives and the students' mastery of past and present concepts and processes.

Anticipatory Set. Early in the lesson you should include an activity that will elicit the students' attention to the day's content and processes. Anticipatory set will:

- focus the students' attention during the period of transition.
- elicit attending behavior and mental readiness for the day's lesson.
- provide a connection between past lessons and the lesson to be taught.
- last long enough to orient students to the immediate objectives and lesson.

Objective and Purpose. This step is one of communicating *to the students* the day's objectives. The objective and purpose statement will:

- inform the students of the day's objectives and outline what they will be able to do at the end of the lesson.
- clarify how and why the lesson is important and useful.

---

you can teach the skills required for cooperative learning.

1. Be sure that students understand the need for group skills.
2. Be sure that students understand the skill and when to use it.
3. Be sure that students have time and situations where they can practice the skills.
4. Be sure that students have the opportunity and procedures for discussing their use of group skills.
5. Be sure that students continue using the skills until they are a natural part of group work.

Since much work in science classes, and later life, is dependent on group work we think the time and effort required to implement cooperative skills will be well spent. There is still a time and place for individual and competitive learning. The coopera-

tive learning model provides an excellent complement to other models used in science teaching.

The Madeline Hunter Model

Over the years Dr. Madeline Hunter of the University of California at Los Angeles Laboratory School has endeavored to develop materials and a teaching model designed to increase instructional effectiveness. Her model is based on psychological theory, primarily behaviorism, and educational research. The model is quite practical. It seems a simple and complete way to integrate many essential aspects of instruction into a teachable plan. This discussion is based on two of Dr. Hunter's books.[23] It should be clear that there is much more to this model (and the others) than can be given here.

The first step is a pre-lesson evaluation. The aim of the evaluation is to place your objectives at the

Instructional Input. Here the teacher actually does something to achieve the objectives. Instructional input will:

- require the teacher to determine the content and processes that relate directly to the objectives.
- select the best means available to facilitate students' learning of the desired objectives.

Modeling. Seeing examples of instructional outcomes is an important aspect of learning. Where appropriate, you should try to provide examples of the science content and processes included in your objectives. Modeling will:

- provide examples of expected learning outcomes.
- give the students visual and auditory input.

Monitoring Student Understanding. Monitoring is evaluation that occurs while the lesson is in progress. You should check for students' understanding of essential information and concepts during the lesson. Monitoring will:

- identify students' understanding.
- provide ways and means to adjust the instructional sequence.
Use sampling, signaling and explaining to monitor student progress.

Practice. Lessons should include opportunities for students to practice the content and processes they have learned. Initial attempts should be teacher guided; later practice can be done on an individual basis. Practice will:

- provide opportunities to apply concepts and processes with your supervision.
- extend student understanding to new situations.

Post-Lesson Evaluation

Sometime after the lesson you will evaluate students' understanding of the concepts and processes. The evaluation is based on the major objectives identified in the pre-lesson evaluation and the specific objectives of the lessons.

---

correct level and best sequence for your students. While this seems simple enough, it is often not done. As a part of this process you may also consider analyzing the task of achieving your objectives and designing an activity to diagnose student understanding before and enroute to your final objective.

Next, design the beginning of your lesson. There are three components to be considered. Some sort of readiness activity, in which the present lesson relates to the learner's past, involves the learner and establishes a relevance of the instructional objectives. Another aspect of the readiness activity is to inform the students of your objective, that is, what they will learn and how you will know if they have learned it.

After the readiness section of the lesson, consider the actual input of information, processes, or skills. For instance, you might review the catalogues of instructional strategies outlined in chapter two and consider which methods will best deliver the material. Teaching efficiency, learning effectiveness, and relativity of facilities, materials, and equipment should be the criteria of evaluation and choice.

Next, there should be some form of assessment. How can you check for student understanding and comprehension? You may wish to sample the class, give a quiz, have a discussion, or ask individual students questions. This need not be as formal as a class quiz, but there should be some type of feedback, for you and the students, concerning the lesson's effectiveness.

Finally, there should be some form of closure for the lesson. It should not just stop. There should be an ending in which you and/or the students summarize what has been learned.

So far the discussion has been on planning the lesson; the obvious next step is teaching it. What is it that will make the lesson effective? Once you have formulated instructional objectives, be sure you *teach to the objective.* Include actions and strategies

The Effective Science Teacher

Dwight Lindbloom
Curriculum and Instruction
State Department of Education
St. Paul, Minnesota

The effective science teacher possesses attitudes and utilizes behavior, that will facilitate learning. I expect the new science teacher to be (or to become) effective. What are the characteristics of an effective teacher? My opinion is based on knowledge I have gained as a districtwide administrator, science teacher, building principal, and teacher-educator. This knowledge has been validated by research and is used in some teacher education programs and by some districts as the basis for staff development.

The Teacher's Attitude. I know of only one teacher attitude that research has consistently shown to relate positively to student learning: the belief that the teacher *does* make a difference. *My* teaching affects the student's learning! This attitude is not only important to learning but without it there is little likelihood that the other expectations can be adequately met.

A second set of attitudes is the enjoyment of teaching and students and the appreciation of science. Students will catch the teacher's enjoyment for science and will adopt an attitude of curiosity and critical thinking if the teacher possesses and models these attitudes.

The Teacher's Instructional Decisions. Three kinds of decisions are made by the teacher as part of the teaching/learning act. These categories of decisions are used as a framework for teacher education by Madeline Hunter in her work at UCLA. Although learning cannot be directly controlled, instructional decisions and behavior are under the control of the science teacher and improved instruction increases the probability that learning will be increased. It is the sound decision and resulting instructional behavior that determine the degree to which learning takes place.

The first instructional decision the teacher must make is content selection or determination of the learning objective. Before entering the classroom, the teacher should have considered answers to the questions: "What should the student learn today?" "What will he/she be able to do at the end of the instructional period that had not been learned earlier?" "Will today's content extend yesterday's learning and prepare the student for tomorrow?" Continuous diagnosis of the student's knowledge and attitudes is important for selecting appropriate content. Once the learning objective has been determined, the teacher should teach to this objective unless he has good reason to make changes.

Having made the content decision, the science teacher must then decide what the student will do to achieve the objective. Can the student learn the specified content best by listening, speaking, questioning, viewing, reading, or experimenting? Does the prescribed "behavior" match the capabilities of the student? Which student behavior is most appropriate to learn the specified content? Students have different learning styles and some can utilize one or more learning strategies better than others.

Selection of methodology is the third

that relate to the objectives. Are your questions, concepts, processes, skills, and activities clearly related to the objective?

As you teach the lesson you will want to *monitor student progress and adjust instruction* accordingly. Monitoring student progress can be done overtly by asking students to do something indicating the degree to which they have learned the material. Or, monitoring can be done covertly by observing student work and listening to student discussions of the assignment. Based on this feedback you will have to make one of several decisions: continue the lesson as planned; alter the lesson; reteach the lesson; or stop the present lesson and prepare a new one.

The 4MAT System

Bernice McCarthy has developed a teaching model based on individual learning styles and right/left-

instructional decision made by the teacher. The new science teacher often decides first what he will do. However, sound decisions regarding teaching methods are possible only after decisions have been made about content and learner behavior. The teacher behavior that is most appropriate is the one that will best facilitate learning. One of my weaknesses as a new science teacher was that I had too few alternatives in my repertoire of behaviors. Many other teachers continue to use a very limited number of methods, often because the content and learner-behavior questions have not been carefully considered first. To make wise decisions about methodology, the teacher must be familiar with the research and theory (e.g., in motivation, reinforcement, and transfer) which focus on the link between teacher behavior and student learning.

A "science" of teaching is available and the new science teacher should have a related base of knowledge in order to teach. The "art" of teaching is the application of this knowledge in the classroom. This application will vary to some degree because of differences among teachers, students, and situations. Only experience *and* practice will translate this knowledge into integrated behavior.

The Teacher as Learner and Professional. A final set of expectations reflects the need for continual growth and development. Our base of knowledge will continue to expand, and all of us need to learn new behaviors which, with practice and assistance, will become integrated and natural. One criterion used to identify a professional is that he takes some responsibility for the behavior of others in the profession. Such responsibility includes a commitment to self-development and to helping others improve.

In summary, for the new science teacher to be effective he must be able to:

1. Reflect the attitudes of "I make a difference," enjoyment of teaching and students, and appreciation for science.
2. Have a good grasp of content and the ability to assess students' knowledge and attitudes to select learning objectives that are appropriate for each student.
3. Select alternative learner behaviors based on learning theory, research, the specified content, and the capabilities of the individual student.
4. Use the method or teacher behavior that will best assist the student in accomplishing a given learning objective.
5. Continually grow, help others improve their instructional decisions and behaviors, and accept help from others.

I believe the teacher's attitudes and growth potential are the most important characteristics in determining whether the new science teacher will become effective. If these two expectations are met, the instructional decisions and behavior can most easily be learned.

---

mode techniques. The 4MAT System is based on the premise that individuals perceive and process experiences and information in different ways. Those ways are referred to as learning styles. There are four identifiable learning styles and each is an equally valid way of learning. Here is a brief summary of learning styles according to McCarthy.

1. Type-one learners are primarily interested in personal meaning.
2. Type-two learners are primarily interested in facts that lead to conceptual understanding.
3. Type-three learners are primarily interested in how things work.
4. Type-four learners are primarily interested in self discovery.

You can probably already see the different aspects of the 4MAT learning cycle. McCarthy claims that all students should be taught in all four styles.

=== **STEPS FOR DESIGNING LESSONS** ===

The 4MAT System

Quadrant One
1. Express the value of the learning experience.
2. The lesson should have personal meaning for the student.
3. Create a learning environment where learners can explore ideas without being evaluated.

Quadrant Two
1. Provide information to the students.
2. Present concepts in an organized way.
3. Encourage students to analyze data and form concepts.

Quadrant Three
1. Provide activities for students.
2. Coach the students as they progress in the activities.

Quadrant Four
1. Allow students to discover meaning and concepts by doing.
2. Challenge students to review what has happened.
3. Analyze experiences for relevance and originality.

That way, students will experience the comfort and success of learning in their preferred mode one quarter of the time and be stretched to develop their learning capacities in other modes the rest of the time.

The 4MAT system moves through a four-step learning cycle in sequence. An additional "style" that McCarthy incorporates is students' preference for right- or left-hemisphere (brain) functioning. The right/left modes are embedded in each of the four steps in the learning cycle.

The first portion of a 4MAT lesson should have the learner move from concrete experience to reflective observation. Begin with a concrete experience and allow students time to discover the meaning that experience has for them. This approach *creates a reason* for learning. The first phase of the 4MAT System is displayed graphically in Figure 18.1.

The second phase is the formulation of the concept. The student moves from reflective observation to abstract conceptualization. Teachers teach in the traditional sense. The second phase is represented in Figure 18.2. This approach gives the big idea.

In the third phase, students move from abstract conceptualization to active experimentation. Students who are common-sense learners do best in this phase. This is the hands-on approach to science. You can tell the students who have this learning style because they need to *try it.* "This is how the idea works" is the result of this phase. They are concerned with finding out how things work. The teacher's role is to provide the materials and opportunity. The

graphic representation of this phase of the 4MAT System is displayed in Figure 18.3.

The final phase is the progression from active experimentation to concrete experience. The students combine knowledge from personal experience and experimentation. They extend the original concepts by asking "What can this become?" They apply the ideas in new and different forms. The quadrant is represented in Figure 18.4.

The entire 4MAT System is represented in "Steps for Designing Lessons, The 4MAT System." This diagram is from Bernice McCarthy's book *The 4MAT System.*[24]

In closing, the 4MAT System is a synthesis of several lines of research. The system is workable and effective, but it is complex, especially for the new teacher.

■ An Instructional Model for Science Teaching

In the early 1960s, J. Myron Atkin and Robert Karplus first proposed a learning cycle.[25] Karplus, Herb Their, and their colleagues later used the learning cycle in the Science Curriculum Improvement Study (SCIS), and based the learning cycle for SCIS on the psychological theories of Jean Piaget. We have extended and elaborated the original design for a teaching model by Atkin and Karplus and have based the model proposed in this chapter on that work.

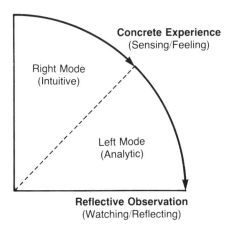

FIGURE 18-1
First phase of the 4MAT system

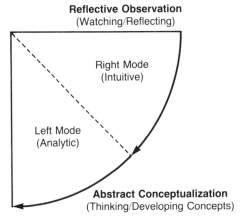

FIGURE 18-2
Second phase of the 4MAT system, abstract conceptualization

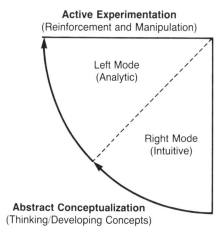

FIGURE 18-3
Third phase of the 4MAT system, active experimentation

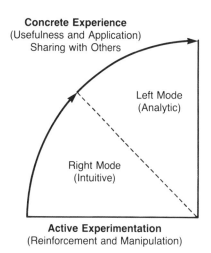

FIGURE 18-4
Final 4MAT system phase, concrete experience

Over the years, many curriculum designers have elaborated, modified, and applied teaching models in different educational programs.[26] The approach in this chapter is first to describe the form and function of a teaching model, then to discuss the psychological basis for the proposed model, and finally to describe the model.

Form and Function

The instructional model has five phases: engagement, exploration, explanation, elaboration, and evaluation. Each phase has a specific function and is intended to contribute to the learning process. We have described the phases in terms of (1) assumptions about the mental activity of students, (2) activities that students would be involved in, and (3) strategies used by the teacher. Later in this section, we shall discuss the five phases in detail.

An instructional model has two functions. A model provides guidance for curriculum developers as they design a program. Depending on the instructional model, curriculum developers can use the model at different levels. One level is equivalent to a year-long sequence; another is equivalent to a unit; and another is equivalent to an activity or series of daily lessons. The second function of an instructional model is to help the classroom teacher improve instructional effectiveness through a systematic approach to and use of strategies closely aligned with educational outcomes.

Psychological Basis

Historically, educators have explained learning by classifying it into one of three broad categories. In simple terms, these are transmission, maturation, and construction (see Table 18.1). In recent years, cognitive scientists and science educators have focused on the constructivist model in their work on the misconceptions of students, differences between novice and expert explanations of phenomena, and naive versus canonical theories individuals hold.[27,28]

In the constructivist model of learning, students reconstruct core concepts, or intellectual structures, through continuous interactions between their own selves and their environment, which includes other people. Applying the constructivist approach to teaching requires the teacher to understand that students *have* conceptions or prior knowledge of the world. Those conceptions may be inadequate (misconceptions) and need further development. In teaching for conceptual change, teachers should be sure that students are focusing on objects or events that engage concepts of interest to the teacher. That is, they are related to science or technology. Then, students can encounter problematic situations that are slightly beyond the current level of understanding. In so doing, the student will experience a form of cognitive disequilibrium. Teachers then structure physical and psychological experiences that assist the reconstruction of core concepts. New constructions can then be applied to different situations and tested against other conceptions of the world.

Educators are beginning to recognize the constructivist view. Doing so requires (1) teaching in a manner that recognizes the students' level of conceptual understanding, and (2) an understanding that the students' construction of knowledge occurs through the confrontation of problem situations and resolution of the confrontation. The key here is that confrontation should be challenging, but within the students' parameters of intellectual accommodation. Challenges that are actually included as instructional strategies are described by terms such as moderate novelty, appropriate dissonance, optimal discord, tolerable mismatch, and reasonable disequilibrium.

An assumption of this model is that using sequences of lessons designed to facilitate the process described above will assist in the students' construction of knowledge. And, concrete experiences and computer-assisted activities will assist in the process of constructing knowledge. The following are general strategies based on the constructivist view of learning.

1. Recognize the students' current concepts of objects or phenomena.
2. Present situations slightly beyond the students' current conceptual understanding. One could also present the student with problems, situation conflict, paradoxes, and puzzles.
3. Problems and situations should be challenging but achievable.
4. Students should present their explanations (concepts) to other students.
5. When students are struggling with inadequate explanations (misconceptions), first help them by accepting their explanations; second by suggesting other explanations of the same phenomena or activities designed to provide insights; and third, by allowing them time to construct their explanations.

The instructional model is based on a constructivist view. Constructivism is a dynamic and interactive conception of human learning. Students redefine, reorganize, elaborate, and change their initial concepts through interaction between the individual and the environment and other individuals. For an individual, the learner "interprets" objects and phenomena and internalizes the interpretation in terms of current concepts similar to the experiences being presented or encountered; that is, changing and improving conceptions often requires challenging the current conceptions and showing them to be inadequate. The instructional and psychological problem is to avoid leaving students with an overall sense of inadequacy. If this occurs, educators have encouraged other psychological problems. If a current conception is challenged, there must be opportunity, in the form of time and expenses, to reconstruct a more

TABLE 18–1
Perspectives on education

Perspective	View of Students	View of Knowledge	Approach to Teaching
TRANSMISSION	They must be filled with information and concepts.	Core concepts are a copy of reality.	External to Internal
MATURATION	They must be allowed to mature and develop.	Emergence of core concepts.	Internal to External
CONSTRUCTION	They are actively involved in learning.	Construction of core concepts.	Interaction between Internal and External

adequate conception than the original. In short, the students' construction of knowledge can be assisted by using sequences of lessons designed to challenge current conceptions and provide opportunities for reconstruction to occur. There is one other factor worth noting. Though not the primary orientation of the instructional model, learning styles are a contributing factor to the learning process. The approaches used in the different phases of the instructional model accommodate varied learning styles as recommended by Paul Kuerbis.[29] You will note that many of the ideas presented earlier—for example, use of textbooks, cooperative learning, and the 4MAT System—are applicable to the instructional model presented here.

The Instructional Model

The model has five phases. The five phases are engagement, exploration, explanation, elaboration, and evaluation. The following sections contain descriptions of the instructional model.

Engagement
The first phase is to engage the student in the learning task. The student mentally focuses on a problem, situation, or event. The activities of this phase make connections to past and future activities. The connections depend on the learning task and may be conceptual, procedural, or behavioral.

Asking a question, defining a problem, and showing a discrepant event are all ways to engage the students and focus them on the instructional task. The teacher's role is to present the situation and identify the instructional task. The teacher also sets the rules and procedures for establishing the task.

Successful engagement results in students being puzzled, and actively motivated in the learning activity. Here, we are using activity in the constructivist and behavioral sense, that is, mentally active. If we combine the external events with the basic needs and interests of the students, instruction contributes to successful learning. Table 18.2 summarizes the engagement phase.

Exploration
Once the unit has engaged the students' interest in ideas, the students need to have time for exploration of those ideas. We have specifically designed the exploration activities so that students in the class have common, concrete experiences that begin building concepts, processes, and skills. Engagement brings about disequilibrium, exploration initiates the process of equilibration. Some of the key words used to describe this phase are concrete and hands-on.

Courseware can be used in the phase, but it should be carefully designed to assist the initial process of reconstruction.

The aim of exploration activities is to establish experiences that a teacher can use later to formally introduce a concept, process, or skill. During the activity, the students have time in which they explore objects, events, or situations.

As a result of their mental and physical involvement in the exploration activity, the students establish relationships, observe patterns, identify variables, and question events.

The teacher's role in the exploration phase is that of facilitator or coach. The teacher initiates the activity and allows students time and opportunity to investigate objects, materials, and situations based on each student's own ideas of the phenomena. If called upon, the teacher may "coach" or guide students. Use of concrete materials and experiences is essential. Table 18.3 summarizes the exploration phase.

Explanation
The word "explanation" means the act or process in which concepts, processes, or skills are made plain, comprehensible, and clear. The process of explanation provides the students and teacher with a common use of terms relative to the learning task. In this phase, the teacher directs student attention to specific aspects of the engagement and exploration experiences. First, students are asked to give *their* explanations. Second, the teacher introduces scientific or technological explanations in a direct and formal manner. Explanations are ways of ordering the ex-

TABLE 18–2
Engagement

Orientation
This phase of the teaching model initiates the instructional task. The activity should: (1) make connections between past and present learning experiences, and (2) anticipate activities and organize students' thinking toward the learning outcomes of current activities.
Students
• Establish an interest in, and develop an approach to, the instructional task.
Teachers
• Identify the instructional task.
Activities
• May vary, but should be interesting, motivational, and meaningful to the students.
Learning
• Initiated by, exposure to and experience with, the concepts, processes, and skills.

TABLE 18–3
Exploration

Orientation
This phase of the teaching model provides the students with a common base of experiences within which current concepts, processes, and skills may be identified and developed.

Students
• Complete activities directed toward learning outcomes.

Teachers
• Facilitate and monitor interaction between students and instructional situations, materials, and/or courseware.

Activities
• Provide mental and physical experiences relative to the learning outcomes. These activities provide an initial context for students' explanations as they have unanswered questions based on the exploration.

Learning
• Directed by objects, events, or situations.

TABLE 18–4
Explanation

Orientation
This phase of the teaching model focuses students' attention on a particular aspect of their engagement and exploration experiences and provides opportunities to demonstrate their conceptual understanding, process skills, or behaviors. This phase also provides specific opportunities for teachers to introduce a concept or skill.

Students
• Describe their understanding, use their skills, express their attitudes.

Teachers
• Direct student learning by clarifyng misconceptions, providing vocabulary for concepts, examples of skills, modifying behaviors, and suggesting further learning experiences.

Activities
• Provide opportunities to identify student knowledge, skills and values, and to introduce language and/or behaviors related to learning outcomes.

Learning
• Directed by teacher and instructional courseware.

ploratory experiences. The teacher should clearly base the initial part of this phase on students' explanations and clearly connect the explanations to experiences in the engagement and exploration phases of the instructional model. The key to this phase is to present concepts, processes, or skills in a simple, clear, and direct manner and move on to the next phase. One should not equate telling with learning. The explanation phase can be relatively short because the next phase allows time for restructuring and extends this formal introduction to concepts, processes, and skills.

The explanation phase is teacher (or technology) directed. Teachers have a variety of techniques and strategies at their disposal. Educators commonly use oral explanations; but, there are numerous other strategies, such as video, films, and educational courseware. This phase continues the process of mental ordering and provides words for explanations. In the end, students should be able to explain exploratory experiences using common terms. Students will not immediately express and apply the explanations—learning takes time. Students need time and experience in order to establish and expand concepts, processes, and skills. That is one reason for the next phase. For a summary of the explanation phase, see Table 18.4.

Elaboration

Once students have an explanation of their learning tasks, it is important to involve students in further experiences that extend or elaborate the concepts,

processes, or skills. In some cases, students may still have misconceptions, or they may only understand a concept in terms of the exploratory experience. Elaboration activities provide further time and experiences that contribute to learning.

According to Audrey Champagne:

> During the elaboration phase, students engage in discussions and information-seeking activities. The group's goal is to identify and execute a small number of promising approaches to the task. During the group discussion, students present and defend their approaches to the instructional task. This discussion results in better definition and gathering of information that is necessary for successful completion of the task. The teaching cycle is not closed to information from the outside. Students get information from each other, the teacher, printed materials, experts, electronic data bases, and experiments they conduct. This is called the information base. As a result of participation in the group's discussion, individual students are able to elaborate upon the conception of the tasks, information bases, and possible strategies for its completion.[30]

Note the use of interactions within student groups as a part of the elaboration process. This is an application of Vygotsky's psychology to the teaching model. Group discussions and cooperative learning situations provide opportunities for students to express their understanding of the subject and re-

TABLE 18–5
Elaboration

Orientation
This phase of the teaching model challenges and extends students' conceptual understanding and skills. Through new experiences, the students develop deeper and broader understanding, more information, and adequate skills.

Students
• Present and defend their explanations and identify and complete several experiences related to the learning task.

Teachers
• Provide an occasion for students to cooperate on activities, discuss their current understanding, and demonstrate their skills.

Activities
• Provide experiences to extend student conceptions, behaviors, and attitudes to new and unique situations.

Learning
• Encouraged through challenges, repetition, new experiences, practices, and time.

TABLE 18–6
Evaluation

Orientation
This phase of the teaching model encourages students to assess their understanding and abilities and provides opportunities for teachers to evaluate student progress toward achieving the educational objectives.

Students
• Examine the adequacy of their explanations, behaviors, and attitudes in new situations.

Teachers
• Use a variety of formal and informal procedures for assessing student understanding.

Activities
• Evaluate the concepts, attitudes, and skills of the students.

Learning
• Repeat different phases of the teaching model in order to improve conceptual understanding and/or skills.

ceive feedback from others who are very close to their own level of understanding.

The phase is also an opportunity to involve students in new situations and problems that require the application of identical or similar explanations. Generalization of concepts, processes, and skills is the goal. Table 18.5 is a summary of the elaboration phase of the teaching model.

Evaluation

At some point, it is important that students receive feedback on the adequacy of their explorations. Informal evaluation can occur from the beginning of the teaching sequence. The teacher can complete a formal evaluation after the elaboration phase. As a practical educational matter, teachers must assess educational outcomes. This is the phase in which teachers administer tests to determine each student's level of understanding. This is also the important opportunity for students to use the skills they have acquired and evaluate their understanding. The instructional model is in close alignment with the actual processes involved in the scientific enterprise. In science, the "methods of scientific inquiry" are an excellent means for students to test their explanations. This is, after all, congruent with science. How well do student explanations stand up to review by peers and teachers? Is there need to reform ideas based on experience? Table 18.6 summarizes the evaluation phase.

Table 18.7 provides more details about what the

teacher does and what the student does at different stages in the instructional model. Note that we have provided descriptions of methods and activities that are both consistent and inconsistent with this model.[31]

In conclusion, the basis of the instructional model proposed for this program is the original learning cycle used in the SCIS program. We have modified and extended this learning cycle and drawn on research in the cognitive sciences—research that deals primarily with student misconceptions. Three factors justify this instructional model: (1) research from the cognitive sciences, (2) concordance of the model with the scientific process, and (3) utility to curriculum developers and classroom teachers.

■ Summary

This chapter describes several instructional models. Although textbooks are used by the majority of science teachers, there has been little effort to use them effectively. Science teachers should recognize that students' use of textbooks is influenced by their prior knowledge (misconceptions) and that this prior knowledge can dominate or distort text material. Some recommendations for using a textbook include the following:

• Direct students' attention for important concepts.
• Challenge students' misconceptions.
• Ask students to construct explanations of everyday phenomena.
• Probe student responses.

TABLE 18–7

Stage of the Instructional Model	What the Teacher Does	
	That Is Consistent With This Model	*That Is Inconsistent With This Model*
Engage	• Creates interest • Generates curiosity • Raises questions • Elicits responses that uncover what the students know or think about the concept/topic	• Explains concepts • Provides definitions and answers • States conclusions • Provides closure • Lectures
Explore	• Encourages the students to work together without direct instruction from the teacher • Observes and listens to the students as they interact • Asks probing questions to redirect the students' investigations when necessary • Provides time for students to puzzle through problems • Acts as a consultant for students	• Provides answers • Tells or explains how to work through the problem • Provides closure • Tells the students that they are wrong • Gives information or facts that solve the problem • Leads the students step-by-step to a solution
Explain	• Encourages the students to explain concepts and definitions in their own words • Asks for justification (evidence) and clarification from students • Formally provides definitions, explanations, and new labels • Uses students' previous experiences as the basis for explaining concepts	• Accepts explanations that have no justification • Neglects to solicit the students' explanations • Introduces unrelated concepts or skills
Elaborate	• Expects the students to use formal labels, definitions, and explanations provided previously • Encourages the students to apply or extend the concepts and skills in new situations • Reminds the students of alternative explanations • Refers the students to existing data and evidence and asks: What do you already know? Why do you think . . . ? (Strategies from Explore apply here also.)	• Provides definitive answers • Tells the students that they are wrong • Lectures • Leads students step-by-step to a solution • Explains how to work through the problem
Evaluate	• Observes students as they apply new concepts and skills • Assesses students' knowledge and/or skills • Looks for evidence that the students have changed their thinking or behaviors • Allows students to assess their own learning and group-process skills • Asks open-ended questions, such as: Why do you think . . . ? What evidence do you have? What do you know about x? How would you explain x?	• Tests vocabulary words, terms, and isolated facts • Introduces new ideas or concepts • Creates ambiguity • Promotes open-ended discussion unrelated to the concept or skill

• Provide accurate feedback to students.
• Construct alternative representations of textbook explanations.
• Select activities that create conceptual conflict.

Another instructional model is the learning cycle. The learning cycle is a three-step instructional sequence that includes

• concept exploration,

• concept introduction, and
• concept application.

Cooperative learning is an effective strategy in the science classroom. The students learn a number of strategies that help them develop and function as a group. Formation of a group, group functioning, formulating understanding of the task, and time to discuss and reform concepts are all important aspects of cooperative groups.

TABLE 18–7
(continued)

What the Student Does	
That Is Consistent With This Model	*That Is Inconsistent With This Model*
• Asks questions, such as: Why did this happen? What do I already know about this? What can I find out about this? • Shows interest in the topic	• Asks for the "right" answer • Offers the "right" answer • Insists on answers or explanations • Seeks one solution
• Thinks freely, but within the limits of the activity • Tests predictions and hypotheses • Forms new predictions and hypotheses • Tries alternatives and discusses them with others • Records observations and ideas • Suspends judgment	• Lets others do the thinking and exploring (passive involvement) • Works quietly with little or no interaction with others (only appropriate when exploring ideas or feelings) • "Playing around" indiscriminately with no goal in mind • Stops with one solution
• Explains possible solutions or answers to others • Listens critically to one another's explanations • Questions one another's explanations • Listens to and tries to comprehend explanations offered by the teacher • Refers to previous activities • Uses recorded observations in explanations	• Proposes explanations from "thin air" with no relationship to previous experiences • Brings up irrelevant experiences and examples • Accepts explanations without justification • Does not attend to other plausible explanations
• Applies new labels, definitions, explanations, and skills in new, but similar, situations • Uses previous information to ask questions, propose solutions, make decisions, design experiments • Draws reasonable conclusions from evidence • Records observations and explanations • Checks for understanding among peers	• "Plays around" with no goal in mind • Ignores previous information or evidence • Draws conclusions from "thin air" • Uses in discussions only those labels that the teacher provided
• Answers open-ended questions by using observations, evidence, and previously accepted explanations • Demonstrates an understanding or knowledge of the concept or skill • Evaluates his or her own progress and knowledge • Asks related questions that would encourage future investigations	• Draws conclusions, not using evidence or previously accepted explanations • Offers only yes-or-no answers, memorized definitions or explanations as answers • Fails to express satisfactory explanations in his or her own words • Introduces new, irrelevant topics

Madeline Hunter's model is described in this chapter. The teaching sequence in this model includes

• anticipating set,
• objectives and purpose,
• instructional input,
• modeling,
• monitoring student understanding, and
• practice.

The 4MAT System designed by Bernice McCarthy is also included. The 4MAT System is based on a synthesis of the research on styles and modes of learning. The four phases that should be included in any lesson are

• concrete experiences to reflective observation,
• reflective observation to abstract conceptualization,

- abstract conceptualization to active experimentation, and
- active experimentation to concrete experience.

The final portion of the chapter presents an instructional model that incorporates many of the findings from educational research and curriculum development. The model has five phases:

- *Engagement*—This phase initiates the learning process. It makes connections to the past and future activities. The activities should be concrete and engaging.
- *Exploration*—Experience that includes the concepts and skills important to the lesson. The students are allowed some freedom to explore problems presented by the teacher.
- *Explanation*—The teacher focuses students on specific experiences and formally introduces concepts.
- *Elaboration*—The experiences in this phase are interrelated to extend the students' understanding or skills. New and different experiences develop deeper and broader understanding.
- *Evaluation*—Activities are used to assess the students' understanding and abilities.

■ References

1. See the entire issue on major questions related to curriculum and instruction in science education. *Journal of Research in Science Teaching*, 20, no. 5 (May 1983).
2. Kevin Wise and James Okey, "A Meta-Analysis of the Effects of Various Science Teaching Strategies on Achievement," *Journal of Research in Science Teaching*, 20, no. 5 (May 1983), p. 434.
3. Iris Weiss, *Report of the 1985-86 National Survey of Science and Mathematics Education* (Research Triangle Park, NC: Research Triangle Institute, November, 1987).
4. Jean Osbourn, Beau Jones, and Marcy Stein, "The Case for Improving Textbooks," *Educational Leadership*, April, 1985.
5. Stephen Jay Gould, "The Case of the Creeping Fox Terrier Clone," *Natural History*, January, 1988.
6. Joseph D. McInerney, "Biology Textbooks—Whose Business?" *The American Biology Teacher*, 48, no. 7 (October, 1986).
7. Audrey Champagne, et al., "Middle School Science Tests: What's Wrong That Could Be Made Right?" *American Association for the Advancement of Science Books & Films*, May/June, 1987.
8. Iris Weiss, 1987.
9. Kathleen Roth and Charles Anderson, "Promoting Conceptual Change Learning from Science Textbooks," in *Improving Learning: New Perspectives*, ed. P. Ramsden (New York: Kogan Page Publishers, 1988).

10. Kathleen Roth, *Conceptual Change Learning and Student Processing of Science Texts*, (Research Series No. 167) (East Lansing, MI: Institute for Research on Teaching, Michigan State University, 1985).
11. Charles Anderson and Edward Smith, *Teacher Behavior Associated With Conceptual Learning in Science*, Paper presented at the annual meeting of the American Educational Research Association, Montreal, Canada, 1983.
12. Roth, *Conceptual Change Learning*.
13. Robert Karplus, "Teaching for the Development of Reasoning," in 1980 AETS Yearbook, *The Psychology of Teaching for Thinking and Creativity*, ed. Anton E. Lawson (Columbus, OH: ERIC Clearinghouse for Science, Mathematics, and Environmental Education, 1979).
14. Howard Birnie, *An Introduction to the Learning Cycle* (Saskatoon: University of Kastachewan Press, 1982).
15. Robert Karplus, et al., "Teaching and the Development of Reasoning" (Berkeley: University of California Press, 1977).
16. John Renner, Michael Abraham, and Howard Birnie, "The Importance of the FORM of Student Acquisition of Data in Physics Learning Cycles," *The Journal of Research in Science Teaching*, 22, no. 4 (1985), pp. 303-326.
17. Renner et al., "The Importance of the FORM," pp. 303-326.
18. Anton E. Lawson, "A Better Way to Teach Biology," *The American Biology Teacher*, 50, no. 5, (May 1988), pp. 266-278.
19. Lawson, "A Better Way to Teach Biology," pp. 266-278.
20. See for example David Johnson, et al., "Effects of Cooperative, Competitive and Individualistic Goal Structures on Achievement: A Meta-Analysis," *Psychological Bulletin*, 89, (1981), pp. 47-62 and Roger Johnson and David Johnson, "What Research Says About Student Interaction in Science Classrooms," in *Education in the 80s: Science*, ed. Mary Budd Rowe (Washington, D.C.: National Education Association, 1984), pp. 25-37.
21. David Johnson, Roger Johnson, Edith Johnson Holubec, and Patricia Roy, *Circles of Learning: Cooperation in the Classroom* (Alexandria, VA: Association for Supervision and Curriculum Development, 1986).
22. Johnson, et al., *Circles of Learning*.
23. Madeline Hunter, *Mastery Teaching* (El Segundo, CA: TIP Publications, 1982), and *Improved Instruction* (El Segundo, CA: TIP Publications, 1976).
24. Bernice McCarthy, *The 4MAT System: Teaching to Learning Styles with Right/Left Mode Techniques* (Barrington, IL: Excel, Inc., 1987).
25. J.M. Atkin and Robert Karplus, "Discovery or Invention?" *The Science Teacher*, 29(1986), pp. 45-51.
26. John W. Renner and Michael Abraham, "The Sequence of Learning Cycle Activities in High School Chemistry," *Journal of Research in Science Teaching*, 23, no. 2 (1986) pp. 121-143.
27. Charles W. Anderson, "Incorporating Recent Research on Learning into the Process of Science Curriculum Development," Commissioned paper for IBM-

supported Design Project (Colorado Springs, CO: Biological Sciences Curriculum Study, 1987).

28. Audrey Champagne, "The Psychological Basis for a Model of Science Instruction," Commissioned paper for IBM-supported Design Project (Colorado Springs, CO: Biological Sciences Curriculum Study, 1987).

29. Paul J. Kuerbis, "Learning Styles and Elementary Science," Commissioned paper for IBM-supported Design Project (Colorado Springs, CO: Biological Sciences Curriculum Study, 1987).

30. Champagne, "The Psychological Basis for a Model."

31. Nancy M. Landes, senior staff associate at the Biological Sciences Curriculum Study (BSCS) is the person primarily responsible for developing this table. It is used here with her permission.

CHAPTER 19

Planning for Effective Science Teaching

Science teachers are especially fortunate because of the many interesting and motivational things connected with science which they can use in their teaching. Examples of natural and scientific phenomena abound. The daily cycle of news events, the endless variety of clouds and weather, the growth of plants and animals, the passage of the seasons—all contribute to an endless store of materials for scientific and technologic discussions. There are rocks and minerals to be collected, flora and fauna in season, and many examples of scientific ideas and technological devices to be used as teaching aids in science classes.

Alert and enthusiastic science teachers do not miss the opportunity to use these things in their teaching plans. Clever use of appropriate items and examples will inject a degree of interest and spontaneity into science classes that are unmatched by other disciplines. How does the science teacher put the things of science to use? Are there meaningful ways to plan for effective teaching? Can the teacher maintain sequence and organization and at the same time stimulate interest? Can the objectives of science teaching be realized while permitting the objects of science to dominate the scene? These are questions teachers must face when planning their yearly and daily work.

At this point, we recommend that you complete at least one of the following activities—"Investigating Science Teaching: Planning a Simple Lesson," "Investigating Science Teaching: Evaluating a Lesson,"—located at the end of this chapter. Doing these activities will provide some initial thought and experience for the following sections of this chapter. In the next sections, we introduce some elements and strategies of effective teaching. These are the "pieces" that science teachers use in designing individual lessons or teaching units. The chapter is structured so you develop an idea of different types of planning for effective science teaching. This chapter presents the practical, "how to" of science teaching—the actual planning of a science program, a teaching unit, and daily lesson plans.

■ Some Elements and Strategies of Effective Science Teaching

Teaching is more than telling. Often individuals approach teaching as the relatively simple task of telling about a scientific fact or concept. As you will see, it is much more. Teaching is not necessarily more difficult. As it turns out, telling is sometimes a difficult way to teach an idea. Effective teaching requires a great deal of thought, preparation, and design. In the next paragraphs, we introduce some ideas that you might keep in mind while designing a lesson, teaching unit, or entire science curriculum.

Before a Lesson or Unit

Several times in this book we have indicated the importance of goals and objectives. They emerge here as the fundamental consideration of the planning process.

Goals and objectives are like maps. They indicate the journey and the day's destination respectively. Goals and objectives indicate where you are going and tell you when you have arrived. In teaching, it is often well to remember that, like travel, the destination defines the trip, and the means of travel accommodates other aspects of the trip, for example, budget, time, and access. We recommend careful thought and identification of goals and objectives at an appropriate level for the individual or class. Once you actually have designed the lesson and begun teaching, it is important to continually direct and redirect teaching to the goals and objectives. To use the trip analogy again, one can have educational side trips, but it is essential to continue in the general direction of your daily objectives and your unit or yearly goals.

After you have identified goals and objectives, you will have to decide on such things as *content, time, pacing, grouping,* and *activities.* These decisions were described in Chapter 2.

Beginning a Lesson or Unit

How you begin sets the stage for the lesson and unit. The beginning of a lesson should achieve several things. First, it should connect what has been learned in the past with what is going to be learned in the present lesson. While the connections may seem obvious to you as the teacher, it is not always as clear to the students. Second, a good beginning can provide a focus or context for the present lesson. Effective beginnings answer the why and what questions that students may have. Third, the beginning should be exciting and engaging. Students should be enthusiastic about what they are going to study.

There are many effective ways to begin a unit of study or a daily lesson. Demonstrations, current events, the confrontation with problems, pictorial riddles, discrepant events, counter-intuitive situations, and challenging questions are but a few ways to begin a teaching sequence.

The Middle of a Lesson or Unit

Once the lesson or unit is underway, there is a lot to do. With experience, more elements and strategies are incorporated into science teaching. Here are a few initial ideas to consider as you design science lessons. Active participation with materials, equipment, and audiovisual aids is a good way to engage the learner's attention and develop the concepts, skills, and values of your objectives. You want to optimize the amount of time students are *engaged* in learning tasks.

There are different means of capturing, maintaining, and enhancing students' attention. These motivational strategies include showing the personal meaning of the lesson to the students' lives. Personal meaning can be provided through a rationale; con-

necting an idea or concept to the students' lives, or answering a personal question. Success is another motivator. New objects and experiences can improve student interest and attention as much as success.

Once you are into the lesson, remember to apply the principles of learning and development. At a minimum, use reinforcement to discourage behaviors that are nonproductive.

When introducing skills, it is often essential to model what you want the students to do. For example, demonstrate how you want them to set up and dismantle laboratory equipment or use the probes of a microcomputer-based laboratory.

Practice is another element of learning. Some ideas, skills, and values are learned because they have great personal meaning. In others, proficiency is achieved through repetition of a task. Don't hesitate to schedule time to practice the skills that you perceive to be important. Sometimes practice can be done with the entire class, usually at the initial stages of learning, other times practice can be individualized and either distributed throughout or clustered at the end of the learning sequence.

As you teach the lesson, it is valuable to monitor student progress. How are they doing? Do they understand what has been taught? If students are not progressing as you had anticipated, it is well worth adapting the sequence or method to better enhance student learning. The assessment can be as simple as spotchecking papers, asking questions, or giving a quiz. The crucial point is to change instruction based on the assessment.

There is another, sometimes illusive, set of factors that are important for planning and teaching. Those factors can be thought of as the classroom climate. What plans should be made to establish a classroom environment that enhances student learning? Planning your lesson or unit should include *communicating expectations of achievement*—your goals, procedures for a *safe and orderly work environment, anticipation and sensible management of disruptive behavior,* and *establishment of cooperative learning.*[1]

Yes, there is a lot that goes into teaching. Some of the factors described above can actually be a part of your planning, others are part of your instructional theory.

Ending a Lesson or Unit

Too often, lessons and units just stop. Plan an ending to your lesson. There should be closure, an opportunity for you or the learners to summarize what has been taught. At the lesson's end, you should be able to indicate how well the objectives were met. The students ought to leave the room with a feeling of accomplishment and closure for the day's lesson or the unit.

After a Lesson or Unit

When a lesson or unit is over, you should have some measure of the lesson and student achievement. The measure can be an informal assessment of "how things went" and "what they learned" or a formal evaluation of the lesson and a quiz or test of student achievement. These procedures are feedback for you and the students. They indicate what might be changed in the instructional sequence and the problems students may be having with the material. The next section is a more complete description of planning for effective science teaching.

■ Designing Programs, Units, and Lessons

This section is designed to have you take the steps toward the practical, everyday matter of science teaching. You just read about some general strategies of effective teaching. Here many of the elements and methods are combined into a sequence of instruction. While there are many models and methods for teaching science, the purpose of this section is to have you begin thinking generally about your science program and specifically about planning science lessons. We take the approach of beginning with the science program, the year-long plan. Although this is probably not your most immediate concern, having the "big picture" of your science program provides the framework for consistent and coherent units and lessons. The sequence is the science program, unit plans, and lesson plans.

The Long-Range Plan: A Science Program

Our goal for this brief section is to have you begin thinking about a full year's science program. The essential elements for this section are discussed in length in the chapters on curriculum. We recommend review of those chapters. To accomplish our goal of conceptualizing a total science program—seeing the forest before looking at trees—you should complete the activity "Investigating Science Teaching: Designing a Full-Year Program," at the end of this chapter.

Designing your science program will be a major challenge. You will have to synthesize many diverse ideas and recommendations into your program. Ob-

jectives, topics, and activities come from a variety of issues. Those sources may include the following:

- science department requirements,
- district syllabi,
- state guidelines,
- textbook organization, and
- national organizations.

Sorting all of these recommendations is not easy. Fortunately, many of the recommendations are more consistent than not. In the end, you will decide on your science program. That is why we encourage to begin thinking about how to organize your program. There are many ways to organize programs. We briefly describe some of those ways in the next section.

Structure of the Discipline
Science disciplines are organized by major conceptual structure. Themes such as thermodynamics in physics, bonding in chemistry, and diversity in biology are examples of conceptual schemes that organize disciplines. Curriculum projects of the 1960s and 1970s were organized by the structure of disciplines.

Nature of Scientific Inquiry
Inquiry refers to the ways scientists within disciplines determine the truth or falsehood, validity or invalidity of knowledge claims. The inquiry includes the processes scientists use—observation, classification, controlling variables, forming hypothesis, and designing experiments. But organizing on the basis of inquiry includes more—the study of how and why scientific propositions are accepted or rejected. If scientists have competing theories, how does one know which is acceptable?

Topics of Science Disciplines
Topics can be used to organize science courses. Electricity, magnets, rocks and minerals, cell division, and photosynthesis are examples of topics.

Issues Related to Science
In recent years, there has been a trend toward using issues to organize courses. In many cases, the issues cut across the science disciplines. If carefully and properly done, organizing a program by issues can be exciting for students and include many important concepts and processes of science. Some issues include air quality and atmosphere, water resources, land use, population growth, food resources, mineral resources, and environmental quality.

Organizing a science program can take the form of a yearly calendar. The calendar indicates the order

TABLE 19–1

Yearly calendar for a course organized by concepts and issues

Unit	Issue	Concepts	Days Allotted
I	Science and Technology in Society	The Nature of Science and Technology	10
II	Air Quality	Cycles	20
III	Land Use	Scale	20
IV	Water Quality	Equilibrium	20
V	Hazardous Substances	Gradient	25
VI	Space Exploration	Systems	40
VII	Population, Resources, Environment	Interactions	45
			(Total 180 Days)

of units and time allotted to the units. Table 19.1 is a calendar for a course organized by both integrating concepts and social issues. Examination of textbooks and state syllabi will provide other examples of yearly calendars.

In preparing this calendar, the order of issues and concepts generally goes from simple to complex. The more complex problems come later in the year and more time is allotted for study of those issues. There are 180 days, the average number of classes a science teacher has in a school year.

The Middle-Range Plan: A Science Unit

Ms. Henderson was a new teacher of tenth-grade physical science at Warren High School. The head of the science department, Mr. Longwell, who had taught the course the previous year, had talked briefly with Ms. Henderson about the objectives and general nature of the course.

No textbook was being used. Mr. Longwell believed that most physical science textbooks tried to cover too many topics in a one-year course. To permit time for greater depth of study, only five major areas were taught in physical science at Warren High: the nature of the atom, the nature of the molecule, nuclear energy, radiant energy, and human applications of physical science. Materials for the course were provided by the purchase of small paperback books on appropriate science topics and the development and photocopying of activities.

When they discussed the objectives of the physical science course, Ms. Henderson and Mr. Longwell agreed that it should serve a dual role: to introduce students to the more rigorous specialized chemistry and physics courses in the eleventh and twelfth grades of Warren High School and to function as a terminal science course for those students who were planning to go into nonscience areas of study. As much as possible, the chosen topics were approached from an activity and laboratory point of view.

With this background for the course, Ms. Henderson decided to outline the year's work. Her first task was to plan the sequence of topics. She decided that the sequence used by Mr. Longwell—atom, molecule, nucleus, radiations, applications—had stood the test of experience and seemed to be a logical sequence; therefore, she would use this sequence the first year and modify it in the future if necessary. With only five areas to study, it seemed feasible to plan about six weeks on each of the first three topics and eight weeks on each of the last two. This schedule would enable the class to finish the third topic at the end of the first semester. Ms. Henderson realized that this schedule might have to be modified but she was prepared to make the necessary adjustments when needed.

Over the next few days, other parts of the long-range plan were finalized. Films were ordered to arrive as near proper times as could be estimated so early in the year. Dates of holidays and examination periods were considered. Some thought was given to a possible excursion or two during classes on applications but the dates were left tentative. The storage room was checked for apparatus and laboratory supplies and seemed adequate, but Ms. Henderson knew that certain unavailable materials might be needed on short notice. She checked with Mr. Longwell and found that expendable items could be obtained within a week from a laboratory-supply house.

Ms. Henderson kept a loose-leaf planning notebook for each of her classes. The long-range plan and schedule were placed in the front of this notebook and space was allotted for notes and modifications.

A beginning teacher is assisted by a teaching-unit plan designed in moderate detail for a period of a month or six weeks. The unit topic is usually a cohesive area of study that fits into the long-range plans and objectives. The teaching unit frequently contains the following sections and characteristics:

1. Title
2. Purpose statement

3. Objectives
4. Content
5. Methods
6. Materials
7. Evaluation
8. Teaching sequence

The *title* is simply an identifying name for the unit. It need not be anything complicated, e.g., "An Introduction To Physics," "Human Ecology," or "Earth Processes: Folds and Faults."

A *purpose statement* is a synopsis of *why* this unit is important and generally *what* will be accomplished by the teaching unit.

The *objectives* should be specific brief statements of purpose for the unit. They should serve as constant reminders to the teacher of the things to be accomplished in the time allotted. They should be practical, timely, and carefully suited to the capabilities of the class. Objectives should be clearly written and testable.

Content refers to the actual material to be taught in the unit. Because this material may be extensive, the teaching-unit plan cannot list all of it in minute detail; however, the plan may list major principles, pertinent facts of major importance, examples and illustrations, and references to specific knowledge in text material deemed important for the unit. An outline form may be used in this part of the unit plan. Because of the chronological nature of the teaching unit, specific content and references to subject matter can be distributed sequentially throughout the unit.

Methods to be used in teaching should be planned as carefully as possible. This is where the use of one, (or a combination), of instructional models is highly recommended. Plan through the sequence of lessons using a model. Based on the model and your objectives, certain parts of the teaching sequence may be taught more suitably by one method than by another. For example, a film may be the most effective teaching agent for an introduction (e.g., engagement, anticipatory set) and a simulation game may be most appropriate as an elaboration of the lesson's concepts. At another time you may deem a discussion or individual project to be the best teaching method.

Materials must be planned with care to ensure their availability when they are needed. In some cases, ordering is necessary a few weeks in advance. Apparatus should be checked to see if it is in working order. Development of the teaching unit will undoubtedly involve hours of work in the library, getting ideas for reading materials and activities. Consideration should be given to the needs of slow and gifted learners and suitable materials should be arranged for them.

Evaluation should be thought of as a continuing process throughout the unit. One of the major functions of evaluation is to keep students informed of their progress and to give them realistic assessments of their own abilities. Assigned work, short quizzes, conferences, and unit tests must be planned in the teaching unit. Not all of the evaluative devices and techniques can be planned in detail in advance but provision for them can be incorporated. Evaluation should be based on the objectives of the unit.

The *teaching sequence* may be outlined for the period of time involved but flexibility for change must be provided. This can be done by arranging for alternative procedures, omitting or adding certain subject matter, and providing for unplanned periods which can occasionally be interspersed to take up slack or give needed time for completing a topic.

The teaching unit should be thought of as a guide for action rather than a calendar of events. Slavish attention to the preplanned schedule can result in ineffective rigidity. On the other hand, reasonable attention to the sequence, objectives, and procedures of the teaching unit can promote better learning and feelings of satisfaction and accomplishment when it is finished. A general outline for a unit is presented here.

Outline for a Science Teaching Unit

Title

Purpose Statement

Outline for a Year Program (Use "Investigating Science Teaching: Designing a Full-Year Program," and indicate where your unit is located in the total program.)

Objectives for the Unit

Weekly Schedule for the Unit (See Table 19.2 for an example.)

Pretest

Daily Lesson Plans (Use a specific model or combination of models.)

Unit Test

Checklist of Requirements for the Science Unit

Your teacher will indicate those things he/she requires for your unit. You can use this checklist to organize your science unit.

_____ 1. *Title Page.* Give the title of the unit, grade level, and whether it is based on a new curriculum. If it uses a modern curriculum, state its name. List your name, the title and number of the course, and leave a space for the unit evaluation.

_____ 2. *Purpose Statement.* Give the reason for the scope and sequence of the unit. Indicate the broad goals to be achieved through the unit.

TABLE 19–2
Example of a weekly schedule for a middle school science class studying environmental change

Content Outline	Class Period	Phase of Teaching Model	Class Activity
Environmental problems in paper	Homework	Engagement	Students collect examples of the newspaper articles dealing with environmental problems, e.g., hazardous substances, or pollution.
Evidence of Environmental Change • Change is common • There are good, bad, and neutral changes	1	Exploration	Class goes outside and gathers evidence of change in local environment. They should find good, bad, and neutral changes.
Factors Related to Environmental Change • Immediate • Delayed • Cycles • Growth	2	Explanation	Film "The Saga of DDT." Use film to focus discussion on key concepts. End class with short lecturing, defining and giving examples of immediate change, delayed change, cyclical change, and change through growth.
Changing Environmental Systems	3	Elaboration	Do silent demonstrations of changes in aquatic and terrestrial ecosystems. Have students identify potential immediate, delayed, cyclical, and growth changes.
Limits to Change in Environmental Systems	4	Elaboration	Do Invitation to Inquiry on "Tragedy of the Commons." Use cooperative groups.
End of Section	5	Evaluation	Quiz on concepts. Students will define concept and give one local and one global example.

_____ 3. *Objectives*. Preferably, these should be stated in behavioral terms.

_____ 4. *Weekly Schedule of the Unit*. A brief one-page survey of what will take place each day as shown in Table 19.2.
  a. Include reading assignments.
  b. Include homework activities.

_____ 5. *Laboratory Exercises*. These should be some of your own laboratory activities including the following:
  a. The subject-matter objectives (concepts) the laboratory will teach.
  b. Critical thinking and problem-solving processes the lesson will develop, indicated in the margin of the activity.
  c. A discussion section preceding the lesson and open-ended possibilities following the lesson.
  d. Other (assigned by your instructor).

_____ 6. *Invitations to Inquiry*. (You are to prepare these invitations.)

_____ 7. *Discussion Questions During or at the End of the Unit*.
  a. List the questions you will ask to determine if the students understood the material studied and if they can apply what they have learned.
  b. When possible, the questions should develop critical thinking and problem-solving processes. The type of mental process the student must use, for example, predicting or inferring, should be placed in the margin to indicate what is required.

_____ 8. *Pictorial Riddles*. The pictures or diagrams for these riddles should be included. Place under them the questions you will ask.

_____ 9. *Demonstrations*. Include only if they are required because of a shortage of equipment or examples of safety reasons.

_____10. *Bulletin Board Display*. Prepare a diagram for at least one bulletin board display, indicating how it will appear.

_____11. *Supplemental Materials*.
  a. Laboratories or investigations
  b. Reading materials

_____12. *Audiovisual Materials*.
  a. Films

b. Film loops and filmstrips

c. Audiotapes

d. Transparencies

e. Models, charts

_____13. *Consideration of Safety Precautions.* What, if any, special considerations should be made about safety?

_____14. *Consideration of Special Students.* You might wish to include the variations on the lesson you would implement if you have special students, e.g., deaf or gifted.

_____15. *Reference or Resource Materials.* Include magazine materials and books you might want to use to improve your knowledge about the topic; may include teacher's manuals.

_____16. *Tests and Evaluation.* All tests should evaluate your objectives.

a. Quizzes—Include at least one quiz.

b. Practicals—These are tests using actual laboratory materials.

c. Unit tests—Include higher-order questions and indicate the course objectives.

_____17. *Self-Evaluation of the Unit.*

a. After compiling this unit outline, go back over it and write what problems you think you will have in teaching.

b. After teaching this unit, evaluate how you think it could be improved. (Leave this space for your information so that you may record your evaluation later.)

The Resource Unit

Many science teachers prepare a resource unit for the different topics they teach. A resource unit is, as the title indicates, a collection of resource materials that can be used for a specified topic, (e.g., acids and bases, the laws of thermodynamics, the rock cycle, or photosynthesis) or various issues, (e.g., population growth, air quality, world hunger, or health and disease). Rather than assemble the resources in a teaching sequence such as we have discussed above, a resource unit is usually arranged by teaching strategies or methods. If you begin organizing resource units now, it will only be a few years before you have an extensive collection of ideas and methods. While you will have to determine the topics or issues for your science program, we can provide some general organizational categories for resource units. You would probably want to develop resource units for each of the major topics you plan to teach.

Organization Categories for Resource Units
• Aims and Goals
• Objectives

• Bulletin Boards
• Computer Software
• Demonstrations
• Discussion Topics
• Field Trips
• Films
• Filmstrips
• Games
• Homework
• Invitations to Inquiry
• Lecture Notes
• Overhead Transparencies
• Projects
• Supplementary Readings
• Tests and Quizzes
• Videos
• Worksheets
• Miscellaneous

You will probably not use all of these categories, and will perhaps add some of your own, but this list should help you begin organizing your resource units. Use of a personal computer and a database or HyperCard program will greatly enhance your organization, filing, and search capacity. Table 19.3 is a more complete description of the categories and examples of materials for a resource unit.

The Short-Range Plan: The Science Lesson

The sequence of topics in this chapter may have seemed unusual to the science teacher facing a first lesson. We think there is added advantage for all teachers who have thought through their year's program and a unit before writing a daily lesson plan. Planning gives direction. A yearly plan guards against disconnected units, and unit plans protect against disconnected lessons. For all teachers planning is an essential component of effective instruction. Approaching a science class with a well-organized plan gives the teacher personal assurance and leaves the students with a sense of confidence in the teacher's abilities.

Thought planning should precede any written plans. Ask yourself questions such as:

• What are my goals?
• How can I best achieve my goals?
• What will motivate the students to learn the concepts? Processes? Skills?
• How can the concepts, processes or skills be presented most effectively?
• What can be done for an effective beginning, middle, and end of the lesson?
• How can I evaluate the lesson's effectiveness?

TABLE 19–3
Resource unit: Examples of categories and contents

Categories	Contents
Aims and Goals	Lists of aims and goals from your local district, state education agency, national organizations, and textbooks.
Objectives	Lists of objectives from your local district, state education agency, national organizations, and textbooks.
Bulletin Boards	Sketches and designs, newspaper and magazine articles, pictures, and maps.
Computer Software	CAI programs, microcomputer-based laboratory, tutorial, simulation, HyperCard, models.
Demonstrations	Collections of good demonstrations from journals such as *Science Scope, The Science Teacher, The American Biology Teacher, The Physics Teacher;* ideas from workshops and college courses.
Discussion Topics	Questions and issues that are successful with students.
Field Trips	Description of where to go, what to do, and who to contact.
Films, Filmstrip, Filmloops	Lists of films from school, local media center, state education agency, good films previewed at conventions, and college courses.
Games	List of games in science department, local media center.
Homework	Unique and interesting homework assignments for the topic.
Invitations to Inquiry	Lists of appropriate invitations from *Biology Teachers Handbook,* invitations you have developed, ideas for invitations.
Lecture Notes	Revised notes from past courses.
Overhead Transparencies	List (by title or content) of transparencies on file.
Projects	Problems and ideas for projects.
Supplementary Readings	Books and articles in media center, your file, or public library.
Tests and Quizzes	Copies of quizzes, tests, and questions.
Videos	List of videos from NOVA, DISCOVERY, etc. for VCR replay.
Worksheets	Masters for worksheets.
Miscellaneous	Other items that will help in the unit.

Since students vary in abilities and interests, plans must provide for these variations. Some method of motivating each student must be found. Only by knowing something of the background of each student can the teacher be effective in this task. This fact argues strongly for taking a personal interest in the students in one's classes.

The small human contacts in a friendly classroom, an interested question here and there, can motivate students better than any other method.

Planning for effective science teaching is more than just making sure that there is something to do for the entire class period. For example, unless it is the very first lesson of the year, it is probable that assignments have been made and that the nature of the subject matter is understood. Thus, the basis for planning has already been established.

To conduct an interesting class period, the teacher must vary the methods from day to day and even within the class period itself. It is eventually

TABLE 19–4
An instructional sequence for planning lessons

Engagement

This phase of the instructional sequence initiates the learning task. The activity should (1) make connections between past and present learning experiences, and (2) anticipate activities and focus students' thinking on the learning outcomes of current activities. The student should become mentally engaged in the concept, process, or skill to be explored.

Exploration

This phase of the teaching sequence provides students with a common base of experiences within which they identify and develop current concepts, processes, and skills. During this phase, students actively explore their environment or manipulate materials.

Explanation

This phase of the instructional sequence focuses students' attention on a particular aspect of their engagement and exploration experiences and provides opportunities for them to verbalize their conceptual understanding, or demonstrate their skills or behaviors. This phase also provides opportunities for teachers to introduce a formal label or definition for a concept, process, skill, or behavior.

Elaboration

This phase of the teaching sequence challenges and extends students' conceptual understanding and allows further opportunity for students to practice desired skills and behaviors. Through new experiences, the students develop deeper and broader understanding, more information, and adequate skills.

Evaluation

This phase of the teaching sequence encourages students to assess their understanding and abilities and provides opportunities for teachers to evaluate student progress toward achieving the educational objectives.

ineffective to use the same pattern of teaching day after day. Even an excellent method can suffer from overuse. With the great variety of methods from which to choose and with the potential excitement of inventing a new technique or of modifying one, the science teacher is in an excellent position to plan a highly effective lesson.

The teaching model described in the last chapter can be used to organize lessons. Recall that the model is designed to promote conceptual change and skill development. You should review Table 19.4 which is a summary of the teaching model.

The written plan should be concise and functional. The format may vary with the situation and individual teacher but most importantly it should be a practical, usable plan. In general, there should be provision for listing *objectives* and the related *con-*

cepts. The learning *activities* and required procedures should be listed. The procedures ought to be in adequate detail, for example, write out questions and directions to ensure a smooth class. All *materials* needed for the class period should be listed and checked. Two last essentials are *assignments* and *evaluation*. A skeletal form for a daily lesson would include the topics listed below.

  I. Objectives
 II. Concepts
III. Activities/Procedures
 IV. Materials
  V. Assignments
 VI. Evaluation

More general formats appear outlined here. We recommend you use one of these for your first lesson. With experience, science teachers often use less detailed plans, but if they are effective, they have thoroughly thought through their plan, no doubt in the detail suggested by these formats.

If you examine the "Teaching Science Activity: An Introduction to Population, Resources and Environment" on pages 469–471 you will see a thorough lesson plan. In this plan we have combined many instructional strategies, methods, and the instructional model to show how these can be pulled together for a teaching lesson. We suggest that you plan at least one lesson in this detail as a portion of your methods course experience. To this end, we recommend completing "Investigating Science Teaching: A Complete Lesson Plan," at the end of this chapter.

During the class hour, a teaching plan should be as unobtrusive as possible, yet referred to when needed. Main ideas, questions, and procedures may be memorized. Be sure the plan is handy if you need it for reference. As we mentioned above, a plan gives direction. You should also "plan" for flexibility. By this we mean realize that you will have to make some decisions about the direction of a particular lesson based on circumstances that arise in class.

After each lesson we recommend evaluating the lesson plan. The experience gained in teaching a lesson should be recorded with brief notations on the written plan, either during the class period or immediately after class. Suggestions for timing, organization, student involvement or modification of a technique can be noted for future use. (See "Investigating Science Teaching: Evaluation of Instructional Skills," at the end of this chapter.)

We will conclude this section with some helpful hints for contemporary lesson planning. Planning lessons that include goals such as problem solving, inquiry, study of controversial science-related social issues, and decision making present certain unique

Lesson Plan Format

Teacher_____   Unit_____
Subject_____   Class_____

     I. Topic: (Title)

    II. Aims: (Long-term goals)

   III. Objectives: (Short-term goals)

   IV. Materials:

    V. Procedures:

   VI. Evaluation:

  VII. Assignments:

 VIII. Resources:

Lesson Plan Format

Teacher:_____   Unit Title:_____
Subject:_____   Class:_____

Major Concepts	Major Processes	Major Skills
1.	1.	1.
2.	2.	2.
3.	3.	3.

Behavioral Objectives
1.

2.

3.

General outline	Activity or method	Phase of teaching model	Materials and equipment	Advance preparation	Evaluation

References:

Assignments:

Special Notes:

Lesson Plan Format

Teacher:_____   Unit:_____
Class:_____   Topic:_____
Date:_____

Purpose Statement:

Activity	Objectives	Method	Materials	Evaluation

Assignments:

Resources:

Notes for Future Lessons:

---

problems. To help advance organize your planning we have listed below some features of lessons for contemporary science teaching.

- Students are involved in broad, open-ended questions related to science, technology and/or social issues related to science and technology. Generally, students do not know the answer to the question.
- Students are required to understand the problem before designing an experiment.
- Students design their own investigations and make their own observations and conclusions.
- Students write their results using the standard protocol of science papers.
- Students extend their findings in several ways: to new problems, methods and experiments; to decisions relative to the issues; and to practical applications for life and living.

Students in contemporary science classes are given much more responsibility in planning experiments and carrying them to completion than has traditionally been the case. Effective handling of this responsibility will depend largely on how well the science teacher can provide experiences that will develop students capable of designing experiments, gathering data, and drawing conclusions from them.

Planning for such experiences should be done with the following points in mind:

1. Students probably have not had many previous opportunities of this type. Some may feel the need for explicit directions. The initial progress made by these students may be disappointing and frustrating, both to student and teacher.
2. Accepting responsibility for one's own learning is a challenge which some students may tend to resist. Passive learning in which the teacher has been the key person for initiating a course of action has probably been ingrained in the student's background.
3. First attempts should be on a small scale, with opportunities for greater choice and greater responsibility increasing as the student gains experience.
4. Rather than acting as a dispenser of information, the teacher should provide situations in which questions are asked. The student should be encouraged to formulate and ask questions of himself, of the experiment, of resource persons, and of library resource materials.
5. Means must be provided for the student to gain experience in analyzing the results of an experiment. The ability to see relationships, to organize data so that meaningful patterns emerge, to draw inferences, and to visualize ways of improving the experiment is a necessary skill which must be developed for effective learning by the inquiry method.

■ Summary

Planning is one of the critical aspects of effective science teaching. When designing a lesson, teaching unit, or total course, you should keep in mind some ideas that are fundamental to effective instruction: use objectives, focus teaching on the objective, be sure students actively participate, apply principles of learning and motivation, and develop lessons with a beginning, middle, and end that are educationally productive.

A variety of methods are used in contemporary science teaching. Some of the key methods are lecturing, questioning, discussing, demonstrating, reading, role playing, presenting reports, doing projects, working in the laboratory, solving problems, taking field trips, showing films and filmstrips, conducting simulations, and debating.

Science teachers can use models of teaching that combine strategies and methods into an instructional sequence. Using teaching models contributes to more efficient design of science lessons, and the synthesis of many elements of instruction into a workable and effective form.

The long-range plan of science teaching is the full-year program. This idea was introduced briefly.

There are at least two kinds of middle-range unit lesson plans. The teaching unit is planned with a time sequence in mind and usually provides for statements of objectives, outlines of content, methods, materials, and evaluation techniques. The resource unit is not usually concerned with chronology but a reservoir that the teacher uses for daily lesson planning. It may contain lists of aims, important knowledge objectives, lists of activities and projects, computer software, suitable demonstrations and experiments, references, films, bibliographies, sample tests, assignments, and other teaching aids.

The lesson plan is a guide for action, not a rigid blueprint to be followed unswervingly. It should be flexible and should be modified when necessary.

Much thought precedes the writing of a lesson plan. Questions of, "What is the purpose of the lesson?" "What major generalizations are to be taught?" "How is the material best presented?" "What kinds of individuals are in the class?" are considered before planning the sequence on paper.

The format of the lesson plan should be functional and comfortable to the teacher. Individual teachers select the format most useful to them. Lesson plans should be as concise as possible within the limitations of effective teaching. While teaching, the lesson plan should be unobtrusive but available for reference.

Planning for contemporary science teaching usually requires a somewhat different approach than more traditional methods. The role of the teacher becomes one of guidance and direction, with the student himself accepting greater responsibility for learning. Plans must provide more time, more questioning, greater variety of materials, and willingness on the part of the teacher to allow individual variations in progress by students.

Thorough lesson planning is a necessary facet of effective science teaching. Good teaching does not happen by accident. It is particularly important that a prospective teacher of science recognizes the values and benefits to be derived from careful, inspired planning in the art of science teaching.

■ References

1. David Berliner, "The Half-full Glass: A Review of Research in Teaching," in *Using What We Know About Teaching*, Philip Hosford (Alexandria, VA: Association for Supervision and Curriculum Development, 1984).

INVESTIGATING SCIENCE TEACHING

ACTIVITY 19–1

Planning a Simple Lesson

1. Select a simple and specific short-range objective for a science class, such as "to develop skill in correct use of the microscope," or "to learn how to use a balance," or "to operate a microcomputer." Plan a lesson to achieve this objective, incorporating the features of a good lesson plan.
2. Using the lesson plan prepared above, or a similar one, teach your classmates the lesson. Invite them to play the role of a secondary science class, with appropriate questions and activities. Solicit their constructive criticisms and comments on your lesson and the effectiveness of your teaching.

ACTIVITY 19–2

Evaluating a Lesson

A lesson plan for an eighth-grade science class is described below. Read through the description of the teacher's preparation and topic and study the teacher's written lesson plan. Then respond to the questions at the end of this section.

Mr. Foster looked forward to planning the eighth-grade science class on Monday morning. The topic for consideration was the simple Mendelian ratio of 1:2:1 for the offspring in the first generation produced by crossing of two pure strains. As he thought of the students in his class, it seemed that he might involve them in class participation and generate enthusiasm by doing a demonstration experiment. He would use the crossing of pure white and pure black guinea pigs as a simple case to illustrate this phenomenon.

In pure strains the genes for coat color in the parents could be represented by BB and ww. The only possible combinations in the first generation offspring would be Bw. These animals would be black but each would carry the gene for white. If animals of this genetic makeup were crossed, the possible combinations in their offspring (second generation) would be BB, Bw, wB, and ww.

To demonstrate the purely statistical nature of the results obtained in this cross and of the effect of dominant over recessive genes, Mr. Foster decided to make a simple arrow spinner that could be attached to the blackboard with a suction cup. Then a circle could be drawn on the blackboard, around the spinner, and labeled as shown in the figure. With this device, he could engage the class in a "game of chance," give them practice in keeping a record of the data, and put across the point of the lesson in an interesting manner.

After constructing the spinner, Mr. Foster decided to give it a trial run to see if it would perform satisfactorily and if the demonstration could be accommodated in the fifty-minute class period. Out of forty trials, the results he obtained in his trial run were

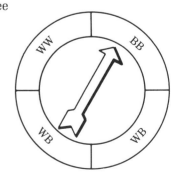

	BB	BW	WB	WW
Trials:	11	8	11	10

It took ten minutes and the results appeared to be close enough to the expected values to illustrate the point. He decided to plan his class period around this demonstration experiment.

On paper, Mr. Foster's lesson plan looked like this:

Life Science 8

Monday, April 20

Topic: Simple Mendelian ratio

Purpose: To show the statistical nature of the Mendelian ratio

Objective: At the completion of this lesson the student should be able to predict the approximate proportions of each gene combination obtained with 100 trials of the spinner.

Introductory remarks and questions (10 min.):

1. What is meant by *dominant gene*? By *recessive gene*?
2. Suppose a pure-bred black and a pure-bred white guinea pig (BB, ww) were mated. What genes have they for color? What would be the color of their offspring?
3. What are the possible combinations of dominant and recessive genes for color of coat? (BB, Bw, wB, ww)
4. What might be the proportions of each of these combinations in the offspring? (1:1:1:1—since Bw and wB are the same, the ratios appear as 1:2:1)
5. How would we show that this is the result of statistical probability?

Activity: Set up the blackboard spinner. Select a volunteer to spin it. Select another volunteer to keep a record on the blackboard under the headings BB, Bw, wB, and ww. Continue for 10–15 minutes.

Discussion (20 min.):

1. What are the actual colors of offspring which have each of the possible gene combinations? (three black and one white)
2. Why aren't the results in an exact ratio of 1:2:1? (change variations when few trials are used)
3. Could we improve the results? (more trials)
4. Student questions (anticipated)

Assignment (a volunteer assignment): Two boys or girls might run this experiment for more trials to see what the results would be.

Evaluation:

Time OK?____ Interest?____ Understanding?____ Student Learning?____

1. How would you improve Mr. Foster's lesson?

2. What pitfalls and precautions would you advise Mr. Foster about?

3. What features would you identify as a well-planned lesson?

ACTIVITY 19–3

Planning A Unit: Preliminary Questions

Suppose you are faced with the task of planning and carrying out a unit of work (e.g. 4–5 weeks) in your teaching area. What questions might you ask yourself? How will you organize your thoughts and plans? Consider each of the following questions:

1. What will be some important factors to take into consideration?

2. How might you involve students in the planning? How much student involvement is desirable?

3. What different levels of planning will probably be necessary?

4. What parts of your plans will you, of necessity, put down in written form?

5. What parts of your plans might you prefer to note mentally but not necessarily write down?

6. How much importance will you grant to a time budget?

7. How will you provide for the anticipated procedure questions and activities of the class? For the unanticipated questions and activities?

8. How will you provide for flexibility so that unexpected events can be handled adequately?

9. What purpose will evaluation serve in subsequent planning?
   a. From the standpoint of knowledge acquired by the students?

   b. From the standpoint of modification of the plans for the next teaching session?

ACTIVITY 19–4

Designing a Full-Year Program

As best you can, design a year's science program. We have found it best to complete the preliminary items as a way of thinking through your ideas. Then, complete the weekly schedule. You may wish to indicate major units within the weekly outline. Finally, complete the questions at the end of the investigation.

Title of Program: Preliminary Textbook:
Discipline: Supplemental Textbook(s):
Grade Level:
Purpose Statement:

Weekly Schedule for an Academic Year: Unit Topics for an Academic Year

1.
2.
3.
4.
5.
6.
7.
8.
9.
10.
11.
12.
13.
14.
15.
16.
17.
18.
19.
20.
21.
22.
23.
24.
25.
26.
27.
28.
29.
30.
31.
32.
33.
34.
35.
36.

Questions:

What was your rationale for the sequence, or order, of topics outlined?

ACTIVITY 19–5

A Complete Lesson Plan

Think through all aspects of a lesson plan. The experience will contribute to your doing this on a less formal basis for future lessons.

Use the general format in "Teaching Science Activity: An Introduction to Population, Resources, and Environment." pages 469-471.

- Topic
- Aims
- Objectives
- Materials
- Instructional Plan
- Evaluation

ACTIVITY 19–6

Evaluation of Instructional Skills

This form is provided for a self-evaluation of a lesson you teach. The evaluation is directed toward the use of strategies, methods, and models discussed in this chapter.

	Highly skilled, superior application and integration	Very skilled, instruction is integrated, evenly consistent, and smooth	Good use of skill but does not apply consistently	Poor application of skill	Unable to observe
Selects appropriate objectives	1	2	3	4	5
Makes objectives and purposes of lesson clear to students	1	2	3	4	5
Teaches to the objective	1	2	3	4	5
1. Asks questions relevant to objective	1	2	3	4	5
2. Provides information relative to objective	1	2	3	4	5
3. Responds to learned questions/ problems related to objectives	1	2	3	4	5
Demonstrates continuity in lesson	1	2	3	4	5
1. Beginning	1	2	3	4	5
2. Middle	1	2	3	4	5
3. End	1	2	3	4	5
Uses different methods	1	2	3	4	5
Applies a model of teaching	1	2	3	4	5
1. Concept Mapping	1	2	3	4	5
2. The Learning Cycle	1	2	3	4	5
3. Cooperative Learning	1	2	3	4	5
4. Madeline Hunter	1	2	3	4	5
5. Textbook	1	2	3	4	5
6. 4-MAT	1	2	3	4	5
Shows continuity of plans	1	2	3	4	5
1. Long Range (year)	1	2	3	4	5
2. Middle Range (unit)	1	2	3	4	5
3. Short Range (daily)	1	2	3	4	5

ACTIVITY 19–7

Student Attention

The following technique can be used to analyze student attention in class. Enlist the aid of another teacher or friend to observe your teaching for a full class period. Provide him with a form similar to the following:

OBSERVATION SHEET

Name_____Class_____

Date_____Time_____

Instructions: (a) At intervals of three minutes, count the class and determine the number of students who are actively paying attention to the lesson or activity. Use your best judgment as to whether a student is paying attention. (b) Keep a record of the types of activities engaged in by the teacher and/or class (e.g., lecture, discussion, demonstration, experiment, film, student report). Note the time of transition from one type of activity to another. Note any major occurrences, such as disciplinary action public address system coming on, entrance of a visitor, or any unusually distracting event. Plot a graph of percent attention versus time for each class observed.

Total attendance_____

Time	Class Count	Percent	Comments
0	_____	_____	_____
3	_____	_____	_____
6	_____	_____	_____
•			
•			
•			
•			
•			

ACTIVITY 19–8

Effectiveness of Methods

The effectiveness of different teaching methods can often be judged by student attention. In this investigation you are provided with a class attention record for a middle school physical science class. The record is for a week and the different activities are noted. You are to review the high and low points of the week and draw conclusions about the different methods used and pupil attentiveness.

- How many methods did the teacher use?
- Which methods seemed most effective?
- What can you tell about transitions between activities?
- If you were to redesign the lessons for this week what would you change?

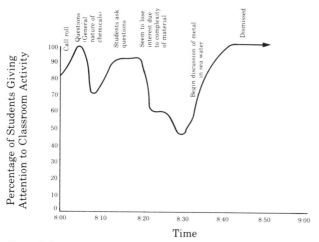

Type of class — Physical Science
Activity — Lecture discussion
   (Nature of chemicals)

# of Students — 12
Monday

Class attention on Monday

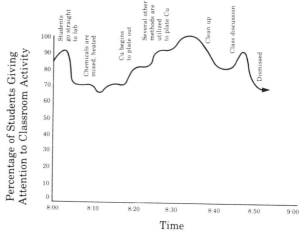

Type of Class — Physical Science
Activity — Lab (reactions)

# of Students — 11
Thursday

Class attention on Thursday

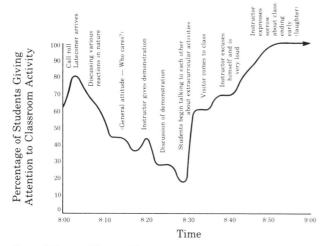

Type of class — Physical Science
Activity — Discussion (Various types
   of reactions)

# of Students — 11
Tuesday

Class attention on Tuesday

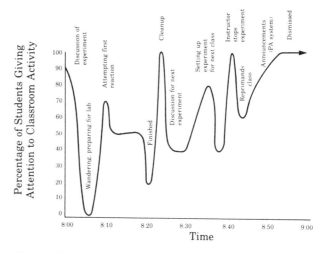

Type of Class — Physical Science
Activity — Laboratory experiments on
   chemical activity of various metals

# of Students — 10
Friday

Class attention on Friday

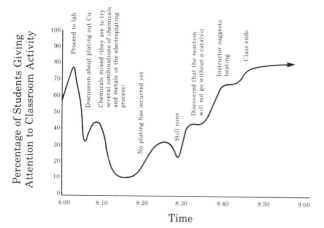

Type of class — Physical Science
Activity — Lab (electroplating)

# of Students — 9
Wednesday

Class attention on Wednesday

CHAPTER 20

Evaluating Classroom Performance

A common perception of evaluation by most teachers is that it is limited to giving tests. The broader aspects of evaluation, including self-evaluation by students, evaluation of laboratory work, diagnostic, formative and summative evaluation, and other aspects of the total evaluation process are sometimes misunderstood by teachers. Most teachers have received little formal training in evaluation and so their evaluation methods have traditionally tended to be formal, concentrating on quizzes and end-of-term tests.

As a result instruction and evaluation are thought of as separate entities. In addition, an adversarial relationship seems to exist between the evaluator and those being evaluated. This minimizes the evaluation's effectiveness and destroys one of the very reasons for doing it—the valid assessment of achievement, attitudes, skill development, and progress. Evaluation should be considered a vital part of instruction and inseparable from it. In this chapter, many illustrations will show the connections between instruction and evaluation.

■ Orientation of Instruction and Evaluation Toward Success

All instruction and evaluation in science classes should be oriented toward success rather than failure. Students respond favorably toward successful experiences whereas they are quickly turned off by repeated failures. This does not require a teacher to sacrifice her standards or "water down" her course work to a meaningless level. It simple recognizes that pupils function better when they have positive concepts about their own worth and class performance.

Therefore tasks should be provided that give the potential for successful accomplishment at some level for all students regardless of their academic abilities. In most cases final achievement is more closely related to one's rate of learning than it is to some questionable I.Q. level.

A dramatic example of the use of success oriented instruction and evaluation is given in an article entitled, "Dear Class, I Love You" by Harry Wong. Excerpts from this article are used to illustrate the main point.

No lesson lasts more than two or three days. The time factor is important because the students have a short attention span. More important, I recognize that the students need frequent successes, because successes are the basis for an improved self-concept. Thus, the first lesson is finished by the second day of school and returned on the third. And when it is, every student dies. They all look at me with shock and suspicion. You can read the 'you've-made-a-mistake; we're-a-class-of-dummies' look. They not only all have A's on their papers, they are praised for their work. They sit there dumbfounded by my praise; a kind word is a rarity in school. But they're happy, and while they're smiling, I slip them the next four pages. An inscrutable Oriental trick!

We live in a society that guarantees everything. The Bill of Rights guarantees us freedom of speech and the right to trial by jury. If we are dissatisfied with a purchase, we take it back to the store and get a refund or replacement. And with the replacement we may get a 90-day guarantee, a one-year guarantee or even a five-year warranty. In other words, we guarantee everything in our society—except for success in school. Not only do we not guarantee success in school, we believe in the failure system, because it is supposed to maintain some nebulous set of standards.

To a baker, the only relevant standard is a perfect loaf of bread. A mechanic only desires to repair each car perfectly. A secretary's goal is to type nothing but perfect letters. But the concept of designing a curriculum in which everyone succeeds is foreign, and even repugnant, in education. Contrary to popular belief, none of my administrators have ever questioned the high percentage of successful students in my classes. Rather, these questions have come from colleagues who suspect that my methods are designed to disgrace their techniques.

If I have succeeded with my students, it is because I believe that a person's self-concept is related to his school achievement. For this reason my entire curriculum is success oriented. There is a continuum of success, reinforced every two or three days. As early as the end of the first week, I have every student hooked on success. In fact, success is guaranteed.

As the successes reinforce each other, I see a definite change in my class. For instance, by the third week of school I no longer see despair and frustration, yet neither do I face a sea of bright smiles. Instead, I see faces that are deliberately holding back. Some thirty students are trying to act like cool cats. They know I will return the papers and follow it with words of praise. They have come to enjoy hearing these words, but they're not going to let on. I hold up my grade book and say, "Look, you've all been great. Everyone's not only turned in the assignments, you have gotten mostly A's and B's. You're a fantastic class and I love you all.[1]

■ The Nature of Evaluation

Evaluation involves the total assessment of students' learning. It includes evaluating their understanding of the process of science, subject matter competence and achievement, multiple talents, scientific attitudes, laboratory skills, and willingness to work. The progress of the students toward the objectives of the course and goals of the school as well as the effectiveness of instruction are considered. Good evaluation indicates the strengths and weaknesses of instruction. Once a teacher has made a thorough assessment, she has an indication of how to improve her teaching. Evaluation acts as feedback in the experimental process of teaching. A teacher must experiment if she is to progress and become more skilled. She must be willing to try new methods and new techniques, and by so doing evolve toward teaching mastery.

Science teachers should be experiment-oriented, not only in the laboratory but in their daily approaches to teaching. An experimental approach assumes collection of data to verify the success of the methods used. The data must come from the evaluation techniques. The better the evaluation instruments, the greater the information available to the teacher for improving her teaching.

There are three types of evaluation usually considered in the teaching area—diagnostic, formative, and summative. These three primary types differ mainly by their chronological position in the instruction sequence. *Diagnostic* evaluation normally precedes instruction but may be used under special circumstances to discover student learning problems. Diagnostic evaluation can provide information to teachers about the knowledge, attitudes, and skills of the students entering a course and can be used as a basis for individual remediation or special instruction.

Formative evaluation is carried on during the instructional period to provide feedback to students and teachers on how well the material is being taught and learned. Since teaching is a dynamic process, formative evaluation can provide useful information that teachers can use to modify instruction and can improve teaching effectiveness for individuals and groups.

The third kind of evaluation, *summative*, is the kind that is used most often by teachers and is primarily aimed toward providing student grades and reports of achievement. It is most frequently based upon cognitive gains and rarely takes into consideration other areas of the intellect.

Recent decades have given educators much information concerning areas of intellectual development, including the cognitive, psychomotor, and affective domains. The cognitive domain has been traditionally the main area of concern by most teachers. Achievement in the form of memorized information, concepts, problem-solving skills, and other aspects of information acquisition has been tested thoroughly and in many forms. The psychomotor and affective domains, however, have not been given the same thorough study. In later sections of this chapter, we will provide recommended procedures in each of the areas that broaden the concept of evaluation and provide increased total assessment information for teacher and student.

Evaluation is an ongoing process and shows evidence of change over the years. Rodney Doran has listed several predicted trends in measurement and evaluation of science instruction. These are given in Table 20.1.

■ The Use of Objectives in Evaluation

Well-stated behavioral objectives include within them statements of the performance expected and

TABLE 20–1

Predicted trends in measurement and evaluation of science instruction

From	To
1. Primarily group-administered tests	A variety of administrative formats including large groups, small groups, and individuals.
2. Primarily paper-and-pencil tests	A variety of test formats including pictorial and laboratory performance tests.
3. Primarily end-of-course summative assessment	A variety of pretest, diagnostic and formative types of measurements.
4. Primarily measurement of low-level cognitive outcomes	The inclusion of higher level cognitive outcomes (analysis, evaluation, critical thinking), as well as the measurement of affective (attitudes, interests, and values) and psychomotor outcomes.
5. Primarily norm-referenced achievement testing	The inclusion of more criterion-referenced assessment, mastery testing, and self and peer evaluation.
6. Primarily measurement of facts and principles of science	The inclusion of objectives related to the processes of science, the nature of science and the interrelationship of science, technology, and society.
7. Primarily measurement of student achievement	The inclusion of measuring the effects of programs, curricula, and teaching techniques.
8. Primarily teacher-made tests	The combined use of teacher-made tests, standardized tests, research instruments, and items from collections assembled by teachers, projects, and other sources.
9. Primarily concern with total test scores	Interest in sub-test performance, item difficulty and discrimination, all aided by mechanical and computerized facilities.
10. Primarily a one-dimensional format of evaluation (e.g., a numerical or letter grade)	A multidimensional system of reporting student progress with respect to such variables as concepts, processes, laboratory procedures, classroom discussion, and problem-solving skills.

Source: Rodney L. Doran, *Basic Measurement and Evaluation of Science Instruction* Washington, D.C., National Science Teachers Association, 1980, p. 13. Used with permission.

the level of achievement to be realized by the students.

Cognitive Domain

As an example of how to use behavioral objectives in the cognitive domain suitable for testing and evaluation purposes, consider the following statement: "The student should be able to state the Third Law of Motion in written or oral form when called upon to do so."

The Third Law of Motion states, "For every action there is an equal and opposite reaction." The evidence for the student's achievement of this objective would be to have the student verbally state in your presence or write for later inspection a correct statement of the Third Law of Motion.

Another example of a cognitive objective is, "The student should be able to describe how a cloud is formed." The evidence of achievement of this objective is either a verbal or written description of the processes involved in formation of a cloud, one which meets satisfactorily all the conditions expected by the teacher.

Cognitive behavioral objectives may be simple or complex, but should be stated in such a way that certain desired knowledge, thought processes, or thinking skills are demanded that meet the general objectives of the instruction. The evaluation of student achievement is simplified when such objectives are carefully formulated.

Psychomotor Domain

Psychomotor objectives are no less important than cognitive ones in science, although less attention has traditionally been paid to them. These objectives refer to certain manipulative skills that are vital to learning in science. Such skills as measuring, calibrating, constructing apparatus, using refined instruments, and many others are important, and as such they deserve the attention of teachers and students.

Psychomotor objectives may be stated similarly to cognitive ones as in the following example: "The student should be able, using a meter stick, to measure accurately the length, height and width of a prescribed object." Evidence for the achievement of this objective is a written record of the measurements obtained with the proper units associated. The degree of success in meeting this objective is an evaluative measure of the student's achievement of this psychomotor skill.

Another example would be, "The student should be able, following written reactions, to focus a laboratory microscope clearly on an object placed upon the microscope stage." Evidence of achieving this objective might be either a direct confirmation of the student's success by the teacher actually looking through the microscope or by having the student draw what he sees and presenting the product to the teacher. In either case, evaluation of the student's progress is provided directly. This represents the important role of behavioral objectives in the evaluation of instruction—progress can be directly observed.

Affective Domain

Affective objectives present a somewhat more difficult problem. These objectives represent legitimate expectations of students in secondary school science classes but until recently have received minimal attention in the overall consideration of teaching outcomes.

One can classify affective objectives in two forms—overt and covert. A sample statement of an overt behavioral objective is, "The student should be able to give evidence of supporting the argument of another student concerning a particular topic under discussion." Overt actions are those which are observable to the teacher or another person. A valid assessment of whether a given overt affective objective is achieved by the student depends upon some voluntary expression. Without this, it is uncertain whether the student is registering an actual behavioral change or is merely attempting to please the teacher for other reasons, such as obtaining a better grade.

The second type of affective objective, the co-vert, is even more difficult to assess. Covert objectives depend upon some form of voluntary self-expression by the student, for example, "The student will be able to give evidence of behavioral change by voluntarily self-reporting that he enjoys working with live animals in the laboratory." Evidence of the achievement of this objective would be obtained by an informal accounting of voluntary, self-reported statements by the student of this, or similar supporting evidence. As in the previous type, the validity of the assessment depends upon registering expressions through noncoercive means. One may go even further and state that any indication that the student is responding to some teacher directive or implied assignment may render the responses suspect.

Evaluating Objectives

Just as there are levels of objectives, there are also levels of testing. Much evaluation does not test for all of the important objectives in science. A teacher attempting to evaluate the quality of her instruction from a purely cognitive test may not discover how well she is teaching. The psychomotor and affective areas need to be considered to give complete feedback to the teacher so she can effectively modify her instructional techniques.

The first rule of test construction is to use your objectives and scientific principles as guides in devising your test. Students tend to learn in the way in which they are tested. If the emphasis is on memorization of facts, they will memorize facts to the satisfaction of the teacher. If the emphasis, however, is on the understanding of principles, development of process skills, creativity, other aspects of inquiry, or investigative types of teaching, these tests will bring forth those types of responses from the student. It is important for the teacher to consider whether the test emphasizes all of the important goals of the course. When tests are given, they should evaluate how well the students have attained these objectives, irrespective of whether they are student- or teacher-defined.

It is relatively easy to write objectives, but to evaluate their achievement is often difficult. Benjamin Bloom identified six levels of cognitive objectives: knowledge, comprehension, application, analysis, synthesis, and evaluation.[2] It follows, therefore, that questions should be devised to evaluate each of these levels. If you write good behavioral objectives and use them as guides for constructing your tests, they probably will provide better examinations than those prepared by teachers who do not.

One way to insure that your test follows your objectives and gives adequate attention to each of the areas desired is to devise a Table of Specifications, such as is shown in Table 20.2, a blueprint of a ninth-grade science examination. It indicates on the left-hand side the six levels of Bloom's taxonomy and across the top the various content or topic areas covered in the course. By using this table of specifications during instruction and noting the amount of time devoted to each of the respective areas and objective levels, and following the table carefully when making a test, (particularly of the summative variety), you will create a test that has better content validity than one that is put together hastily from memory or based upon the teacher's recollection of time spent on each area.

Although the Table of Specifications shown in Table 20.2 is designed to analyze the cognitive domain, it can be easily modified to include the affective domain by adding another category on the left entitled "Affective Domain."

Constructing and analyzing tests using this grid helps to insure your growth in writing tests that evaluate the higher levels of learning. Teachers who do not evaluate all their objectives or classify their test questions in some way similar to the preceding grid tend to evaluate for the lowest levels of Bloom's taxonomy. Research reported in 1960 found that the major emphasis in chemistry tests produced by teachers in four year high schools was on factual knowledge.[3] Application, analysis, and synthesis were virtually neglected.

■ Levels of Testing

The lowest rung on the ladder in the hierarchy of Bloom's taxonomy is the *knowledge* level. This emphasizes simple recall or recognition and represents the lowest level of learning, requiring only memo-

rization of information. Teaching mainly for recall is the lowest level of instruction, but teachers have often devoted excessive amounts of time to this because recall questions are simple to write. A rule of thumb is that no more than 20 percent of any test should consist of simple recall questions.

The next level is the level of *comprehension*. It is sometimes considered the first level of understanding. Students may know something about a topic, be able to follow a process, or know how to write an equation without understanding it fully. Comprehension questions require the student to (1) interpret a statement, (2) translate or describe a process or idea in their own words, (3) extrapolate, i.e., go beyond the data, or (4) interpolate, i.e., supply intermediate information. Comprehension questions are not difficult to write but require some thought on the part of the teacher to be worded in a form that demands a higher level of thinking than simple memorization.

The third level is *application*, which can best be described by comparing it with comprehension. A comprehension problem requires that the student know an abstraction well enough to correctly demonstrate its use when specifically asked to do so. Application, on the other hand, requires a step beyond this. Given a new problem, the student can apply the appropriate abstraction without having to be shown how to use it in that situation. In comprehension, the student shows that he can use the abstraction when its use is specified. In application, the student shows that he can spontaneously use the abstraction correctly.

The fourth level of Bloom's taxonomy is *analysis*. It is related to both comprehension and evaluation. Analysis emphasizes breaking down the material into its constituent parts and detecting the relationships of these parts in the organization. It is

TABLE 20–2
Blueprint of grade nine science examination, 1965

Objectives	Topic or Content Area									Emphasis %
	Matter and Energy Force, Work & Power	*Mechanics*		*Chemical Reactions*	*Heat*	*Light*	*Transportation*	*Measurement**	*Science as Inquiry**	
		Machines	*Fluids*							
1. Knowledge										
2. Comprehension										
3. Application										
4, 5, and 6— Analysis, Synthesis and Evaluation										
Emphasis %										

*Note: The topics "Measurement" and "Science as Inquiry" cut across Content Areas. The latter category will be used for items that involve more than one content area or that involve inquiry as, for example, Items 6 to 10 under Analysis.
Source: "Summary Description of Grade Nine Science Objectives and Test Items, Revised Edition," The High School Entrance Examination Board, Department of Education, Edmonton, Alberta, March, 1965. Reprinted with permission.

also sometimes directed at the techniques or devices used to convey a meaning or establish a conclusion.

The fifth level, *synthesis*, involves putting together elements and parts to elucidate a previously poorly defined pattern or structure. This procedure usually involves combining previous experience with new material, constructing a more or less well integrated whole. It is a creative act. This category is in the cognitive domain and may not always involve free creative expression since the student is usually expected to work within the limits set by the particular problem, materials, or methodological framework.

The highest level of the taxonomy is *evaluation*. This is the process of judging the extent to which ideas, solutions, methods, and materials satisfy criteria. It also involves using criteria as standards for appraising the extent to which particular items are accurate, effective, economical, or satisfying. Such judgments may be either quantitative or qualitative and the criteria may be determined by the student or may be provided.

■ Quantitative Terms in Tests

All sciences use mathematics to ensure more accurate communication. Mathematics brings exactness to science where vagueness once flourished. When we describe phenomena, we may do so by use of dichotomous or metrical terms. A dichotomous explanation is of the "either-or" type: Something is tall (or short), small (or large), heavy (or light). Science strives to escape from such explanations because they are ambiguous; what may be tall to one person may be short to another. Scientific explanations are usually given in metric terms. Instead of saying a person is tall, a scientist says he is 1.8 meters tall. Instead of stating, "Place some glucose in water," he is more likely to say, "Place 10 grams of glucose in 100 cm³ of water." The use of quantitative, metric terms ensures exactness.

Exactness in science is important for ensuring better communication and for replicating research. It is the nature of the scientific enterprise to have one scientist check the results of another, which would be impossible without the use of exact metric terms. The following examples underline the obviousness of this statement.

A nonquantitative explanation: "A small amount of penicillin was injected into a human organism suffering from a bacterial infection. The infection was cured in a short time."

A quantitative explanation: "Sixty subjects and ten control patients infected with streptococcus were administered 500,000 units of penicillin. On the third day, forty of the patients no longer evidenced the infection in the nasalpharyngeal passages."

The importance of quantitative terms can be easily pointed out to a class by holding up an eraser and having them describe it so completely that it could be produced by someone who had never seen one. Students will often write a description without giving exact dimensions. An instructor can then discuss the necessity of giving the dimensions, thereby emphasizing the place of mathematics in science. There are other uses of mathematics in science aside from those discussed here, but the important points are that mathematics become a part of each examination and that students gain insight into association with science.

Using Graphs in Testing

One quantitative tool used to a considerable extent in science is graphing. Graphing has the following advantages: (1) it gives a tremendous amount of information in a small space (try to describe verbally all the information depicted by a curved line on a graph and this point immediately becomes apparent); (2) it helps the viewer to quickly see relationships which are not as apparent when one looks at a set of numbers; and (3) a pictorial representation of data is more easily retained by students than are other forms of data. Below are examples of graphing exercises used in secondary science.

Graph Interpretation

Exercise 1. The following graph represents data collected on *E. coli* bacteria in the laboratory. *E. coli* is found internally in a symbiotic relationship with man.

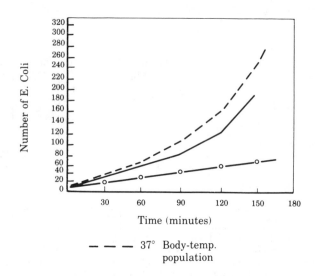

– – – 37° Body-temp. population

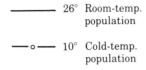

——— 26° Room-temp. population

—o— 10° Cold-temp. population

1. From the data given in the graph, what are your conclusions about the effect of temperature on *E. coli* population?
2. At 375°C, approximately how long does it take for *E. coli* to double its population? at 10°C?
3. Why do you think *E. coli* is successful in its relationship with man?
4. What would be the approximate population of *E. coli* in four hours at 37°C? at 26°C?
5. Each population is in 100 ml of nutrient. What could you predict about the eventual curve of bacteria populations at 37°C? at 10°C?
6. Which of the three populations will reach its maximum growth development first? Why?

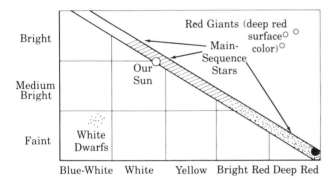

Exercise 2.
1. The graph preceding indicates that which of the following is not true?
   A. The sun is an exceptional star.
   B. The sun is a medium bright star.
   C. The sun is between yellow and white in color.
   D. The sun will some day become a red giant star.
2. Which of the following is true of the information found in the graph?
   A. Red giant stars are faint.
   B. The sun is a main sequence star.
   C. White dwarf stars are brighter than red giants.
   D. Deep red stars and red giant stars have the same weight.

Exercise 3. A flask of sterile beef broth was inoculated with a single species of bacteria. The flask was not sealed; thus, mold spores were able to enter. The growth patterns for the bacteria and mold are shown here in a graph.

Using the graph, answer the following questions:

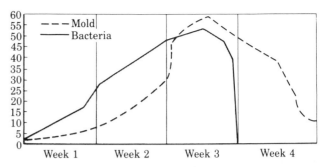

1. Why do you think the bacteria flourished at first and then all died by the end of the third week?
2. Why do you think the mold population decreased so rapidly during the fourth week?
3. Notice the shape of the growth curve for the mold during the first two and one-half weeks. What important concept of growth rate does this illustrate?

Exercise 4. Answer the following questions in relation to conclusions that can be drawn from the graphs. Before being tested for germination, corn seeds represented in Graph A were soaked 0 hours, in Graph B, 24 hours, and in Graph C, 72 hours.

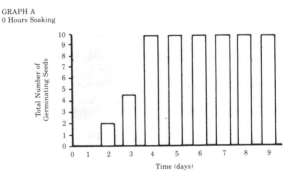

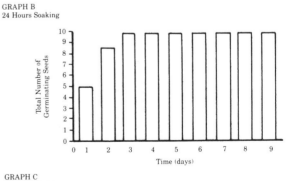

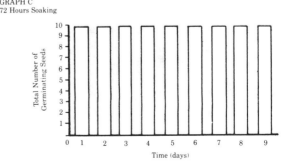

1. Farmer Brown wants to plant corn seeds and have them germinate as soon as possible. From the graphs, how long would you advise him to soak the seeds prior to planting? (a) 0 hours, (b) 24 hours, (c) 72 hours.
2. Which of the graphs shows maximum germination after three days? (a) Graph A, (b) Graph B, (c) Graph C.
3. How many days does it take for 50 percent germination of seeds soaked for 24 hours? (a) 1 day, (b) 2 days, (c) 4 days, (d) 10 days.
4. Moisture applied to seeds for 24 hours before planting has a greater effect on seed germination than soaking them: (a) 0 hours, (b) 36 hours, (c) 72 hours, (d) 100 hours.
5. In the graphs, which group of seeds would be considered the control? (a) That in Graph A, (b) That in Graph B, (c) That in Graph C.

Graphing Data

Another way to determine students' understanding of graphing is to have them complete a graph. Exercises such as the ones here can be used for regular assignments or homework.

Exercise 1. The following graph applies to the red-fox population on an island which is ten miles long and twenty miles wide. It is located in the center of a very large lake in Canada. This island supports several species of animals; however, detailed population studies have been conducted only on the fox population. These population studies began in 1958 and continued for six full years.

During part of the year, October to May, the lake is frozen, allowing a fluctuation in the fox population due to immigration and emigration across the ice. The breeding population for each year was determined in late May, as soon as the lake thawed. The young are born early in June and are counted in early July.

Total population counts were continued for six full years. These counts were always made in late September by elaborate trapping methods. Immigration and emigration counts were determined by tagging the foxes as they were trapped and counted.

In September of 1958 the total population of foxes was 27. In September of 1959 it was 31. Data compiled for each one-year period from September 1959 to September 1964 appear in the table in Exercise 2.

Exercise 2. From the data below, compute the total population for each year and complete the following questions:

	9/59– 9/60	9/60– 9/61	9/61– 9/62	9/62– 9/63	9/63– 9/64
Breeding population	20	14	8	22	41
Natality	24	17	16	26	59
Mortality	11	16	4	6	43
Immigration	1	0	7	16	3
Emigration	9	5	3	6	15
TOTALS	25	10	24	52	45

1. Plot your computed populations on the graph for each year and then complete the graph by drawing the line from point to point.
2. What was the density of foxes in September of 1960?
3. From September 1961 to September 1963, there is an increase in population; however, you notice that there is a very high rate of mortality during the same period of time. Can you offer a valid conclusion about this high mortality rate? What would the graph probably look like if the population studies had been continued for ten more years?

Drawing Graphs

Another way to test for understanding of graphs is to require the students to devise a graph. For example, students could be given these instructions: "Graph the rate expansion of copper for temperatures 10°C to 100°C" or "Draw a graph showing the rate of absorption of the red wavelengths of light in water."

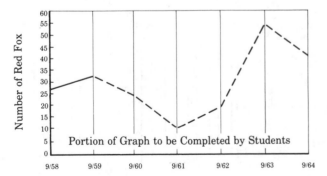

=========================== REFLECTING ON SCIENCE TEACHING ===========================
Evaluating Graphs

1. Devise three questions involving understanding of graphing.
2. What are the steps you should take in writing a question requiring application of knowlege? Write three examples of this type of question.
3. Write two questions requiring a student to use his creative ability.

■ General Considerations in Test Construction

This section contains some suggestions for constructing tests. They are not exhaustive but they are fundamental.

True-False Tests

If the examination is limited to true or false questions, statistics show that 75 or more items are necessary to overcome the guessing factor. On a 100-question true-or-false test, students should be able to answer about 50 questions correctly merely by guessing. Some instructions eliminate this problem by subtracting the number of wrong answers from the number of right ones to determine the score; they penalize for guessing. This procedure is not recommended because students usually think the instructor is using this technique maliciously. It is also undesirable because the student is penalized for guessing; in science we wish to have students make hypotheses, that is, good guesses.

Avoid overbalancing the test with too many true or too many false questions. Try to make them fairly even in number, so that a student who knows a little about the material cannot get a high score simply by assuming that more questions are true (or false).

Avoid using statements that might trick students.
Do not use the same language as in the text or students will tend to memorize.
Do not use double negatives in a statement.
Avoid ambiguous statements. For example, do not write, "Erosion is prevented by seeding."
Avoid using complex sentences in your statements.
Do not use qualitative language if you can possibly avoid it. Do not write, for example, "Good corn grows at a slower rate than hybird corn," or "The better metals conduct electricity faster."
Arrange your statements in groups of ten to twenty. This procedure relieves excessive tension for students.

Put answer blocks on one margin so that they can be easily checked using a key.

Multiple-Choice Tests

A multiple-choice test is composed of items having more than three responses. If there are not at least four possible responses to each question, a correction formula should be used. A multiple-choice test differs from a multiple-response test in that only one answer is correct for each question in the first type of test.

In a multiple-choice test, make all responses plausible.
All answers should be grammatically consistent.
Try to keep all responses about the same length.
Randomize the correct answers so that there is no pattern in the examination. Students often look for a pattern.
Remember that the correct response often can be determined by a process of elimination as well as by knowing the correct answer. Try to prevent this in phrasing the answers.
Present first the term or concept you wish to test for.
Test for the higher levels of understanding as much as possible.
Require a simple method for the response. Provide short lines for the answers along one margin of a page so they can be easily keyed.
Group your items in sections. This system makes it easy to refer to various sections of the test and helps break the monotony in taking the test.
Group together all questions with the same number of choices.

Completion and Matching Tests

Since completion and matching tests usually emphasize recall and are often verbally tricky, they should be minimized.

If matching questions are used, they should be grouped. When there are more than fifteen matching items in a group, the test becomes cumbersome.

Number your questions and use letters for your answers, or the reverse, but be consistent.

Have more matching choices than questions to minimize obtaining answers by elimination.

Although matching tests have traditionally stressed simple recall, they can be used to test for recognition or application principles. Three sample matching questions follow:

_____ 1. A machine which would require the least amount of friction to move it twenty feet.

_____ 2. A machine which could best be used to pry open a box.

_____ 3. Which of the listed devices is made up of the greatest number of simple machines?

A. Pliers
B. Wheelbarrow
C. Ice tongs
D. Seesaw
E. Doorknob
F. Pencil sharpener
G. Saw

Self-Tests

A self-test is similar to any other test in its construction but is taken by the student mainly as a learning device. It usually has questions on one side of a page and the answers on the other. The student takes the test, then turns the page and checks his answers. The instructor can use the completed tests as a means of stimulating discussion.

Teachers usually set up self-tests on ditto masters and run off enough copies for their students. A suggested format is shown in Figure 20.1. The back page should contain a detailed explanation for each answer so that students learn from the test. The student folds under the answers on the right side of his page. His answers are then next to the correct answers and explanations on the left margin of the back page making it easy to correct the test.

Problem Tests

This kind of test presents a problem and asks the students to work on it. It is similar to an invitation to inquiry except that it is done by an individual student. The test usually contains a series of questions which the students must answer to solve the problem. A problem test can be constructed with relative ease if it is based on a problem that has actually confronted a scientist. These problems can be easily obtained from a scientific journal. Give the students information about the problem and have them devise their own hypotheses, research designs, or methods of collecting and recording data. A problem test can best be used to acquaint students with scientific processes. The tests may have an answer sheet similar to that for a self-test or they may be used to stimulate discussion. Open-ended scientific problems are preferable for this kind of test.

Some examples of problems that might be used in constructing a test of this nature are:

1. How would you reduce the amount of pollution from a smoke stack?
2. A citizen thought the local river was polluted; how could he find out? What experiments could he do?
3. A scientist thought fungus might produce a chemical that inhibits the growth of bacteria. What kind of experiments must he conduct to verify his hypothesis?
4. What are some general considerations to be kept in mind when making a true-false, a multiple-choice, and a completion test?
5. Prepare a picture or problem test.

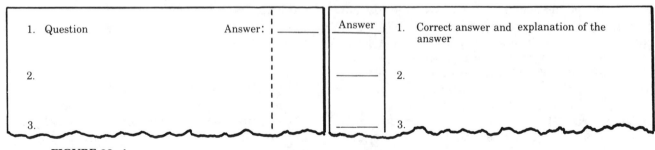

FIGURE 20–1
Format for self-test

Diagrams or Picture Types of Tests

Most science tests evaluate more for reading than they do for science. Many students understand the science principles but because they have verbal difficulties, such as reading and interpreting what they have read, they do poorly on tests. Studies indicate that many students do significantly better on tests consisting mainly of pictures and requiring them only to check the correct responses.[4] The BSCS, in preparing a special course in biology for the mentally retarded, found when evaluating achievement by using 35-mm slides that both the teachers and specialists were amazed at how well the students did.[5]

Student Correction of Tests

Student correction of tests can be done in several ways. A student can act as an aide using a key prepared by the instructor. An instructor can pass the tests to students at random, read the answers to the class, and have them correct and compute scores. Students may be given a key after they have taken the test; they then correct their own tests. For wrong answers, they should write on the back of the test or on a separate paper an explanation for their incorrect responses. These explanations can be analyzed to determine the questions that should be modified or eliminated in future testing.

■ Self-Evaluation

One of the important values of instructional evaluation is that it provides feedback to students. Included in this aspect should be the component of student self-evaluation with respect not only to her feelings and concerns regarding the class but also concerning her understanding of her own progress in the course. One of the objectives for which we strive in education is to teach students to establish aims and objectives for themselves and then carry out the necessary procedures to achieve these aims or objectives. Self-evaluation is a natural and necessary part of this process, and students should be

encouraged to acquire the habit early. All individuals from time to time look introspectively upon their own progress and achievement; it is natural that such opportunities ought to be provided in the classroom with respect to their instruction as well.

Research by Hofwolt, Tillery, Duel, and others during the 1950s and 1960s has established that students can do a reliable and valid job of evaluating themselves.[6-8] However, student self-evaluation and the importance of giving students opportunities to make self-judgments about their gains during the course of instruction have only recently been emphasized.

To be effective in providing self-evaluation opportunities for students in the classsroom, teachers must be aware of certain guidelines to promote best results:

1. Students must know what the class objectives are and how they are to be met.
2. Students must be able to relate to specific tasks, e.g., discussions, class projects, tests, attendance, book reports, etc.
3. Students should have repeated practice in evaluating themselves.
4. A Likert scale or some other form of continuum should be used instead of a letter grade.
5. Ratings on the continuum should be explained and clarified.
6. Students should know the purpose for which the evaluation is to be used.
7. The teacher has the final responsibility for evaluation. Student self-evaluation can assist in this task.
8. There must be good rapport and a trusting atmosphere.
9. The teacher should be knowledgeable about the students' attitudes toward the class.
10. Self-evaluation should not be used in conjunction with other traditional evaluations.
11. Substantive, not trivial, questions should be assessed.
12. A variety of self-evaluation methods should be used, e.g., checklists, semantic differential scales, interviews, picture symbols, etc.
13. A low pressure, nonthreatening situation should prevail.

=== **REFLECTING ON SCIENCE TEACHING** ===
Self-Evaluation Inventories

1. Why would you want to use a self-evaluation inventory in class?
2. Prepare a self-evaluation inventory for a unit.

14. Results on the self-evaluation should be kept confidential.
15. The teacher should provide for administration of the self-evaluation procedure on suitable days, e.g., avoiding Mondays and Fridays.
16. The teacher should consider the individuals and class temperament on the day of self-evaluation.
17. The student should be able to see some value in the self-evaluation for his own benefit or improvement.
18. Skill in self-evaluation should be developed over a period of time, not in a one-time effort.
19. Research shows a satisfactorily high correlation between self-evaluation ratings and teacher grading scores.
20. Self-evaluation ratings should not be used directly for grading.

■ Evaluation and the Learning Cycle

In Chapter 18, you read about a modification of the Learning Cycle which includes a fourth phase, that of evaluation. At some point in the learning cycle, it is important to provide feedback to students concerning their understanding of concepts and process skills. The results of the evaluation should provide the teacher with information about the students' understandings and competencies in the processes of gathering information in investigative lessons.

Among the techniques of evaluation that can be used in the fourth phase of the Learning Cycle are self-evaluation, peer evaluation, quizzes, tests, and other formal methods. In addition, simple techniques of asking questions, initiating discussions, and observing classroom and laboratory behaviors are also effective means of evaluation in this phase. Evaluation using all of these techniques should focus on giving feedback to the students about their conceptual understandings and abilities to use skills and processes of science. Formal evaluations for the purpose of giving grades should be given late in the learning cycle after ample opportunities have been afforded to explore, develop concepts, apply information, formulate new problems, and evaluate one's own progress.

Some specific suggestions for the evaluation phase of the learning cycle are:

1. Test for reasoning as well as content memorization.
2. Ask students to justify their answers.
3. Help students who are reasoning at lower levels to employ higher level reasoning skills such as analysis, synthesis, and evaluation.
4. Devise ways of evaluating skill and process development as well as cognitive accomplishments.

In general science, the teacher might arrange for a laboratory period in which the students can use rulers, calipers, graduated cylinders, and balances to determine the volumes and masses of objects of widely differing shapes and various materials for plotting graphs of volume vs. mass. Using a Science Activity Evaluation Checklist such as is described later in this chapter would enable the teacher to evaluate the skill and process achievement level of the students.

In earth science, the teacher might arrange for the class members to operate a small weather station with which they are able to gather data on temperature, pressure, humidity, and wind information for a period of time. Skills of graphing could be developed and evaluated during this time, as well as informal assessments of concept understandings achieved by the students.

In biology, a museum trip might be arranged where students are able to select exhibits that enable them to observe fossils, study geologic history, look for relationships between climatic changes and changes in populations of organisms. Another evaluative activity could involve providing students with chalk and meter sticks, along with a list of important events in geologic and archeological time, for the purpose of constructing a time line indicating the relative occurrence of various historical events. Observation of student performance, accomplishment of specific tasks or process skills, and informal assessments of concept understanding could take place at this time. The basic plan is to give students an opportunity to perform rather than simply to regurgitate information on some type of paper and pencil test.

In physics, students could engage in a laboratory experiment in which they used air tracks, springs, weights, timing tapes, flexible ramps, Polaroid cameras, strobe lights and stop watches to observe accelerated motion under various conditions. These activities provide perfect opportunities to evaluate both skill development and understanding of concepts in an informal setting.

As can be seen, the evaluation phase of the learning cycle is an important aspect of this learning and teaching strategy. Not only is it important for student assessment, but also to provide guidance and feedback to the students while they are in the process of learning new concepts and developing new skills of learning. An additional bonus in this type of evaluation is that it largely removes the threat and intimidation often experienced by students faced with the

======   REFLECTING ON SCIENCE TEACHING   ======

Evaluating Laboratory Work

1. How would you evaluate laboratory work?
2. Design five questions that test mainly for the science process.

---

prospects of being evaluated, especially if such evaluations culminate in a grade with all the usual connotations that grades bring to the foreground.

■ Evaluation of Laboratory Work

Broad concepts of evaluation include giving attention to all of the activities in which students are engaged during their secondary-school years. With increasing time and emphasis devoted to laboratory work, it becomes necessary to devise suitable methods for evaluating this activity. As with all evaluation, the goals of the activity or teaching method must be identified before the actual procedures to be used in evaluation are determined. For laboratory work, a suggested list of goals is:

1. To develop skills in problem-solving through identification of problems, collection and interpretation of data, and drawing conclusions
2. To develop skills in manipulating laboratory apparatus
3. To establish systematic habits of record keeping
4. To develop scientific attitudes
5. To learn scientific methods for solving problems
6. To develop self-reliance and dependability
7. To discover unexplored avenues of interest and investigation
8. To promote enthusiasm for the subject of science

Specific activities in which students are usually involved in laboratory work include:

1. Planning an experiment and forming hypotheses
2. Planning an excursion for collecting purposes
3. Setting up apparatus
4. Constructing materials and apparatus
5. Observing natural phenomena
6. Observing a process in an indoor laboratory
7. Searching for authoritative documentary information on the topic
8. Gathering and recording data
9. Collecting specimens
10. Classifying and organizing materials
11. Modifying equipment
12. Reading instruments
13. Calibrating apparatus
14. Drawing charts and graphs
15. Analyzing data
16. Drawing conclusions from the data
17. Writing a report of the experiment
18. Describing and explaining an experiment to someone else
19. Identifying further problems for study
20. Dismantling, cleaning, storing, and repairing apparatus

These activities and the general results of laboratory work may be evaluated in several ways, such as practical tests, use of unknowns, achievement tests, direct observation of laboratory techniques, written reports, individual conferences, and group conferences. (For an example of such evaluation, see the "Teaching Science Activity: Evaluating Laboratory Work," on p. 471-472.)

Practical Laboratory Tests

In a practical test, a student may be directed to perform a certain laboratory task. The teacher may observe the techniques used, the correctness of procedures, and the results obtained. Procedures such as identification of unknown chemicals, a common practice in qualitative analysis in chemistry, might be extended to earth sciences, biology, and physics. Achievement tests, designed to assess understanding of course content, are an important evaluative technique for laboratory work because of the concern that correct knowledge be obtained through laboratory methods. Pure recognition and recall tests are not usually suitable forms for achievement tests of laboratory experience. Tests that depend on accurate observation, recognition of pertinent data, and ability to reason logically are more suitable for measuring results of laboratory work.

Laboratory work involving the testing of materials, determining unknowns, recognizing and classifying organisms, and outlining experimental procedures is valuable. The problem with practical laboratory examinations is that they take a great deal of time to set up. Student laboratory assistants or one or two A students can be very helpful in setting up the examination before or after school.

Laboratory Reports

The written report, a frequently used method of evaluating progress and understanding in the laboratory, must be scrutinized. Too often the written report becomes a stereotyped form that loses its value as an instrument of evaluation. Each student is required to use a standard form that leaves little opportunity for creativity and flexibility.

The following characteristics of a good experiment report point out the essential items required yet leave room for initiative and creativity on the part of the student. In this type of report, the student begins with a blank sheet of paper. As he writes, he keeps the following criteria in mind:

1. The reader can tell exactly what the student is trying to determine.
2. The reader can "see" the procedure the student is using to arrive at an answer to the problem. The description is clear, concise, and complete.
3. The data collected are well organized and easily understood.
4. All measurements are shown with their proper units.
5. Diagrams, if used, are clear and carefully labeled. Diagrams are useful only for making the experiment clearer to the reader.
6. Graphs, if used, are titled, labeled, and neatly drawn. The purpose of a graph is to show relationships between data obtained, so that conclusions may be drawn.
7. Conclusions should answer the problem, using the data obtained in the experiment.
8. The report should help the student, in reviewing the course, to recall exactly what the experiment was about and what conclusions he reached.
9. The main criterion for evaluation of this experiment report is: Is this report written clearly enough that an uninformed person could read it, know exactly what was being attempted, how it was done, and what conclusions were reached, and if necessary, could he duplicate the experiment himself, using this report alone as a guide?

Recording Student Performance

A convenient form for recording student performance of activities associated with laboratory work is shown in Figure 20.2. It should be used as a sampling technique rather than as a daily record form, which would be too time-consuming for large classes. Students' names are written in on the diagonal lines above the chart. In the cells of the chart, evaluations are recorded (0 = low; 5 = high).

Occasionally the laboratory work might be scrutinized carefully. At other times it might be skimmed. The form could be referred to at the end of the quarter or semester as an aid in determining grades for the laboratory aspect of science classes.

■ Evaluation of Mastery Learning

Mastery learning is an area of instructional strategy that relates to the processes of evaluation. It refers to the student's mastery of certain prescribed objectives at identified levels.

In the 1950s a series of studies indicated that in the United States, the difference between the highest and lowest achievement means obtained by students in schools across the nation was approximately one standard deviation. This implies that in some states it required 12 years of schooling to attain the same level and achievement scores as required only 8 years in other states. The implications of this led a number of researchers to consider the ideas of mastery learning. The first of these was John B. Carroll of Harvard University, who in 1960 developed a model using the element of time as the central instructional variable in the learning process. It was his premise that, given sufficient time and perseverance to complete the task, students should be able to reach a desired criterion level of achievement. While rates of learning would vary from student to student, the final outcome would be the same. Carroll identified five factors that influence learning: (1) aptitude, (2) ability to understand instruction, (3) quality of instruction, (4) time allowed for learning, and (5) perseverance.

In 1974, Benjamin Bloom developed a plan for mastery learning based on the findings of Carroll. He theorized that under favorable conditions 95 percent of the students in our schools should be capable of attaining the level of achievement now reached by only the top 20 percent. Bloom criticized present educational evaluation methods when he warned that one of the most destructive effects of modern education is basing students' performance standards on the traditional distribution of grades based upon the normal curve. The result, he stated, is that only a small proportion of students are provided with a successful educational experience. He also stated that efforts in education can be judged unsuccessful to the extent that student achievement is distributed normally. This tells us that practically all students have the ability to learn what we propose to teach them in the secondary schools. The difference lies in the amount of time it takes and in the difficulty in accommodating these varied rates of learning within the traditional time structure of our school day.

Bloom has observed that the initial work done on mastery learning was in subjects in which there are few prerequisites, such as algebra and science. When subjects rely heavily on previous course learning, it is unlikely that many students will attain mastery within a normal course time schedule. Science is one of those areas in which the mastery learning concept can be used favorably. Science content areas meet the requirements of being both closed and sequential. This means that they require a minimum of prior learning, are sequentially learned, emphasize convergent thinking, and are closed insofar as they possess a finite set of ideas and cognitive behaviors upon which teachers can usually agree.

Bloom has defined five provisions that the instructor in a mastery learning class must fulfill successfully to be effective:

1. The students must be informed of the course expectations, usually through the use of learning objectives.
2. Standards for mastery are set in advance and grades are assigned in terms of performance.
3. Short diagnostic tests, called formative tests, are used for each unit.
4. Additional learning to help students reach the criterion level is prescribed at appropriate points.
5. Additional learning time is provided for students needing it.[9]

Bloom is critical of ideas of competition that are sometimes used as justification for the traditional evaluation system and "preparation for life." He cautions that much learning and development may be destroyed if competition is the primary basis for motivation. Instead students should be given a performance standard and grades denoting success should be awarded to all who attain the criterion level. In the past we have usually based the mastery level standard upon what has historically been A and B achievement levels in our classes. Typically, this refers to mastery of 75-85 percent of the tasks required in a particular series of objectives.

The most important elements in Bloom's mastery learning strategies are the feedback/correction procedures, which are a product of formative testing. Formative tests are given periodically throughout the instruction and are used to provide feedback to the students as well as to the teachers. They are not graded, and students may repeat the tests enough times to reach the mastery level. The rationale for this is that patterns for learning should be structured as part of a cyclic process whereby students can test their knowledge and then be given feedback necessary to direct their learning efforts in their attempt to master the subject.

Traditional methods of giving a summative test at the end of the chapter do not serve the needs of students for learning because they are not apprised of the results and no attempt is made to relearn the material that was missed. Summative tests measure only achievement and fail to identify the areas of weakness. We are forced to give grades in most school systems, and summative tests should be limited to that purpose, as quantitative adjuncts to a more holistic student evaluation.

One way to look at mastery teaching is to consider that a course consists of two types of concepts, one type that outlines the core objectives of the subject and represents the minimal expectations required of all, and another that outlines noncore objectives that go beyond the minimal requirements. Bloom maintains that spending extra time within the same calendar period to reach the same level of achievement as classmates gives the student a feeling that she is doing well. This is a reasonable expectation, as long as the time required is not inordinately long so that students begin to experience frustration and decreased motivation for school.

In summary, it has been found that mastery learning can be implemented with practically any course content. The major constraint is the time and the dedication necessary to specify the learning outcomes and to develop the criterion-referenced measures to assess achievement. The teacher is faced with the task of refining test items and objectives and developing new materials as situations change.

Mastery-based learning is not an educational panacea. It demands an equal and perhaps greater amount of time on the part of the teacher and the learner than traditional classwork. However, studies show that attitudes remain generally positive, achievement levels increase, and enthusiasm for the learning process does not diminish. These are substantial and notable gains to experience in a learning process in our school systems.

■ Using Science Tests with Different Culture Groups

Problems in interpreting and using tests frequently occur in classes in which pupils of different cultural backgrounds are present. The results of such tests are usually suspect when there are wide differences in

SCIENCE ACTIVITY EVALUATION CHECKLIST

Class_____ Unit_____ Date_____ File_____

Objectives: Student should be able to:

a.

b.

c.

(student's name)

Affective														
Values														
Cooperation, sharing														
Respect for materials														
Respect for peers, acceptance of ideas														
Neatness and organization														
Efficiency in using time														
Interest Curiosity														
Active participation														
Enthusiasm														
Attitudes Scientific														
Scholarly														
Psychomotor														
Manipulation and Articulation Setting up apparatus														
Dismantling and storing apparatus														
Uses measuring instruments properly														
Drawing illustrations														
Naturalization Dexterity, hand-eye coordination														
Expression, dramatization														

FIGURE 20–2
Form for evaluating performance in the laboratory

home environments, which may not provide opportunities to learn the types of tasks included on the tests. These differences may include children from disadvantaged homes, those who are not highly motivated by school work, those children with weak reading skills, or in families in which English is a second language, and those children with emotional problems.

In addition, there are differences in motivation, attitude toward testing, competitiveness, rates of reading, writing, and thinking, practice in test taking, and variations in opportunities to learn the skills and knowledges being tested.

Some of the techniques a science teacher can use to minimize the differences in test results because of the cultural or psychological differences mentioned above are as follows:

1. Nonverbal tests can be prepared, using diagrams and pictures familiar to the various culture

SCIENCE ACTIVITY EVALUATION CHECKLIST
Continued

Cognitive

Knowledge

Use of correct terminology

Evidence of recall and recognition

Understanding symbols

Understanding purpose

Comprehension
Understanding symbols

Understanding diagrams

Application
Predicting results

Comparing and contrasting properties

Graphing

Analysis
Interpreting graphs

Problem-solving

Synthesis and evaluation
Forming judgments

Drawing conclusions

Laboratory reports (e.g., neatness, organization)

Verbal reports (e.g., post-laboratory discussions)

Process Skills

Organizes work

Initiates Actions

Records data properly

Comments:

FIGURE 20–2
Continued

groups being tested. In the case of language difficulties, use of translations might be considered.

2. Attempts can be made to use items that are intrinsically interesting to the students, to encourage motivation. Selection of items that have relevance to the experiences of the test takers will increase the likelihood of success.

3. Time is made less of a factor, to provide less emphasis on speed as an important condition for success on the test.

4. Test procedures are kept simple and clear instructions are given.

5. The content of the test is based on intellectual skills and knowledge that is familiar to the group being tested. Of course, this is good advice in the preparation of tests for students at any time.

Some examples of types of test items that minimize verbal responses are those that require understanding of a series, that is, selection of the item that comes next in a series; those of classification where it is necessary to select the item that does not belong with the others; those which use matrices where the pupil is required to select the item that completes a matrix; and those with conditions where one is to match the conditions in a sample design with those of several alternative designs.[10]

■ General Guidelines for Using Tests

When you are confronted with the prospect of preparing a test, there are several methods that will contribute to appropriate, effective evaluation. Some guidelines for testing are listed here.

1. Use tests humanely as learning and diagnostic devices. Give students opportunities to demonstrate that they have learned what they missed on a test; adjust the grade.
2. Never use a test as a punishment.
3. Minimize the use of completion and matching questions.
4. Use tests or self-evaluational inventories to evaluate all of your behavioral objectives, including the science processes and attitudes.
5. Spend time with each student going over the questions he missed. This may be done while the class is involved in laboratory work.
6. Remember that tests are only a sample of what has been learned and probably not a very good one. Therefore, they should not be used as the only means of evaluation. Take into consideration all the things students have done in class to develop their multitalents.
7. Test for all levels of Bloom's Taxonomy and use a test analysis grid to see that this is done.
8. Ask questions to determine how students feel about the material being used.
9. Place the easier questions at the beginning of the test so students gain confidence and minimize their frustration and nervousness.
10. Consider the time factor. How long will it take students to complete the test? Some students will finish much sooner than others. What will you do with them? If you do not have some work outlined, they are likely to present discipline problems.
11. Design the test to be easily scored. Leave a space for all the answers on one margin.
12. Rather than having the students write on the test, have them place their responses on an answer sheet. This procedure ensures ease of recording and saves paper since the test may be used for more than one class.

Encourage honesty. Remove the temptation to copy by spreading students out or by making two versions of the same test and alternating them when you pass out the tests. You may wish to try the honor system; some instructors in high school have used this with success. Caution students as soon as you see anyone cheating. It is usually better not to mention the name of the culprit at the first infraction. You might just say, "I see cheating" or "Some people

are looking at other students' papers." If you really stress honesty in the first tests your task of trying to prevent dishonesty will be lessened during the rest of the term. Set a pattern of honesty immediately in your classes. Be present while students take tests and discipline a pupil if he is guilty of continued dishonesty.

■ Alternatives to Traditional Grading

The evaluating process in itself is neither negative nor positive. Its function depends on how the instructor uses it. He can use it to diagnose his teaching and student achievement or to compare one student with another.

Unfortunately, most teachers use testing to obtain a class range in which some students are identified as high and others as low as determined by achievement scores. These scores are then used to grade students. Increasingly, educators are questioning the desirability of using tests for this purpose and even if grading should be used. They argue that grading establishes a competition system which is bound to depreciate and demean the self-concepts of many students. It is true that competition may be a motivating force for some people; however, an individual will compete only if he knows he has a chance of winning. The "hierarchy game," placing one person above another, is bound to contribute to the beliefs of some students that they are trapped in a system in which they have few opportunities for success. If this is true, it is no wonder that the newspapers frequently carry stories about young vandals breaking into schools and destroying thousands of dollars worth of equipment. The general reaction of the public is that these children are "bad" and must be punished. But what made them bad? Why do they hate and strike out at the school? Certainly it is human nature to avoid harming the things you love. The facts are that the American school system has a high percentage of dropouts. The individuals who drop out often leave because they do not have feelings of success and thereby opportunities to enhance their self-concepts in the school environment.

Teachers aware of the problems in using evaluation to establish student achievement hierarchies have devised various approaches to deemphasize the importance of testing and grading. Some of these methods are:

1. Self-motivation, where the student evaluates himself and than decides, in cooperation with the instructor, where he needs to improve.
2. Performance criteria, where the teacher outlines what materials must be completed for a certain

grade. The teacher may also use certain performance criteria to see if the student has achieved a certain level.

3. Written evaluations, where the instructor writes a summary of the achievements and weaknesses of the student, preferably with the student.

4. Pass-fail, where students are given pass or fail as a grade. This system reduces competition but does not recognize excellence.

5. Giving all students the same grade. This system eliminates competition but usually is not well received by all students, particularly if a grade less than an "A" is given.

6. Grading secretly, where the teacher gives grades but doesn't tell the student what his grade is except that he is doing above or below average work. A disadvantage of this approach is that a student may experience anxiety over the instructor's feelings about him.

7. Student-teacher contract, where the teacher, in cooperation with the students, establishes the amount of work that must be done to receive a grade of A, B, C, etc.

Many years ago, Dr. Arthur Combs became concerned about the negative aspects of grading. As a result, he devised a contract system which he has continually modified and tested with students over the past fifteen years. A brief summary of his system is outlined below.[11] Although his system has been tested mainly with university students, it has many components that could be modified for use in the secondary school.

A desirable grading system should:

1. Meet college and university standards of effort, performance, and excellence.

2. Evaluate the student with his/her personal performance rather than in competition with his fellow students.

3. Permit students to work toward their personal goals.

4. Provide the broadest possible field of choice for the student.

5. Challenge students to stretch themselves to their utmost.

6. Eliminate, as much as possible, all sources of externally imposed threat.

7. Actively involve the student in planning for his own learning, placing the responsibility for this learning directly and unequivocally on his shoulders.

8. Free the student as much as possible from the necessity of pleasing the instructor.

9. Provide maximum flexibility to meet changing conditions.

Combs states: "To meet these criteria my current practice is to enter into a contract with each student for the grade he would like to achieve. Each student writes a contract with his instructor indicating in great detail: (a) the grade he would like to have, (b) what he proposes to do to achieve it, and (c) how he proposes to demonstrate that he has done it. Once this contract has been signed by the student and instructor, the student is free to move in any way he desires to the completion of his contract. When the contract has been completed 'in the letter and in the spirit' the student's grade is automatic."

■ Summary

Evaluation means that the teacher makes a total assessment of a student's learning. Science teachers evaluate students mainly by tests and laboratory reports. Just as there are levels of learning, so are there levels of testing.

Modern teacher-made tests should stress the higher cognitive levels of Bloom's Taxonomy and the affective domain more than recall questions. Tests should be constructed from an instructor's list of behavioral objectives so that she evaluates what she considers most important in the learning process. A test is only a sample of what is being learned. Other means of evaluation should also play a major part in determining the achievement and development of the student's multiple talents. Self-evaluation inventories should be used frequently in assessing a student's achievement. The student is best able to determine what he is learning and how he feels about it. Teachers should ask students to judge their own achievement. One way to do so is to give the students a list of objectives for a unit or course and have them judge what they know or felt about the course before and after studying the material. This method has been shown to be a valid measuring technique and gives a better indication of actual growth than does the typical test.

Because mathematics and graphing are so much a part of science, tests should incorporate many graphs and mathematical data. A good technique for determining if students understand graphing is to have them complete or devise a graph.

Each test should contain questions that will enable the teacher to evaluate the student's understanding of scientific methods. Students should know how to recognize a problem, make hypotheses, interpret data, draw valid conclusions, and devise experiments.

Certain features of each type of test must be considered before tests are constructed. Completion and matching tests, because of their emphasis on recall, are to be discouraged. Self-tests and problem tests place more emphasis on self-instruction and can be used to motivate class discussions. A teacher should consider how long a test will take and should provide assignments for those who finish before the class ends, to avoid discipline problems. Cheating must be strongly discouraged early in the term.

Mastery learning provides an additional challenge in evaluation. Criterion referenced tests must be devised which provide clear levels of performance. Satisfactory grades are given for successful performance.

Good test construction requires considerable sophistication if sole dependence on memorization is to be discouraged; therefore, teachers are urged to acquire further training in this very important part of their professional competence.

■ References

1. Harry K. Wong, "Dear Class, I Love You," *Learning* (December 1972), pp. 20-22.
2. Benjamin S. Bloom, *Taxonomy of Educational Objectives* (New York: David McKay Company, Inc., 1956).
3. Dale P. Scannel and Walter R. Stillwagen, "Teaching and Testing for Degrees of Understanding," *California Journal of Instructional Improvement* (March, 1960) pp. 88-94.
4. Leonard B. Finkelstein and Donald D. Hammill, "A Reading-Free Science Test," *The Elementary School Journal* (October 1969) pp. 34-37.
5. Richard R. Tolman and James T. Robinson, "Formative Evaluation of Unit 1, Digestion and Circulation," *BSCS Newsletter* 9, no. 43 (1971) p. 7.
6. This self-evaluational section is based on material prepared by Dr. Clifford A. Hofwolt of Vanderbilt University, Nashville, TN.
7. James H. Duel, "A Study of Validity and Reliability of Student Evaluation of Training" (Ed. D. dissertation, Washington University, Seattle, 1956).
8. Bill W. Tillery, "Improvement of Science Education Methods Courses Through Student Self-Evaluation" (Ed. D. dissertation, Colorado State College, 1967).
9. Gary E. Dunkleberger and Henry W. Heikkinen, "Mastery Learning: Implications and Practices," *Science Education*, 67, no. 5 (1983), pp. 553-560.
10. Norman E. Gronlund, *Measurement and Evaluation in Teaching*, 5th ed. (New York: Macmillan and Company, 1985), pp. 308-309.
11. Arthur W. Combs, "A Contract Method of Evaluation" (Gainesville, University of Florida, no date).

=========== **INVESTIGATING SCIENCE TEACHING** ===========

ACTIVITY 20–1

Preparing a Test

1. Prepare a test to evaluate some of your behavioral objectives.

2. Classify your questions acording to Bloom's Taxonomy and determine the percentage of questions for each of his categories.

ACTIVITY 20–2

Preparing a Unit Test

1. Write a comprehensive summative achievement test for a unit or semester of work in a high school science class of your choice.
2. Before constructing the test, design a Table of Specifications for the unit of instruction to be tested. Follow the guidelines for constructing such a table that are discussed in this chapter.
3. Your achievement tests should have the following features:
   a. At least 35 questions or approximately enough for a one hour test, depending upon the grade level.
   b. Describe the class for which the test is designed—level, subject, composition and any special characteristics that describe the class.
   c. Use a variety of test question types—objective, essay, problem solving, etc.
   d. Approximately 70 percent of your questions should be of high level items, i.e., comprehension, application, analysis, synthesis, or evaluation.
   e. Accompany your test with an answer key both for the objective and subjective test questions.
   f. Describe how you will assess the psychomotor and affective objectives of your instruction.
   g. Tell why you believe your test is a good one, with good content validity and reliability.

CHAPTER 21

Resolving Conflicts in the Science Classroom

Two major concerns for beginning science teachers are student discipline and classroom management. You have probably asked yourself, "How will the students behave?" "Will they do what I tell them to do?" "What can I do if a student is disruptive in science class?" In this chapter we hope to provide some answers to such questions.

Your concern about discipline is not unique. The American public has consistently indicated that "lack of discipline" is one of the most important problems facing the public school. What about science teachers? Do they perceive discipline as an important problem? Actually very few science teachers perceive discipline as a serious problem. In a 1986 survey, Iris Weiss found that only 9 percent of teachers in grades 7-9 and 6 percent of teachers in grades 10-12 reported "difficulty in maintaining discipline" as a serious problem in their school. If you include "lack of student interest in science," those percentages are increased by an additional 14 percent and 16 percent respectively.[1]

Exactly what is considered "lack of interest" and what is meant by "maintaining discipline" is impossible to surmise from these data. There are probably many answers to these questions. In this chapter we discuss "conflicts" and direct attention to their resolution. Our discussion is primarily directed to conflicts between teachers and students and to the constructive resolution of conflicts.

Before proceeding in this chapter, you should complete the first two activities in "Investigating Science Teaching." Those activities are "Conflicts: What Would You Have Done?" and "Resolving Conflicts." Completing these two activities will give you some

personal information and a useful perspective for the rest of the chapter.

■ Classroom Conflicts

A classroom conflict exists when the activities of one or more individuals are incompatible. As such, the conflict can be interpersonal or intergroup. An action that is incompatible with another action interferes, obstructs, or reduces the effectiveness of the action.[2] For the most part, we can discuss conflicts between teachers and students since a teacher must often take some action, even when two students are in conflict. In most classrooms the interface between compatible and incompatible activities is defined by rules, policies, or expectations of behavior. A classroom conflict usually results in disruption of normal activities and educational objectives.

The preceding definition is neutral. We have not defined rules or passed judgment on whether certain rules or expectations of behavior are good or bad. Science teachers have a wide range of rules and expectations for students. Students, likewise, have a remarkable ability to adapt to different teachers and classroom situations. Rather than trying to define rules, we think it better to focus on the inevitable conflicts within the classroom and suggest ways that science teachers can either prevent conflicts or resolve them constructively.

Let us begin by presenting two views of the same conflict. First is the report of a student teacher who had eight weeks of experience; the second is the report of the student teacher's supervisor, a science teacher with ten years of experience.

═══════ GUEST EDITORIAL ═══════

Reflections on Student Teaching

Mark Helpenstell, Student Teacher
Northfield Middle School
Northfield, Minnesota

When I first thought about being a science teacher, the question I most often asked myself was, "How can I possibly create enough material to keep students interested for an hour, every day, all week?" I was sure that my greatest problem would be finding enough things to do to fill an hour-long class and still keep all of the focus on one concept or topic. I knew that I could use filmstrips, overheads, group discussions, movies, laboratory exercises, worksheets, textbooks, and so on, but the problem was how to create an ordered and cohesive exercise without losing the interest of most of the students.

As I approached student teaching, the focus of my apprehensions changed. I found myself worrying less about gathering together enough materials and thinking more about my personal capabilities, strengths, and weaknesses. Could I do it? Did I really have the ability to "teach" (whatever that meant)? This was, for me, probably the hardest part of preparing to be a science teacher. I experienced some days of strong confidence and other days of dread and foreboding, when I was quite sure that I could never be an adequate teacher.

When I actually found myself in a classroom, the problems changed perspective drastically. Suddenly, I was out of time and overloaded with resources. Out of the milieu of possible subjects, aids, references, and texts, I had to "narrow down" the usable material to fit it into a one-hour class. The problem was not filling the hour but picking the very best methods and an interesting means of conveying the material available. I was faced with several possible ways of presenting a topic, trying always to make the class as interesting as possible for the students.

I found that I had the capability to teach but that I was very unsure of myself. The knowledge was there, and the ability to "teach," it was there too—it just needed to be brought out, trained, and refined.

Once I realized that I had the capability to be a science teacher, I found that it was much easier to be objective about what was happening in my classroom. I began to be more critical of my own teaching methods, and when things didn't go as I had expected them to, I could usually figure out for myself several possible factors which could have affected these "failures." I began asking myself, "How well am I doing? How well can I do? How well can these particular kids do? What things can I change to help increase their understanding? How effectively am I able to 'get to' these kids?"

Perhaps the biggest challenges I faced as a

The Student Teacher's Perceptions

A new seating chart was set up for the class. In the shuffle a student (the most openly aggressive and hostile student/person I've ever seen) started to swing at a student sitting behind him. I'm not sure of the reason, but I suspect that the boy behind him had his feet sticking out under the desk and the student either kicked him or tripped over him or slid his chair into his feet, and words were exchanged. I was close enough to verbally stop him and then collar him and send him up to the front of the class. My words were something like, "Alright, you're moved, right now, up to the front, turn forward and don't turn back around or away from the chalkboard or you'll be out of here immediately. If you can't get along with the people around you then you can sit by yourself with no privileges until you're ready to be part of the class." I thought for a minute he was going to explode (both mentally and physically), but he moved, sat and did nothing, very belligerently withdrawn, incredibly strong, and negative.

The Teacher's Perceptions

A new seating chart was established in the class. As one student took his newly assigned seat he appeared to be belligerent but not verbally. Another student immediately behind made a comment and he responded by turning around and pushing the table, and made a comment which I did not hear. The action was bad enough to get the attention of the majority of the class. The instructor (student teacher)

student teacher were those problems related to discipline. Sure, I'd been in some education classes and spent some time thinking about, and discussing, discipline problems and in some cases even reacting to specific "classroom situations." Somehow, though, being in the actual classroom created a totally different atmosphere. Dealing with disciplinary problems in class added new aspects of tension and challenge. Suddenly the student was challenging me before the other students, and although I knew that my response should be cool, carefully thought out and rational, more often than not many other factors intervened: defending my own ego before the class, cooling an initially very angry reaction (either mine or the student's), responding to an irrational student action, dealing with intense emotional tensions—all of these facts created a completely different atmosphere than any preparatory discussions or readings were able to develop. Responding to the situation, while trying to maintain an effective "learning atmosphere" was the greatest challenge I faced as a student teacher.

What did I learn from student teaching? A few things that I now find very important in teaching are: (1) Don't look for an ego trip— although teaching can be very gratifying at times,

it also contains more than its share of disillusion, frustration, and disappointments. (2) Always try to show off the students' knowledge, not your own— they know that *you* know it—what they need is the gratification of finding out that *they* know it. (3) Don't set your expectations and goals too high, either for yourself or the students—better to be pleasantly surprised than to be disappointed. (4) LET GO!!! This is probably the most difficult part of teaching, but if you can really drop your own inhibitions in front of your students, they will respond by doing the same thing. Although this may at times cause problems, I found that the benefits more than outweighed the disadvantages in the long run.

In summary, I found myself dealing with two major issues in the classroom: (1) how do I create a positive atmosphere in which topics are presented in a way that will keep the students' interest, and (2) how do I minimize the effect of disciplinary problems on the classroom experience. Although student teaching has not fully answered these questions, it has helped me to develop some personal means and methods of meeting these challenges, and it has given me new insights into some aspects of their resolution.

---

responded by giving the student a seat at a lone table in the front corner of the room. He took the seat but refused to do any work in class for the next three days. Whenever he attempted to turn or communicate with others, he was told to turn around. The student remained belligerent during this entire three-day period. After corrections or comments were made to him he, usually, unknown to the instructor, had some obscene comment or verbal reaction to the correction.

Teachers' perceptions of the same situation can vary. Likewise, teachers' perceptions of students can influence the way they interact with the student as the conflict is resolved. This conflict was not unique as classroom conflicts go—it was short, resolved by the teacher, and ended with little difficulty.

We can continue by looking at another typical classroom conflict. What is unique about this conflict is that it has been described by *both* the student and the teacher.

The Student's View

I was sitting at a table in the science laboratory with a few friends. We had finished our work and were engaged in normal conversation. The teacher approached our table and told us to get some work out, "You can't just sit there and talk."

I ignored her, and after she left our presence, we resumed our conversation. She came back soon after that, a bit more perturbed, and repeated her previous order. This time I spoke and told her I must be responsible enough to know when and how to do my schoolwork since I had an A average in school. "So," I said, "I don't need you to supervise my study habits." I reminded her we weren't being noisy, just talking among ourselves; that we weren't bothering anyone.

She became angry. She told us we were bothering others and stated that there was a rule of no talking in the science laboratory. In general, she tried to control the situation with power and authority instead of tact and reason. I, in turn, got a little indignant, lost my temper, and smarted off. She then kicked me out of science for the remainder of that day.

The Teacher's View

It was about halfway through the period when I noticed three boys sitting at a table talking. I went over to the table and told them that this was a science class and they should finish their science laboratory. I said they should do something besides talk.

I went about my business until, a few minutes later, I noticed that the boys were still talking. So I went to the table again and explained that they should be working. I hadn't even finished what I was saying when one of the boys said he was "smart enough to take care of himself so you can just leave me alone."

At this I told the boy that a few students do not have the right to talk and disturb other students who wanted to work. The boy got angry and said, "The hell with you and the other students." At this, I asked the boy to leave the room and he did.

This situation is a typical classroom conflict in several respects. The context was related to undefined time in class, apparently the conflict lasted only four to five minutes, and there apparently was a rule governing conduct for the situation.

The reports described above reveal several other factors common to school conflict. The perceptions of the individuals in conflict were very different, as is clear in the descriptions of the confrontation. Communication was somewhat accurate at the beginning but deteriorated as the situation continued to the point of threats, name-calling, and assertion of power. Characteristics of a trusting attitude were lacking. Finally, each party to the conflict thought he or she was correct; thus, the problem belonged to the other person. Note also that the conflict ended but was not resolved. Left the way it was, there is every reason to suspect that future problems would occur between the student and the teacher, and in fact they did in the latter case.

All conflicts are not the same. Table 21.1 outlines different levels of student behavior that may result in classroom conflicts. Understanding differ-

TABLE 21–1
Levels of school conflicts

LEVEL I Normal conflicts for individuals of this age and stage. While the behavior may have violated rules of the school or major norms of peers or society, the conduct is not a typical pattern for the individual.

Active	*Passive*
• Mischievous	• Aloof
• Temperamental	• Sulky
• Overeager	• Slow to warm up

LEVEL II Occasional conflicts for the individual. The conflicts are violations of minor school policies, classroom rules and age appropriate societal norms. There may be an emerging pattern that is subtle and can be overlooked.

Active	*Passive*
• Clowning	• Dawdler
• Impulsive	• Shy
• Acting Out	• Dreamer
• Seeks affirmation	• Alienated

LEVEL III A pattern of behaviors that persistently conflict with minor school policies, classroom rules and age appropriate societal norms. The pattern is clear, but the major rules and basic rights of others are seldom violated.

Active	*Passive*
• Disobedient	• Avoidant
• Oppositional	• Shut down
• Negativistic	• Withdrawn
• Provocative	• Alienated

LEVEL IV A pattern of behaviors that persistently violate major school policies, classroom rules, and the basic rights of others. The pattern is clear to school personnel and peers.

Active	*Passive*
• Aggressive	• Depressive
• Destructive	• Self-destructive
• Angry	• Substance abuse

LEVEL V Episodes of behaviors directed toward the physical harm of self, others, or property.

Active	*Passive*
• Violent	• Substance addiction
• Vandalism	• Suicidal

ent student (and teacher) behaviors that lead to conflict situations can help prevent some conflicts and gives direction and guidelines on the intervention and resolution of others. Also, such understanding clarifies how conflicts escalate; that is, each party "moves" to a higher level, hoping the other party will back down. In some unfortunate cases, simple conflicts can escalate to violent and destructive episodes within the school.

Causes of Conflicts

Understanding the origins and causes of disruptive behavior can provide you with responses that prevent many conflicts. The causes discussed below are arranged from origins common to almost all adolescents to the beginnings of unique disorders suffered by a few adolescents.

The Junior High/Middle School Student

The fifth- through ninth-grade student is going through the most difficult period of early adolescence. Students at the early adolescent period are sometimes mature and reflective; they are also sometimes immature and impulsive. They sometimes want to separate themselves from adult authorities, such as science teachers, and they sometimes want to be directed by adults. They sometimes want to be treated as individuals who can make decisions and act responsibly, and they sometimes want to be told what to do and when to do it. It is difficult for a science teacher to know the appropriate way to respond.

The junior high/middle school teacher should take into account the developmental needs of early adolescents. The classroom can be a place where there is a certain amount of testing of "adult" roles and learning to be responsible. The result can be great bursts of energy for learning science and, also, great energy sinks. Frustrating? Yes. What can you do? First and foremost you must understand that these behaviors are part of the developmental process and more often than not should not be internalized as something directed at you, your teaching, or science. Second, you must establish the limits of tolerable activity for your class. The limits vary from teacher to teacher and so we cannot say what your limits should be. But, you must have limits and it is in your interest to identify them and make them known to your students.

Discipline for this age level is largely a matter of instilling controlled self-discipline. Thus, limited freedom must be permitted so that self-discipline can be exercised. Students will not develop self-discipline and reliability if they are never given the opportunity to practice them. Overly rigid, authoritarian control, in which the primary motivation for good behavior is fear of the teacher's reprisal, will not develop the kind of student who is capable of self-discipline. At the same time, you cannot permit chaos to develop by allowing uncontrolled behavior. An environment must be provided in which students can show initiative and be responsible for their own actions within a framework of supervisory control by the teacher.

Early adolescents are usually quite responsive and sensitive to their peers. Therefore a positive approach to discipline is to show them that their actions influence the actions of other members of the class. If they misbehave and take up valuable class time, they are infringing on the study time of classmates. As a result, they are likely to lose the favor of peers and be seen as troublemakers; their status will correspondingly deteriorate.

The junior high/middle school science teacher can use peer pressure to bring about improved classroom behavior. This is not to be done by sarcastic remarks or public humiliation of the student. Rather, the teacher should constantly refer to the need for cooperation, the value of class time, the real purposes of the study of science, and mutual obligations to one's classmates.

The Senior High School Student

There is no sharp character difference between the junior high/middle school student and the senior high student. One can easily find younger students who are as mature as those in the senior high school. The reverse is also true. In general, however, as the students mature, one finds more inhibition and less boisterous behavior in the classroom. This change is a natural result of the student's approach to adulthood. More thought is given to future plans, vocational choice, or choice of advanced education.

From the standpoint of discipline, this increased maturity is salutary. The frequency of classroom incidents requiring disciplinary measures usually decreases. The student is more likely to respond to treatment normally accorded adults and, because of the student's sensitiveness in this regard, the most effective measures the teacher can use in disciplinary matters are those that treat the student as an adult, with responsibilities for adult behavior.

Some students cause discipline problems because they are bored with the activities and they have nothing else to do. Although you may think that science is interesting and exciting, the students may not. Many students may not understand the concept being discussed or demonstrated, but some may. These difficulties cause boredom and subsequent behaviors that lead to conflicts. Gearing class activities to the needs and interests of a wide range of students is certainly desirable. Likewise, having interesting and relevant lessons is recommended. Still, you may wish to have optional activities and projects from which students can choose.

"Negative attention is better than no attention at all" is the motto for some students. Often students who are not successful academically, athletically, musically, and so on become the "class clowns" or show other behaviors that result in minor conflicts with the science teacher's activities. Attention-seeking behavior is often hard for teachers to change because the responses that teachers think reduce or eliminate the disruptive behavior are the very responses that reinforce the students' behavior.

The best way to reduce this behavior is to give the student attention in educationally constructive ways. Give recognition for the types of behavior you desire and try (even though it is very difficult) to ignore the attention-seeking behaviors you do not wish to have reoccur.

We can return to Abraham Maslow's hierarchy of basic needs—food, water, sleep, safety and security, love and belongingness, and self-esteem—for another source of discipline problems. Sometimes students' basic needs have not been fulfilled and the result is inappropriate behavior. The teacher's response is to try and fulfill those needs in the best way possible.

In other cases students can be frustrated with the amount of effort required in science versus the amount of learning and the rewards they receive. Other problems can be students' resistance to required subjects; that is, they feel forced to do activities they are not interested in or do not like, and they occasionally must comply with rules that conflict with personal preferences, e.g., wearing safety goggles.

We are not suggesting that you provide a frustration-free environment. But, if frustrations are mounting, you can change the pace, switch activities, take a break, let the students have a "discussion day," and so on. Forcing a tense situation can result in a conflict that could have been avoided.

We turn to the origin of one of the more persistent and difficult discipline problems, alienation. Simply defined, alienation is a feeling of being separated or removed from one's group or from society. There is also a weakening of the social bond between the individual and society or the school system as a subsystem of society. The latter problem results in the student's rejection of school and the appropriate behaviors for those in school. Melvin Seeman, a sociologist, has written a classic paper in which he suggests five components which influence alienation.[3] We will discuss the components in terms of the science classroom.

First, there is *powerlessness*. This is the individual's belief that he is unable to influence his life under the present rules. This feeling was described by Mary Budd Rowe[4] as fate control. Control over one's life is directed by something besides the individual. Here, science teachers can show individuals that they can achieve and that there are positive results for appropriate behavior.

Second, there is *meaninglessness*. This is the absence of a clear set of values and "connections" between the individual and society. We have heard this problem discussed as relevance of instruction and the curriculum. Trying to present the concepts and processes of science in a context that is meaningful to the student helps reduce this particular problem.

Third, *normlessness* is a reduction in the regulatory power of social rules and laws over individual behavior. To overcome this problem, the science teacher should make classroom rules clear and enforce them consistently and fairly. Let the students know that there are rules, that you intend that they be obeyed, and that all students are subject to the same rules and consequences for rule violation.

Fourth is the feeling of *isolation*. Here the individual feels left out of the group, class, or school. This problem occurs most frequently in large and impersonal schools and classes. Be sure students know that you care for them, you want them in your classroom, and you show some personal attention to their work.

Finally is *self-estrangement*. The individual comes to rely on external rewards and is easily frustrated when they are not received. The individual lacks self-confidence. This problem suggests a need for experiences where the student's confidence in completing a task is supported and he learns that there are some internal rewards for learning science.

Our discussion of the origin of students' discipline has been general. There are more specific descriptions and recommendations concerning behavior problems of adolescents. Too often, science teachers construct their own explanations for adolescent behavior and they do not consult individuals or resources who are knowledgeable. Science teachers provide explanations of adolescent behavior that is disruptive with "theories" such as "He only wanted attention," "She comes from a broken home," or "They associate with the wrong group." While these are explanations, they are also incomplete and hold every possibility of having misconceptions about the causes of adolescent behavior. If you do not think you have an adequate understanding of adolescent behavior; if you are having trouble with a particular student; or, if you think something is seriously wrong; please consult a counselor, school psychologist, or a reference such as those listed in Table 21.2. If you are wondering about a student's behavior, ask yourself these questions.

- Is there a *pattern* of behaviors? Does the student behave the same way in other classes?
- Does the student continually demonstrate inappropriate behaviors for his/her age?

TABLE 21–2
Understanding adolescent behavior

James M. Kaufman, *Characteristics of Children's Behavior Disorders (3rd)*. Columbus, OH: Merrill, 1985.
> One of the best books available describing the origins of behavior disorders and outline of four facets of behavior disorders. Although this is written for special educators, it will provide the science teacher an initial understanding of behaviors that are hyperactive, aggressive, withdrawn, or delinquent.

Betty C. Epandien and James L. Paul, *Emotional Problems of Childhood and Adolescence*. Columbus, OH: Merrill, 1987.
> An introduction to the definition and assessment of different disorders. Chapters are written by experts in the field.

Mary Margaret Kerr, P. Michael Nelson and Deborah L. Lambert, *Helping Adolescents with Learning and Behavior Problems*. Columbus, OH: Merrill, 1987.
> This book takes a decidedly educational approach. There are chapters on assessment, strategies for solving school problems, and special issues, such as drug abuse and juvenile justice. There are many practical guides that could help the science teacher.

Henry R. Reinert and Allen Huang, *Children in Conflict*. Columbus, OH: Merrill, 1987.
> This is an excellent introduction to emotional disturbances. After an overview of approaches (biophysical, psychodynamic, behavior, ecological), the authors concentrate on classroom application.

- Are the basic rights of others (including you) consistently violated?
- Is there the possibility of personal harm, either to the student in question, or to others?

If you find yourself answering yes to these, or similar questions, you should consult an authoritative source because the behaviors are probably not in the acceptable range for your classroom and school. There is no need to try and solve the problem yourself. Many of your colleagues in the school system—special educators and school psychologists—are immediate resources.

Discipline Problems and the Science Classroom

The nature of science classes affects some types of discipline problems and the methods of control. On the positive side, we find that science has numerous applications to the daily lives of students. Every student has had contacts with the environment that reveal scientific relationships. Thus, motivation can be an easier matter than in a more abstract course.

Science classes also have the advantage of many demonstration devices and laboratory equipment that stimulate interest. Students may find themselves drawn away from unruly influences and toward scientific interests in spite of themselves. Furthermore, for students whose poor behavior may stem from lack of recognition, science classes may offer opportunities to gain prestige in the eyes of their peers.

On the negative side, certain unique problems exist in science classes. The laboratory by its very nature offers freedom of movement that may lead to discipline problems. Students without self-discipline will find many opportunities to cause trouble. The teacher's control must be completely effective, although not rigid, or the learning opportunities of the laboratory will be sacrificed. Learning requires considerable self-direction and attention to the task, and the laboratory, under skillful guidance of the teacher, can help develop self-discipline. Completing "Classroom Discipline" in the "Investigating Science Teaching" section is highly recommended.

■ Conflict Resolution and Regulation

In recent decades social psychologists have learned a great deal about the resolution and regulation of conflicts. *The Resolution of Conflict* by Morton Deutsch is probably the single most important accumulation of these research findings.[5] For this reason we rely on Deutsch's ideas in this discussion.

We assume that conflicts will occur in the science classroom. Likewise we assume that you are interested in their *constructive* resolution. Further, we assume that in those rare situations of intense conflict, you are interested in *regulating* the conflict so that the results are not destructive to yourself or others.

Avoiding Destructive Conflicts

Destructive conflicts tend to escalate from minor encounters to major events in the classroom. Involved persons increasingly rely on power and authority to resolve, regulate, and finally control the situation. As the conflict takes a destructive course, threats, coercion, and demonstrations of power steadily displace open discussion and the processes of peaceful resolution. The destructive course is set once: (1) the conflict is defined as a win-lose situation; (2) communication is decreased and thus misperceptions increase; and (3) commitments for personal and social consistency decrease. We can look to the opposite of these three ideas for some means to avoid destructive classroom conflicts. We suggest that you consider the following in order to avoid destructive conflicts:

1. Encourage cooperation.
2. Communicate clearly.
3. Commit yourself personally and socially to resolve the conflicts peacefully.

Encouraging Constructive Resolutions

Conflicts will take a constructive course when science teachers use a creative problem-solving model for intervention. This model would include (1) motivation to resolve the problem, (2) finding conditions to redefine the problem, and (3) suggesting ideas that might solve the problem. Here are some suggestions that will contribute to constructive resolutions of conflicts:

1. Define the conflict as small.
2. Resolve the problem as soon as possible.
3. Focus on the problem, not the person.
4. Reduce the conflict to several smaller problems and resolve them.
5. Emphasize similarities and common goals.
6. Be sure all parties agree on the problem.
7. Acknowledge that a conflict exists.
8. Use a neutral third party to help resolve the conflict.

But what should one do when conflicts cannot be resolved? On some occasions problems persist and for many reasons cannot be easily resolved. When a situation such as this exists, you should try to regulate the conflict so it does not take a destructive course.

Regulating Classroom Conflicts

Regulating conflicts is an attempt to set limits or boundaries on the interaction between conflicting parties. Regulating conflicts is obviously harder than resolving them. Both parties are often on a "thin edge" leading to destruction. There is little doubt about teachers fearing for their safety and having intense emotional responses. The same is true of students who find themselves in these situations. Although we must accept the legitimacy of these human resources, we must also guard against the detrimental consequences of a destructive conflict. What can a science teacher do? The following recommendations will help regulate conflicts:

1. Wait until parties are calm, rational, and organized and then start talking about the conflict.
2. Demonstrate the legitimacy of all parties to the conflict.
3. Reach agreement on the limits of interaction.

4. Use new and different approaches when old ones have failed.
5. Develop a sense of community for all parties.
6. Make sure rules are known, clear, and unbiased.
7. Remedy rule violations as soon as possible.
8. Use counselors for third-party regulation when necessary.

This is an excellent time to complete the "Investigating Science Teaching" activity "Resolution and Regulation of Conflicts" at the end of this chapter.

■ Some Recommendations for Science Teachers

Developing Self-Discipline

The goal of all discipline training should be the development of responsible self-discipline. Students should reach a point where they have inner motivation to complete learning tasks. Discipline of this type is positive and self-rewarding.

To reach this goal, numerous opportunities must be provided for students to practice self-discipline or peer-group discipline. As with the development of any skill, there must be time to practice.

Teaching science by inquiry methods provides a setting for developing self-discipline. Individual work in the laboratory or on projects carried out in the classroom or at home gives many opportunities to develop good work habits and qualities of self-reliance, persistence, and reliability.

The following suggestions may assist the science teacher in providing an environment in which student self-discipline can be developed.

1. Capture interest through activities, experiments, projects, and other student-oriented learning methods.
2. Allow a degree of unstructured work commensurate with the maturity and experience level of the students.
3. Give suitable guidance to students who require direction and external control, until it is no longer needed.
4. Treat students as adults from whom you expect mature behavior and evidence of self-discipline.

Developing Techniques to Influence Behavior

Every teacher has several techniques that are designed to influence student behavior. In light of earlier discussions of conflicts, many of these techniques are "early warning signals" for the student. In this respect, the actual conflict is prevented, usually because the student responds to the signal.

Here are some suggestions you may consider.

1. Nonverbal signals such as staring, clearing your throat, shaking your head, or stopping discussion and waiting.
2. Influencing behavior by your physical closeness or proximity control. While continuing the discussion, move to the part of the room where the disruptive student is seated.
3. Use humor to let the student know that enough is enough. Use gentle humor, however; it should not be sarcastic or personal.
4. Ask the disruptive student a simple and direct question that will bring him into the discussion.
5. Provide help for particularly difficult problems, laboratories, or assignments. Some students may disrupt class because they do not understand the material.
6. Help the students through "transitional periods" in class. Shifting from a laboratory to seat work takes a few minutes of adjustment; you can provide the time and be sure not to expect "immediate" response.
7. As much as possible, establish patterns for laboratory work, cleanup, and other routine or common activities in the classroom.
8. Modify routines such as attendance and distributing papers at the first indication that they are conducive to misbehavior.
9. You can help prevent some misbehavior by removing particularly "seductive" laboratory equipment from the students.
10. The most effective techniques for influencing behavior are to have well-prepared lessons, to use a variety of instructional methods, and to show a personal interest in students.

Developing Means of Resolving Classroom Conflicts

The following recommendations may help avoid serious conflicts and bring about constructive as opposed to destructive consequences.

1. Try to recognize the consistent patterns of behavior that can result in conflicts (see Table 21.1).
2. Clarify classroom rules. This may require mentioning particular rules relating to daily activities.
3. Clarify each person's perceptions of the conflict situation. "How does this situation seem to you?"
4. Maintain communication. You should be able to keep the lines of communication open for several minutes by avoiding personal insults, threats, or the use of power.
5. Define the conflict as a mutual problem. "Look, you would like to visit and I would like it quiet so the students can work. How can *we* resolve this?"
6. Avoid using power to resolve the conflict. This can escalate the conflict and/or end it without resolution.

Developing a Discipline Policy

One of the strongest recommendations we can make to beginning teachers is to develop a discipline policy. Having a policy will result in consistency and clear expectations for both you and your students. Once you have developed a set of rules (and we suggest you do this *with* the students), the following suggestions should be considered when there are rule violations or conflicts.

1. Request that the student stop the behavior and remind the student of the rule he/she is violating.
2. If the behavior continues, inform the student that the behavior must stop and that "we will have to resolve the problem."
3. Establish what the problem is and what can be done to resolve it.
4. Help establish the new rules and procedures for the student's behavior; make the consequences for any further rule violations very clear. Avoid using personally or physically harsh or abusive measures. Be consistent with the rules and consequences you have *both* agreed to. Be kind and firm. Being kind shows respect for the student; being firm shows respect for yourself as a person and as a science teacher.

Meeting Parents to Solve a Discipline Problem

Occasionally it is necessary to meet with parents concerning their child's behavior in school. As a first step we recommend that you do a thorough assessment of the student's discipline problems, the steps for which are outlined in Table 21.3. Scheduling a meeting with parents indicates a high level of concern about the student, and this suggests the need for information, documentation, and understanding of the problems and their potential resolution.

As you approach the meeting there are several things to keep in mind. First, have the information

TABLE 21–3
Steps in assessment of a discipline problem

Understand the Problem
- What happened in the last 48 hours of the adolescent's life?
- What were the circumstances of the problem?
- What patterns of behavior are identifiable?

Clarification of Current Difficulties
- What is the nature of present *school related* problems?
- What is the duration of all problems, i.e., academic, behavioral, with peers?
- Have there been any recent changes in behavior? Achievement? Friendships?

Review of Background
- What is the relevant family background?
- What is the student's relation to peers?
- How has the student related to other teachers? Administrators? Counselors?

Identification of Coping Style
- How does the student handle stress?
- What triggers a discipline "event"?
- How does the student think he/she could avoid problems?
- What resources are available to help the student avoid difficult situations?

Assessment of Psychological and Developmental Status
- What is the student's mood?
- What are the student's cognitive, moral, social and emotional levels of development?

List All Current Problems
- What are the present problems as perceived by (1) the student, (2) school personnel, and, if appropriate, (3) parents?
- Which problems have highest/lowest priority?

Establish Help That Is Required
- What does the student want (or agree) to do?
- What does school personnel want done?
- What will all parties agree to?
- Should anyone else be involved?

Develop a Contract
- What terms are acceptable to student, school personnel and parents?
- Who is responsible for doing what? When? How?

(and examples) concerning the student's problems with you. Second, realize that you have two goals, to gain further understanding of the student's background and role in the family, and to join with the family in a cooperative approach to intervene and improve the student's behavior.

Outside of the natural nervousness about meeting with parents, there are other challenges to bear in mind. The family will usually be very concerned and often quite defensive about being called to school. In order to work effectively you must have the cooperation of other school personnel. Finally, in order to develop a plan of action that will be im-

plemented you will have to identify and work with the central decision makers in the family.

Here we list some suggestions for a meeting with parents to solve a discipline problem. We would also point out that some of the ideas in this section are applicable to any meeting with parents concerning school-related problems, whether academic, social, or behavioral.

1. *Be sure the meeting is scheduled.* Don't plan to just see the parents after school, or stop by their house unannounced.
2. *Have data, documentation and examples.* The more specific you can be, the more the parents will realize the seriousness of the problem.
3. *Try to recognize and overcome the parents' anxiety and defensiveness.* Some simple statements such as "I'm sure you are concerned about your child's problems" will help. You can also be clear on the point that the parents know about their child and can contribute to the problem's resolution.
4. *Define and clarify the current problem.* Present the problem in a clear and concise manner. Direct the discussion toward actual behaviors and avoid derogatory comments relative to the student.
5. *Allow the parents to respond.* If the parents do not respond, then review the problems to impress on them their seriousness. If the parents seem confrontive, then direct their attention to the problem and not side issues, such as the personalities of school personnel. If the parents are cooperative, then develop a list of means that might be used to help them resolve the problems.
6. *Develop a Plan of Action.*
   - Identify the behaviors to be increased/decreased.
   - Are there other problems that should be attended to, e.g., reading difficulties, learning disabilities?
   - Identify the consequences of inappropriate behaviors. A logical-consequence approach often works very well.
   - Decide on who, what, when, where, and how the plan will be implemented.
   - Clarify the responsibilities of school personnel, parents, and others.
   - Determine what all parties would see as improvement.
   - Schedule other meetings to review progress.

■ Summary

The matter of class control is of primary concern to the beginning teacher. The multiple problems of class preparation, devising suitable teaching methods, and keeping the class orderly are frequently overwhelming.

The actual statistics indicate that most science teachers do not perceive "maintaining discipline" as a problem. Likewise, they do not think they need assistance with this problem. Although statistics indicate that discipline problems are not a major concern, it is nonetheless true that there will inevitably be conflicts in the science classroom. Conflicts occur when the activities of one individual or group are incompatible with the activities of another individual or group.

The causes of conflicts vary, but some of the more prevalent origins of conflicts are adolescent need for separation and individuation, boredom, the need for attention, frustration, tension, and alienation. It is also true that the very nature of the science classroom can cause some problems.

Conflicts can be resolved using a few simple procedures: define the conflict as small, work to resolve the conflict immediately, focus on the problem, reduce the problem to smaller parts, be sure there is agreement on the problem, use a third party if necessary. If conflicts are headed in a destructive direction you should wait until all parties are calm; recognize legitimacy; reach limits on interactions; use new approaches if old ones do not work; make rules clear, known, and unbiased; and, again, use a third party if necessary.

There are many possible ways to resolve conflicts in the classroom. For the students, an important first step is to develop self-discipline. A second step is developing a set of techniques that can prevent or resolve a conflict before it develops. Next, it is recommended that the teacher use the various means of resolving conflicts. Finally, each teacher must develop a discipline policy. Such a policy will result in a fair and consistent pattern of conflict resolution in the science classroom. All of these methods converge in the recommendation to be firm, friendly, fair, and consistent in your interactions with disruptive students.

■ References

1. Iris Weiss, *Report of the 1985-86 National Survey of Science and Mathematics Education* (Research Triangle Park, NC: Research Triangle Institute, November, 1987).
2. Morton Deutsch, *The Resolution of Conflict* (New Haven: Yale University Press, 1973).
3. Melvin Seeman, "The Meaning of Alienation," *American Sociological Review*, 24 (December 1959) pp. 783-91.
4. Mary Budd Rowe, *Teaching Science by Continuous Inquiry* (New York: McGraw Hill, 1979).
5. Deutsch, *The Resolution of Conflict*.

========================= INVESTIGATING SCIENCE TEACHING =========================

ACTIVITY 21–1

Conflicts: What Would You Have Done?

The following three incidents were recorded by student teachers. The incidents occurred in science classrooms and represent discipline situations you might encounter. Read each incident and decide what *you* would have done had you been in the situation. After this you might share your response with other students in class to see what they would have done.

Incident 1

I was tutoring seven students who had fallen behind in their ninth-grade general-chemistry class. As I proceeded, two male students made sly remarks which related to my subject material. I laughed at first, but then said, "OK, fun is fun, but let's get down to business." Since they did not take this as a warning, I told them that if they did not keep quiet and listen, they would have to return to the classroom. At this point I realized that I had "threatened" them in the form of a warning—the old "do or die" situation.

The two students continued this behavior, so I asked them to leave and just stand and wait. It was tough for me since I really did not want them to leave. They needed the help I was there to provide but they infringed on the learning opportunity of the five other students. Class went well after the two boys left.

What would you have done in this situation?

Incident 2

This was a conflict between two students during a laboratory period. I stepped in to try to resolve it before it grew out of control.

The laboratory required a perch made of books. One student borrowed a book from a laboratory partner that was large enough to meet his needs. However, the partner decided he wanted to have the book available for reading during the period and asked for his book back. The first student didn't want to move his setup since it was all prepared and checked, so he refused the other's demands. The partner was slowly losing patience when I stepped in. Since the problem wasn't very grave to me, I told the two that we could easily solve the conflict and asked for the student's help in exchanging the book and rechecking the setup while the partner cooled off. The tension subsided and they were able to work together during the period.

What would you have done in this situation?

Incident 3

I passed out a test. An A+ student forgot to do one section of the test. I graded all the tests. This student received a B+. She is a talkative student, always making some jokes or puns in class to gain attention. After I returned the test, she said *nothing* in class for two days.

On the second day, I approached the student to help her on some problems in balancing equations. She had some trouble, so I was able to help her. After class she came up to me and insisted that I change her grade. I listened to her explain her mistake. Then I asked her what she thought should be done. She said I should change her grade. She decided that it would be fair to give her a better grade.

What would you have done in this situation?

ACTIVITY 21–2

Resolving Conflicts

There are many factors that influence the direction and resolution of a conflict. In this activity we are going to have you examine your preferred methods for resolving problems. In other words, how do you typically try to resolve conflicts with other people? The insights you gain from the exercise will be beneficial when you have to resolve conflicts with students in your science class.*

The following sayings can be thought of as descriptions of different ways individuals resolve conflicts. Read each of the statements carefully. Using a scale of 1 through 5, indicate how typical each saying is of your actions in a conflict situation.

5—Very typical of the way I act in a conflict
4—Frequently typical of the way I act in a conflict
3—Sometimes typical of the way I act in a conflict
2—Seldom typical of the way I act in a conflict
1—Never typical of the way I act in a conflict.

_____ 1. Soft words win hard hearts.
_____ 2. Come now and let us reason together.
_____ 3. Arguments of the strongest have the most weight.
_____ 4. You scratch my back, I'll scratch yours.
_____ 5. The best way of handling conflicts is to avoid them.
_____ 6. If someone hits you with a stone, hit the person with a piece of cotton.
_____ 7. A question must be decided by knowledge and not by numbers if it is to have a right decision.
_____ 8. If you cannot make a person think as you do, make the person do as you think.
_____ 9. Better half a loaf than no bread at all.
_____10. If someone is ready to quarrel with you, the person isn't worth knowing.
_____11. Smooth words make smooth ways.
_____12. By digging and digging, the truth is discovered.
_____13. One who fights and runs away lives to run another day.
_____14. A fair exchange brings no quarrel.
_____15. There is nothing so important that you have to fight for it.
_____16. Kill your enemies with kindness.
_____17. Seek till you find, and you'll not lose your labor.
_____18. Might overcomes right.
_____19. Tit for tat is fair play.
_____20. Avoid quarrelsome people—they will only make you unhappy.

Some insights about your typical style of resolving conflicts can be gained by adding the responses to different sayings. Add your typical responses to the sayings as indicated.

Sayings		*Total*	*Response Style*
1, 6, 11, 16	=	_____	Smoothing
2, 7, 12, 17	=	_____	Negotiating
3, 8, 13, 18	=	_____	Forcing
4, 9, 14, 19	=	_____	Compromising
5, 10, 15, 20	=	_____	Withdrawing

Science teachers are concerned with two goals as they resolve conflicts. One goal is personal and involves achieving, gaining, or maintaining something; for example achieving an educational goal, gaining personal recognition, or maintaining one's sense of security in the science classroom. The second goal has to do with preserving or changing the relationship with the conflicting party. In the science classroom this usually means preserving the relationship with a student, while changing the patterns of behavior.

The five different response styles to conflicts have direct bearing on the personal and relational goals of science teachers. We describe briefly the results of typical conflict responses relative to personal and relational goals of teachers.

Withdrawing

Withdrawing from a conflict fulfills neither the personal nor the relational goals. Essentially it is a lose/lose approach to conflict resolution since the educator gives up whatever educational goals he or she had and does not try to maintain the relationship with the student. In brief it is:

PERSONAL—LOSE
RELATIONAL—LOSE

Smoothing

Smoothing over the conflict gives highest priority to maintaining the relationship, often at all costs, including giving up personal goals. This is a resolution that usually results in:

PERSONAL—LOSE
RELATIONAL—WIN

Forcing

Here, personal goals are achieved at any cost. The cost is often to give up a personal relationship with the students. So we have a situation of:

PERSONAL—WIN
RELATIONAL—LOSE

Compromising

The educator gives up some personal goals, and some relational goals are modified in order to resolve the conflict. All parties to the conflict give up something and are often dissatisfied with the results. The grounds for resentment by both educators and students have been established. The amount of resentment will depend on the perceived amount of compromise by each party to the conflict. In essence this is a resolution of:

PERSONAL—TIE
RELATIONAL—TIE

Negotiating

Educators and students resolve conflicts through cooperative problem solving. Though some changes occur, essentially the goals of both educators and students are achieved and relationships are maintained. This approach is one of:

PERSONAL—WIN
RELATIONAL—WIN

There are times when each of the different means of resolving conflicts is an appropriate course of action. Science teachers should understand this and make judgments concerning the situation, student, their personal and relational goals.

Think of a classroom situation where each of the response styles would be appropriate.

Withdrawing:

Smoothing:

Forcing:

Compromising:

Negotiating:

You might observe some actual classroom or school conflicts and examine the teachers' response style. Go back and review your responses to the conflicts presented in "Investigating Science Teaching: Conflicts." Would you try to use a different response style?

*This activity is based on ideas from P. Lawrence and J. Torsch, *Organization and Environment: Managing Differentiation and Integration* (Cambridge, MA: Division of Research, Graduate School of Business Administration, Harvard University, 1967), and from David Johnson, *Human Relations and Your Career: A Guide to Interpersonal Skills* (Englewood Cliffs, NJ: Prentice-Hall, 1978).

ACTIVITY 21–3

Classroom Discipline

One of the best ways for you to gain an understanding of conflicts in the science classroom is to analyze a situation that you perceive to be a serious discipline problem. You will have to spend some time observing in a science classroom or recall a situation from earlier experience.

Incident.   Describe the actual behaviors and statements between the science teacher and the student during a conflict incident. This should be an objective statement. What did the teacher say and do? What did the student say and do?
After describing the incident complete the following:

Grade Level_____   The conflict was between: Teacher   Student
School_____   Male_____   Male_____
Class_____   Female_____   Female_____
Other (specify)_____

How long did the conflict last?

_____Less than one minute   _____7–10 minutes

_____1–3 minutes   _____Longer than 10 minutes

_____4–6 minutes   _____Indicate how long _____

Most classroom conflicts involving individuals can be categorized at one of the levels described in Table 19-1. Indicate the individual student's behaviors in terms of the categories outlined:

1. Affirmation _____ Alienation _____

2. Assertion _____ Withdrawal _____

3. Aggression _____ Depression _____

4. Violence toward others _____ Violence toward self _____
Was this incident part of a recurring or consistent pattern of behavior for the student?

Yes _____ No _____ Don't know _____

Context. Describe the classroom setting, circumstances, and origin of the conflict. What preceded the conflict?

Complete the following questions concerning the context of the conflict.
1. Was the situation during: Comments

_____ Teacher presentation, e.g., lecturing

_____ Class discussion, e.g., teacher leading

_____ Class presentation, e.g., film

_____ Group work, e.g., laboratory

_____ Individual work, e.g., reading

_____ Student presentation, e.g., discussion of project

_____ "In-between time," e.g., between a laboratory activity
and class discussion.

_____ Free time in class, e.g., after a test before bell

_____ Free time in school, e.g., hall, cafeteria

_____ Free time outside of building, e.g., after school

_____ Other (specify)

2. Were there any unusual circumstances which should be noted?

3. What was the rule, policy, or expectation of behavior?

4. Was the rule, policy, or expectation presented or enforced as:

_____ Prohibitive (e.g., You should not . . .)

_____ Prescriptive (e.g., You should . . .)

_____ Benefit to group (e.g., You must, so we can . . .)

_____ Benefit to individual (e.g., We must, so you can . . .)

_____ Other (specify)

5. To your knowledge was the rule, policy, or expectation:

Stated _____ Unstated _____ by either party to the conflict?

Written _____ Unwritten _____ prior to the conflict?

Known _____ Unknown _____ to the accused?

Comments:

Resolution: Describe how the conflict was ended or resolved. Would you say the resolution was:

_____ Mutual, e.g., agreed on by both parties

_____ Coercive, e.g., one party got the other to stop through warnings

_____ Assertive, e.g., one party threatened the other

_____ Aggressive, e.g., one party physically did something to the other

What happened in the brief period (3–5 minutes) after the conflict ended or was resolved?

Did the behaviors change for the persons directly involved in the conflict?

How did behaviors change for those indirectly involved i.e., the other students?

Were there any other consequences of the conflict/resolution?

Interpretation

How would you interpret the conflict you have described?

What general statements can be made concerning the conflict?

Recommendations

What could be done to avoid further conflicts such as the one you described?

What would you do if you had to resolve a similar conflict?

If the entire methods class completed this investigation, it may be interesting to compile the observations and discuss you findings.

ACTIVITY 21–4

Resolution and Regulation of Conflicts

In this exercise we present some conflicts that may occur in science classrooms. Based on the earlier discussions of conflict resolution and regulation you are to suggest what should be done: First, list what you would do. Then join with other members of your class and share ideas about the resolution or regulation of the conflicts.

Incident 1

At the beginning of class, the last period of a Friday afternoon, the students came in talking and laughing. They didn't settle down when the bell rang. The teacher didn't say anything for a while, just watched the students with an amused half-smile on her face. After about a minute she said something like, "How much time are you going to waste? You've already wasted 45 seconds, and you're going to have to stay after class for 45 seconds to make up for it."

What would you do?

Incident 2

Mary Beth was extremely withdrawn in science class. When I talked to her she would say, "Leave me alone and go away." Yet she was failing class, mostly due to not completing her assignments.

What would you do?

Incident 3

Gil was always causing a disturbance. He would continually clown around in class. His antics would disrupt the other students and my teaching. I must admit that he was occasionally funny.

What would you do?

Incident 4

Glen had a "chip on his shoulder" from the first day he entered earth science. This one day we were cleaning up and he dropped a beaker of sand. I told him to clean it up and he responded, "I don't feel like it." I then said he had spilled it and he had to clean it. He replied, "Make me."

What would you do?

Incident 5

This wasn't the first time Jane had been in trouble. She just could not follow the rules. It didn't ever seem serious, at least until this incident. Well, she came into class and was chewing gum. I told her to get rid of the gum. Then she started talking to her neighbor. I told her to pay attention. Then she started making remarks about my discussion. I was at my wit's end.

What would you do?

## CHAPTER 22

Student Teaching and Professional Growth

A student nearing the end of her teacher training grows increasingly anxious to get "on the job." She may look forward with anticipation to "trying her wings" as a full-fledged teacher in charge of a class. At the same time, she is apt to feel somewhat apprehensive at the prospect of facing a roomful of students. Will she be able to hide her nervousness? Will her knowledge of her subject be adequate for the task? Will she be able to handle discipline problems? These questions and many others may give her concern as she faces the future—a future that will see her transformed from a "science student" to a "teacher of science."

■ Why Student Teach?

The student-teaching experience is designed to smooth the transition from the role of student to that of teacher. It is the student's opportunity to test her liking for the teaching task. She will discover whether she really enjoys teaching the subject for which she has prepared herself. She will learn through her close contacts with children whether she is really interested in teaching children of the particular age level for which she is assigned. Most important of all, she will, hopefully, find a genuine enthusiasm in the teaching task, an enthusiasm sufficient to convince her that this should be her chosen vocation.

At the same time, the student-teaching assignment will give the training institution an opportunity to evaluate the student's teaching capabilities. A successful student-teaching experience, under the supervision of a qualified classroom teacher, will enable the training institution to place its stamp of approval on the student teacher's work, with reasonable assurance of her future success.

The prospective science teacher can confidently expect to gain the following values from her student-teaching experience. These values will not accrue automatically. Much of the responsibility rests with the student teacher herself as she attempts to profit from this culminating experience in her teacher training.

1. *Improvement in Confidence.* Actual experience with a science class will take away the fear of the unknown that everyone experiences when faced with a new situation. Many of these fears may turn out to be groundless. The experience will actually prove to be fun and exhilarating once the initial uneasiness is overcome. Psychologists have learned that the way to overcome "the butterflies" of fear of the unexpected is to become deeply involved in the experience. The immediacy of the routine problems then supercedes the anticipated difficulties.

2. *Putting Theories into Practice.* Here the new teacher will be able to test what she has learned in methods classes (and in other classes) about ways of handling various problems. Handling individual differences among students, discipline cases, techniques of presenting science material, laboratory methods, working with small groups, etc. will provide situations in which the student teacher can apply educational theories to classroom reality.

3. *Learning About Student Behavior.* Firsthand, responsible relationships with students will give the student teacher the chance to study them, observe their behavior under a variety of con-

ditions, and learn about motivation, competition, enthusiasm, boredom, and many other factors which make up the "climate" of a typical classroom.

4. *Testing Knowledge of Subject Matter.* Regardless of the student teacher's self-assurance and confidence in her own knowledge of the subject she is planning to teach, there is likely to be a certain amount of apprehension about her ability to transmit this knowledge to others. The responsibility of teaching enthusiastic and sometimes critical students can be unnerving and is certain to convince the student teacher of the necessity of knowing her subject thoroughly and of preparing for her contacts with the class. One frequently hears the comment, even among experienced teachers, "I really learned my subject when I had to teach it."

5. *Receiving Constructive Criticism.* At no other time in a teacher's experience will she have the benefit of prolonged, intensive observation of her teaching by an experienced teacher who can be constructive in her criticism and advice. This value is not to be taken lightly. If the criticism and suggestions are taken receptively, with the intention of putting them into practice, this experience can be the most valuable part of the student teacher's assignment. It is important, therefore, to select one's supervising teacher wisely. The chance to observe and be observed by a master teacher in an atmosphere of mutual respect and helpfulness is immeasurably worthwhile.

6. *Discovering Teaching Strengths and Weaknesses.* The student teacher will have the opportunity to discover her own strong and weak points in the handling of science classes. She may find that performing demonstrations results in the most successful teaching and gives her the most pleasure. It may be that organizing classes into effective discussion groups brings about maximum learning under her direction. The questioning technique and the Socratic method of carrying on teacher-pupil discussions may be most successful under her guidance. On the other hand, these same activities may be the least

A new practice teacher tries out her teaching skills.

effective for her. Knowing these facts early in her career will enable her to improve her weaknesses and capitalize on her strengths. It is certainly to the advantage of a science teacher to be highly competent in many methods of teaching, but it is equally important to recognize that individual teachers have certain innate teaching strengths and should use techniques that capitalize on these strengths.

7. *Gaining Poise and Finesse.* Because teaching is as much an art as a science, experience should improve ways of handling classes, such as anticipating student questions and problems, timing, exploiting enthusiastic and dramatic classroom events, sensing the proper time for introducing a new activity, and commending good work. These factors will contribute to smoother functioning of class activities and generally more effective learning. It is important to recognize, of course, that this kind of improvement will continue as long as a teacher teaches and that rarely, if ever, does a teacher reach complete perfection in the art.

Selecting Your Supervising Teacher

Frequently, a certain amount of latitude is allowed the prospective student teacher in her choice of school, subject, and teacher under whom she wishes to work. The extent of this freedom will vary with the institution and circumstances in which the student-teaching program is operated, and it is entirely possible that assignments may be made quite arbitrarily. However, it is more likely that, within certain limitations, the wishes of the student will be taken into consideration.

Therefore, it is to the advantage of the student teacher to make a careful selection of school, subject, and supervising teacher. Often, new teachers feel that their student-teaching assignment was the most valuable experience in their training program. This can be true if the selection is well made and the experience fulfills its potential.

The prospective student teacher should obtain the maximum advantage by teaching in her major field. It is this area for which she is best prepared and in which she will probably feel the greatest confidence. If the situation permits, teaching in her minor field also, under a different supervising teacher, may be advantageous; she will benefit from constructive help from two experienced teachers. This experience may be analogous to an actual situation as a full-time teacher in a small or medium-sized school system.

It would be wise to visit several classes in a number of schools in the quarter or semester before the student-teaching assignment. Arrangements can be made through the principal of the school, and advance notice can be given to the teachers involved. If the purpose of the visits is explained, the prospective student teacher will probably be favorably received, particularly if it is a school in which student teachers have customarily been supervised.

The advantages of the visit can be manifold. The student will be able to refresh her memory of the atmosphere and activities of a high school classroom. She will be able to observe an experienced teacher in action. She will mentally attempt to project herself into an equivalent situation as a teacher in charge of a class, a desirable step in preparation for her actual student-teaching assignment. She may be able to talk briefly with the teacher at the close of class to gain further insight into the teaching situation. After several such visits to a variety of classes, including several outside the field of science, the prospective student teacher will be able to choose more intelligently the kind of teaching situation she wishes to select for her student-teaching experience.

Some suggestions of criteria to look for in the teaching situation are:

1. Is the teacher well prepared, and is she teaching in her major field?
2. Does the teacher have good control of the class?
3. Do the students appear to be alert and interested in the activities?
4. Is there a genuine atmosphere of learning?
5. Do the facilities and materials appear to be adequate for the kind of science being taught?
6. Does it appear that the teacher is a person from whom one can learn valuable teaching techniques?
7. Is there opportunity for a certain degree of flexibility in carrying out one's teaching plans?
8. Does the teacher have a moderate work load, thus affording time for constructive help for a student teacher?
9. Does the teacher appear to be interested in serving as a supervisor for a student teacher in his or her charge?

Meeting Your Supervising Teacher

Once the assignment is made for a particular school, class, and teacher, it is imperative that the student teacher arrange for a short interview before attendance at the first class. This interview can be brief but preferably should be a day or two in advance and by appointment. You will then avoid incurring the displeasure of the supervising teacher by intruding

In student teaching, theory meets practice.

on her last-minute preparation for class and will give an opportunity for an interchange of questions and answers by both parties.

At the interview, the student teacher should be punctual, interested, enthusiastic, and suitably dressed. The purpose of the interview is to become acquainted and to exchange ideas and information. The supervising teacher is interested in knowing the background and preparation of the student teacher. She is also interested in any special qualifications the student teacher may have, such as ability to handle audiovisual equipment, take charge of a science club, or talk on travel experiences. The student teacher is interested in learning what her role is to be in the classroom, what meetings she should attend, what text materials are in use, etc.

The supervising teacher will probably suggest a period of class observation, perhaps a week or two, at the outset. There may be certain room duties to perform such as roll-taking, reading announcements, and distributing materials. Each of these tasks will enable the student teacher to learn the names of pupils quickly, a necessary step in establishing rapport with members of the class. The student teacher will probably be encouraged to prepare a seating chart immediately. Text materials may be discussed and the teacher's long-range objectives clarified. The student teacher will probably be asked to read certain assignments so that she will be acquainted with the students' present studies. She will find it imperative to do this regularly, so as to be of maximum assistance to students who call on her for help.

Facilities and apparatus available for teaching the science class may be shown to the student teacher during the interview. Location of the library and special preparation rooms may be pointed out. The place in the classroom where the student teacher may observe the activities of the class may be designated. (In one school, it was customary for the student teacher to sit next to the demonstration desk, facing the class. In this way, she learned to recognize pupils more quickly; but, more importantly, this arrangement enabled the student teacher to see the expressions on the faces of the pupils as they responded to questions or watched a demonstration, as they showed perplexity or registered insight into problems under discussion.)

Students who intend to teach in urban-area schools are advised to seek out student-teaching experiences that will give them the best possible preparation for such an assignment. Such an experience might involve student teaching in a school similar to the type they wish to be teaching in ultimately.

■ Being a Student Teacher

Your First Days in the Class

Observing pupils in the science class can be a profitable experience the first few days or weeks. The student teacher has an advantage in this situation because she is not preoccupied with teaching plans and conducting the class, as is the regular teacher. The alert student teacher can, in fact, be of assistance to the regular teacher in recognizing incipient discipline problems, lack of interest, or special conditions which might lead to better teaching if recognized early. The student teacher may wish to engage in a systematic program of observation to become familiar with all members of the class. For this purpose, a checklist of individual differences is suggested. Place a check mark in the column opposite the observed characteristic. The numbers represent individual pupils observed.

The first days in the student-teaching class should afford opportunities to give individual help to pupils who need it. Do not answer questions directly but use inquiry methods, that is, ask guiding questions. It is wise to confer with the supervising teacher about the extent of such help. There may be some reason to withhold assistance on certain assignments. At the same time, contact with students on an individual basis is an excellent way to gain confidence in your ability to explain, teach or convey information. The student teacher should capitalize on every possible opportunity to develop this skill.

Recognizing Individual Differences in a New Class During the First Few Weeks[1]
Things to observe and consider:

	Pupils			
	1	2	3	4
1. Health	___	___	___	___
2. Physical defects and differences	___	___	___	___
3. Personality	___	___	___	___
4. Basic skills	___	___	___	___
5. Relationships with fellow pupils	___	___	___	___
6. Relationship with teacher	___	___	___	___
7. Class participation	___	___	___	___
8. Class attitude and co-operation	___	___	___	___
9. Dependability	___	___	___	___
10. Probable ability combined with effort	___	___	___	___

If the science class is one in which laboratory work plays a large part, (i.e. chemistry, physics, biology, or earth science), there will be many opportunities to give individual help. The student teacher can also be of significant help to the regular teacher in preparing laboratory apparatus and supplies. In this situation the student teacher will realize that teaching a laboratory science requires extensive planning and attention to detail.

Because the initial period of observation may be rather brief, perhaps only a few days or a week, the student teacher will do well to begin thinking about the choice of a teaching area or unit. Such a choice may have already been made in conference with the supervising teacher. It will certainly depend on the subject-matter goals of the course during the semester or quarter of the assignment. In anticipation of her student teaching, the student will wish to

gather appropriate materials and to prepare general plans. Some of the details of the preliminary planning are considered in the next section.

Preparing to Teach a Lesson

Some of the problems involved in lesson planning are detailed in Chapter 19. However, a brief review of the salient factors may be worthwhile.

A teacher facing a class for the first time may expect to accomplish far too much in a given amount of time. Although it is not necessarily wasteful to overplan a lesson, it is a mistake to try to teach everything on the lesson plan just because it is there. Sometimes the learning pace of the pupils does not allow the entire lesson plan to be completed. You must constantly be in tune with your class, sensing the proper pace and modifying your presentation as the situation demands.

A second common fault of the beginning teacher is the tendency to teach beyond the students' comprehension. This fault may be a result of recent contact with college courses, in which the level is very high, or the inability to place abstract ideas into concrete terms for comprehension by secondary school students. The problem is important enough that it is worth extra consideration by the beginning teacher to make certain that her presentation is at the appropriate level for the class involved. Perhaps she could try a few "test trials" with individual students to acquire a realistic sense of the proper difficulty level before she teaches the entire class.

Construction of unit and daily lesson plans is an important task at this stage (see Chapter 19 for suggested formats). It is important to have a clear idea of what you wish to accomplish in the allotted time and what specific objectives are to be met. The student teacher should attempt to place herself in the position of a science pupil who is learning about the material for the first time. She should consider factors of interest, motivation, individual differences, time limitations, facilities, and equipment; she should try to anticipate the kinds of problems which may occur and prepare possible solutions. When she has considered these elements, she will feel more secure and will have fewer discipline problems.

The beginning teacher should also anticipate questions from the class. First attempts at planning tend to neglect preparation for handling these questions and fail to provide enough time for dealing with them in the class period. Yet the frank interchange of ideas between teacher and students which is provoked by questions can be an effective teaching technique and should not be ignored. In planning, try to anticipate the kinds of questions students may ask.

Student Teaching in Science

Melinda Bell
Student Teacher, Northfield Senior High School
Northfield, Minnesota

"We never learn as much with a student teacher."

"The student teachers are always nervous, lack confidence, and can't keep the classes under control."

"The student teachers expect us to be like college students because that is what they are most familiar with."

These comments were generated by high school students in the school where I am doing my student teaching. I think it is important to take them seriously, although I will rapidly deny that they characterize each and every student teacher. Sure, we're all bound to be a little nervous and to be somewhat unsure of how to discipline or how to present material so it is clear, understandable, and interesting to the students. But that doesn't mean we have to be bogged down by those things!

There is so much else that we, as student teachers, have going for us. We are well armed with a knowledge of our subject and a delightful artillery of ways in which we can present our material. We are bright and enthusiastic and willing to try things in new, innovative ways. We have taken a science teaching methods course which has hopefully prepared us in some other ways. We even have students who will see advantages in our being there!

"Student teachers are young and don't seem as fuddy-duddy as the regular teacher."

"Student teachers are more on our level so they are easier to approach."

"Sometimes the student teacher can explain things in a different way than the regular teacher so more students understand it."

All of these things don't make student teaching "easy"; rather they make it an exciting challenge and an opportunity for you to practice your skills, accepting the lesson plans that don't work and the feeling of accomplishment and pride when your lesson goes over well and the students get excited about something which you taught them! Not all of your students are going to enjoy you as a teacher, but some will welcome you openly, along with the fresh change and enthusiasm you bring to the classroom.

Some of my friends are amazed by the amount of enjoyment I get out of student teaching.

"Don't you get bored teaching the same material over and over?" is a question commonly asked. Once I've recovered from the shock of picturing myself "bored," I reply that I can teach the same or similar materials in such a variety of ways that it remains interesting to me. In fact, the personalities of each class are generally so

If you remember that the students may be encountering the subject matter for the first time, it is not too difficult to foretell what questions may come to their minds. These probable questions should be jotted down on the lesson plan with suitable answers or with suggested procedures for finding the answers if the questions come up. Time spent in this manner is not wasted, even if the specific anticipated questions do not arise. The beginning teacher will gain confidence in her own understanding of the subject matter and in her ability to provide suitable answers.

A final point for consideration is that of proper pacing and timing of the class period. The written lesson plans may have suggested time allotments for various activities, but the actual class is certain to deviate to some extent from these plans. The important thing is to be flexible enough to accommodate

minor variations within the class period. However, to avoid gross miscalculations of time requirements for certain activities, it is well to rehearse them in advance. A short lecture, for example, can be tried out on one's roommate, who will be able to give critical comments on clarity and organization, as well as timing. In the case of student activities or laboratory work, it is usually advisable to allot about 50 percent more time than appears adequate for the teacher herself to do the work. This leeway is also recommended in giving written tests.

At all stages of planning for the first day of teaching, it is imperative that the student teacher keep the supervising teacher informed of her plans, solicit advice and assistance, and in general plan in such a way as to make the transition from regular teacher to student teacher as smooth as possible.

varied that the "best" way of presenting the material to one class might be the "worst" method for another. Gauging the class correctly and presenting the material in a suitable manner for that class is the challenge in making the lesson a successful one.

My friends also worry that teaching will not be intellectually satisfying enough for me. After all, it is only high school material! That is the *least* of my worries! I really "learned" about DNA when I had to understand it thoroughly enough to answer the students' questions on it and when I had to be able to explain what newspaper articles meant when they talked about genetic engineering. To make DNA relevant, I had to ensure that it touched something which they are conscious of as happening in the world today. That holds for whether we are talking about DNA and test-tube babies or about photosynthesis and the greenhouse effect. If it doesn't make sense to them and if they don't find it relevant, it will be rapidly forgotten.

The intellectual challenge for me is to keep up on the recent advances in different areas of science and understand how these advances are applicable to the students' world today.

Some people are curious as to why I am going into education when I could go on into research or

a medical profession. Selfishly, it is because I hope that I will be an influence through teaching and other aspects of my life in helping people to understand that every decision they make is a reflection on how they look at the world. And science to me has an important message for everyone. Science is a way of looking at the world and dealing with the world on a physical level. Science gives us a method we can use for finding solutions to problems that come up in everyday life. It is unfortunate that science, for many people, is an object to be feared or held in mystified awe. Science is not magic. It is merely a way of putting curiosity and creativity together to come up with reasonable explanations for unanswered questions.

Not everyone has the capacity to become a nuclear physicist, but everyone can learn what processes a scientist goes through in his thinking and can apply these same methods to areas of his own life. If I can get that across to my students, I will feel that I have accomplished something.

Because I believe in science and because I am excited about the things we can learn from it, I want to share that with others. My own interest in it causes me to be enthusiastic and to remain involved myself.

The First Day of Teaching

If the student teacher has had frequent opportunities to work with individuals and small groups before her first day of actual teaching, she will find the new experience a natural extension of these tasks and a challenging opportunity for growth in the art of teaching.

A good introduction will get the class off to an interesting start. A brief explanation of the purpose of the lesson and the work at hand, followed immediately by plunging into the class activities, will convey to the students an appreciation of the tasks to be accomplished. A forthright and businesslike manner by the student teacher will elicit cooperation of the class and leave no doubt about who is in charge.

Attention should be given to proper speech and voice modulation. A good pace should be maintained; and, above all, genuine enthusiasm must be displayed. This enthusiasm will normally be infectious and will secure an enthusiastic response from the class. If possible, students should be encouraged to participate. Questions from students should be encouraged and a relaxed atmosphere maintained for free interchange of ideas.

It is usually advisable, especially with junior high school classes, to vary the activity once or twice during the class period. Perhaps a short lecture can be followed by a brief film and the period concluded with a summarizing discussion. Or a demonstration by the teacher might be followed by a period of individual experimentation. It is true that planning and execution of a varied class period requires more work on the part of the teacher, but they will pay dividends in the form of enthusiasm, alert attention, and better learning by the pupils.

The last five or ten minutes of a class period are often used to summarize the major points of the lesson and to make appropriate assignments. It is important to recognize that students need to have a feeling of accomplishment and progress to keep their motivation high. A final clarification of what is expected of them in preparation for succeeding lessons is worth a few minutes at the close of a class period.

Completion of the first day of teaching by the student teacher should be followed as soon as possible by reflection on the successes and failures of the class period and an effort to diagnose any problems which may have arisen. This evaluation can usually be done profitably in conference with the supervising teacher and can be a useful follow-up to the day. Any required adjustments in future plans can be made at this time, necessary additional materials can be gathered, and the stage can be set for a new day of teaching to follow.

Your Responsibilities

The opportunity to student teach in a given school system under a competent supervising teacher should be considered a privilege. Contrary to an apprentice in a typical trade situation, the "apprentice teacher" is not working with inanimate materials such as wood and metal but with live human beings of infinite worth. She must never forget her responsibility to provide the best possible education for the students and to avoid possible harmful measures.

It is, therefore, extremely important to make lesson plans with care, to consider individual differences in interest and ability, and to conduct the class in an atmosphere of friendly helpfulness. Each student should be considered a potential learning organism with capabilities for infinite growth. The teacher's responsibility is to develop this potential to the maximum extent.

The student teacher's responsibility to the supervising teacher rests in the area of recognition of authority and respect for experience. Certainly disagreements about teaching methods of approach may exist, but the final authority in the matter is that of the supervising teacher, who is officially responsible for the class. At the same time, an alert student teacher can be of great help by anticipating the needs of the class, suggesting materials, preparing materials, and in general earning the title of "assistant teacher," which is used in some school systems. The varied backgrounds of student teachers and their

willingness to share experiences and special talents can make the science classroom more interesting and educationally effective.

The responsibility of the student teacher toward herself and her potential as a science teacher is also important. It would be relatively easy to sit casually by, waiting for things to happen in the student-teaching assignment. The student teacher who gains the most, however, from the standpoint of personal growth, will be the one who enters into the experience with a dynamic approach, intent on learning everything she can in the time allotted. She will participate, when permitted, in meetings of the school faculty, in attendance and assistance at school athletic events, in dramatic and musical productions of the school, and other functions relating to school life. In this way she will see her pupils in many roles outside of the science classroom and will gain insight into the total school program. She will be able to achieve a balanced perspective of her own role as a teacher of science among the other academic disciplines and curricular activities of the school. Such experience will enable her to become a mature teacher of science and will complete the metamorphosis from the role of college science student.

Concerns of the Student Teacher

A questionnaire listing nine areas of preparation was distributed to forty student teachers of secondary science at the University of Northern Colorado. They were asked to indicate those areas in which they felt the need of greater preparation.

Four areas receiving the greatest number of responses were: evaluating students and grading, handling discipline problems, answering students' questions, and stronger preparation in subject matter, in that order. Other areas of consideration were: lesson planning, record keeping, extracurricular activities, demonstrations, and handling laboratory work.

In the same survey, when asked to suggest improvements in the methods courses in physical and biological sciences, the following suggestions were made:

1. Put more emphasis on discipline, problems and on answering students' questions.
2. Have more discussion on techniques for handling slow and fast learners.
3. Do more demonstrations and experiments.
4. Emphasize methods of evaluation.
5. Provide opportunities to hear the experiences of recent student teachers.

6. Evaluate the texts and materials of the new secondary curriculum projects.
7. Provide more opportunities to speak in front of a group and do demonstration teaching.
8. Cover a greater variety of topics, including test construction, extra-credit work, interest development, grouping of students, policies regarding student failures, science fairs and exhibits, etc.
9. Provide opportunities to observe several teachers in one's field.
10. Acquire more information on specific source-books of activities, demonstrations, and experiments.

Becoming a Professional

The science teacher today is a member of a dedicated group of professional educators which includes classroom teachers, supervisors, coordinators, administrators, and other educational specialists. This group has the responsibility for developing curriculum plans and effectively teaching the youth of the nation.

Science teachers greatly influence the nation's youth. Science courses are regarded as respectable academic subjects in any secondary curriculum, along with such courses as mathematics, English, foreign languages, and social sciences. The science teacher, by virtue of his choice of subject, is viewed with respect by other teachers and by laymen of the community.

The young science teacher cannot help but feel pride in being a part of the science teaching profession. Science holds the spotlight in many of our country's schools. It is an exciting time to be a science teacher and the rewards are abundant. Along with a favorable focus of attention comes responsibility for dedication to the task and for self-improvement as a teacher. It is for this reason that attention is directed in this chapter to the preparation of the professional science educator.

The prospective science teacher in an undergraduate program at a college or university is nearing her goal of becoming a qualified specialist in her subject. In most cases her decision to prepare herself as a teacher of a particular science subject was made early in her college career, on the basis of interest, environmental background, previous training, and prospective rewards in the teaching field. As she approaches the end of her training, the prospective teacher looks forward to an interesting and productive career as a professional educator in a challenging field of teaching. She is concerned that her training has been adequate for the task and that she will be successful in meeting the challenges ahead.

Even if you obtain the best undergraduate preparation available to the prospective science teacher, it is a mistake to assume that the goal has been reached when the bachelor's degree is granted. Because of the rapid and continuing pace of science achievements and the ever-changing pattern of teaching methods and curriculum organization, the science teacher must constantly be alert to new knowledge and new techniques. For this reason, a conscientious science teacher will consider that her education is never finished as long as she wishes to remain an effective contributor to her profession.

■ Securing a Teaching Position

Recent years have shown a fluctuating job market for teachers. The prospective teacher must work diligently at finding a suitable position. Competition is high, and she must use all of the available avenues to secure a satisfactory teaching job.

Getting Ready to Look for a Job

As preparation to enter the job market, there are several necessary steps. The prospective employee of a school system will wish to secure several recommendations from her college instructors in her major and minor fields, her methods instructors, and perhaps others of her own choosing. Be sure to obtain permission to use an instructor's name for a reference and request the recommendation personally, either by letter or by personal conversation. Remember that instructors are asked to write many recommendations, and a thoughtful instructor will put in a reasonable amount of time in writing a good one. To make the job as easy for her as possible, supply her with specific information about yourself. For example, give her information on your hobbies and on your experiences in working with children such as coaching, camp counseling, summer recreation programs, Sunday school teaching, etc. Tell her about any special competencies that you have such as the ability to handle a photography club, or special knowledge of rocks and minerals, or model airplane building, or any other relevant experiences. Give specific evidence of the kinds of experiences that would qualify you to be a good science teacher. This kind of information will pay dividends and will secure for you the immediate attention of a thoughtful school administrator.

When requesting a recommendation, if the

contact with the instructor is several months old, it is a good idea to supply her with a snapshot of yourself which will refresh her memory as to your presence in her classes. Below is a sample recommendation request form that will supply the instructor with the kind of information she needs to do a thorough job.

Using Placement Services

You will probably wish to use one or more teacher placement services to secure a satisfactory position. Most teacher-training institutions have placement offices. There may be an enrollment fee for this service. You would be well advised to get all of your required materials in early, usually by January 1, because the placement offices begin to make appointments with school administrators early in the new year to interview applicants for positions. If you are conscientious about submitting all of your requirements, you will be eligible to meet with prospective employers.

Second, many state departments of education have placement bureaus. It is wise to contact them and give them the necessary information so that they can assist you in locating vacancies within the state where you plan to teach.

Letters of Application

Once you have been notified of a suitable vacancy for which you wish to apply, you must prepare a letter of application that will be considered favorably by the recipient. If you plan to type your own application letter, it is a good idea to check with a secretary to refresh your memory on style and form. In many cases, your letter of application will merely bring forth a standard application form from the school to which you apply. In this case, give the complete information required by the school.

If possible, have your letter of application typed by a secretary. This adds quality and dignity to the correspondence and you will impress the recipient. The receipt of a poorly constructed letter with typographical errors, erasures, and other evidence of carelessness is almost certain to result in the letter being tossed into the reject file.

In your letter of application, be sure to include all of the necessary information to give a clear picture

---

Personal Recommendation

Name _____

Classes from me _____

_____

Grades _____

Because many of you will be applying for teaching jobs (or other jobs in the near future), you will be required to obtain letters of recommendation for your files at the Office of Appointments. If requested to write such a recommendation, I shall be happy to oblige but I should like to have some further information about you to include in the recommendation. It is my belief that the following types of information can be very meaningful to a prospective employer and may make the difference between being hired and not being hired.

Please give information on the following points.

1. Any experience you have had working with young people in any capacity other than practice teaching, such as scout leader, Sunday school teacher, swimming instructor, camp counselor, or other. Give specific information.

2. Any scientific hobbies or specialties you may have (past or present) such as specimen collecting, lapidary, ham radio, model airplane building, amateur telescope making, special reading in a topic, expertise with computers, etc.

3. Any travel you have done which may have been scientifically broadening or educational, such as Carlsbad Caverns, Grand Canyon, Yellowstone Park, or any others.

4. Any other experiential information which may be important for a prospective employer to know.

of your qualifications for the job for which you are applying. Include your major and minor teaching areas, information on special competencies, such as ability to handle specific types of clubs, and information on your familiarity with new teaching trends such as inquiry teaching, team teaching, individualized instruction, new curriculum projects, open-school concepts, and other current trends.

You might conclude the letter by volunteering your willingness to meet the superintendent for an interview at a mutually convenient time. Following is a sample letter of application you might use as a guide:

The Job Interview

If you are interviewed by the principal or superintendent of schools, you will wish to present yourself in the best possible manner. Be sure to arrive on time, dress appropriately, and be well groomed. Allow the employer to conduct the interview at his own pace and in his own manner. Supply information about yourself as requested. If asked, discuss your philos-

ophy of teaching briefly, tell about your training and special competencies, and inform him of your professional memberships, such as the National Science Teachers Association, Academies of Science, National Association of Biology Teachers, and other organizations to which you belong.

You will have the opportunity to ask questions. You will want to know some of the details of the position, such as the level of the class, its probable size, the text materials that are used, and the availability of supplies. You perhaps will want to ask questions about the community such as the availability of housing, churches, and recreation facilities. Let the interviewer supply you with information on the prospective salary and other fringe benefits associated with the job.

After Obtaining the Job

Securing a position as a new teacher is a major accomplishment and may give you the feeling that your teaching career is set for all time. However, this would be a short-sighted view. Of course it should

---

January 12, 1986

Dr. Harold Oglesby
Superintendent of Schools
Wichita Falls, Missouri

Dear Dr. Oglesby:

I wish to apply for the position as teacher of junior high school science announced as a vacancy in your school system. The placement office at Webster State College, Webster, Kansas, will send my complete credentials.

My major teaching area is junior high school science and my minor is mathematics. In addition, I have secured a teacher's permit for driver education and am qualified to give the driver education course for the state of Missouri.

Photography has been a hobby and a vocation of mine for many years and I would be interested in supervising a junior high school photography club.

I shall be happy to come for a personal interview at your convenience.

Sincerely yours,

John Tryst

be your intention to remain on the job with the expectation of doing excellent work, but you should also recognize that you may want to move upward professionally. Therefore, it is a good idea to keep your placement file up to date. Keep in contact with the placement office by informing them of any new course work that you have taken, such as institutes or summer school attendance. Have updated transcripts supplied to the placement office, which may include the completion of a new degree or additional course work. When you are ready to apply for a new position, be sure to get recommendations from your principal and supervisor.

■ Characteristics of a Good Science Teacher

Administrators and supervisors constantly evaluate teachers, for salary increments, promotions to department chairman, differentiated staffing, and other reasons. Unfortunately, many evaluations are made on the basis of superficial characteristics or personal qualities that happen to please or displease the evaluator, rather than on more basic characteristics that exemplify good teaching. Following is a question checklist that can be used by an administrator, supervisor, or by the science teacher herself for self-evaluation (prepared by Lawrence Conrey, University of Michigan, Ann Arbor, Michigan).

Question Checklist

1. Is she enthusiastic about what she is doing and does she show it?
2. Is she dynamic and does she use her voice and facial expression for emphasis and to hold attention?
3. Does she use "gadgets" or other illustrative devices extensively to make each new learning experience as concrete as possible?
4. Does she show originality in making teaching materials from simple objects or "junk"?
5. Does she have a functional knowledge of her subject so that she can apply what she knows to everyday living?
6. Does she possess the ability to explain ideas in simple terms regardless of the extent of her knowledge?
7. Does she stimulate actual thought on the part of her students or does she make parrots out of them?
8. Is she a "have to finish the book" type of teacher or does she teach thoroughly?
9. Does she maintain calm and poise in the most trying of classroom circumstances?

10. Does she use a variety of teaching techniques or is it the same thing day after day?
11. Does she exhibit a feeling of confidence and are the students confident about her ability?
12. Does she encourage class participation and questions and does she conscientiously plan for them?
13. Does she maintain a good instructional tempo so that the period does not drag?
14. Does she use techniques to stimulate interest at the beginning of new material or does she treat it merely as something new to be learned?
15. Does she concentrate on key ideas and use facts as means to an end?

Of a more formal nature is the Stanford Teacher Competence Appraisal Guide.[2] It may be used to assist the individual teacher in assessing her strengths and weaknesses or it may be used for formal evaluation purposes. For rating, each item may be evaluated on the basis of eight points and totaled for a cumulative score. The ratings are:

0	Unable to observe	4	Strong
1	Weak	5	Superior
2	Below average	6	Outstanding
3	Average	7	Truly exceptional

Stanford Teacher Competence Appraisal Guide

Aims
1. *Clarity of aims.* The purposes of the lesson are clear.
2. *Appropriateness of aims.* The aims are neither too easy nor too difficult for the pupils. They are appropriate and are accepted by the pupils.

Planning
3. *Organization of the lesson.* The individual parts of the lesson are clearly related to each other in an appropriate way. The total organization facilitates what is to be learned.
4. *Selection of content.* The content is appropriate for the aims of the lesson, the level of the class, and the teaching method.
5. *Selection of materials.* The specific instructional materials and human resources used are clearly related to the content of the lesson and complement the selected method of instruction.

Performance
6. *Beginning the lesson.* Students come quickly to attention. They direct themselves to the tasks to be accomplished.
7. *Clarity of presentation.* The content of the lesson is presented so that it is understandable to the pupils. Different points of view and specific illustrations are used when appropriate.

8. *Pacing of the Lesson.* The movement from one part of the lesson to the next is governed by the students' achievement. The teacher "stays with the class" and adjusts the tempo accordingly.
9. *Pupil participation and attention.* The class is attentive. When appropriate, the students actively participate in the lesson.
10. *Ending the lesson.* The lesson is ended when the students have achieved the aims of instruction. The teacher ties together chance and planned events and relates them to long-range aim of instruction.
11. *Teacher-student rapport.* The personal relationships between students and teacher are harmonious.

Evaluation

12. *Variety of evaluative procedures.* The teacher devises and uses an adequate variety of procedures, both formal and informal, to evaluate progress in all of the aims of instruction.
13. *Use of evaluation to provide improvement of teaching and learning.* The results of evaluation are carefully reviewed by teacher and students to improve teaching and learning.

Professional

14. *Concern for professional standards and growth.* The teacher helps, particularly in her specialty, to define and enforce standards for (1) selecting, training, and licensing teachers, and (2) working conditions.
15. *Effectiveness in school staff relationships.* The teacher is respectful and considerate of her colleagues. She demonstrates awareness of their personal concerns and professional development.
16. *Concern for the total school program.* The teacher's concern is not simply for her courses and her students. She works with other teachers, students, and administrators to bring about the success of the program.
17. *Constructive participation in community affairs.* The teacher understands the particular community context in which she works and helps to translate the purposes of the school's program to the community.

■ Research on Science Teacher Characteristics

In 1980 Cynthia Druva and Ronald Anderson carried out a research project, using the principles of meta-analysis of research, that focused on science teacher characteristics.[3] The results were reported by displaying correlations between these identified teacher characteristics, teacher behavior, and student outcomes. The meta-analysis was conducted of research studies that used characteristics of gender, course work, I.Q., and so forth as independent variables and as dependent variables (1) teaching behavior in the classroom such as questioning behavior and teaching orientation, and (2) student outcome characteristics such as achievement and attitudes toward science. The subject population was chosen from teachers and students in science classes throughout the United States from kindergarten through 12th grade.

With respect to the relationships between teacher characteristics and teacher behavior, the following outcomes were reported:

1. Teaching effectiveness is positively related to training and experience as evidenced by the number of education courses, student teaching grade, and experience in teaching.
2. Teachers with a more positive attitude toward the curriculum that they are teaching tend to be those with a higher grade-point average and more teaching experience.
3. Better classroom discipline is associated with the teacher characteristics of restraint and reflectivity.
4. Higher level, more complex questions were employed more often by teachers with greater knowledge and less experience in teaching.

With respect to the relationships between teacher characteristics and student outcomes, several relationships were discovered:

1. Student achievement is positively related to teacher characteristics of self-actualization, heterosexuality, and masculinity. It is also related positively to the number of science courses taken and attendance at academic institutes.
2. The process skill outcomes of students are positively related to the number of science courses taken by teachers.
3. The outcome of a positive attitude toward science was positively associated with the number of science courses taken by teachers and the number of years of teaching experience.

One of the implications of the study is that there is a relationship between teacher preparation programs and what their graduates do as teachers. Science courses, education courses, and overall academic performance are positively associated with successful teaching.

For the student teacher, the research reported above is significant because it gives direction and guidance to his career and goal preparation. While the results may seem to be natural, common-sense results, it is significant that data now show that teachers with better preparation in science as well as in the pedagogical areas do a better job of teaching. Also significant is the finding that a positive attitude toward their task relates to better results for the students in their charge.

One of the difficulties brought about by the daily routine of hard, laborious work in teaching—the incessant planning, paper grading and all such work—is that this sometimes has a debilitating effect on young teachers. It may cause them to become cynical and skeptical of the results they are achieving. Many times they will tend to blame the students or the system when in fact it may be the negative attitude which they themselves bring to the teaching task that is at least partially responsible for their poor results.

It is very important to maintain zest for teaching. In no other profession is it as important to exhibit a positive and enthusiastic relationship with individuals. Young minds in your charge are vulnerable to your attitudes and enthusiasm as well as your obvious background of preparation and experience. A caring teacher is able to overcome many shortcomings in background and preparation but an uncaring teacher cannot be successful though he or she may have excellent preparation in terms of subject matter and teaching techniques.

■ Opportunities for Professional Growth

Among the opportunities for professional growth while on the job are graduate work during the summer or at night, depending on the available opportunities; inservice workshops and institutes; government- or industry-sponsored summer institutes; committee activity on curriculum revision or evaluation; membership in professional organizations, with accompanying attendance at regular meetings and participation in committee work; reading professional journals, scientific publications, and current books in science and teaching; writing for professional publications; keeping up to date on new materials, teaching resources, education aids, etc.

Graduate Work

The National Science Foundation reported that 39 percent of science and mathematics teachers in the United States have master's degrees and that over 75 percent hold credits for at least ten semester hours of graduate work.[4] Twenty percent had completed at least one National Science Foundation summer institute.

There are many opportunities for graduate work. The usual requirement for completion of a

Exchanging ideas with other teachers stimulates professional growth.

master's degree in education is one year or four summers of course work. Theses are generally not required, but comprehensive examinations in a major and minor field usually are. The monetary rewards for science teachers with master's degrees are well worth the time and expense involved in obtaining the degree. Most school systems have a salary differential of several hundred dollars for holders of master's degrees; furthermore, opportunities for higher-paying jobs are greater and a better selection of teaching positions is available for the applicant who holds a master's degree.

Inservice Training and Institutes

Inservice workshops and institutes are usually sponsored by public school systems for improvement of the teachers within that system. Degree credit may or may not be offered, depending on the arrangements with the colleges or universities from which consultant services are obtained. Such workshops and institutes often have objectives designed to stimulate curriculum improvement or to improve teacher competencies in subject-matter understanding and teaching techniques. The new teacher is encouraged to avail herself of these opportunities to familiarize herself with broad problems of curriculum improvements and to benefit from the experience of older teachers in the system.

Government- or industry-sponsored summer and inservice institutes provide excellent opportunities to grow professionally. Although fewer of these institutes are available now than before, the usual requirement is three years of teaching experience; however, this rule is frequently relaxed for one reason or another.

Committee Work

Committee activity is an excellent way to develop a professional attitude and become aware of the many problems facing the science teacher. Active school systems frequently have a curriculum committee, a professional committee, a salary and grievance committee, a textbook-selection committee, or other committees of temporary nature as the need for them arises. Participation on one or more of these committees can be enlightening and can contribute to the professional growth of the new teacher; however, committee responsibilities mean extra work, and the new science teacher should consider her total work load and weigh carefully the ultimate benefits of participation.

Professional Organizations

There are many professional organizations serving the science teacher. They are listed here along with their respective journals.

1. American Association of Physics Teachers—the *American Journal of Physics* and *The Physics Teacher*
2. The American Chemical Society—the *Journal of Chemical Education*
3. The National Association of Biology Teachers—*The American Biology Teacher*
4. The National Science Teachers Association—*The Science Teacher, Science and Children, Science Scope,* and *The Journal of College Science Teaching*
5. The School Science and Mathematics Association—*School Science and Mathematics*
6. The National Association for Research in Science Teaching—*Journal of Research in Science Teaching*
7. The American Association for the Advancement of Science—*Science*
8. Council for Elementary Science, International—*Science Education*

Membership in a professional organization brings benefits which are proportional to the member's active participation in the organization. Attendance at periodic meetings develops a sense of cohesiveness and shared objectives, the stimulation of meeting professional coworkers, and the absorption of new ideas. Voluntary participation as a panel member or speaker at a discussion session is a highly beneficial experience. It is not necessarily true that a teacher must have many years of experience before she can be considered worthy of a presentation at a professional meeting. A young, enthusiastic science teacher with a fresh approach to a problem can make a definite contribution to a meeting of this type.

Professional journals provide another source of teaching ideas. A science teacher should personally subscribe to one or two and make it a habit to regularly read others that may be purchased by the school library. Occasional contribution of teaching ideas for publication in a professional journal is highly motivating and is to be encouraged. The professional benefits of such a practice are unlimited because it helps one to become known in science teaching circles and to make valuable contacts.

Professional journals usually contain feature articles on subject-matter topics of current interest; ideas for improvement of classroom teaching techniques; information on professional meetings; book

Dedicated science teachers invest energy and time in professional meetings.

reviews; information on teaching materials, apparatus, and resource books; information on career opportunities for secondary school students in science; and information on scholarships and contests for students and teachers.

■ Self-Inventory for Science Teachers

The National Science Teachers Association Commission on Professional Standards and Practices has published a Self-Inventory for Science Teachers.[5] The NSTA has summarized its beliefs concerning the professionalism of science teachers. "The professional science teacher: (a) is well educated in science and the liberal arts, (b) possesses a functional philosophy of education and the technical skills, (c) continues to grow in knowledge and skill throughout his career, (d) insists on a sound educational environment in which to work, (e) maintains his professional status, (f) contributes to the improvement of science teaching, (g) takes a vital interest in the quality of future science teachers."

This is the first time that a science teachers' organization has developed a set of standards against which science teachers can measure themselves and which provides stimulation and motivation for improving their professional practices.

■ Evaluation of Teachers

Increasingly, teachers are faced with periodic evaluations by principals, their peers, and students. Such evaluations are for the purpose of comparisons, retention, merit pay, salary increments, promotion,

and/or tenure. Teacher evaluation is defined as "the process of an external observer (administrator or supervisor) gathering information regarding a teacher's instructional performance to determine the value and worth of that teacher."[6]

In 1987, a study of a teacher evaluation was reported by two researchers at McGill University, William Searles and Naile Kudeki. From the results of their study it was possible to develop a profile of an outstanding science teacher as follows:

The profile of an outstanding science teacher obtained from this study describes a person who is able to maintain a classroom with a pleasant atmosphere where learning can occur, one who is sure of the subject matter being taught, and presents the material to be learned in a clear and effective manner. This person is concerned about the students and ensures that they understand the concepts of science they are being taught by relating new knowledge to that which they already know. This instructor's teaching shows evidence of creativity and resourcefulness by utilizing various materials and methods of teaching as deemed necessary. The teaching is definitely "pupil-centered" for an outstanding science teacher is able to perceive then make provisions for the needs and abilities of the individual student. The teacher is a person who is available after school for those students who need extra help. As an interested, enthusiastic science teacher, the instructor tries to develop the students' interest in science by varying instructional methods to keep up-to-date with contemporary developments in the teaching of science. An outstanding science teacher presents thought-provoking laboratory activities and encourages the students to develop hypotheses and theories. As a self-confident person, the science teacher attempts to develop the attributes of self confidence and motivation in the students. Such an individual is consistently fair and emotionally calm when enforcing the rules of the school, has a good sense of humor, and is respected by the students.

Outside of the classroom, the outstanding science teacher cooperates with colleagues, consults with them in case of difficulties, is interested in academic self-improvement, and keeps up-to-date with scientific developments by reading journals and taking refresher courses.[7]

■ Summary

Student teaching is the most important phase of the prospective teacher's training. Entered into with enthusiasm and a willingness to learn, the experience will be a valuable culmination of college preparation for teaching.

The selection of subject, school, and supervising teacher are enhanced by visits to schools before the semester or quarter of student teaching. It is advisable to do one's student teaching in the major field of preparation to capitalize on one's strength of subject-matter competency.

The usual pattern of preparation is to spend several days or a week observing the class one is going to teach. Such observation can be done on a systematic basis and may enable one to achieve real insight into the individual differences present in the class. The student teacher can be an "assistant teacher" in the truest sense if she is alert to developing problems, anticipates future activities of the class, and prepares herself accordingly.

Taking over the class to teach a lesson or a unit will be completely successful if the student teacher plans adequately in consultation with the supervising teacher and makes her preparations carefully. Advance rehearsal for the first day of teaching is an advisable procedure, particularly if the time budget is questionable or if class questions are anticipated. An immediate followup of a day of teaching with a brief conference with the supervising teacher is advisable. Necessary changes in lesson plans can be made at this time.

A desirable arrangement is to follow the student-teaching quarter with a final quarter on the college campus before graduation. At this time, seminars in special problems of teaching can be most profitable, and the student teacher can reflect on the teaching experience. The opportunity to give maximum attention to the important choice of a first teaching position in the light of the recent experience in student teaching is thus afforded.

Today's science teacher is in a position of respect and responsibility. The demand for well-prepared science teachers has never been greater and the rewards are exceptional.

Proper education of the science teacher in this fast-moving scientific age is a matter of increasing concern. A suitable balance of general education, subject-matter preparation, and professional training must be achieved. The current trend is toward strengthening all of these areas, particularly subject-matter preparation. Attainment of a bachelor's degree does not end the science teacher's education. More and more, graduate work, up to and beyond the master's level, is being demanded. From a financial standpoint, it is generally to the teacher's advantage to obtain this advanced training as soon as possible. Better-paying jobs with other attractive features frequently await the applicant who has additional training.

The science teacher can grow professionally in many ways. Graduate course work, inservice institutes and workshops, summer institutes, committee involvement, membership in professional organizations, a program of reading, participation in meetings, and writing for professional journals are but a few. It is important to realize that continual growth and experience are necessary if one is to be an enthusiastic, productive science teacher.

The professional educator of today faces a challenging future. Investment in superior preparation and recognition of the need for continual professional growth can return rich dividends: a citizenry better educated in the area of science.

■ References

1. Checklist from Lawrence A. Conrey, University of Michigan, Ann Arbor.
2. "Stanford Teacher Competence Appraisal Guide" (Stanford, CA: Stanford Center for Development in Teaching).
3. Cynthia Ann Druva and Ronald D. Anderson, "Science Teachers Characteristics by Teacher Behavior and by Student Outcome: A Meta-Analysis of Research," *Journal of Research in Science Teaching*, 20, no. 5 (1983), pp. 467-479.
4. NSTA, "Secondary School Science and Mathematics Teachers," NSF Bulletin 63-10 (Washington, DC: U.S. Government Printing Office, 1963), p. 4.
5. *The Science Teacher*, 37, no. 9 (December 1970), p. 37.
6. G.D. Bailey, "Teacher Self-Assessment: in Search of a Philosophical Foundation," *National Association of Secondary School Principals Bulletin*, 62, no. 422 (1978), pp. 64-70.
7. William E. Searles and Naile Kudeki, "A Comparison of Teacher and Principal Perception of an Outstanding Science Teacher," *Journal of Research in Science Teaching*, 24, no. 1 (1987), pp: 1-13.

===== INVESTIGATING SCIENCE TEACHING =====

ACTIVITY 22–1

Individual Differences

1. In your observation of a science class use the checklist like the one on page 357 to discover the individual differences present in the class. At the end of a week, discuss your observations with the teacher. How does the student's achievement appear to correlate with your observations of study habits and classroom behavior?
2. List the traits you would like to see in the supervising teacher with whom you wish to do your practice teaching. Using this list as a guide, objectively analyze your own traits and compare them. Do you think similar or opposite traits are preferable or that a judicious blend of both is preferable?

ACTIVITY 22–2

Applying for a Job

1. Write a letter of application for a teaching position.
2. Briefly describe your qualifications, special areas of interest, and teaching field.
3. Volunteer to make an appointment for an interview at a mutually convenient time.
4. Write a short description of your philosophy of education. This need not be included in the letter of application but should be held in reserve for an appropriate time when called for.

ACTIVITY 22–3

Being a Professional Science Teacher

1. Write to the department of education in your state and obtain a summary of the current salary schedules in the major cities. Compare the starting salaries for teachers with bachelor's degrees and master's degrees. Compare the annual salary increase and the number of years required to reach maximum salary.
2. Obtain a copy of *Guidelines for Preparation Programs of Teachers of Secondary School Science and Mathematics* from the American Association for the Advancement of Science, Washington, D.C. Compare the training you have received with that recommended by this group.
3. Prepare a critical analysis of two professional journals, such as *The Science Teacher, School Science and Mathematics, The American Biology Teacher,* and *The Physics Teacher.* Examine the feature articles, the classroom teaching tips, the articles contributed by teachers in the field, the book reviews, and other parts of the publications.
4. Prepare a critical review of two research-oriented professional science teaching journals such as *Science Education* and *Journal of Research for Science Teaching.* Report on the results of one research study published in each of the journals reviewed.

CHAPTER 23

Being a Science Teacher

Throughout this book we have used the theme "Becoming a Science Teacher" to bring unity and clarity to the organization and presentation of chapters. Here, we are switching to the theme "Being a Science Teacher."

Becoming is the process of developing suitable or appropriate qualities needed for science teaching. Becoming, then, represents a change from that which you were to that which you are now. It is your coming to be all that you potentially can be as a science teacher, given the time and constraints of this textbook, your life, the methods course, etc.

Being is the existence of a particular state or condition, in this case, that of a secondary school science teacher. The title of this chapter signifies that you are one step closer to actually being a science teacher. In many ways you have probably already developed many qualities and attitudes of science teachers. Paradoxically, you will always be some degree of both becoming and being a science teacher. For example, during the science methods course you have been involved with a variety of experiences, all contributing toward your becoming a science teacher. Simultaneously, you have developed a set of interests and attitudes similar to those of science teachers. Perhaps you imagined yourself as a science teacher and, on occasion, actually experienced this position through teaching a class and working with students. We are referring to your own attitudes and values and your own interest and desire to be a science teacher. These are the most significant variables in the becoming-being equation.

If we had to identify one symbolic point at which the percentage of becoming and being shifted in favor of being, it would be the first day of your first job. Throughout the practice-teaching experi-

ence, becoming and being will probably be about equal. However, there has been some degree of being a science teacher from the moment of your career decision and there will be some degree of continually becoming a better science teacher throughout your career.

These two situations summarized in "Investigating Science Teaching: Fulfillments and Frustrations," at the end of this chapter, are two ends of an emotional continuum for science teachers. There are indeed frustrations and fulfillment, and both are a part of becoming and being a science teacher. For some reason, more time is devoted to the frustrating aspects of science teaching than to the fulfillments; yet, without a doubt, the latter occur each day and in many ways. Science teaching is a source of personal fulfillment because it contributes to the development of students and ultimately to society. Occasionally we lose sight of this simple fact because

Helping students learn science is personally and professionally fulfilling.

of the daily frustrations, dissatisfactions, and challenges.

■ Personal Fulfillment

In Chapter 4 we discussed Abraham Maslow's hierarchy of motivational needs. The context of that presentation was the fulfillment of student needs. Here, the emphasis is on teachers' needs. The fulfillment of needs can lead to one's personal growth as a science teacher.

Safety and Security

Some teachers have a very real need for safety. Fortunately the numbers are small and the school systems are working very hard to change this situation. In Chapter 21 we offered suggestions for alleviating concerns about safety and control in the science classroom.

Science teaching is generally a very secure career. From time to time budget cuts and other economic problems make it difficult; there are, too, occasional reductions in the teaching force. These are short-term problems; our society always needs good teachers. Further, science teachers will be important as long as science and technology have a central role in society.

Love and Belongingness

Love and belongingness needs can also be fulfilled through science teaching. At the secondary level, however, students do not express their closeness as clearly and unabashedly as at the elementary level. Adolescents are in their quest for separation from authorities and for development of their own identity, which makes their closeness and expression of appreciation toward an authority figure, such as a science teacher, particularly difficult. Often the students who like you the most will demonstrate it the least. Still, the picture is not all gray. Science teachers can and do earn the respect and affection of their students. It is often subtle, oblique, and obtuse. But it is there. You can contribute to the feelings of belongingness by establishing a climate of caring in your science classroom, thus fulfilling both your needs and those of the students.

Self-Esteem

What about the self-esteem of the science teacher? If self-esteem is equated with having material posses-

sions, which in turn relates to a high salary, then the prospects for fulfilling this need are not very encouraging. There is prestige within the educational community for science teachers and there is a long tradition of respect for teachers in our society. Although education is frequently criticized, it is also looked to as a source of remedy for many problems. There is deserved, earned esteem in knowing you have helped young people understand more about the world in which they live, thus helping their personal development and improving society.

It would be nice if we could simply state that all of your needs would be met through science teaching and you would experience continued growth as a professional and as a person. Such is not the case. We can say that this is possible, in fact even probable, but part of the task will be your own contribution. For everything that Maslow did say about motivation and personal growth, he *never* said that it was easy.

Fulfilling Needs

How does an individual know which needs are important? Knowing this, how does one proceed to fulfill personal needs in the context of a science classroom? The first question is most directly answered by you. Our contribution to the answer has been to provide activities that direct you to reflect on various aspects of science teaching. Self-awareness is essential if you wish to know more about your needs and possible ways to fulfill them.

Once you have some insights concerning your personal needs as a science teacher, there are many ways to fulfill them. Here are a few suggestions listed under Maslow's categories.

Safety

1. Establish rules for the science classroom.
2. Clarify consequences of rule violation.

Security

1. Talk to your principal or personnel director about future goals, budgets, etc.
2. Work to develop a strong science program.

Belongingness

1. Have personal conferences with students.
2. Evaluate the class to see how it might be improved.
3. Have the students work on cooperative projects.
4. Spend more time talking to the students on a personal level during class.

Esteem

1. Conduct a workshop on a topic of interest to the rest of your school staff, e.g., energy, pollution, nutrition.
2. Attend a local or national meeting of science teachers.
3. Present a talk on science to a community group.
4. Join a local committee that is working on a science-related problem.

These are a few simple suggestions that can stimulate your thoughts about change and growth as a science teacher. The list is not unique; most of the ideas are simply a part of being a science teacher.

■ Professional Challenges

It is hard to identify all of the trends and issues that will affect science teaching in the years to come. We can assure you there will be new challenges. Here we discuss a few challenges that will face science teachers in the 1990s.

Enrollments

Enrollments in secondary schools increased during the 1950s, 1960s, and 1970s. However, in the 1980s, they declined. Principals surveyed in the NSF studies confirm the importance of declining enrollments by ranking it fourth among all problems in science and mathematics education. However, science teachers did not rank low enrollment in courses as one of their most important problems.

According to the National Science Board Commission, enrollments will begin to rise again in the early 1990s. In light of the recent decline in student enrollment it should be noted that there is not a shortage of secondary school science teachers, and there will not be until the mid-1990s.

Equality of Educational Opportunity

The issue of equality of educational opportunity has resulted in a conflict between educational practices and democratic principles. To date, it seems that the confrontation has been subtle and beneficial to neither teachers nor students. The confrontation centers on the Fourteenth Amendment rights of students and the pedagogic practices of teachers. Since *Brown vs. Board of Education* (1954) there have been increasing legislation and regulation requiring that the handicapped, minorities, children from low-income families, and women be allowed an education.

The impact of these requirements on science education is not clear. Science teachers encounter a dichotomy between their belief in the principle of human rights as guaranteed in the Constitution and the concrete facts of the need to modify their teaching style and adapt their curricula to the individual needs of students.

Facilities and Equipment

Science equipment and supplies, or the lack of them, greatly influence science teaching. Funds for the purchase of science supplies is, obviously, a major factor 181 science programs. In light of these statements, 26 percent of science teachers rate inadequacy of facilities as a serious problem and 42 percent as somewhat of a problem. To some degree, facilities are a problem for 68 percent of science teachers.

Curriculum

In the early 1980s a number of reports on education recommended increasing graduation requirements by adding another year of science. While most applaud such requirements, there are implications not generally recognized by those making the recommendations. Who will take the extra courses? What are the curricular implications? Who will teach the courses? To answer the first question, students who have decided *not* to take any more science will now be required to take at least another course. The curricular implication is related to the inappropriateness of existing courses for the group of students now required to take another year of science. The result will be a need for new curriculum materials. Finally, increasing the requirements will increase the need for science teachers. There is the possibility of unqualified teachers teaching the newly required courses, and the need for inservice programs to better qualify the science teachers.

Instruction

In 1978, 13 percent of secondary science teachers were teaching at least one class for which they did not feel qualified. Most of these teachers were referring to courses within science and not a course such as mathematics or history.

Disruptive Students

Student discipline and classroom management are concerns of science teachers. Junior high science teachers think their students are not well behaved. An estimated 5 percent of science teachers indicated that maintaining discipline was a serious problem and 24 percent indicated that it was somewhat of a problem. These data are consistent with a NIE report, *Violent Schools—Safe Schools*.[1] There are higher levels of violence (in intensity and numbers) at the junior high level. Approximately 8 to 10 percent of schools see violence and disruption as a serious problem. Interestingly, one study showed that less than 10 percent of teachers, principals, and district program respondents indicated that maintaining discipline was a serious problem.

Careers

Although it is seen in various forms, the recent emphasis on career education is being felt in science education. In the 1970s a concern for vocational or career skills and knowledge became increasingly important. This change is, in part, a response to public opinion. When teachers, parents and science coordinators were asked about vocational goals of science courses, they agreed that science courses should be more vocationally oriented; yet, the majority would select a good general education over a vocational program if they had to select between them.

Science teachers should be aware of the continuing need for scientists and engineers. They should also be aware that career choices are often made based on experiences in science classes. We think most science teachers understand these two points. A more difficult issue is the fact that science teachers contribute to a filtering process that eliminates significant numbers of individuals from the talent pool of scientists and engineers. The imbalance is one of historical record, and one that eliminates not on the basis of intelligence and ability, but in large measure on the basis of sex, race, handicap, and cultural advantage.

In the early 1980s an estimated 30 percent of all teachers currently teaching science and math in secondary schools were either completely unqualified or severely underqualified to teach those subjects.[2,3]

When asked about the areas of greatest need, science teachers listed several items directly related to instruction. Approximately 66 percent of all teachers surveyed (science, mathematics, and social studies) indicated that they needed information about instructional media. Sixty-one percent indicated a need for assistance in learning new teaching methods. Fewer than 50 percent of teachers surveyed feel they are not competent enough to implement the discovery/inquiry approach. They felt they needed the

assistance of a coordinator or other resource person. Forty-eight percent of all science, mathematics, and social studies teachers indicated they would like assistance in the use of manipulative materials. This need may relate to the fact that manipulative materials are generally used less than once a week in most science, mathematics, and social studies classes.

Funding

Funding is perceived to be a major problem facing science teachers. An estimated 66 percent of science teachers indicated that funding is, to some degree, a problem. It is evident that there is a need for improving the financing of science education or addressing this problem in some way.

These are some of the challenges that lie ahead. They are not insurmountable, but they can cause frustration. One thing is certain; they will not be reduced without the cooperation of all school personnel and others working within the science education community.

■ Decision Making

During any single class period a science teacher makes many decisions about students and the lesson. Often science teachers are unaware of these decisions. "Shall I tell John to be quiet?" "What is Pat doing?" "Do the students understand density?" "Should I use a different example of convection currents?" "Would it be best for the students to work in groups of two or three on this laboratory project?" The decisions may not seem that important, but they all add up to effective instruction and classroom management.

Teaching science is simultaneously directed and flexible. Decision making in science teaching is the process of synthesizing your planned direction with the instantaneous and spontaneous factors in the classroom.

Direction in teaching science is provided in two ways: first, through the organization of textbooks, curriculum guides, lesson plans, and objectives and, second, from the science teacher's own instructional theory. When situations emerge in the classroom the teacher evaluates the situation, the goals, the curriculum, and the consequences of choices and then decides on a course of action. One important, though seldom considered, variable in the decision-making process is the direction suggested by the science teacher's own instructional theory.

An instructional theory helps establish a frame of reference for decisions, gives consistency of responses, and provides a general direction as science teachers encounter different classroom situations. With the aid of an instructional theory, science teachers are in a better position to make instruction effective and fulfilling. In the final analysis, the individual science teacher is the one who can best relate the possible directions to the actual situations when it comes to different students, classrooms, and schools.

An instructional theory provides an underlying direction that transcends immediate classroom problems. Being able to go beyond the immediate situation affirms one's ability as a science teacher. Clarifying one's long-term goals and intentions helps provide an organizational pattern that slowly becomes a personal style of teaching. The power of an instructional theory is in the direction it provides. There must be another component, that is, the freedom to deviate from the direct path in response to different classroom situations. This is the spontaneity and flexibility required in science teaching.

Effective science teachers are able to deviate from the lesson. The degree of flexibility varies with the teacher's goals, students' needs, and environmental contingencies. The problems described in "Investigating Science Teaching: What Would You

Do—Now?" at the end of this chapter are similar to those presented earlier. This time, however, no solutions, directions, or ideas are suggested—you must resolve the incident on your own.

When confronted with problem situations such as those described in "Investigating Science Teaching: What Would You Do—Now?" science teachers usually respond: "I would have to know more," "I would have to be in the situation," or "It depends; every teacher would probably do something different." This is precisely the point. The individual science teacher must decide the course of action in response to the classroom situation. Science teachers intuitively know that they are the primary source for effective education when they ask questions as, "When should I answer the student's question if I am teaching by inquiry?" There is usually an implicit tone of voice that says, "There is no direct answer except as the individual teacher responds to the situation."

Science teachers enter the classroom with knowledge, techniques, plans, textbooks, and curriculum materials. It is also the teacher who combines all of them and builds a helping relationship with the students. In the classroom, the helping relation-

The creative and perceptive science teacher can maintain direction but can also meet the unexpected demands of students with spontaneity and flexibility. (Photo by Lloyd Lemmerman.)

ship is characterized by situations requiring the teacher to react spontaneously. Science teachers must think critically, diagnose, decide, and respond to conditions in the teaching environment. The creative, insightful, and perceptive science teacher does react effectively to the instantaneous needs and demands of the children, classroom, or school.

Developing a consistent direction through an instructional theory and flexibility in classroom situations will evolve into a personal teaching style that can help overcome frustrations and contribute to your fulfillment as a science teacher.

■ Becoming a Better Science Teacher

As discussed in the Introduction to this text, part of being a science teacher is engaging in the process of becoming a better science teacher. In this chapter, we will use a self-evaluation inventory to examine some of the immediate concerns of science teachers. (See Activity 23-4, "Improving My Science Teaching," at the end of this chapter.) Although concentrating on improving various aspects of science teaching, the feedback will also contribute to your becoming a better educator and more fulfilled as a person.

Remember, you do not have to be a bad science teacher to become a better one. Science teachers want to improve, as is shown by their continued involvement in workshops, college courses, attendance at conventions, etc. The responsibility for improving is yours; likewise, the means of developing as a science teacher is unique to your preferences, problems, and potential. Based on the categories in the self-evaluation inventory, several possible means are suggested.

Scientific Knowledge

There are a number of relatively easy ways to update and/or keep abreast of scientific developments.

1. Read an introductory textbook in the area you feel needs improvement.
2. Enroll in science courses at a local college or university.
3. Contact the district or state science supervisor and see if a workshop can be organized.
4. Subscribe to the American Association for the Advancement of Science and read their journals, *Science* or *Science '90* (the figure changes with year of publication). The editorials will keep you up-to-date on social concerns and scientific developments.

5. Read *Scientific American* or purchase offprints of articles or the monographs of accumulated articles on important topics.
6. Join the National Science Teachers Association and read one of the journals: *Science and Children*, *The Science Teacher*, *Science Scope* or *Journal of College Science Teaching*.
7. Subscribe to and read *Science News* or *Science World*.
8. Attend local, state, regional, and national conventions of scientific societies, academies of science, science teachers, and teachers.
9. Make a point of watching television programs on scientific issues. "Nova" is a science program sponsored by the National Science Foundation and is shown on the Public Broadcasting System.
10. Read the science sections of weekly magazines such as *Time* or *Newsweek*.
11. Go to local museums and planetariums.

Planning and Organization

If this is a concern, part of the problem can be improved through personal effort toward better lesson planning and classroom organization.

1. Read the chapters on planning in any teaching-methods textbook.
2. Find a colleague who is well organized and ask if the two of you could spend some time planning classes together.
3. Ask the science supervisor to look over your science program and suggest ways to improve the organization.
4. Have a colleague observe your teaching and make suggestions concerning your lesson plans and class management.

Teaching Methods

Teachers often find it difficult to break old teaching habits and try new methods of teaching, but you can do it. Here are some suggestions.

1. Read chapters on different methods in any science methods textbook and then imagine how the different approaches could work in your classroom.
2. Look over journals such as *Science and Children*, *The Science Teacher*, *The American Biology Teacher*, *The Physics Teacher*, and *Journal of Geological Education* for new approaches to science teaching.

3. Take a "professional day" and observe several science teachers who use methods that you are interested in adopting.
4. Read *Models of Teaching* by Bruce Joyce and Marsha Weil. This is an excellent book that presents many teaching methods.
5. Team-teach with another science teacher who uses different methods.
6. Request a student teacher; they often have new and different approaches to science teaching.

Interpersonal Relations

This is an area that is essential to effective science teaching, yet often neglected in the education of science teachers. Some suggestions that may help include the following:

1. Practice active listening when students talk.
2. Use questions that encourage students to express their ideas on certain issues.
3. Read and apply ideas from *Questioning and Listening* by Robert Sund and Arthur Carin.
4. Attend a workshop or course on human relations.
5. Read and apply ideas from *Teacher Effectiveness Training* by Thomas Gordon.
6. Read and apply ideas from *Human Relations and Your Career: A Guide to Interpersonal Skills* by David Johnson.

Personal Enthusiasm

If you lack enthusiasm for teaching science, the problem is difficult, but not impossible, to resolve. The reason for the difficulty is that the problem involves a very personal dimension of your teaching. We can recommend an introspective route to improvement.

1. Think about your original interest and excitement in science and teaching. What made you choose science teaching? Now, think about what you know about yourself and teaching science. What is lacking? Where did the spark of enthusiasm go?
2. List your frustrations with teaching. What are the problems you have encountered as a science teacher? What caused a "burnout" or your change of interest in science teaching?
3. Attend meetings of science teachers such as NSTA or NABT. This often can inspire enthusiasm through new ideas and new colleagues.
4. Form a group to improve teaching in your school.

You will probably find others who share your problem, and the discussion and support can certainly assist you in developing your enthusiasm for teaching.
5. Take a professional day and visit other science teachers who are dynamic and enthusiastic.
6. Request a sabbatical.

■ Being a Person, Educator, and Science Teacher

Young children are often surprised to find that their teacher does not live at school. Older students think it is funny to meet their teacher shopping or on a picnic. Students often perceive the science teacher and not the person. We are all, however, first and foremost persons. What does this mean? Being a person means we share qualities with all other persons: we struggle with decisions; we are sad and happy; we succeed and fail; we make mistakes and get things right; we are frustrated and fulfilled. Too often students do not see us as persons. Students should understand that we belong to the community, and have hobbies, interests, and ideas that go beyond science teaching.

As an educator, science teachers are in the helping professions. Their identity is with people more than objects. Their goal is to help people improve their health, education, and welfare. There are aspects of science teaching that are shared with other helping professionals such as doctors, counselors, social workers, nurses, and psychologists. The shared qualities have to do primarily with the interpersonal relations, that is, the personal dimension of science teaching, those qualities that contribute to effective interactions between persons, and eventually contribute to one person facilitating the other's personal development.

The science teacher has elected to help others through a better understanding of the physical and biological world, the methods of gaining knowledge about this world, and the role of science in society. Here the qualities of the person, the educator, and the science teacher should unite to achieve the dual goal of furthering the personal development of students and society through science education.

Much time, money, and effort have been expended on improving the science curriculum. Most science curricula have carefully structured texts and materials so the science teacher will have the maximum opportunity for a good teaching experience. The contribution of new programs and textbooks has been invaluable. But, although curriculum materials are necessary and can account for some success in

======== **GUEST EDITORIAL** ========

Empathy, Understanding, and Science Teaching

Eric Johnson, Science Teacher
Northfield Middle School
Northfield, Minnesota

The best teachers are those who aren't boring. They challenge us with the quality of classwork, encourage extra work, and are available out of class to provide help. This type of teacher cares that we learn, listens actively, and is open-minded.

Having summarized the feelings of four of my high school science students on what makes an excellent teacher, I would like to suggest two key traits that we, as science teachers, need to strive constantly to develop: the first is empathy for students and the second is an understanding of science based on experience rather than books.

Webster defines empathy as "intellectual or emotional identification with another," and science as "systematized knowledge derived from observation, study, etc." Since neither empathy nor scientific involvement is fully attained by completing an undergraduate program culminating in earning a teaching certificate, how can the beginning teacher actively pursue these two important goals? Moreover, how can these goals be pursued while handling several laboratory preparations, five classes, and 150 students?

I shall begin with the question of understanding and experiencing science since

increased empathy can follow from it. One type of active encounter with science can be found in the many summer programs run by colleges and universities. Those courses specifically designed for teachers may not necessarily involve problem identification and data collection, but the best combine factual updating with experience in scientific process. Those courses established as summer programs for graduate students in research, such as the university biological field stations, are geared entirely to "systematized knowledge derived from observation." A teacher returning to class in the fall after engaging in this type of scientific challenge will approach classwork and students differently. There will be a closer "intellectual or emotional identification" with the role of students and with the processes of science. Empathy can be a side benefit.

Another major area of teacher experience that can enhance the quality of student learning is in applying lessons from the summer programs to the biology, chemistry, or physics class. In biology the connection might be a natural area near the school. Annual studies by students of soil or water conditions, of phenology with wildflowers, or growth rates in trees, or of chemical changes downstream of a sewage-treatment plant provide

the classroom, they are not sufficient; they cannot account for effective and successful science teaching. The science teacher is still the crucial variable and the one person who must pull all the pieces together for effective teaching.

A review of the research literature on good, ideal, effective, or successful teaching reveals that it is impossible to identify any particular set of variables that amounts to "the good teacher." Yet, we all have had good science teachers, we know good science teachers, and, most importantly, we want to be good science teachers. Rather than looking at the research and concluding that we can't identify the characteristics of good science teaching, perhaps we can take a different view and thus form a different conclusion. Perhaps good science teachers have developed their potential, their talents, their attributes, all of which give them a unique, identifying style of

teaching. It is understandable then that our research efforts cannot find common characteristics, for the answer is to be found in uniqueness, not commonality.

Being a science teacher means improving. Science teachers want to improve, and science teachers can improve. Even an especially good science teacher can become a better one. Often science teachers complain, "I just didn't seem to be effective today; the students seemed confused and frustrated. I didn't get the concept across." However, they never finish the statement with, "and if you think I was bad today—wait until tomorrow. I'll really be much worse!" Unfortunately, just the desire to improve is not enough; there must be a commitment to becoming a better science teacher through changing or altering your personal teaching style.

Critics of education have done much to point

immediate application of concepts, a respect for the comparative value of data, and an opportunity to contribute to an understanding of local habitats. In chemistry class, students in farming communities might analyze drinking water from various local sources, looking for nitrate levels. Urban schools might collect rain or snow samples for pH studies of combustion-related acid precipitation.

A physics class could measure the solar constant throughout the year and relate its change to the distance of the sun, angle of incident light, or recent volcanic activity. Application of solar-energy studies in home heating could be conducted by comparing energy use in a gas- or electric-metered home on a sunny versus a cloudy day in winter. The difference in the quantity of energy used each day is a measure of the effectiveness of solar gain through windows. Whose home is most effective? Is every home a solar home to some extent? These and other questions can make the process of learning science pertinent, memorable, and exciting for teacher and students.

Knowing that investigations can be conducted by students on local subjects sets a tone early in each school year that suggests that science involves practicing, not just reading and memorizing, and that contributions are needed to sustain the momentum of past work. Students experiencing science in this way will continue to look for ways to apply what they've learned. The rate of technological change will intimidate them less. Critical-thinking skills will more often be applied to problems beyond the classroom.

To succeed with this process of actively becoming involved in science, the teacher must include the scientific process in each aspect of the class, including laboratories, field trips, and discussions, must be committed to taking risks in the process of learning, and must be convinced that the course is relevant. Beyond the content benefits, a teacher following the active-participant role will necessarily show increased empathy for students by being more closely attuned to what is challenging and exciting. In addition, the teacher organizing her class in this way will not become bored teaching the same course time and again: discovery of new patterns and problems will continue to present fresh challenges for investigation. Most important, we who use this approach can view each new year with the expectation that we will acquire further insights into our subject, our students, and ourselves.

---

out the wrongs of education and little to give direction. One result of this critical confrontation has been defensiveness by many teachers and administrators. Displacing blame is one manifestation of this defensiveness, the "let's blame somebody or something else" syndrome: "We would if we had money." "I have thirty-five children in my class." "Well, what do you expect?" "The home has more influence than the short time students are in my classroom." The "let's try something new" syndrome is another manifestation. Teaching machines, contract performance, accountability, competency-based programs, and the open classroom are examples of this approach. The ideas presented in this chapter center on the science teacher developing as a person and as an educator. Our theme might be, "Let's get with it as persons and perform as professionals." You can be in any classroom, with any children, and with any curriculum to develop your competency as a science teacher. The ideas presented are not easy; they deal, for the most part, with personal improvement and fulfillment.

Start being a science teacher by looking at your potential and not your limitations. Becoming aware of the importance of the suggestions for improvement and translating them into actual practice can result in your development as a science teacher. The process of becoming a better science teacher is long, and it takes courage to overcome the many small barriers to personal and professional growth. It is not something that can occur through the purchase of a new set of science materials, a single workshop, or reading one methods textbook. Being a science teacher requires continuous personal development aimed toward the ideal of being a great educator, and for those who say, "I can't be a great science teacher," we reply, "If not you—then who?" We all have much more potential than we are now using. It is the actualization of this potential that will help you become a better science teacher, educator, and person.

Summary

In this chapter we changed from the theme of *becoming* to a theme of *being*. Becoming is changing and moving toward a goal, which was the orientation of most of the book. Being is a state or a condition. In this instance, it is that of a science teacher. The title tells you that student teaching and your first job are very near. And, subsequently, it is time to think in terms of being a science teacher.

Being a science teacher has its professional frustrations and motivational needs; safety, security, love and belongingnss, and self-esteem are ways of thinking about levels of fulfillment in your job. Some of the professional challenges of the 1990s are the basics movement, competency and accountability, facilities and equipment, curriculum and instruction, funding, disruptive students, and career education.

Decision making is a crucial aspect of being a science teacher. The particular focus of decision making is on two seemingly paradoxical aspects of teaching—that one must maintain a direction and that one must demonstrate flexibility. The balance between these variables is set by the science teacher's decisions. A personal theory of instruction will help guide the science teacher's decisions and develop a consistent pattern of responses to the instantaneous demands of the classroom.

Being a science teacher is more than signing your first contract or teaching your first class. It is more than your knowledge of science, capacity to plan, ability to use different methods, and your enthusiasm for teaching. Although these attributes are included, being a science teacher means:

1. *Courage* to continue your professional growth
2. *Commitment* to doing a better job tomorrow
3. *Competence* to fulfill your professional duties
4. *Compassion* toward your students
5. *Caring* for your own dignity, integrity, and worth *and* for the dignity, integrity, and worth of those in your care

References

1. David Boesel, *Violent Schools—Safe Schools*, 1 (Washington, D.C.: National Institute of Education, 1978).
2. Bill G. Aldridge and Karen L. Johnston, "Trends and Issues In Science Education," in *Redesigning Science and Technology Education* 1984 NSTA Yearbook, eds. R. Bybee, J. Carlson, and A. McCormack (Washington D.C.: National Science Teachers Association, 1984).
3. James A. Skymasnky and Bill G. Aldridge, "The Teacher Crisis in Secondary School Science and Mathematics," *Educational Leadership* (November 1982).
4. Don Cosgrove, "Diagnostic Rating Of Teacher Performance," *Journal of Educational Psychology*, 50, no. 5 (1959), pp. 200-204.
5. Rodger Bybee, "The Teacher I Like Best: Perceptions of Advantaged, Average and Disadvantaged Science Students," *School Science and Mathematics*, 62, no. 5 (May 1973), pp. 384-390.
6. Rodger Bybee, "Science Educators' Perceptions of the Ideal Science Teacher," *School Science and Mathematics*, 78, no. 1 (January 1978), pp. 13-22.

=== **INVESTIGATING SCIENCE TEACHING** ===

ACTIVITY 23–1

Fulfillments and Frustrations

Joan is approaching your desk. "Look, I solved the chemistry problem. It was easy after you explained the difference between ionic and covalent bonding." Then, with a warm smile, she said, "I really appreciate the extra time you spend helping me; you are a good teacher and I'm glad I decided to take chemistry." What would you do?

1. Ask her if she has solved the other chemistry problems.
2. Say nothing, smile, and go on with your work.
3. Tell her that it is just part of your job.
4. Smile and thank her for the compliment.
5. Tell her you are glad she asked you about the problem.

You have just sat through one more insufferable faculty meeting. The results of the meeting: your clerical work will increase due to a new grading system; your budget has been reduced by 50 percent (and the price of science materials, equipment, and textbooks has gone up 25 percent); your new duty is to supervise the cafeteria; your new class will be a "difficult, but small" group of students; your salary increase for next year will be 3 percent below the present rate of inflation. What would you do?

1. Quit.
2. Go to the next NEA of AFT meeting and demand a change in contracts.
3. Ignore the situation because one-fourth of the problems will be changed in the next two weeks; one-fourth of the changes will never be implemented; you can ignore one-fourth of the problems, and the remaining one-fourth are "part of the territory."
4. Make an appointment with the principal and politely, but firmly, inform her that she has asked too much of you.
5. Talk over the problems with several colleagues.
6. Go to a psychotherapist to see if you or the school system is sick.

Once you have selected the option closest to what you think, you might discuss it with a partner. What else would you do?

ACTIVITY 23–2

Developing an Instructional Theory

The idea of an instructional theory was introduced in Chapter 2. Now it might be a good idea to return to this idea. To help you develop your instruction theory, complete the following exercise.

1. What is the aim of your science teaching? What is the broad goal you would hope to achieve through your interaction with students in the science classroom?

   a. What is your primary goal?

   b. What are your secondary aims?

2. Based on the understanding of yourself, students, science, and society, what are your justifications for the goal and aims cited above?

   a. Why are these and not other aims to be the focus of science education?

   b. In a broad sense, what is to be done or not done to achieve these aims?

3. What are your conclusions about what to do, and how and when to achieve these aims?

   a. By what specific instructional methods or processes are the aims developed?

   b. What is your science curriculum?

   c. Is there any sequence in your instructional theory?

   In sum, you should: first, state what your aims are; second, justify why these aims are important; and third, explain how you plan to achieve these aims through your science curriculum and instruction.

ACTIVITY 23–3

What Would You Do—Now?

Based on your sense of direction and flexibility, what would you do as a science teacher in these situations?

1. You are introducing a biology lesson on predator/prey relationships. The chameleons and crickets you ordered for the students to observe have not arrived.

   What would you do?

2. You are teaching a physical-science lesson on energy. The class was supposed to read the chapter on energy in the book. You suddenly realize that several of the students cannot read at the level of your textbook.

   What would you do?

3. During an earth-science lesson on the planets a student informs you that he has talked with a visitor from another planet—called Xerob. He describes the visitor in detail. The class is interested and starts asking the student questions.

   What would you do?

4. The unit is on health, the lesson on smoking. A student tells about a person she knows who is 85 years old and very healthy. This person has smoked two packages of cigarettes a day for over sixty years. In addition, the person drinks, eats candy, and does not watch his diet.

   What would you do?

ACTIVITY 23–4

Improving My Science Teaching

What are your strengths and weaknesses? How do you think you should improve as a science teacher? Following is a self-evaluation inventory designed to provide answers to these questions. We don't know how you would like to become more effective as a science teacher. Of course, the answers to these questions vary from person to person. The inventory will provide you with insights concerning some of your own characteristics as a science teacher. The self-evaluation inventory is based on items used in a study of teacher effectiveness[4] and later modified for the study of science teaching.[5,6] Only selected items are used here.

The following statements are descriptions of various facets of science teaching. Read each of the statements carefully. Using the scale, indicate how each statement presently characterizes you as a science teacher.

5   Very characteristic of me. This is a real strength of my teaching.
4   Frequently characteristic of me. This is a good aspect of my science teaching.
3   Sometimes characteristic of me. I should evaluate this aspect of my science teaching.
2   Seldom characteristic of me. I should improve this aspect of my science teaching.
1   Never characteristic of me. I really need to improve.

As a science teacher, I:

_____   1. Am well read in science
_____   2. Have a well-organized science course
_____   3. Adjust my teaching to the class situation
_____   4. Have a good rapport with my science students
_____   5. Enjoy teaching science to students
_____   6. Have a thorough knowledge of science
_____   7. Have always planned and am prepared for science class
_____   8. Use a variety of techniques in teaching science
_____   9. Recognize the unique needs of my science students
_____   10. Am enthusiastic about teaching science
_____   11. Present science concepts that are current and relevant
_____   12. Recognize the need to modify daily and unit plans
_____   13. Facilitate different types of student activities in science
_____   14. Relate well with students on the individual and group level
_____   15. Become excited when students learn science
_____   16. Am well informed in science-related fields
_____   17. Have thought about the long-range goals of my science class
_____   18. Use different curriculum materials and instructional approaches to teach science
_____   19. Am sincere while helping my science students
_____   20. Make an extra effort to help students learn science
_____   21. Am knowledgeable concerning science-related social issues
_____   22. Have a continuity of course material in science
_____   23. Provide adequate opportunity for active work by science students
_____   24. Listen to student questions and ideas
_____   25. Am excited and energetic when teaching science

Now go back and add up your responses for the items listed below in the left column. Divide the total by 5. The result should be a number between 1 and 5 for each of the categories listed. Refer back to the five-point scale for your evaluation.

Items		Average	Category
1, 6, 11, 16, 21	=	_____	Knowledge of science
2, 7, 12, 17, 22	=	_____	Planning and organization
3, 8, 13, 18, 23	=	_____	Teaching methods
4, 9, 14, 19, 24	=	_____	Personal relations
5, 10, 15, 20, 25	=	_____	Enthusiasm

All five categories—knowledge of science, planning and organization, teaching methods, personal relations, and enthusiasm—are important for effective science teaching. The rating system should have helped you identify categories where you are strong and ones you would like to improve. Ideally, all categories would have ratings of 5; really, there are few (if any) science teachers that good. Since science teachers are continually improving, suggestions for improving teaching within the different categories of this survey seem appropriate.

## CHAPTER 24

Science-Technology-Society (S-T-S) A Vision for Science Teachers

As we approach the year 2000 most people living in industrial societies are enjoying a quality of life unprecedented in history. Children survive traumas and diseases of premature birth and early childhood that would have been fatal a few decades ago. The elderly live longer and enjoy the benefits of health and well being. Personal living is more convenient and pleasant and our natural and human environments enrich our lives. Science and technology are largely responsible for these and many other benefits that enhance life and living.

The year 2000 is also growing near for three quarters of the world's population not living in industrialized societies. These people still await the benefits of science and technology that promise to ease their pain, feed their hungry, and reduce their burdens of labor. Science and technology could also contribute to improving their quality of life. But as yet the promises have not come to fruition.

Until recently, one could not have written these paragraphs about the benefits and promises of science and technology. The degree to which science and technology influence our lives and transform societies is only now being realized. For two centuries science and technology have increasingly shaped the character of American society. Throughout most of history the interaction and significance among science, technology, and society went unrecognized. During this time, however, the interaction continually changed. Citizens became aware of the promises of science and technology. Government became

involved in the support of research and development. Science evolved from "little" to "big." Technology also became larger and more sophisticated. With little fanfare, science and technology slowly moved to center stage in society.

A paradox has also recently emerged. Scientific advances and technological innovation have contributed to *both* social progress and cultural problems. And, many of the same citizens who became aware of the scientific and technological promises also became aware of the problems. While science and technology moved to center stage, the stage was also being set for a conflict between science, technology and democratic participation. How is the conflict to be resolved? Enter here the increasing role of public policy debates.

Many critical decisions related to the role of science and technology have to be made by the nation. The decisions will be made relative to many local and regional issues—land use, acid rain, atmospheric conditions, carbon dioxide, toxic waste dumps, energy shortages, preservation of endangered species, and water resources to name only a few examples. Decisions will also be made concerning budgets for research and development, and the role of public and private institutions' support of science and technology. Who should make decisions about problems, research, development, or applications? The federal government? Scientists? Citizens? On what basis should these decisions be made? Economic? Moral? Contributions to the public health and social welfare of the nation? Increasing knowledge for knowledge's sake? Fulfilling the needs of humanity? General recognition of these questions has brought about problems concerning the public's ability to participate in decision

Portions of this chapter are revisions of the following work. R.W. Bybee, "Science-Technology-Society: An Essential Theme for Science Education," 1985 Yearbook for Association for Education of Teachers of Science (Columbus, OH: AETS, March, 1986), pp. 3-15.

making and policy development within American society.

Several factors underlie the general problems of public participation in science- and technology-related issues. Democratic participation is more widespread, *but* the groups often have a single issue orientation. Public interest in participation has increased, *but* the public often lacks the ways and means to influence decisions. There has been greater reliance on experts to explain complex issues related to science and technology, *but* the experts often do not agree and, in addition, many have ventured beyond facts into the domain of ethics and values. The media have increased public awareness of science- and technology-related issues, *but* public understanding of the concepts, values, and processes involved in contemporary issues is lacking.

These and other factors converge on the need to identify appropriate means of directing science and technology while simultaneously maintaining the independence of scientists and engineers to pursue their research and development and the freedom of the public to participate in decisions and policies affecting their lives. With time, this fundamental tension between scientific independence and social control will only increase. A careful balance must be reached in the coming years. Achieving a balance between the values of science and society suggests the need for citizens to be well informed concerning social issues and the facts and values related to the costs, benefits and consequences related to decisions made about science, technology, and society (S-T-S). There is need for a new scientific and technologic literacy. Recognizing and responding to this need means there will be a fundamental reform of science education.

This is a general introduction to more specific themes and discussions of this chapter. First, there is a science education context for later discussion. A second section is on the historical contributions of science and technology to society. Next is a section describing some significant science-related social changes that have occurred since the Sputnik-inspired curriculum reform era. Finally there is a section outlining the contemporary challenges of science and technology in society.

■ A Science Education Perspective

The date October 4, 1957, was historic in science education. The Soviet Union launched Sputnik on that day and a curriculum reform movement that was already in progress was propelled forward with both spiritual and fiscal support. Twenty-five years later, October 1982, was an occasion to ask about the con-dition of science education. Upon examination, the public found that science education was in a state of crisis.

Questions about the curriculum reform movement were pointed. Did the reform movement of the 1960s and 1970s fail? If the new science programs were a success, then why is there a crisis? What was wrong with the new science programs? All of these are legitimate questions and should be answered.

First of all, it can be said that the initial goals were achieved. Thousands of scientists and engineers were brought into the work force. A national goal and appropriate technology landed men on the moon and returned them safely to Earth. In the process, science and mathematics programs and teachers' backgrounds were updated.

Second, why is there a crisis? The answer can be stated directly—the goals for past social challenges are not adequate for present social challenges. The "golden age" of science education has passed. Many of the "new" science programs soon will be twenty-five-years-old! Now is the time to develop a perspective suitable for the 1990s and beyond.

Third, at least one mistake was made in the 1960s that is related to the present situation in science education. An implicit question to the reform movement was—"What does a student need to know and do in order to be a scientist or engineer?" The answer—the student should understand the structure of science disciplines and processes of scientific investigation. With these answers, science educators developed programs that appealed primarily to students bound for colleges and universities and eventually for careers in research and development. The mistake was to purge programs of any emphasis on a citizen's use or understanding of science and technology. Teachers continued to claim they were "preparing students for life," but failed to characterize it as the life of a scientist or engineer. This is not an argument about what was done, or what should have been done, if the goal was preparation for careers in science and engineering. This goal was, and continues to be, inappropriate for the majority of our students and inconsistent with the historical goals of public education. The new S-T-S thrust in science education is toward what was *not* done in the 1960s and 1970s, and what must be done in the 1990s. We should provide an education appropriate to needs and concerns of students as future citizens which will enable them to live, work and participate in a society which is increasingly scientific and technological. There is a need to reinstate personal and societal goals that were eliminated in the 1950s and 1960s. Additionally, we need to update science education to include changes in S-T-S that have occurred in the past decades.

This discussion and brief analysis of science and technology in part serves as a context for the following discussions of S-T-S. It also establishes the position that this chapter is also a rationale and justification for the S-T-S theme.

■ Contributions of Science and Technology to Society

Bertrand Russell's 1952 book, *The Impact of Science on Society,* stands as a particularly cogent early analysis of the interactions among science, technology, and society. Russell suggests that the effects of science have taken several different forms. Science has had *intellectual effects,* for example, a greater stress on empirical observations and the scientific method; *technological effects,* for example, in industry and war, work is more efficient and nations are more powerful; *social organizational effects,* for example, control is more centralized and experts can gain more power; and *philosophical effects,* for example, a new pragmatic philosophy has developed based on utility rather than on truth which ultimately could have disastrous consequences for society. The next paragraphs describe some of the details relative to these contributions.

The first influence science had on society was *intellectual.* Stress on empirical observations and use of scientific methods have served to dispel such things as beliefs in witchcraft and demons. The result has been a mechanistic world view with the following ingredients:

1. *Observation versus authority.* The resolution of matters concerning the natural world can be ascertained through observation and not through appeal to authorities.
2. *The physical world conforms to natural laws.* There is no need to invoke external forces, such as deities, to explain the movement of objects. The causes for certain effects in the natural world are found in the natural world itself. We have Galileo and Newton to thank for this world view.
3. *Dethronement of "purpose."* While there is human purpose, there is not room for purpose in scientific explanation. Darwin's theory of evolution through natural selection is a good example of the scientific dethronement of purpose as an explanation.
4. *Human place in the world.* There are two aspects to this intellectual influence. One was the humbling of human perceptions about their place in the universe. Kepler and Copernicus contributed to this changed world view. On the other hand, humans gained a degree of power to cause

changes. Prior to the scientific world view, prayer and humility were thought to influence change. This view was replaced with one that encouraged acquiring knowledge and understanding natural laws. The power of the latter was found to be greater and more reliable.

Technology has a long history of important contributions to society. Russell uses two discoveries of the late Middle Ages—gunpowder and the mariner's compass—as critical in the interaction between technology and society. Gunpowder gave military power to governments. The long development and escalation of weapons of war have continued to this day. The compass opened the age of discovery. After these important technologies there was a long period with relatively few applications of knowledge to more efficient ways of doing things. Most people are familiar with other major technological contributions such as the cotton gin, electricity, and the internal combustion engine.

Invention of the telegraph influenced social organizations. Messages could travel faster than people; subsequently, governments had more power to enforce law and order. Power could be located in a central position in governmental and private organizations. This observation is true of many technologies. Power is centralized in a few, and the power is greater than it had been historically.

A very important point about the contributions of technology to society is that technology increases the interactions and interdependence among social systems. In a word, societies become "organic." Russell discusses this point:

> The most obvious and inescapable effect of scientific technique is that it makes society more organic, in the sense of increasing the interdependence of its various parts. In the sphere of production, this has two forms. There is first the very intimate interconnection of individuals engaged in a common enterprise, e.g., in a single factory; and secondly there is the relation, less intimate but still essential, between one enterprise and another. Each of these becomes more important with every advance in scientific technique.[1]

Russell is correct on this point. Witness the more "organic" nature of society as new techniques for information dissemination have developed. There is an additional point worth noting. Since 1950, when Russell wrote these essays, the society has extended to a global community that is interdependent in large measure due to technology. The size and power of social organizations have grown to international, in fact global, dimensions.

In a later chapter on "Democracy and Scientific

Technique," Russell returns to this "organic" theme and makes a point related to public participation, a point that is common to discussions of S-T-S themes in education. Here is Russell's view.

> The main point is this: Scientific technique, by making society more organic, increases the extent to which an individual is a cog; if this is not to be an evil, ways must be found of preventing him from being a mere cog. This means that initiative must be preserved in spite of organization. But most initiative will be what may be called in a large sense 'political,' that is to say, it will consist of advice as to what some organization should do. And if there is to be opportunity for this sort of initiative, organizations must as far as possible be governed democratically. Not only so, but the federal principle must be carried so far that every energetic person can hope to influence the government of some social group of which he is a member.

The message to educators is clear. The means to preserving personal initiative is through educating people about the ways and means of participating in the democratic process. This seems especially applicable in the context of science- and technology-related social issues. This point is even more relevant today than in the 1950s when Russell wrote his essay.

Russell's fourth contribution about philosophy argued strongly that John Dewey's pragmatism ultimately would not be beneficial. Russell maintained that substituting the value of utility for truth was inappropriate.

Additionally, the pragmatic philosophy shifts the balance of science and technology toward technology, due to the emphasis on application and utility. No effort will be made to resolve the philosophical point here. Suffice it to note that different philosophies do prevail and do influence the public's perceptions about science and technology in society.

In his book, Russell identified many contemporary issues that are discussed in the next two sections. In a chapter entitled "Can a Scientific Society be Stable?", he concludes with a set of conditions that a scientific society must fulfill if it is to be stable. These are mentioned here because they are ideal precursors to discussions in the next section on "Contemporary Challenges of Science and Technology in Society." Conditions put forth by Russell included not using soil and raw materials faster than scientific and technological progress can replace the loss. Population growth must be controlled at levels lower than the rate of food production. Finally, he suggested the need for a general diffusion of prosperity, a single world government, provisions for individual initiative in work and play, and a diffusion of power compatible with the maintenance of political and economic frameworks.

All through this discussion of the contributions of science and technology to society, a tension exists between the potential goods and possible evils. From gunpowder to atomic weapons, there is simultaneously security and insecurity. In the centralization of power and authority, there is efficiency and loss of personal freedom. These issues are not unlike those we confront today as a society. One point is different from the Middle Ages, or even the 1950s when Russell wrote. Science and technology are much more influential. They are powerful forces for social transformation and the need for public understanding—scientific and technological literacy—is even more urgent.

■ Science and Technology: A Social Perspective

Significant social changes have occurred since Bertrand Russell wrote *The Impact of Science on Society* and Sputnik was launched. Examples particularly important to science and technology education will be used to highlight some of the fundamental social changes that have occurred in the past two and a half decades.

Silent Spring[2] was published in 1962. This powerful book directed the world's attention to the detrimental effect of chemicals. Rachel Carson warned that the indiscriminate use of chemicals could "linger in the soil," "slow the leaping of fish," and "still the song of the birds." If society continued contaminating the environment, then one day society would experience a silent spring. Carson did go beyond the available evidence and was criticized for the book's alarming message. But, the book became a symbolic figure and the environmental movement was born. Carson's basic conviction was stated in a Congressional hearing when she urged that this generation must come to terms with nature. For the remaining years of the decade, society began coming to terms with our effect on the environment. We witnessed the establishment of many public policies: In 1965 Congress passed the Clean Air Act (and subsequently in 1970 and 1975) and the Solid Waste Disposal Act. In 1966 the Species Conservation Act was passed, and in 1969 the National Environmental Policy Act was passed.

In 1969 the world witnessed the achievement of the greatest technological challenge in human history. Men landed on the moon and returned safely to Earth. Clearly, this was a decade that closed with scientific success. But, other societal issues had occurred during this period. Protests began against the war in Vietnam. And in the United States, urban problems generated social concerns. Comparisons of money spent on space programs versus poverty-related problems were reported and debated. Technological advances were identified both with space exploration and the power of destruction in war. The advantages of industrial growth were weighed against the disadvantages of pollution. By the end of the 1960s, some of the science-related issues that were so important at the beginning of the decade were achieved, resolved, or forgotten, and entirely new problems had emerged. But the reader should note that many themes identified in Russell's analysis of science and society were clearly evident.

In the 1970s past ideas and values about growth were questioned. High technology was challenged in the specific form of the supersonic transport (SST). After a long Congressional battle, support for the SST was terminated. In 1972 the public heard that we needed to recognize *The Limits to Growth*[3] and we had *Only One Earth*.[4] In the event that people had missed the messages of these books, the Organization of Petroleum Exporting Countries (OPEC) made it explicit clear through the oil embargo of 1973-74. The embargo brought the issue of energy to the public's attention and it has been there ever since.

During the decade 1970-80, Congress passed a number of bills related to the environment, including the Water Pollution Control Act (1972), the Endangered Species Act (1973), the Toxic Substances Control Act (1976), and the Clean Air and Clean Water Acts (1977). But, as the decade drew to a close, the Three Mile Island incident further underscored the impact of technology on society and brought the themes of science, technology, and society to the public consciousness. This incident symbolizes the ambivalence between society and science that had developed for two decades. There was, simultaneously, the hope for cheap energy and the disillusionment with technology; the need for energy and the questioning of nuclear power; the possibility of unlimited energy and profound vulnerability based on science and technology.

Many themes of the 1960s and 1970s were substantiated in the 1980s and extended from local or national levels to global concerns. The *Global 2000 Report to the President: Entering the Twenty-First Century* serves as an example. Here is a summary of the major findings and conclusions:

> If present trends continue, the world in 2000 will be more crowded, more polluted, less stable ecologically, and more vulnerable to disruption than the world we live in now. Serious stresses involving population, resources, and environment are clearly visible ahead. Despite greater material output, the world's people will be poorer in many ways than they are today.
>
> For hundreds of millions of the desperately poor, the outlook for food and other necessities of life will be no better. For many it will be worse. Bar-

ring revolutionary advances in technology, life for most people on earth will be more precarious in 2000 than it is now—unless the nations of the world act decisively to alter current trends.[5]

In the twenty-five years since Sputnik and thirty-five years since Russell's book, there has developed an environmental movement, a growing concern about the role of science and technology in society, a recognition that the rate and direction of social growth must change, and a realization of the global dimensions of problems and the interdependence of human beings with each other and their environment.

■ Contemporary Challenges of Science and Technology in Society

Economic growth results from the combination of labor, capital, and land (natural resources) for the production of social goods and services. Science and technology contribute to economic growth in several different ways. There is the creation of new products and services with the resulting expansion of consumer choice. Science and technology also contribute to more efficient (less expensive) production of goods and services. And, finally, the resources used for economic growth are extended through better extraction and processing and through development of synthetic substitues that can replace natural resources which are too expensive and/or not available. In the example of economic growth, one can see the symbiotic relationship that has been established within science, technology, and society. Support for research and development contributes to economic progress which, in turn, provides more support for scientific investigation and technological innovation.

While this makes sense, many people know that all is not well in industrialized societies. There are many characteristics of industrial societies such as advanced technology, complex social organizations, and rapid social transformation. However, it is worth directing our attention to the characteristic mentioned above, namely a commitment to continued economic growth. In *Problems of an Industrial Society*,[6] William Faunce suggests that we are witnessing problems *of* an industrial society as opposed to problems *in* an industrial society. That is, there are problems unique to and inherent in the social structure and function of industrial societies. There are some problems common to all societies—crime and poverty, for example. But there are some problems only found in contemporary industrial societies. What are these problems? And, more importantly, how are they related to science and technology? Here is William Faunce's list of problems: resource depletion, environmental degradation, individual alienation, and threats to personal freedom. Two of these problems, resource depletion and environmental degradation, are very closely related to science and technology. Alienation and loss of freedom are indirectly related through large bureaucratic organization, mechanization, and lack of participation in public policy. Science educators are more concerned about resources and the environment because they pose a more fundamental threat to long term social stability. Recommendations for a S-T-S emphasis in education programs include public participation which, at least partially, recognizes the problems of alienation and loss of freedom.

The Industrial Revolution was based on the use of fossil fuels to run machines. Very importantly, these fossil fuel resources (such as various metals) were also basic to the industrialization of society. Along with the perception of unlimited resources, there was an apparently unlimited environment for waste disposal. With these perceptions, and the advances of science and technology, the economy prospered. But now we realize that resources and environments are finite. These are the related challenges for science and technology.

Science and Technology: Promises and Dangers in the Eighties[7] outlines four challenges to future expectations for science and technology. The first two are external to society. The primary challenge is *limited resources*—physical, social, and economic restraints on growth. The second external challenge is from a *changing world order*—emergence of Third World powers and interdependence of nations. There are two challenges from within society. One is *public participation* in science policy making—institutional forms and legislation. And, second, an *understanding of the increasing complexity of the science and society relationship*—scientific and technologic literacy.

Limited resources are seen by many as the most critical challenge because resources essential to traditional economic growth are diminishing. As resources continue to decrease, prices of goods and services will increase, and science and technology will strain to extend the limited resources through new discoveries. But there are inevitably going to be diminishing returns. And, as noted earlier, the symbiotic relationship between science, technology, and society could be broken due to decreased financial support on the one hand, and fewer innovations to spur economic growth on the other.

Other social concerns such as the national debt and the rising cost of government are outside the scientific and technologic enterprise, but do affect it. There are, however, constraints directly related to science and technology. The cost of doing research has increased enormously in recent decades. And, when you consider that physics and chemistry are no longer the only major research areas (there are also the life, earth, and social sciences), then it is fairly easy to see that fewer dollars are being spread further, to cover increased costs. And, all of this is done with higher expectations for economic returns from investments in research and development.

The paradox in this situation is that investments in science and technology are critical if society is to move beyond the present situation. Vital resources are found within the community of scientists and engineers that can help with natural resource problems, policy options, and economic and political choices.

Without much notice, we have become a global community. This constitutes the second challenge. After World War II, the United States was a world leader in science and technology. In the decades since the war, Western Europe and Japan have also become world leaders. In addition to this, Third World countries have emerged with coalitions of power that influence the economies of other more developed countries. The 1973 OPEC oil embargo serves as a good example of this challenge (and the one of limited resources).

After World War II, there were increased numbers of countries with the basic skills for labor. They possessed equal abilities to manufacture products at less cost. The result has been a shift of production of goods and services to other countries. The balance of foreign trade shifted as the U.S. bought more from and sold less to other countries. To this scenario one can add the development of multi-national corporations and the fact that they use natural and human resources from other countries, often Third World, and one can easily see the significance of the new world order.

How does this relate to science and technology? Several examples may make this relationship clear. Most scientists and engineers reside in developed countries and pursue the research and development priorities of their countries. These priorities are seldom aligned with the real human needs of the developing world, and there is a problem with the transfer of technologies to the Third World. When technologies are transferred, they are often either inappropriate or maintained for an elite group. Other examples include development and sale of armaments and use of resources.

The complexity of science and technology and its powerful influence in society, combined with greater citizen participation in decisions and policy, forms the third challenge. Many decisions concerning science and technology—and issues related to science and technology—will have to be made in the 1990s and in future decades. Who should make the decisions? On what basis should decisions be made? And, how should the decisions be made in a democratic society?

There is increased public participation in various forms which is significantly related to science and technology. Debates over the siting of nuclear power plants and recombinant DNA technology serve as two examples. The use of computers, issues of privacy, and problems involving risk and uncertainty have also brought public attention.

Tension is growing between the necessary freedom of scientific enterprise and the requirement of public participation in a democratic society. This is related to the fourth challenge, scientific literacy. There is a strand of logic that connects this challenge to all of the others. An imperative in today's world is for individuals to understand the impact of the science and technologic enterprise on their *personal* lives in relation to important *social issues*. That is, they need to know *about* the history, philosophy, and social role of science and technology as well as the concepts, processes, and skills of science. Finally, there is a need to introduce students to the ways and means of democratic participation in the context of science- and technology-related social issues.[8,9] The interaction and significance of science and technology in society is clear. That science and technology education is related to, but not reflective of, the needs of individuals and of society is cause for concern and the basis for a contemporary reform of science education.

■ The Contemporary Reform of Science Education

It is difficult to identify the exact time when the need for curricular reform became recognized as important. When the Department of Education's report *A Nation At Risk* was published in 1983, the debate became widespread. Other books and reports on general education followed—*Action for Excellence*,[10] *Making the Grade*,[11] *The Paideia Proposal*,[12] *High School*,[13] and *A Place Called School*.[14] Science education was a prominent theme in the literature on the need for educational reform.

One of the first indicators of a need for change in science education came in a 1980 report jointly prepared by the National Science Foundation and the Department of Education—*Science and Engineering Education for the 1980s and Beyond*. There were concerns about student achievement, lack of participation in science and mathematics courses, low standards, and inadequate requirements. There was

also concern about science curricula and programs, namely, that the science curricula gave little attention to students who were not intent on careers in science and engineering and that this was the majority of students.

> . . . There is a great mismatch between the content of secondary school science and mathematics courses and the needs and interests of students for whom these courses will contribute their entire formal scientific education. With few exceptions, these courses are not directed toward personal or societal problems involving science and technology; nor do they offer any insight into what engineers and scientists do; nor do they have vocational relevance except for the chosen few.[15]

The report recommends that curriculum materials be developed that will motivate students to take science beyond tenth grade, and that will emphasize the special needs of minorities, women, and the disabled. The recommendation also included a focus on the scientific and technologic basis of national problems such as energy, natural resources, and health.

Other reports followed. In 1981 the recommendations of Project Synthesis were published.[16] Project Synthesis was a major effort to bring together the best information available on the present state and future direction of science and technology education. The curricular recommendation was congruent with that discussed so far—there is a need for science programs for *all* students, ones that include an emphasis on personal, social, and career goals.

In 1982 the National Science Teachers Association issued a position statement entitled "Science-Technology-Society: Science Education for the 1980s."[17] Again, the theme was that of the title—science and technology education should focus on literacy for all the students. Recommendations for the curriculum included

* Development of scientific and technological process and inquiry skills
* Provision of scientific and technologic knowledge
* Use of skills and knowledge of science and technology as they apply to personal and social decisions
* Enhancement of attitudes, values and appreciation of science and technology
* Study of interactions among science-technology-society in context of science related societal issues

A prestigious National Science Board report, *Educating Americans for the 21st Century*,[18] furthered the reform. In particular, one aspect of the

=== **GUEST EDITORIAL** ===

Science Teaching in a New Key

Paul DeHart Hurd
Professor Emeritus, Stanford University, Palo Alto,
California

Educators, scientists, and people at large increasingly sense that science must be taught in a new key to bridge the gap between the search for knowledge and its utilization. Science and technology have a significant capacity to shape nearly every aspect of human experience, including the social structure and personal and cultural values. The educational issue we face is a reconstruction of science teaching for making wise use of knowledge to improve the quality of life and living.

In the history of science teaching, every age has its own preoccupations. New advances in theory influence what should be taught. At the turn of this century, for example, the works of Mendel, Einstein, and Mendeleev had this effect. As industrialism grew in the United States, topics on farm machinery, the internal combustion engine, and steelmaking were added to science textbooks. The rapid growth of "big science" and technology at midcentury threatened America with a possible shortage of scientists and highly trained engineers and technicians. Thus it became important to develop science courses that stressed the basic theories and principles of a discipline which, if properly taught, might attract students to careers in science or technical fields. Today, because science and technology have become central to our social, political, and economic process, science teaching takes on a new perspective that binds science, technology, and values to human welfare—a new key for the teaching of science.

Throughout history, intellectual, social, and cultural events have, at times, accumulated to produce a major turning point in human affairs. The introduction of agriculture, the industrial revolution, and the development of modern science mark such times. Again we find human beings challenged with a plethora of circumstances, events, and innovations in sociotechnical systems that assure us that our future will not be like our past, no matter how we deal with them. Thus the 1990s represent a critical juncture for all humankind. The intellectual context and substance for science teaching are equally critical.

The major educational issue that we face has developed from our extraordinary ability to generate new knowledge. In the 400 years of modern research in science, the amount of new knowledge introduced into human experience has been astronomical. It continues to grow exponentially. No longer can we legitimately conceive of a science course, at any level of schooling, as sampling the total knowledge of a discipline or even its underlying principles and

report outlined new goals under the provocative title "A Revised and Intensified Science and Technology Curriculum Grades K-12 Urgently Needed For Our Future." There were recommendations for a proposed curriculum. Though some recommendations are for lower grades, we think it appropriate to give the entire list.

- Science and technology education should be taught daily in every pre-college year
- Emphasis in grades K-6 on phenomena in the natural environment, collecting and processing data, and a balanced physical and biological sciences program
- Emphasis in grades 7-8 on biological, chemical, and physical aspects related to the personal needs of adolescents and to development of quantitative analysis skills
- Emphasis in grades 9-11 on the application of science and technology to improvement of the community, local and national
- Options in grades 11-12 for discipline-oriented career preparation courses, preferably with several disciplines taken each year rather than one science subject each year
- Grades K-11 program be an integration of science and technology and practical mathematics
- Introduction of concepts of technology, such as feedback, along with concepts of science
- Curriculum be organized around problem-solving skills, real-life issues, and personal and community decision making

theories. For most disciplines, this would require a lifetime of learning. Researchers in science first sought to resolve this situation by specializing and then by using an integrated team attack on problems. But the complexity of modern problems in science, technology, and society is rapidly exceeding human capacities for dealing with them. There is too much to know. Technologies have had to be developed to serve as multipliers of the mind, technologies such as computer-based information-storing systems and systems for synthesizing and interpreting knowledge, popularly known as "artificial intelligence." The impact of the growing knowledge base of science portends the need for new goals for science teaching.

The magnitude of the knowledge transformation in our time will influence the cultural and social arrangements of people throughout the world. Primarily, the difference between a developed and an undeveloped country is a capacity to produce and use knowledge, particularly that which is a product of science. These conditions also influence people as individuals. In the United States we are rapidly dividing into two groups of people: the knowledge-poor and the knowledge-rich. The knowledge-poor are those who are unable to tap, manage, and use the continuous flow of new knowledge that might enrich their lives. In recent years a major goal of science teaching has been the discovery or creation of new knowledge in science. The information revolution of the 1980s represents pressures to extend the sphere of science-derived knowledge into areas of personal utilization and social problem-solving. Science teaching under these conditions seeks to develop the insights and skills that link the creation, diffusion, and utilization of knowledge for the common good.

The goal of science teaching for this new age of information is to discover how we can best use what knowledge we now have as a means to learn more. The learning task is one of knowing how to obtain and decipher information that already exists to further improve our knowledge base and our ability for making informed decisions. Much of what we need to know in life cannot be perceived during the years of schooling. What can be learned, however, are the skills for tapping knowledge sources at any time in life.

The complexity of science-based personal and social problems is so great that we cannot comprehend all knowledge. Science teaching must focus on knowing what to do with what is known and must cultivate the ability to translate knowledge into wise action.

* Research in teaching and learning be applied to identify desirable characteristics of curricular materials and teaching methods
* Coverage of what is basic in contemporary science and engineering concepts and methods
* Provision for interaction with the community and with informal education centers
* Implementation of the above curriculum in stages as new material and qualified teachers become available[19]

The National Science Teachers Association (NSTA) Yearbooks also expressed the need for curricular reform. The 1983 Yearbook, *Science Teaching: A Profession Speaks*,[20] conveyed the practical, program, and policy concerns of the science education profession. The 1984 Yearbook, *Redesigning Science and Technology Education*,[21] expressed the fact that we are in the process of change. The first section of this yearbook reviewed several of the contemporary reports mentioned at the beginning of this section. Other chapters addressed the essential components of science and technology education— requirements and standards, curriculum, instruction, teacher education, and research and leadership. The last section outlined an agenda for action based on the yearbook chapters. According to this agenda, science and technology education's curriculum should include the following:

* integrate science-technology-society themes, problems, and issues;

- present a multidisciplinary analysis of science- and technology-related problems;
- provide opportunities for informal learning;
- demonstrate relevance to the student's world; and
- include computer literacy in the context of science knowledge, skills, and values.

The science-technology-society theme has been prominent in the recent literature on reform in science education.[22] The guest editorial by Paul DeHart Hurd and Table 24.1 provide overviews of changes in science education and the S-T-S theme. In the next sections of this chapter we discuss scientific and technologic literacy and the S-T-S theme.

TABLE 24–1
Science education past, present and future

Past to 1950s	1960s to Present	1990s to . . .
1. Personal/social goals were somewhat recognized.	1. Personal/social goals were largely unrecognized.	1. Relationships among science, technology, and society will be the organizational core of curriculum.
2. Scientific knowledge was presented in a logical progression.	2. Scientific knowledge is presented as the "structure of the discipline."	2. Scientific knowledge will be presented in the context of science-technology related social issues.
3. Scientific method was presented as a specific-procedure—"the scientific method."	3. Scientific methods are presented as inquiry and discovery processes designed to involve students in "pure" science.	3. Scientific methods will be presented as inquiry into personal, environmental, and social problems to acquire information for decisionmaking.
4. Laboratory work was to demonstrate, visualize, or confirm knowledge.	4. Laboratory exercises are to develop inquiry skills and to "discover" knowledge (mostly reductive analysis).	4. Laboratory exercises will provide opportunities to solve technologic problems, to learn scientific inquiry (both reductive and holistic), and to develop decision-making skills.
5. Science programs determined primarily by textbooks and authors.	5. Science programs determined by curriculum developers and scientists.	5. Science programs determined by teachers, curriculum developers, supervisors, national organizations, and textbooks.
6. Textbook was the curriculum.	6. Textbook and laboratory are the curriculum.	6. Textbook, laboratory, simulation games, community experiences, electronic media, and other informal educational resources will be the curriculum.
7. Science related to technology much of the time.	7. Science-technology relationship is largely neglected for "pure" science.	7. Interdependence of science, technology, and society will be stressed.
8. Science was presented as established knowledge.	8. Science is presented as ever-changing body of knowledge that is updated through inquiry processes.	8. Science will be presented as an ever-changing body of knowledge having important influences on society. Updating and using the knowledge for democratic participation will be underscored.
9. Disciplinary and multi-disciplinary (within scientific disciplines, e.g., general science) approach was used.	9. Disciplinary approach is used.	9. Interdisciplinary approach will be used. (Extending beyond natural sciences and including social sciences, humanities, philosophy and history)
10. Careers were represented by stereotyped male scientists in the laboratory.	10. Career information in science largely ignored; the programs were primarily directed toward science and engineering.	10. Career information will be directed to multiple scientific and technological occupations for all citizens.

Source: This first appeared in: R. Bybee, "Citizenship and Science Education," *The American Biology Teacher*, 44, no. 6, (September, 1982), p. 344. The current form is a modification of the original table.

■ "What Should the Scientifically and Technologically Literate Person Know, Value and Do—as a Citizen?"

Answering this question sets the task for the following sections. Science educators have developed admirable, and in many ways adequate, answers to the question that heads this section. For example, Paul DeHart Hurd has long argued that personal and social goals are essential to scientific literacy.[23,24,25] Other science educators and organizations have made various contributions to the theme of scientific and technologic literacy.[26-37] Several things ought to be made explicit about the perspective presented in this chapter.

The last phrase of the heading—as a citizen—is a controlling statement concerning the reformulation of goals. The aim is to assure that science teaching contributes to the student's personal development and to his or her realization as a citizen; that is, a person with civic duties, rights and obligations. Included also in this formulation of goals is the important aim of all public education—informed and rational participation in the democratic process. This includes the development of individual sensibilities about science, technology, and society. The word sensibilities incorporates intellectual, ethical and emotional responses to conditions and events. Our perspective for scientific and technologic literacy is concerned with citizens' receptivity and responsiveness to science and technology as an important cultural enterprise with influences ranging from the individual to global dimensions.[38] How can we help citizens respond sensibly to the personal, environmental and public policy issues involving science and technology? Obviously, there is need for students to understand something about the nature of science and technology. And, they should understand the limits and possibilities of science and technology as a force for social change.

The question "What should the scientifically and technologically literate person know, value and do—as a citizen?" implies that all knowledge, attitudes, and skills concerning science and technology are not essential. Science teachers are being called on to ask and answer for the 1990s a contemporary and expanded version of Herbert Spencer's 1859 question—"What knowledge is of most worth?" Spencer's answer was science. But, then, what science is of most worth to the citizen? Considering the social, scientific and technologic situation in the 1990s it seems reasonable to suggest that some essential topics might include: population growth, air quality and atmosphere, water resources, land use, world hunger and food resources, hazardous substances, human health and disease, and war technology.[39,40,41] In addition to this list, other vital topics are: quality of life, transportation, space exploration, microelectronics and biotechnology.

All of this is to say that one must answer the question in a contemporary context. If it were the 1890s when the United States was in the process of transformation from an agricultural to an industrial society, the question would be the same, but the answer would be quite different. Likewise, in A.D. 2010 the question would be the same, but the answer will undoubtedly vary.

The question considers *both* science and technology. Recently, science has been the primary concern of most education programs. Yet, citizens actually experience more technology than science. To be sure, science is basic to technology, but technology is a part of each citizen's direct and daily experience, and generally, science is not. However, technology is not a part of education programs. It seems reasonable to recommend that acquiring knowledge about technology be included in educational goals.

There is an attitudinal dimension of scientific and technologic literacy. Public attitudes affect social policies as much as knowledge and skills. And, when asked, the public demonstrates attitudes toward basic and applied science—be they informed or ill-informed, accurate or inaccurate perceptions.[42-45] Citizens are called on to understand and evaluate the uses and consequences of science and technology in society. They must decide to support or reject programs having to do with basic and applied research, and to help establish public policies that enhance or protect the quality of life. Concluding the need for recognition and enlarged understanding of attitudes as a part of science and technology educations seems, at this time, obvious.

■ A Framework for Scientific and Technologic Literacy

While developing a conceptual framework for scientific and technologic literacy we came upon an excellent 1975 essay by Benjamin S.P. Shen, "Science Literacy: The Public Need." In this paper, Shen writes about three distinct, but related, forms of scientific literacy: practical, civic and cultural. Practical literacy is defined as "the possession of the kind of scientific and technical knowledge that can be immediately put to use to help solve . . . the most basic human needs (of) health and survival . . . practical science literacy has to do with just those needs." The aim of civic science literacy is to increase citizens' awareness of science and technology as they relate to social problems so that they and their representatives can bring common sense to bear on the issues.

TABLE 24–2

A conceptual framework for knowledge, skills and values of scientific and technologic literacy

Acquisition of Knowledge	Utilization of Learning Skills	Development of Values and Ideas
Related to	*Based on*	*About*
Science and technology	Scientific and technologic inquiry	Science and technology in society
through study of	*by means of active participation in*	*through investigation of*
Personal matters	Information gathering	Local issues
Civic concerns	Problem solving	Public policies
Cultural perspectives	Decision making	Global problems

Cultural science literacy is directed toward the citizen's understanding of science and technology as major human achievements. Practical problems and civic issues are not necessarily solved by cultural literacy, but it helps bridge the gap between "the two cultures."[46]

Table 24.2 is a conceptual framework for scientific and technologic literacy. The framework is based on the main categories of the question that heads this section—knowledge, skills and values. Secondly, the framework identifies three essential themes, science and technology *concepts;* the process of *inquiry;* and *science-technology-society* interactions. Under each of the three main categories we suggest general areas of emphasis, participation and study. Each column does fulfill several important criteria for the translation of the concepts, processes and attitudes to curriculum programs.

Note that any program based on this framework would progress from personal to cultural, information gathering to decision making, and local issues to global problems. In general, the framework goes from simple to complex, concrete to abstract, immediate to past and future perspectives. Tables 24.3, 24.4, and 24.5 further elaborate some concepts, skills and ideas for the conceptual framework.

The acquisition of knowledge related to science and technology continues to be a central purpose of science teaching. Ten sets of general concepts are presented in Table 24.3. The concepts are consistent with the personal, social, and world view essential to contemporary life and living. One of the main criteria for including these, as opposed to other concepts, is that they unify the apparent disparate content areas of science, technology and society. That is, the concepts are integrative. Undoubtedly there are other important concepts. This set should provide an initial overview of the knowledge component of scientific and technologic literacy.

Inquiry skills based on science and technology are described in Table 24.4. Initial curiosity and questioning by students about the natural world around them is the basis for these skills. Questioning and searching for information combined with observing and organizing information are processes of informal inquiry emphasized in elementary science education that set the stage for formal inquiry during secondary science education. Measuring, classifying, comparing, conserving, analyzing and synthesizing skills are also included. Problem solving includes the identification and description of problems, hypothesizing and predicting outcomes of experiments, situations and events. Separation and control of variables is central to the design of scientific experiments, development of technologies and analysis of policy issues. Finally, inquiry skills are extended to the realm of decision making—the exploration and evaluation of decisions to be made and actually making and acting on the choice.

Themes important to the development of ideas and values about science and technology in society are outlined in Table 24.5. Simple definitions of science, technology and society are presented first. From this point various combinations of interactions are described, e.g., science, technology, science and society, society and technology and so on.

This section outlines a general framework for scientific and technologic literacy. In doing so, our purpose is to answer the question—what should the scientifically and technologically literate person know, value, and do—as a citizen?—and to provide concrete examples of some knowledge skills and values appropriate for science education. This is a framework, not the final structure. The complete structure will have to be developed by science teachers, science supervisors and curriculum developers as they answer the central question in the context of their students, schools and communities. Some dis-

TABLE 24–3
Unifying concepts for science-technology-society

Systems and Subsystems

Systems are groups of related objects that form a whole. A system is also a collection of materials isolated for the purpose of study. Subsystems are systems entirely within another system. Elements of a system, and systems, often interact. There is usually evidence for the interaction. Evidence of interactions provide opportunities for identification and analysis of causal relationships.

Organization and Identity

Systems have characteristics that give them identifiable properties. There are boundaries, components, flow of resources, feedback and open and closed aspects of systems organization. Changes in systems may alter some properties but maintain the system's identity. Some changes of systems result in different identities.

Hierarchy and Diversity

Matter, whether nonliving or living, natural or manmade, is organized in hierarchical patterns and systems. There are hierarchical levels of organization from subatomic to the cosmologic levels. There is also increasing complexity in physical, biological and human systems. Diversity can result in stability of systems.

Interaction and Change

Components within systems, and systems, interact. There is usually evidence of the interaction. All things change over time. The course of change may be influenced in such a way to modify the properties, organization and identity of systems.

Growth and Cycles

Growth is an increase in size, number, complexity or value. Linear growth changes by a constant amount over a time interval. Exponential growth occurs by an increasing rate at a constant percentage for identifiable periods of time. Some systems change in regular sequences, or in cycles, in time and/or space. There are biogeochemical cycles essential to life and living.

Patterns and Processes

Interactions, change, growth and cycles often occur in observable patterns and as a result of identifiable processes.

Probability and Prediction

Some changes are more predictable than others. Statistical calculations allow some degree of accuracy—a probability—in the prediction of future events.

Conservation and Degradation

Matter and energy are neither created nor destroyed. Both may be changed to different forms. This is the first law of thermodynamics. Considered as a whole, any system and its surroundings will tend toward increasing disorder or randomness. This is the second law of thermodynamics.

Adaptation and Limitation

All systems—nonliving, living and social—exhibit a range of capabilities in responding to environmental or cultural challenges. There are limits to environmental, organismic and social changes. Adaptations may be biological, physical, technological, social, political, economic or human.

Equilibrium and Sustainability

Components of a system acting with one another in ways that maintain a balance. Due to adaptation, growth, and change all systems exist on a continuum of balanced to unbalanced. The extent of the equilibrium or disequilibrium observed at any point is a function of the system's capacity to carry the load created by factors operating in and on the system. Sustainability describes a human system that has adapted its economic and social systems so that natural resources and the environment are maintained within the limits of adaptation.

cussion of goals based on the categories of emphasis, participation and study are described in the next sections.

Science and Technology in Personal Matters

One of the most fundamental aspects of education for scientific and technologic literacy is the practical use of knowledge, skills and understandings that will help citizens in personal matters. Examples are plentiful in which some basic information could help improve the quality of life. For example, the United States could reduce its infant mortality rate by providing basic health and nutrition information through education. Knowledge of basic developmental needs of children would result in better parenting, thus reducing the possibility of problems such as abuse and neglect.

TABLE 24–4
Inquiry skills based on science and technology

Questioning and Searching
Curiosity and questions about the world are basic to inquiry skills. Thus locating or discovering information based on questions is essential. Informal inquiry—questioning and searching—are first steps toward scientific and technologic problem solving and personal and social decision making.
Observing and Organizing
One or more senses are used to gather information about objects, events or ideas. Once observed and gathered there is need to group information in relation to space, time, and causal relationships.
Measuring and Classifying
Counting objects or events, establishing one to one correspondence and organizing objects according to numerical properties. Quantifying descriptions (e.g. length, width, duration) of objects, systems and events in space and time. Forming meaningful groupings. Putting objects or events in order by using a pattern or property to construct a series (seriation). Classifying includes defining similarities and identifying subsystems based on a property and arranging subsystems and systems in a hierarchy.
Comparing and Conserving
Identifying similarities, differences and changes in objects and systems in space (local to global) and time (past, present, future). Understanding that quantitative relationships between materials and systems remain the same even though they have undergone perceptual alterations.
Analyzing and Synthesizing
Reducing information to simpler elements for better understanding of the organization and dynamics of objects, systems, events and ideas. Analysis includes describing components, clarifying relationships among systems or subsystems and identifying organizational principles of systems. Where analysis stresses reduction and parts, synthesis stresses construction and the whole. Bringing together information to form unique organizations, patterns or systems. Understanding the whole is greater than the sum of parts.
Identifying and Describing
These skills extend those of gathering information to problem solving. Problem identification and description are first steps in formal inquiry. Included are identification of personal and/or social problems, gathering information and describing what is known and unknown about a problem.
Hypothesizing and Predicting
When confronting a problem, making reasonable guesses, or estimates based on information. Making statements of conditionality—"If . . . then . . . " concerning a problem. Predicting possible conclusions. Inductive (specific to general) and deductive (general to specific) thinking as well as propositional thinking are included.
Separating and Controlling
Applying logical patterns of reasoning, whether to the design of formal experiments, analysis of data, solution of problems or evaluation of policies is based on the skill of separating and controlling variables. Making clear how a condition or event is similar to or different from other conditions or events. Identifying factors and all possible combinations of factors relative to a problem. Control factors and change are variable to determine how it influences reactions. Use hierarchical thinking such as building classification keys.
Exploring and Evaluating
Describing decisions to be made, using skills developed earlier to identify and gather information, converting information to alternatives and examining the consequences of different decisions are all part of the exploration of a decision. Evaluating consists of making value judgments based on the internal consistency of information and clearly defined external criteria such as costs, risks and benefits of alternatives.
Deciding and Acting
Selecting from among alternatives, making an intelligent and responsible choice. Using available information and justifying the decision. Also, identifying ways and means of taking responsible action to reduce or eliminate problems.

TABLE 24–5
Themes of science-technology-society interaction

Science
A systematic, objective search for understanding of the natural and human world. A body of knowledge, formed through continuous inquiry, having significant interactions with technology and society. Science is characterized by use of an empirical approach, statements of generality (e.g. laws, principles, theories) and testing to confirm, refute or modify knowledge about natural and human phenomena.

Technology
The application of knowledge to solve practical problems to achieve human goals. Body of knowledge available to a culture that can be used to control the environment, extract resources, produce goods and services and improve the quality of life.

Society
The collective interactions and relationships among human beings at local, regional, national and global levels. Human groups that are differentiated from other human groups by mutual interests, distinctive relationships, shared institutions and common culture. The human setting in which the scientific and technologic enterprise operates.

Science and Technology
Knowledge generated by the scientific enterprise contributes to new technologies.

Science and Society
Scientific knowledge has a practical influence on the quality of life and on the collective perceptions and actions of those in society. The knowledge produced by science and the processes used by scientists influence our world views—the way we think about ourselves, others and the natural environment. There may be functional and dysfunctional social consequences of scientific knowledge. The impact of science on society is never entirely beneficial nor uniformly detrimental. The impact varies with persons, populations, places and times. Science and society controversies usually center on issues of research priorities and proprietorship of knowledge.

Technology and Science
New technologies influence the scientific enterprise, often determining research problems and the means employed to solve research problems. Technological developments can lead to improved methods and instruments for scientific research.

Technology and Society
Technology influences the personal quality of life and how people act and interact locally, nationally and globally. Technological change is accompanied by social, political and economic changes that may be beneficial or detrimental for society. The impact of new technology is never entirely beneficial nor uniformly detrimental. The impact varies with persons, populations, places and times. Technology and society controversies usually center on issues of efficiency, equitability, benefit, risk and regulation.

Society and Science
Society is often the source of ideas and problems for scientific research. Research priorities are influenced by requests for proposals, grants and funding through public and private sources. The social context (dominant social paradigms) affects the reception of new ideas and social factors within the science community (dominant scientific paradigms) influence the research undertaken and the acceptance of new findings. Social control over science is seen in public demands for the assessment of research priorities.

Society and Technology
Social needs, attitudes and values influence the direction of technological development. Technologies often arise as expressions of cultural values and serve the needs of dominant social groups. Social control over technology is seen in increased demands for the assessment of new technologies.

Science and Technology in Society
Personal and social systems are subject to complex interactions among science, technology and society. There is a history and future of science and technology in social development from the local to global levels.

Some examples of topics that will help translate the goal to practice concerning the application of science and technology in personal matters: appropriate personal diets, adequate health practices, increasing energy efficiency in a house, conservation, short- and long-term effects of inappropriate food, air and water on personal health and welfare, evaluation of practical problems of living.

Science and Technology in Civic Concerns

Citizens need to comprehend environmental and resource problems. Before citizens can participate in the democratic process there must be some minimal level of comprehension of civic concerns. An estimated half of legislative bills are related in some way to science and technology. Unfortunately, many citizens think that science is beyond their grasp. Science- and technology-related civil concerns can be presented in clear and precise ways. From this point, the common sense, rational judgments and practical awareness of decisions and consequences can be considered. Environmental and resource issues are too important to be left to bureaucrats and technocrats. Sample topics of this goal might include: renewable and nonrenewable resources; short-, middle- and long-range proposed solutions to the energy problem; the limits of population growth and the consequences of exceeding the limits to growth; environmental quality for home, school, community and globe; and the role technology has had in increasing and decreasing resources.

Science and Technology in Cultural Perspectives

Understanding science and technology as a human endeavor and appreciating the limits and possibilities of science and technology are also important for citizens. This type of literacy is directed toward knowledge and attitudes *about* science and technology in society. There are some essentials for citizens concerning science and technology: the relationship between research and development and social progress; the connection between technological innovation and employment; problems within and outside the realm of science and technology. Topics such as these and others related to historical-philosophical and social-political perspectives of science and technology are important. Other topics might include: interrelationships among science, technology and society; the connection between science, technology

and social change; basic research and applied research; the social role of science and technology in matters such as energy, armaments and mining; and the role of science and technology in developing countries.

Scientific and Technologic Inquiry for Information Gathering

We live in an information society. A goal of obtaining and using information is not something new or unusual for science education. It has been a long-standing aim of science. For contemporary purposes the goal includes not only gathering information from observations of nature; but, also gathering information from various sources that exist in society. Traditional topics include: questioning, observing, organizing, measuring and classifying. New goals might include: knowing various sources of information, gaining access to information and using different information about retrieval systems.

Scientific and Technologic Inquiry for Problem Solving

Problem solving in a personal-social context is a goal that has been unrecognized for over two decades of science teaching. Replacing a once important goal requires only building on the essential structure of problem solving. Identifying problems, hypothesizing, predicting, and separating and controlling variables are commonly recognized goals of science teaching. But which problems are worth solving? Those of personal and social concern to citizens. Addition of the personal-social theme is clearly recognizable in the framework presented throughout this essay.

Scientific and Technologic Inquiry for Decision Making

The goal is new to science teaching. It is, however, a logical extension of problem solving in a personal and social context. Once one has information, and attempts to resolve problems, decision making cannot be avoided. This is true for problems related to science and technology; it is equally true for life and living. Some practical objectives are: describing a decision to be made; utilizing various information gathering skills; clarifying alternatives; assessing costs, risks, and benefits of various alternatives; and choosing the best alternatives.

===== GUEST EDITORIAL =====

Superconductivity: A Revolution in Physics

Paul Chu, Ph.D.,
Program Director
Solid State Physics Program

To illustrate the excitement of working on the frontiers of science, I would like to share some of my experiences in the recent discovery of "high temperature" superconductors.

Unlike ordinary electrical conductors, in which some of the useful electrical energy is always lost as heat, superconducting materials can carry a current with no loss, and so if a current were set up in a loop of superconducting wire, the current would go around and around forever.

Kamerlingh Onnes discovered superconductivity in 1911. While exploring the properties of matter at very low temperatures, Onnes found that wires of frozen mercury became superconducting at about $-275°$ C. By the start of 1986, the highest superconducting temperature known was only about $-251°$ C. Because such a temperature is difficult to produce and maintain, these superconductors were useful only when the alternatives were even more difficult and expensive.

Late in 1986 all this began to change. Georg Bednorz and Alex Mueller, who both work at the IBM research lab in Zurich, Switzerland, found that a compound of barium, lanthanum, copper, and oxygen superconducts at about $-240°$ C. I first learned of their discovery in November, 1986, when I saw an article they had published. I became excited, because I too had worked with metal oxides of this type, and my experience told me that it should be possible to make similar compounds and perhaps raise the temperature for superconductivity even higher. The goal was $-196°$ C because it is relatively easy to cool to that temperature using liquid nitrogen. We knew that if we would make a $-196°$ C superconductor, it would have many revolutionary uses. Of course, other scientists had also read the article by Bednorz and Mueller. I now know that a group in Tokyo was on the same track I was. My group quickly managed to find superconductivity at $-223°$ C. When the reports of our work and of similar work by the group in Tokyo were given in December at a meeting in Boston, even more scientists became interested. By this time everyone knew that to be first would require hard work, good intuition, and a bit of luck. We were in a race with the best. On January 29, 1987, our group observed superconductivity above $-184°$ C in a yttrium-barium-copper oxide sample with a structure different from the compound studied by Bednorz and Mueller. We immediately knew that we had opened the door to widespread applications of superconductivity.

Every year in March the American Physical Society holds a meeting devoted to solid state physics. The new discoveries in superconductivity had occurred too late to be included in the scheduled program, but we nevertheless presented our discoveries at a special session, dubbed the "Woodstock of Physics," that started at 7 P.M. and lasted until 3 A.M.. The excitement and enthusiasm evident at that special session have continued, with everyone working hard to achieve still higher temperatures than before and to get a theoretical understanding of the new superconductors. Much remains to be done to make practical use of these materials. They are, as yet, difficult to form into useful films and wires, but with luck we will soon see superconducting computers, loss-free electricity transmission, and trains that "float" in a magnetic field.

Developing Ideas and Values About Science-Technology-Society Interactions in Local Issues

This goal combines with the other goals of science and technology in personal matters and the skills of information gathering. The exact nature of personal matters and local issues will vary with science teachers' locations. Likewise the magnitude and seriousness of the topics will vary. Emphasizing local issues for the clarification and development of S-T-S themes seems an appropriate starting point. Topics will certainly relate to larger concerns, but from a developmental perspective they are much better introduced at the personal and local levels. Examples of topics include: pollution, energy resources, waste disposal, erosion, recycling, ground water and food production.

Developing Ideas and Values About Science-Technology-Society Interactions in Public Policies

The interactions among science, technology and society can be illustrated through education about public policies. Issues of public policy also provide opportunities for teaching basic science concepts and a forum for introducing the theme of civic participation. Where earlier study was directed toward local issues, the study of public policies can include that level, but extends the study to state, regional and national levels. Topics such as conservation and utilization of the environment, resources and population could be included.

Developing Ideas and Values About Science-Technology-Society Interactions in Global Problems

Because many problems related to science and technology have global dimensions, there is a need for students to develop a global perspective. Recent surveys I have completed (Bybee, 1984 a, b) identify important global problems and suggest the need for education concerning these issues. I might also note that the theme of citizenship is equally applicable at this level (Bybee, 1982). Topics of study include: world hunger and food resources, population growth, air quality and atmosphere, water resources, war technology and human health and disease.

■ Summary

Educators at all levels, pre-school to graduate school, are keenly aware of the scientific advances and social problems as we progress toward the twenty-first century. And, more than most, we recognize the disparity between the needs of society and appropriateness of our programs. At the same time education is beset with budget cuts, staff reductions, disruptive students and numerous new requirements. Other unsettling issues render the daily task of teaching difficult at best and impossible at worst. Reluctance to reform programs is understandable but so are the reasons and responsibilities to change. We have a choice. We can give in to the forces acting on us, or we can continue our educational mission. Science and technology education awaits our new initiative. We cannot have a failure of will and professional

obligation at this crucial period in history. Citizens have a genuine need to understand science and technology in our society. Educators have a responsibility to meet this public need. And so, again, we question—what should the scientifically and technologically literate person know, value and do—as a citizen?

■ References

1. B. Russell, *The Impact of Science on Society*. (London: Unwin Books, 1952).
2. R. Carson, *Silent Spring* (Boston: Houghton Mifflin Company, 1962).
3. D.H. Meadows and D.L. Meadows, *The Limits to Growth* (Washington, D.C.: Potomac Associates, 1972).
4. B. Ward and R. Dubos, *Only One Earth* (New York: W.W. Norton, 1972).
5. G. Barney, *The Global 2000 Report to the President: Entering the Twenty-First Century* (Washington, D.C.: U.S. Government Printing Office, 1980).
6. W. Faunce, *Problems of an Industrial Society* (New York: McGraw Hill, 1981).
7. G. Watts, *Science and Technology: Promises and Dangers in the Eighties* (Englewood Cliffs, NJ: Prentice-Hall, 1980).
8. R.W. Bybee, "Global Problems and Science Education Policy" in *Redesigning Science and Technology Education*, 1984 Yearbook of the National Science Teachers Association, eds. R.W. Bybee, J. Carlson, and A. McCormack (Washington, D.C.: NSTA, 1984a).
9. R.W. Bybee, "The Restoration of Confidence in Science and Technology Education," *School Science and Mathematics*, 85, no. 2 (1985), pp. 95-108.
10. Task Force on Education for Economic Growth, *Action for Excellence* (Denver, CO: Education Commission of the States, 1983).
11. Twentieth Century Fund, *Making the Grade* (New York: Twentieth Century Fund, Inc., 1983).
12. M. Adler, *The Paideia Proposal: An Education Manifesto* (New York: MacMillan Publishing, 1982).
13. E. Boyer, *High School* (New York: Harper and Row, 1983).
14. J. Goodlad, *A Place Called School* (New York: McGraw Hill, 1984).
15. National Science Foundation and the Department of Education, *Science and Engineering Education for the 1980's and Beyond* (Washington, D.C.: U.S. Government Printing Office, 1980), p. 5.
16. N. Harms and R. Yager, *What Research Says to the Science Teacher*, Vol. III (Washington, D.C.: National Science Teachers Association, 1981).
17. Committee on NSTA Position Statement, "Science-Technology-Society: Science Education for the 1980's" (Washington, D.C.: National Science Teachers Association, 1982).
18. The National Science Board Commission on Pre-College Education in Mathematics, Science, and Technology, *Educating Americans for the 21st Century:*

Source Materials (Washington, D.C.: National Science Foundation, 1983).

19. The National Science Board Commission on Pre-College Education in Mathematics, Science, and Technology, *Educating Americans for the 21st Century* (Washington, D.C.: National Science Foundation, 1983).

20. F.K. Brown and D. Butts, eds., *Science Teaching: A Profession Speaks, 1983 NSTA Yearbook* (Washington, D.C.: National Science Teachers Association, 1983). R.W. Bybee, J. Carlson, and A. McCormack, eds., *Redesigning Science and Technology Education, 1984 Yearbook* (Washington, D.C., National Science Teachers Association, 1984).

21. R.W. Bybee, J. Carlson, and A. McCormack, "Redesigning Science and Technology Education: An Agenda for Action," in the 1984 NSTA Yearbook, *Redesigning Science and Technology Education* (Washington, D.C.: National Science Teachers Association, p. 246, 1984).

22. R.W. Bybee, ed., *Science-Technology-Society*, in the 1985 NSTA Yearbook (Washington, D.C.: National Science Teachers Association, 1985).

23. P.D. Hurd, "Scientific Enlightenment for An Age of Science," *The Science Teacher*, 37, no. 3 (1970).

24. P.D. Hurd, "Emerging Perspectives in Science Teaching for the 1970's" *School Science and Mathematics*, 72, no. 3 (December, 1972).

25. P.D. Hurd, *Reforming Science Education: The Search for A New Vision* (Washington, D.C.: Council for Basic Education, 1984).

26. M. Agin, "Education for Scientific Literacy: A Conceptual Frame of Reference and Some Applications," *Science Education*, 58, no. 3 (1974).

27. M. Pella, "The Place and Function of Science for A Literate Citizenry," *Science Education*, 60, no. 1 (1976).

28. J.J. Gallagher, "A Broader Base for Science Teaching," *Science Education*, 55, no. 3 (1971).

29. A. Champagne and L. Klopfer, "Actions in A Time of Crisis," *Science Education*, 66, no. 4 (1982).

30. R. Anderson, "Are Yesterday's Goals Adequate for Tomorrow?" *Science Education*, 67, no. 2 (1983).

31. G. Berkheimer and G. Lott, "Science Educators' and Graduate Students' Perceptions of Science Education Objectives for the 1980's," *Science Education*, 68, no. 2 (1984).

32. R. Miller, "Science Teaching for the Citizen of the Future," *Science Education*, 68, no. 4 (1984).

33. D. Zeidler, "Moral Issues and Social Policy in Science Education: Closing the Literacy Gap," *Science Education*, 68, no. 4 (1984).

34. D. Chen and R. Novik, "Scientific and Technological Education in An Information Society," *Science Education*, 68, no. 4 (1984).

35. National Science Teachers Association, "School Science Education for the 1970's," *The Science Teacher*, 38, no. 3 (November, 1971).

36. National Science Teachers Association, "Science-Technology-Society: Science Education for the 1980's," an NSTA Position Statement (Washington, D.C.: National Science Teachers Association, 1982).

37. "Scientific Literacy," *Daedalus*, 112, no. 2 (Spring 1983).

38. R.W. Bybee, "Citizenship and Science Education," *The American Biology Teacher*, 44, no. 6 (September, 1982).

39. R.W. Bybee, "Global Problems and Science Education Policy," in *Redesigning Science and Technology Education, 1984 NSTA Yearbook*, eds. R.W. Bybee, J. Carlson, and A. McCormack (Washington, D.C.: National Science Teachers Association, 1984).

40. R.W. Bybee and R. Bonnstetter, "Science, Technology, and Society: A Survey of Science Teachers" in *Science-Technology-Society*, 1985 Yearbook of the National Science Teachers Association, ed. R.W. Bybee (Washington, D.C.: NSTA, 1985).

41. R.W. Bybee, *Human Ecology: A Perspective for Biology Education* (Reston, VA: National Association of Biology Teachers, 1984b).

42. National Science Board, *Sciences at the Bicentennial: A Report from the Research Community* (Washington, D.C.: U.S. Government Printing Office, 1976).

43. National Assessment of Educational Progress, *Attitudes Toward Science* (Denver, CO: Education Commission of the States, 1979).

44. R.W. Bybee, N. Harms, B. Ward, and R. Yager, "Science, Society, and Science Education," *Science Education*, 64, no. 3 (1980).

45. J. Miller, *The American People and Science Policy* (New York: Pergamon Press, 1983).

46. B. Shen, "Science Literacy: The Public Need," *The Sciences*, 27, no. 6 (January-February, 1975).

===== **INVESTIGATING SCIENCE TEACHING** =====

ACTIVITY 24–1

Curriculum Priorities for Science- and Technology-Related Social Issues

Many public policy problems confront citizens. And, many of these public policy problems have a significant scientific or technologic component. As a science teacher who has to design new curriculum programs it may be of interest to you to see how you would rank some of the common science/technology/society related policy issues.

The easiest way to rank the twelve issues is to first rank those items you think are most important (i.e., 1,2,3,4). Then rank the *least* important items (i.e., 12,11,10,9). Finally, rank the *middle* options from most to least important (i.e., 5,6,7,8).

_____ **Air quality and atmosphere** (acid rain, CO_2, depletion of ozone, global warming)
_____ **Energy shortages** (synthetic fuels, solar power, fossil fuels, conservation, oil production)
_____ **Extinction of plants and animals** (reducing genetic diversity)
_____ **Hazardous substances** (waste dumps, toxic chemicals, lead paints)
_____ **Human health and disease** (infectious and noninfectious diseases, stress, diet and nutrition, exercise, mental health)
_____ **Land use** (soil erosion, reclamation, urban development, wildlife habitat loss, deforestation, desertification)
_____ **Mineral resources** (nonfuel minerals, metallic and nonmetallic minerals, mining, technology, low grade deposits, recycling, reuse)
_____ **Nuclear reactors** (nuclear waste management, breeder reactors, cost of construction, safety)
_____ **Population growth** (world population, immigration, carrying capacity, foresight capability)
_____ **War technology** (nerve gas, nuclear development, nuclear arms threat)
_____ **Water resources** (waste disposal, estuaries, supply, distribution, ground water contamination, fertilizer contamination)
_____ **World hunger and food resources** (food production, agriculture, cropland conservation)

Now that you have ranked these items it may be of interest to discuss some of the following questions with other students or colleagues.

- How much do you know about each of the twelve science related social issues? Quite a lot? Some? Very Little? Nothing?
- How important is it to study these issues as a part of science courses in middle, junior high, or high school? Very Important? Fairly Important? Not too Important? Not Important at all?
- How do you think each of the science related problems will change by the year 2000? Will the individual problems be Much Better? Better? About the Same? Worse? Much Worse?
- What does your response to these questions mean for you as a citizen?
- What are the implications of your responses for the science curriculum you will teach?

Teaching Science Activities

An Introduction to Scientific Inquiry

Aims   To develop a fundamental understanding of, and ability to use, the methods of scientific investigation

Objectives   At the completion of this lesson the student should be able to:

1. Identify and state a simple problem
2. Collect data relative to a simple problem
3. Draw conclusions relative to data
4. Form hypotheses based on observations and data
5. Design a simple experiment to confirm/refute an hypothesis

Materials
1. Dice (or small cubes with numbers 1–6 on different sides), one die for each pair of students.
2. "Mystery Boxes" (small closed boxes with objects inside. Each box may contain a different object), one box for groups of 3–4 students.

Procedures

Anticipatory Set:
1. Ask students, to review what they think scientists do (investigate, solve problems, inquire)
2. Which goal of science is important? Why? How does the process of inquiry apply to them?

Objective and Purpose
1. Today's lesson is an introduction to scientific inquiry.

Instructional Input
1. *Introductory Exploration*
   Prior to your discussion place a die on each desk. Give very clear directions that they are *not* to touch the die.

   - A problem exists relative to the die. What is it? (Let them give their ideas.)
   - Direct discussion to the identification of a problem. (What is on the bottom?)
   - Focus discussion on assumptions, data, inference, etc.
2. *Explanation* of Inquiry
   - Systematic approach to problems
   - Collection of data (not assumptions)
   - Form hypothesis based on data
   - Confirm or refute hypothesis
   - Design of experiments
   - Present the information supporting your conclusion, i.e., writing a scientific paper.
   - Have students summarize the process of inquiry in terms of their observations of the die. How would they best support the case for their hypothesis of what is on the bottom, e.g., adding sides of the die, sequence of numbers, the missing number and so on. Ask them to show how they could systematically approach the problem, collect data, form hypotheses, confirm or refute hypotheses and design an experiment to support their hypothesis. Have the students write a short paper based on this activity. They should use the scientific protocol for the paper's organization.
3. *Extension* of Ideas to a New Problem
   - Present mystery box
   - Allow students to state problem, collect data, form hypothesis, design experiment and present final conclusions.

Evaluation of Objectives:
1. Present a new problem, that you have designed.
2. Have the students collect information, etc. and write a "scientific paper."
3. Evaluate the "scientific paper" and provide feedback relative to the student's understanding of the inquiry process.

Effects of Acid Rain on the Life Cycle of Fruit Flies

Activity Overview

Students investigate the effects of varying levels of acid mist on egg, larval, and pupal stages of the life cycle of *Drosophila melanogaster*. The teacher coordinates a research project for which different teams of students accumulate data on aspects of the problem. All the student teams report their results at a scientific meeting. Students are then confronted with the task of summarizing the results across the entire research effort. Finally, there is a discussion of recommendations for other experiments and recommendations based on accumulated data. Estimated time for the project is two weeks.

Science Background

The design of the activity is such that students gain some understanding of scientific investigation using the life cycle of a simple organism and the problem of acid rain.

Some of the problems related to scientific inquiry are modeled in the activity. Design of experiments, separation and control of variables, observing, graphing, and reporting data are all aspects of the activity. There is another dimension that teachers can introduce. Science is an enterprise that accumulates and evaluates new knowledge, and this is often done at scientific meetings. By having each group of students study one small part of the problem and share their results, the students can gain a better understanding of science.

The activity extends beyond the mere reporting of results. People are required to act on the best information available on a given problem. Often the information is not clear, and seldom does it provide all the answers. Students are asked to make recommendations for the control of acid rain based the available information. Essentially, they are asked to determine harmful levels of acid precipitation for one organism. The lack of clarity of data, the fact that lower phyla organisms were studied and the weight or strength of evidence in decision making will become evident in the final stages of the activity.

Major Concepts

- The effects of logrithmic differences in acidity
- Susceptibility of different stages in the life cycle of fruit flies to acid precipitation
- Separation and control of variables in scientific experiments
- The influence of chronic low intensity changes in the environment
- Limiting factors in the life cycle
- Effects of lethal and sublethal doses of a pollutant
- Science progresses through the accumulation of information

Student Objectives

After this activity students should be able to

- Use the processes of scientific investigation, specifically to
    Design an experiment with a suitable control and single variable
    Observe changes
    Record data
    Report data to fellow students
    Analyze significance and limitations of class results
    Suggest the next logical experiment

- Use data analysis in making a recommendation on what standards should be set as tolerable limits on acid precipitation
- Use the *Drosophila* life cycle to represent organisms generally that have varying sensitivity to acid precipitation during their lives
- Describe observable effects of acid rain on organisms
- Calculate logrithmic differences in pH scale
- Identify difficulties in making decisions based on scientific information

Vocabulary

pH	Lethal dose
Life cycle stages	Control
Egg	Variable
Larva	Quantitative data
Pupa	Lethal
Adult	Sublethal
Viability	Scientific meeting

Materials

- Petri dishes—5 per lab group designated as follows:
    Control with no added water
    Control with pH = 7 water (boiled and cooled) sprayed
    Experimental with assigned pH sprayed during the egg stage
    Experimental with assigned pH sprayed during the larval stage
    Experimental with assigned pH sprayed during the pupal stage
- Nutrient agar prepared with standard materials
- Simple grid to simplify counting

- Stock acid solutions (sulfuric or nitric) of pH 2.6, 3.6, 4.6, 5.6, and 7.0 in plastic spray bottles
- Data tables and graphs drawn by students prior to collecting data. (See examples.)

Procedures   (Note: A step by step *and* daily sequence are indicated)

Beginning on a Monday, spraying containers through the 13 day life cycle.

Day 0
1. Gather 5 nutrient filled Petri dishes and label each appropriately (see materials).
2. Introduce a fertilized female *Drosophila* to provide eggs. Leave female in dish for 24 hours.
3. Prepare stock solutions and adjust sprayers to give uniform amounts of mist.

Day 1   4. Remove female *Drosophila* and use grid to help count the number of eggs in each Petri dish. Record numbers.

5. Spray appropriate solutions into one control and 1st experimental Petri dish to simulate a light rain.

Days 2 & 3   6. Repeat Step 5.

Days 4–7   7. Spray appropriate solution into the 2nd experimental Petri dish to simulate a light rain.

Days 8–11   8. Spray appropriate solution into the 3rd experimental Petri dish to simulate a light rain.

Day 12   9. Count and record the number of adult *Drosophila* in each of the 5 Petri dishes.

10. Divide the number of adult *Drosophila* survivors by the original (day 0) number of eggs to obtain a percentage of survivors under your pH conditions.

11. Have the class simulate a scientific meeting at which each group will report its data and learn about the research of fellow scientists. Report data to class indicating which stage was most affected by your simulated acid rain.

12. Suggest what experiments should be done next to learn more about the effects of acid rain on organisms.

Questions, Discussion and Extension

The discussion of student work can be based on:

1. A standard lab report
2. Participation in the scientific meeting
3. Suggestions on the next steps needed to further study acid precipitation
4. Participation in an optional second set of experiments based on 3
5. Extension and elaboration of this study to the scale of a science fair project

This experimental approach could be expanded in many ways including:

1. Use other species of flora and fauna.
2. Changing a second factor such as temperature or light to test for synergistic effects.
3. Vary the amount or frequency of simulated acid precipitation.
4. Use different acids but the same pH range.
5. Observe organisms daily to note sublethal effects such as differences in activity patterns or levels of activity.
6. Expand the number of acid solutions in the range this experiment shows to be harmful. Try to more specifically pinpoint a critical or lethal concentration for each stage.

References

Demerec, M. and Kaufmann, *Drosophila Guide* (Washington, D. C., Carnegie Institute of Washington, 1965).

Sample Student Data Table

pH = _____

Egg #		Day 1	Egg 2	3	Larva 4	5	6	7	Pupa 8	9	10	11	Adult— 12	Adult #	% Surviving
____	Petri Dish 1														
____	2													___	___
____	3			Use X to indicate spraying schedule										___	___
____	4													___	___
____	5													___	___

Sample Class Data Table

	% Egg Survival	% Larval Survival	% Pupal Survival
pH 7			
6.6			
5.6			
4.6			
3.6			
2.6			

Geologic Time

Activity Overview

Students complete a scale model of geologic time. The primary goal of the activity is to give them a concept of the immensity of geologic time. Secondary to this, they are introduced to geologic periods and the record of life as recorded in rocks. The activity should last for two class periods.

Science Background

There are two primary methods of determining the age of materials and thus establishing a time scale. The first is an ordering of events, simply determining what happened first, second, third, and so on. In this method the dating is *relative*. The second method establishes a specific time of an organism, event, or rock stratum. This is an *absolute* method of dating materials. Geologists have used the relative method of dating materials for years. It is represented classically in the time scale constructed in this activity.

William Smith, working in the nineteenth century, is credited with formally establishing the practice of ordering geologic events. He observed that rocks revealed an orderly succession of life; that is, older species were represented in older rocks (bottom layers) and as these species disappeared from the rock record fossils of new species appeared. This is called *faunal succession*—groups of fossils succeed each other in sedimentary rock layers in such a way that the sequences of rocks are predictable. It should be noted that Smith did not develop the idea of evolution—the biological implication of his observations. He was only concerned with the fossils as chronological indicators. The method used by Smith also allowed him to correlate groups of rocks that were some distance apart. The assumption here is that similar fossils in rocks at two different locations means the rocks were deposited in the same period.

Nineteenth century geologists succeeded in ordering many formations of the world's rocks. The order was based on relative dates, since absolute dating methods had not been developed. Though there are inconsistencies and problems with this method of dating rocks it does represent a good introduction to geologic time and the record of past life and events in the rocks.

Understanding the immensity of geologic time gives students some perspective relative to our time and influence on earth. Compared to other organisms our time has been short and our impact can be viewed with mixed reactions; we probably represent the highest, most complex form of life and we have done the most to endanger our own existence and the existence of other species. It is well for students to understand the perspective of geologic time for these reasons as well as the knowledge contained about the earth's history in the rock record.

Major Concepts

- Environments can change and conserve their identities.
- Environments change because living and nonliving matter interact.
- The earth is very old, geologic time is immense.
- Interpretation of rocks and fossils provide a record of the earth's history.
- Geologic time is subdivided on the basis of natural events in the evolution of life.

Objectives

At the completion of this activity the student should be able to:

- Describe the immensity of geologic time
- Relate the relative ages of some geologic events.
- Identify his/her location in the scale of geologic time.

Materials

- Meter stick
- Colored pencils
- Adding machine tape (6 meter strips for each group of two)

Vocabulary

Geologic time (you may wish to include the names of geologic eras)

Procedures

1. Divide the students into groups of 2.
2. Each group should have a piece of adding machine tape 6 meters long, a meter stick, and a pencil.
3. Mark off a line about 5 centimeters from one end of the tape. Label this line NOW (today's date).
4. Using the meter stick and the ages given in Table 1, plot the different times on the adding machine tape. Indicate that the students should start by using the scale 1 meter = 1 billion years.

(NOTE: As the activity progresses the students will have difficulty with the scale of 1 meter = 1 billion years. They will have to change the scale in order to include recent events on their tape. The frustration of this change and the realization of the difference between 1 year, 100 years, 1000 years, 1 million years, and 1 billion years is as much a part of the lesson as the geologic periods. Let them struggle with the new scale. It may help to point out that 1 millimeter equals a million years on a scale where 1 meter equals a billion. Or, one billion = 1000 million.)

5. After the activity, discuss the problem of scale and how the students resolved it. Usually they decide to change the scale for the last meter and make 1 meter equal 1 million. Still, recent events are very hard to plot. Again, this is part of the realization of the immensity of geologic time.

Evaluation Tasks

The students can use their tapes to explain some of the earth's history. Ask the students to explain *why* they had trouble plotting recent events. How did they overcome the problem?

Extending the Activity

The students can do a report on one geologic period.

TABLE 1
Approximate Age in the Earth's History

1. Earth's beginning	4.5 billion years ago
2. Oldest rocks	3.3 billion years ago
3. First plants (algae)	2.0 billion years ago
4. First animal (jellyfish)	1.2 billion years ago
5. Cambrian Period (abundant fossils)	600 million years ago
6. Ordovician Period	500 million years ago
7. Silusian Period	440 million years ago
8. Devonian Period	400 million years ago
9. Mississippian Period	350 million years ago
10. Pennsylvanian Period	305 million years ago
11. First reptiles	290 million years ago
12. Permian Period	270 million years ago
13. Triassic	225 million years ago
14. First mammals	200 million years ago
15. Jurassic	180 million years ago
16. First birds	160 million years ago
17. Cretaceous Period	135 million years ago
18. Paleocene	70 million years ago
19. Eocene	60 million years ago
20. Oligocene	40 million years ago
21. Miocene	25 million years ago
22. Pliocene	11 million years ago
23. First humanlike mammals	2 million years ago
24. Pleistocene	1 million years ago
25. Humans make tools	.5 million years ago
26. Last Ice Age	10,000 years ago
27. Calendars used in Egypt	4234 B.C.
28. Pythagoras proposes theory of mountain origin	580 B.C.
29. Eratosthenes measures Earth circumference	200 B.C.
30. Mount Vesuvius eruption at Pompeii	79 A.D.
31. First U.S. satellite	1958 A.D.
32. Mount St. Helens eruption	1980 A.D.

Activity for Middle-level Students: How Can Hardness be used to Identify Minerals?

1. Obtain the following materials: Steel file, copper penny, table knife, piece of glass, collection of minerals.
2. Discussion:
   a. What will scratch glass? Wood? A penny?
   b. How can hardness be used to identify minerals?
   c. A substance's resistance to scratching is called its *hardness*. If calcite scratches gypsum, which is harder? If calcite scratches both talc and gypsum, which is harder, talc or gypsum? How could you find out?
3. Investigation:
   a. Obtain a collection of minerals from a geology department. Make a list of minerals a fingernail will scratch, a file will scratch, a knife will scratch, and a copper penny will scratch. Which minerals are hardest?
   b. Find out about Moh's Hardness Scale. What is the hardness of a knife blade on Moh's Scale? A penny? A steel file? A fingernail?
   c. Using the hardness number of the knife blade, penny, file, and fingernail, determine the Moh number for each mineral in your collection. Record your results. Obtain a mineral from your classmate without finding out its name. Using your new knowledge, can you identify the mineral from its hardness?
4. Teacher's Information:

Moh's Hardness Scale

1. Talc	1.	Fingernail scratches it easily
2. Gypsum	2.	Fingernail scratches it
3. Calcite	3.	Penny scratches it
4. Fluorite	4.	Knife scratches it
5. Apatite	5.	Knife scratches it
6. Feldspar	6.	It scratches glass
7. Quartz	7.	It scratches glass
8. Topaz	8.	It scratches most minerals
9. Corundum	9.	It scratches topaz and most all minerals
10. Diamond	10.	It scratches all other minerals

Challenges to Thinking for Gifted Students
Discovery Demonstration: Bottle and Key—Put the Key in the Bottle

1. Prepare a box as shown in the diagram. The materials needed are listed below.
2. Demonstrate the device. Have each student look into the peephole while the teacher opens the trapdoors on the top alternately. Have students go back to their desks and try to draw a diagram of the outside and inside of the box, so that the images they see would be formed properly and in the right locations.

Materials

1. Two shoe boxes, cut diagonally on one end at 45° angle
2. Piece of window glass, cut to fit the diagonal cut of the shoe boxes
3. Masking tape
4. Black rubber tape for light seal around trap doors
5. Bottle of red-colored liquid
6. Red rubber stopper of same color as the liquid
7. 25-watt light bulb mounted above trap door B

What is the problem (or problems)? Is it a real problem to the students? What makes the device work? How is it built? What parts does it have?

What might be some explanations? It has mirrors. It is built like this (draw diagrams on the board). It has glass. (Try to select the most reasonable explanation after logical thinking.)

We need more information. (Let one student look the device over carefully and report the data to the class. We need accurate observations here.)

Draw conclusions about construction of the device. Draw conclusions about its operation.

Test the conclusion with something else (piece of mirror, piece of window glass, piece of one-way glass).

Explanation:
The eye responds to the light having the strongest intensity.

Other applications:
Why do you cup your hands around your eyes to look outside at night from a lighted room?

Some sunglasses are partially silvered mirrors. Why?

Some rear view mirrors on cars can be adjusted when the lights from a car behind cause too much glare. Can you devise a way for such a mirror to work using what you have learned from this demonstration?

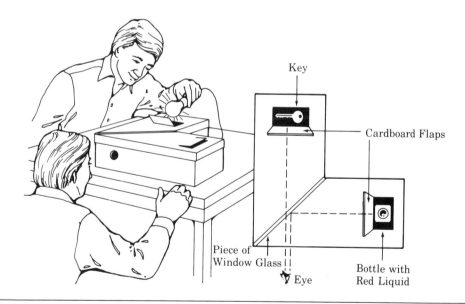

Activities in Science for Gifted Students

Development of various talents among students requires providing for opportunities to practice these talents and abilities. Gifted students are usually quite self-reliant and resourceful. Following are several examples of activities a teacher can provide for them to give practice in self-development.

To develop organizing abilities:

Plan a terrarium
Plan a garden
Plan a vegetable party
Plan a unit of study on seeds
Plan a landscaping project for trees, shrubs, and lawns
To develop divergent production:

List the ways you can use a specific fact to help you

To develop fluency and flexibility:

Have students discuss why being fluent and flexible would be an advantage for a scientist

To develop use of similes:

Discuss a scientific field such as biology. Analyze science specialties in terms of similarities and differences.

To develop perception:

Compare human sensations to animal sensations by analyzing the nervous systems of each. Describe how signals are transmitted.

To develop abilities to analyze codes:

Ask students to make a code. What codes are used in science? Why? Are there any international scientific codes?

To develop convergent production:

Have students bring in objects of nature such as leaves, pine needles, pebbles, shells, etc., and categorize them

To develop the ability to see trends:

Write an invitation to inquiry

To develop the ability to give and follow directions:

Have students write their own directions for doing an experiment

Have one group give oral directions to another group for performing a science experiment, testing a theory, or showing a cause and effect relationship

To develop the ability to hypothesize:

Answer the question, "What would happen if—?"

There were no gravity?

There was no action-reaction principle?

Instead of discrete particles, matter was continuous?

To develop the ability to compare and contrast:

Have students plan a zoo. What animals would be put together and why? What animals would definitely be kept apart and why?

To develop the ability to make decisions:

Answer the questions, "What was the world's most important discovery and why?"

What is the best way to test a principle? Give your reasons

Consider different climates. Which do you prefer and why? What type of soil and crops do you prefer? Why?

To develop creativity:

Invent new words for common objects

Invent new names of plants and animals. Give reasons for your choices

---

Mathematics in Science: How will Specific Gravity Help to Identify Minerals?

1. Obtain the following materials: Spring balance, string, can or jar of water, iron small object, aluminum small object, piece of glass, collection of minerals

2. Discussion:
   a. State the following: "Mary had a rock that weighed different amounts at different times. The rock has not changed in any way."
   b. What ideas do you have about how this may happen?
   c. Have you ever picked up a large rock under water and then carried it out of the water? Was it heavier in water or out of water?
   d. How could we make sure of our answer?

3. Suspend a rock on a spring balance with a length of string. Record its weight. Immerse the rock in water. Record its weight under water. How much more or less does it weigh now?

4. Specific gravity is a way to help identify minerals. Specific gravity is found by comparing the weight of a mineral in air to the amount of weight the mineral loses in water. Specific gravity may be found as illustrated in the following example:

Weight of rock in air	35 grams
Weight of rock in water	15 grams (subtract)
Loss of weight in water	20 grams

$$\text{Loss of weight in water} \overline{\left| \frac{\text{Specific gravity}}{\text{Weight of rock in air}} \right.}$$

$$20 \overline{\left| \frac{1.75}{35} \right.}$$
$$\underline{20}$$
$$150$$
$$\underline{140}$$
$$100$$
$$\underline{100}$$

The specific gravity of the rock is 1.75.

How can specific gravity be used to identify minerals?

5. What is the specific gravity of the rock you weighed in and out of water? Record your answer and show how you obtained it.

6. Obtain a piece of iron, aluminum, glass, and other objects. Using the method above, find their specific gravity. Compare your results with those of your classmates.

7. Make a list of the minerals in your collection and find the specific gravity of each. Record the specific gravity of each in a column beside the name of the mineral.

Teacher Information

The table below lists average specific gravities for common minerals.

Material	Average Specific Gravity		
Pyrite	5.0	Magnetite	5.2
Halite	2.2 (dissolves in water)	Limonite	4.3
Fluorite	3.2	Talc	2.7
Quartz	2.7	Mica	2.8
Calcite	2.7	Gypsum	2.3
Graphite	2.3	Glass	2.13–2.99
Galena	7.5	Feldspar (orthoclase)	2.6
Hematite	5.3	Feldspar (plagioclase)	2.7

Mathematics Challenge:
Using Simple Materials to Find the Earth's Magnetic Field

1. Obtain the necessary materials and set up the apparatus as shown in the diagram.

Materials

1. Dry cell
2. Resistance box
3. Milliammeter (0–1 am. range)
4. Cardboard cylinder
5. Small sewing needle
6. Ten feet of No. 24 insulated copper wire
7. Protractor
8. Connecting wire
9. Knife switch
10. Terminal posts
11. Cellophane tape
12. Wood base

Construction as shown in Figure

Experiment (see Figure)

Align the magnetometer so that the needle which is pointing north-south will be parallel to the base line of the protractor. Make the connections as shown and throw the knife switch. If the needle makes a full ninety-degree turn, R must be increased to that the magnetic field H_c of the magnetometer is less strong. Adjust R so that the needle comes to rest somewhere between zero and ninety degrees. Read the milliammeter and the angular deflection of the needle (θ). Take several trials.

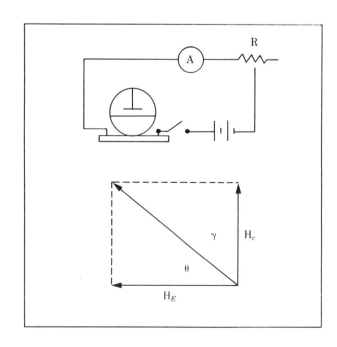

Calculations:

To find H_c, use $H_c = \dfrac{2\pi NI}{10r}$ where N = number of coils

I = current in amperes

r = radius of coil in cm.

H_c = magnetic field strength of coil in oersteds

H_E = magnetic field strength of earth in oersteds (to be found)

To find H_E, use $H_E = H_c \tan \gamma \ \square$ where $\gamma = 90° - \theta$

Your result should be in the neighborhood of 0.2 oersted for H_E at 40 degrees latitude. The values of H_E in the United States range from 0.13 oersted at Gull Island in Lake Superior to 0.28 oersted near Brownsville, Texas. The higher values are at lower latitudes because it is the *horizontal* component which is being measured.

2. Where is mathematics needed in this experiment?
3. What could you learn about the magnetic field of the earth without the use of mathematics?
4. How much more can you learn using mathematics?

Stimulating Mathematics Usage in Science Classes

The laboratory provides the opportunity for many data-gathering problems. The student may practice measuring, keeping records, and graphing. Analysis of experiments gives additional practice in using mathematics. The PSSC exercise entitled "Analysis of an Experiment" is an example. The data given in the exercise show a record of the time required to empty a can of water through a hole punched in the bottom.

TABLE 1
Amount of time to empty (in seconds)

d (in em)	h (in em)			
	30	10	4	1
1.5	73.0	43.5	26.7	13.5
2.0	41.2	23.7	15.0	7.2
3.0	18.4	10.5	6.8	3.7
5.0	6.8	3.9	2.2	1.5

Students are told to plot graphs of the data to analyze the relationships between emptying times and two other variables, diameter of the hole (d) and height of water in the can (h). Types of graphs suggested are one showing time vs. diameter for a constant height and one showing time vs. square of diameter. Graphs for different heights are also suggested. Typical questions asked in this exercise are:

1. From your curve, how accurately can you predict the time it would take to empty the same container if the diameter of the opening was 4 cm.? 8 cm.?
2. Can you write down the algebraic relation between t and d for the particular height of water used?
3. Can you find the general expression for time of flow as a function of both h and d?*

This exercise illustrates clearly how using mathematics gives a student practice in analyzing the results of an experiment and demonstrates the integral nature of mathematics in science.

Senior high school science students should learn the limitations of measurement, the sources of quantitative errors, and standards of accuracy. How accurate is a meter stick? To how many significant figures can a measurement be made? Of what value are estimated units? How accurate is a volume computation made from linear measurements which have estimated units? What are possible sources of error in an experiment? To what degree of precision are certain measurements made? How does one express the degree of precision recording data?

Knowledge of significant figures is particularly important in chemistry and physics, where physical measurements are made frequently in laboratory experiments.

*Physical Science Study Committee, *Laboratory Guide for Physics* (Boston: D.C. Heath).

Using Microcomputers in Interdisciplinary Problems

The introduction of microcomputers poses the problem of where to fit them into the curriculum. Even before the advent of this new discipline, there has been increasing demand on schools to provide coverage of new subjects:

drug education, driver education, environmental studies, various ethnic studies, etc.

Now computers can help to settle some of these competing demands through meaningful interdisciplinary problem solving. While not essential for interdisciplinary activities, they can make problem solving more interesting, more realistic, and more useful to students.

The sciences are the most fertile source of problems for use of microcomputers. For example, many of the laws of physics involve the relationship between the speed of a wave, its frequency, and its wavelength. Speed (v) equals the frequency (f) times the wavelength (l), $v = f \times l$. This law involves simple multiplication or division similar to problems students do in routine problem sets.

A program for junior high students using this equation could begin by showing the definitions of speed, wavelength, and frquency. Several waves might be displayed simultaneously, with a chart showing v, f, and l. Students could change one variable, while holding the others constant and watch the change in the third. Students might then be asked to solve multiplication and division problems involving one of the variables as an unknown. The program could be written to display the results in tabular form as shown below:

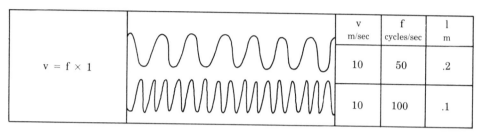

$v = f \times l$		v m/sec	f cycles/sec	l m
		10	50	.2
		10	100	.1

This table could then be used as a basis for interdisciplinary problem solving. Some students could study sound waves, solving problems of the design of musical instruments. Others could study ocean waves, determining where to place a wave barrier to prevent wave erosion, etc.

One of the attractions of the computer as an educational tool is the relative ease with which most students can learn to write simple programs. Interdisciplinary problems provide an ideal opportunity for students to develop their own learning materials through programming.*

*Peter Kelman, et al., *Computers in Teaching Mathematics*, Addison-Wesley Publishing Co., Reading, MA, 1983, p. 22. Reprinted with permission.

Using the Microcomputer to Model Solutions to Problems
The Coffee Cup Problem*

How long will it take a cup of coffee to cool? Specifically, how long will it take the coffee to cool from 190 degrees to 104 degrees if it sits undisturbed at 70 degrees Fahrenheit?

We would expect the rate of cooling to change with temperature of the cup. Newton's Law of Cooling states that the rate of cooling is directly proportional to the difference in the temperature of the room and the temperature of the cup. This can be expressed as:

Rate = K (temp. of cup – room temp.)

This problem can be solved by a method called *iteration*, using a small time interval as the iteration interval. For example, if the iteration length is set at 0.1 minute, the approximate cooling rate for the short interval can be calculated at 190° F. The degrees of cooling resulting from this cooling rate approximation would then be subtracted from 190 and a new cooling rate calculated for the next 0.1 minute interval. This procedure would be repeated until the endpoint of 104 degrees is reached; the sum of the 0.1 minute intervals required to reach this point would be the approximate answer of how long it would take the coffee cup to cool to 104 degrees F.

The teacher or students could write a program like the following to perform all the calculations and print out the results.

```
10 REM . . Coffee Cooling Simulation Using New-
   ton's Law
30 TE = 190
50 K = 0.09:DT = 0.1
60 PRINT "TIME", "TEMP", "CHANGE"
70 FOR T = 1 TO 200
80 TC = K* (7C – TE)
100 TE = TE + TC * DT
110 IF INT (T/5) () T/5 THEN 130
120 PRINT T/10, INT (100 * TE)/100, INT (100
    *TC)/100
130 NEXT T
```

*Peter Kelman, et al., *Computers in Teaching Mathematics*, Addison-Wesley Publishing Co., Reading, MA, 1983, p. 84. Reprinted with permission.

How Can You Use Questions to Solve Problems?
Discovery Demonstration: Kelvin's Waterdropper Electrostatic Generator

1. Construct the apparatus as shown in the diagram. Demonstrate it to the class in a slightly darkened room. Ask the following questions:

Materials

1. Two small juice cans
2. No. 2½ can (reservoir)
3. Two short pieces of glass tubing, tapered at one end
4. Two 12 in. sections of rubber tubing
5. Coat-hanger wire shaped as shown in Figure
6. NE-2 neon lamp (0.25 watt)
7. Two blocks of paraffin
8. Blocks of wood for base and upright
9. Two small metal rings soldered to coat-hanger wire as shown

Procedure

Fill the reservoir can with water. By siphon action, start water flowing through each outlet tube. Adjust lower cans and rings so water falls through the rings into the cans.

Adjust spark gap so it is about one millimeter in width.

Watch the neon bulb for intermittent flashes. In a darkened room these flashes will be visible to a whole class.

Questions

1. What did you observe as the apparatus was put into operation?

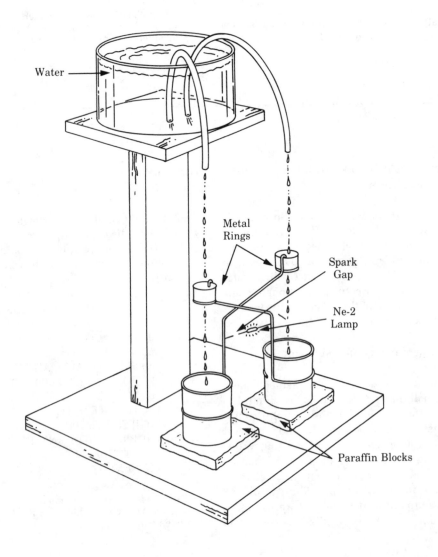

Water

Metal Rings

Spark Gap

Ne-2 Lamp

Paraffin Blocks

2. How long did it take for the first flash?

3. How much time elapses between flashes?

4. What happens to the length of time if the gap distance is changed?

5. What happens when the gap is eliminated entirely?

6. What is causing the flash?

7. Where does the electricity come from?

8. What kind of charged particles are in water?

9. Suppose you were to construct an apparatus like this. Would each half of the apparatus (small can, coathanger wire, and metal ring) be likely to have exactly the same initial charge?

10. Suppose the side labeled A had a slightly negative charge as compared to B. What kinds of charges would be attracted to A?

11. But these charges fall into side marked B. What kind of charge do they give to B?

12. By similar action, what charge does A acquire?

13. For how long will these charge accumulations go on?

14. What is the likely charge distribution after the flash?

15. What is the complete explanation of the operation of this "water-dropper" generator?

Explanation

One side of the apparatus will have a slightly greater initial negative charge. The other side will have a slightly higher initial positive charge. This is an assumption but an extremely good one.

Ions in the water will be attracted to the metal rings differentially, with positive ions going toward the negative ring and negative ions going toward the positive ring.

But these ions do not neutralize the rings. Instead they fall *through* the rings and contribute to buildup of like charge in the cans.

Potential difference between the two halves of the apparatus increases until a small spark occurs at the gap. At this instant, the neon bulb flashes.

The process repeats cyclically. Widening the gap delays the discharge. Closing the gap completely prevents any build-up of potential difference. Consequently, there is no flashing.

2. How many different types of questions did you (could you) ask to arrive at an understanding of how this device operates?

3. Will simply asking the right questions finally solve the problem? What else might be needed?

Effects of Acid Rain on Seed Germination

Activity Overview

Students investigate the effects of acid rain on seed germination by conducting an experiment with bean seeds, or locally available seed, under varying pH conditions. The estimated time for this activity is one class period to organize groups and set up the experiment. Then, take a few minutes at the start of every other class for approximately two weeks to water and measure seed growth, and to record data on individual and class groups.

Major Concepts

• Seed germination is dependent upon proper conditions of pH.

• Increases of acidity due to acid rain may inhibit seed germination and plant growth.

Student Objectives

After the activity students should be able to:

• Measure the growth of bean seed.

• Record data on an individual graph and on a class graph.

• Draw the bean seed before seed germination and each day that growth measurements are taken.

• Make a summary graph of individual graphs.

• Compare data to establish the optimum pH for the germination of a bean seed.

Materials

• Petri dish

• 4 bean seeds (preferably seeds grown locally: alfalfa, pea, bean, etc.)

• Water solutions ranging in pH from 2–7 (boiling will be necessary to drive off CO_2 and raise pH to 7)

• Rain water (optional)

• Absorbent paper towels

• Transparent metric ruler

• Graph paper

• Colored chalk or magic markers

Procedures

Preparation of bean seed:

1. Assign each student a pH solution to "water" their bean seeds. A couple of students should be assigned

distilled or rain water for a control. The class as a whole should represent increments on a pH scale ranging from 2–7.
2. Cut four paper discs the size of a petri dish from the absorbent paper towel.
3. Dampen the paper discs with appropriate pH or rain water solution.
4. Place two discs at the bottom of the petri dish.
5. Measure the seeds and average them.
6. Arrange seeds in the petri dish and cover with the two remaining paper discs.
7. Replace lid on petri dish and label with student name.
8. Each student should hypothesize what they believe will be the ideal pH on a piece of paper.

Preparation of Graph

1. Obtain a piece of 8 × 11 graph paper.
2. Set up graph as follows: Horizontal axis, age of seed in days; Vertical axis, length of seed in mm.

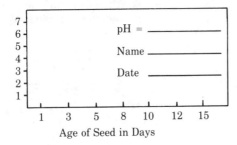

Straight Length of seed in mm.

pH = _____
Name _____
Date _____

Age of Seed in Days

Procedures for Alternate Days

The students will be taking measurements of seed growth and recording data on individual and class graphs.

- Take measurements and plotting data on individual graphs.
- Remove lid from petri dish.
- Sketch the shapes of the four seeds. Note the color of the seeds.
- Use transparent ruler to measure the straight length of seeds.
- Take the average straight line length increase and plot it on your graph. (It is important to plot the increase of

seed growth because seeds are different lengths before germination takes place.)
- Make sure paper towel is still moist. If not, add more pH solution (be sure pH solutions are not mixed).
- Replace lid on petri dish.
- Construct class graph on chalkboard or large piece of white construction paper on visible wall or board and saved throughout experiment. The graph should use same layout as individual graphs.
- Assign each pH a particular color (chalk or magic marker).
- More than one student may be experimenting with the same pH solution. These students should average their results of seed length.
- Have one student representing each pH record data on the board using the code color that represents pH used. (example: a pH of 3 is represented by the color green; a pH of 7 is represented by the color purple).
- After a few recordings have been plotted, students should draw a line connecting points of same pH.

Discussion Questions

- What appears to be the first optimal pH solution for successful seed germination and growth? The least ideal?
- How does the local rainwater used compare to the other pH solutions used?
- From the data expressed on the class graph, what pH do you think the rainwater has?

Evaluation

Each student should prepare a report that includes:

- Brief description and purpose of experiment
- Data collected, individual graphs, and seed drawings
- Analysis of individual class results:
  1. Ideal pH
  2. Least ideal pH
  3. Comparison of rainwater to other pH solutions
- Discussion questions: What impact on local crops might an increased acidity have? Do you think there is a reason for concern?
- A concrete example of how acid rain and its effect on seed germination could make an effect on food crops grown in the nearest agricultural area

---

How Long Can You Boil Water in a Paper Cup?

Teacher's note: This is a junior high level inquiry lesson. Sections I through III are for the teachers only and Sections IV and V are to be duplicated for the student.

I. *Concepts*
A flame is a source of radiant heat.
Water, when heated, expands and gives off water vapor.
Water can absorb a considerable amount of heat.

Before a substance will burn, its kindling temperature must be reached.
The kindling temperature is the temperature at which a substance will first start to burn.

II. *Materials*
Nonwaxed paper cup
Bunsen burner, propane torch, or alcohol burner

Ring stand
Ring clamp
Wire screen

III. *Prelaboratory Discussion*
Processes:

Hypothesizing   1. What do you think will happen to a paper cup when you try to boil water in it?

Hypothesizing   2. What do you think will happen first, the water boiling or the cup burning?

Hypothesizing   3. How do you think you could get a paper cup containing water to burn?

Designing an investigation   4. What should you do to find out?

IV. *Pupil Discovery Activity*
Processes:

Collecting materials   1. Obtain the following equipment: A nonwaxed paper cup, torch or burner, ring stand, ring clamp, and screen.

Designing an investigation   2. How could you use this equipment to find out if you can boil water in paper cup?

Teacher's note: The students should place the paper cup, containing not more than 5cm³ of water, on the wire screen as indicated in the diagram and heat it from below with the burner.

Following directions   3. If you can think of no other ways to test your hypothesis, set up the equipment as indicated by your teacher's diagram.

Observing   4. What happens when you try to heat the water in the cup?

Inferring   5. What do you think the ring clamp and screen do to the heat from the flame?

Inferring   6. What can you say about the heat energy entering and leaving the water as you try to heat it to the boiling point?

7. Why does the water level in the cup change?

8. What effect does water in the cup have on its temperature as it is being heated?

9. Keep heating the cup until all the water is evaporated. Record your observation and conclusions.

V. *Open-ended Questions*
Processes:

Hypothesizing   1. If you took paper, cloth, wood, and charcoal and heated them, in what order would they start to burn? Why?

Criticizing   2. If you were going to repeat the preceding experiment, what would you do to obtain better data?

Hypothesizing   3. How would varying the amount of heat energy differ if you used a Styrofoam cup?

Hypothesizing   4. How would varying the amount of heat energy applied to the cup change the results?

Hypothesizing   5. How would the results vary if there were a different liquid in the cup such as a cola, syrup, etc.?

Hypothesizing   6. In what way would the results vary if the cup were supported by a ring clamp and screen?

Designing an investigation   7. What other experiments does this investigation suggest?

Discovery Demonstration: Inquiring into Falling Bodies

Construct the apparatus as shown in the diagram. Demonstrate it several times. Let several students try to demonstrate it.

Materials

1. 3-foot piece of board (1 × 2 in.)
2. 2 small plastic cups (1-in diam.)
3. Bearing ball (1-in. diam.)

Procedure

Put the ball in the cup at the end of the stick. Raise the stick to an angle of about thirty degrees. Drop the stick. The ball transfers to the other cup.

Questions

Why does the ball transfer to the other cup?

Is there a problem here? Is there anything out of the ordinary? Does it have an easy answer?

How did the ball get out of the first cup? Don't the ball and cup fall at these same rate of acceleration?

Something must be accelerating faster than gravity here. What is it? How can this happen?

Suppose you tossed a tumbling board over a cliff. Would all parts of it be accelerating downward at the same rate? What part of it accelerates at thirty-two feet per second per second?

What part of the stick in this demonstration accelerates at thirty-two feet per second per second? Where is this point?

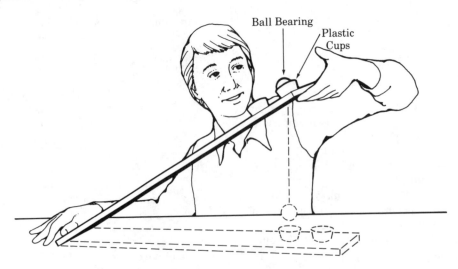

Explanation

The cup at the end accelerates faster than thirty-two feet/sec/sec. The ball accelerates only at thirty-two ft/sec/sec. The point on the stick which accelerates at thirty-two ft/sec/sec is the "center of percussion" which is two-thirds of the way from the pivot end to the end with the cup.

1. What parts of the inquiry demonstration represented problem identification?
2. What part involved making hypotheses?
3. What part represented data-gathering?
4. What was concerned with drawing conclusions?

Astronomic Distances

Activity Overview

In this activity the students complete a scale model of astronomic distances. The goal is to have the students conceptualize the vastness of space. This activity should take two class periods.

Science Background

A light year is an astronomic measure of distance. The words "light year" as said quickly may not capture the immensity of the distance involved. Try completing the following exercise so you will have an understanding of the astronomic distance. You can have the students do the same activity. Light travels about 298,000 kilometers per second (186,000 miles per second).

$$\begin{array}{r} 298,000 \text{ kilometers per second} \\ \underline{\times\ 60} \quad \text{km per minute} \\[4pt] \underline{\times\ 60} \quad \text{km per hour} \\[4pt] \underline{\times\ 24} \quad \text{km per day} \\[4pt] \underline{\times\ 365} \quad \text{km per year} \end{array}$$

There are some terms and symbols in the activity (see Table 1) about which students may ask. Some of these are defined for you:

Cluster—a group of stars or galaxies often identified by the constellation in which they are located
Galaxy—a group of stars
M—this stands for Messier number, a way astronomers catalogue stars
Milky Way—the galaxy in which our solar system is located
Nebula—a cloud of dust and gas

This activity should give students a new perspective relative to the earth in time and space. Our earth is small and insignificant in the scale of astronomic time and distance. Yet, our earth is the most important astronomic object as far as our existence is concerned.

Major Concepts

The average distance between stars in space is incredibly large. Stars are made of hot gases, but they differ in temperature, mass, size, luminosity, and density.

Objectives

At the completion of this lesson the student should be able to:
Describe the immensity of astronomic distance
Indicate that stars have different distances from earth
Identify his/her location in the scale of steller space
Define a light year as the distance light travels in a year

Materials

Meter stick
Colored pencils
Adding machine tape (6 meter strips for each group of 2)

Vocabulary

Astronomic	Quasar
Stellar	Star
Distance	Nebula
Galaxy	

Procedures

1. Divide the students into groups of 2–3.
2. Each group should have a piece of adding machine tape 6 meters long, a meter stick, and pencils.
3. Mark off a line about 5 centimeters from one end of the tape. Label this line EARTH.
4. Using the meter stick and the distances given in Table 1 plot the distances to the various stellar objects on the adding machine tape. Tell the students they should start by using the scale 1 meter = 1 billion light years. (Note: When the students start plotting distances closer to the earth, millions of miles, they will find it impossible to use the scale of 1 meter = 1 billion light years. Frustration will be evident as they try to figure out how far a million is on their scale and finally how to get so many stellar objects located in such a small distance. This is the realization that is essential to the lesson. They will have to change the scale to 1 meter = 1 million light years and then they will still have difficulty with the last few distances.)
5. Discuss the problems students had with the scale 1 meter = 1 billion light years. Ask them "How did you resolve the problem?" "How does this distance make you feel in the scale of the universe?"

Evaluation Tasks

The students can use their tapes to explain the immensity of space.

Extending the Activity

The students can report on some of the stellar objects named in Table 1.

TABLE 1
Distances to selected objects in the celestial sphere

Celestial Object	Distance in Light Years
Quasar—3c 295	4.5 billion
Hydra Cluster of Galaxies	3.9 billion
Quasar—3c 273	1.5 billion
Gemini Cluster of Galaxies	980 million
Ursa Major I Cluster of Galaxies	720 million
Cygenus A—radio source	500 million
Pegasus II Cluster of Galaxies	470 million
Hercules Cluster of Galaxies	340 million
Coma Cluster of Galaxies	190 million
Perseus Cluster of Galaxies	173 million
Pegasus I Cluster of Galaxies	124 million
Fornox A—radio source	60 million
Virgo Cluster of Galaxies	38 million
M49 in Virgo	11.4 million
M81	4.8 million
M31 in Andromeda	2 million
Leo II Galaxy	710 thousand
Fornox Galaxy	390 thousand
Megellanic Clouds	170 thousand
Center of Milky Way	30 thousand
Owl Nebula	12 thousand
Ring Nebula	4.5 thousand
Deneb—star	1.6 thousand
Regil—star	900 light years
Polaris—star	680 light years
Vega—star	26.5 light years
Sirius—star	8.7 light years
Alpha Centauri—star	4.3 light years
Sol—our sun	8 light minutes

Using a Demonstration to Initiate Discussion
Discovery Demonstration: The Rubber Band Wheel

Construct the rubber band wheel as shown in the diagram. Set up the apparatus as shown. Without explanation, shine a bright light on the wheel.

Materials

1. Shoe box

2. Cardboard wheel made of corrugated cardboard, 6 in. in diameter
3. Knitting needle
4. Four fresh rubber bands, all of equal length and thickness
5. Strong light source, preferably a 150-watt spotlight

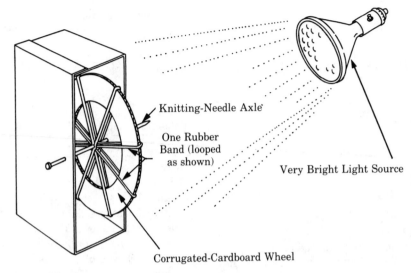

Knitting-Needle Axle

One Rubber Band (looped as shown)

Very Bright Light Source

Corrugated-Cardboard Wheel

Conclusion

There are usually exceptions to most scientific generalizations.

Demonstrate the action of the rubber band wheel. Ask several questions to initiate discussion.
a. What do you observe?
b. What did you expect to happen?
c. What direction does the wheel turn? Is it always the same?
d. What would happen if the light came from the opposite side?
e. What would happen if the wheel were mounted in the open so light could strike all parts of it?
f. What would happen if the light were moved farther away?
g. What are some possible hypotheses or explanations?
h. Suspend a weight on a single strand of a rubber band fastened to a support. Shine the light on the rubber band. What happens to the weight?
i. How does this new information help explain the action of the rubber band wheel?

Explanation

Rubber bands in the light (heat) contract and pull the center of rotation toward the right. This makes the left side of the wheel heavier than the right side, and it turns counterclockwise.

Fact: Rubber bands under tension contract when heated, expand when cooled.

Principle: In general, solids expand when heated, contract when cooled, but rubber bands under tension are an exception.

Small Group Problem Solving

Small group discussions have the advantage of providing an atmosphere that is conducive to drawing out shy and reticent students. The setting is less threatening and the topics may be more easily controlled. Some guidelines for this variation of the discussion method follow:

1. Form groups of 3–5 persons
2. Present a problem
   a. Demonstration
   b. Story
   c. Social issue
   d. Dilemma
3. Each group appoints a spokesman
4. Allow discussion to continue 5–10 minutes
   a. Clarify the problem
   b. Suggest hypotheses for solution
   c. Discuss hypotheses
   d. Obtain consensus in the group
   e. Draw conclusions
5. Assemble as a large group
6. Spokesmen present the group conclusions
7. Discuss as a large group using guidelines discussed earlier

Using a Demonstration to Motivate Students—The Diffusion Cloud Chamber

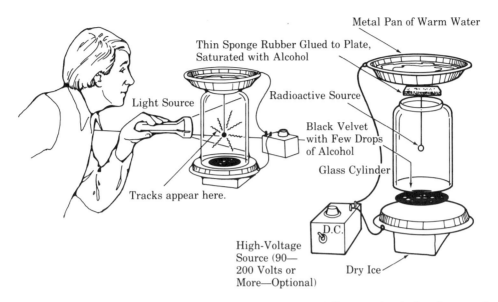

Metal Pan of Warm Water

Thin Sponge Rubber Glued to Plate, Saturated with Alcohol

Radioactive Source

Light Source

Black Velvet with Few Drops of Alcohol

Glass Cylinder

Tracks appear here.

High-Voltage Source (90—200 Volts or More—Optional)

Dry Ice

D.C.

1. Construct a diffusion cloud chamber as shown in the diagram. Students can help you obtain the necessary materials and may want to participate in actual construction of the device. This is one of the best ways to motivate science students!

2. After successfully demonstrating the device, you may want to suggest other activities and extensions as followup for students who become motivated and show interest in learning more about radioactivity.

   a. What materials are radioactive?
   b. What does it mean to be radioactive?
   c. What radioactive particles are probably producing the tracks you see?
   d. What is the purpose of having dry ice on the bottom and warm water on the top of the cloud chamber?
   e. Read about radioactivity in an encyclopedia. Find out what materials are naturally radioactive.
   f. Find out about the benefits of radioactivity. Also find out about the dangers of excessive exposure to radioactivity.

Materials

1. Cylindrical glass container, with top and bottom removed
2. Two aluminum pie tins
3. Flat sheet of sponge rubber
4. Circular piece of black velvet.
5. Light source—e.g., slide-projector bulb
6. Dry ice (small cakes several inches square)
7. Methyl alcohol
8. Glue
9. D.C. high-voltage source (90–200 volts) (desirable but not absolutely necessary)
10. Radioactive source (Old parts from luminous clock face will do)

The diffusion cloud chamber can be used to give evidence of the existence of radioactive particles such as alpha particles, beta particles, gamma rays, and cosmic particles.

A radioactive source can be obtained by taking a small fragment of a luminous dial or number of a watch or clock face which has been discarded. Also, it is possible to use a small pin coated with a radioactive salt.

Principle

Radioactive particles traveling through a supersaturated area will cause small droplets to form by creating charged ions on which the droplets can condense.

Setup

Suspend the radioactive source as shown about three-quarters of an inch from the velvet at the bottom. Saturate the sponge rubber with methyl alcohol and place a few drops on the black velvet. Set the whole cylinder on a cake of dry ice, which may be in chunk form or crushed. Place a little warm water in the pan on top. Shine the light directly at the source near the bottom of the container. Wait about thirty seconds for supersaturation to occur. You should be able to tell that this has happened because of the appearance of a light "snow" falling slowly in the bottom inch or so of the container. It is in this region that the cloud tracks will appear. They will occur suddenly as a streak and will then disappear by evaporation in a moment or two. A bit of persistence will bring great satisfaction in the appearance of these very fascinating cloud tracks of radioactive particles.

Evaluation of Student Understanding of a Basic Physical Principle*

Each student is to be given a mimeographed sheet containing the following information:

Part 1

1. The demonstration material is set up as indicated in Diagram 1. A beaker of water is filled, and when the instructor is ready to start the demonstration, he pours water in the thistle tube labeled "X". The water will then flow from tube "Y".

Diagram 1

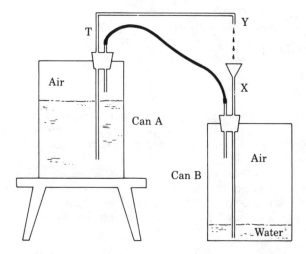

2. The students are next given a mimeographed sheet resembling Diagram 2 and asked to describe what they think the apparatus looks like within the can.

Diagram 2

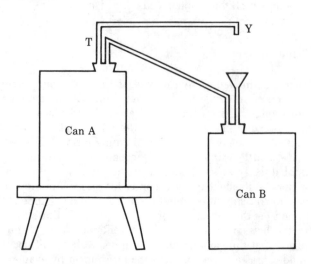

3. In a few sentences, they are to explain why the water started to run and why it continues.

4. They are also asked to write the basic principles involved in the demonstration and how long they think the water will continue to run.

Part 2

After students have answered the questions, they are given a copy of Diagram 1 and asked to take the following test. They are to assume (1) that can "A" and can "B" are identical and (2) that all parts of the apparatus remain unchanged unless a change is specified in the statement they are considering.

Directions:
In the blank to the right of each statement place an X in the column indicating the effect which the given change would have on the rate of flow.

How would the rate at which the liquid flows from the glass tube be affected if:

	No Flow	Slower	Same Rate	Faster
1. The top of the funnel was only one-half as far above can "B" as it was in the diagram?	___	___	___	___
2. Can "B" was lowered until the top of can "B" was level with the bottom of can "A"?	___	___	___	___
3. The glass tube "T" was lengthened so that it extended twice as far above can "A"?	___	___	___	___
4. The funnel was replaced by a thistle tube extending to the same height above can "B" but having a bulb volume three times as great?	___	___	___	___
5. The tip "Y" of the glass tube from which the water is flowing was lengthened until it was level with the top of the funnel?	___	___	___	___
6. Kerosene, which is less dense than water, was used instead of water? (Neglect differences in viscosity and vapor pressure.)	___	___	___	___

	No Flow	Slower	Same Rate	Faster
7. The volume of can "B" was doubled while its height "H" remained constant?	___	___	___	___
8. The bottom of can "A" and can "B" were at the same level?	___	___	___	___
9. The funnel tube was cut off at "X" and did not extend below the stopper in can "B"?	___	___	___	___
10. The glass tube in can "B" to which the hose is fastened was extended to the bottom of the can?	___	___	___	___

Part 3

After students have marked their papers, the instructor leads the class in discussing their answers. What types of process thinking are required in this type of demonstration?

*This demonstration and evaluation guide prepared by Dr. Gene F. Craven, Department of Science Education, Oregon State University, Corvallis.

Using an Identification Key

Overview

In this activity students use a simple identification key to classify several animals. The activity is designed for middle/junior high school levels. This activity can be adapted and programmed for use on a microcomputer.

Objectives

At the completion of this activity students should be able to:

1. Use a simple identification key
2. Describe the usefulness of classifying organisms
3. Apply the identification key to identify an unknown organism

Materials

1. A variety of common organisms. The organisms should represent different phyla in the animal kingdom (see key for examples). In general organisms commonly found in life science classrooms can be used.
2. A key for each student or groups of students (see below).
3. Common references for information about organisms of different phyla.

Procedures

1. Divide the class into groups of students. The size of groups should be determined by the number and variety of organisms available.
2. Provide 3–4 organisms for each group of students.

3. Distribute and introduce the key to the students. Some of the points to make are
   - The key is made up of a series of questions that can be answered by either YES or NO.
   - The answer leads to the next question or identification of the organism.
   - Go through the key and identify one organism at a time.
4. Have the students proceed to identify their organisms.
5. The students should look up information about the organisms they have identified.
6. As a follow-up evaluation have the students go out of doors and identify an "unknown" organism.

A Classification Key

1. Does the animal have a backbone? If your answer is YES go to 1a. If it is NO, go to 2.
   1a. Does the animal have hair or fur on its body? If YES, it is a MAMMAL. If NO, go to 1b.
   1b. Does the animal have feathers? If YES, its scientific name is AVES. If NO, go to 1c.
   1c. Does the animal have smooth skin and lay its eggs in water? If YES, it is an AMPHIBIAN. If NO, go to 1d.
   1d. Does the animal have scaly skin and lay its eggs on land? If YES, it is a REPTILE. If NO, go to 1e.
   1e. Does the animal have scaly skin and lay its eggs in water? If YES, it is an OSTEICHTHYES. If NO, return to question 1 and check to be sure the animal has a backbone.
2. If the animal does not have a backbone begin here. Does the animal have a hard, outside covering *and* jointed legs? If YES, it is an ARTHROPOD—go to 2a. If NO, go to 3.

2a. Does the animal have three pairs of legs? IF YES, it is an INSECT. If NO, go to 2b.

2b. Does the animal have four pairs of legs and two body sections? If YES, it is an ARACHNID. If NO, go to 2c.

2c. Does the animal have at least 5 pairs of legs and a hard covering? If YES, it is a CRUSTACEAN. If NO, go to 2d.

2d. Does the animal have many body sections with a pair of legs on each section? If YES, it is a CENTIPEDE. If NO, go to 2e.

2e. Does the animal have many body sections with 2 pairs of legs on each section? If YES, it is a MILLIPEDE. If NO, return to 2.

3. Does the animal have spines covering its skin? If YES, it is an ECHINODERM. If NO, go to 4.

4. Does the animal have a hard shell covering a soft body? If YES, it is a MOLLUSK. If NO, go to 5.

5. Does the animal have a long, wormlike body with many sections? If YES, it is an ANNELID. If NO go to 6.

6. Is your animal wormlike with a smooth tapered body? If YES, it is a NEMATODA. If NO, go to 7.

7. Does the animal have a flat ribbonlike body? If YES, it is PLATYHELMINTHES. If NO, go to 8.

8. Does the animal have tentacles around the mouth opening and a soft body? If YES, it is a COELENTERATE. If NO, go to 9.

9. Does the animal have openings, called pores, all over its body? If YES, it is a PORIFERA. If NO, go back to question 1, 2, or 3.

The Moon

Activity Overview

Students make observations of the changing phases of the moon over a two month period. After a summary of their observations, the phases of the moon are demonstrated using a simple classroom demonstration.

Science Background

The moon travels around the earth in an elliptical orbit. The moon travels from *west to east* around the earth. (Due to the earth's rotation the moon *appears* to rise in the east and move toward the west.) The average distance of the moon from the earth is 384,000 kilometers (240,000 miles). The lunar month is actually 27½ days; but, the earth is traveling through space in its orbit around the sun, so the time from one full moon to the next is just over 29 days. The moon rotates on its axis west to east, the same direction that it revolves around the earth. The period of rotation is exactly the period of revolution for the moon.

The moon appears larger when rising because we see it in comparison to other objects such as buildings and trees. It also appears yellow or orange when rising or setting. This is because the reflected light from the moon must pass through longer sections of the earth's atmosphere; in doing so the blue rays are reflected and scattered by dust particles. This is the same phenomenon that causes red sunsets.

As the moon travels around the earth we see different amounts of the half of the moon that is in sunlight. During the lunar month the moon goes through a continuous change from complete darkness (new moon) to complete light (full moon) and then back to complete darkness. As the moon goes from new moon to full moon we term the phase *waxing*. The moon's change from full to new is called *waning*.

Outside of the romantic, aesthetic, and mythic qualities of the moon one of the important societal implications is that it causes tides on the earth. Tides result because the moon's pull of gravity makes a bulge in the water on the earth's side facing the moon. Tides have been proposed as one potential source of energy.

Major Concepts

Phases of the moon and lunar eclipses depend on the relative positions of the sun and moon as viewed from the earth.

The earth and moon can be thought of as a system.

Objectives

At the completion of this activity the student should be able to:
   Identify the phases of the moon
   Describe the phases of the moon as a relationship among the earth-moon-sun system
   Describe the cycle of lunar phases

Materials

Bulletin board calendar of two months
Duplicate of bulletin board calendar for students' notebooks
Globe
Styrofoam ball
Light source

Phases of the Moon— Observations

FIGURE 1
Phases of the moon—observations

Phases of the Moon— Demonstration

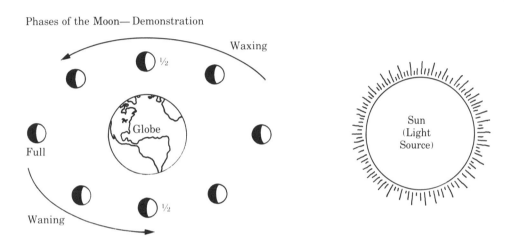

FIGURE 2
Phases of the moon—demonstration

Vocabulary

Lunar	Waning
Phases	Crescent
Waxing	

Procedures

1. Place a calendar on the bulletin board. Each day on the calendar should have a space available for one student to draw in a record of the moon as it was observed that day/night. The students should record similar observations on a daily calendar in their notebooks. Starting with a full moon is strongly recommended.
2. Continue the calendars for two full cycles of the moon. (There are 29 days from one full moon to the next.)
3. After continuing the observations for about 2 months, plan on a period of discussion in which the students summarize their observations. Use Figure 1 for the summary *after* the students have given their observations.
4. On a class period after the discussion of student observations plan on completing a demonstration using a light source, globe, and styrofoam ball.

5. Darken the room and place the light source in a position where it will shine on the globe. Move the styrofoam ball around the globe in such a way as to demonstrate the moon's phases (Figure 2).

Evaluation Tasks

Give the students figures similar to Figure 2 above, without the phases of the moon completed. Have them fill in the phases and label the diagram.

Set up different sun-earth-moon configurations and have the students predict the moon's phase.

Extending the Activity

This activity can be extended to show how lunar and solar eclipses occur. Usually the moon passes above or below the earth's shadow so there is not a lunar eclipse. And, the shadow projected by the moon does not cross the earth; but, when it does there is a solar eclipse along the shadow's path. These eclipses can be demonstrated and discussed with the materials and procedures of this activity. Students can also complete reports on the moon.

Teaching Inquiry Skills

Grade level

Junior high

Objectives

To gain practice in the skills of (1) measurement, (2) record-keeping, (3) graphing

Subject

Forces produced by springs

Problem

How does the length of spring depend on the force exerted on it?

Procedure

Work in pairs, or do as a student demonstration with all students recording the data and drawing the graph. Set up the spring and weights as shown in Figure 1. Add weights one at a time and check the readings each time.

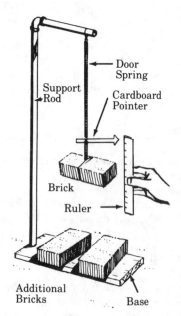

FIGURE 1
Demonstration setup

Record the results as shown in Table 1. Graph the results as shown in the graph.

Materials

Door springs
Several bricks
Ruler
String

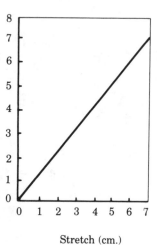

Table 1

Weight (Bricks)	Stretch (cm.)
1	1.5
2	3.0
3	4.5
4	6.0

FIGURE 2
Results recorded in table and graph form

Conclusion

The change in length of a spring is directly proportional to the change in the force exerted on it—if the spring is not stretched beyond its elastic limit.

Probable skills developed

1. Setup and adjustment of apparatus (manipulative)
2. Observation of initial conditions and changes due to experimental factors (acquisitive)
3. Recording of data (organizational)
4. Graphing and analysis of data (organizational and communicative)
5. Drawing conclusions (organizational)

Evaluation

Can the student
1. Set up the apparatus for use?
2. Devise a plan of procedure?
3. Read a scale to the limits of its accuracy?
4. Record data in a tabular form?
5. Plot a graph?
6. Interpret a graph?
7. Draw conclusions from the experiment?
8. Recognize sources of error?
9. Report his results lucidly?

Weather: Air Masses and Fronts

Activity Overview

Students observe weather reports on television over a period of a week. The concepts of air masses and fronts are then presented in a lecture-discussion format by the teacher. Weather maps are studied for the final section of the activity. Students watch weather reports on the evening news for one week. Spend one class period on lecture-discussion. This activity is for grades 6–8.

Science Background

The movement of large air masses and the influence of more localized fronts determine the majority of daily weather. An air mass is a large body of air that originates in a particular location and then moves across the earth's surface. The important characteristic of air masses is that they acquire the properties (temperature and humidity) of the region in which they originate. Air masses are either tropical or polar and either continental or maritime. The major air masses and their origins are shown in Figure 1.

Continental polar air masses are cold and dry. Maritime tropical air masses are warm and moist. Continental tropical air masses are warm and dry. Maritime polar air masses are cold and moist. The different characteristics of the air masses greatly influence local weather.

A cold front is the phrase applied to the leading edge of a cold dense air mass. Since the air is cold and dense it wedges under lighter, warmer air and forces some air up into the atmosphere. As the warm air is lifted it cools and has a reduced capacity to hold moisture. As this occurs clouds form and precipitation falls. Cold fronts are often identified by a line of storm clouds (see Figure 2).

Air Masses Influencing the Continental United States

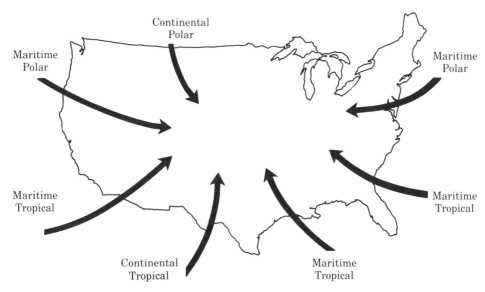

FIGURE 1
Air masses influencing the continental United States

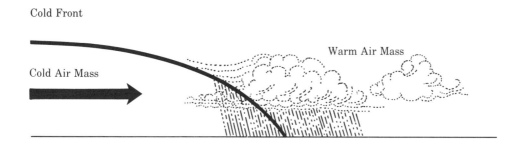

FIGURE 2
Cold front

A warm front results when warmer, lighter air pushes behind colder, denser air. The result is that warmer air moves up over the colder air producing a long area of precipitation as the warm air rises and cools. High cirrus clouds can precede the front by several days (see Figure 3).

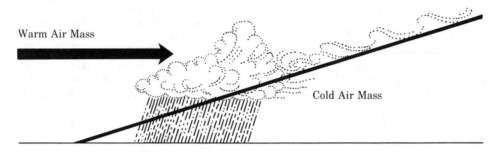

Warm Front

Warm Air Mass

Cold Air Mass

FIGURE 3
Warm front

We are influenced daily by the weather. Yet, many know little about the dynamics of this daily phenomenon. The implications of weather range from moisture for agriculture to severe weather that threatens human life.

Major Concepts

Atmospheric motion occurs on many scales.
Air masses have characteristics of the place of origin.
The interaction of warm and cold air results in different patterns of weather called *fronts*.

Objectives

At the completion of this activity the student should be able to:
   Identify a warm front
   Identify a cold front
   Describe the characteristics and influences of different air masses

Materials

Prepare overhead transparencies for Figures 1, 2, and 3.
Chalkboard
Old weather maps (from the newspaper or weather station)

Vocabulary

Cold front   Air masses
Warm front
Weather

Procedures

1. Present the concepts of air masses and fronts in a formal manner (15–20 minutes).
2. Have the students apply their observations to the presentation during a discussion period.
3. In the final section of the activity have the students look at weather maps and see if they can discover the concepts of air masses and fronts as they have actually been recorded.

Evaluation Tasks

Use figures 1, 2, and 3 *without* labels and have the students identify air masses and fronts.
Tell the students to observe weather forecasts for the next week and summarize their observations in terms of air masses and fronts.

Extending the Activity

Have the students look up occluded fronts and report on their characteristics.
Have a meteorologist (a local TV weather person) visit class and tell about predicting the weather.
The students can study the instruments used in recording atmospheric conditions.

The Evolution Simulation Game*

Activity Overview

The following game simulates the process of evolution. It clearly demonstrates the role of mutations, adaptations, and chance in this process. The game can also be used as an introduction to food chains, the effects of competition within an environment, the effects of pollution, or man's role in relation to environmental issues. It is designed for high school students, but with some modifications it could be played with junior high school students.

Science Background

Charles Darwin's theory of evolution states that every species on the earth is undergoing constant, gradual change controlled by natural selection. Today it is generally accepted that these changes are caused by genetic mutations. Those mutations that are harmful are weeded out by the low survival rate of their carriers. Conversely, those mutations that are beneficial gradually become more common due to the high survival rate of their carriers. Whether a given mutation is beneficial or detrimental is determined by the organism's environment: temperature, precipitation, competition, predators, and pollution.

Additional Sources

Darwin, Charles, *On the Origin of Species* (Harvard University Press, Cambridge,, 1964).
Darwin, Charles, *The Illustrated Origin of Species* abridged and introduction by Richard E. Leakey (Hill and Wang, New York, 1979).
Moody, Paul Amos, *Introduction to Evolution* (Harper and Row, New York, 1970).
Moore, Ruth E., *Evolution* (Time, Inc., New York, 1964).

Major Concepts

- Mutations occur at random and their results cannot be predicted; organisms do not choose to mutate.
- Some mutations help a species adapt and survive in its environment.
- Just how helpful a mutation will be depends on the environment.
- Organisms with characteristics well suited to the environment in which they live will be able to adapt and survive.

Student Objectives

After this activity students should be able to:

*This activity was developed and field tested by Ms. Kathy James, Carleton College, Northfield, Minnesota. It is used with her permission.

- Describe the relationship between mutations and adaptations.
- Explain how natural mutations facilitate evolution.
- Describe the role the environment plays in evolution.
- Identify ways in which evolution is continuing today.

Vocabulary

Mutation
Adaptation

Materials

- Handout stating rules of the game and describing the original organism
- Overheads listing the mutation for each round (1–41)
- Cards stating the environmental changes (1–19)
- A map of the region (see below)

Rules of the Game

All players begin as the same organism (described below) in the same geographic location (square K)

The game will be organized into rounds that represent periods of roughly one million years. These rounds will be organized as follows:

- At the beginning of each round each player picks up to two mutations from a list prepared by the teacher. The mutations for each round should be displayed on an overhead. Suggested rounds are listed below.
- Do not allow students to see the list of mutations for future rounds. Most mutations will appear in more than one round. New mutations will be added each round.
- Each mutation is permanent to the player's species and will be effective in all the following rounds.
- Any new mutation replaces any contradicting traits. These contradictions are explained in brackets [ ] after the mutation.
- Some mutations require previous mutations, which are listed in parenthesis ( ) after the mutation.
- In any round, any student may choose to migrate one square in any direction as one of his mutations, but the species must have adapted to survive any changes in climate caused by the migration. (See The Region for a more detailed explanation.)
- After all mutations have been chosen, an environmental change is picked. This can be done by randomly drawing from a hat, thereby emphasizing the role of chance in evolution, or the sequence of mutations can be chosen by the teacher, allowing for the emphasis to be on the effects of specific environmental changes.
- The environmental changes only have an effect in the round in which they are chosen; no points will be gained or lost for past environmental changes.

- Students can be allowed to debate whether an environmental change was beneficial to their organism. Guidelines are included below, but these are only guidelines.

Scoring

Each student begins with five points. A score of zero represents extinction and the player is out of the game. Players attempt to survive and increase their scores.

If an environmental change is beneficial, +1

If an environmental change is detrimental, −1

Optional: After the first four rounds, competition may become a factor in scoring. See The Region for an explanation of the scoring if competition is included.

The Original Species: A Salamander

Color: red
Skin: moist, soft
Size: 6 inches long
Body temperature: cold blooded
Diet: Algae, swallowed whole
Reproduction: Attracts mate by smell
Mates on land
Lays eggs in shallow pools of water
Does not care for young in any way
Behavior: Does not hibernate
Low endurance—must rest after running or swimming 150 yards
Poor swimmer—is carried away by a current flowing faster than half a mile per hour
Poor jumper—can jump only one inch vertically
Moderate runner—runs at the speed of the average house cat
Rests at night in holes in the ground, under logs, or wherever it can find some shelter
General: Mute
Body and eggs absorb salts from salt water so it cannot survive in a saltwater environment

The Region

The map and descriptions of the various regions on the map allow the teacher to include competition as a factor influencing the course of evolution. After the first five rounds, if there are three or more players in a given square each player loses a point. If two players are in a square and a third player then moves in that square, making a total of three players in the square, only the player moving into the square loses a point. (The maximum limit per square will need to be increased to 3 if more than 15 students are playing.)

These migrations will force players into new environments, which are described below. Players must have adapted to survive the conditions they will encounter before moving into an environment. For example, a player cannot migrate away from the river until he can reproduce on dry land.

This aspect of the game is optional. If it is included, tell the students about the environments they will encounter in each square, and discuss the adaptations necessary to survive in each environment before the game begins.

Square A is a northern region. It is well forested, with a wide variety of trees, plants, and animals. But six months a year the ground is covered with snow, making plant life very hard to find and a fur coat a necessity. Cold-blooded animals cannot survive here, nor those who lay their eggs in water, since pools of water are scarce. Seasonal coloring, allowing an animal to be white in the winter but brown or green in the summer, is necessary here. Hibernation is also beneficial and would eliminate the need for seasonal coloring.

Squares B, E, and F are similar, but the winters are less severe. A fur coat and seasonal coloring will be helpful, but they are not a necessity.

Squares C and G are open prairie. There is little or no tree cover, but a wide variety of plants grow here. Many small birds and animals live in the grasses. Winters are cool, but snow rarely accumulates.

Square D is a desert. Days are hot and dry, but nights can be very cool. It never snows here. Water is sometimes hard to find, but desert plants are common. Some desert animals can be found here.

Squares L and P are salt water regions. Those animals whose skin is permeable to salt cannot survive here.

Squares O and N are cut off from the rest of the region by the river, so only flying predators will affect species living there. To live in this region, species must develop the ability to cross the river, which requires increased endurance and webbed feet (or three times the original endurance if webbed feet are not added).

All other squares, H, I, J, and K, represent forested regions bordered by a large river. There is plenty of plant and animal life to support other forms of life. Winters are not severe; snow rarely accumulates.

Mutations

1. dryer skin
2. develops scales (1)
3. develops hair (1, 2) [cancels 4]
4. develops shell-like exterior (2) [cancels 3, 36]
5. develops brown pigment, producing reddish brown color [cancels 8,10]

6. increases brown pigment, producing solid brown (5)
7. develops white pigment, producing spotted white [cancels 6, 10]
8. increases white pigment, producing solid white in color (7)
9. develops green pigment, producing spotted green [cancels 6, 8]
10. increases green pigment, producing solid green color (9)
11. seasonal color changes (5, 7, or 9) [cancels 12]
12. variety in pigment allowing color to change to fit environment, chameleon coloring (5, 9) [cancels 11]
13. variety in pigment so that mates are attracted by coloring (5, 7, or 9) [replaces use of scent to attract a mate so scent is lost]
14. skin becomes impermeable to salts found in salt water

Changes in Diet

15. develops small molars, allowing organism to chew plants
16. adds enzyme in the digestive track, allowing digestion of insects swallowed with the water
17. adds small canines, allowing organism to eat mice-sized rodents (16)
18. develops larger canines, allowing the organism to eat larger prey (17)
19. develops claws
20. develops a frog-like tongue, which allows the organism to catch flying insects (16)

Changes in Body Temperature and Habitat

21. becomes warm blooded (1)
22. becomes nocturnal (21)
23. builds a den/nest
24. spends part of its waking hours in trees (19)
25. nests in trees (23, 24)
26. borrows, nesting under ground (19)

Changes in Means of Reproduction

27. develops a protective covering on eggs
28. lays eggs on land (27)
29. develops pigment in egg shell which acts as a camouflage (27)
30. cares for young after eggs hatch
31. becomes a marsupial (30)
32. carries young to term (30)
33. uses voice to attract mates [replaces scent used to attract a mate]

Changes in Locomotion

34. changes in circulatory system increase endurance
35. develops webbed feet

36. leg length doubles, producing longer legs in proportion to body size, and allowing for swifter running—twice as fast as before
37. develops stronger leg muscles, allowing for greater jumping ability—twice as high as before [initial jumping ability was one inch]
38. loses limbs [cancels 35, 36, 37, 39]
39. develops fins (35) [cancels 37, 38]

Other Changes

40. increases size 50 percent (34)
41. lives in water continually (34, 35)

Environmental Changes

1. Flies begin to be seen in the area [helps 16 + 20]
2. Temperatures drop; only severe in region A, where temperatures are now consistently below freezing and snow accumulates [little effect]
3. Small green land plants become common [helps 15]
4. Worms and slugs become common [helps 16]
5. Drought: small pools dry up and the river level drops 2 feet [hurts those without 28, 31, 32]
6. A herbivorous turtle moves into the region by the river [hurts those without 15, 16, 17, or 20]
7. Rabbits begin to populate the region [helps those with 18, hurts those with 15]
8. The population of song birds in the region increases [little effect]
9. A population of freshwater carnivorous turtles moves into the river [hurts those without 28 and those with 41]
10. A population of freshwater fish that eats eggs laid in the water moves into the river [hurts those without 28 unless they also have 30, helps those with 18 that still live in or near the river]
11. A snake similar to a rattlesnake develops in the region; snakes locate their prey by warmer body temperatures [hurts those with 21 unless they have 40]
12. Hawks migrate into the region [hurts those without some form of protective coloring]
13. A weasel moves into the region; weasels locate their prey by scent [hurts those without 13 or 33; helps those with 18 and 40 four times]
14. A flood washes away regions near the river [hurts those in squares I, J, K, L, M, N, O who are without 24]
15. Sewage dumped into the river contaminates the river downstream from square J [hurts all in squares, J, K, N, O, L, P]
16. An oil spill contaminates the saltwater sea [hurts all those in squares L, O, P]
17. Prairie fire sweeps across square C [hurts those in square C without 16 and 17, helps those in square C with 16 and 17]
18. People begin to hunt species over 15 inches long [hurts those with 40 four or more times]
19. Squares I and M become a game refuge [helps all in those squares]

Tips for Playing the Game

1. Keep a simplified copy of the rules and a description of the original species where it will be visible to all the students throughout the time that the game is played. The easiest way to do this will probably be to give each student his or her own copy.
2. Have each student record his or her species evolution by writing down his or her choices of mutation and the environmental changes of each round.
3. After the first three or four rounds have been played, stop to discuss how the students' species have evolved to this point. What do they look like now? What advantages do they have that help them survive? Where can they best survive? Is there anywhere they could not survive? What additional changes might help them even more? Is it possible that evolution really happened this way?
4. Spend one full class period introducing and playing the game. Additional games/rounds can be played later with less preparation time. One round a day can be played, using the environmental changes as a means of focusing attention on the lesson topic. Or it may be useful on those days when the film you planned to show fails to come in or you did not have time to write up a lesson plan for the substitute teacher.
5. There is no limit to the number of rounds that can be played. Listed are 19 environmental changes, but these can be repeated or the list can be expanded.

6. Currently, the mutations will not allow a species to fly or walk erect. These advances involve an incredible number of mutations. It might be a good idea to tell students this when the game begins.
7. There are no predators other than those introduced as environmental changes. Do not tell the students what types of predators these will be.

Suggested Mutation Choices

Round 1: 1, 5, 9, 15, 16, 17, 21, 27, 28, 34, 35, 40
Round 2: 7, 10, 14, 15, 16, 19, 21, 27, 29, 30, 36, 40
Round 3: 2, 3, 12, 15, 20, 22, 26, 28, 30, 33, 34, 39
Round 4: 6, 8, 11, 18, 19, 23, 29, 31, 36, 38, 39, 41
Round 5: 1, 3, 4, 5, 13, 15, 16, 24, 32, 34, 35, 36
Round 6: 2, 14, 19, 20, 21, 26, 28, 30, 33, 37, 39, 40
Round 7: 6, 7, 10, 11, 17, 18, 22, 23, 24, 32, 36, 38
Round 8: 4, 8, 9, 19, 29, 31, 34, 36, 37, 39, 40, 41
Round 9: 2, 3, 5, 13, 22, 33
Round 10: 13, 14, 35, 36, 39, 40
Round 11: 11, 14, 23, 32, 38, 39
Round 12: 3, 4, 27, 29, 40, 41
Round 13: 15, 24, 26, 30, 37, 39
Round 14: 13, 16, 22, 29, 36, 40
Round 15: 23, 26, 32, 33, 35, 41
Round 16: 4, 18, 22, 26, 40, 42
Round 17: 1, 12, 16, 34, 35, 41

Technology and the Quality of Life

Activity Overview

Each student will report on a technology that he or she feels will be pivotal in improving the quality of life. Examples of such technologies in history are the wheel, the automobile, and television. Students should learn how important technology is in their lives and become familiar with careers related to significant technologies. This activity can be scheduled to occupy three to five class periods and make extensive use of library resources.

Science Background

Technology affects the way we spend our time and even the way we think. Quality of life would be somewhat different without the sophisticated technologies that we have come to depend on. Recognizing the importance of certain technologies such as computers and biotechnology will enable students to form a clearer picture of how

technology interacts with our society. Career exploration may also prove useful as students learn about occupations that will be important in the future.

Innovations have often been instrumental in creating revolution in lifestyles. The wheel opened possibilities of transportation, the gun changed the nature of war, and the telegraph opened up the world to communication across thousands of miles. The common denominator in all of these technologies is that they improved the quality of life for some people in some way. In other words, these technologies have made some aspect of life easier or better.

Today, the dominant technologies include microelectronics and biotechnology. Microelectronic computers make possible efficient processing of great volumes of information. Biotechnology works wonders in replacing body parts and performing delicate surgery. Many careers are related to technologies such as these, and people with training in these areas are likely to be in demand in the future. For example, health technology careers include medical and biological researchers, laboratory technicians, and surgeons. New discoveries in all areas will probably eliminate some old jobs and create many new jobs in the next century.

Major Concepts

- Technology is an integral part of society.
- Many technologies revolutionize society by improving the quality of life.

Objectives

After completing this activity, students should be able to:

- recognize that technology has direct impact on our lives
- identify some technologies that are likely to prove instrumental in determining the directions that our society takes
- define quality of life
- describe the relationship between quality of life and technology

Materials

Library resources
Career information resources

Vocabulary

Innovation
Quality of Life
Technology
Microelectronics
Biotechnology

Procedure

1. Have students look around the room and ask them to point out objects that illustrate the use of technology. Possible answers include computers, audiovisual materials, fluorescent lights, etc.
2. Define technology and discuss with the class what it is and how it affects all goods that are produced. Explain that sometimes a new technology may greatly affect people's lives and that this is related to the general concept of quality of life. Give examples such as the wheel, plow, electric light, etc.
3. Each student should decide on a recent innovation that he or she believes will improve the quality of life in the future. Encourage diversity in the topics. Some general topics are health, genetic engineering, food, communication, and media technologies.
4. The students should spend at least three class periods researching their topics in the library. They should concentrate on how the technology improves the quality of life and should also investigate at least one occupation related to the technology.
5. Each student should write a three-to-four-page report on his or her findings. These reports may be handed in and evaluated or reported orally and discussed.

Extension

Find primary sources that discuss technologies of the past that have proven to be instrumental in improving the quality of many people's lives. For example, read a 1948 or 1950 article about television. How did people feel about it at the time? Did they recognize how important television would be? Lead a class discussion on this topic or have students do individual research projects on these past technologies.

Evaluation

Have students write short answers to these questions:

- Are there any technologies that seem to be dominant today?
- How does technology affect, for example, medical care?
- How did the invention of the telephone, for example, improve the quality of life? Were there any tradeoffs?

Evaluating Food Choices

Activity Overview

Students keep a record of the food they eat for one day. By means of a graph, the students evaluate their food choices. This activity is designed for middle/junior high school.

Science Background

Nutrients can be defined as the different substances in foods that function specifically to keep the body healthy, active, and growing. Some of the major nutrients needed by the body include protein, fats, carbohydrates, vitamins, and minerals.

Protein is the body's building material. It contains nitrogen, which is necessary for all tissue building. Protein is essential for maintaining body structure, for providing substances that act as body regulators, and for producing compounds necessary for normal body functions. Milk products, meat, fish, poultry, eggs, legumes, and nuts are good sources of protein.

While protein can also provide energy for the body, *fats* and *carbohydrates* are the major food substances that provide the body with calories for heat and energy. If the body lacks sufficient amounts of fats and carbohydrates, or if there is an excess of protein in the diet, the body will use protein for heat and energy. Fats are normally consumed from margarine, butter, mayonnaise, salad dressings, and meat. Carbohydrates are found in grain products, fruit, and sugar-sweetened foods.

Although vitamins and minerals are needed in smaller quantities than are protein, fats, and carbohydrates, they remain essential to normal body functioning. Our discussion is limited to those often lacking in the diets of adolescents.

Vitamin A is important for vision. Night blindness, an inability of the eye to adjust to dim light, can result from a lack of vitamin A in the diet. Yellow, orange, and dark green vegetables, and fruits contain vitamin A (sweet potatoes, carrots, squash, spinach, broccoli, melon, apricots, and peaches).

Vitamin C contributes to the formation of a substance called *collagen*, which holds body tissue together and encourages healing. Vitamin C also strengthens blood vessel walls and helps the body utilize calcium in making bones and teeth. Scurvy, a disease characterized by swelling and tenderness of joints and gums, loosening of teeth, hemorrhaging, and puffiness can result from severe lack of vitamin C. Citrus fruits, broccoli, spinach, greens, potatoes, tomatoes, melon, cabbage, and strawberries contain this vitamin.

Iron is a mineral that is essential to *hemoglobin*, the substance of the blood that carries oxygen. Oxygen is necessary for all cells. A diet that fails to supply a sufficient amount of iron may lead to anemia. This condition is characterized by a tired and listless feeling due to a lack of energy. Although liver is a major source of iron, greens, beans, beef, pork, prunes, and raisins are also good sources.

Calcium is the bone and tooth building mineral. It forms the structure of teeth and bones and helps keep them strong. Milk products are good sources for calcium.

Major Concept

Individuals should develop eating patterns that contribute to wellness.

Objectives

By the end of this activity, the students should be able to: Analyze and evaluate food choices in terms of the Recommended Daily Allowance (RDA) of protein, energy, and selected vitamins and minerals

Materials

"Comprehensive List of Foods" booklet with nutritive values and percent of U.S. RDA for 139 foods, available from the National Dairy Council. Contact the office serving your area or write: National Dairy Council 630 North River Road Rosemont, Illinois 60018.

Vocabulary

anemia	minerals	Recommended
calories	night blindness	Daily Allow-
carbohydrates	nutrient	ance (RDA)
fats	proteins	scurvy
		vitamins

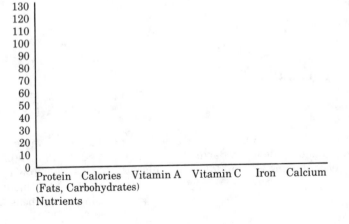

Graph of
Food Choices for
One Day
(expressed as % of U.S. RDA)

Percent of U.S. Recommended Daily Allowance

130
120
110
100
90
80
70
60
50
40
30
20
10
0

Protein   Calories   Vitamin A   Vitamin C   Iron   Calcium
(Fats, Carbohydrates)
Nutrients

Procedures

1. Have the students keep a complete record of all foods eaten for one day.
2. Using the "Comprehensive List of Foods," the students should then determine the nutritive values and graph the percent of RDA that chosen foods contained. (See sample graph.)

3. Upon completion of the bar graphs, invite the students to answer the following questions:
   Is the percentage of calories (energy) in your daily diet too low, about right, or too high?
   Nutrients I need more of are _____.
   Which foods could provide these nutrients?
   Foods I ate that had a lot of calories (energy) but not many other nutrients are _____.
   How can I improve my diet?

An Introduction to Population, Resources, and Environment

Aims

To develop a general understanding of the technology, economics, environmental effects and social issues related to finding and extracting resources

- Describe the role of technology, economics and environmental effects on the extraction and use of resources
- Describe the difficulties in making decisions about the distribution of limited resources

Objectives

At the completion of this lesson the participant should be able to:
- Describe the relationship between population growth and resource use
- Define resource
- Describe the difference between reserves and resources

Materials

Pennies (300)
Tweezers
Toothpicks
Other items commonly available in classrooms
Riddle of lily pond
Handout of worksheets

Instructional Plan

A. Exploration
   1. Use riddle to focus attention and introduce relationship between population and resources.

   > There is a lily pond that has a single leaf.
   > Each day the number of leaves doubles.
   > On the second day there are two leaves.
   > On the third day there are four leaves.
   > On the fourth day there are eight leaves.
   > On the thirtieth day the pond is full.
   > When was the pond half full?

   Set

   2. Show film "World Population".
   3. Purpose statement and transition to activity
   4. Explain the activity.

   Purpose

   - The activity simulates the exploration and extraction of earth materials needed by individuals and society.
   - Students first *explore* the room to assess the availability of resources (pennies).
   - Report on resources that were observed and introduce definitions. Summarize data on overhead.
   - Have the students actually "mine" the resources. Students must record the number of pennies found each minute.
   - Students must use objects to extract pennies.
   - Students will have 10–15 minutes to obtain pennies.
   - Complete a graph of the pennies found each minute.

5. Do the first exploration. Have the students spend 3 minutes looking around the room to determine how many pennies there are. (Review rules: they cannot touch, turn over, change furniture, and they cannot collect any pennies)   } *Active Participation*
6. Return to groups. Have the groups report on their findings. Record observations on overhead.

B. Explanation
7. Define reserves, resources, and technology.   } *Information Input*
8. Have the students actually "mine" the resources.   *Active*
9. Provide time to complete graphs.   *Participation*
10. Summarize and discuss resource activity.
   • What happened as their extraction of resources continued?
   • Did they find all the resources?   } *Reinforcement*
   • How close were the estimates of the resources?
   • What problems did they experience with time? Extraction? Location?
   • How is this activity like the actual extraction of resources?   } *Transfer*
   • What is the relationship of technology to your activity? Of economics? Of population? Of environment?   } *Assessment*

C. Extension
11. Introduce the simulation game involving the distribution of resources.
12. Have participants complete the individual and group decisions.
13. Discuss the distribution simulation.
   • What was the basis for your individual and group decision?   } *Transfer*
   • What other information would you have requested?
   • Would you change your decisions if more units of resources were available?   } *Decision Making*
   • How could more resources be obtained?   } *Values*
   • What lifestyle changes, price increases, environmental effects, etc. would you be willing to tolerate in order to have more resources?   } *Personal Meaning*

D. Evaluation
13. Conclude with a discussion of the interrelationship of population, resources, and environment.   } *Closure*

Definitions

Reserves:
The amount of a particular resource in known locations that can be extracted at a profit with present technology and prices.

Resources:
The total amount of a particular material that exists on earth.

Technology:
A) The application of science, especially to industrial or commercial objectives
B) The entire body of methods and materials used to achieve industrial or commercial objectives
C) The body of knowledge available to a civilization that is of use in fashioning implements, practicing manual arts and skills, and extracting or collecting resources

Groups	1	2	3	4	5	6	7
Reserves							
Estimates of Resources							
Actual Resources							

Data Sheet for Distributing Resources

Your problem is to decide how to distribute resources among three groups who have requested your help. For this activity we are using the term resources to include many different things such as food, minerals, fuels, and other items needed by people. Here is the only information you have to make your decisions:

   You have 300 units of resources
   You presently use 200 units of resources
   You can survive on 100 units of resources

Three groups want some of your resources. Here are their situations:

   Group 1 — needs 250 units of resources to survive
            — wants 250 units of resources
   Group 2 — needs 100 units of resources to survive
            — wants 200 units for survival *and* improvement
   Group 3 — needs 50 units for survival
            — wants 100 units for improvement
   Group 4 — needs no units for survival
            — wants 200 units for improvement

Your problem is to decide how you will distribute the resources.

Complete the chart below.

Individual Decisions

Distribution of Resources	Group 1	Group 2	Group 3	Group 4
Reasons for Decision				

Group Decisions

Distribution of Resources	Group 1	Group 2	Group 3	Group 4
Reasons for Decision				

Evaluating Laboratory Work: Experiment—Why is the Sky Blue? Why is the Sunset Red?

1. Have students form groups of four for this experiment.
2. Have each group follow the suggested procedure for doing the experiment.
3. As the experiment progresses, circulate among the groups and note the following: (A check list such as found in chapter 20 might be used.)
   a. Ability to follow directions
   b. Ability to use proper safety precautions
   c. Keeping a record of observations
   d. Working cooperatively with other members of the group
   e. Ability to form hypotheses
   f. Ability to make predictions
   g. Ability to draw conclusions from the observations and data
   h. Care in using the materials, assembly, cleanup and storage
4. What kinds of process objectives were realized in having students do this experiment? What cognitive objectives were achieved? What affective objectives?

Materials

Each group should have the following materials:
1. 12 in. or 14 in. rectangular aquarium (clear glass)
2. Flashlight
3. Concentrated sulfuric acid (H_2SO_4)
4. Sodium thiosulfate; may use sodium hyposulfite (photographic fix)
4. Water
6. White screen or white sheet of paper

Purpose

To demonstrate the effect of the atmosphere on the sun's rays. As white light passes through the atmosphere, various colors are removed by scattering and show up in the color of the sky. Violet is removed with smallest particles; blue, with next smallest; green, with next; and so on for yellow, orange, red, etc.

Procedure

An illustration clarifies the procedure. Mix thiosulfate, 10 grams per gallon of water (not critical) in the aquarium. Project light through aquarium to screen. Add a few drops of concentrated sulfuric acid and stir with glass rod.

Questions

At the beginning, what color is the water when the flashlight shines through it? What color is the light of the flashlight when looked at directly?

How does the color of the water change as time goes on? How does the color of the light from the flashlight change? To what is this analogous in nature?

What causes the water to change color?
What causes the light source to change color?
What is the final color of the water? Why?
What is the final color of the light source? Why?
To what natural sky condition is this analogous?

Explanation

Reaction of the acid on the sodium thiosulfate releases very fine particles. Only very fine particles in the atmosphere cause the rays to scatter. This can be shown by the fact that smoke blown across a beam of light appears bluish, but chalk dust gives no coloration at all. This is because the chalk particles are too large.

The scattering effect first removes the violet and blue end of the spectrum, and later the red end as the particles grow larger. Observe the color of the "sky" water and also the color of the "sun" flashlight which remains. Color of the sun goes from white to yellow to orange to red to blackness, where it is not visible at all.

In nature the sunlight becomes redder near the horizon because the light passes through more atmosphere with larger particles when the sun is about to set.

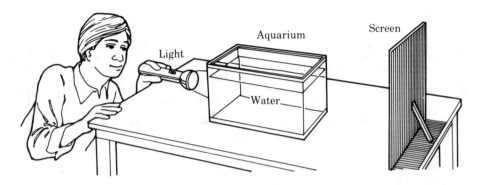

Teaching Concepts

Light travels in waves.
White light contains all colors.
Short waves are scattered more than long waves.
Short waves are scattered by smaller particles than
    are long waves.
Scattering subtracts colors from a beam of white
    light.

Subtracting blue from white leaves yellow; therefore, the sun appears yellow.

Additional Principle

Use a Polaroid sheet and look at the beam from the side
and turn your sheet through a ninety-degree angle. Observe the fact that scattered light is polarized.

Genetic Engineering: A Splice of Life

Overview:
How do scientists create new combinations of genetic material? What are the benefits of these new
combinations? Should scientists avoid or prohibit any combinations? In this activity the students will
simulate the process of engineering bacteria capable of producing human growth hormone. Then they will
discuss the ethical implications of genetic engineering.

Scientific Principles:

- Genetic engineering is the manipulation of a genotype to alter an organism's phenotype.
- Gene splicing is a set of processes by which scientists incorporate the DNA for a specific protein into the
  DNA from another cell. The host organism will express this new information.
- Ethics enters into scientific endeavors. While genetic engineering may solve a variety of problems, it
  nevertheless may create other problems. Consequently, scientists and nonscientists must prepare
  themselves to make decisions about these issues.

Student Outcomes: Upon completion of this activity, the students should be able to

- Describe and simulate the processes involved in genetic engineering.
- Understand how molecular biologists use bacteria to manufacture proteins for human use.
- Support a rational point of view.

Skills:
Interpretation, Analysis

Related Disciplines:
Technology, Ethics

Time Frame:
Splicing Bits & Pieces   45 minutes

Opening Pandora's Box   45 minutes

Materials and Advance Preparation

Splicing Bits & Pieces

Materials:

- One set of colored paper clips per lab group. Each set of clips should contain:
  35 black paper clips
  27 white paper clips
  46 red paper clips
  46 green paper clips
   9 silver paper clips
- Tape, 4 small pieces per lab group

Before class:

- Gather colored paper clips and divide them into sets so that each group of students has one set. You may want to store individual sets in plastic bags.

Opening Pandora's Box

Materials:

- 4 index cards
- Paper, 1 sheet per student

Before class:

- Prepare the 4 index cards as indicated in *Opening Pandora's Box*, step 2.
- Make a student worksheet based on the questions raised in *Opening Pandora's Box*, step 6
- Copy the student worksheet, 1 per student.

Splicing Bits & Pieces

NOTE: This activity is for students who have a solid understanding of genetics. Students should be familiar with information transfer, DNA, RNA, and the genetic code. In addition, the students must clearly understand protein synthesis to be successful with this activity.

1. Review with your students the role of DNA in the human body. In particular, remind the students that genes code for proteins, such as hormones.
2. Sometimes people are unable to produce certain hormones. Two examples of hormone deficiencies are diabetes and human growth hormone (hGH) deficiency. To give your students a perspective on these two problems, relate the following information:

   Diabetics are unable to regulate sugar, and more than 3 million diabetics in the U.S. must receive insulin daily. Until recently, the only sources of insulin were swine and cattle pancreases; but this supply has dwindled as hog and cattle production has declined. Some diabetics develop an immune reponse to porcine or bovine insulin and so are unable to continue using it.

   Children who produce an insufficient amount of hGH have extremely short stature; they may never grow more than one meter tall. About 2,500 children in the U.S. suffer from this deficiency. For many years, the only sources of hGH were sheep brains or the pituitary glands of human cadavers; it takes 500,000 sheep brains to collect 5 mg of this hormone. Pituitary glands are also very scarce, so doctors could treat only the most severely affected children. In addition, some pituitary glands came from individuals who had died of Creudzfelt-Jacob disease, a slow, degenerative brain disease caused by a virus. Because of this contamination, human cadaver pituitary glands have not been used as a source of hGH in the U.S. since May 1985.

   Today, recombinant DNA technology—genetic engineering—makes it possible to produce unlimited quantities of these two hormones. Biosynthetic insulin, called Humulin, has been available since 1983. Genentech, a major commercial biotechnology firm, produces a synthetic growth hormone called Pro-tropin, which was approved for public use in 1985; and the U.S. Food & Drug Administration recently approved the marketing of another biosynthetic growth hormone called Humatrop, which is produced by Eli Lilly.

3. Define the term *recombinant DNA technology* for your students (see *Background for the Teacher*).
4. Using the information that follows, explain the basic processes of genetic engineering to your students.

   To synthesize a particular substance in a new organism, a scientist must:

a. Locate the gene that codes for the production of the desired protein, such as insulin or hGH. This requires finding a specific sequence of DNA bases among the 3 billion bases that comprise the human genetic code.

b. Isolate the specific gene.

c. Insert the isolated gene into a plasmid, and ensure that the proper regulatory sequences are intact.

d. Introduce the altered plasmid to a host cell, usually a bacterium, such as *E. coli*.

e. Cultivate the *E. coli*, and produce the desired protein.

5. Divide the class into small groups and distribute a set of colored paper clips to each group. Explain to the students that they are going to simulate the steps in the recombinant DNA process. Write the following key on the board:

  A = adenine—black
  T = thymine—white
  C = cytosine—red
  G = guanine—green
  U = uracil—silver

On the board, beside the key, write the 37 pairs of DNA bases listed below. This is a small section of the gene for human growth hormone, which actually has 573 pairs of DNA bases.

Partial sequence of the hGH gene:

```
1   2   3   4   5   6   7   8   9   10  11  12
A - A - G - C - T - T - A - T—G—G—C— T
T - T - C - G - A - A - T - A - C—C—G— A
13  14  15  16  17  18  19  20  21  22  23  24
A—C—A—G—G—C—A—T—C—G—T— C
T—G—T—C—C—G—T—A—G—C—A— G
25  26  27  28  29  30  31  32  33  34  35  36  37
C—C - G - G - A—C—G—A—A—G - C - T - T
G—G - C - C - T—G - C—T—T—C - G - A - A
```

6. Tell the students that this is a short piece of the hGH gene. They will use the top strand—the sense strand—of the DNA sequence to construct the complementary strand of mRNA for this sequence of the hGH gene. Remind the students to substitute uracil for thymine in the mRNA strand.

7. The mRNA strand the students create has extraneous genetic information in it called an *intron*, which scientists remove chemically. Most bacteria do not have the enzymatic systems required to remove introns. Bases 19, 20, 21, and 22 comprise the intron in this strand. Have the students remove the intron and reconnect the remaining pieces, or *exons*.

8. Now have the students use the 33 base mRNA strand to create a double-stranded DNA molecule for hGH. Creating this strand is a two-step process. First, the students code for a DNA strand based on the existing mRNA. Second, they create a complementary strand of DNA based on the first strand of DNA. In a lab, a scientist would use the enzyme *reverse transcriptase* to accomplish the task of copying a DNA molecule from the mRNA strand.

9. Check the students' work and then ask them to lay this representation of the hGH gene along the top of their desks.

10. Now the students need to create a paper clip model of a plasmid. Using the same color key, ask the students to create the following double-stranded DNA sequence:

```
1   2   3   4   5   6   7   8   9   10
G - G - A - T - C - C - T - G - A —C
C - C - T - A - G - G - A - C - T —G
11  12  13  14  15  16  17  18  19  20
A —C —C —G —G —A —A —C —G —T
T —G —G —C —C —T —T —G —C —A
21  22  23  24  25  26  27  28  29  30
C —A —A —G —C —T —T —C —C —C
G —T —T —C —G —A —A —G —G —G
```

11. Because plasmids are circular, have the students attach base 1 to base 30 in each strand of the plasmid sequence. They should mark the point of attachment with a piece of tape. Ask the students to lay the double-stranded circles on their desks. The students are now ready to recombine DNA molecules.

12. To insert the gene for hGH into the plasmid, both the hGH gene and the plasmid need "sticky ends" (complementary bases) that will attach to each other. To create these sticky ends, genetic engineers cut gene sequences with very specific restriction enzymes. These enzymes will only cut DNA in specific places, as shown below, and only if the entire sequence is present.

Ask the students which of the enzymes listed below will cut both the hGH gene and plasmid in sites that leave the hGH gene intact:

Enzyme	Cutting Site		
BAM 1	G	GATC	C
	C	CTAG	G
Hind III	A	AGCT	T
	T	TCGA	A
Hpa II	C	CG	G
	G	GC	C

13. After the students have discovered that Hind III is the only restriction enzyme that will cut the gene and the plasmid at appropriate sites, instruct them to "cut" their genes and plasmids and connect the spliced gene to the plasmid. Mark these places with tape to represent the en-

zyme *ligase*, which "pastes" complementary sticky ends together in nature and in the lab.

14. In a lab, scientists would next insert altered plasmids into many bacteria, which would reproduce and create identical bacteria containing altered plasmids. Because these bacteria contain altered plasmids, they are capable of producing hGH. Use the Figure to review this entire process with your students.

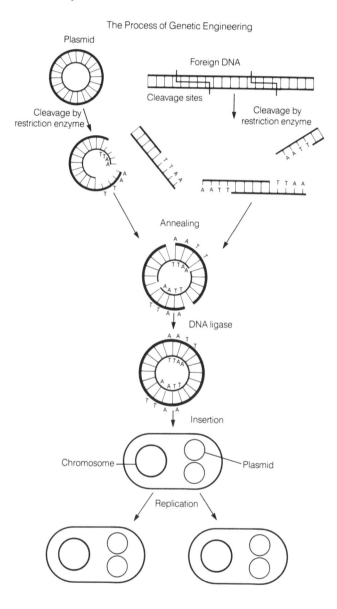

The Process of Genetic Engineering

Opening Pandora's Box

1. Explain to your students that although scientists can easily use bacterial hosts to clone recombinant DNA and produce large amounts of a desired protein, many difficult questions arise. Because bacteria divide so rapidly, there is virtually no limit to the synthesis of new genetic combi-

nations. For people in need of a steady supply of insulin or human growth hormone, the products of this type of genetic engineering are invaluable. But what happens if, as in the case of hGH, a person wants to take the readily available biosynthetic growth hormone just to attain greater height? After such a large investment in research and development, the companies that manufacture the biosynthetic growth hormone might be happy to expand their market beyond hGH deficient children. Should physicians prescribe biosynthetic growth hormone to anyone who wants to be taller? Though these questions point out that in certain situations most everyone accepts genetic engineering, that is, the production of recombinant molecules, however, many questions remain about how to regulate the resulting product.

2. Write the following viewpoints on separate index cards:

   • You are the CEO of the company that developed and produced biosynthetic hGH. Your board of directors and stockholders expect this product to make a profit for the company. Even if every patient who needs hGH bought your product, the company would not recoup its investment in the development of the hormone. To whom will you market this product?

   • As a pediatrician who treats children who have insufficient amounts of hGH, you are aware of the potential side effects of the biosynthetic hormone (glucose intolerance, hypertension, abnormal bone development, and enlargement of the heart, which may lead to heart failure). Some parents have asked you to prescribe hGH for a child of average height because they know that height is a desirable characteristic in our culture. What will you do?

   • You are a basketball player in junior high school. You are quite good, but want to improve your chances for playing basketball in high school, in college, and maybe even professionally. If you were just a little bit taller, you would really stand out on the team. A biosynthetic growth hormone could add those centimeters, but you may develop diabetes; end up with elongated hands, feet, and chin; or even suffer heart problems. What do you think? Would you try a little hGH?

   • You are the parent of a child who has an hGH deficiency. Your child has a moderate deficiency and will probably be 15-20 centimeters shorter than average when grown. Because this biosynthetic hormone is very new, no one knows what the long-term side effects may be. If your son takes biosynthetic growth hormone, he has a 50-50 chance of reaching average adult height. What will you do?

3. Divide the class into four groups and distribute one card to each group. Ask the students to discuss the hGH issue from the point of view presented on their card.

4. After each group has developed a rationale representing its view of the issue on the card, ask each group to present its issue and conclusions to the rest of the class. Do any of the groups want to reconsider their positions based on the new information?

5. Genetically altered bacteria can bear new and unforeseen genetic combinations. Release of these bacteria into the environment poses problems that concern scientists, bioethicists (people who address the ethical, legal, and public policy issues raised by the biomedical sciences), and the general public.

   Explain to your students that genetic engineers are working on a variety of projects other than the two hormones already mentioned. Scientists have developed prenatal diagnostic tests that use restriction fragment length polymorphisms (RFLPs) to check for disorders, such as sickle-cell anemia, thalassemia, and hemophilia. Genetic technology has resulted in the ability to use viral vectors to carry genes as a possible treatment for metabolic disorders and has resulted in the use of recombinant interleukin-2 to treat cancer. Scientists are also developing and using techniques to improve crop yield, the nutritional value of seed crops, and the resistance of crop plants to pests, pathogens, and environmental damage. All of these techniques or products raise ethical dilemmas.

6. To encourage your students to think about these ethical issues, distribute a copy of the following questions to each student. Ask the students to answer the questions, on a separate sheet of paper, in the following manner: read the first question, think about it, and then write the answer to the question. The answer should be short and take only one minute to write. Do the same for the rest of the questions.

   a. If the results of genetic technology create a real conflict between benefits and risks, what price should we be willing to pay for new knowledge?

   b. Should we allow scientists to alter bacteria genetically and release them into the environment without being certain of the end result? If so, in what cases?

   c. Should we allow scientists to control the evolutionary destiny of any organism? What limits, if any, should we place on scientific research?

   d. Should representatives of the lay public be involved in determining the direction of genetic technology? Why or why not? How will people determine the direction of this type of scientific research?

7. After all the students have answered the questions, discuss their answers. Are there clear "right" and "wrong" answers to these questions? How do we decide what is "right" or "wrong"?

Resources for the Classroom
This activity was adapted from *Advances in Genetic Technology*, developed by BSCS, published by D.C. Heath & Co., Lexington, MA, 1988. [For more activities, including laboratory investigations, please refer to this book.]
BSCS. *Basic Genetics: A Human Approach.* Dubuque, IA: Kendall Hunt Publishing Co., 1983. [A six week module on basic genetics for high school students.]
BSCS. *Genes and Surroundings.* Dubuque, IA: Kendall Hunt Publishing Co., 1983. [A six week module on basic genetics for middle school students.]
The Industrial Biotechnology Association has a number of flyers and films available related to biotechnology. [Contact K. Sherrod Shim, Director of Communications, IBA, 1625 K Street, N.W., Suite 1100, Washington, D.C. 20006, or 202/857-0244; FAX: 202/857-0237.]

Background for the Teacher
The Sphinx, the Minotaur, and the Chimera—Greek mythology is full of such hybrid creatures. In the real world, natural barriers normally prevent the exchange of genetic information between unrelated organisms, but recombinant DNA technology has made it possible to breach genetic barriers by excising a DNA segment from one organism and joining it to a DNA segment of an unrelated species. The breaking and rejoining of DNA molecules from unrelated organisms result in recombinant DNA molecules.

Scientists use bacteria to clone recombinant DNA molecules. Some bacteria contain plasmids—small, circular, double-stranded DNA molecules that are distinct from chromosomal DNA. In the early 1970s Annie Chang and Stanley Cohen succeeded in isolating and purifying plasmid DNA molecules. These small *extrachromosomal* elements can replicate inside the bacterium and independently of the bacterial chromosome. Because they are self-replicating entities, plasmids will propagate indefinitely in the *E. coli* bacterial culture. By the same token, any foreign DNA spliced into the plasmid DNA will replicate as well. Because bacteria divide every 20 minutes, they can produce, within a day; billions of organisms carrying hundreds or thousands of plasmids. In this manner, foreign genes are amplified—cloned—yielding large quantities of purified genes.

Many people have concerns about genetic engineering. Even though E. coli is part of the normal human intestinal flora, critics of recombinant DNA technology fear that scientists might inadvertently allow E. coli that bear new genetic combinations to escape from the laboratory. For example, some people fear that a human could become accidentally infected with the E. coli strain that synthesizes human growth hormone. The hormone would pour into the intestine, unregulated by the body, upset the body's chemical balance and possibly result in death. Or they fear that someone might produce an E. coli strain that secretes a deadly toxin. Other concerned people think that genetic recombinants might produce adverse effects on human, animal, or plant populations.

Scientists also recognize the potential risks of genetic engineering. In 1973, concerned scientists wrote two letters that raised the question of regulating this type of research. As a result of the publication of these letters, in 1975 a group of scientists met in Asilomar, California, to discuss the risks of using recombinant DNA technology, as well as to discuss benefits and possible mechanisms for regulation. The scientists agreed to use voluntary guidelines to regulate experimentation. They decided that they could use physical containment in many experiments, such as glove boxes and laminar flow hoods, to prevent the escape of novel organisms and to protect laboratory workers. The researchers also suggested that they might genetically "cripple" cloning vectors (plasmids) and E. coli hosts and thus provide a form of biological containment.

Today, the Recombinant DNA Advisory Committee at the National Institute of Health must approve all genetic research funded by the federal government. Many industrial scientists voluntarily seek the approval of this committee for their work. Few other areas of scientific research are as heavily regulated as genetic engineering. Some scientists feel that this heavy amount of regulation is excessive and impedes scientific research. Others feel this amount of regulation prevents abuse. Many countries have regulations more relaxed than those in the U.S. This inequity puts the U.S. at a disadvantage in international competition. How much regulation is enough? Who should decide? What are the costs and benefits of such regulations? Clearly, there are many questions for scientists and nonscientists to answer; but only the well-informed can answer these questions.

■ References

Benjamin, M., et al. Short children, anxious parents: Is growth hormone the answer? *Hastings Center Report.* 14(2):13; 1984.

Brill, W. J. Safety concerns and genetic engineering in agriculture. *Science.* 227(4685):381; 1985.

Farber, F.E. Unpublished handout from *Biology 10.* Northfield, MN: Carleton College, 1980.

Office of Technology Assessment, *Genetic Technology: A New Frontier,* Boulder, CO: Westview Press, 1982.

Tangley, L. Engineered organisms in the environment? Not yet. *BioScience.* 33(11):681; 1983.

Superconductivity: A New School of Thought

Overview: In 1987, an exciting discovery piqued the interest of the scientific community: scientists synthesized new high-temperature materials that could conduct electricity with no loss of energy. This discovery marked new progress on the intellectual and technological frontiers of superconductivity. In this activity, the students will learn the scientific principles that underlie superconductivity, experience the excitement of a scientific frontier, and appreciate the political and financial implications of one of the most important scientific discoveries of the twentieth century.

Scientific Principles:

- A superconductor is a material through which an electrical current can flow without resistance.
- Resistance in a conductor causes heat; this heat occurs because free electrons collide with imperfections in the conductor's crystalline structure.

- A material can become a superconductor if, when cooled below the transition (or critical) temperature, not enough collisions with sufficient energy occur (on average) to disrupt the coherent binding of electrons that makes superconductivity possible.
- New discoveries in science often occur when scientists take a radically new approach to a problem.
- The application of scientific research does not occur independently of politics or economics.

Student Outcomes: Upon completion of this activity, the students will be able to

- Explain the differences between a nonconductor (insulator), a conductor, and a superconductor.
- Describe the principles of superconductivity.
- Chronicle the history of developments in superconductivity research.
- Describe why superconductivity has excited so many scientists.
- List at least two political or economic issues related to superconductivity.

Skills:
Reasoning, Understanding models, Applying information, Making decisions

Related Disciplines:
Economics

Time Frame:
Conducting Lessons   45 minutes

In a Class of Its Own   45 minutes

Materials and Advance Preparation

Conducting Lessons

Materials:

- 9 volt battery, 1 per lab group
- Flashlight bulb, 1 per lab group
- Socket, 1 per lab group
- 3, 30 cm lengths of wire, 1 set per lab group
- A variety of conductors and nonconductors, 1 set per lab group
- Immersion heater, 1 per lab group
- Styrofoam cup, 1 per lab group
- Thermometer, 1 per lab group
- 100 ml graduated cylinder, 1 per lab group

Before class:

- Draw a diagram on the board to illustrate a conductivity-testing apparatus made from a battery, a bulb, a socket, and three pieces of wire.

In a Class of Its Own

Materials:

- Borax, 1 g per lab group
- Cobalt (II) chloride or Nickel (II) chloride, .5 g per lab group
- 6 inch nichrome wire loop, 1 per lab group
- Mortar and pestle, 1 per lab group
- Bunsen burner, 1 per lab group
- Dictionary
- Overhead projector
- Hammer

Conducting lessons

1. Review electrical conductivity with the students. Have each lab group assemble the conductivity testing apparatus illustrated on the blackboard (see *Materials and Advance Preparation*), and test the conductivity of the conductors and nonconductors gathered for this activity. Next, let the students test articles of their own choosing, such as pencils, belt-buckles, or rings.
2. Explain why metals conduct electricity and

other materials usually do not. Include a description, such as the following, of how a conductor differs from an insulator.

The difference between metals (conductors) and insulators is essentially the ability of the highest energy electrons to move around the materials. In an insulator, the "energy band" containing the outer electrons is completely filled; consequently, those electrons cannot carry current. In a metal, the uppermost "energy band" is *partially* filled, enabling those electrons to carry current. Because the uppermost energy band is not filled, the electrons in a conductor can move in response to an electrical field. Although the electrons are free to roam, they cannot move from one end of a conductor to the other. Instead, they run into phonons (nuclear vibrations), impurity atoms, and other electrons, transferring kinetic energy to one another. Each collision results in resistance to the flow of current, and produces heat energy at the expense of electrical energy. (See *Background for the Teacher* for more information.)

3. Have the students perform the following experiment to determine how much heat a conductor loses. In this case, the conductor is an immersion heater—a wire with an electric current running through it.
   a. Measure 100 ml of water into a styrofoam cup.
   b. Measure and record in degrees Celsius the temperature of the water.
   c. Insert the immersion heater into the water for two minutes. Record the amount of time the heater is in the water.
   d. Remove the heater.
   e. Measure and record in degrees Celsius the temperature of the water after heating.
4. Discuss with the students the results of the experiment in terms of the model of conduction of electricity. Discuss heat loss as both a desirable and a nondesirable product of conduction.

In a Class of its Own

1. Define the term superconductivity for your students (see *Background for the Teacher*). Include a description of the differences between the free electrons of a conductor and the bound pairs of electrons in a superconductor and the way in which each conducts an electrical current. Stress that in previously known superconductors the pairing of electrons was dependent upon very low temperatures and strong electron-ion attractions. The most promising superconductors belong to a new class of ceramic materials. Although ceramics are usually thought of as insulators, there is a class of ceramics, the oxygen-defect perovskites, that are well-known to the solid state chemistry and physics communities. The metallic nature of these ceramics is due to the vacancies left by removing electrons from the uppermost energy band of the oxygen atoms. Some scientists currently think that interactions between the electrons' spins cause the pairing of electrons at higher temperatures. Recall that, at lower temperatures, the presence of

ions is thought to be responsible for electron pairing (see *Background for the Teacher*).

2. Have the students work in lab groups of three or four, and prepare a ceramic material as follows:
   a. Using a mortar and pestle, grind together 1 g of borax and .5 g of Nickel (II) chloride or Copper (II) chloride.
   b. Heat a nichrome wire loop in the flame of a Bunsen burner.
   c. Dip the heated wire into the borax mixture. Be sure to get only a very small amount of the mixture on the wire. Return the wire to the flame. Repeat this process, each time picking up only a small amount of the borax mixture until the loop contains a glassy material.
   d. Observe and describe the material.
3. Discuss the appearance and physical properties of the ceramic material. Ask the students if they think it appears to be conducting or nonconducting. Ask the students to look up the definition of "ceramic" in a dictionary. Read the definition aloud: hard, brittle, electrical insulators, requires high-temperature processing, and is formed from powders. Explain to the students that it was only when scientists abandoned metals and turned to an entirely different kind of material—ceramics—that the field of superconductivity progressed. Stress that new frontiers in science often occur when scientists take a radically new approach to a problem.
4. Discuss with students the factors that currently affect the use of superconductors. Besides the extremely low temperatures required to maintain a material in a state of superconductivity, fabrication is also a problem. Ask students how they would form a ceramic material into a wire-like strand. Demonstrate the brittle nature of a ceramic by using a hammer to hit the glassy material formed at the end of one of the student's nichrome loops. Scientists are proposing that the ceramic material be put into a thin, hollow, silver wire or into copper/nickel tubes. Even if those wires can be made, scientists are not sure that the wires will be able to carry a large enough current or have the necessary mechanical strength for some applications. The use of superconducting film in integrated circuits (computer chips) is an intriguing idea, but engineers will have to find ways to integrate the film with semiconductor technology, which cannot tolerate the high temperatures required to produce the superconducting films.

Another problem with the new materials is that they are unstable: a chunk of fired Y-Ba-CuO that is impure will dissolve completely if left in a glass of water overnight; even a pure pervoskite will eventually dissolve in water. It is not clear whether perfect crystals will react the same way, but devices made from the superconducting material may need a coating of an impermeable substance to prevent deterioration. Scientists are studying the limitations of the new ceramic materials and trying to figure out ways to make the materials easier to use. Even with the large number of scientists working on high-temperature superconductors, it will be at least five years before thin films of superconductors are in computers, and up to twenty years before superconductors are used in bulk applications, such as magnets or power lines.

5. Brainstorm potential future uses of room-temperature superconductors. Use *Background for the Teacher* as a guide. Students will be able to think of others.

Background for the Teacher
NOTE: This information reflects events in the field of superconductivity as of August 1987. The developments in this field are occurring so rapidly that by the time you read this activity, portions of this background probably are out of date. Check recent periodicals for more current information.

Early in 1987, a scientific breakthrough occurred that was so exciting it was the cover story for the May 11 issue of *Time* magazine,[1] and it generated standing-room-only crowds at the American Physical Society and the American Chemical Society meetings. What phenomenon has graduate students and Nobel Prize hopefuls alike clamoring to be involved? The answer is *superconductivity*.

Hypothetical Models
What makes a material a superconductor? To understand the currently accepted model for how superconductors work, it is helpful to look at the model for how nonsuper conductors work. These conductors are usually pictured as consisting of fixed nuclei with electrons that are essentially free to roam about the metal because the uppermost energy band is not completely filled. Electrons move in response to the electric field that is created when an external voltage is applied to the metal. However, the electrons are not truly "free"— they run into phonons (vibrations of the nuclei). Because of these collisions, metals have resistance to the flow of a current and they heat up when a current flows through them.

At certain temperatures, many materials become *superconductors*. It is possible for two electrons to experience an attractive force that leads to superconductivity at a given temperature (the critical temperature or T_c). This attraction is possible if a positively charged ion assists the process by "over-screening" the normal repulsion that the two electrons experience. The electrons thus form bound pairs. This leads to superconductivity because the electrons no longer behave like electrons. Normal electrons obey the Pauli Exclusion Principle, which says that no two electrons can exist in the same quantum-mechanical state; the wave functions of the electrons do not overlap. In a superconductor with bound pairs of electrons, the wave functions of the pairs overlap considerably. As a result of this overlap, all the pairs in a superconductor behave much more like a single unit; they move as one.

Superconductivity Time Line

1911	Dutch physicist Heike Kamerlingh Onnes discovers superconductivity at 4K in mercury.
1950	Scientists discover alloys that keep their superconductivity in the presence of a strong magnetic field.
1960	Manufacture of large superconducting magnets becomes standardized.
1970s	Scientists discover superconductivity in polymers and organic materials. They achieve transition temperatures near 8K.
1973	Scientists discover that an alloy of niobium and germanium superconducts at 23K.
1983	Karl Alex Mueller and Johannes Georg Bednorz begin to examine metallic oxides (ceramics) as possible superconductors.
1985	Mueller and Bednorz find superconductivity in Ba-La-CuO at 35K.
1986	Bell Labs researchers find a similar conductor at 38K.
Jan. 1987	University of Houston scientist Paul C. W. Chu finds another member of the copper oxide ceramic family, Y-Ba-CuO, superconducts at 98K.
June 1987	Researchers at the University of Houston and University of California, Berkeley, develop a material that retains superconducting properties at temperatures between 280 and 300 degrees Kelvin (78° F).
Aug. 1987	Colorado State University researcher Walajabad Sampath isolates bits of material that show evidence of superconductivity at room temperature—70°F.

Some collisions still take place, but they do not have sufficient energy to break up the electron pairs and the overlapping nature of the electron wave functions. Due to the overlapping nature of the electron wave function, there is no resistance, and no energy is lost through heat. Although a large number of electrons are not in a superconductive state, they do not produce heat, because they are "shorted out" by the superconducting state. This is similar to having a resistor with finite resistance and a resistor with zero resistance in a parallel circuit; the current will always take the zero resistance path, thus "shorting out" the finite resistor.

This model predicts that materials not normally thought of as good conductors will make good superconductors. A crucial aspect of the hypothesis is that electrons must be able to form bound pairs. In the superconductors known before 1986, electrons formed these bound pairs only with the help of an interaction with ions, making materials with strong electron-ion attraction good candidates. However, materials in which electrons and ions interact strongly are normally thought of as poor conductors. This led Bednorz and Mueller to study ceramics, which are normally insulators. In an interesting twist of events, however, it now appears likely that the superconductivity of the new higher temperature superconductors (23K and above) is not caused by electron-ion (phonon) interaction. Present thinking focuses on spin-mediated pairing. This means the interactions between spins cause the pairing of electrons and an ion is not necessary.[2]

Marketplace Applications

Why all the fuss over superconductors? The discovery of nitrogen-cooled superconductors could be a boon to utilities, industry, electronics, transportation, medicine, and research.[3] But one must be careful not to oversell the promise of new discoveries. All new technologies must compete with existing technologies that are continuously being improved. Present technologies produce billions of dollars of revenue, a good percentage of which corporations use to hire excellent scientists and engineers, both of whom work to extend these technologies as long as possible.

- Power companies could use superconductive transmission lines to send current hundreds of miles from a distant generating center without energy losses. Power distribution grows at a very slow rate (slightly more than one percent per year in the U.S.) so it may not be cost effective to use this technology in developed countries. In third world countries that do not have extensive power distribution networks in place, however, it may be very reasonable.

Resources for the Classroom

Breathed, B. "Bloom County" cartoon, Sunday, 21 June 1987.
Gleich, J. In the Trenches of Science. *The New York Times Magazine*. 16 August 1987: p. 28. [An excellent review of some of the controversies and competition related to superconductivity research.]
Grant, P. Do-It-Yourself Superconductors. *New Scientist*. 30 July 1987: pp. 36-39. [This article describes a complex laboratory activity in which high school students actually made a superconductor.]
Hudson, R.L. Scientific Saga: How Two IBM Physicists Triggered the Frenzy over Superconductors. *The Wall Street Journal*. 19 August 1987: p. 1.

- Densely-packed microchips made of superconductive materials would not produce heat and could be packed more closely together in a computer. This would allow for a decrease in the size of computers. These smaller computers would work faster than present machines because the signals would have less distance to travel between components.
- Trains, like the Japanese levitated train, but much simpler and less expensive to operate because of the nitrogen-cooled superconductive magnets, could fly at 300 miles per hour on a frictionless magnetic support. This application would be most important to nations without a railroad system or nations that are very dependent on public rail transportation.
- Magnetic resonance imaging (MRI) machines use powerful magnets to make images of tissues inside the body. Currently, relatively few hospitals can support the use of the helium-cooled machines, which cost about $500,000. New MRI scanners made with high temperature superconductors cooled with liquid nitrogen would be less complex and less expensive than the helium-cooled machines. This would require superconducting wire, however, which poses other difficulties.
- Physics research could benefit from the use of new superconductors in the super-magnets that constrain the flight paths of high-speed particles in particle accelerators, and safely contain the hot plasma in which nuclear fusion reactions take place.

It is no wonder that scientists have been losing sleep over superconductivity. Leading industrial nations have recognized the potential of the new superconductors and have subsidized research in the public and private sectors. Scientists view the new superconductors in the same light as lasers and transistors.[4] Competition among institutions is great: "I'm a standard American scientist," says theoretical physicist Marvin Cohen. "My definition of science is to discover the secrets of nature—before anybody else."[5]

It is important that people realize that the first application of superconductivity is already occurring, and was unanticipated. This application is the demonstration of superconductivity in the schools. High school students have been able to create high temperature superconductors in their classrooms (see *Resources of the Classroom*). This may be the first time high school students and teachers have been able to repeat one of the great scientific findings of this century. The social impact of having emergent technological and scientific principles accessible to young scientists could renew enthusiasm for careers in science and technology.

Consultants
Paul Grant
Research Staff Member
Manager, Magnetism and Cooperative Phenomena
IBM Almaden Research Center
San Jose, CA
Joseph Serene
Research Scientist
National Science Foundation
Washington, D.C.

■ End Notes

1. Superconductors! *Time.* 129(19):65-75; 1987.
2. Mueller, K.A.; Bednorz, J.G. The Discovery of a Class of High-Temperature Superconductors. *Science.* 237(4819):1133-1139; 1987.
3. Dagani, R. Superconductivity: A Revolution in Electricity is Taking Shape. *Chemical and Engineering News.* 65(19):8; 1987.
4. Superconductors! *Time.* 129(19):65; 1987.
5. Ibid, p. 68.

A Place in Space

Overview:

Without technology, the exploration of space would be impossible. As we increase the possibility that humans will one day live and work in space, we also increase the need for more sophisticated technology. In this activity, the students identify the basic needs of living things, examine a variety of self-contained biospheres designed to support life and construct a simple model of a space station. Through these experiences, the students will realize some of the challenges that scientists and engineers face when exploring the frontier of space.

Scientific Principles:

- The basic needs of living things include oxygen, carbon dioxide, water, light, food, and protection from extreme heat and cold.
- Artificial biospheres rely on technology to provide the basic needs of resident organisms.
- Engineers use scale models to help them in the design of complex systems.
- A closed system is an isolated system; neither energy nor material can pass through its boundaries.

Student Outcomes: Upon completion of this activity, students will be able to

- Identify the basic needs of a living organism.
- Construct a biosphere for a simple organism such as a plant.
- Recognize different models of complex biospheres.
- Use scale models to design larger objects.

Skills:
Analyzing, Discussing, Constructing models

Time Frame:
Life Under Glass   45 minutes
A Human Terrarium?   45 minutes

Materials and Advance Preparation

Life Under Glass

Materials:

• Large potted plant
• 2-liter soft-drink bottles
• 1 small plant, no more than 8″ tall, for the demonstration terrarium
• Large scissors, 1 pair per lab group
• Potting soil, 10-pound bag
• Newspaper, enough to cover desks
• Seeds, 5 per student (suggested seeds: radish, marigold, alfalfa)
• 500 ml beaker of water, 1 per lab group
• Duct or electrical tape, 15 cm per lab group
• Masking tape, 30 cm per lab group

A Human Terrarium?

Materials:

• Terrarium with small plant (from Life Under Glass)
• Overhead projector

Little Plans for Big Ideas

Materials:

• Meter stick or metric tape measure
• Graph paper with metric divisions, 1 sheet per student
• Scissors, 1 per lab group
• Metric rulers, 1 per student
• Masking tape

Related Disciplines:
Life science, Earth science, Physical science, Mathematics

Little Plans for Big Ideas   45 minutes

Before class:

• A week in advance, ask the students to bring in empty, rinsed, clear 2-liter soft-drink bottles. You will need one per student.
• Organize materials for lab groups.
• Make a soft-drink bottle terrarium using a small plant instead of seeds. This will serve as the demonstration terrarium. (See *Teaching Strategies*, Life Under Glass, step 3.)

Before class:

• Make transparencies of the Figures on pages 484 and 485.

Before class:

• Write the dimensions of the space module on the chalkboard. (See *Teaching Strategies*, Little Plans for Big Ideas, step 2.)

Life Under Glass

1. Display a large plant and ask the students to explain what this organism needs to stay alive. List the students' responses on the chalkboard, and assist them in identifying needs that are basic to the plant's survival: minerals, water, air, and light.
2. Display the demonstration terrarium containing a small plant. Review the students' lists of basic

needs. Will this plant stay alive? Why or why not? Have the class explain how each basic need of the plant is being met.
3. Divide the students into lab groups and distribute materials so students can construct terraria by doing the following:
   a. Use the large scissors to cut off the top of each plastic bottle.

b. Separate the colored base from the rest of the bottle by tugging on it vigorously.

c. Use the duct or electrical tape to seal the holes in the base from the inside. Do this carefully to make the base water-tight.

d. Fill the base with soil.

e. Add 50 ml of water to moisten the soil. *Do not overwater.* Stir the soil.

f. Use a pencil to poke five holes in the soil, and then plant a seed in each hole. Gently cover each seed with soil.

g. Invert the clear plastic part of the bottle to create a dome to cover the base. Use masking tape to seal the base and dome. Record names on the tape.

4. Keep the students' terraria in a warm place until the seeds germinate (two to three days), and then place the terraria in sunlight. After the majority of the seedlings are well sprouted, ask the students to evaluate the varying success of individual terraria. Have the students discuss how the basic needs of the plants are, or are not, being met. Your students may want to design and conduct experiments to test the relative importance of different factors on plant life in a terrarium.

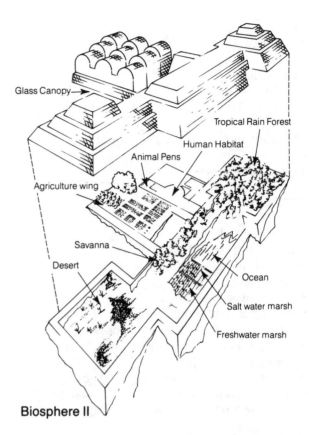

Biosphere II

A Human Terrarium?

1. Instruct the students to reexamine the terrarium containing the small plant. Ask the students if they think humans could live in a terrarium. Discuss the needs of humans, and list these needs on the chalkboard. Ask the students to decide which of the items listed are biological needs that are basic to the survival of humans (oxygen, light, water, food, protection from heat and cold) and which are psychological needs (companionship, entertainment, recreation). Have the class discuss how the biological needs could be met in a closed system like a terrarium.

2. Define a closed system for your students. In a closed system, the total amount of water and air remains constant. In addition, no new food or nutrients can enter the system, so food and nutrients must cycle through the system for plants and animals to use them again. The earth is a closed system, energy is the only resource that reaches the system from the outside. Sunlight is necessary to heat air and supply energy for various cycles.

3. In the Arizona desert, scientists are currently building an artificial, closed biosphere—or a human terrarium—called Biosphere II. Modeled after the biosphere of the earth (Biosphere I), Biosphere II will be a self-supporting ecosystem containing five biomes: a savanna, a marsh, a desert, a tropical rain forest, and an ocean 35 feet deep. Four men and four women will inhabit the two-acre structure for two years beginning in 1989. The $30 million project could serve as a prototype for orbiting space stations or planetary outposts, and as a model for improved resource management.

Use a transparency of the Figure to present the Biosphere II project in Arizona, and discuss the project, asking the students to consider the following:

a. What are the objectives of the project? (According to the planners, there are two: to develop technology for settlements on the moon and Mars, and to improve human stewardship of earth by learning how to manage such things as human wastes.)

b. What problems require solutions if Biosphere II is to become self-sustaining? (Some suggestions are: how to seal the glass roof so that no air can escape or enter; how to cool the air temperatures, which could peak at 156° F, without using conventional methods that draw air from the outside; how to handle water purification and air quality; how to make sure there is adequate vegetation to sustain all life forms; and, how to make sure that none

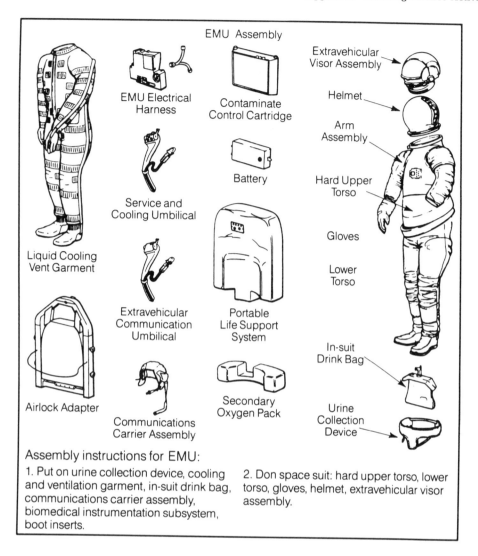

EMU Assembly

EMU Electrical Harness

Contaminate Control Cartridge

Service and Cooling Umbilical

Battery

Liquid Cooling Vent Garment

Extravehicular Communication Umbilical

Portable Life Support System

Airlock Adapter

Communications Carrier Assembly

Secondary Oxygen Pack

Extravehicular Visor Assembly

Helmet

Arm Assembly

Hard Upper Torso

Gloves

Lower Torso

In-suit Drink Bag

Urine Collection Device

Assembly instructions for EMU:

1. Put on urine collection device, cooling and ventilation garment, in-suit drink bag, communications carrier assembly, biomedical instrumentation subsystem, boot inserts.

2. Don space suit: hard upper torso, lower torso, gloves, helmet, extravehicular visor assembly.

of the selected life forms will be a hazard to the ecosystem.)

c. What would it be like to live in Biosphere II? What kind of people would be appropriate to include in the group of eight Biosphereans? What skills should they have?

d. What will be the social dynamics of the Biosphereans? What strains will the Biosphereans encounter during their two-year stay in Biosphere II? Would the students like living for two years with seven other people in a closed system?

4. Another life-supporting biosphere model is the extravehicular mobility unit (EMU) used by astronauts in space. NASA developed the EMU to enable astronauts to work in space without the support of a space craft. An attachable manned maneuvering unit (MMU) allows astronauts to work untethered in space and return safely to the spacecraft. By providing the atmospheric pressure and oxygen necessary for human life as well as insulation from the sun's heat, the EMU protects the astronaut from the hostile environment of space. The technology involved in the EMU is complex; astronauts preparing to work in space must carry all of their life-support systems with them. Use a transparency of the Figure to illustrate an EMU. Have the students identify the basic needs of an astronaut and describe how the EMU meets those needs.

Little Plans for Big Ideas

As we push back the frontiers of space, we must create self-supporting biospheres. Most people call these artificial biospheres *space stations*. In 1984, President Ronald Reagan directed NASA to develop a permanently occupied space station within a decade. Scientists once envisioned a collection of modules that would form huge, spoked wheels that would spin through space.

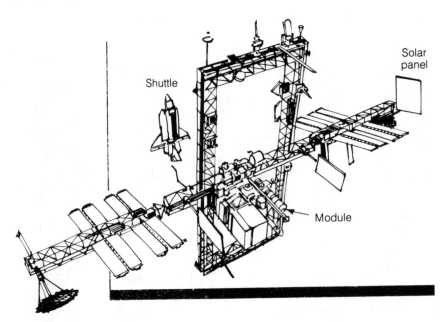

Shuttle

Solar panel

Module

Current U.S. plans for the station, however, describe a structure that includes four pressurized, cylindrical modules, in the center of a huge supportive structure. Two of these modules will provide living space, and the other two will provide a working area. The space station will house a crew of six, with replacement crews arriving every 90 days.

1. If space is available, have the students measure the dimensions of one module on the classroom floor. Instruct six people to stand within the boundaries of the module, and ask the students to imagine living in that space for 90 days at a time. Remind the students that they would have only two modules available for sleeping, eating, recreation and relaxation.

2. Currently, plans for the space station are only on paper. Because something as large as a space station is difficult to design, engineers use scale models. Scale models are small two- or three-dimensional renderings of a large object. With the advent of sophisticated computers, computer modeling has replaced paper and pencil drafting in the design of complex objects. In a scale model, the relative sizes of the parts of the model are the same as those of the larger object; all the proportions are identical. Introduce the students to the concept of a scale model. Use familiar examples, such as airplane models and architectural plans. Ask the students to make a three-dimensional scale model of one of the cylindrical modules.

   a. Review the dimensions with students:
      Diameter of module = 4.2 meters
      Length of module = 12.1 meters

OPTIONAL: The module is cylindrical. In order to draw the module two-dimensionally and then roll it into a correctly scaled cylinder, ask the students to calculate the circumference of the module. Review with the students the formula for calculating the circumference of a circle from its diameter: circumference = π d. If students are not familiar with the formula for calculating the circumference, include the circumference (13.2 meters) in the dimensions.

   b. Ask the students to convert the measurements of the module from meters to centimeters, using the scale of 1 cm = 1 m. In this way, one centimeter on paper will be equivalent to one meter on the module.

   c. Supply each student with one sheet of graph paper with metric divisions. Ask the students to draw on the graph paper the scaled dimension they had calculated (length × circumference). The finished drawing will be a rectangle.

   d. Instruct students to cut out the rectangle with scissors, and tape the two short sides together to form a cylinder. This cylinder is proportionally accurate and resembles the proposed module. Each dimension is 1/100 of the size of the real module, making the scale model, with its three dimensions, 1/1,000,000 of the size of the real module.

   e. The students can use a metric ruler to check their model by measuring the diameter of the cylinder. Being careful to maintain the cylindrical form, the students should measure the diameter as approximately 4.2 cm.

Going Further

- Have the students write a letter from space, describing where they live, what they do, and how they feel about living on a space station.
- Ask the students to search their school or local libraries for science fiction that includes predictions of how humans will live in space.
- Have the students conduct research on plans for the industrialization of space. Ask the students to find out the results of various projects on shuttle flights and what industrial applications may be suited for a space station.
- Have the students draw a scale model of one room of their house. Ask them to measure the room's size and the furniture, and to draw a two-dimensional plan with all parts of the room in relative proportion.
- Have the students investigate the numerous spin-offs produced by the space program, such as teflon, velcro, and temperfoam. Information on the products is available in the library or from the U.S. Government Printing Office (address listed under *Resources for the Classroom*).
- Encourage the students to study the history of space exploration. What happened when? How did the explorations benefit life on earth? When did the first animal, man, or woman orbit the earth, walk on another planet, or travel past the moon?
- Let the students explore the accomplishments of the U.S. and U.S.S.R. in space. Why is there so much competition between these nations? When have they cooperated? What other nations have active space programs?

Resources for the Classroom

Freundlich, N.J. Biosphere. *Popular Science.* 229(6):pp. 54-56; 1986.

Maranto, G. Earth's First Visitors to Mars. *Discover.* 8(5):28-43; 1987.

NASA. NASA Facts: Waste Management. JSC-09696 (Rev. A) Washington, D.C.: U.S.G.P.O.; undated.

NASA. NASA Facts: A Wardrobe for Space. JSC-09378 (Rev. Ad.) Washington, D.C.: U.S.G.P.O.; 1984.

Scobee, J.; Scobee, D. An Astronaut Speaks. *Science and Children.* 23(6), reprint; March 1986.

Taylor, P. *The Kid's Whole Future Catalog.* NY: Random House, Inc; 1982.

Government documents can be ordered from the Superintendent of Documents, U.S. Government Printing Office, Washington, D.C. 20402. Many fliers are free, even in bulk quantities.

A Teacher's Companion to the Space Station: A Multi-disciplinary Resource, as well as other materials, is available at the NASA Teacher Resource Centers listed below:

Alabama Space and Rocket Center
Huntsville, AL 35807
Serves Alabama.

NASA Ames Research Center
Moffett Field, CA 94035
Serves Alaska, Arizona, California, Hawaii, Idaho, Montana, Nevada, Oregon, Utah, Washington, and Wyoming.

NASA Goddard Space Flight Center
Greenbelt, MD 20771
Serves Connecticut, Delaware, District of Columbia, Maine, Maryland, Massachusetts, New Hampshire, New Jersey, New York, Pennsylvania, Rhode Island, and Vermont.

NASA Jet Propulsion Laboratory
4800 Oak Grove Drive
Pasadena, CA 91109
Serves inquiries related to space exploration and other JPL activities

NASA Johnson Space Center
Houston, TX 77058
Serves Colorado, Kansas, Nebraska, New Mexico, North Dakota, Oklahoma, South Dakota, and Texas.

NASA Kennedy Space Center
Kennedy Space Center, FL 32899
Serves Florida, Georgia, Puerto Rico, and the Virgin Islands.

NASA Langley Research Center
Hampton, VA 23665
Serves Kentucky, North Carolina, South Carolina, Virginia, and West Virginia.

NASA Lewis Research Center
Cleveland, OH 44135
Serves Illinois, Indiana, Michigan, Minnesota, Ohio, and Wisconsin.

NASA Marshall Space Flight Center
Tranquillity Base
Huntsville, AL 35812
Serves Alabama, Arkansas, Iowa, Louisiana, Missouri, and Tennessee.

National Space Technology Laboratories
NSTL, MS 39529
Serves Mississippi.

The United States Space Foundation, 1522 Vapor Trail Drive, Colorado Springs, CO 80916, also has many teacher and student resource materials.

Background for the Teacher

Space stations orbiting earth, space travellers living in artificial, enclosed biospheres, and shuttles transporting people between earth and Mars—are these just science fiction images, or is the space program bringing us to the reality of settlements beyond earth?

NASA has been working toward the settlement of space for many years. With President Ronald Reagan's directive in 1984 to "develop a permanently manned space station—and do it within a decade,"[1] NASA has been able to put form to its concepts and deadlines to its timetable. An occupied space station requires a self-supporting biosphere—a closed, complex system in which organisms support and maintain themselves. Because human survival in space requires oxygen, water, food, light, protection from temperature extremes and a shield from cosmic and solar radiation, scientists and technologists have several complex problems to solve.

The *Challenger* disaster in January 1986 changed NASA's schedule for launching a space station. Originally, NASA planned to build a station in space over the course of 18 months, taking up materials with 12 shuttle flights.[2] Because of the problems with *Challenger*, NASA decided to reduce each shuttle's cargo capacity from 65,000 pounds per launch to 40,000 pounds, thus changing the timetable for building the station. Current plans call for construction of a modest station, which NASA can enlarge later. Shuttle flights will ferry the modules for living and working, and, after 11 flights, a crew of four will occupy the station. The station will be complete in 1996 and will have required a total of 32 flights.[3]

For centuries, humans have been curious about the worlds beyond our planet. Why do we want to explore beyond the confines of earth? Why do we need to? What do we hope to accomplish?

Research in space will help answer numerous scientific questions. Aboard the space station, specialists will conduct astronomical studies, such as mapping Venus with the Magellan probe, which has high-resolution radar equipment. There is widespread interest in manufacturing in space, because the micro-gravity environment eliminates heat convection, hydrostatic pressure, sedimentation and buoyancy, and enables the fusion of mixed particles into homogeneous composites that are impossible to make on earth.[4] Private industries hope to use the space station to purify pharmaceutical and biological products, such as erythropoietin, a kidney hormone that controls the production of red blood cells. Other products include nearly flawless glass-like linings for artificial hearts that would prevent clotting, and

membranes coated with antibodies that could filter the blood of an AIDS patient.[5] The computer industry hopes to improve high-speed computers by growing high-quality gallium arsenide crystals in space. Researchers also would like to develop new polymers and catalysts, to process improved fiber optics, and to create new metal alloys not produced on earth.

The scientific purpose of space travel is the pursuit of new knowledge. Scientists, however, are not the only people interested in space travel. Others also see space as an avenue to pursue their goals. The National Commission on Space has said, in its rationale for exploring and settling the solar system, that exploring the universe is a goal that will encourage increased world cooperation and will be a peaceful mission with respect for the integrity of planetary bodies and alien life forms.[6] The ratio of funding for space projects, however, is tipped heavily in favor of the armed services. The defense budget helps to build technological infrastructures and underwrites expensive high-tech science.[7] The existence of the Strategic Defense Initiative (SDI) as an impetus for space research underscores that there may not be unity of purpose in space exploration. Space is a large frontier; how and why the United States ventures into it will determine the benefits derived from its exploration.

Consultant
Victoria Duca
Director of Special Projects
U.S. Space Foundation
Colorado Springs, CO

■ **End Notes**

1. Anderson, D.A. Space Station. EP-211 Washington, D.C.: U.S.G.P.O.; undated, p. ii.
2. National Commission on Space. *Pioneering the Space Frontier.* NY: Bantam Books, Inc.; 1986:p. 120.
3. Biddle, W. NASA: What's Needed to Put It on Its Feet? *Discover.* 8(1): 31-49; 1987.
4. Space Industries. Manufacturing facility in space cited in *The Futurist.* 21(3):33; 1987.
5. Biddle, p. 45.
6. National Commission on Space, p. 4.
7. Biddle, p. 45.

Dirty Water: Who Needs It?

Overview:

Life as we know it is not possible without water. Despite its importance, water has become improperly managed, seriously depleted, and contaminated by toxic materials. In this activity, students examine the distribution of water, investigate pollutants and treatment methods, and consider their roles in the water problem, thereby recognizing that we face a frontier in maintaining this valuable resource.

Scientific Principles:

- The world's supply of water remains constant, but the supply is neither readily available for human use nor distributed uniformly.
- Specialized treatments can remove impurities and pollutants from water, but those impurities and pollutants are not removed from the earth's closed system. There is no such place as *away*.

Student Outcomes: Upon completion of this activity, students will be able to

- State the percentage of water resources readily available for human use.
- Describe the steps used in water treatment and explain the results.
- Identify ways they contribute to the water pollution problem.

Skills:
Observing, Investigating, Measuring, Comparing, Discussing, Evaluating

Related Disciplines:
Environmental science, Life science, Mathematics, Chemistry

Time Frame:

Water, Water Everywhere	15 minutes	Where is Away?	15 minutes
Pollution Solution?	45 minutes	Who, Me?	30 minutes

Materials and Advance Preparation

Water, Water Everywhere

Materials:

- 7 *clear* containers—2 one-liter containers; 5 smaller containers, one of which is plastic
- 1 plate
- Overhead projector
- Masking tape
- Marking pen
- One liter of water
- Salt—34 grams
- Sand—approximately 250 ml
- Blue food coloring
- 1000 ml graduated cylinder
- One eye dropper

Before class:

- Gather all materials
- Fill one small container with sand.
- Fill a one-liter container with water, add 4 drops of blue food coloring, and stir.
- Label the other 5 containers as follows:
  —a one-liter container *oceans*
  —a small plastic container *polar ice*
  —a small container *deep ground water*
  —a small container *fresh water*.
- Make a transparency of the Figure Distribution of the World's Water Supply.
- Measure and set aside 34 grams of salt.

Pollution Solution?

Materials:

- Gravel, approximately 250 ml
- Sand, approximately 250 ml
- Soil, approximately 250 ml
- Salt, approximately 250 ml
- 1000 ml beaker, 1 per lab group
- 250 ml beaker, 1 per lab group
- 500 ml beaker, 1 per lab group
- Glass stirring rod, 1 per lab group
- Granulated alum (KAl (SO$_4$)^2 · 12H$_2$O), approximately 0.5 g per lab group
- Coffee filter, 1 per lab group
- Rubber bands
- Masking tape
- Household bleach (sodium hypochlorite, NaOCl), 10 ml
- Eye dropper, 1 per lab group
- Balance, 1 per lab group
- Tray for evaporation, 1 for the class
- Distillation setup, 1 for the class (optional)

Before class:

- Divide the students into lab groups.
- Prepare one liter of "polluted" water for each lab group by putting approximately 25 ml each of gravel, sand, soil, and salt into one liter of tap water.
- Write the directions for water treatment on the chalkboard or on a transparency (see *Teaching Strategies*).

Where Is Away?

Materials:

- All Pollution Solution materials (from completed activity above)
- Salt residue from evaporation experiment

Before class:

- Complete Pollution Solution? activity. Keep water and treatment materials.
- Complete evaporation experiment. (See *Teaching Strategies* for details.)

Who, Me?

Materials:

- Overhead projector

Before class:

- Make a transparency of the Water Treatment Process.

Substance	MCL*
Arsenic	0.05 mg/l
Lead	0.05 mg/l
Mercury	0.05 mg/l
Silver	0.05 mg/l
Fluoride	2.4 mg/l
Sodium	20 mg/l
*maximum contaminate level	

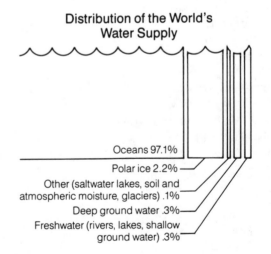

Distribution of the World's
Water Supply

Oceans 97.1%
Polar ice 2.2%
Other (saltwater lakes, soil and atmospheric moisture, glaciers) .1%
Deep ground water .3%
Freshwater (rivers, lakes, shallow ground water) .3%

Water, Water Everywhere

The world's supply of water covers more than 70 percent of the earth's surface. Although the supply of water remains constant, it is not distributed evenly. Nearly 98 percent of the water is in the earth's oceans, where salinity makes it unavailable for many human uses. The remaining 2 percent of the earth's water is underground, or in polar ice, lakes, rivers, and the atmosphere.

Perform the following class demonstration to help students visualize the distribution of the earth's water resources:

a. Display the seven containers prepared for this activity (see *Materials and Advance Preparation*).
b. Display a transparency of p. 490, lower right. Use a graduated cylinder to distribute the one liter of water into the five empty containers according to the percentages indicated in the figure. (For example, 97.1 percent of the water on the earth is found in the oceans. Because one liter contains 1000 milliliters, 97.1 percent of one liter is 971 milliliters. Therefore pour 971 milliliters into the container marked *oceans*.)

   NOTE: The percentages in the figure are rounded-off to facilitate this demonstration. Take care to measure accurately so you have three milliliters of water left over. Also, these percentages will vary from source to source depending on the method of calculation and the divisions used. It may be an interesting project for students to examine a variety of sources that contain data about the distribution of water.

c. After you have filled the empty containers with the appropriate amounts of water, continue with the demonstration, as follows:
   • Add 34 grams of salt to the *ocean* container; this will match the salinity of the water sample with the salinity of the earth's oceans (3.5 percent).
   • Place the plastic *polar ice* container in a freezer.
   • Set the *other* container aside. We do not have access to this water.
   • Pour the *deep ground water* into the container of sand.
   • Ask the students which of the containers represents fresh water that is readily available for human use. (They should easily see that only the jar marked *fresh water* has the readily available supply.) Initiate a discussion on the limits of fresh water supplies, the problems of population distribution, and the contamination of existing supplies (refer to *Background for the Teacher*). Only a small part of this fresh water (.003 percent of the earth's total water supply)

is accessible. The rest is too remote (found in Amazon or Siberian rivers) to locate, too expensive to retrieve, or too polluted to use. Hold a plate in front of the class and dramatically drop the usable portion of fresh water onto it. (Represent this portion as one drop of water from an eye dropper.)

Pollution Solution?

Faced with dwindling water resources, people have concentrated on two methods of alleviating the shortage problem. One is conservation, which includes management of toxic waste. The second method is treatment of already-contaminated water. The technology exists to purify polluted water, but economics often determines whether we use the technology. To complicate matters, the pollutants removed from the water in the purification process still exist, and handling the toxic materials creates another pollution problem.

Ask the students to work in teams of two or three and to clean a prepared sample of contaminated water as follows:

a. Fill a one-liter glass container with a well-stirred contaminated water sample (see *Materials and Advance Preparation*). Observe and record the water's color, clarity, and particulate pollution. Stir the sample and immediately pour 250 ml of the sample into a beaker. Determine and record the density of the 250 ml sample by measuring its mass and dividing mass by volume: density = grams of material/volume of material. Set this sample aside as a control.
b. Add approximately 0.5 g of alum to the water sample. Stir with a glass stirring rod for three to five minutes. Aluminum hydroxide particles (floc) will develop.
c. Allow the water to settle for 10 to 15 minutes. Observe and record the water's color, clarity and particulate pollution.
d. Place a coffee filter over a 500 ml beaker and secure it with a rubber band or masking tape. Allow room for 250 ml of water between the bottom of the filter and the bottom of the beaker.
e. Carefully pour approximately 250 ml of the water through the filter, leaving the particles behind in the one-liter container. (Be careful not to stir up the settled particles as you pour.) Observe and record the filtered water's appearance. Determine and record the density of the 250 ml of filtered water and compare it to the density of the 250 ml control set aside in step a.

f. Add one drop of household bleach to the filtered sample and stir the solution.

g. Observe the final sample and compare its appearance to the 250 ml control set aside in step a.

h. Keep all water and treatment materials for reference in the next activity, *Where Is Away?*

Help the students identify the four steps of water treatment used in this activity: flocculation, sedimentation, filtration, and sterilization. See the figure below for an illustration of a water treatment process. Different treatment plants use different processes. One important process that students did not encounter in *Pollution Solution?* is biological treatment, during which microorganisms digest certain impurities. Encourage students to find out about the water treatment processes used in their community.

Identify the "pollutants" you used to prepare the water sample: gravel, sand, dirt, and salt. These materials are actually impurities, not pollutants. In this activity these impurities represent pollutants like sewage, dissolved minerals, and toxic chemicals. Ask the students if they think the treatment methods they used removed all the pollutants. They may suggest that the salt still remains in the water, and may ask to taste the water; but they should follow the universal laboratory rule: Don't taste. Instead, ask your students how they might test for salinity without tasting. Focus their suggestions on procedures they are capable of conducting. Measuring the mass of the polluted water and comparing its density to a sample of clean water of the same volume is one option; or, using a distillation process may also be a viable method.

Before dismissing the students for the day, have them set up the procedure they intend to use for testing for the presence of salt, and also have them pour a small amount of the treated water into a shallow tray so that complete evaporation will have taken place before the next class meeting.

Where Is Away?

Ask students to observe the results of the evaporation of the water sample from the previous day. What do they think is there? (The residue at the bottom of the tray does contain salt.)

Display the water and treatment materials saved from the previous activity, *Pollution Solution?* Ask the students to focus on each step of the water treatment process. Did they notice that although the water became cleaner with each step, the amount of waste material (flocculent debris, waste filter paper, salt residue) increased? Ask the students if they think we can depend on our current technology to remove pollutants and impurities completely from contaminated water. Can technology completely remove pollutants from the earth?

Introduce the concept of *away*. Ask students where they think *away* is. When they throw something *away*, where does it go? When a pollutant is washed *away*, where does it go? After a treatment plant has treated the water, have the impurities gone *away*? Is there really a place called *away*? If students are ready, raise the issue of ground water pollution. What happens to the ground water when pollutants are thrown *away*?

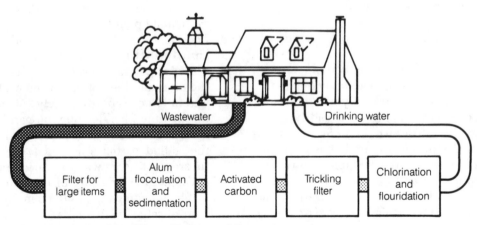

One Example of the Water Treatment Process

Who, Me?

With an understanding that pollution can never go *away*, your students should see that the most powerful solution to the problem of contaminated water supplies is to prevent contamination in the first place. Ask your students who they think contributes to the contamination of water supplies. Frequent answers will involve industry and agriculture. Students should be aware that, although industry and agriculture do contribute substantially to the contamination of water, individuals who use hazardous products in the home also contribute to pollution. Ask students what happens to household products that are dumped down the toilet or sink. Where is *away* in this case?

Materials are hazardous if they are toxic to living things, flammable, explosive, or corrosive. Display page 494 on an overhead projector covering up the third column, and ask the students to identify which hazardous products they have in their homes. Where are these products found?

Uncover the third column and discuss with the students the substitutes available for hazardous materials in the home. Ask students if they see any problem with using the substitutes instead of the hazardous products. Why don't more people use these safer substitutes? What are the trade-offs of using these alternatives? How would our lifestyles change if we used "elbow grease" to clean ovens and no strong chemicals? When is the trade-off worth the consequence? Can action on the household hazardous waste front make a difference in the war against contamination of water? Why or why not?

Have students write a summary of their lessons on water. Ask them to identify the current "water crisis," some of its causes, how pollution of water is measured and then treated, and how the water crisis is closer to home than they might have expected.

Resources for the Classroom

League of Women Voters. *A Hazardous Waste Primer*. Pub. No. 402. Washington, D.C. Available from: League of Women Voters, 1730 M. Street, NW, Washington, D.C., 20036. [A short, unbiased survey of the issue of hazardous waste.]
Concern, Inc. *Groundwater: A Community Action Guide*. Washington, D.C.: Concern, Inc.
Consultant
Stephen W. Almond
Division Chemist
Halliburton Services
Oxnard, CA

Background for the Teacher

Water is a vital resource. Human beings can live almost a month without food, but cannot survive more than two or three days without water. There are five properties that make water so essential: (1) high boiling point, (2) high heat of vaporization, (3) high heat capacity, (4) lower density as a solid than as a liquid, and (5) its solvency.[1]

Water is the universal solvent. It holds and transports, in solution, nutrients that nourish plant and animal systems. Water's powerful solvency also makes it an excellent cleanser, because it dissolves and dilutes so many substances. Unfortunately, this capacity for dissolving a wide variety of substances makes water easy to pollute.

Many different things pollute water: wastes that demand oxygen (sewage, manure); disease-causing agents (bacteria, viruses); inorganic chemicals (acids, salts, metals); organic chemicals (pesticides, plastics, detergents); fertilizers (nitrates, phosphates); sediments from land erosion; radioactive substances; and heat.[2] Most of these pollutants result from human activities. Water pollution is a serious problem because the supply of usable water is small, the distribution is uneven, the demand for use is high, and the rate of water's replenishment is low.

Although water covers more than 70 percent of the earth, less than 1 percent is considered fresh water.[3] Because much of this fresh water is either too expensive to retrieve, too remote to reach, or too polluted to use, it turns out that only .003 percent of the earth's total water supply is available for human use.[4] This small amount of fresh water comes from both surface waters and ground water. In the United States, we draw about 75 percent of our water from lakes and rivers and 25 percent from ground water.[5] There are exceptions, however, to these average figures. For instance, the Greater New York area obtains two percent of its water from subsurface sources and 98 percent from surface sources;[6] yet Tucson, Arizona and San Antonio, Texas are completely dependent on ground water supplies.[7]

Traditionally, water policies have been left to the states and, until recently, the federal government has been reluctant to become involved in this issue. Nevertheless, ground water issues became serious enough for the Reagan administration to acknowledge the need for limited federal action, and Environmental Protection Agency director, Lee Thomas, has urged the creation of a combined state and federal ground water program.[8]

In the United States, industry, agriculture, and our personal lifestyles depend on huge

TOXIC HOUSEHOLD PRODUCTS

PRODUCT	COMMENTS	ALTERNATIVES
CLEANERS		
• Drain Cleaner	Contains caustic poisons	Plunger, boiling water, plumber's snake
• Oven Cleaner	Contains caustic poisons, some are carcinogenic	Salt, self-cleaning oven, "elbow grease"
• Toilet Cleaner	Contains strong acid	Mild detergent, mix of Borax and lemon juice
• Window Cleaner	Contains toxic chemical compounds, sometimes carcinogenic, may cause birth defects	vinegar and water
• Spot Remover	Contains poisonous solvents, some are carcinogenic	Wash fabric immediately with cold water and detergent
AEROSOL SPRAYS		
• Most aerosol sprays	Contain highly toxic poisonous petroleum distillates, some are carcinogenic. Most are flammable and toxic when inhaled.	Non-aerosol Products
• Hair Spray		Setting Lotion/Gel
• Shaving Cream		Brush & Shaving Soap
• Air Fresheners		Ventilation, open bowl of fragrant spice
• Furniture Polish	Contains poisonous solvents, some are carcinogenic	Paste waxes, carnauba wax in mineral oil
PAINT PRODUCTS		
• Paint (Oil or Alkyd	Contains poisonous solvents, some are carcinogenic	Latex paint
• Spray Paint	Contains toxic solvents and propellants	Non-aerosol paint Mineral Oil
• Wood Finishes	Most contain harmful solvents	
• Paint Strippers	Contains poisonous solvents some are carcinogenic	Heat gun with ventilation, hand or electric sander and wear respirator
OTHERS		
• Moth Balls	Contain poisonous chemical compounds, may be carcinogenic	Cedar closet, store woolens in plastic
• Insect Repellent	Can be lethal if ingested	Protective clothing
• Disinfectants	Many extremely toxic	Soap, detergent, hydrogen peroxide

quantities of water. Per capita use is now up to 200 gallons per day.[9] This is the amount of water it takes per day to produce all the goods, grow all the food, and meet all the personal needs of each individual in the country. In contrast, countries with comparable levels of social and economic development use far less water; for example, per capita use in Germany is 37 gallons per day; in Sweden, 54 gallons per day; and in the United Kingdom, 53 gallons per day.[10]

This high level of use in combination with the unequal distribution of resources and the pollution of water sources has made the continued availability of clean water one of the prominent environmental issues in the world. As a result, we must advance the scientific and technological frontiers that deal with water issues. In addition, people must seriously consider their roles in conserving clean water. What can we find out about water, its sources, how it cycles, and how it becomes polluted? What technological advances produce pollution? What technologies can we develop to clean up the dirty water? What is each person doing to contribute to water problems and water clean-up? How can we adjust our lifestyles to preserve our most valuable resource?

■ End Notes

1. Miller, G.T. *Living in the Environment* 2nd ed., Belmont, CA: Wadsworth Publishing Co.; 1979:p. 337.
2. Ibid, p. 357, 359.
3. Purdom, P.W.; Anderson, S.H. *Environmental Science* 2nd ed., Columbus, OH: Merrill Publishing Co.; 1983: p. 214.
4. Miller, p. 339.
5. Chiras, D.D. *Environmental Science*, Menlo Park, CA:Benjamin/Cummings Publishing Co.; 1985:p. 280.
6. Brown, L.R., et al. *State of the World 1987*, NY: W.W. Norton & Co.; 1987: p. 51.
7. Schmitz, G. Poisons Simmer in Nation's Aquifers. *The Denver Post*, 9 August 1987:D-3.
8. Ibid, p. 10.
9. Sheets, K.R. War Over Water: Crisis of the '80s. *U.S. News & World Report*, 95(18):57.
10. Rogers, P. The Future of Water. *The Atlantic Monthly*, 252(1):80-92; 1983. [This article discusses water issues and discusses possible solutions.]

INDEX

About the Authors

Leslie W. Trowbridge has taught science and science education classes since 1941 at all levels from junior high school to university graduate courses. His undergraduate degree was obtained from Central State Teachers College in Stevens Point, Wisconsin. His master's degrees were earned at The University of Chicago and The University of Wisconsin. His doctorate in science education was earned at The University of Michigan in 1961.

Dr. Trowbridge taught for twenty-one years at The University of Northern Colorado, chairing the Department of Science Education for fourteen years until the reorganization of the university in 1983. He has taught at Texas A & M University, National Taiwan Normal University, and The University of Northern Iowa and in 1987 returned, as a tenured professor, to The University of Northern Colorado where he presently teaches.

He has been active professionally in the National Association for Research in Science Teaching (NARST), the Association for the Education of Teachers of Science (AETS), and the National Science Teachers Association (NSTA), of which he was president in 1973-74.

Dr. Trowbridge is the author or co-author of fifteen books in the fields of science activities, meteorology, methods of teaching secondary school science, and elementary school science.

Rodger W. Bybee is associate director of the Biological Sciences Curriculum Study (BSCS), The Colorado College, Colorado Springs, Colorado. Dr. Bybee is principal investigator for two new National Science Foundation (NSF) programs; an elementary school program entitled *Science for Life and Living: Integrating Science, Technology, and Health* and a middle school program entitled *Science and Technology: Investigating Human Dimensions*. His work at BSCS also includes chairing the curriculum and instruction study panel for The National Center for Improving Science Education (NCISE). Prior to joining the BSCS staff in August 1985, Dr. Bybee was professor of education at Carleton College in Northfield, Minnesota. He received his Ph.D. degree in science education and psychology from New York University. He received his B.A. and M.A. from the University of Northern Colorado in Greeley, Colorado. As an undergraduate, Dr. Bybee majored in both biology and fine arts and minored in earth science. As a master's candidate, he majored in science education and minored in earth science and psychology. He has taught science at the elementary, junior, and senior high school levels.

Dr. Bybee has been active in education for more than twenty years. He is a member of the National Science Teachers Association, National Association of Biology Teachers, National Association of Research in Science Teaching, and the American Association for the Advancement of Science, among other organizations. Throughout his career, Dr. Bybee has written widely, publishing in both education and psychology. Over the years, he has received awards for Leader of American Education and Outstanding Educator in America, and in 1979 was recognized as the Outstanding Science Educator of the Year.

WE VALUE YOUR OPINION—PLEASE SHARE IT WITH US

Merrill Publishing and our authors are most interested in your reactions to this textbook. Did it serve you well in the course? If it did, what aspects of the text were most helpful? If not, what didn't you like about it? Your comments will help us to write and develop better textbooks. We value your opinions and thank you for your help.

Text Title _____ Edition _____

Author(s) _____

Your Name (optional) _____

Address _____

City _____ State _____ Zip _____

School _____

Course Title _____

Instructor's Name _____

Your Major _____

Your Class Rank _____ Freshman _____ Sophomore _____ Junior _____ Senior

_____ Graduate Student

Were you required to take this course? _____ Required _____ Elective

Length of Course? _____ Quarter _____ Semester

1. Overall, how does this text compare to other texts you've used?

_____ Superior _____ Better Than Most _____ Average _____ Poor

2. Please rate the text in the following areas:

	Superior	Better Than Most	Average	Poor
Author's Writing Style	_____	_____	_____	_____
Readability	_____	_____	_____	_____
Organization	_____	_____	_____	_____
Accuracy	_____	_____	_____	_____
Layout and Design	_____	_____	_____	_____
Illustrations/Photos/Tables	_____	_____	_____	_____
Examples	_____	_____	_____	_____
Problems/Exercises	_____	_____	_____	_____
Topic Selection	_____	_____	_____	_____
Currentness of Coverage	_____	_____	_____	_____
Explanation of Difficult Concepts	_____	_____	_____	_____
Match-up with Course Coverage	_____	_____	_____	_____
Applications to Real Life	_____	_____	_____	_____

3. Circle those chapters you especially liked:

1   2   3   4   5   6   7   8   9   10   11   12   13   14   15   16   17   18   19   20

What was your favorite chapter? _____

Comments:

4. Circle those chapters you liked least:

1   2   3   4   5   6   7   8   9   10   11   12   13   14   15   16   17   18   19   20

What was your least favorite chapter? _____

Comments:

5. List any chapters your instructor did not assign. _____

6. What topics did your instructor discuss that were not covered in the text?_____

_____

7. Were you required to buy this book? _____ Yes _____ No

   Did you buy this book new or used? _____ New _____ Used

   If used, how much did you pay? _____

   Do you plan to keep or sell this book? _____ Keep _____ Sell

   If you plan to sell the book, how much do you expect to receive? _____

   Should the instructor continue to assign this book? _____ Yes _____ No

8. Please list any other learning materials you purchased to help you in this course (e.g., study guide, lab manual).

_____

9. What did you like most about this text? _____

_____

10. What did you like least about this text? _____

_____

11. General comments:

May we quote you in our advertising? _____ Yes _____ No

Please mail to: Boyd Lane
                  College Division Research Department
                  P. O. Box 508
                  Columbus, Ohio 43216-0508

Thank you!